Emerging Technologies and Applications in Data Processing and Management

Zongmin Ma
Nanjing University of Aeronautics and Astronautics, China

Li Yan
Nanjing University of Aeronautics and Astronautics, China

A volume in the Advances in Data Mining and
Database Management (ADMDM) Book Series

Published in the United States of America by
    IGI Global
    Engineering Science Reference (an imprint of IGI Global)
    701 E. Chocolate Avenue
    Hershey PA, USA 17033
    Tel: 717-533-8845
    Fax: 717-533-8661
    E-mail: cust@igi-global.com
    Web site: http://www.igi-global.com

Library of Congress Cataloging-in-Publication Data

Names: Yan, Li, 1964- editor. | Ma, Zongmin, 1965- editor.
Title: Emerging technologies and applications in data processing and
    management / Zongmin Ma and Li Yan, editors.
Description: Hershey, PA : Engineering Science Reference, [2019] | Includes
    bibliographical references.
Identifiers: LCCN 2018054313| ISBN 9781522584469 (h/c) | ISBN 9781522584476
    (eISBN) | ISBN 9781522585053 (s/c)
Subjects: LCSH: Database design. | Geospatial data. | Aerospace
    engineering--Data processing. | JSON (Document markup language)
Classification: LCC QA76.9.D26 E44 2019 | DDC 005.74/3--dc23 LC record available at https://lccn.loc.gov/2018054313

This book is published in the IGI Global book series Advances in Data Mining and Database Management (ADMDM) (ISSN: 2327-1981; eISSN: 2327-199X)

British Cataloguing in Publication Data
A Cataloguing in Publication record for this book is available from the British Library.

For electronic access to this publication, please contact: eresources@igi-global.com.

Advances in Data Mining and Database Management (ADMDM) Book Series

David Taniar
Monash University, Australia

ISSN:2327-1981
EISSN:2327-199X

MISSION

With the large amounts of information available to organizations in today's digital world, there is a need for continual research surrounding emerging methods and tools for collecting, analyzing, and storing data.

The **Advances in Data Mining & Database Management (ADMDM)** series aims to bring together research in information retrieval, data analysis, data warehousing, and related areas in order to become an ideal resource for those working and studying in these fields. IT professionals, software engineers, academicians and upper-level students will find titles within the ADMDM book series particularly useful for staying up-to-date on emerging research, theories, and applications in the fields of data mining and database management.

COVERAGE

- Web-based information systems
- Neural Networks
- Data Analysis
- Enterprise Systems
- Database Security
- Sequence analysis
- Cluster Analysis
- Profiling Practices
- Text Mining
- Predictive Analysis

IGI Global is currently accepting manuscripts for publication within this series. To submit a proposal for a volume in this series, please contact our Acquisition Editors at Acquisitions@igi-global.com or visit: http://www.igi-global.com/publish/.

Titles in this Series

For a list of additional titles in this series, please visit: www.igi-global.com/book-series

701 East Chocolate Avenue, Hershey, PA 17033, USA
Tel: 717-533-8845 x100 • Fax: 717-533-8661
E-Mail: cust@igi-global.com • www.igi-global.com

Table of Contents

Detailed Table of Contents

Chapter 1

Ruizhe Ma, Georgia State University, USA

Azim Ahmadzadeh, Georgia State University, USA

Soukaina Filali Boubrahimi, Georgia State University, USA

Rafal Angryk, Georgia State University, USA

Initially used in speech recognition, the dynamic time warping algorithm (DTW) has regained popularity with the widespread use of time series data. While demonstrating good performance, this elastic measure has two significant drawbacks: high computational costs and the possibility of pathological warping paths. Due to the balance between performance and the tightness of restrictions, the effects of many improvement techniques are either limited in effect or use accuracy as a trade-off. In this chapter, the authors discuss segmented-DTW (segDTW) and its applications. The intuition behind significant features is first established. Then considering the variability of different datasets, the relationship between specific global feature selection parameters, feature numbers, and performance are demonstrated. Other than the improvement in computational speed and scalability, another advantage of segDTW is that while it can be a stand-alone heuristic, it can also be easily combined with other DTW improvement methods.

Chapter 2

Zhen Hua Liu, Oracle, USA

Being a simple semi-structured data model, JSON has been widely accepted as a simple way to store, query, modify, and exchange data among applications. In comparison with schema-oriented relational data model to store, query, and update application data, JSON data model has the advantage of being self-contained, free from schema evolution issues, and flexible enough to enable agile style development paradigm. Therefore, during the last 5 years, SQL/JSON standard has been established as foundation for managing JSON data in SQL standard and there have been JSON functionalities added into RDBMS products to support SQL/JSON standard to various degree. In this chapter, the authors will analyze the strength and weakness of using JSON as the data model to manage data for applications. For use cases where JSON data model is ideal, they present the design approaches to store, index, query, and update JSON in the kernel of RDBMS to support SQL/JSON standard defined operations effectively and efficiently.

Chapter 3

The World Wide Web is a bunch of interlinked documents full of information and knowledge where people search sources to interpret relevant information. As the modern web is becoming more interactive and data-centric, it is necessary to focus on how to exchange data efficiently, easily, and quickly. There are several ways to exchange data among web services like XML and JSON. JSON is one of its kind of emerging data-interchange format. Its data model maps the type system of many programming languages is recommended for web development, especially Java scripting language. Previously, JSON was the focus by NoSQL community, but presently, the relational database community also claims to manage both relational and JSON data in one platform efficiently. This chapter focuses on various approaches to use JSON stores with NoSQL and relational database systems. The study reveals work accomplished so far to identify the working of JSON Stores as NoSQL stores and role relational system plays to enhance the power of JSON stores.

Chapter 4

Along with the rapid development of ICT technologies, new areas like Industry 4.0, IoT, and 5G have emerged and brought out the need for protecting shared resources and services under time-critical and energy-constrained scenarios with real-time policy-based access control. To achieve this, the policy language needs to be very expressive but lightweight and efficient. These challenges are investigated and a set of key requirements for such a policy language is identified. JACPoL is accordingly introduced as a descriptive, scalable, and expressive policy language in JSON. JACPoL by design provides a flexible and fine-grained ABAC style (attribute-based access control) while it can be easily tailored to express other access control models. The design and implementation of JACPoL are illustrated together with its evaluation in comparison with other existing policy languages. The result shows that JACPoL can be as expressive as existing ones but more simple, scalable, and efficient. The performance evaluation shows that JACPoL requires much less processing time and memory space than XACML.

Chapter 5

As a data format, JSON is able to store and exchange data. It can be mapped with RDF (resource description framework), which is an ontology technology in the direction of web resources. This chapter replies to the question about which techniques or methods to utilize for mapping XML to JSON and RDF. However, a plethora of methods have been explored. Consequently, the goal of this survey is to give the whole presentation of the currents approaches to map JSON with XML and RDF by providing their differences.

Chapter 6

Safa Brahmia, University of Sfax, Tunisia
Zouhaier Brahmia, University of Sfax, Tunisia
Fabio Grandi, University of Bologna, Italy
Rafik Bouaziz, University of Sfax, Tunisia

The JSON Schema language lacks explicit support for defining time-varying schemas of JSON documents. Moreover, existing JSON NoSQL databases (e.g., MongoDB, CouchDB) do not provide any support for managing temporal data. Hence, administrators of JSON NoSQL databases have to use ad hoc techniques in order to specify JSON schema for time-varying instances. In this chapter, the authors propose a disciplined approach, named Temporal JSON Schema (τJSchema), for the temporal management of JSON documents. τJSchema allows creating a temporal JSON schema from (1) a conventional JSON schema, (2) a set of temporal logical characteristics, for specifying which components of a JSON document can vary over time, and (3) a set of temporal physical characteristics, for specifying how the time-varying aspects are represented in the document. By using such characteristics to describe temporal aspects of JSON data, τJSchema guarantees logical and physical data independence and provides a low-impact solution since it requires neither updates to existing JSON documents nor extensions to related JSON technologies.

Chapter 7

Zhangbing Hu, Nanjing University of Aeronautics and Astronautics, China
Li Yan, Nanjing University of Aeronautics and Astronautics, China

As a ubiquitous form of data in human natural life, time has been widely used in military, finance, medical treatment, environment and other fields. Therefore, temporal data models used to express the dynamic development process of data have been proposed constantly. Currently, the main research achievements focus on temporal database and temporal XML. With the rapid development and popularization of network technology, the requirement of efficiency and security is getting higher and higher. JSON, a new generation of data exchange language, has been widely used because of its lightweight, fast parsing and high transmission efficiency. However, modeling temporal information with JSON has not been studied enough. The chapter proposes a temporal data model based on JSON. What is more, the temporal query language and the JSON Schema is also mentioned.

Chapter 8

Luyi Bai, Northeastern University, China
Nan Li, Northeastern University, China
Chengjia Sun, Northeastern University, China
Yuan Zhao, Northeastern University, China

Since XML could benefit data management greatly and Markov chains have an advantage in data prediction, the authors study the methodology of predicting uncertain spatiotemporal data based on XML integrated with Markov chain. To accomplish this, first, the researchers devise an uncertain spatiotemporal data model based on XML. Then, the researchers put forward the method based on Markov chains to predict spatiotemporal data, which has taken the uncertainty into consideration. Next, the researchers apply the prediction method to meteorological field. Finally, the experimental results demonstrate the advantages the authors approach. Such a method of prediction could broaden the research field of spatiotemporal data, and provide a significant reference in the study of forecasting uncertain spatiotemporal data.

Chapter 9

Guanfeng Li, Ningxia University, China
Zongmin Ma, Nanjing University of Aeronautics and Astronautics, China

With the popularity of fuzzy RDF data, identifying correspondences among these data sources is an important task. Although there are some solutions addressing this problem in classical RDF datasets, existing methods do not consider fuzzy information which is an important property existing in fuzzy RDF graphs. In this article, we apply fuzzy graph to model the fuzzy RDF datasets and propose a novel similarity-oriented RDF graph matching approach, which makes full use of the 1-hop neighbor vertex and edge label information, and takes into account the fuzzy information of a fuzzy RDF graph. Based on the neighborhood similarity, we propose a breadth-first branch-and-bound method for fuzzy RDF graph matching, which uses a state space search method and uses truncation parameters to constrain the search. This algorithm can be used to identify the matched pairs.

Chapter 10

Xiangfu Meng, Liaoning Technical University, China
Lulu Zhao, Liaoning Technical University, China
Xiaoyan Zhang, Liaoning Technical University, China
Pan Li, Liaoning Technical University, China
Zeqi Zhao, Liaoning Technical University, China
Yue Mao, Liaoning Technical University, China

Existing spatial keyword query methods usually evaluate text relevancy according to the frequency of occurrence of query keywords in the text information associated to spatial objects, without considering the degree of preference of users to different query keywords, and without considering semantic relevancy. To deal with the above problems, this chapter proposes an interactive personalized spatial keyword querying approach which is divided into two stages. In the offline processing stage, Gibbs algorithm is adopted to estimate the thematic probability distribution of text information associated to spatial objects, and then an LDA model is used for semantic expansion of spatial data set.

Chapter 11

Wei Yan, Liaoning University, China

The kNN queries are special type of queries for massive spatial big data. The k-nearest neighbor queries (kNN queries), designed to find k nearest neighbors from a dataset S for every point in another dataset R, are useful tools widely adopted by many applications including knowledge discovery, data mining, and spatial databases. In cloud computing environments, MapReduce programming model is a well-accepted framework for data-intensive application over clusters of computers. This chapter proposes a method of kNN queries based on Voronoi diagram-based partitioning using k-means clusters in MapReduce programming model. Firstly, this chapter proposes a Voronoi diagram-based partitioning approach for massive spatial big data. Then, this chapter presents a k-means clustering approach for the object points based on Voronoi diagram. Furthermore, this chapter proposes a parallel algorithm for processing massive spatial big data using kNN queries based on k-means clusters in MapReduce programming model. Finally, extensive experiments demonstrate the efficiency of the proposed approach.

Chapter 12

In order to solve the problem of storage and query for massive XML data, a method of efficient storage and parallel query for a massive volume of XML data with Hadoop is proposed. This method can store massive XML data in Hadoop and the massive XML data is divided into many XML data blocks and loaded on HDFS. The parallel query method of massive XML data is proposed, which uses parallel XPath queries based on multiple predicate selection, and the results of parallel query can satisfy the requirement of query given by the user. In this chapter, the map logic algorithm and the reduce logic algorithm based on parallel XPath queries based using MapReduce programming model are proposed, and the parallel query processing of massive XML data is realized. In addition, the method of MapReduce query optimization based on multiple predicate selection is proposed to reduce the data transfer volume of the system and improve the performance of the system. Finally, the effectiveness of the proposed method is verified by experiment.

Chapter 13

The resource description framework (RDF) is a model for representing information resources on the web. With the widespread acceptance of RDF as the de-facto standard recommended by W3C (World Wide Web Consortium) for the representation and exchange of information on the web, a huge amount of RDF data is being proliferated and becoming available. So, RDF data management is of increasing importance and has attracted attention in the database community as well as the Semantic Web community. Currently, much work has been devoted to propose different solutions to store large-scale RDF data efficiently. In order to manage massive RDF data, NoSQL (not only SQL) databases have been used for scalable RDF data store. This chapter focuses on using various NoSQL databases to store massive RDF data. An up-to-date overview of the current state of the art in RDF data storage in NoSQL databases is provided. The chapter aims at suggestions for future research.

Chapter 14

Development and wide acceptance of data-driven applications in many aspects of our daily lives is generating waste volume of diverse data, which can be collected and analyzed to support various valuable decisions. Management and processing of this big data is a challenge. The development and extensive use of highly distributed and scalable systems to process big data have been widely considered. New data management architectures (e.g., distributed file systems and NoSQL databases) are used in this context. However, features of big data like their complexity and data analytics demands indicate that these concepts solve big data problems only partially. A development of so called NewSQL databases is highly relevant and even special category of big data management systems is considered. In this chapter, the authors discuss these trends and evaluate some current approaches to big data processing and analytics, identify the current challenges, and suggest possible research directions.

Chapter 15

Joan Maso, CREAF, Spain
Alaitz Zabala Torres, Universitat Autonoma de Barcelona, Spain
Peter Baumann, Jacobs University, Germany

Map browsers currently in place present maps and geospatial information using common image formats such as JPEG or PNG, usually created from a service on demand. This is a clear approach for a simple visualization map browser but prevents the browser from modifying the visualization since the content of the image file represents the intensity of colors of each pixel. In a desktop GIS, a coverage dataset is an array of values quantifying a certain property in each pixel of a subdomain of the space. The standard used to describe and distribute coverages is called web coverage service (WCS). Traditionally, encoding of coverages was too complex for map browsers implemented in JavaScript, relegating the WCS to a data download, a process that creates a file that will be later used in a desktop GIS. The combination of a coverage implementation schema in JSON, binary arrays, and HTML5 canvas makes it possible that web map browsers can be directly implemented in JavaScript.

Chapter 16

Palanivel Kuppusamy, Pondicherry University, India

Electronic learning or e-learning is the use of technology to enable learners to learn from anywhere and anytime. The delivery involves the use of electronic devices in some way to make available learning contents. Today, e-learning has drastically changed the educational environment. The e-learning methodology is a good example of green computing. Green computing refers to the study and practice of using computing resources in an eco-friendly manner. It is the practice of using computing resources in an energy efficient and environmentally friendly manner. In order to reduce costs, education services can be provided using cloud technology. The green cloud computing solutions save energy, reduce operational costs, and reduce carbon footprints on the environment. Hence, the objective is to provide a green cloud architecture to e-learning solutions. This architecture is addressing the issues such as improving resource use and reducing power consumption.

Chapter 17

Palanivel Kuppusamy, Pondicherry University, India

Smart education is now a typical feature in education emerging from information communications technologies (ICT) and the constant introduction of new technologies into institutional learning. The smart classroom aims users to develop skills, adapt, and use technologies in a learning context that produces elevated learning outcomes which leads to big data. The internet of things (IoT) is a new technology in which objects equipped with sensors, actuators, and processors communicate with each other to serve a meaningful purpose. The technologies are rapidly changing, and designing for these situations can be complex. Designing the IoT applications is a challenging issue. The existing standardization activities are often redundant IoT development. The reference architecture provides a solution to smart education for redundant design activities. The purpose of this chapter is to look at the requirements and architectures required for smart education. It is proposed to design a scalable and flexible IoT architecture tor smart education (IoTASE).

Preface

In recent years, advances in Web technology and the proliferation of sensors and mobile devices connected to the Internet have resulted in the generation of immense data sets available on the Web. To satisfy the need of application domains, we have witnessed *some emerging paradigms* for data processing and management such as XML (eXtensible Markup Language), JSON (JavaScript Object Notation), RDF (Resource Description Framework) and NoSQL (Not Only SQL) in addition to the classical databases. All these paradigms are required to manage not only massive data but also *some emerging data types* such as time series data, temporal/spatial/spatiotemporal data, and uncertain data. Given that diverse massive data need to be managed and processed effectively and efficiently, many *emerging technologies* have been developing and applying in the context of wide applications as well.

To manage and process diverse massive data organized in various paradigms, the technologies of Big Data and artificial intelligence have been widely investigated. In particular, some efforts have devoted to combine Big Data and artificial intelligence together towards big data intelligence. The research, development and application of data processing and management in Big Data and artificial intelligence environments are receiving increasing attention. By means of novel computing technologies, diverse massive data can be processed and managed, and this can support various problem solving and decision making effectively and efficiently. Emerging technologies and applications in data processing and management are the fields which must be investigated by academic researchers together with developers. Nowadays a lot of efforts have been devoted to the research and development of data processing and management in the emerging applications. As a result, some emerging technologies of data processing and management are investigated by researchers all around the world on the one hand. On the other hand, diverse massive data in many application domains are managed and analyzed in the emerging applications.

This book covers a fast-growing topic in great depth and focuses on emerging technologies and applications in data processing and management. It aims to provide a single record of emerging technologies and applications in data processing and management. The objective of the book is to provide state of the art information to academics, researchers and industry practitioners who are involved or interested in the study, use, design and development of advanced and emerging information technologies with ultimate aim to empower individuals and organizations in building competencies for exploiting the opportunities of the data and knowledge society. The book presents the latest results in technology research, design implementation and application development. The chapters of the book have been contributed by different authors and provide possible solutions for the different types of technological problems.

This book consists of seventeen chapters, covering several emerging technologies and applications in data processing and management.

The Dynamic Time Warping algorithm (DTW) has regained popularity with the widespread use of time series data. While demonstrating good performance, this elastic measure has two significant drawbacks: high computational costs and the possibility of pathological warping paths. The effects of many improvement techniques are either limited in effect or use accuracy as a trade-off. Ruizhe Ma *et al.* discuss segmented-DTW (segDTW) and its applications. They first establish the intuition behind significant features and then, considering the variability of different datasets, demonstrate the relationship between specific global feature selection parameters, feature numbers, and performance. Other than the improvement in computational speed and scalability, another advantage of segDTW is that while it can be a stand-alone heuristic, it can also be easily combined with other DTW improvement methods.

JSON (semi-structured) data model has been widely-accepted as a simple way to store, query, modify and exchange data among applications. In comparison with schema-oriented relational data model, JSON data model has the advantage of being self-contained, free from schema evolution issues and flexible enough to enable agile style development paradigm. Therefore, during the last 5 years, SQL/JSON standard has been established as foundation for managing JSON data in SQL standard and there have been JSON functionalities added into RDBMS products to support SQL/JSON standard to various degree. Zhen Hua Liu analyzes the strength and weakness of using JSON as the data model to manage data for applications. For use cases where JSON data model is ideal, he presents the design approaches to store, index, query and update JSON in the kernel of relational database management systems to support SQL/JSON standard defined operations effectively and efficiently.

As the Web is becoming more interactive and data centric, it is essential to exchange data on the Web efficiently, easily and quickly. There are several ways to exchange data among Web services like XML and JSON. JSON is a kind of emerging data-interchange format, which can map the type system of many programming languages recommended for Web development especially: Java Scripting language. Initially, JSON is only the focus of NoSQL community. Recently, relational database community also claims to manage both relational and JSON data in one platform efficiently. Lubna Irshad *et al.* focus on various approaches to store JSON with NoSQL and relational databases. They reveal the research works accomplished so far to identify working of JSON stores as NoSQL stores and relational systems, which can enhance the power of JSON stores.

New areas like Industry 4.0, IoT and 5G have emerged and brought out the need for protecting shared resources and services under time-critical and energy-constrained scenarios with real-time policy-based access control. To achieve this, the policy language needs to be very expressive but lightweight and efficient. Hao Jiang and Ahmed Bouabdallah investigate these challenges and identify a set of key requirements for such a policy language. They introduce JACPoL as a descriptive, scalable and expressive policy language in JSON. They illustrate the design and implementation of JACPoL together with its evaluation in comparison with other existing policy languages. The result shows that JACPoL can be as expressive as existing ones but more simple, scalable and efficient. The performance evaluation shows that JACPoL requires much less processing time and memory space than XACML.

Data model conversion is primordial since the data exchange on the Web is numerous. The trend is to get better application services for users, and easily manage data and involve data formats conversion for the web developers. JSON (JavaScript Object Notation) at first visual perception is engendered to supersede XML (Extensible Markup Language), which is able to store and exchange data. In addition, RDF (Resource Description Framework) is a meta-data model with semantics for web resources. Currently, a number of methods have been explored to map different data models. Gbéboumé Crédo Charles

ADJALLAH-KONDO and Zongmin Ma try to provide a survey on the techniques/methods that have been utilized for mapping XML to JSON and RDF. The goal of their survey is to present a whole presentation of the currents approaches for mapping JSON with XML and RDF by providing their differences.

JSON Schema language lacks explicit support for defining time-varying schemas of JSON documents. Existing NoSQL databases (e.g., MongoDB, CouchDB) do not provide any support for managing temporal data also. Safa Brahmia *et al.* propose a disciplined approach, named Temporal JSON Schema (τJSchema), for the temporal management of JSON documents. τJSchema allows creating a temporal JSON schema from (i) a conventional JSON schema, (ii) a set of temporal logical characteristics, for specifying which components of a JSON document can vary over time, and (iii) a set of temporal physical characteristics, for specify how the time-varying aspects are represented in the document. By using such characteristics to describe temporal aspects of JSON data, τJSchema guarantees logical and physical data independence and provides a low-impact solution since it requires neither updates to existing JSON documents, nor extensions to related JSON technologies.

Time is a ubiquitous form of data in real life and temporal data representation and processing have been widely investigated in diverse application domains. Temporal data models used to express the dynamic development process of data have been proposed constantly, including temporal database model and temporal XML model. With the rapid development and popularization of Web technology, JSON, being a new generation of data exchange language, has been widely used because of its lightweight, fast parsing and high transmission efficiency. However, few attentions have been paid to modeling temporal information with JSON. Zhangbing Hu and Li Yan propose a new temporal data model based on JSON, including the temporal JSON document and Schema. They further develop the JSON temporal query language.

Considering that XML can benefit data management greatly and Markov chain has an advantage in data prediction, Luyi Bai *et al.* investigate the methodology of predicting uncertain spatiotemporal data based on XML integrated with Markov chain. To accomplish this, they devise an uncertain spatiotemporal data model based on XML and then put forward a method based on Markov chain to predict spatio-temporal data, which has taken the uncertainty into consideration. They apply the proposed prediction method to meteorological field. The experimental results demonstrate the advantages of their prediction approach, which could contribute to broad field of spatiotemporal data and provide a significant reference in forecasting uncertain spatiotemporal data.

With the popularity of uncertain data, identifying correspondences among fuzzy RDF data sources is an important task. Although there are some solutions addressing this problem in classical RDF datasets, existing methods do not consider fuzzy information which is an important property existing in fuzzy RDF graphs. Guanfeng Li and Zongmin Ma apply fuzzy graph to model fuzzy RDF data and propose a novel similarity-oriented RDF graph matching approach. Their approach makes full use of the 1-hop neighbor vertex and edge label information and meanwhile takes the fuzzy information of fuzzy RDF graph into account. Based on the neighborhood similarity, they propose a breadth-first branch-and-bound algorithm for fuzzy RDF graph matching, which uses a state space search method and truncation parameters to constrain the search. Then the proposed algorithm can be used to identify the matched pairs.

Existing spatial keyword query methods usually evaluate text relevancy according to the frequency of occurrence of query keywords in the text information associated to spatial objects. These methods do not consider the degree of preference of users to different query keywords, and do not consider semantic relevancy also. To deal with the above-mentioned problems, Xiangfu Meng *et al.* propose an interactive personalized spatial keyword querying method. Their method is divided into two stages. At the first stage of offline processing, they adopt Gibbs algorithm to estimate the thematic probability distribution of text information associated to spatial objects. At the second stage, they apply LDA (Latent Dirichlet Allocation) model for semantic expansion of spatial data set.

The k nearest neighbor queries (kNN queries) are special type of queries for massive spatial big data. In cloud computing environments, MapReduce programming model is a well-accepted framework for data-intensive application over clusters of computers. Focusing on kNN queries based on Voronoi diagram-based partitioning using k-means clusters in MapReduce programming model, Wei Yan proposes a Voronoi diagram-based partitioning approach for massive spatial big data. Based on Voronoi diagram, he presents a k-means clustering approach for the object points. He further proposes a parallel algorithm for processing massive spatial big data using kNN queries based on k-means clusters in MapReduce programming model. Extensive experiments demonstrate the efficiency of the proposed approach.

To solve the problem of massive XML data storage and query, Wei Yan proposes a method of efficient storage and parallel query for massive XML data with Hadoop. With his method, the massive XML data is divided into many XML data blocks and loaded on HDFS and then, by using parallel XPath queries based on multiple predicate selection, the results of parallel query can satisfy the requirement of query given by the user. For this purpose, he proposes the Map logic algorithm and the Reduce logic algorithm based on parallel XPath queries by using MapReduce programming model, and then realizes the parallel query processing of massive XML data. Particularly, he proposes the method of MapReduce query optimization based on multiple predicate selection to reduce the data transfer volume of the system and improve the performance of the system. The effectiveness of the proposed method is verified by experiments.

The Resource Description Framework (RDF) is a model for representing information resources on the Web. With the widespread acceptance of RDF as the de-facto standard recommended by W3C (World Wide Web Consortium) for the representation and exchange of information on the Web, a huge amount of RDF data is being proliferated and becoming available. Nowadays, massive RDF data management is of increasing importance and has attracted more attentions in the database community as well as the Semantic Web community. Currently much work has been devoted to propose different solutions to store massive RDF data efficiently. To manage massive RDF data, NoSQL ("not only SQL") databases have been used for scalable RDF data store. Zongmin Ma and Li Yan concentrate on using various NoSQL databases to store massive RDF data. They provide an up-to-date overview of the current state of the art in RDF data storage in NoSQL databases, aiming at suggestions for future research.

Volume of diverse data can be collected and analysed to support various valuable decisions. Management and processing of this Big Data is a challenge. The development and extensive use of highly distributed and scalable systems to process Big Data have been widely considered. New data management architectures (e.g. distributed file systems and NoSQL databases) are used in this context. However, features of Big Data like their complexity and data analytics demands indicate that these concepts solve Big Data problems only partially. A development of so called NewSQL databases is highly relevant and even special category of Big Data Management Systems is considered. Jaroslav Pokorny and Bela Stantic discuss these trends and evaluate some current approaches to Big Data processing and analytics, identify the current challenges, and suggest possible research directions.

To demonstrate how JSON can be used to represent and transmit coverage information in standard way, Joan Maso *et al.* present and extend the work done in the elaboration of the version 1.1 of the Coverage Implementation Schema (CIS) released as a conceptual model and three encodings, one of them in JSON. They present a successful stress test that demonstrates the applicability of the generic rules for directly derive JSON from UML class diagrams proposed in the Testbed. The JSON encoding for CIS is able to represent gridded and discrete as well as continuous coverages as defined by CIS. The data model covers the definition of the array of values (rangeSet) together with the description of the rules to generate the domainSet from axes or directly to individual geometries, and the semantics of the values (rangeType), plus any additional metadata. The JSON objects are instances of the UML class model.

e-Learning enables learners to learn from anywhere and anytime, which has drastically changed the educational environment. The e-Learning methodology is a good example of green computing. Green computing refers to the study and practice of using computing resources in an eco-friendly manner. K. Palanivel and T. Chithralekha design a green cloud architecture to e-Learning solutions, which can decrease the energy consumption of clouds without affecting the service providers' objectives. The proposed architecture includes the architectural roles and the components. This architecture complies with a standard cloud architecture, considering the classical SaaS, PaaS and IaaS layers and supporting components such as energy consumption, the infrastructure monitor and etc. They address the energy efficiency of the architecture at all layers of the cloud software stack during the complete lifecycle of a cloud application.

The use of ICT (Information and Communications Technology) techniques in learning/teaching has a very positive influence on a student's learning capabilities. K. Palanivel explains the need and significance of IoT (Internet of Things) as well as its applications with a specific focus on smart education. He presents an education model and proposes an e-learning architecture with smart objects. Aiming to use e-Learning architecture with smart objects, he designs complex learning scenarios, which keep track of the learner's learning experience. This architecture grants interoperability between standards and to provide context-aware activities to learners. However, IoT in smart learning is progressing very fast and so.

Acknowledgment

The editors wish to thank all of the authors for their insights and excellent contributions to this book and would like to acknowledge the help of all involved in the collation and review process of the book, without whose support the project could not have been satisfactorily completed. Most of the authors of chapters included in this book also served as referees for chapters written by other authors. Thanks go to all those who provided constructive and comprehensive reviews.

A further special note of thanks goes to all the staff at IGI Global, whose contributions throughout the whole process from inception of the initial idea to final publication have been invaluable. Special thanks also go to the publishing team at IGI Global. This book would not have been possible without the ongoing professional support from IGI Global.

The idea of editing this volume stems from the initial research work that the editors did in past several years. The research work of the editor was supported by the *National Natural Science Foundation of China* (61772269, 61370075 & 61572118).

Zongmin Ma
Nanjing University of Aeronautics and Astronautics, China

Li Yan
Nanjing University of Aeronautics and Astronautics, China
April 2019

Chapter 1
Segmented Dynamic Time Warping:
A Comparative and Applicational Study

Ruizhe Ma
Georgia State University, USA

Azim Ahmadzadeh
Georgia State University, USA

Soukaina Filali Boubrahimi
Georgia State University, USA

Rafal Angryk
Georgia State University, USA

ABSTRACT

Initially used in speech recognition, the dynamic time warping algorithm (DTW) has regained popularity with the widespread use of time series data. While demonstrating good performance, this elastic measure has two significant drawbacks: high computational costs and the possibility of pathological warping paths. Due to the balance between performance and the tightness of restrictions, the effects of many improvement techniques are either limited in effect or use accuracy as a trade-off. In this chapter, the authors discuss segmented-DTW (segDTW) and its applications. The intuition behind significant features is first established. Then considering the variability of different datasets, the relationship between specific global feature selection parameters, feature numbers, and performance are demonstrated. Other than the improvement in computational speed and scalability, another advantage of segDTW is that while it can be a stand-alone heuristic, it can also be easily combined with other DTW improvement methods.

DOI: 10.4018/978-1-5225-8446-9.ch001

INTRODUCTION

Different data and applications usually require different distance measures. Generally speaking, distance measures can be categorized as either a lock-step measure or an elastic measure. Lock-step measure commonly refers to L_p-norms, meaning that the i-th element from one sequence is always mapped to the i-th element in the compared sequence. Since the mapping between the two sequences is fixed, lock-step measures are sensitive to noise and misalignments (Ranacher et al., 2014). The elastic measure, on the other hand, allows one-to-many, or even one-to-none mappings (Wang et al., 2013). A suitable distance measure should be chosen based on the data and task at hand.

With the improvement of data storage capability and processing power, more and more data are now being collected and used in the form of time series. Time series data is widely applied in a variety of domains, such as voice recognition, the stock market, solar activities, medical research, and many other scientific and engineering fields where measurements in the temporal sense are important. Time series data enjoys its popularity because it records details that can be overlooked by the summarization of data. At the same time, small temporal discrepancies and unequal length are very common in time series sequences. This length difference means lock-step distance measures are not as effective as elastic measures when identifying similarities in time series data (Ranacher et al., 2014).

A widely used elastic measure is the Dynamic Time Warping (DTW) algorithm (Serra et al., 2014). The warping path, or shortest global route, for DTW is identified based on the computation and comparisons of several options at each step. While this contributes to the general success of the DTW algorithm's performance with time series data, the large- scale computations make DTW a very time-consuming algorithm. Another common issue to run into when using DTW is the occurrence of pathological warping path, which happens when the warping path tries to compensate value differences by making wild and improbable mappings, as shown in Figure 1 (a). When the path is found in a greedy manner and never readjusted, the optimal warping path could be permanently missed. The root cause of pathological warping paths is that the decision at each step does not take significant global similarities into consideration; in other words, the bigger picture is neglected in standard DTW. In application, we can often observe the warping path between two time series does not match the expected intuitive mapping. Previously, it has been found that segmentation of time series based on feature peaks can alleviate this problem (Ma et al., 2018). Global similarity can be identified by adding a layer of peak identification, which acts as a form of restraints, then the focus on local similarity is found by mapping the points and computing the distances of each corresponding segments.

Figure 1 shows the mapping comparison between the standard DTW algorithm and an example of segDTW with peaks. Here the standard DTW is showing signs of pathological warpings, which does not match our intuitive expectations. In contrast, by identifying two peaks and segmenting the two time series into three paired segments, the mapping provides more intuitive results. Theoretically, any feature extracted from the data that could meaningfully segment time series can be used. When features are identified and paired, not only do we obtain a more intuitive mapping, but also makes it possible and exceptionally easy to parallelize DTW computation within a time series sequence. This segmentation makes our method scalable and sets segDTW apart from other DTW improvement heuristics.

Achieving speedup by segmenting one computation into several pieces of simultaneous computations is to be expected. Therefore, in this chapter, we establish the meaning and importance of intuitive segmentation, by comparing peak and valley segmentation against equal-window segmentation. This

Figure 1. A comparison between standard DTW and segDTW, (a) is the mapping of standard DTW, which is computed linearly and is showing signs of a pathological warping path, (b) shows the mapping results of segDTW with peak identification, and each segment can be simultaneously computed. Hence, segDTW can generate faster and more intuitive results.

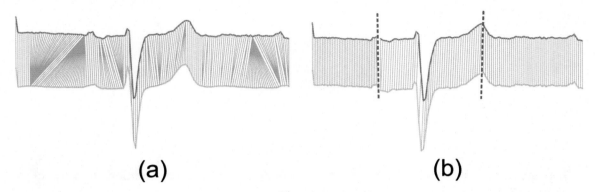

(a)   (b)

comparison is also proof that only meaningful segmentation is useful for segDTW. Our next focus is the accuracy performance of segDTW. Due to the vast difference between different datasets, it is near impossible to obtain a set of universally good parameters for segmentation. As such, we examine the performance of different datasets when different applied segmentation parameters and show the best results specific to each dataset. When used as a stand-alone heuristic, segDTW can avoid most pathological warping path, obtain intuitive mappings, and speed up the computation. Furthermore, segDTW can also be combined and layered with other DTW improvement techniques to obtain further enhancement. The balance between the tightness of constraints and computation efficiency should be user dependent.

The rest of this chapter is organized as follows: Section 2 gives the background on DTW improvement methods; Section 3 presents segDTW and the feature pairing technique; Section 4 shows the effectiveness of segDTW, how the performance of segDTW is associated with feature selection and demonstrates how it can be used in conjunction with other methods; finally, Section 5 concludes this chapter.

BACKGROUND

Dynamic Time Warping

Dynamic Time Warping (DTW) was originally used in speech recognition (Sakoe et al., 1978), human speech is regarded as a form of sequential data. Later it was introduced to the computer science community and was adapted to various real-world data mining problems. By allowing one-to-many mappings, DTW can measure the similarity between two temporal sequences which may vary in time or speed. This added elasticity to similarity measure allows computers to mimic shape identification, and can, therefore, find an optimal mapping between two given sequences.

Given two time series sequences Q and C, with $Q = \left\{q_1, q_2, \ldots, q_i, \ldots, q_n\right\}$ and $C = \left\{c_1, c_2, \ldots, c_j, \ldots, c_m\right\}$, Equations 1 and 2 show the computation for Euclidean and DTW distances respectively, with Euclidean only applicable for equal length sequences (i.e., $n = m$), while DTW is applicable for sequences of both equal and unequal length.

$$dist\left(Euclidean\right) = \sqrt{\sum_{i=1}^{n}\left(q_i - c_i\right)^2}$$

(1)

$$D\left(i,j\right) = dist\left(q_i - c_j\right) + \min\begin{cases}D\left(i, j-1\right)\\ i-1, j-1\\ i-1, j\end{cases}$$

(2)

There are three basic conditions in the DTW algorithm: the boundary condition, monotonicity, and continuity (Müller, 2007). The boundary condition means that the first and last components from two compared sequences are always mapped, and because DTW only allows one-to-many mapping and not one-to-none mapping, every element has to have a mapping component. Mapping within a pair of time series cannot cross, because it would not make sense on the time scale. Monotonicity means time can only proceed in one direction and that the warping path cannot go back in time. The continuity constraint is also known as the step pattern constraint; it is where the warping path can only follow the predetermined steps patterns and cannot make any jumps. The continuity constraint is also a form of eliminating one-to-none mapping and implies monotonicity.

The standard DTW algorithm first constructs an m-by-n matrix, which contains the distance information between all the elements from the two time series. Each axis of the matrix represents the time in one time series; this matrix is referred to as the cost matrix. An example of such a matrix is illustrated in Figure 2 (Salvador et al., 2007). An entry of this matrix, $D\left(i, j\right)$, is the minimum-distance warping path that can be constructed from time series $Q = \left\{q_1, q_2, \ldots, q_i\right\}$ and $C = \left\{c_1, c_2, \ldots, c_j\right\}$. $D\left(n, m\right)$ denotes the minimum-distance warping path between Q and C. An optimal warping path, denoted as w_k, can then be found based on the constructed matrix. Starting from the last constructed point of the matrix which is $D\left(n, m\right)$, assuming $D\left(i, j\right)$ is already chosen to be a part of the optimal path, and the three allowed candidate steps are: $D\left(i, j-1\right)$, $D\left(i-1, j-1\right)$, and $D\left(i-1, j\right)$. The step with the minimum value will be added to the warping path, to satisfy the objective of keeping the cost of the warping path minimal.

This continues until the point $w_1 = D\left(1,1\right)$ is reached. The optimal warping path for this example is shown as the black line that passes through the matrix in Figure 2 (a), which connects the bottom-left cell to the top-right cell. This path, as a proximity measure between the time series, can be interpreted as the warping path passing through entry $D\left(i, j\right)$, where the point q_i is mapped to point c_j in such a way that the total cost of such warping is minimal. While there are exponentially many warping paths, only the minimized path is of interest (Keogh et al., 2001). A trivial minimal warping path would be formed as a straight diagonal line when the two time series are identical, which would then become the Euclidean distance.

The above example illustrates the elasticity of the DTW measure. Shown in Figure 2 (a), when the warping path forms a vertical line, it means a single point in Q is mapped to multiple points in C. Conversely, when the warping path is horizontal, multiple points from Q are mapped to a single point in C. While the effectiveness of DTW can be attributed to this elasticity, it can also cause low efficiency. When a large number of consecutive points from one time series is mapped with one single point from the other time series to the point it no longer represents the actual situation, it could lead to singularity and create a pathological warping path.

The major bottleneck of DTW computation is the time and space complexity. Calculation of the cost matrix requires $n \bullet m$ operations that can be done in constant time, hence $O\left(n^2\right)$, where $N = n = m$. As in many datasets, such as sensor-based data, stock market time series, etc., the sequences of interest are relatively lengthy, meaning the quadratic time complexity becomes nontrivial. Also, since DTW requires the entire cost matrix to construct the optimal warping path, the space complexity of the algorithm is also quadratic, $O\left(n^2\right)$. This high complexity is particularly important since time series are high-dimensional data and the polynomial space complexity would quickly exhaust gigabytes and even terabytes of memory. In the next section, we review some of the well-known approaches that deals with the problems of DTW.

Existing DTW Improvement Methods

By allowing elastic mapping, DTW provides more intuitive alignments between sequential data such as time series. However, despite its general success, DTW often attempts to explain the variability on the

Figure 2. An example of the standard DTW for time series Q and C, with respective lengths m and n. The identified warping path passing through $D\left(1,1\right)$ and $D\left(n,m\right)$ is represented as the black line passing through the matrix. At each step, the allowed mapping choice which introduces the minimal dissimilarity value to the overall warping path is chosen, thus satisfying the objective of keeping the cost of the warping path minimal.

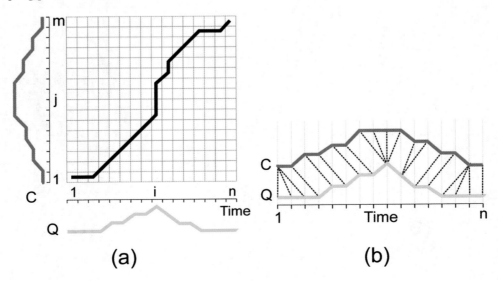

(a)   (b)

y-axis of the similarity matrix by warping on the x-axis. This compensation is the cause of the undesirable phenomenon of singularity and could lead to pathological warpings (Keogh et al., 2001). When pathological warpings occur, the DTW algorithm can no longer provide us with sensible or reliable results.

For DTW algorithm improvement both quality-wise and efficiency-wise, many methods have been proposed. Overall, time series data analysis can be categorized as whole-sequence-analysis and sub-sequence analysis. Whole sequence analysis improvement techniques can be further categorized as global constraints and approximations. The goal of global constraints is the attempt to place restraints on the warping path, and shortening the processing time by eliminating computations. Time series data are high- dimensional and approximations are the attempt to manipulate the input time series as a means to lower data dimensionality and cut-down on the number of comparison computations. In the extreme case, one time series sequence can be abstracted to one number, such as the mean or median of the sequence; this type of statistical abstraction is commonly used in traditional non-time series data analysis. Here we discuss some of the more commonly applied DTW improvement methods for whole sequence analysis.

Windowing is a global constraint and has been used by different researchers before it was formally summarized by Berndt and Clifford (Berndt et al., 1994). Windowing effectively prunes the corners of the distance matrix, where the warping path are not allowed to venture to, meaning the potential warping path is restrained to a fixed region. This method can alleviate some of the singularity problems but cannot prevent it (Biba et al., 2011). Two of the well-known global windowing constraints are shown in Figure 3, including the Sakoe-Chiba Band (Sakoe et al., 1978), which is a slanted diagonal window, and Itakura parallelogram (Itakura, 1975), which is a parallelogram-shaped window. The window sizes can be adjusted according to user requirements. When the windows are minimum in size where only the straight diagonal path is allowed, and DTW becomes the Euclidean distance.

Figure 3. DTW windows: (a) Sakoe-Chiba Band and (b) Itakura Parallelogram, only the colored cells will be computed, thus improving efficiency. Additionally, since the warping path is constrained, the occurrence of pathological warpings can be reduced.

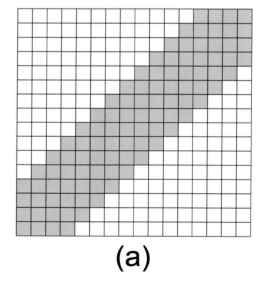

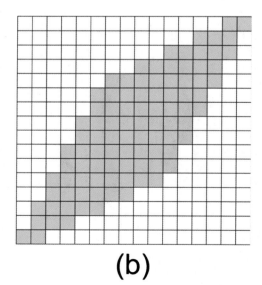

(a)   (b)

Slope weighting encourages the warping path to remain close to the diagonal. When a weighting factor is generally applied to the whole sequence, it is a global constraint. Depending on the specific weighting factor, it reduces the frequency of singularities (Kruskall, 1983). The weight factor would depend on user specifications.

Step pattern is a global constraint approach which encourages changes to the warping path to avoid pathological paths. Based on symmetry and slope bounds, Sakoe and Chiba proposed *symmetric1*, *symmetric2* (Sakoe et al., 1978), and *asymmetric* (Sakoe et al., 1973) approaches. The first is a basic step pattern. The second favors the diagonal warping path similar to slope weighting, and the third limits time expansion to a factor of two. Rabin and Juang introduced *rabinerJuangStepPattern* (Rabiner et al., 1993) based on the continuity constraint, slope weighting, and the state of being smooth or Boolean. We will be using the symmetric1 step pattern for segDTW and all the experiments supporting this chapter.

Lower bounding is another global constraint for improving the DTW algorithm. By defining tight and fast lower bounding functions, sequences that cannot provide a better match in the process of finding the warping path are pruned. The idea is to favor the execution time needed for calculating the similarity matrices on large datasets. While Yi et al. (Yi et al., 1998) gave an approximation for indexing, the lower bounding function introduced in LB_Kim (Kim et al., 2001) was the first to define exact indexing. Compared to the earlier works, LB _Keogh (Keogh et al., 2005) had an overall greater pruning power and could also give tighter bounding measures. Their lower bounding function is defined based on U and L, the two new time series generated from the reference time series Q, such that $U_i = \max\left(q_{i-r}, q_{i+r}\right)$ and $L_i = \min\left(q_{i-r}, q_{i+r}\right)$. Where $j - r \leq i \leq j + r$ and r is used to define the allowed warping range. Having the bounding envelope defined by U and L, the lower bounding function is defined as "the squared sum of the distances from every part of the candidate sequence C not falling within the bounding envelope, to the nearest orthogonal edge of the bounding envelope" (Keogh et al., 2005).

Among other variants of the DTW method, PDTW (piece-wise DTW) (Keogh et al., 2000), DDTW (derivative DTW) (Keogh et al., 2001), and shapeDTW (Zhao et al., 2018) are some other methods which attempt to manipulate the input time series to improve either the warping path or the processing time. The primary achievement of PDTW is to increase the speed factor by one to two orders of magnitude on average, while maintaining the accuracy of DTW, by utilizing a piece-wise approximated representation of the time series instead of the raw data. Similarly, DDTW utilizes an approximated

Figure 4: Step Patterns: (a) symmetric1 is the basic step pattern, (b) symmetric2 favors the diagonal warping path, (c) asymmetric limits time expansion to a factor of two, and (d) rabinerJuangStepPattern has attributes local continuity constraint type, slope weighting, and the state of smoothed or not.

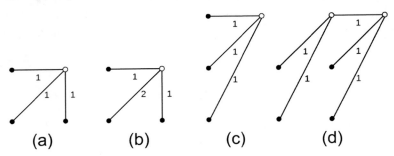

derivative of the time series to work on a higher level of similarity between two time series. A similar approach is also used in shapeDTW. Zhao et al. represented each temporal point q_i of a time series Q by a shape descriptor which encodes the structural information of a fixed-width neighborhood of q_i. The choice of the descriptor depends on the general structure of the time series and the user requirements. Some of the widely used descriptors are the slope, piece-wise aggregate approximation (PAA), discrete wavelet transform (DWT), and the histogram of oriented gradient for 1-D time series (HOG1D).

The methods discussed so far are based on either the constraints, data abstraction, or indexing (Salvador et al., 2007). Windowing, slope weighting, and step pattern approaches fall into the constrained group, whereas heuristics such as DDTW, shapeDTW, and pDTW, belong to the data abstraction group. The idea behind the constraints group is to avoid pathological warpings by trying to encourage the warping path to stay close to the diagonal rather than to stray excessively vertical or horizontal. While the abstraction family of methods uses coarsely granulated data to avoid detail pitfalls that could potentially cause pathological warpings. The third category revolves around lower bounding is also referred to as indexing. The methods which utilize indexing are different from the other two in the sense that they are mainly focused on speeding up the algorithm. It is important to note that constraints and data abstraction improve the time and space complexity only by a constant factor since they still have to deal with the cost matrix, which results in both the time and space complexity to remain quadratic. However, the third group made a significant contribution in this aspect by bringing the computation time and space down to $O(N)$ using different indexing methods (Kim et al., 2001) (Keogh et al., 2005).

Regardless of the elimination of certain calculations or data abstraction, to the best of our knowledge, the computation of each pair of time series in other DTW improvement heuristic is done linearly. Which means the computational time is proportional to the length of the given time series, and therefore the extent of speedups is limited. Our previous work introduced the segDTW heuristic, in this chapter we perform a more comprehensive evaluation as well as introducing the applicational aspect of segDTW (Ma et al., 2019). In the following section, we explain how segDTW can break the computation linearity and achieves scalability.

Segmented Dynamic Time Warping: segDTW

The tightness of global constraints for DTW is an issue not often discussed. Generally, it is not easy to determine the tightness of constraints or the level of dimensionality reduction in DTW improvement methods. For example, when the window constraint becomes too tight, DTW degenerates to the Euclidean distance. Alternatively, when the dimension of time series is reduced too much, the significance of using time series data is dissipated. segDTW differs from previous works in the sense that it is designed to break the linearity barrier and parallelize the computation of DTW. Through detecting time series' data features and segmenting accordingly, a layer of approximation is added prior to DTW distance computation. While this idea is straightforward, it is extremely effective in providing scalability and improving speed.

TIME SERIES SEGMENTATION

The problem with a global optimal solution for DTW improvement is that it often misses the big picture of global similarities in time series. If a global constraint is too tight, it can hurt the overall performance and in the more extreme cases, render the use of time series futile. segDTW, on the other hand, can divide the problem of finding the global optimal mapping into smaller, more manageable pieces.

The pairing of corresponding features is used for segmentation. Figure 5 (a) shows the standard DTW mapping between two time series Q and C, peaks a, b, c, a', b', and c' can be considered as significant feature peaks. However, with standard DTW, various points around a are mapped to a', the same is true for b and b'. Being a variant of DTW, the basic conditions of boundary, monotonicity, and continuity are also applicable for segDTW. As an effect of the boundary condition for segDTW computation, endpoints for each segment are specifically mapped. This method can alleviate singularities, minimize mismatches and avoid pathological warping paths. Next, the optimal DTW mapping is found for each subsequence, and the distances of all the sub-sequences are aggregated to obtain the overall distance between two time series sequences.

Another way to understand segDTW is to consider it as a form of dynamic windows. When the three peaks are identified a, b, and c are mapped to a', b', and c' respectively, as is shown in Figure 5 (a), they correspond to the three dots in Figure 5 (b). The paired peaks define the colored squares which can be seen as dynamic-warping windows. Mappings outside these sub-windows do not need to be computed, and this is extremely important since not only does it speed up the computation, but also provides more intuitive results. The computations pruned off by the segDTW model is not done for the sole purpose of achieving a lower computational cost, but more importantly, the choice is justified by intuitive mapping. Based on the behavior of time series sequences, the detected global similarities place a coarse constraint. Compared to global constraints, segDTW allows more freedom for a warping path to develop within each sub-window (segment pair). In practice, depending on user requirements and preferences, traditional warping windows can be layered within the sub-windows for further speedups.

Figure 5. (a) Standard DTW mapping where the three pairs of identified peaks are not all cleanly mapped. (b) Dissimilarity matrix needed for segDTW with identified peaks.

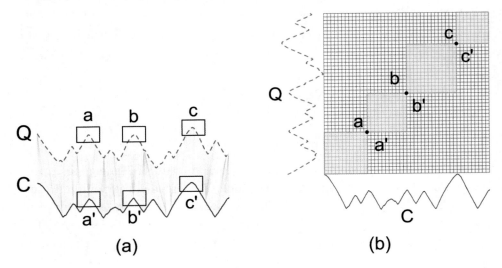

(a)   (b)

Here we reiterate the peak/valley feature detection heuristic. The naive definition of a peak is formulated as follows: the temporal index i corresponds to the peak c_i, if $c_i > c_{i-1}$ and $c_i > c_{i+1}$, and c_i is referred to as candidate peaks. Similarly, a valley can be formulated as the temporal index i corresponds to the valley c_i, if $c_i < c_{i-1}$ and $c_i < c_{i+1}$, and c_i is referred to as candidate valley. This simple definition equipped with peak/valley selection parameters t, d, and n form a peak/valley detection method that provides the criteria necessary to distinguish a set of selected peak/valley used in segDTW referred to as significant peaks/valleys.

- t: Threshold on the frequency domain. Any candidate peaks below t will be ignored for peak detection, and any candidate valley above t will be ignored for valley detection.
- d: The minimum peak/valley radius. For any identified peak/valley, any adjacent peak/valley within a radius of d will be considered as either noise or insignificant.
- n: The maximum number of features to be taken into account. Since the values of features are sorted before being analyzed, only the top n features that have met the other criteria will be considered.

For simplicity, Algorithm 1 only shows the selection for feature peaks, but the conditions can simply be changed according to the previous description for valley detection. Initially, all candidate peaks are found and sorted based on their values. Then, the threshold t on the frequency domain is applied, and all the candidate peaks below the threshold will be removed from the list. For the remaining peaks, the neighboring peaks within the radius of d temporal indices will then be removed. The algorithm processes the peaks in a top-down fashion. This is to guarantee that the presence of a smaller peak will never justify the removal of a larger peak. Finally, the top n peaks can be optionally picked among the remaining peaks in the list.

In the worst scenario, the time complexity of segDTW, if implemented as described, is

$$\max\left\{O\left(\left\lceil \frac{\left(p \bullet \left(p+1\right)\right)}{2} \right\rceil\right), s\right\}$$ where p is the number of candidate peaks/valleys and s is the time bound

of the utilized sorting algorithm. The worst case refers to the situation where $d = 0$, $n = \infty$, and $t = \min\left(C\right)$. However, by taking the order of the indices into account, in addition to the order of the values, the time complexity would only be determined by the sorting step. Hence, the worst-case running time would be decreased to $O\left(n \bullet \log\left(n\right)\right)$ which reflects the complexity of a sort algorithm such as merge or heap sort.

FEATURE PAIRING

Once the features are identified, we need to pair the detected features. The mapping method in such a situation plays a crucial role in achieving sensible results. A prerequisite condition for segDTW is that it has to satisfy all the basic requirements of DTW, namely boundary, monotonicity, and continuity conditions. This can be extended to the condition that no set of paired features in segDTW could cross another pair of features, as this would be a violation of the monotonicity requirement of DTW. Since

Algorithm 1 Time Series Peak Selection

Input: $C = \left\{ c_1, \cdots, c_m \right\}$ **time series data,**

t: the minimum threshold on the frequency domain,

d: the minimum radius from a selected peak,

n: the maximum number of peaks allowed.

Output: the list of peaks with both their indices and values.

procedure *FIND PEAKS*

$significant.peaks$, $candidates \leftarrow list()$

for all $c_i \in C$ **do**

if $((c_i > c_{i+1})$ **&** $((c_i < c_{i-1})$ **then**

$candidates.add\left(\left(i, c_i \right) \right)$

end if

end for

$peaks \leftarrow sortByValue \left(candidates \right)$

for all $\left(i, c_i \right) \in peaks$ **do**

if $c_i < t$ **then**

$peaks.remove\left(\left(i, c_i \right) \right)$

end if

end for

$indices \leftarrow peaks.getIndices()$

for all $i \in indices$ **do**

for all $j \in \left\{ i - d, \cdots, i + d \right\}$ **do**

if $peaks.hasIndex\left(j \right)$ **then**

$peaks.remove\left(\left(j, c_i \right) \right)$

end if

end for

end for

$significant.peaks \leftarrow peaks.getNFirstElements\left(n \right)$

return $significant.peaks$;

end procedure

segDTW is made up of standard DTW, when boundary and continuity requirements are satisfied for each time series segment, they are automatically satisfied as a whole.

The mapping of features, in many situations, is a subjective task and it is not always possible to agree on any ground truth even when visually analyzing the time series. Therefore, we set our goal to minimize the total distances of the pairs. To this end, we employ the Hungarian algorithm (Kuhn, 1955) in order to achieve a global optimum feature pairing. This is a generalized choice, depending on the situation, this choice can be alternated with any other user preferred method that potentially suits the dataset or task at hand.

The Hungarian algorithm is a well-known assignment problem which is regarded as a relative of the traveling salesman problem. The assignment problem is formulated as follows: given an n by n matrix $R = \left(r_{ij} \right)$ of non-negative integers, the objective is to find the permutation $\left\{ j_1, j_2, \cdots, j_n \right\}$ of the integers $\left\{ 1, 2, \cdots, n \right\}$ such that it minimizes the sum $r_{ij_1} + r_{ij_2} + \cdots + r_{ij_n}$. The Hungarian method utilizes linear programming to tackle this problem. Although the assignment problem can always be reduced to the case where R takes only ones and zeros, representing paired and non-paired integers, it is not limited to this binary case. In addition, the problem can be easily extended to the non-square matrices. Thus, this approach is a natural choice and is well suited for our feature-pairing problem. The sequence of the integers, in this context, is the temporal indices of the features in the two time series, Q and C, and the permutation of interest is the mapping between the features of one time series with the other. The entries of the assignment matrix R for our problem can be defined as follows:

$$r_{ij} = \text{temporal distance between} \, \hat{q}_i \, \text{and} \, \hat{c}_j$$

where $\hat{q}_i$ and $\hat{c}_j$ are the i-th and j-th feature in the time series Q and C, respectively. The objective here is to find a permutation that minimizes the total temporal distance of the features.

Two important adjustments to the original Hungarian algorithm need to be made to fully customize this solution to fit the task of pairing significant features. Our main objective here in adjusting the feature pairing method is to mimic the human decision-making process. First, the algorithm must avoid situations where two pairs of features are mapped in reverse temporal order. The mapping of one pair crossing the mapping of another pair of features is a violation of the monotonicity requirement of DTW. Coincidentally, this also ensures the algorithm to drop the more costly feature mappings. Second, when the number of significant features is different in the two time series, which occurs more often than not, only those contributing to the global optimum are selected. The pairing of features are high-level decisions that must be made even when a practitioner is assigned to tackle subjective tasks of this kind, and in most cases, the most optimal decision is the one that aligns with our intuition.

Experiments

When the peak selection radius d is large or when the peak threshold t is large, generally fewer peaks are identified, which means fewer sub-sequences. In the extreme case, when no peaks are detected, and no segmentation is imposed, segDTW degenerates to standard DTW. In contrast, when the peak detection radius is small or when the peak threshold is low, there are more peaks and sub-sequences, which leads to more segments and potentially shorter processing time. However, more segments in time series sequences introduce risks of identifying false peaks, which could lead to lower accuracy performance.

We demonstrate our findings with datasets from the UCR time series archive (Chen et al., 2015). The original train-test split is well suited for 1-nearest-neighbor classification. Although the time series length in all the datasets is uniform, segDTW can be applied toward time series of different lengths just as DTW can. All the measurements, DTW, DDTW, and segDTW are used as is, with no further optimization methods applied. This holdback means we purposefully slowed down the experiments to ensure fair comparisons. There is no parallelization on the time series event level for any of our experiments. When using any distance measurements, the computation between each training and each testing events can always be distributed to different cores. In other words, the parallel computation of time series events can be done for any DTW based method. Therefore, we take away that factor and utilize multiple processor cores for computation only when time series are segmented. In other words, parallelization occurs only within sequences, and never between sequences, and our experiments are overall slowed to a controlled state of having one single factor: segmentation.

The experiments are executed in four sections. First, we explain the significance of meaningful features for segmentation, by comparing peak and valley segmentation with equal-window segmentation. This will show the importance of significant features and intuitive mapping. Then we demonstrate the most prominent feature of segDTW: efficiency. As well as the influence of segmentation parameters, and the relationship between feature numbers and performance. In the last section of our experiments, we discuss the applicational aspects of segDTW. While segDTW can be used as a stand-alone DTW improvement method, and it can also be an additional tool to be combined with other methods.

GLOBAL FEATURES OF SEGDTW

We first explore the importance of significant features by comparing global features peak and valley with equal window segmentation. Instinctively, by segmenting one computation into several pieces and processing simultaneously would improve the overall time cost. However, in order to obtain meaningful results in sequential comparison, the segmentation would also have to be meaningful. Being meaningful cannot be precisely defined but insinuates that the segmentation corresponds to human interpretation. Figure 6 shows the segDTW with peaks as features, valleys as features, and the same number equal-width segments respectively. The two time series in Figure 6 (a) are both divided into three segments based on the two peaks identified as significant features, and the accumulated segDTW distance is 16.16. One significant valley and one miniature valley are found in Figure 6 (b), and the accumulated segDTW distance is 18.75. When time series are segmented into equal-width segments, as is the case in Figure 6 (c), the accumulated segDTW distance is 22.14. Although the processing time is approximately the same for the three cases, the segmentation for the last one with equal-width window does not have any meaning. This situation could be worsened as the number of equal-width segments grow, and in the extreme case for equal length time series, when each window has the width of 1, segDTW with equal-width segment degenerates to the L_p-norms Euclidean distance.

Figure 6. Two time series computed with segDTW with (a) peak, with distance 16.16 (b) valley, with distance 18.75, and (c) equal-window, with distance 22.14 respectively.

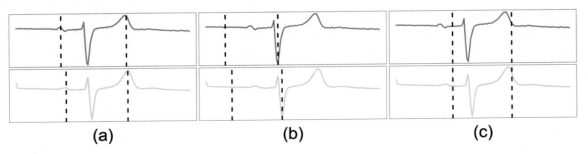

(a)　　　　　　　　(b)　　　　　　　　(c)

Both peaks and valleys are easily distinguished and can be used for sequence segmentation; either could be more effective depending on the dataset and application. In the following experiments, we are solely using peaks as it is easy to recognize and simple to utilize for most datasets.

EFFICIENCY OF SEGDTW

While any segmentation of time series would improve computation efficiency, it is the quality of segmentation that is our focus. Although general parameters can help us gain some insight into the data, for optimum performance, specialized parameter settings should be applied for specific datasets.

The number of identified features change when different segmentation parameters are applied. Figure 7 shows how the number of peaks and accuracy change with different peak selection parameter settings. The horizontal axis is the permutations of parameter settings $d = 1 / 2, 1 / 4, 1 / 8, 1 / 16, 1 / 32, 1 / 64, 1 / 128$ of data length L, and t with values of the first quantile ($Q1$), median (M) and the third quantile ($Q3$); here no n imposed. The left-y-axis is the accuracy, and the right-y-axis is the average number of paired peaks. The orange line corresponds to the accuracy, and the blue line corresponds to the number of peaks. The accuracy range for each dataset is varied; in order to show detailed accuracy fluctuation, we did not use uniform accuracy range. While the results are distinct from dataset to dataset, there are some identifiable trends. For datasets shown in (d), (k), (l), and (p), accuracy does not fluctuate much based on the number of peaks. The relationship between accuracy and the number of peaks is positive in ratio for datasets (b), (c), and (g). While the relationship between accuracy and the number of peaks is inverse in ratio for datasets (i) and (n). For some datasets, the maximum accuracy occur for a low number of paired peaks, while others occurs specifically for a high number of paired peaks. In short, similar to the no free lunch (NFL) theorem, parameter setting, and the number of paired features differ drastically depending on the datasets.

Figure 8 (a) shows the computation time in seconds, and Figure 8 (b) shows the accuracy for standard DTW, DDTW, and segDTW, with datasets on the horizontal-axis ordered by the length in the ascending order. Due to the different data length and number of identified peaks, the general processing time varies drastically from dataset to dataset. Therefore, for a more clear illustration, the time-scale is depicted on the logarithmic scale. Generally, DDTW is more efficient than standard DTW, and segDTW is more efficient than DDTW. Out of the 38 datasets, there is only 1 case where segDTW did not outperform the standard DTW and 2 cases where segDTW did not outperform DDTW, all of which occurred for the 3 datasets with the shortest data length. There are also 19 cases where compared to the standard DTW, segDTW had over ten-times increase in processing time. Since the scalability of segDTW is segment dependent, it makes sense for this advantage to be more apparent for datasets with longer time series sequences; when the overhead of the time spent on segment computation becomes less relevant compared to the linear calculation time spent on an entire sequence pair. For the two longest sequence datasets, we saw an over 40-times increase in computation speed. Without using any other DTW improvement methods, segDTW performed the same or better in accuracy for 31 out of 38 datasets.

Figure 7. The relationship between the number of peaks and the accuracy of 16 datasets. The parameter settings are the permutations of $d = 1/2, 1/4, 1/8, 1/16, 1/32, 1/64, 1/128$ of data length L, and t with values of the $Q1$, M and $Q3$.

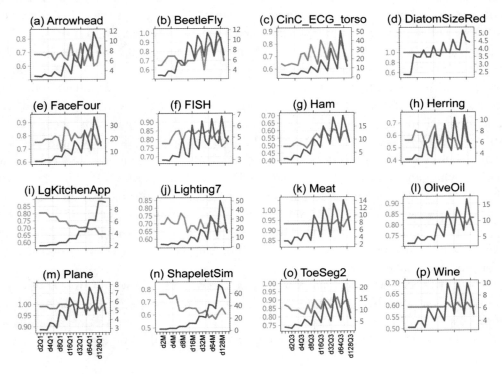

Figure 8. Datasets are in ascending order of time series length, (a) shows the processing time in seconds for standard DTW, DDTW, and segDTW on the logarithmic scale, with segDTW speedup becoming more apparent as time series length increases; (b) shows the corresponding accuracy performance

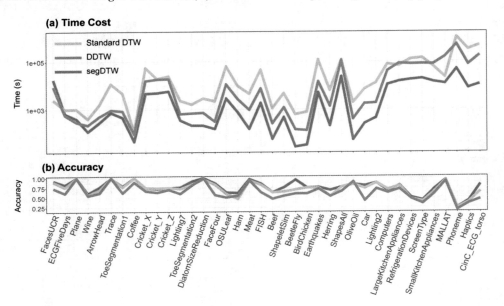

APPLIED SEGDTW

As we have mentioned, segDTW does not have to be a stand-alone heuristic. Due to its unique divide-and-compute structure, segDTW can be combined with almost any existing DTW improvement approach. Here we will demonstrate segDTW combined with global warping windows. Table 1 shows the performance of segDTW with the Itakura warping window compared to the standard DTW and segDTW. In general, segDTW with warping window is more efficient than the segDTW alone. However, there is a slight decrease in the accuracy of segDTW with window; this can be attributed to the tightness of constraint, as there is always a risk of over-constraining the warping path when we pursue efficiency.

For a more visual understanding, Figure 9 is an example of the warping path for the standard DTW (Figure 9 (a)), segDTW (Figure 9 (b)), and segDTW combined with the Itakura warping window (Figure 9 (c)). Each orange cell corresponds to a pairwise computation. In this example, segDTW identifies two peaks, and the white area outside the dynamic windows are pruned. segDTW with the Itakura warping window has the least amount of computation. The warping paths are drawn in red, and compared to the standard DTW, segDTW avoided some pathological warpings. While segDTW combined with the Itakura warping window provides a very tight constraint for the warping path. In practice, segDTW would also work with methods such as slope weighting, step-pattern, lower bounding, approximation, shape descriptor, early abandonment, and more.

The trade-off between efficiency and performance can be observed with many DTW improvement method. With little or no restraints, the warping path may stray pathologically, which also adds to the computation cost of the similarity matrix. When the restraints are too tight, we risk missing the optimal warping path, threatening on the Euclidean distance and missing the point of using elastic measures entirely.

CONCLUSION

In this chapter, we extensively tested segDTW, a DTW improvement heuristic. Unlike its predecessors, it is scalable and easy to parallelize; this merit is especially apparent for time series datasets with long sequences. While all segmentation can speed up computation, only meaningful segmentation can contribute to performance improvement. Under optimum feature selection, we achieved an overall speedup

Table 1. segDTW with Itakura Warping Window Performance

Dataset	DTW Time	DTW Accuracy	segDTW Time	segDTW Accuracy	segDTW & Itakura Time	segDTW & Itakura Accuracy
DiatomSizeReduction	2851.152	0.967	209.814	1.000	200.943	0.938
FaceFour	2184.636	0.830	150.442	0.773	140.988	0.761
Ham	9517.044	0.467	755.781	0.581	755.268	0.543
Lighting7	2313.384	0.726	348.706	0.712	324.118	0.721
Meat	4426.224	0.933	148.530	0.933	133.588	0.933
ToeSegmentation2	1606.704	0.838	211.372	0.877	215.616	0.631

Figure 9. Warping path of (a) standard DTW, (b) segDTW, and (c) segDTW combined with the Itakura warping window

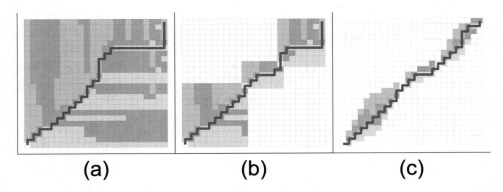

and saw an increase of over 40x in speed for two of the longest datasets. In addition, segDTW can also avoid pathological warpings, produce more intuitive warpings, and improve the accuracy performance in most cases. As we have demonstrated, segDTW is not an alternative to existing DTW speed-up methods. Instead, it can be combined with existing techniques. Depending on feature selection and dataset, the segDTW efficiency performance lies between standard DTW (when no feature is selected) and Euclidean distance (when each point in the sequence is a feature). For optimum performance, segDTW should be fine-tuned according to the characteristics of the processed dataset.

As we have demonstrated, segDTW should only be applied for speed improvement purposes when the overhead of segmentation does not outweigh DTW time. For example, if time series sequences are very short, or if there are a very limited number of processor cores, segDTW would be more costly than the standard DTW. However, segDTW would provide more intuitive mapping than the standard DTW. In application, when we are dealing with very long time series sequences, and have multiple processor cores at our disposal, using segDTW can definitely speed up computation and provide better quality results. While all DTW computation between time series can be parallelized, segDTW expands the limit of possible utilized processor cores by introducing parallelization within time series. The major contribution of segDTW is that by using feature selection to segment time series sequences and perform parallel elastic measure calculation, we can break the linearity barrier and obtain scalability with the otherwise linear DTW sequence computation.

REFERENCES

Berndt, D. J., & Clifford, J. (1994, July). Using dynamic time warping to find patterns in time series. In KDD workshop (Vol. 10, No. 16, pp. 359-370). Academic Press.

Biba, M., & Xhafa, F. (Eds.). (2011). *Learning Structure and Schemas from Documents* (Vol. 375). Springer. doi:10.1007/978-3-642-22913-8_1

Chen, Y., Keogh, E., Hu, B., Begum, N., Bagnall, A., Mueen, A., & Batista, G. (2015, July). *The ucr time series classification archive*. Retrieved from www.cs.ucr.edu/~eamonn/time_ series_data/

Itakura, F. (1975). Minimum prediction residual principle applied to speech recognition. *IEEE Transactions on Acoustics, Speech, and Signal Processing, 23*(1), 67–72. doi:10.1109/TASSP.1975.1162641

Keogh, E., & Ratanamahatana, C. A. (2005). Exact indexing of dynamic time warping. *Knowledge and Information Systems, 7*(3), 358–386. doi:10.100710115-004-0154-9

Keogh, E. J., & Pazzani, M. J. (2000, August). Scaling up dynamic time warping for datamining applications. In *Proceedings of the sixth ACM SIGKDD international conference on Knowledge discovery and data mining* (pp. 285-289). ACM. 10.1145/347090.347153

Keogh, E. J., & Pazzani, M. J. (2001, April). Derivative dynamic time warping. In *Proceedings of the 2001 SIAM international conference on data mining* (pp. 1-11). Society for Industrial and Applied Mathematics.

Kim, S. W., Park, S., & Chu, W. W. (2001). An index-based approach for similarity search supporting time warping in large sequence databases. In *Proceedings 17th International Conference on Data Engineering* (pp. 607-614). IEEE.

Kruskall, J. B. (1983). *The symmetric time warping algorithm: From continuous to discrete*. Time warps, string edits and macromolecules.

Kuhn, H. W. (1955). The Hungarian method for the assignment problem. *Naval Research Logistics Quarterly, 2*(1-2), 83-97.

Ma, R., Ahmadzadeh, A., Boubrahimi, S. F., & Angryk, R. A. (2018, December). Segmentation of Time Series in Improving Dynamic Time Warping. In *2018 IEEE International Conference on Big Data (Big Data)* (pp. 3756-3761). IEEE. 10.1109/BigData.2018.8622554

Ma, R., Ahmadzadeh, A., Boubrahimi, S. F., & Angryk, R. A. (in press). A Scalable Segmented Dynamic Time Warping for Time Series Classification. In *International Conference on Artificial Intelligence and Soft Computing Proceedings of the 18th International Conference on Artificial Intelligence and Soft Computing (ICAISC '19)*. 397-408.

Müller, M. (2007). *Information retrieval for music and motion* (Vol. 2). Heidelberg, Germany: Springer. doi:10.1007/978-3-540-74048-3

Rabiner, L. R., Juang, B. H., & Rutledge, J. C. (1993). *Fundamentals of speech recognition* (Vol. 14). Englewood Cliffs, NJ: PTR Prentice Hall.

Ranacher, P., & Tzavella, K. (2014). How to compare movement? A review of physical movement similarity measures in geographic information science and beyond. *Cartography and Geographic Information Science, 41*(3), 286–307. doi:10.1080/15230406.2014.890071 PMID:27019646

Sakoe, H., & Chiba, S. (1973, December). Comparative study of DP-pattern matching techniques for speech recognition. *Tech. Group Meeting Speech, Acoust. Soc.*

Sakoe, H., & Chiba, S. (1978). Dynamic programming algorithm optimization for spoken word recognition. *IEEE Transactions on Acoustics, Speech, and Signal Processing, 26*(1), 43–49. doi:10.1109/TASSP.1978.1163055

Salvador, S., & Chan, P. (2007). Toward accurate dynamic time warping in linear time and space. *Intelligent Data Analysis*, *11*(5), 561–580. doi:10.3233/IDA-2007-11508

Serra, J., & Arcos, J. L. (2014). An empirical evaluation of similarity measures for time series classification. *Knowledge-Based Systems*, *67*, 305–314. doi:10.1016/j.knosys.2014.04.035

Wang, X., Mueen, A., Ding, H., Trajcevski, G., Scheuermann, P., & Keogh, E. (2013). Experimental comparison of representation methods and distance measures for time series data. *Data Mining and Knowledge Discovery*, *26*(2), 275–309. doi:10.100710618-012-0250-5

Yi, B. K., Jagadish, H. V., & Faloutsos, C. (1998, February). Efficient retrieval of similar time sequences under time warping. In *Proceedings 14th International Conference on Data Engineering* (pp. 201-208). IEEE.

Zhao, J., & Itti, L. (2018). Shapedtw: Shape dynamic time warping. *Pattern Recognition*, *74*, 171–184. doi:10.1016/j.patcog.2017.09.020

KEY TERMS AND DEFINITIONS

Classification: A supervised learning method in machine learning, which is used to identify unknown instance categories based on known instances.

Dynamic Time Warping: An elastic similarity measure for temporal sequences alignment.

Euclidean Distance: The ordinary straight-line distance between two points in the Euclidean space.

Hungarian Algorithm: A combinatorial optimization algorithm used to find maximum-weight matchings, which can be used to solve the assignment problem.

K-Nearest Neighbors: A method applied in classification and regression for pattern recognition, where the input consists of the k closest examples in feature space.

Parallel Process: A computation process in which one computation can be broken into several computations and processed simultaneously.

Time Series Data: An indexed series of data points taken at equally spaced points in time in a sequential order.

Chapter 2
JSON Data Management in RDBMS

Zhen Hua Liu
Oracle, USA

ABSTRACT

Being a simple semi-structured data model, JSON has been widely accepted as a simple way to store, query, modify, and exchange data among applications. In comparison with schema-oriented relational data model to store, query, and update application data, JSON data model has the advantage of being self-contained, free from schema evolution issues, and flexible enough to enable agile style development paradigm. Therefore, during the last 5 years, SQL/JSON standard has been established as foundation for managing JSON data in SQL standard and there have been JSON functionalities added into RDBMS products to support SQL/JSON standard to various degree. In this chapter, the authors will analyze the strength and weakness of using JSON as the data model to manage data for applications. For use cases where JSON data model is ideal, they present the design approaches to store, index, query, and update JSON in the kernel of RDBMS to support SQL/JSON standard defined operations effectively and efficiently.

JSON DATA MODEL AND ITS APPLICATION USE CASES

Why JSON Database?: Merits of Using JSON Data Model

Relational model (Codd, 1970) in RDBMS is based on 'schema first, data later' paradigm. Database users are required to design a relational schema before data can be stored. The schema is based on Entity-Relationship design practices (Chen, 1977) where an entity is composed of a set of attributes. Entities are related to each other through reference keys. Each entity is modeled as a table and every attribute of an entity becomes a column of the table. Each reference relationship is enforced as primary key and foreign key constraint. Foreign key columns of a table store reference keys to support reference relationship. To achieve update efficiency by avoiding data duplication, normalization rules (Fagin 1979) are followed so that there is no duplicated storage of the same data.

DOI: 10.4018/978-1-5225-8446-9.ch002

The issue with 'schema first, data later' paradigm is that when database applications evolve to add new attributes to an entity, the table for that entity must be altered to add new columns. This schema evolution issue becomes burden for database application developers who have to constantly request database administrators to evolve schema. Therefore, relational model is ideal for supporting highly structured data whose schema is relatively static.

In pure RDBMS, each column of a table is of a particular simple scalar datatype, such as integer, varchar, date, timestamp, etc. A complex type needs to be decomposed into multiple columns, each of which maps to a simple scalar datatype. An address type, for example, must be physically decomposed into three columns: street name, city name, zip code as the underlying storage columns. Furthermore, each column cannot be of an array type. An array type needs to be decomposed into two storage tables with reference relationship enforced by primary key and foreign key integrity constraint. Although object relational DBMS (ORDBMS) (Stonebraker, 1986) relaxes the simple datatype requirement by allowing complex datatype, including the array datatype, as a datatype of a column, the complex datatype definition, known as structured user defined type definition in SQL 99 (Melton, 2003), needs to be defined first so that columns of that complex datatype can store complex data. Therefore, schema evolution in the form of evolving structured user defined datatype definition with their implied physical storage structures remains. Furthermore, in ORDBMS, it is still true that each row of a table must have same number of columns and each column must be of same datatype whether it is complex type or not.

In contrast with the time when relational model and RDBMS were built, we are living in the big data age when there are variety of data to manage so that it is not practical to expect application users to design schema first before their application data are storable, indexable, queryable and manageable. In particular, for data that has loose structures, typically referred as semi-structured data, an alternative paradigm, known as 'data first, schema later', becomes more attractive. Two common semi-structured data models are XML and JSON. Native XML and JSON database systems are built based on the philosophy of 'data first, schema later' paradigm. MarkLogic and MongoDB are representatives of pure XML and JSON databases respectively. In particular, due to popularity of JavaScript, JSON, which represents the persistent data of JavaScript programming language, is a very simple semi-structured data and thus has gained its popularity during the last decade. JSON is a simple way to model an entity with flexible attributes. Each attribute can be of scalar type, object type, array type.

Compared with RDBMS, Native JSON database systems are based on document-object model instead of relational model. Native JSON DBMS supports concept of collection which is analogous to the concept of table in RDBMS. Each JSON document stored in a collection is analogous to a row stored in a table in RDBMS. Each JSON document is of document-object model. There can be variable number of attributes of various datatypes, including complex types, array types within each JSON document. Therefore, each JSON collection has flexible schema with variety of attributes that can be stored in each JSON document. Such schema flexibility in JSON database, in comparing with rigid schema requirement in RDBMS, really enables agile development style for application users who want a developer friendly instead of DBA friendly database system to manage their data. This trend has pushed RDBMS to embrace JSON capabilities as a schema-less development paradigm for application developers (Liu et al., 2014).

In summary, Table 1 shows the comparison between classical RDBMS and JSON native DBMS.

Table 2 shows an example of a JSON collection storing a set of JSON documents describing purchase orders.

Table 1. Comparison between classical RDBMS and JSON DBMS

	Classical RDBMS	**JSON DBMS**
Philosophical Approach	Schema First/Data Later	Data First/Schema Later
Entity	Each row must have same number of columns. Same column in different rows must of same datatype.	Each document may have different attributes. Same attribute in different JSON document may of different datatype.
Attribute of an Entity	Simple scalar datatype, complex datatype must be decomposed into simple scalar type	Simple and complex datatype are allowed and stored inline within the JSON document.
Array attribute of an Entity	Decompose array into a child table linked with parent table enforced by primary-foreign key constraint. Each row in a child table represents an array item.	Array data are stored inline within the JSON document without decomposition.
Schema evolution	Running alter table DDL to add/drop new columns, change column datatypes.	No need to run alter table DDL statements. Just add new JSON document with new attributes.

To store the same amount of information in a pure RDBMS, we need to create a set of tables: purchaseOrder, lineItems, Parts, DiscountItems, DiscountPart (See Table 3, 4, 5, 6, 7 respectively) so that each JSON document is decomposed into rows and columns stored in the five tables.

The biggest challenge with JSON object decomposition is that the underlying table structures need to be evolved to accommodate schema evolution of JSON data. Therefore, supporting schema flexible data is the key differentiation between JSON DBMS and RDBMS. This is also one of the critical tensions between SQL and NoSQL database systems (liu et al., 2015). Another advantage of using JSON database is that JSON is a de-normalized model so that retrieval of one JSON document can be done without joining multiple tables through chasing foreign key references. For a small to medium size of JSON document that fit within a single storage unit, it can be retrieved very efficiently.

Any Shortcomings of JSON Database?

Although not enforcing schema for storing JSON data has great advantage for data ingestion, JSON data model, which is a single hierarchical based data model, is not a general purpose data model compared with entity-relationship based relational model. In fact, both XML and JSON data models are conceptually the same as that of hierarchical data model supported in IBM IMS (Information Management System) DBMS. There are much data that do not fit well into a single hierarchical data model.

Consider the classical many-to-many relationship use case that requires managing student class enrollment. In such use case: A student may enroll into a set of classes. A class is enrolled by many students. Using JSON data model, there are two JSON collections: a student collection that tracks a set of classes taken by each student; a class collection that tracks a set of students enrolled into a class. In relational model, there are three tables: student table, class table and a third course-enrollment table that records enrollment by mapping a student id with a class id. It is much easier to simply change the course-enrollment table to support student class enrollment change in comparison with changing of two JSON collections that updating both student JSON document and class JSON document. This update flexibility from entity-relationship modeling stems from the commonly practiced normalization rule in

Table 2. One JSON collection: PurchaseOrder

DID	JDOC
1	{"purchaseOrder":{"id": 1, "podate": "2014-09-08", "items": [{"name":"phone", "price": 100, "quantity": 2}, {"name":"ipad", "price": 350.86, "quantity": 3}]}}
2	{"purchaseOrder":{"id": 2, "podate": "2015-03-04", "items": [{"name":"table", "price": 52.78, "quantity": 2}, {"name":"chair", "price": 35.24, "quantity": 4}]}}
3	{"purhcaseOrder":{"id": 3, "podate": "2015-06-03", "foreign_id": "CDEG35", "items": [{"name":"TV", "price": 345.55, "quantity": 1, "parts": [{"partName": "remoteCon", "partQuantity": "1"}, {"partName": "antenna", "partQuantity": "2"}] }, {"name":"PC", "price": 546.78, "quantity": 10, "parts": [{"partName": "mouse", "partQuantity": "2"}, {"partName": "keyboard", "partQuantity": "1"},] }]}}
4	{"purchaseOrder":{"id": 98, "podate": "2015-07-04", "items": [{"name":"CD", "price": 5.55, "quantity": 10, }, {"name":"DVD", "price": 6.78, "quantity": 20, }], "discount_items": [{"dis_itemName": "CPH", "dis_itemPrice": 105.52, "dis_itemQuanitty":2, "dis_parts": [{"dis_partName": "phonejack", "dis_partQuantity": 3}, {"dis_partName": "plug", "dis_partQuantity": 2},] }, {"dis_itemName": "Printer", "dis_itemPrice": 121.33, "dis_itemQuanitty":9, "dis_parts": [{"dis_partName": "toner", "dis_partQuantity": 5}, {"dis_partName": "paper", "dis_partQuantity": 20},] }] }}

Table 3. Purchaseorder_rel table

Id	Podate
1	2014-09-08
2	2015-03-04
3	2015-06-03
4	2015-07-04

Table 4. lineItems table

fid_po	Name	Price	quantity	Item_id
1	Phone	100	2	1
1	Ipad	356.86	3	2
2	Table	52.78	2	3
2	Chair	35.24	4	4
3	TV	345.55	1	5
3	PC	546.78	10	6
4	CD	5.55	10	7
4	DVD	6.78	20	8

Table 5. Parts table

fid_item	partName	partQuantity
3	remoteConn	1
3	antenna	2
4	mouse	2
4	keyboard	1

Table 6. DiscountItems table

fid_po	dis_itemName	dis_itemPrice	dis_itemQuantity	DistIem_Id
4	CPH	105.52	2	1
4	Printer	121.33	9	2

Table 7. DiscountPart Table

dis_partName	dis_partQuantity	Fid_distitem
phoneJack	3	1
Plug	2	1
Tonner	5	2
paper	20	2

RDBMS that avoids duplicated data storage. **JSON using de-normalized model suffers from duplicated record updating problem when the data does not fit naturally into single hierarchical data model.**

Fundamentally, entity-relationship based relational model design forces database users to decompose data into its fundamental pieces of scalar data types and their relationships through key references. Querying JSON data requires query access path always following the single hierarchical path in the JSON document. On the other hand, querying relational data can start from any table following any directions by traversing the key references. Comparing with JSON database system, RDBMS has its advantage of being able to modeling any relationships instead of supporting just single hierarchical relationship. **Thus relational model not only has fine-grained update advantage but also has query flexibility advantage in terms of being able to model data of any relation shapes and querying them starting at any fundamental piece. JSON data model, however, loses such update and query flexibility in exchange for ease of data ingestion and schema evolution flexibility.**

Another shortcomings of JSON data model is due to lack of central schema management that forces data applications to embed the knowledge of underlying JSON data schema inside queries that are scattered in various pieces of data application code. In contrast, in RDBMS, the entity-relationships is centrally managed as data dictionary in one place. It is easy to query data dictionaries to discover the structure of the relational data. Therefore, JSON database needs to support capability of deriving schema from JSON collections. The 'schema later' aspect of 'Data First/Schema Later' paradigm needs to be compensated via automatic schema derivation capability from the loaded data in the system. After all, schema describes the shape and structure of the data that makes the data more queryable. **Using schema to determine the storage structure of JSON data is inflexible whereas using schema to guide querying of the JSON data is essential.**

In summary, we extend Table 1 with additional comparisons between classical RDBMS and JSON native DBMS shown in Table 8.

The Need to Integrate: Supporting JSON Data Management in RDBMS

The pros and cons comparison between classical RDBMS and JSON DBMS has led to the development of JSON capability inside RDBMS.

Table 8. Additional comparison between classical RDBMS and JSON DBMS

	Classical RDBMS	JSON DBMS
Modeling Relationships	Flexible enough to support any relationships through key references. Very efficient and effective to support many-to-many relationship.	Single hierarchical relationship, very good at one-to-many parent-child relationship. Not very effective to support many-to-many relationship.
Queryablity expressing join	Flexible enough to support any join relationship beyond just parent-child relationship.	Simple hierarchical path traversal is very efficient. No need to do explicit join between parent-child hierarchical relationship.
Update	Avoid duplicated data update anomaly via high-degree of normalization.	Need to support duplicated data update due to de-normalized storage
Schema Management	Centralized and managed and queryable in one place	Maybe scattered in various places of the application code.

The strong use case of JSON Data Model is to support rapid data application development without breaking down data into fine grained relational elements by storing and retrieving the whole JSON document as one unit. There are large volume of JSON data generated from JavaScript language that promote such use cases. Most of these data are either read only or intensive read and write for a period of time but become read only in the long run. The structure of JSON data may range from highly structured data to loosely structure data. Therefore, it is important for RDBMS to manage JSON data without forcing a relational model to decompose JSON data.

The key to support JSON data management in RDBMS is to embrace the concept of 'data first/schema later' through the idea of 'schema-less for write, schema-rich for query'. Fundamentally, this boils down to the key insight that positioning data schema as logical concept instead of physical concept. That is to say, **instead of forcing users to define schema to determine the physical storage structures of data, computing schema from data on behalf of users so that computed schema can be used to guide users on how to query the data [14].** This is a new concept in classical RDBMS. Applying this concept to JSON data management, RDBMS enables storage of JSON documents into JSON collection without a priori schema definition, that is, 'schema-less for write'. However, RDBMS derives the schema from the JSON collection and lets users to query over the JSON collection based on the derived schema, that is, 'schema-rich for query'.

The main benefit of integrating JSON data with RDBMS is that from the perspective of database users is that they have a single DBMS to manage all of their data. Within a single DBMS, users have choice of applying either 'schema first/data later' or 'data first/schema later' paradigm. Even if users choose 'data first/schema later' paradigm, it is the underlying DBMS that is able to manage and compute schema on behalf of users and assist users to query data without up-front schema definition. Since all data is managed by one system, there is no data replication, synchronization among different DBMSs. Furthermore, many mature database practices, such as concept of transaction can be applied to JSON data management. Querying both relational data and JSON data can be done in one system instead of writing mid-tier code to query different DBMS systems. As there is no apparent dis-advantage of integrating and supporting JSON functionalities into RDBMS products, major RDBMS vendors and open source RDBMS products have all extended their RDBMS kernels to support JSON data management.

In the remaining sections of this chapter, we focus on the perspective of supporting JSON data management in RDBMS.

SQL/JSON FOR DECLARATIVE QUERYING, UPDATING JSON AND BI-DIRECTIONAL MAPPING BETWEEN JSON AND RELATIONAL DATA

Querying JSON Data Model Declaratively

SQL is a declarative language to query relational model. It is based on set algebra that models a table as a set of elements and each element of the set is a row. It is natural to leverage the set oriented SQL language to apply to a JSON collection as a set of elements and each element of the set is a JSON document. However, each JSON document is a complex object that can be queried declaratively using a native JSON path language (Liu et al, 2015). That is, we leverage SQL as an inter-JSON document query language and create a new hierarchical path based language as an intra-JSON document query language. This is the fundamental design idea of SQL/JSON standard. It defines a SQL/JSON path language over a single JSON document. The SQL/JSON path language is then embedded inside a set of new SQL/JSON operators that can be used in various clauses of SQL.

SQL/JSON Path Language

Since JSON data model is a hierarchical tree model, a hierarchical path language is the most nature way to query it. So SQL/JSON path language syntax is based on the XPath for JSON language that adopts JavaScript syntax. Semantically, SQL/JSON path language is composed of a sequence of path steps. Each path step is either an **object member access** using object field name or an **array member access** using a zero based array index. Each step can be attached with a set of boolean predicates as filters. The SQL/JSON path language expression results in SQL/JSON sequence data model that is **closed** under the expressions. The following is a description of important properties of SQL/JSON Path language that is designed to handle schema-free JSON document collection.

1. **SQL/JSON Sequence Data Model:** There are JSON object, JSON array and JSON scalar of atomic type: number, string, Boolean, null, defined in JSON data model. However, to define closure property of SQL/JSON path language expression, it is required to define SQL/JSON sequence data model that represents the result of a SQL/JSON path expression language. For example, applying path step expression '*$.purchaseOrder.**' on JSON document with did = 1 in Table 2 results in a sequence of three items: the JSON object *{"id":1}*, the JSON object *{"podate": "2014-09-08"}*, the JSON array *"items": [{"name":"phone", "price": 100, "quantity":2}, {"name": "ipad", "price": 350.86, "quantity":3}]*. Therefore, just as XQuery/XPath 2.0 [17], SQL/JSON sequence data model is defined to consist of a sequence of items. An item can be either a JSON object, or a JSON array, or a JSON scalar of atomic type. The sequence data model does not support nested sequence. A singleton item is equivalent to a sequence of that singleton item. Note that JSON array is not the same as that of the sequence data model because a JSON array may be a valid item in the sequence data model. For example, Path expression '*$.purchaseOrder.items*' results in a sequence of one item, which is the JSON array: *[{"name":"phone", "price": 100, "quantity": 2}, {"name": "ipad", "price": 350.86, "quantity":3}]*. On the other hand, Path expression '*$.purchaseOrder.items[*]*' results in a sequence of two items: the *{"name":"phone", "price": 100, "quantity":2}* JSON object item and the *{"name": "ipad", "price": 350.86, "quantity":3}* JSON object item.

2. **Path Step Expression and Predicate Filter Expression:** Each path step expression results in an instance of SQL/JSON Sequence data model. The sequence data model instance may consist of a sequence of items. The predicate filter expression attached to the path step is applied as boolean predicates to filter each item within the result sequence from the path step expression.

3. **Default Lax Mode when applying Path Step:** Each path step has auto-wrapping and unwrapping capability on results from its previous path step. For example, both path expression '*$.purchaseorder.items[*].name*' and '*$.purchaseorder.items.name*' applying to JSON doc (did = 1) in Table 2 results in a sequence of two JSON scalar items: *"phone"* and *"ipad"*. For the first path step '*$.purchaseorder.items[*]*' that results in a sequence of object items, it is expected to apply *'name'* object member access step on each object item. For the second path step '*$.purchaseorder.items*' that results in a sequence of a single array item, the evaluation of *'name'* path step is intelligent enough to know that if the previous result item is an array, it automatically unwraps the array to apply *'name'* path step to each element of the array. **This is a very crucial semantics to support**

27

querying a set of JSON documents in a JSON collection that may not have homogenous shapes for each JSON document. For example, in one JSON document of a JSON collection, the items might be a JSON array, in another JSON document of the same JSON collection, the items might be a JSON object. However, there is no need to change path query when querying the JSON collection. When an array member accessor is applied to a JSON object item, a singleton item is implicitly wrapped as an array of that item. When an object member accessor is applied on a JSON array item, the array is implicitly unwrapped so that the object member accessor is applied to each item of the JSON array. Applying this lax mode to predicate filter expression, then path expression '*$.purchaseOrder.items?(@.price > 200 && @.quantity == 3)*' and '*$.purchaseOrder. items[*]?(@.price > 200 && @.quantity == 3)*' yield the same result because evaluation of path step '*price*' and '*quantity*' in the predicate does the same auto-unwrapping operation of applying the object member access '*price/quantity*' to each element of the '*items*' array.

4. **Default Lax Mode for Error Handling:** The SQL/JSON path language is more forgiving of errors by returning false in filter expressions instead of raising error. Such forgiving behaviour is important to handle the weak-typed JSON collection. Consider applying the JSON path expression '*$.purchaseOrder.items?(@.price > 200)*' to a JSON document with the value of *"price"* is '*unknown*' which is not convertible to a number. Rather than raising a type conversion error, this results in false for the predicate evaluation for the lax mode, which is the default mode. Combined with point 3, SQL/JSON path language has intelligent default lax mode to handle the semi-structured nature of a JSON collection.

5. **SQL Datatype Conversion Functions:** Although JSON data model does not have date, timestamp, binary float or double datatypes, SQL does have those scalar datatypes defined. Therefore, SQL/ JSON path language have introduced SQL datatype conversion functions into SQL/JSON path language to construct JSON scalar atomic value of SQL scalar datatypes. The type conversion function is used at the end of the path step. For example, path expression '*$.purchaseOrder?(@. podate.date() >= date("2014-09-08"))*' converts the JSON scalar value for a *"podate"* field to a SQL date datatype and then does range comparison based on date datatype.

SQL/JSON Query Operators and Table Function

1. **IS JSON** predicate is used to verify if the input SQL expression contains a valid JSON document. This predicate is commonly used in column check constraint to validate DML of the column yields a valid JSON document.

2. **JSON_EXISTS**(<json_expression>, '<sql_json_path_language>') predicate is used to apply a SQL/JSON path language over an input JSON document to see if the result is an empty sequence or not. If the result is empty sequence, it returns SQL false whereas non-empty sequence result resulting in SQL true. JSON_EXISTS() predicate is typically used in SQL where clause to searching JSON documents satisfying certain search criteria.

3. **JSON_VALUE**(<json_expression>, '<sql_json_path_language>' returning <sql_datatype>) is used to apply a SQL/JSON path language over an input JSON document to extract a leaf scalar value which is the result of the last step of the path expression. JSON_VALUE() by default is NULL ON ERROR, that is, if the last step of the SQL/JSON path language does not result in a JSON scalar value or the JSON scalar value is not convertible to the desired sql datatype, it returns SQL NULL instead of raising error. ERROR ON ERROR option can also be specified to raise error.

This reflects the same design property of having default lax mode to handle schema-free JSON data.

4. **JSON_QUERY**(<json_expression>, '<sql_json_path_language>') is used to apply a SQL/JSON path language over an input JSON document to extract a JSON fragment and wrap it as a JSON document.

5. **JSON_TABLE()** is used in the SQL FROM clause to convert arrays within JSON object instances into a virtual relational table. The SQL/JSON path language can be used in both row and column expressions of JSON_TABLE().The typical use case of JSON_TABLE() is to expand a JSON array within a JSON object into a set of relational rows, each of which corresponds to an element within the array.

SQL/JSON Query Examples Over JSON Collection

Table 9 shows a list of SQL/JSON Query examples. Q8 and Q9 show how to use JSON_TABLE() to un-nest JSON array elements into a set of relational rows. Since JSON is a de-normalized model, it is common to embed JSON array in a JSON document to capture a set of related detail items for a particular master item. JSON array is nestable. That is, each element of the JSON array can be another JSON array. Therefore, to un-nest an array of array, NESTED PATH construct is available in JSON_TABLE() to support such master-detail-detail array expansion. Q9 in Table 9 is used to expand a set of items within each JSON document, for each array element in the items array, it expands a set of parts.

Table 10 shows the result of Q8

SQL/JSON Generation Functions Over Relational Data to Construct JSON

JSON_OBJECT(), JSON_ARRAY() SQL operators are used to construct a JSON object or a JSON array from a set of SQL expressions. JSON_OBJECT() accepts a series of KEY and SQL VALUE expressions to construct a JSON object with each KEY mapping to the result of SQL value expression. JSON_ARRAY() accepts a series of SQL value expressions to construct a JSON array with each SQL value expression as an element of the JSON array. Q10 in Table 9 shows a query that constructs a JSON document with a nested JSON array from each row of lineItems table.

JSON_OBJECTAGG(), JSON_ARRAYAGG() are **SQL AGGEGRATE** operators to construct a JSON object or a JSON array object from a set of SQL rows. In Q11 of Table 9, JSON_OBJECTAGG() is a SQL aggregation function over a correlated sub-query that selects relational rows from *lineItems* table (see Table 4) for each purchase order id from the outer driver table *PurchaseOrder_rel* (see Table 3) table. This is the typical pattern to construct de-normalized JSON document by constructing and embedding JSON array into the resulting JSON document. The result of this query is the same as that of content of the Table 2. This shows that SQL/JSON generation function that converts from relational data to JSON data while SQL/JSON query function that converts JSON data into relational data. JSON_OBJECTAGG() and JSON_TABLE() are inverse operations so that when they are used together, they effectively cancel each other.

Table 9. SQL/JSON query example

Query #	Query
Q1	SELECT did FROM purchaseOrder WHERE **JSON_EXISTS**(jdoc, '$.purchaseOrder.foreign_id')
Q2	SELECT did, **JSON_VALUE**(jdoc, '$.purchaseOrder.podate') FROM purchaseOrder WHERE **JSON_EXISTS**(jdoc, '$.purchaseOrder.items?(@.name == "TV")')
Q3	SELECT JDOC FROM purchaseOrder WHERE **JSON_VALUE**(jdoc, '$.purchaseOrder.poid' returning number) = 4567
Q4	SELECT did FROM purhcaseOrder WHERE **JSON_VALUE**(jdoc, '$.purchaseOrder.podate' returning date)) = DATE('2018-03-04')
Q5	SELECT did, **JSON_QUERY**(jdoc, '$.purchaseOrder.discount_items') FROM purchaseOrder WHERE **JSON_EXISTS**(jdoc, '$.purchaseOrder.discount_items?(@.dist_name == "Printer")')
Q6	SELECT did, jdoc FROM purchaseOrder WHERE **JSON_EXISTS**(jdoc, '$.purchaseOrder.items?(@.price > 100.34 && @.quantity >= 2)')
Q7	SELECT did, **JSON_VALUE**(jdoc, '$.purchaseOrder.podate') FROM purchaseOrder WHERE **JSON_EXISTS**(jdoc, '$.purchaseOrder.items?(@.name == "TV" && @.parts.partQuantity >= 2)')

Q8	SELECT PO.DID, JT.*
	FROM PO, **JSON_TABLE**(JCOL, '$.purchaseOrder.items[*]'
	  COLUMNS
	  Name varchar2(8) PATH '$.name',
	  Price number PATH '$.price',
	  Quantity number PATH '$.quantity') JT

Q9	SELECT PO.DID, JT.* FROM PO, **JSON_TABLE**("JCOL" FORMAT JSON, '$' COLUMNS "JCOL$id" number path '$.purchaseOrder.id', "JCOL$podate" varchar2(16) path '$.purchaseOrder.podate', "JCOL$foreign_id" varchar2(8) path '$.purchaseOrder.foreign_id', **NESTED PATH** '$.purchaseOrder.items[*]' COLUMNS ("JCOL$name" varchar2(8) path '$.name', "JCOL$price" number path '$.price', "JCOL$quantity" number path '$.quantity'), **NESTED PATH** '$.parts[*]' COLUMNS ("JCOL$partName" varchar2(16) path '$.partName', "JCOL$part Quantity" varchar2(1) path '$.partQuantity'))) JT

Q10	SELECT **JSON_OBJECT**(
	    KEY 'id' VALUE li.fid_po,
	     JSON_ARRAY(li.name, li.price, li.quantity))
	FROM lineItems li

Q11	SELECT po.Id as DID,
	    JSON_OBJECT (
	KEY 'id' VALUE po.Id,
	KEY 'podate' VALUE po.podate,
	KEY 'items' VALUE
	     SELECT **JSON_OBJECTAGG** (
	    JSON_OBJECT (
	                KEY 'Name' VALUE E.Name,
	        KEY 'Prcie' VALUE E.Salary
	        KEY 'Quantity' VALUE E.Quantity)
	FROM lineItems E
	WHERE E.fid_po = po.Id)) AS JDOC
	FROM PurchaseOrder_rel po

Table 10. Result of Q8 of Table 9

DID	Name	Price	Quantity
1	Phone	100	2
1	Ipad	350.86	3
2	Table	52.78	2
2	Chair	35.24	4
3	TV	345.55	1
3	PC	546.78	10
4	CD	5.55	10
4	DVD	6.78	20

Note that result of Q8 is identical to the content of lineItems table (except Item_id column) in Table 4. This reflects that the intension of JSON_TABLE() as a mechanism to convert from JSON Document-Object Data Model into relational mode.

Future Enhancements to SQL/JSON Standard

SQL/JSON standard will continuously be enhanced based on user feedbacks. Two major enhancements will most likely be supporting JSON update and supporting native storage of JSON in a binary format. With introduction of JSON_UPDATE() function, JSON update enhancement will enable partial update of JSON document without fully replacing the JSON document. Native storage of JSON in binary format is able to support the binary JSON atomic value type, such as date, timestamp, that is defined as valid JSON item in a SQL/JSON sequence data model. Furthermore, JSON storage using JSON binary format performs more efficiently than JSON text model. (See section 3 discussion below). The binary storage of JSON will make partial update of JSON document feasible physically inside database kernel. When updating a large JSON document with small patch, it is efficient to update the desired portion without fully updating the entire document. The work is similar to that of supporting efficient update of XML using native XML storage (Liu et al., 2012).

JSON STORAGE, INDEXING AND IN-MEMORY PROCESSING STRATEGIES FOR SUPPORTING EFFICIENT EVALUATION OF SQL/JSON

Binary JSON Storage Format for Supporting Efficient SQL/JSON Path Evaluation

In classical RDBMS, binary row format is designed so that column projection from the row is done efficiently through directly jumping to the desired column value based on column offset table at the beginning of the row header (Stonebraker, 1976). The same design idea is applicable to binary JSON storage. Although JSON text can be stored and evaluation of SQL/JSON path language over JSON text can be done via JSON text parsing during run time, such text based evaluation strategy is inevitably slower than storing a post-parsed binary representation of JSON and using the persistent binary representation of JSON to support efficient evaluation of SQL/JSON path language.

There are conceptually two ways of encoding JSON into a binary format for storage: an **event stream based encoding format** and a **tree jump navigation friendly based encoding format**. The pure event stream based encoding format essentially records token event streams from JSON text parsing. Although evaluation of JSON path expression by processing post-parsed event tokens saves the cost of parsing JSON text, it does not have a fast sibling navigation capability. All descendants of a JSON object has to be streamed through before the next sibling of the JSON object is reached. That is, event stream processing does not have the capability of skipping contents that are irrelevant to the query. Therefore, performance improvement based on pure event based binary encoding of JSON is limited compared with JSON text parsing. An improved event stream encoding, such as BSON encoding, is that each JSON object container records the aggregated size of its descendants so that it is feasible to directly jump to its next sibling by skipping the aggregated size of its descendants.

However, recall that each step of SQL/JSON path language (section 2.1.1) is either an object member field access based on a field name or an array member access based on an array index. Therefore, the binary JSON format needs to support these two common operations very efficiently. To support quick object member field access given an object name, a binary search based on field name is required and thus children of an object are typically sorted based on their field names when they are stored in a binary JSON format. Oracle OSON (Liu et al., 2016), MySQL's binary JSON format, Postgres binary JSON format, STREED binary row format (Z. Wang et al., 2017), Sinew (Tahara et al., 2014) all have such tree jump navigation friendly capability that is fully exploited to efficiently evaluate SQL/JSON path expressions. Therefore, **tree jump navigation friendly based encoding format** is a preferred binary JSON storage format.

Now the question is whether we can avoid doing binary search using field name but rather using field id that is more efficient for binary search. In classical RDBMS that is schema based, each row has known number of columns and each column has a pre-assigned column id stored in global schema dictionary, therefore, column format in a classical RDBMS can use column id instead of column name to locate column content (Stonebraker 1976). To support schema-free JSON format, we cannot rely on global schema dictionary to describe JSON, therefore, each JSON document encoding must be self-contained. JSON text is self-contained, **binary JSON encoding format needs to be self-contained** to be schema free. Sinew (Tahara et al., 2014) and (Z. Wang et al., 2017), have a separate schema file for a JSON collection. Rather than relying on existence of such global schema dictionary or file, OSON (Liu et al., 2016) binary format establishes a local dictionary mapping between a field name and a field id within each OSON document so that each OSON document is completely self-contained in every tier. There is no need to attach global schema into each OSON instance when it is shipped in and out of DBMS boundary.

The field name dictionary ensures that each field name string occurs just once in the binary representation, and replaces the name with a small numerical id that's efficient to search for. The tree node structure allows for rapid navigation within the document without the need to read through the bytes of content that is irrelevant for the query. Each parent maintains an array of sorted field ids. For each field id, there is an offset to the child with that field id. The sorted field id array is binary searched using the field id of the field name. To access a member of a JSON array using an array index, an offset jump table for each array element is also established.

Furthermore, another advantage of binary encoding of JSON is that its encoder and decoder can be executed at client side. BSON has client side encoding and decoding library. It saves DBMS CPU cycles to encode the JSON document into binary format and thus improves document ingestion time. On the way out, decoding JSON binary into JSON text can be done at client side to save DBMS CPU cycles as well. Furthermore, client may consume the binary JSON via client side JSON DOM navigation API without the need to decode it into JSON text.

JSON Collection Indexing

As document instance storage format, path query navigation friendly JSON binary format speeds up document instance processing time, however, the ultimate query performance boost for searching JSON documents within a JSON collection using JSON_EXISTS() and JSON_VALUE() as predicate in SQL WHERE clause is to establish index over the JSON collection.

One indexing approach is 'schema-aware indexing' approach and the other indexing approach is 'schema-agnostic indexing' approach.

Schema-Aware Indexing Approach

Schema-aware indexing approach enables users to index leaf values of a specific path expression. Although JSON collection may store a set of heterogeneous documents with variety of schema, however, there are some common schema, in the form of common path expressions, that are shared in the JSON collection. There are frequent queries to search JSON documents using these common path expressions. For example, in the purchaseOrder collection example in Table 2, '*$.purchaseOrder.id*' and '*$.purchaseOrder.podate*' are common path expressions that are commonly searched for.

Users are able to create following two functional indexes over the JSON collection using JSON_VALUE() to extract the leaf scalar value and casting it to SQL number and date datatypes.

```
CREATE INDEX poid_idx ON purchaseOrder (JSON_VALUE(jdoc, '$.purchaseOrder.id'
returning number));
CREATE INDEX podate_idx ON purhcaseOrder(JSON_VALUE(jdoc, '$.purchaseOrder.po-
date' returning date));
```

Q3 and Q4 in Table 9 will be able to use index poid_idx and podate_idx respectively.

Both *poid_idx* and *podate_idx* are single value functional indices. That is, there is only one index value derived from each JSON document. To index array element in JSON, however, we need multi-value functional index that can index an array of scalar values derived from each JSON document.

Since JSON document may have an array or even multiple arrays, therefore, path expression may select values from an array. Furthermore, each array element can be an object with common attributes. Users may request range query search over array elements using JSON_EXISTS() queries as shown Q5, Q6, Q7 in Table 9. One approach is to exploit a common schema of purchaserOrder that has items as an array with each array element having *(price, quantity)* as scalar values to answer Q6. In this case, we need to create multi-value functional index. Multi-value functional index implies there can be multiple values derived from each JSON document. Most of the JSON enabled RDBMSs do not have multi-value functional index capability. Instead, a domain index or DML synched materialized view defined using json_table() can be used to emulate multi-value functional index. Either the domain index or DML synched materialized view internally creates and maintains an internal relational table. This internal relational table is kept consistent with the base JSON collection as it is updated whenever there are DML operations on the JSON documents. This is shown below:

```
Create materialized view lineItem_itab(pdid,price, quantity) DML SYNCHED as
SELECT PO.DID AS pdid, JT.price as price, JT.quantity as quantity
```

```
FROM PURCHASEORDER PO, JSON_TABLE(JCOL, '$.purchaseOrder.items[*]'
COLUMN
     Price    number  PATH '$.price',
Quantity number PATH '$.quantity') JT;
CREATE INDEX price_idx ON lineItem_itab(price);
CREATE INDEX quantity_idx ON lineItem_itab(quantity);
```

The internal table lineItem_itab is populated using JSON_TABLE() expression as shown in Q8 in Table 9. It has a column pdid to be joinable with the base JSON collection PurchaseOrder table in Table 1. There are two secondary indices price_idx and quantity_idx on the lineItem_itab table.

```
For Q6 in Table 9:
SELECT did, jdoc
FROM purchaseOrder
WHERE json_exists(jdoc, '$.purchaseOrder.items?(@.price > 100.34  && @.quan-
tity >= 2)')
JSON query rewrite transforms Q6 into the query below which replaces the JSON_
EXISTS() predicate operator by an EXISTS() subquery on table lineItem_itab.
SELECT did, jdoc
FROM purchaseOrder
WHERE EXISTS (SELECT 1 FROM lineitem_itab il WHERE price > 100.34 AND quantity
>= 2 AND il.pdid = purchaseOrder.did)
```

The rewritten query is evaluated efficiently using B+ tree indices name_idx, price_idx, quantity_idx and semi-join with base table purchaseOrder.

The problem of schema-aware index approach in general is that the index definition expression is subject to schema evolution issue. Therefore, applicability of schema-aware index is restricted for indexing commonly searched relative static components of JSON documents in a JSON collection. For ad-hoc search query without assuming a priori the schema of JSON collection, a schema-agnostic indexing approach is desired.

Schema-Agnostic Indexing Approach

The strength of schema-agnostic indexing approach over a JSON collection is that it does not make any assumption of specific schema of each JSON document stored in a JSON collection. The schema-agnostic indexing approach essentially does vertical partition of each JSON document based on its path from root to the node of leaf scalar value and fills in a path-value-index table for all JSON documents in a JSON collection. The principle is the same as that of Indexing XML without schema information in RDBMS (S. Pal et al., 2004). The path-value-index table consists of 4 columns (path, value, docid, dewey encoding key). For each path from the JSON document root to the node that is of scalar value, a row containing 4 columns: the path, the leaf value and the id of JSON document, the dewey encoding key, is inserted into the path-value-index table.

Table 11 shows the content of a path-value index table for purchaseOrder collection. To save space, we only include following paths (purchaseOrder.id, purchaseOrder.items.price, purchaseOrder.items. quantity).

Q6 query in Table 9 can be answered using following equivalent query leveraging the path-value-index table and the secondary B+ tree index on (path, to_number(value), docid) that is created on the path-value-index table.

```
--Q6-query-rewrite using path-value-index table
SELECT did, jdoc
FROM purchaseOrder
WHERE EXISTS(SELECT 1 FROM PATH_VALUE pv1, PATH_VALUE pv2
      WHERE pv1.path = `purchaseOrder.items.price` AND to_number(pv1.value) >
100.34
      AND pv2.path = `purchaseOrder.items.quantity' AND to_number(pv2.value)
>=2
      AND pv1.docid = pv2.docid AND pv1.docid = purchaseOrder.did)
AND common_dewey_parent(pv1.dewey, pv2.dewey))
```

Table 11. Path-value-index table for PurchaseOrder collection

path	Value	docid	Dewey Encoding Key
purchaseOrder.id	1	1	1.1
purchaseOrder.id	2	2	1.1
purchaseOrder.id	3	3	1.1
purchaseOrder.id	98	4	1.1
purchaseOrder.items.price	100	1	1.3.2
purchaseOrder.items.price	350.86	1	1.4.2
purchaseOrder.items.price	52.78	2	1.3.2
purchaseOrder.items.price	35.24	2	1.4.2
purchaseOrder.items.price	345.55	3	1.4.2
purchaseOrder.items.price	546.78	3	1.4.3
purchaseOrder.items.price	5.55	4	1.3.2
purchaseOrder.items.price	6.78	4	1.4.2
purchaseOrder.items.quantity	2	1	1.3.3
purchaseOrder.items.quantity	3	1	1.4.3
purchaseOrder.items.quantity	2	2	1.3.3
purchaseOrder.items.quantity	4	2	1.4.3
purchaseOrder.items.quantity	1	3	1.4.3
purchaseOrder.items.quantity	10	3	1.4.4
purchaseOrder.items.quantity	10	4	1.3.3
purchaseOrder.items.quantity	20	4	1.4.3

The execution plan is to do semi-join of path table with purchaseOrder table. The path table is probed using B+ tree index on (path, to_number(value), docid) . Note we must use common_dewey_parent() operator to make sure the required path and value are in the same document. This is because within a JSON document, *items* is an array, the *price* and *quantity* may not be under the same item array element.

The Path-value-index table layout here is still a logical table design. Physically, there are strategies to keep the table small (S. Pal et al., 2004). A unique id is assigned for each distinct path so that a small integer representing the path id is stored instead of the full path in string form. B+ tree index prefix compression can be applied to (pathid, to_number(value)) to keep the B+ tree index size small. A columnar store of the path-value-index table can fully leverage the columnar compression of columns having many repetitive values to make path-value-index table small. In general, the path-value index table is still quite large in size especially for JSON documents that have many arrays. The fan-out ratio defined as number of rows per JSON document can be quite high. Maintaining schema-agnostic index in-synch with DMLs on the JSON collection has significant I/O overhead. In general, the disadvantage of path-value index table design is that the index size can be even bigger than the original JSON collection. Therefore, to reduce the space consumption of path-value index, both JSON inverted index (Liu et al., 2014) and Schema-agnostic index (D. Shukla et al., 2015) have leveraged the idea of inverted index structures from information retrieval to reduce the size of schema-agnostic index. We will discuss them in section 4.

In summary, here is comparison between schema-aware indexing and schema-agnostic indexing approach

SQL/JSON Query In-Memory Processing

Classical RDBMS keeps data in buffer cache the same format as that of on-disk storage format. Recent approach of in-memory query processing is to populate data in memory in a more query friendly format than the disk storage format. Oracle in-memory columnar processing converts row-storage persistent data into a columnar format in memory so that OLAP query processing can scan in-memory columnar format efficiently (T. Lahiri et al., 2015). Since OLAP queries are ad-hoc in nature and may run various predicates over many columns, so users usually have to maintain multiple indices on those columns. Consequently, this slows down DML performance due to many indices maintenance. It has been shown

Table 12. Comparison between schema-aware and schema-agnostic indexing over JSON collection

	Schema-Aware Indexing	Schema-Agnostic Indexing
Suitable use case	More homogeneous JSON collection with known query predicates	More heterogeneous JSON collection with ad-hoc query predicates
Size	Small	large
Schema Evolution	Less flexible. It can be used to index stable common part of the schema of a JSON collection	Fully flexible without any schema dependency
Indexing maintenance overhead for DML	Less overhead	More overhead
Index based Query Performance	Equivalent to B+ tree index applied to schema-based relational tables.	Less optimal compared with schema-aware index, however, still provide reasonable performance

that leveraging SIMD scanning over columnar in-memory format is fast enough so that there is no need to maintain multiple B+ tree indices to answer OLAP queries. However, few B+ tree indices remain to be useful for OLTP point queries. The idea of disk memory dual format is reflected in-situ query processing (S. Idreos et al., 2011).

SQL/JSON query In-memory processing leverage the same idea. For external textual JSON data, one approach is to apply Mison (Li et al, 2017) technique. Using a SIMD driven fast JSON parser to establish in-memory structural index over each textual JSON document and then pushing down JSON projection and selection into the JSON parser by leveraging the in-memory structural index.

The other approach is to load OSON as in-memory format from parsing JSON text document once and keeping OSON in-memory by leveraging dual format architecture (T. Lahiri et al., 2015). As discussed in section 3.1, OSON supports efficient evaluation of any SQL/JSON operators and JSON_TABLE() table function. Recall that OSON format encodes JSON into three segments: dictionary, navigation tree, leaf value. When multiple OSON instances from a set of JSON documents in a JSON collection are populated in memory, the commonality among the three segments can be shared to reduce overall memory consumption. For example, common dictionary and common leaf value are extracted and shared to create set OSON format upon loading in memory.

Whether it is Mison (Li et al, 2017), OSON (Liu et al., 2016) or CSV indexing structures (S. Idreos et al.,., 2011), they are all binary row in-memory structures that speed up query at each document level. To speed up query over a set of JSON documents via SMID scan of the data, we need columnar layout for JSON. Dremel (Melnik, 2010) and STREED columnar layout (Wang et al., 2017) are examples of JSON columnar encoding formats. However, both of them assume a JSON collection is a homogeneous collection having uniform schema so that re-assembling of original JSON document through columnar decomposition of the data is feasible via storing only the repetition and definition level to track original hierarchical positions. Therefore, for homogeneous JSON collection, it is feasible to load columnar JSON in memory to speed up SQL/JSON queries. A de-generated case for homogeneous JSON collection is that if the JSON scalar is not in array, that is, it has one occurrence for each JSON document, then such value can be projected out as a virtual column of the JSON collection table using JSON_VALUE() expression and then leveraging in-memory caching of virtual column expression yields the best performance (Mishra et al., 2016). For example, for JSON collection in Table 2, placing pre-computed value using *JSON_VALUE(jcol, '$.podate' returning DATE)* expression in memory as a columnar format can speed up predicates of *JSON_VALUE(jcol, '$.podate' returning DATE) between DATE('2018-06-01') and DATE('2018-06-05')*.

For a heterogeneous JSON collection, it is feasible to store tree jump navigation friendly binary JSON on disk with an **in-memory JSON indexing**. Recall that schema-agnostic indexing discussed in section 3.2.2 has built a path-value-index table with secondary composite B+ tree indexes on top of the path-value-index table. This schema-agnostic indexing approach has significant DML maintenance overhead. Therefore, the idea is to make path-value-index table to be an in-memory entity only. The in-memory format for path-value-index can be significantly smaller than disk based equivalent.

JSON DATAGUIDE, SCHEMA DISCOVERY, FULL TEXT SEARCH

JSON DataGuide for Schema Discovery of JSON Collection

Although proposed JSON schema can be used to build JSON schema validator to validate JSON data following JSON schema, relying on JSON schema to store, index and query JSON data cause schema evolution issues that slow down the agile style data management enabled by JSON. Therefore, 'Data First/Schema Later' approach applied to JSON management (Liu et al., 2014) requires the underlying DBMS to compute schema for users so as to guide them on how to query the data. Similar to JSON schema discovery work (Izquierdo et al., 2013), a JSON dataguide (Liu et al., 2016) can be computed from a JSON collection. A JSON DataGuide for a single JSON document instance is computed by extracting the container node skeleton of the JSON data model. Leaf scalar values are replaced by their data type. A JSON DataGuide for a JSON collection is simply a merge of the instance DataGuides across all documents in the collection. This is very similar to the path-value table in schema-agnostic index discussion in section 3.2.2. The JSON DataGuide representation for the purchaseOrder collection in Table 1 is presented in Table 13 below.

Table 13. JSON DataGuide for purhcaseOrder JSON collection

Path	Type
$.purchaseOrder	object
$.purchaseOrder.id	number
$.purchaseOrder.podate	string
$.purchaseOrder.items	array
$.purchaseOrder.items.name	array of string
$.purchaseOrder.items.price	array of number
$.purchaseOrder.items.quantity	array of number
$.purchaseOrder.items.parts	array of array
$.purchaseOrder.items.parts.partName	array of string
$.purchaseOrder.items.parts.partQuantity	array of string
$.purchaseOrder.foreign_id	string
$.purchaseOrder. discount_items	array of array
$.purchaseOrder. discount_items.dis_parts	array of array
$.purchaseorder. discount_items.dis_parts.dis_partName	array of string
$.purchaseOrder. discount_items.dis_parts.dis_partQuantity	array of number
$.purchaseOrder.discount_items.dis_itemName	array of string
$.purchaseOrder.discount_items.dis_itemPrice	array of number
$.purchaseOrder.discount_items.dis_itemQuanitty	array of number

Based on this computed JSON DataGuide by the DBMS, users may use them as guide to write SQL/JSON path language expressions to formulate SQL/JSON queries (example queries in Table 9) to query the JSON collection. Furthermore, RDBMS with JSON data management is able to provide utility tools for users to derive JSON_TABLE() views to view the JSON collection relationally. For example, relational views, materialized or not, Q8 and Q9 in Table 9 can be generated by tools using the computed JSON DataGuide on behalf of users. Relational views over JSON collection is very popular because it provides a bridge between hierarchical data and relational data so that users are able to query JSON collection as if there were stored relationally. The dataguide capability in general has accomplished the 'schema-less for write, schema-rich for query' functionality for JSON data stored and managed by RDBMS (Liu et al., 2016).

The key idea is that JSON DataGuide computation can be supported as a new SQL aggregation function **JSON_DATAGUIDE()**. The flexibility of running JSON DataGuide as a SQL aggregation function is that users have the flexibility of adding other SQL constructs, such as predicates and group by expression to selectively compute JSON DataGuide among different groups of JSON documents that are stored in one JSON collection. Queries in Table 14 show how to compute JSON DataGuide on demand. The output of JSON_DATAGUIDE() is a JSON document that are queryable via SQL/JSON path language. Table 15 shows the result of query Q1.

JSON Full Text Search With JSON Search Index

In section 3.2, JSON collection indexing, we have focused on indexing JSON collection from the perspective that JSON collection is data centric instead of document centric. That is, the leaf scalar data of a JSON collection is merely scalar string data that are typically range searchable, sortable, joinable. However, there are leaf string data that may represent textual paragraph that full text search is more applicable way to query it. Therefore, JSON_TEXTCONTAINS() usable as a predicate in SQL WHERE clause is helpful for user to do full text search within a SQL/JSON path language. For example, a new JSON purhcaseOrder document with "description" field is added into the JSON collection.

To process JSON_TEXTCONTAINS() queries efficiently, there is need to integrate classical inverted index for full text search with hierarchical document object that uses path to express document context to search. To extend inverted index architecture to support full text search capability over JSON collection, we need to index not only on text tokens within leaf string value of a JSON node but also index on

Table 14. JSON_DATAGUDIE() aggregation query example

Query #	Query
Q1	SELECT **JSON_DATAGUIDE(jdoc)** as jdataguide FROM purchaseOrder
Q2	SELECT **JSON_DATAGUIDE(jdoc)** as jdataguide FROM purchaseOrder Where JSON_EXISTS(jdoc, '$.purchaseOrder.foreign_id')
Q3	SELECT JSON_VALUE(jdoc, '$.purchaseOrder.orderDate' return date) as podate, **JSON_DATAGUIDE(jdoc)** as jdataguide FROM purchaseOrder GROUP BY podate

Table 15. Result of Q1 in Table 14

```
[
{
"o:path":"$.purchaseOrder",
 "type":"object",
 "o:length":512
},
{
"o:path":"$.purchaseOrder.id",
 "type":"number",
 "o:length":2
},
{
"o:path":"$.purchaseOrder.items",
 "type":"array",
 "o:length":128
},
...
{
"o:path":"$.purchaseOrder.items.price",
 "type":"number",
 "o:length":8
},
{
"o:path":"$.purchaseOrder.items.quantity",
 "type":"number",
 "o:length":2
},
......
{
"o:path":"$.purhcaseOrder.foreign_id",
 "type":"string",
 "o:length":8
}
]
```

Table 16. New JSON Document amendable for full text search

5	{"purchaseOrder":{"id": 98, "podate": "2015-07-04", **"description": "this is holiday sale discount for Independence Day"** "discount_items": [{"name":"Text Book", "price": 5.57, "quantity": 8, "discount_rate": 0.1 }, {"name":"DVD", "price": 6.78, "quantity": 5, "discount_rate": 0.25 }] }

JSON object field names and their hierarchical relationships (Liu et al., 2014). The principle of building JSON full text search index is the same as that of building XML full text search index (Liu et al., 2014).

However, unlike a standard text indexing tokenizer, the JSON search indexer consumes the JSON event streams from the underlying JSON data. The JSON event stream consumer in the JSON indexer assigns each JSON object field name fetched from the event stream with an interval of starting and ending offset position. The interval of starting and ending offset position of an object field name is always contained by the interval of its parent object field name so that a hierarchical containment relationship

Table 17. SQL/JSON query with JSON_TEXTCONTAINS() example

Query #	Query
Q1	SELECT did FROM purchaseOrder WHERE **JSON_TEXTCONTAINS**(jdoc, '$.purchaseOrder.description', "holiday NEAR discount")
Q2	SELECT did, JSON_VALUE(jdoc, '$.purchaseOrder.podate') FROM purchaseOrder WHERE JSON_EXISTS(jdoc, '$.purchaseOrder.discount_items?(@.discount_rate > 0.1)') AND **JSON_TEXTCONTAINS**(jdoc, '$.purchaseOrder.description', "holiday NEAR discount")
Q3	SELECT JDOC FROM purchaseOrder WHERE JSON_EXISTS(jdoc, '$.purchaseOrder.discount_items?(@.discount_rate > 0.2 && @.quantity >= 4)') AND **JSON_TEXTCONTAINS**(jdoc, '$.purchaseOrder.description', "Independence Day NEAR discount")

between object field names can be determined via testing the within interval bound relationship. JSON scalar string is tokenized as a set of keywords to facilitate full text search. Each keyword is assigned an offset position that is contained by the interval of the parent JSON object field name.

Each JSON object member name is indexed with a posting list consisting of the DOCIDs of JSON objects that contain the object member name and their list of intervals. Each keyword in the leaf data of a JSON object member content is indexed with a posting list consisting of the DOCIDs of JSON objects that contain the keyword and their list of offset positions. By performing an pre-sorted merge join of the posting lists for both keywords and JSON object member names, we can facilitate full text query with JSON path navigation. The containment test between two path steps is done by testing containment of their intervals. The containment test between the keyword and the leaf path step is done by testing containment of the keyword offset position contained within the interval of the leaf path step. This is the underlying mechanism on how JSON_TEXTCONTAINS() in Q1, Q2, Q3 of Table 17 can be efficiently processed using JSON full text search index.

To process Q2 and Q3 of Table 17, however, there is additional need to process range predicates in JSON_EXISTS(). So logically JSON search index shall have two components: indexing the full text and JSON field names through inverted index to evaluate JSON_TEXTCONTAINS(), indexing the leaf scalar value to evaluate JSON_EXISTS(), then join the index results together returned from each index probe. The main cost of maintaining JSON schema-agnostic search index is the DML maintenance overhead (Shukla et al., 2015) So it uses Bw-Tree (Levandoski et al, 2013) as the physical implementation of the "write" data structure. Using principle of log-structured merge-tree (O'Neil et al., 1996) to keep in-memory indexing tree to keep up with fast ingestion of documents and then periodically sync the in-memory indexing with on-disk indexing structure is the general guideline.

CONCLUSION

We are living in an interesting time where E.F Codd's relational model that relies on the existence of static data schema to store, query and index data is being challenged by new style agile application development that does not scale with "schema first, data later" approach imposed by classical RDBMS. This chapter has presented sate of art and practices to address the challenge by extending RDBMS to support schema-less development styles using JSON data model in conjunction with the classical schema-oriented development styles. The storage, query, indexing, schema discovery practices illustrated in this chapter have brought new milestones to support "data first, schema later" based agile application development. The approach of leveraging declarative power of SQL to be applied to query both relational and JSON is natural to SQL users. The principle of storing, indexing JSON data without schema and discovering schema from JSON data for query have been practiced in JSON DBMS products.

Future research and industrial work shall include but not limited to:

- SQL/JSON standard enhancement to support JSON datatype and partial update of JSON datatype declaratively in SQL.
- Supporting efficient partial updatable of binary JSON data storage format to support new enhancements to SQL/JSON standard.
- Enabling more in-memory JSON data processing in conjunction with relational data.
- Maintaining schema-agnostic JSON indexing strategy to reduce DML overhead.
- New approach to schema discovery to manage data without being schema imposed while supporting using JSON schema as a way to validate JSON data.
- Adding more capabilities to integrate relational and JSON data processing more tightly to genuinely realize the advantage of having both "schema first/data later" and "data first/schema later" application development styles hosed by one DBMS product.

We are living in an exciting time to bridge the gap between the schema rigid RDBMS world and the new style schema flexible RDBMS world (Liu et al., 2015).

REFERENCES

Cánovas Izquierdo, J. L., & Cabot, J. (2013). Discovering implicit schemas in JSON data. *Proceedings of ICWE, 2013*, 68–83.

Chasseur, C., Li, Y., & Patel, J. M. (2013). Enabling JSON Document Stores in Relational Systems. *Proceedings of WebDB, 2013*, 1–6.

Chen. (1977). The entity-relationship model: a basis for the enterprise view of data. *AFIPS '77 Proceedings*, 77-84.

Codd, E. F. (1970). A Relational Model of Data for Large Shared Data Banks. *Communications of the ACM, 13*(6), 377–387. doi:10.1145/362384.362685

Fagin, R. (1979). Normal Forms and Relational Database Operators. *ACM SIGMOD International Conference on Management of Data*.

Idreos, S., Alagiannis, I., Johnson, R., & Ailamaki, A. (2011). Here are my Data Files. Here are my Queries. Where are my Results? *CIDR, 2011*, 57–68.

Lahiri, T., Chavan, S., Colgan, M., Das, D., Ganesh, A., Gleeson, M., ... Zaït, M. (2015). Oracle Database In-Memory: A dual format in-memory database. *ICDE, 2015*, 1253–1258.

Levandoski, J. J., Lomet, D. B., & Sengupta, S. (2013). The Bw-Tree: A B-tree for new hardware platforms. *ICDE, 2013*, 302–313.

Li, Y., Katsipoulakis, N. R., Chandramouli, B., Goldstein, J., & Kossmann, D. (2017). Mison (2017). A Fast JSON Parser for Data Analytics. *PVLDB, 10*(10), 1118–1129.

Liu & Gawlick. (2015). Management of Flexible Schema Data in RDBMSs - Opportunities and Limitations for NoSQL. *CIDR 2015*.

Liu, Z. H., Chang, H. J., & Sthanikam, B. (2012). Efficient Support of XQuery Update Facility in XML Enabled RDBMS. *ICDE, 2012*, 1394–1404.

Liu, Z. H., Hammerschmidt, B., & McMahon, D. (2014). JSON data management: supporting schemaless development in RDBMS. *SIGMOD Conference 2014*, 1247-1258. 10.1145/2588555.2595628

Liu, Z. H., Hammerschmidt, B., McMahon, D., Lu, Y., & Chang, H. J. (2016). Closing the functional and Performance Gap between SQL and NoSQL. *SIGMOD Conference*, 227-238. 10.1145/2882903.2903731

Liu, Z. H., Lu, Y., & Chang, H. J. (2014). Efficient support of XQuery Full Text in SQL/XML enabled RDBMS. *ICDE, 2014*, 1132–1143.

Melnik, Gubarev, Long, Romer, Shivakumar, Tolton, & Vassilakis. (2010). Interactive Analysis of Web-Scale Datasets. *VLDB 2010*.

Melton, J. (2003). *Advanced SQL, 1999: Understanding Object-Relational and Other Advanced Features*. Morgan Kaufmann.

Mishra, A., Chavan, S., Holloway, A., Lahiri, T., Liu, Z. H., Chakkappen, S., ... Marwah, V. (2016). Accelerating Analytics with Dynamic In-Memory Expressions. *PVLDB, 9*(13), 1437–1448.

O'Neil, P. E., Cheng, E., Gawlick, D., & O'Neil, E. J. (1996). The Log-Structured Merge-Tree (LSM-Tree). *Acta Informatica, 33*(4), 351–385. doi:10.1007002360050048

Pal, S., Cseri, I., Schaller, G., Seeliger, O., Giakoumakis, L., & Zolotov, V. V. (2004). Indexing XML Data Stored in a Relational Database. *VLDB, 2004*, 1134–1145.

Shukla, D., Thota, S., Raman, K., Gajendran, M., Shah, A., Ziuzin, S., ... Lomet, D. B. (2015). Schema-Agnostic Indexing with Azure DocumentDB. *PVLDB, 8*(12), 1668–1679.

Stonebraker, M. (1986). Object Management in a Relational Data Base System. *COMPCON, 1986*, 336–341.

Stonebraker, M., Wong, E., Kreps, P., & Held, G. (1976). The Design and Implementation of INGRES. *ACM Transactions on Database Systems, 1*(3), 189–222. doi:10.1145/320473.320476

Tahara, D., Diamond, T., & Abadi, D. J. (2014). a SQL system for multi-structured data. *SIGMOD Conference 2014*, 815-826

Wang, Z., Zhou, D., & Chen, S. (2017). An Analytical Database System for TrEE-structured Data. *PVLDB, 10*(12), 1897–1900.

KEY TERMS AND DEFINITIONS

JSON DataGuide: A summary of all possible JSON paths and leaf value domain type for a collection of JSON documents to assist formulation of query to the JSON collection. It is conceptually the computed schema of the JSON collection.

JSON Search Index: A schema-agnostic indexing approach over a JSON collection that does not make any assumption of specific schema JSON documents. It speeds up ad-hoc SQL/JSON path value and keyword search queries over JSON collection.

OSON: Oracle optimized binary JSON encoding format that is capable of running jump navigation to drastically support SQL/JSON path language evaluation and is capable of doing piece-wise update of OSON bytes to avoid full document replacement.

Chapter 3
A Survey on JSON Data Stores

Lubna Irshad
Nanjing University of Aeronautics and Astronautics, China

Zongmin Ma
 https://orcid.org/0000-0001-7780-6473
Nanjing University of Aeronautics and Astronautics, China

Li Yan
Nanjing University of Aeronautics and Astronautics, China

ABSTRACT

The World Wide Web is a bunch of interlinked documents full of information and knowledge where people search sources to interpret relevant information. As the modern web is becoming more interactive and data-centric, it is necessary to focus on how to exchange data efficiently, easily, and quickly. There are several ways to exchange data among web services like XML and JSON. JSON is one of its kind of emerging data-interchange format. Its data model maps the type system of many programming languages is recommended for web development, especially Java scripting language. Previously, JSON was the focus by NoSQL community, but presently, the relational database community also claims to manage both relational and JSON data in one platform efficiently. This chapter focuses on various approaches to use JSON stores with NoSQL and relational database systems. The study reveals work accomplished so far to identify the working of JSON Stores as NoSQL stores and role relational system plays to enhance the power of JSON stores.

INTRODUCTION

The formal international standard for JSON is RFC-4627 (Request for Comments). Douglas Crockford, the discoverer of the JSON (JavaScript Object Notation) specification, describes JSON as "a lightweight data-interchange format" (Introducing JSON, n.d.). As a part of well-defined ECMA (European Computer Manufacturers Association)-262 that is widely followed, makes it flexible to use. It consists of attributes (name/value) pairs, list of values and objects that is easy to understand, develop and integrate. Initially JSON was the focus of the NoSQL (Not only SQL) community providing native JSON Stores like

DOI: 10.4018/978-1-5225-8446-9.ch003

MongoDB (MongoDB, n.d.), CouchDB (Apache CouchDB, n.d.) and many more (Beyer et al., 2005). However, due to its swift acceptance by Web developers, it has gained attention in RDBMS (Relational Database Management System) to embed it as a part. JSON's "No-schema" nature helps the developer to start working with data in no time without the hassle of schema design (Liu, Hammerschmidt, & McMahon, 2016). It is self-describing and has independent text format that exists in almost every significant programming language (Introducing JSON, n.d.). JSON is a format that fills a particular niche to integrate multiple services across many platforms and require no prior knowledge. There are several ways to exchange data among Web Services; JSON is one of its kind of emerging data-interchange format as compared to XML and many other NoSQL document stores.

XML (Extensible Markup Language) and JSON both are hierarchical, human readable and have the support of many programming languages. JSON has replaced XML for data serialization (Yan Betts, 2014) as XML is heavy, more complex and requires more bytes for transfer even for a smaller task. XML required parser while JavaScript function can parse JSON easily without any additional parser. Format of JSON is concise as compared to XML that has lengthy tags and namespaces (Haq, Khan, & Hussain, 2015). JSON is semi-structured hierarchal NoSQL data model as described in Figure 1. It is among one of the most popularly used categories of NoSQL Database System.

NoSQL database is an alternative approach as compared to traditional Relational Database Management Systems (RDBMS). In traditional RDBMS, it is mandatory to design schema carefully before storing/adding data in the tables and creating relations (Liu, Hammerschmidt, & McMahon, 2016). NoSQL databases is a technology that helps to design a database that encompasses a variety of data models like document databases, key-value pair stores, columnar stores and graph formats stores (Chandra, 2015). NoSQL databases deal with a large volume of structured, semi-structured, and unstructured data that is scalable and vary from time to time (MongoDB, n.d.). Data can be validated using validation rules (MongoDB, n.d.). In today's development where time to market is crucial, agile development is gaining much popularity and NoSQL databases are fulfilling these challenges very well as compared to RDBMS.

RDBMS is a packet full of features that include native query language, efficient query processing techniques, indexes for quicker data retrieval, virtual tables to store and query sensitive data (views), triggers for predefined actions, multilevel user access control permissions, data recoveries in case of disaster, ACID (Atomicity, Consistency, Isolation, Durability) safety guaranteed transactions and many more. RDBMS provides immediate data access, stiff data consistency and quick data retrieval for transactional enterprise applications but in many applications quick developments, scalability prevails over everything.

JSON Document Stores besides pulses have some minuses too as compared to relational databases. Major limitations of these NoSQL Document Stores are lacking powerful native query like SQL, missing ACID transaction capability and challenging for data analysis/processing (Chandra, 2015). This trend leads to increase complexity of the management of data with polyglot persistence (Fowler & Sadalage, 2012). On one hand, by using JSON developers gains the benefits of reducing development overhead, costs and improves the quality of service. On the other hand, loses the power of rich native query processing constructs, indexes for quicker data retrieval, safety guaranteed transactions and many more.

This paper focuses on JSON document Storage and up-to-date review of various approaches to store JSON document in NoSQL and Relational Database System. In addition, we have discussed the advantages of using JSON in NoSQL and Relational Databases.

The main theme of this paper has three folds. The first section discusses the background that apprehends JSON data model, its comparison with XML, JSON schema that describes and validate JON document, support of JSON in NoSQL databases and relational databases along with their structural differences. It will help to understand the tradeoffs and appropriate approach under certain circumstances. The second section describes existing approaches for JSON data management with NoSQL document databases like MongoDB and CouchDB. It also designates schema-less and schema-based JSON support in RDBMS. It describes major support, limitations, and application in real time system of various approaches in NoSQL and relational databases. Section three consists of Conclusion and future guidelines. It concludes all major mentioned approaches of NoSQL and relational databases to support JSON along with future guidelines. Future guidelines identify research areas to enhance the power of JSON document store in combination with traditional relational databases. This paper does not include all the approaches that have been adapted so far for JSON data management, as it is cumbersome to discuss all in one paper. Although the most popular and adopted are discussed.

BACKGROUND

JSON is one of the types of data model that maps the type system of many programming languages that is frequently in use for Web development these days, especially with JavaScript language (JS). JavaScript is one of the most commonly used languages for Web and mobile applications. JavaScript along JSON (JavaScript Object Notation) Data Model is going to become leading standard and gaining much popularity. It is semi-structured hierarchal NoSQL data model. XML is also a document based semi-structured data use for serialization but it has many constructs, it is complex and heavy weighted for data transfer as compared to JSON. XML and JSON both are hierarchical, document-oriented, semi-structured data serialization format. However, JSON is a lightweight data serialization format that maps object literals of many programming languages, especially JavaScript. Being easy to understand by human as well as by machine it has been gaining much popularity to send and receive API (application Programming Interface) request over HTTP protocol. API is a part of a server that receives a request and sends a response to the client (listen and reply to a client).

JSON Data Model

It consists of four primitive types String, Number, Boolean and Null and two structured types I-e Objects and Arrays. The object is a collection of pairs of attributes/key and their values where pairs can again be a JSON Object (Bourhis, Reutter, Su´arez, & Vrgoˇc, 2017) Attribute/key is of String type and value can hold any type (number, string, Boolean, null). Arrays are order lists of values. Objects and Arrays can be any of primitive type or can have hierarchically structured values too. In short, the JSON data model processes following properties:

- Hierarchical Data with nested objects and array
- Attributes or keys with Dynamic Types in objects or collection
- Number of attributes vary from objects to objects
- No predefined data structure or dynamic data structure

Figure 1. Sample of JSON document

```
Employee :{

          {   "name": "John",
              "height": 5.8,
              "prosecuted ": False
              "address": {"country" :"UK"
                          "city": "London",
                          },
              "kid": ["Zain", "Jacky"]
          },

          {   "name": "Smith"
              "height": "short",
              "prosecuted": True
          }
      }
```

JSON vs. XML

For serialization, the rate of data transfer and performance depends upon data interchange format (Haq, Khan, & Hussain, 2015) that encodes metadata to support structural attribute of information (Chen, 2002). XML and JSON both are data exchange format and both are hierarchical, human readable and have the support of many programming languages.XML had been the most famous and widely adapted data exchange format but JSON has taken lead on XML as it is simple, flexible, compact format and

Table 1. Companion of JSON and XML

JSON	XML
Simple syntax based on key/Value pair	Complex Syntax based on tags
Lightweight object serialization	Heavy Weight Object Serialization due to size
Smaller Data Exchange Format	Bigger Data Exchange Format
Compact data due to key-value pair	Huge data size due to tags and namespace
Almost all Browser Support	All new browsers supports but cross-browser XML parsing is a bit tricky.
Speedy de-serialization in JavaScript	Slower de-serialization in JavaScript
Simple API for JS and many other languages	Complicated APIs for JS and other languages

light weighted. There are certain query languages designed for JSON (JSONiq, JAQL) and for XML (XQuery). However, XQuery was designed for XML but can also be used for JSON (Bamford et al., 2009). A few major differences that are making JSON more adaptable as compared to XML are mention below

Unlike JSON, a XML document contains parent root node that encompasses other nodes/values and maintains tree-like structures (Khan & Rao, 2001). To send out small information XML required opening and closing tags each time that is redundant information and requires a lot of bytes as compared to JSON. Simple Syntax and light weighted in nature are the main two reasons for the quick acceptance of JSON as a new format. As said by Crockford "JSON is a fat-free alternative to XML".

JSON Schema

Traditional application development and data analysis it is vital to have some notion of structure or schema (Klettke, St¨orl, & Scherzinger, 2015). JSON Schema specifies a format to define the structure of JSON data for validation, documentation, and interaction control (JSON: Schema and metadata, n.d.). JSON Schema is not some algorithm, script or a computer program, data in it is also a JSON document (JSON-based). It is just a declarative format for "describing the structure of other data" (JSON data) (Droettboom et al., 2015). It not only validates JSON documents, but also describes and defines their attributes and types. JSON Schema is the description of JSON document; it affirms valid JSON document by describing attributes with types, mandatory attributes, the hierarchy of attributes and their relationship. There are many online free validators are available to check the validity of JSON document w.r.t JSON Schema. Also, free online converters based on IETF (Internet Engineering Task Force) Draft are available to generate JSON Schema from JSON Document and vice versa like (Wright &Lu_, 2016)

There are certain rules to construct defined in drafts of JSON Schema that specify concepts, syntax and validation rules (Wright & Luff, 2016). However, there are some online tools available to construct the basic building block of JSON Schema. Mandatory parameters for requesting through APIs are handled through "required" property. Like relational systems, handling JSON Document along with Schema is very easy. There is a provision of "allOf", "anyOf", "oneOf" constructs to handle multiple data types of same attributes or to combine multiple schemas (Pezoa, Reutter, Suarez, Ugarte, & Vrgo˘c, 2016). There

Figure 2. Example of JSON schema

```
{
  "$schema": "http://json-schema.org/draft-04/schema#",
  "type": "object",
  "properties": {
                "name": { "type": "string" },
                "height": { "type": "number"  },
                "prosecuted": { "type": "boolean" },

                "address": { "type": "object",
                            "properties": { "country": {"type": "string" } } },

                "kid": { "type": "array",
                        "items": [ {  "type": "string" } ] }
              },
    "required": [ "name", "height", "prosecuted" ]
}
```

are certain assertions that adds constraints on an instance to make it a valid instance like "minItems", "maxItems", "uniqueItems", "minProperties", "maxProperties" and "required" etc.

Yet when accessing this data programmatically, it is vital to have some reliable notion of its structure or schema. This holds for traditional application development, as well as when analyzing large scientific data sets: Without knowing the general structure of the data, and in particular its structural outliers, it becomes virtually impossible to do any pragmatic application development or meaningful data analysis.

NoSQL Document Store

Database management systems that store data as JSON documents is a JSON document store or document-oriented databases. NoSQL database incorporates variety of data models like document databases, key/value pair stores, columnar stores and graph formats stores for structured, semi-structured, and unstructured data that may vary from time to time. Their detail is as mentioned below in the Table.

Relational Databases

RDBMS platforms follow the relational data model (Melton, 2003) based on "schema earlier, data afterward "approach. It proposes simplified manipulation logic based on tables to store data and their relationships. It maintains and enforces certain data relationships between tables in the forms of unique keys. Entity/Relationship (E/R) modeling (Chen, 2002) that defines the master-detail join pattern (Liu et al., 2014) is an effectual way to break down entities into tables and relations, where relations link multiple tables using the primary and foreign key. In a table, the sequence of columns and rows is in-

Table 2. Types of NoSQL databases

Key-value Model	It is the simplest type of NoSQL databases. It consists of key values pair and stores data in a schema-less way.
Column Store	The wide-column store is more like an invertible table, which stores data column wise. This model achieves high performance and scalability by sectioning out columns.
Document Database	It is more like a structured database but still uses the key-value concept and a bit complex. Each document in this type of database has its own data and unique key. It uses a unique key to retrieve it. It is a good choice for managing document-oriented data
Graph Database	It contains interconnected data presented in the form of a graph, where nodes and edges represent information. *Nodes* are the entities in the graph with attributes (key/value). Edges are the relationship between entities. A relationship always has a direction, a type, a *start node*, an *end node* two and nodes can share any number or type of relationships without sacrificing performance (Fowler & Sadalage, 2012).

Table 3. NoSQL Document stores possess BASE transaction properties. Features of BASE Properties are as mentioned below

Basically Available	The database system does guarantee Availability. It states that a failure may disrupt access to a segment of data but not a complete database.
Soft State	The state of the system may change over time so the copies of a data item may be inconsistent
Eventually Consistent	Eventually consistent is just as it means. Once all input has received, the system will ultimately become consistent and propagate changes but the system will not check the consistency before every transaction.

Table 4. ACID transaction description

Atomicity	Atomicity of transaction follows the all-or-nothing approach. Database transaction is either completely successful or fully failed, keeps RDBMS in a valid state. It cannot be partially complete
Consistency	The **consistency** of transactions guarantees that the database will remain in a valid state throughout data transaction that is from one valid state to another. In case of failure, the entire transaction will rollback by keeping RDBMS in a valid state
Isolation	Isolation is insulation of one client's transaction from all others interacting with the same RDBMS at the same time
Durability	Durability ensures persistence of completed or successful transaction. Any kind of system failure, power loss, and other system, breakdowns do not affect the data stability.

significant which helps to simplify query and retrieve data in any order along with various sequences from multiple tables. Hallmark of relational databases that take it ahead from any other databases is the ACID (Atomicity, Consistency, Isolation, and Durability) model and its more powerful flexible querying language SQL. Features of ACID Model are as mentioned below.

NoSQL Document Stores Vs Relational Databases

Database technology mainly divided into two categories SQL and NoSQL or in other words relational and non-relational. The categories on the bases of their build, storage, data organization, and querying mechanism. As there is, no one-size-fits-all solution of every problem so both can use as per requirements in different scenarios. However, before opting any of two databases one must be cautious and fully aware of their legitimate limitations and issues that are associated with them. A few basic differences between these two systems are as mentioned below

EXISTING APPROACHES FOR JSON DATA STORES

JavaScript Object Notation is the current hotspot for developers. It is unstructured, flexible and readable by humans and machine at the same time. Many database management systems support JSON format to store, retrieve and organize JSON as NoSQL Document Stores and Relational Databases. Furthermore, JSON functions and operators provide validation and fast retrieval. So now, JSON documents can be stored as text in key-value stores (NoSQL) or in relational database systems as JSON Datatype. However, storing JSON data in NoSQL or RDBMS differs in many folds.

JSON in NoSQL Document Store

Increasing demand in modern application resulted in a generation of NoSQL databases that includes a wide variety of databases technologies; a document store is the most popular and used once. JSON Document store is one of the types of NoSQL Databases. JSON document has made it easy to store and manage application data. It is flexible to serialize objects containing information in the form of document. Each document is a sort of object/instance but unlike object/instance it can hold varies attributes in each object (missing or null attributes). In the broader expect, document stores are JSON objects composed of native data types of many programming languages. Indexes support faster queries and can include keys from embedded documents and arrays. Query result of NoSQL databases with JSON can

Table 5. A few major differences between NoSQL and relational databases

Data Structure
The basic difference between both the systems is the structure for which they have designed. NoSQL database handles unstructured or semi-structured data while relational database deals with structured data. RDBMS, in addition, requires a clear normalized structure to store and organize data as per defined normalization forms. NoSQL, on the other hand, can manage text, videos, images, emails, social media, documents and any kind of unstructured or semi-structured data without a prior definition of structure.
Data Model
Relational model adopts "Schema first – data later" approach while NoSQL model embraces "data first-schema later or never" approach. It is easy to manage data in RDBMS if the structure of data is predefined. However, NoSQL is flexible, easy and fast for development, if requirements vary with time.
Transaction Capability
The relational databases strongly follow the ACID (Atomicity, Consistency, Isolation, and Durability) properties while the NoSQL databases follow BASE (Basically Available, Soft State, Eventual consistency) principles (Chandra, 2015). The major issue in BASE property is lacking consistency feature in databases; it is the responsibility of the developer. So ACID is simple code, robust database and BASE is complex code, simple database. Features of ACID and BASE transaction properties are as mentioned below in Table 2.
Querying Capability
NoSQL database has begun its journey without a universal query language like relational databases. MongoDB and CouchDB use a query language but it still has many limitations and provides simple DML and some other operation. Many NoSQL database models have defined their own declarative query language that uses MapReduce job (Google's MapReduce or Hadoop Distributed File System or Hadoop MapReduce etc.) for aggregation and multiple collections access. For advance query, it is an overhead on a developer to code for the retrieval of data. RDBMS use SQL (Structured Query Language) to manage and administer the huge amount of data. It stores, update, retrieve, analyze and manage all relational data efficiently and easily.
Scalability
Scalability is handling of a large volume of reading and writing operations in databases at low latency that have high request rates. It spread data on multiple servers or clustered so that multiple hosts can work simultaneously. It not only enhances storage space but also improves performance. The biggest edge of NoSQL over RDBMS is scalability. In traditional RDBMS, scalability in the read operation is not a big issue but write operation is difficult. Scalability in the write operation is keeping all clusters up-to-date and flush out write on the disk before any response. This overhead is due to the ACID model, which is the building block of RDBMS. However, the BASE model of NoSQL is flexible and data can easily scaled-out to too many nodes. Data might not be consistent or up-to-date all the time but becomes consistent eventually, as per definition of the BASE model.
Rapid Development/Frequent Updates
In today's development where time to market is crucial, agile development is gaining much popularity and NoSQL databases are fulfilling these challenges very well as compared to RDBMS. With NoSQL, developers can quickly start work without prior defining schema. It is cost-effective, reduces development overhead and improves quality of service. Another side of picture RDBMS required predefined normalized structure to manage data in advance to start development.

Figure 3. JSON document store vs relational databases

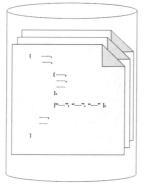 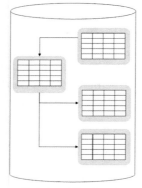

JSON Document Store   Relational Databases

parse easily by almost all programming languages, as its data models maps the type system of many programming languages. They distribute data across the cluster of machines easily as compared to relational DB; where for distribution hardware requirement is very high. Many database systems that are specially designed to handle document stores include MongoDB, CouchDB, DocumentDB, MarkLogic, OrientDB, BaseX and many more.

MongoDB

MongoDB is an open-source NoSQL document database. It provides high performance, high availability, and automatic scaling (MongoDB, n.d.). It supports dynamic schema and collection of documents that reduces expensive joins like in relational databases. Its main features along with schema-less in nature include horizontal scaling, indexing, aggregation support, and multiple storage engines, etc. It stores data in the form of groups called collections with unique identifiers. The collection is a combination of documents or key-value pair that is retrieved by a unique identifier. The value can Boolean, integer, float, date, string and binary types, an array of documents or key-value pairs. MongoDB stores data in BSON (binary JSON) format that is light weighted, fast and traversable.

MongoDB supports a rich query language to support CURD (Create, Update, read, Delete) operations, Data Aggregations, Text Search and Geospatial Queries (MongoDB, n.d.). Simple query construct is easy and flexible and easy for those who understand SQL. For complex aggregation MapReduce job is required that is a bit tricky to handle. Support for high-performance data persistence provides embedded data models that help to reduces I/O activity on database system in addition with indexes on keys. Find Function of MongoDB facilitates to return an array of JSON Document by taking two parameters (filer and projection). Filter parameter selects JSON documents and projection parameter returns the selected the part of the document (Bourhis et al., 2017).

Replication model manages fail-overs and data redundancy automatically, known as "Replica Set". A replica set is a group of MongoDB servers that maintain the same data set, providing redundancy and increasing data availability (MongoDB, n.d.). MongoDB supports dynamic queries with automatic use of indices, like RDBMSs (Cattell, 2011).

Key feature of MongoDB is Sharding or horizontal scaling. With the increase in data, scaling has been becoming the greatest challenge and MongoDB provide it through Sharding technique. Sharding is a process of distributing data across multiple machines that is a tedious task. It requires proper division of data and management of reading/writing operations between different machines. Last but not the least it is platform independent, can works with Windows, UNIX, Linux, etc.

Eliot Horowitz, CTO, and Co-Founder of MongoDB claimed in his document published on Feb 2018 to support multi-document transactions in MongoDB 4.0, making it the only database to combine the speed, flexibility, and power of the document model with ACID data integrity guarantees. Through snapshot isolation, transactions provide a globally consistent view of data and enforce all-or-nothing execution to maintain data integrity" (Horowitz, 2018). MongoDB is picking up where they left off by combining key relational database capabilities with the work that internet pioneers have done to address the requirements of modern applications (MongoDB, n.d.).

MongoDB is a NoSQL distributed key-value database that designed for the storage of big data at Social Networks like Facebook. Its main advantage is to save data in the form of one document; supports document-oriented features and use MapReduce for complex querying. It uses key-value mechanism to query that is faster than the relational query. Another big advantage is horizontal scaling that allows adding more machines with the growth of data and traffic to maintain availability and responsive speed. With auto-sharding and auto-failover provision, it evenly distributes data to different nodes when exceeds to its threshold. Besides user can define its own threshold limit.

Limitations of MongoDB

MongoDB is good for handling big data but on the other side, it is challenging to maintain the relationship between data. It is not a good choice for related data like a bank with account etc. Due to lack of atomicity feature, it cannot use for transactional data where it is compulsory to update many records simultaneously like in banking, business applications and many more. It is not good in handling multiple linked document, therefore it requires the user to store all its data in one document. Similarly, being all data in one document it requires multiple queries to perform join operation. Another important issue with MongoDB is RAM (Random Access Memory) limitation in Operating system. MongoDB uses memory mapped file and uses virtual memory provided by the operating system and hardware only. Like in a 32-bit machine, the operating system will use 2GB and leave 2GB for MongoDB memory mapped files. It results in insertion failure without any warning. It may also corrupt data by giving unclean shutdown detect warning on memory mapped file. We can say it is not one solution to fit in all problems.

Applications of MongoDB

MongoDB is an open source cross-platform compatible database. It is good for many applications and can use with many existing frameworks. It is suitable for applications where the design may change rapidly. It is an excellent choice for applications that require fast and flexible data access. Power of handling unstructured data, horizontal scaling and fast iteration makes it best suited for fast mobile application development. It affirms a variety of data types, stores and incorporates multimedia, tweets, comments and more that makes it more reliable for Content Management Applications (CMA). It has a special function for location-based data analytics and operations that helps in extraction of information with ease for Geospatial data. It is also good for E-Commerce and other applications however, it is not suitable for highly coupled or transactional system.

CouchDB

Apache has been handling his CouchDB has project early 2008 (Cattell, 2011). CouchDB stores document data in the JSON format. CouchDB is somewhat similar to MongoDB. It is schema-less, lockless, provides indexes on collections, facilitates scalability and provides a document query mechanism. Document query mechanism handle document like attachments and fields consists of text, numbers, Boolean and lists. Like document stores it. To save, update, retrieve and delete operations on JSON Document it uses the RESTful HTTP API.

CouchDB querying is a bit complex and is possible only on predefined views. These views facilitate to filter documents, retrieve data in a specific order, and creating indexes. It uses MapReduce for defining views, data indexing, searching and aggregation that is cumbersome and not much easy. Map reduce has two folds. First, it looks at all of the documents. Second, it creates a mapping of document for further processing. Mapping is a onetime process and occurs again only if document updates.

Figure 4. CouchDB vs MongoDB data model

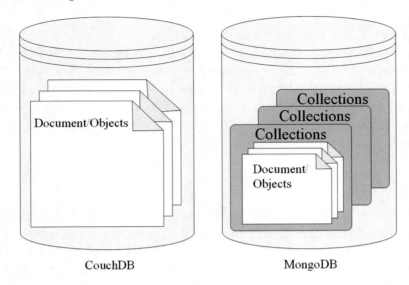

CouchDB   MongoDB

Like MongoDB, it provides replication model named *"Eventual Consistency"*. *In* this model changes copies to a node of document one by one without affecting other node and eventually all nodes syncs while MongoDB replication model is not for scalability it is for failovers. Regarding updating each document, with a commit, all updates flush on the disk by writing updates to the end of a file that lower the risk of conflicts. It provides master-master and master-slave replication. Developer can select replication and filter document, to copy on a specific device, which helps in optimizing the memory usage of mobiles. Many platforms recommend CouchDB for mobile application due to less memory utilization. By using this mechanism along with MVCC CouchDB has claimed to achieve Document level ACID semantics.

Limitations of CouchDB

CouchDB is also a NoSQL distributed key-value database. CouchDB is also good in handling big data but like MongoDB, it cannot use for transactional data where it is required to update many records simultaneously and partial update may cause disaster. CouchDB stores document as JSON BLOB that can be infinitely large and nested, however large document degrades performance. Good thing about CouchDB is maintaining a log of all create, edit and delete operations on documents, although it requires all views to process these changes (What Every Developer Should Know About CouchDB. (n.d.)). It requires MapReduce views for querying that optimizes the data. Although, every change in a document, requires the view to change or refresh as well. All queries can perform on some pre-defined view therefore, arbitrary queries are difficult to handle. The temporary view is required to create for a random query that does not have a predefined view. It allows as many views as require on a single document but more views degrade performance. It stores and indexes views in design docs and changing or deleting view require to index all of the views again that also degrades performance if happens frequently. Besides, MapReduce is a powerful but complex MapReduce may affect performance.

Applications of CouchDB

CouchDB is a best-fit solution for many applications. It can use standalone or with many renowned frameworks. CouchDB is mostly suited for online interactive document or Web applications due to its HTTP interface. It uses HTTP API for communication that makes it more suited for Web applications. It is excellent for Web and Offline Mobile Applications: It is compelling for offline mobile application development due to its high performance and reliability that it provides through Replication Protocol model and network infrastructure. MapReduce Replication also helps for data optimization and management. It is like an API that saves a lot of time.

Summary

JSON Document Stores like MongoDB (Liu, Hammerschmidt, & McMahon, 2014) and CouchDB (Liu et al., 2014) stores and retrieve JSON Objects in their primary format. In other words, MongoDB and CouchDB uses JSON to store its records in the form of JSON BLOB. An efficient binary format, query language, and secondary indices are making MongoDB lead the race of NoSQL document store as compared to CouchDB (Chasseur, Li, & Patel, 2013a). Couchbase Server 4.0 has also introduced N1QL, a powerful query language that extends SQL to JSON, enabling developers to leverage both the power of SQL and the flexibility of JSON (Petkovi´c, n.d.). The document stores generally do not provide explicit locks and have weaker concurrency and atomicity properties than traditional ACID-compliant databases (Cattell, 2011). However, the recent version of CouchDB claimed to be ACID compliant of transactions as far as a single document is concerned that is a big achievement. On the other hand, CTO and Co-Founder of MongoDB also broadcast the news that in the latest release of MongoDB there will be provision of ACID data/transaction guarantee. MongoDB's team is focusing to leverage the capabilities of traditional relational databases to make their design more mature. ACID compliance in NoSQL Document stores will is going to be an added benefit for data collected or generated.

Table 6. Comparison of a few prominent features

	MongoDB	**CouchDB**
Storage Format	Stores Document in a binary format called BSON.	Stores JSON in binary format with a special JSON type
Querying Language	It provides simple query construct that is close to SQL. For complex aggregation uses MapReduce.	Querying is possible only on predefined views and uses MapReduce function. Uses N1QL query language, a bit complex.
Indexes	For efficient querying indexes are mandatory otherwise, it slows down the read process. With indexes it provides much faster read as compared to CouchDB	Views in CouchDB are similar to indexes in SQL, used for efficient indexing and representing relationships between the documents. B-tree index structure keeps all the results of these views.
Replication	Replication model manages fail-overs and data redundancy automatically. Only master-salve replication is provided	Eventual Consistency model copy changes to all nodes one by one without affecting other node. Offers master-master and master-slave replication.
ACID Compliance Transaction	Provided for single document only	Will be available in the new release
Analysis	If the database is growing and maximum throughput is required MongoDB is a best choice	If replication, durability and mobile development are requirement then CouchDB is best

JSON in Relational Databases

Being Simple, easy and close to the type system of many programming languages JSON gain popularity in no times. JSON Document Store (NoSQL Document Stores) came in the ground to replacing traditional databases. NoSQL and RDBMS now both can handle JSON Document well depending upon the application requirement. In applications where consistency does not matter much, JSON Document Store is very small and not many operations or analysis is required NoSQL can be used. However, RDBMS is the best option if consistency, performance, ACID transaction, analytical processing is required. To gain the best of both worlds, traditional databases have leveraged JSON to benefit developers and database administrators.

Schema-Based Development of JSON in RDBMS

"Enabling JSON store in Relational System" (Chasseur et al., 2013a) is an approach that suggests to breakdowns JSON objects into a path-value vertical relational table based on their primitive types. It uses Automated Mapping Layer: Argo on the top of traditional RDBMS. It provides application/user direct access of JSON data into a relational model along with SQL-based query language for JSON querying i.e. called Argo/SQL (Chasseur et al., 2013a). It uses all the ease-of-use benefits of JSON in addition to highly useable query language and other RDBMS features. To prove his concept authors have also specified a "NOBENCH" benchmark by executing several queries successfully and efficiently using Argo/SQL.

The author has defined an approach named "Argo" to overcome all the limitations and to provide ACID semantics using relational command. It consists of two major parts "Argo Mapping Layer" and "Argo/ SQL". Argo Mapping Layer maps JSON Document to Relational Database and uses Argo/SQL for querying JSON Data. Therefor Argo provides a layer to fill a gap between JSON data and relational system by mingling JSON's flexible schema-less nature with the efficient query constructs and ACID transactions of traditional relational systems (Chasseur et al., 2013a). A NOBENCH benchmark has also defined that uses Argo/SQL on a prescribed model and returns results successfully

Argo Mapping Layer not only fulfills all JSON Standards by handling schema flexibility, sparseness, hierarchical data, and dynamic types but also stores JSON data in relational system to provide ACID Semantics. It decomposes JSON objects into a relational format. It uses vertical Table Format Approach inspired by (Petkovi´c, n.d.) to creates a distinct table for primitive types (String, Number Boolean) for collection of JSON. Each table has a standard objid, keystr as well as key-value column based on each data type. Attributes from the document stores in all three tables based on the type of attributes' value (Chasseur et al., 2013a). Each object holds a unique id that is common in all three tables as depicted in Figure 4. For hierarchical data like objects and array key flattening approached has used. Parent key along with separator character "." stores the nested objects and arrays. Arrays are stored with indexes (enclosed by square brackets) to keep a record of its position like in many object-oriented languages as described in Figure 4. Main advantage of this approach is that it stores hierarchical data in a single key-space.

Argo/SQL works on the top of Argo Mapping layer and uses insert, select and delete statements. It provides support for (=, !=, <, <=, >, >=, LIKE, NOT LIKE) operators for pattern matching of strings. A SELECT statement uses attribute/column names or * for all attributes and a predicate (optional) in a WHERE clause to retrieve the specific record. Like SQL DELETE statement with optional where clause removes or delete objects. It identifies type from the literal value to categorize which table to

Figure 5. Decomposition of JSON Object into Argo/3 relational format

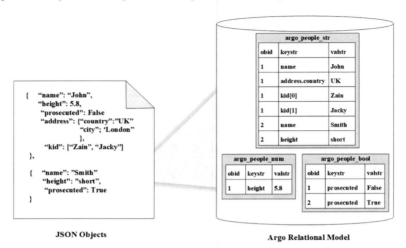

Figure 6. Decomposition of JSON object into argo extended format

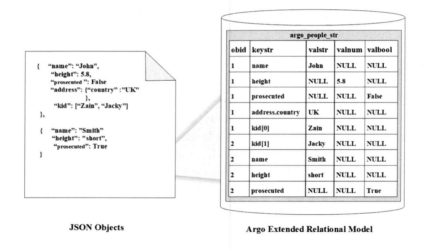

query. After selection of table to query, match the keystr with attribute and gets objid for further query. For Array as predicate use "ANY" keyword to match values.

Another approach proposed in "Extended approach: Enabling JSON store in Relational System" is, to map the whole JSON document in one table (Chasseur, Li, & Patel, 2013b). The idea anticipated is, to map JSON Document into one table with attributes, all primitive types and unique identifier as columns (a single 5-column table). Attributes stores as keystr and their value stores in basic JSON types as columns valstr for TEXT, valnum for DOUBLE PRECISION, and valboolean for BOOLEAN. If the value of any of three types does not exist the value columns of that type contains Null (Chasseur et al., 2013b). Argo/SQL stores objects into created tables. For queries, they have introduced language named "Argo/SQL" that underneath converts SQL queries to JSON format to store and retrieve JSON Objects. It uses insert, select and delete statement to perform operations along with joins for selection.

Limitations of Schema-Based Development of JSON in RDBMS

The first Argo Layer approach is good; however, if the document contains complex hierarchy, it requires complex path expression for querying that will be very difficult to resolve. Besides, long hierarchal objects with large attributes names may also exceed the column limit of the database. The biggest challenge of extended approach is storing all attributes; values in one table may not only increase in the size of the table but also cause wastage of storage space due to null values in each row. As for each attribute, there will be many columns with null values. If the document is of large size, it may cause big wastage of space that is not a good approach in development. However, this approach may use for the small document but not recommended.

Summary

JSON Schema-based Relational approach "Argo" recommends shredding JSON Object into vertical relational tables, one table (for each primitive data type) with columns key-path, value along with unique identifier. Some substantial issues may arise in this approach. If JSON instance contains the large nested hierarchy with long attribute key names, the path value will require large capacity that may exceed column design limit of RDBMS and querying underlying data will become more complex and inefficient. Extended approach suggests to create one table for all primitive types and to manage hierarchical objects and array through key-path value in a single table. This approach is good if instances of JSON Document holds multiple types of values against one attribute property. On the other hand, storing all in one table may not only increase in size of the table but also cause wastage of storage space due to null values in each row. Nested objects and arrays may cause complex key-path value and difficult to retrieve. However, a similar approach can use to generate a relational schema from the JSON Schema. An alternative approach is using the same technique as mentioned in (Chasseur et al., 2013a) to create a relational schema from JSON Schema rather from JSON Document. First, validate JSON Document from JSON Schema. Secondly, create a relational schema from a JSON Schema with the vertical table approach. Parse and creation Relational Schema from JSON Schema will remove many concerns related to multiple data type and will help to integrate multiple JSON Document. Lastly, a simple algorithm will query data using SQL and return information in JSON format. This is our proposed solution and we will discuss it in detail later in our upcoming paper.

JSON Schema-Less Development in RDBMS

RDBMS provide support for the systems where structure and contents can be clearly defined and separated. Change in data is not possible without the structural change in metadata that requires DDL operations. Therefore, without schema data cannot be changed or even uploaded. A JSON object can be shredded and stored in relational DB with Schema-less approach but there are many issues related to it like

- Attributes vary in a collection of objects
- Data types may differ in instances
- A cardinality of attributes that may vary from singleton to multiple over the time
- Recursive structure.
- Large hierarchal structure is difficult to manage

With all these issues, shredding and saving JSON Object is not only tedious but also requires a lot of time. Key idea is to store JSON as an Object along with a unique id for the identification of each instance. Schema will grow dynamically with the increase of JSON Instances. JSON Schema-less to relational database is a new paradigm that has opened new doors for fast efficient development. Being relational still does not require confirmation to a rigid schema, structured data, and strict data type enforcement. The biggest edge of using a relational model for JSON Data is that the capabilities of database servers like fast tuning, high scalability, and refined optimization techniques can apply on JSON Data to achieve high performance (Beyer et al., 2005).

"JSON Data Management – Supporting Schema-less Development in RDBMS" (Wright & Luff, 2016) approach emphasize on the management of both relational and JSON data under one umbrella of RDBMS where SQL after implantation of JSON Path query language can serve for both structured and unstructured data. It proposes to save native JSON Objects into relational databases without shredding it into a relational model. Therefore, the JSON Object instances stores in relational schema without a formal definition of a schema. This JSON data Management support has provided in Oracle release 12c that enables users to store, index and query JSON data along with a relational data- (Oracle Database 12c Release 1 (12.1) JSON in Oracle Database, n.d.).

Authors in this approach have suggested encompassing Schema-less approach in relational databases and utilizing the rich powers of SQL query. JSON data model can work hand-in-hand with relational Data model without proper definition of a schema. Main theme is to Store valid JSON instances as a whole in a binary or text column and used the latest SQL/JSON constructs for its management. These will reduce functional, performance and conceptual gap between SQL and NoSQL worlds.

Almost all Database Titans Oracle, MySQL, and PostgreSQL, etc. are providing JSON data type (binary) and Textual type for storing JSON data. JSON data type only stores valid JSON Document according to JSON validation rules (JSON Types, 2018). Here in this paper, we will only discuss the provision of JSON in Oracle, MySQL and PostgreSQL with respect to storage, indexing, and querying

Support of JSON Data Type

Oracle Database has not defined a new type to store JSON Document instead; it uses SQL data type. VARCHAR2 to store JSON in text format, CLOB and BLOB for binary format. BLOB is preferable as CLOB takes more storage space (almost double than BLOB) and VARCHAR required special indices for retrieval of JSON data. Oracle Database supports JSON natively with relational database features, including transactions, indexing, declarative querying, and views. Oracle with JSON support has explained in (Oracle Database 12c Release 1 (12.1): JSON in Oracle Database. (n.d.)) In addition, usage of indexes for different queries have explained in Oracle documentation (Indexing JSON Data in Oracle Database 12c Release 1 (12.1.0.2), n.d.).

MySQL has provided JSON data type as described in RFC 7159 for efficient access to data in JSON documents (MySQL 8.0 Reference Manual-The JSON Data Type, 2018). JSON data type is an optimized binary format, provides quicker retrieval of data as compared to textual format along with automatic validation. Maximum size allowed by JSON data type is almost the same as LONGBLOB or LONG-TEXT and cannot be indexed directly. Detail of usage of JSON with MySQL has described at (MySQL 8.0 Reference Manual-The JSON Data Type, 2018).

PostgreSQL also contains powerful JSON data types "JSONB and "JSONB" for blending the power of relational and NoSQL databases. The JSON Data Type facilitates to store data in text format and parse it on every execution while JSONB converts and stores input in binary format. JSONB have slower input but fast to process due to the elimination of reparsing and indexing support. It also eliminates white space, duplicate object keys and order of object keys by keeping the last one. The flexibility of the JSONB data type offers many benefits without the complexity of having two separate databases (Halliday, 2018). For detailed usage of JSON Data type with PostgreSQL, the link is (PostgreSQL 9.4.18 Documentation: Data Types, n.d.)

JSON Document Storage Mechanism

Oracle reduces the functional gap by storing JSON Document without static schema by a logical dynamic soft schema in Oracle (Wright & Luff, 2016) that act as a bridge between schema and schema-less world. The JSON format needs no central schema for column meta-data and gives column data access that is close to a schema encoded row format (Wright & Luff, 2016). It stores JSON Object instances in BLOB/VARCHAR data type along with unique object_id for reference and IS_JSON constraint, without defining complex static schema with many columns. It uses"IS_JSON" constraint to ensure that column values are valid JSON Objects. Every instance stores in a separate row with a unique object_id. IS_JSON constraint makes sure that JSON instance fulfills all syntactic requirements as describes in ANSI SQL/JSON standard initial draft (Petkovi´c, 2017a). Oracle encodes JSON textual data in UTF-8 or UTF-16 character-set automatically.

In MYSQL JSON Object can be stored and extracted without any unique key but for indexing auto key generated column is required. Indexing is not possible directly on the binary column. It provides automatic validation of JSON documents stored in JSON columns. Generates errors for invalid JSON Object (MySQL 8.0 Reference Manual-The JSON Data Type, 2018). Most important, normalization of valid JSON Document is achievable by removing duplicate values (suggested by RFC 7159 standard) and discarding of whitespace between keys, values, elements along with some other features by internally optimized formatting. This optimized format helps the server to search in a nested hierarchy of JSON data by array indexing or directly by key without reading the whole document (MySQL 8.0 Reference Manual-The JSON Data Type, 2018). Character set utf8mb4 and utf8mb4_bin collation has implemented to store a string. Detail of usage of JSON with MySQL has described at (MySQL 8.0 Reference Manual-The JSON Data Type, 2018).

Functions/Operations for Querying JSON Objects

Oracle query JSON textual data by encoding JSON, supported by SQL/JSON language along with many functions provided, hence reduces Query Performance Gap. SQL functions (JSON_VALUE, JSON_QUERY, AND JSON_TABLE) or conditions (JSON_EXISTS, IS JSON, IS NOT JSON, AND JSON_TEXTCONTAINS) are provided for querying textual data of JSON (Petkovi´c, 2017a). All function use path expressions for JSON to a relational form. Although update for a single value in JSON Document does not works. It replaces the whole instance with a new one. Handling attribute with different data type in multiple JSON instances is a bit tricky. To avoid errors and get full results it requires error handling and some additional constructs in the statements like WITH ARRAY WRAPPER, ERROR ON ERROR, WITH CONDITIONAL ARRAY WRAPPER- (Hammerschmidt, 2015), etc.

MySQL provides assorted SQL functions for multiple operations on JSON Document, to check existence, for searching values, for modification and many more. For creation (JSON_ARRAY, JSON_OBJECT, JSON_QUOTE etc). For searching of JSON Document like JSON_CONTAINS, JSON_CONTAINS_PATH, JSON_TYPE, JSON_EXTRACT, JSON_KEYS etc. There is also a provision of "->" operator to extract values. Detail discussion on all functions in this paper is dingy it can be checked directly from manual. JSON column can be updated by optimizer by using JSON_SET(), JSON_REPLACE(), or JSON_REMOVE() functions that update the column contents instead of replacing the whole instance with the new one. Comparison Operators =, <, <=, >, >=, <>, !=, and <=> are provided. Composing and merging multiple JSON Document has provided through functions. Detail is available at (MySQL 8.0 Reference Manual-JSON Functions, 2018).

PostgreSQL provides "->" and "->>" to query JSON Object by key and text respectively. It also provides aggregate functions such as MIN, MAX, AVERAGE, and SUM (PostgreSQL 9.4.18 Documentation: Functions and Operators, n.d.-a). Various JSON functions and operators provide assorted operations on JSON Document (JSON Types, 2018) with a little variation as compared to others. PostgreSQL use function-based indexing technique that search key/value pair efficiently in JSON Document also known as "GIN Indexing" (Petkovi´c, 2017b). Explanation of functions/operations are at (PostgreSQL 9.4.18 Documentation: Functions and Operators, n.d.-b). PostgreSQL detail to querying JSON documents is at (Querying JSON in PostgreSQL. (n.d.))

Indexing Mechanism

Indexing is a data structure technique applied to keys/attributes to retrieve data from the database efficiently and speedily. Like its name suggests it about numbering something like in books. One or more indexes apply on specific columns of a table where more searching is required. Indexing creates data structure (B+ Tree or hash table) that holds value and pointer to an attribute/record. It distributes data in the form of a tree with an equal level of nodes. This data structure then gets sort by Binary Search. It facilitates searching by comparing branches of data and avoiding a full scan of a table. With no indexing, querying will cause a full table scan and with indexing only a few rows. It is substantial for large data to define correct indexes to speed up data retrieval. It allows almost direct access to searched data; like a book index guide us directly to the specific page number. However, if the data is small then it can be an overhead too. There are various types of indexing techniques. Indexing applies on columns and on conditions too. All DB Vendors providing JSON Data Store also have indexing facility.

Oracle does not have a distinct data type for JSON. It facilitates indexing for JSON as for any other data type. It provides two types of indexing on searching. The first one is Functional based on columns and on condition. The second one is on the entire JSON Document.

MySQL does not support indexing directly on JSON Document. It uses another column for indexing called generated column indexing. It is about generating a special column to keeps information of other columns, calculations or expressions. Pick values from JSON Document and use them to generate a new column, apply indexing on the generated column; it is like indexing a JSON field. It is a bit different from other RDBMS but it can achieve almost similar indexing through this technique. Detail is available at (Abdullah Alger. (2017).

PostgreSQL uses GiN (Generalized Inverted Index) Indexing Technique for JSON Document. It uses especially for indexing arrays and documents. It stores the key information in index entry and uses posting tree to the store mapping information. It also uses B-Tree Searching methodology.

Figure 7. Example of JSON stores in Oracle RDBMS

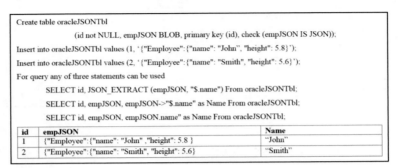

Figure 8. Example of JSON Objects in MySQL

id	empJSON	Name
1	{"Employee":{"name": "John" ,"height": 5.8 }	John
2	{"Employee":{"name": "Smith", "height": 5.6}	Smith

All Types of indexes are useful and improves data retrieval. Although, indexes improves query performance but also slows down DML operations to any table due to the overhead of maintenance. For big Document, it will be great but for small, it is an overhead.

JSON Document Projection

The best advantage of using JSON inside Oracle is that we can select data inside JSON documents as if they were relational data by using the prefix "." to go down the JSON path hierarchy (Nedov, 2016). However, there is another way to use functions, like json_value () and json_query () for the retrieval of scalar data from a JSON object with the support of other functions. Return type for this function must define before while creating indexes using JSON_VALUE function.

MySQL provides variety of functions for searching value, path or whole JSON Document with JSON_CONTAINS, JSON_CONTAINS_PATH(), JSON_TYPE(), JSON_EXTRACT, JSON_KEYS etc. There is also provision of "->" operator to extract values. Function or operators both uses for value extraction.

In PostgreSQL, projection of JSON- to-Relational and Relational-to-JSON Document is carry out by operators (->, ->>) and row_to_json function vice versa. "->" is use to retrieve JSON Object and "->>" to return Text for the projection of JSON in Relational form. Relational-to-JSON is extraction of data from a relational table into JSON format using quotation marks and curly braces etc. A short Example given below for JSON-to-Relational storage and retrieval.

Figure 9. Example of JSON objects in PostgreSQL

```
Create table postgresJSONTbl (id INT, empJSON JSONB);
Insert into postgresJSONTbl values (1, '{"Employee":{"name": "John" ,"height": 5.8 }'});
Insert into postgresJSONTbl values (2, '{"Employee":{"name": "Smith", "height": 5.6}'});
Select id, empJSON, empJSON ->'employee'->>'name' as Name From postgresJSONTbl;
```

id	empJSON	Name
1	{"Employee":{"name": "John" ,"height": 5.8 }	"John"
2	{"Employee":{"name": "Smith", "height": 5.6}	"Smith"

Limitations of JSON Schema-Less Development in RDBMS

Almost all database vendors provide support of JSON in binary format and text format with the recommendation to use Binary format. However, most of the APIs work well with text/String format. Updating JSON document or part of JSON document vary in all RDBMS with a lot of restrictions and limitations. JSON specific functions are not standardized like SQL functions and may vary for all vendors. Querying and handling of a similar attribute with multiple values also required a lot of embedded constructs to avoid errors. Besides, handling recursive structure, a variation of the number of attributes, change in cardinalities among attributes and large hierarchal structure is difficult to manage too.

Summary

Although, NoSQL databases are the game changer in the data-centric world but Relational Databases has shown that they did not give up and they are going to stay in one form or the other by enhancing its power in all means. Relational Databases have adapted salient features of schema-less databases that is a win-win situation for the developer. Almost all big RDBMS companies have provided support of JSON data. Although text and binary data types both are support for managing JSON Document but with the recommendations to use binary data type with provided JSON-Specific functions. Almost all used the same approach on front-end by storing JSON Document instances in binary format, querying by using JSON-specific function and JSON Formatted data retrieval. To parse path hierarchy, JSON instance data can be accessed like relational data by the use of the prefix "." or "->, ->>" notation in different relational systems. However, updating JSON document vary in all of them with some restrictions. A bit complex part is JSON-Specific functions; being new and not very well understood it requires a lot of knowledge as compared to traditional SQL statements for new developers. Querying and handling of the same attribute with multiple values also required a lot of embedded constructs as a part of the query for full data retrieval and to avoid errors. Last but not the least there are many API readily available to work with JSON but in general, API works well with text/String rather than binary data, forces Web developers to do a lot of coding. SQL/JSON is standard to query JSON data but no standard document released by SQL Standardization committee so far. Oracle, MySQL, PostgreSQL all use functions of SQL/JSON with different naming wrappers, behind the scene functionality is the same. At the end, RDBMS have provided JSON Data management, that is not much challenging but require time to hands-on it.

Table 7. Features of JSON Stores in RDBMSs

	Oracle JSON	**MySQL JSON**	**PostgreSQL JSON**
License	Commercial	Open Source	Open Source
Storage Format	BLOB, CLOB, VARCHAR2 (BLOB Recommended)	Binary	Binary (JSON,JSONB) (JSONB recommended)
Update Individual Value	Not Available	Available (size constraint, new data must be of same or less then replaced data size)	Available (locks whole row and later replaces the whole object with the new data)
Query Data	JSON-specific functions	JSON-specific functions	JSON-specific functions
Result set	JSON Format	JSON Format	JSON Format

CONCLUSION AND FUTURE GUIDELINES

JSON is the most powerful data serialization technique and research hotspot these days. RDBMS and NoSQL both are struggling to provide efficient support for JSON Data Management. Both have their own boundaries for JSON Data Management. One is influential in storing data and other is dominant in retrieving or querying data. One follows the BASE and other permit ACID transaction properties. One is good in handling multiple data types other require complex constructs.

NoSQL Document Store is an especial designed for the management of JSON Document Stores, and doing its job really well. However, there are certain concerns like, relational database systems have been the main building blocks of many applications so code, procedures, routines, triggers, etc. are reusable to speed up the development process. Secondly, eventually-consistency transactional state of data in NoSQL does not appreciate in most of the applications like a business and analytical processing applications. Using RDBMS for transaction sensitive business and analytical applications and NoSQL for other applications required to have hands-on expertise on both (might be a big task for developer). Although, NoSQL stores have gained much popularity; however, learning and adapting new tool requires time and may affect reusability in terms of code, routines, functions, API, and processes too. Although, if no time constraint, learning new technology is always amusing for developers.

On the other side, many RDBMS have provided support of JSON Document Stores by introducing JSON (Binary) Data type, JSON specific functions/operations, querying using SQL/JSON language at the backend. Most of the APIs work well with textual data especially in Web development so conversion from binary to text may also require extra coding. Provided JSON specific functions and operations are not standardize through some draft by any organization and vary from one relational system to other in term of storing, updating, retrieving and handling attributes with multiple data types in JSON Document. It requires time to hands-on all these functions, operations and binary to textual conversion to store and query JSON Object. However, standardization of SQL/JSON language may play a great role in gathering all relational systems on the same platform for the management of JSON Document.

To gain the best of all, application programs may use and integrate multiple platforms efficiently. Relational database systems, main building blocks of many applications evolved and enhanced through decades of continued research have standard powerful query language SQL, many skilled experts, abundant utilities, libraries, API, etc. Data can manage and organize well by using a relational database with JSON. Database server features and framework can use to provide security, consistency, and atomicity. Once SQL functions to support JSON gets standardize, the power of SQL will enhance too. Defining, learning and improving new technologies to support JSON is cumbersome as compared enriching the existing technology with additional features. Combining the best features of both JSON and Relational Systems can lead us to the new peak of efficiency along with consistency. Using JSON for fast development, RDBMS for data consistency and SQL for efficient querying can play an important role for developers to achieve their targets appropriately at the time.

One idea that has not instigated yet is the usage of JSON Schema in cross platforms. JSON Schema plays a vital role in describing and validating JSON Document however, it can assist to create a relational schema too by using some simple algorithms. A layer of an algorithm can play a big role to create a relational schema from JSON Schema. Conversion of user query into SQL parameters for retrieval of information will make querying efficient. It can also help in complex querying and analytical processing. Additionally, queried results can display in relational and JSON Format. Being Simple and close to Relational DB architecture, it can be easy to query JSON data by using traditional SQL operators from defined tables with less overhead. Hidden powers of JSON Schema can help as a bridge to fill the gap between NoSQL Document Stores and Relational Systems We hope by this manner both relational and JSON can complement each other within applications efficiently and with great ease.

REFERENCES

Abdullah Alger. (2017). *MySQL for JSON: Generated Columns and Indexes*. Retrieved from https://www.compose.com/articles/mysql-for-json-generated-columns-and-indexing/

Apache Software Foundation. (n.d.). *Apache CouchDB*. Retrieved from http://couchdb.apache.org

Bamford, R., Nasoi, S., Zacharioudakis, M., Borkar, V., Brantner, M., Fischer, P. M., ... Muresan, D. (2009). XQuery Reloaded. *Proceedings of the VLDB Endowment International Conference on Very Large Data Bases*, 2(2), 1342–1353. doi:10.14778/1687553.1687560

Beyer, K. (2005). System RX: One Part Relational, One Part XML. In *Proceedings of the 2005 ACM SIGMOD International Conference on Management of Data* (pp. 347–358). ACM. 10.1145/1066157.1066197

Bourhis, P., Reutter, J. L., Su'arez, F., & Vrgoc, D. (2017). JSON: Data Model, Query Languages and Schema Specification. In *Proceedings of the 36th ACM SIGMOD-SIGACT-SIGAI Symposium on Principles of Database Systems* (pp. 123–135). ACM. 10.1145/3034786.3056120

Cattell, R. (2011). Scalable SQL and NoSQL Data Stores. *SIGMOD Record*, 39(4), 12–27. doi:10.1145/1978915.1978919

Chandra, D. G. (2015). BASE Analysis of NoSQL Database. *Future Generation Computer Systems*, 52, 13–21. doi:10.1016/j.future.2015.05.003

Chasseur, C., Li, Y., & Patel, J. M. (2013a). Enabling JSON Document Stores in Relational Systems. In *Proceedings of the 16th International Workshop on the Web and Databases 2013, WebDB 2013, (Vol. 13*, pp. 14–15). Academic Press.

Chen, P. P.-S. (2002). Entity Relationship Model—Toward a Unified View of Data. In *Software Pioneers* (pp. 311–339). Springer. doi:10.1007/978-3-642-59412-0_18

Droettboom, M. (2015). *Understanding JSON Schema*. Available on: http://spacetelescope. github.io/ understandingjsonschema/UnderstandingJSONSchema. pdf

Fowler, M., & Sadalage, P. (2012). *NoSQL Database and Polyglot Persistence*. Retrieved from http:// martinfowler.com/articles/nosql-intro-original.pdf

Halliday, L. (2018). *Unleash the Power of Storing JSON in Postgres*. Retrieved from https://blog.code-ship.com/unleash-the-power-of-storing-json-in-postgres

Hammerschmidt. (2015). *New SQL/JSON Query Operators (Part 2: JSON_QUERY)*. Retrieved from https://blogs.oracle.com/jsondb/the-new-sqljson-query-operators-part2:-jsonquery

Haq, Z. U., Khan, G. F., & Hussain, T. (2015). A Comprehensive Analysis of XML and JSON Web Technologies. *New Developments in Circuits, Systems, Signal Processing, Communications and Computers, 102–109.*

Horowitz, E. (2018). *MongoDB Drops ACID*. Retrieved from https://www.mongodb.com/blog/post/ multi-document-transactions-in-mongodb.

Indexing JSON Data in Oracle Database 12c Release 1 (12.1.0.2). (n.d.). Retrieved from https://oracle-base.com/articles/12c/indexing-json-data-in-oracle-database-12cr1

Introducing JSON. (n.d.). Retrieved from https://www.json.org/

JSON. (n.d.). *Schema and Metadata*. Retrieved from https://en.wikipedia.org/wiki/JSON#JSONSchema

JSON Types. (2018). Retrieved from https://www.postgresql.org/docs/devel/static/datatype-json.html

Khan, L., & Rao, Y. (2001). A Performance Evaluation of Storing XML Data in Relational Database Management Systems. In *Proceedings of the 3rd International Workshop on Web Information and Data Management* (pp. 31–38). Academic Press. 10.1145/502932.502939

Klettke, M., Störl, U., & Scherzinger, S. (2015). Schema extraction and structural outlier detection for JSON-based NoSQL data stores. *Datenbanksysteme für Business, Technologie und Web.*

Liu, Z. H., Hammerschmidt, B., & McMahon, D. (2014). JSON Data Management: Supporting Schema-Less Development in RDBMS. In *Proceedings of the 2014 ACM SIGMOD International Conference on Management of Data* (pp. 1247–1258). ACM. 10.1145/2588555.2595628

Liu, Z. H., Hammerschmidt, B., McMahon, D., Liu, Y., & Chang, H. J. (2016, June). Closing the functional and performance gap between SQL and NoSQL. In *Proceedings of the 2016 International Conference on Management of Data* (pp. 227-238). ACM. 10.1145/2984356.2985239

Melton, J. (2003). *Information Technology-Database Languages-SQL-Part 14: XML-Related Specifications (SQL/XML) (ISO/IEC 9075-14: 2003)*. OASIS.

MongoD. B. (n.d.). Retrieved from https://www.mongodb.com/

MySQL 8.0 Reference Manual-JSON Functions. (2018). Retrieved from https://dev.mysql.com/doc/ refman/8.0/en/json-functions.html

MySQL 8.0 Reference Manual - The JSON Data Type. (2018). Retrieved from https://dev.mysql.com/doc/refman/8.0/en/json.html

Nedov, L. (2016). *JSON in Oracle Database 12c*. Retrieved from http://www.redstk.com/json-in-oracle-database-12c

Petkovi'c, D. (2017a). JSON Integration in Relational Database Systems. *International Journal of Computers and Applications, 168*(5), 14–19.

Petkovi'c, D. (2017b). SQL/JSON Standard: Properties and Deficiencies. *Datenbank-Spektrum Springer, 17*(3), 277–287. doi:10.100713222-017-0267-4

Pezoa, F., Reutter, J. L., Suarez, F., Ugarte, M., & Vrgoc, D. (2016). Foundations of JSON Schema. In *Proceedings of the 25th international conference on World Wide Web* (pp. 263–273). Academic Press. 10.1145/2872427.2883029

Postgre, S. Q. L. 9.4.18 Documentation: Data Types. (n.d.a). Retrieved from https://www.postgresql.org/docs/9.4/static/datatype-json.html

Postgre, S. Q. L. 9.4.18 Documentation: Functions and Operators. (n.d.b). Retrieved from https://www.postgresql.org/docs/9.4/static/functions-json.html

QueryingJ. S. O. N. in Postgres. (n.d.). Retrieved from https://link.springer.com/article/10.1007%2Fs13222-017-0267-4

Why NoSQL Database. (n.d.). Retrieved from https://www.couchbase.com/resources/why-nosql

Wright, A., & Luff, G. (2016). *JSON Schema Validation: A Vocabulary for Structural Validation of JSON* (Tech. Rep.). IETF Standard 2016. What Every Developer Should Know About CouchDB. Retrieved from https://www.dimagi.com/blog/what-every- developer-should-know-about-couchdb/

Yan Betts. (2014). *How JSON sparked NoSQL – and will return to the RDBMS fold*. Retrieved from https://www.infoworld.com/article/2608293/nosql/how-json-sparked-nosql----and-will-return- to-the-rdbms-fold.html

KEY TERMS AND DEFINITIONS

ACID: ACID means four properties, which are (A)tomcity, (C)onsistency, (I)solation and (D)urability. ACID is the type of transaction processing done by the relational database management system (RDBMS).

CAP: CAP Theorem means three properties, which are consistency, availability, and partition tolerance.

Data Store: A data store is a repository for persistently storing and managing collections of data. Typically, we have database-based repositories and file-based simpler store types.

JSON: JSON (JavaScript Object Notation) is a binary and typed data model which is applied to represent data like list, map, date, Boolean as well as different precision numbers.

NoSQL Databases: NoSQL means "not only SQL" or "no SQL at all". Being a new type of non-relational databases, NoSQL databases are developed for efficient and scalable management of big data.

Relational Databases: A relational database is a kind of databases that is based on the relational model of data. A relational database consists of relations and a relation is a two-dimensional table, which rows and columns are called tuples and attribute values, respectively.

XML: XML (Extensible Markup Language) defined by the W3C (World Wide Web Consortium) is a markup language, which can be used for data representation and exchange on the web.

Chapter 4
A JSON–Based Fast and Expressive Access Control Policy Framework

Hao Jiang
New H3C Technologies Co. Ltd., China

Ahmed Bouabdallah
IMT Atlantique, France

ABSTRACT

Along with the rapid development of ICT technologies, new areas like Industry 4.0, IoT, and 5G have emerged and brought out the need for protecting shared resources and services under time-critical and energy-constrained scenarios with real-time policy-based access control. To achieve this, the policy language needs to be very expressive but lightweight and efficient. These challenges are investigated and a set of key requirements for such a policy language is identified. JACPoL is accordingly introduced as a descriptive, scalable, and expressive policy language in JSON. JACPoL by design provides a flexible and fine-grained ABAC style (attribute-based access control) while it can be easily tailored to express other access control models. The design and implementation of JACPoL are illustrated together with its evaluation in comparison with other existing policy languages. The result shows that JACPoL can be as expressive as existing ones but more simple, scalable, and efficient. The performance evaluation shows that JACPoL requires much less processing time and memory space than XACML.

INTRODUCTION

Policies represent sets of properties of information processing systems (Clarkson&Schneider, 2010). Their implementation mainly rests on the IETF architecture (Yavatkar et al., 2000) initially introduced to manage QoS policies in networks. It consists in two main entities namely the PDP (Policy Decision Point) and the PEP (Policy Enforcement Point). The first one which is the smart part of the architecture acts as a controller the goal of which consists in handling and interpreting policy events, and deciding in

DOI: 10.4018/978-1-5225-8446-9.ch004

accordance with the policy currently applicable, what action should be taken. The decision is transmitted to the PEP which has to concretely carry it out.

Access control policies are a specific kind of security policies aiming to control the actions that principals can perform on resources by permitting their access only to the authorized ones. Typically, the access requests are intercepted and analyzed by the PEP, which then transfers the request details to the PDP for evaluation and authorization decision (Yavatkar et al., 2000). In most implementations, the stateless nature of PEP enables its ease of scale. However, the PDP has to consult the right policy set and apply the rules therein to reach a decision for each request and thus is often the performance bottleneck of policy-based access control systems. Therefore, a policy language determining how policies are expressed and evaluated is important and has a direct influence on the performance of the PDP.

Especially, in nowadays, protecting private resources in real-time has evolved into a rigid demand in domains such as home automation, smart cities, health care services and intelligent transportation systems, etc., where the environments are characterized by heterogeneous, distributed computing systems exchanging enormous volumes of time-critical data with varying levels of access control in a dynamic network. An access control policy language for these environments needs to be very well-structured, expressive but lightweight and easily extensible (Borders et al., 2005).

In this work, the authors investigate the relationship between the performance of the PDP, the language that is used to encode the policies and the access requests that it decides upon, and identify a set of key requirements for a policy language to guarantee the performance of the PDP. The authors argue that JSON would be more efficient and suitable than other alternatives (XML, etc.) as a policy data format in critical environments. According to these observations, the authors propose a simple but expressive access control policy language (JACPoL) based on JSON. A PoC (Proof of Concept) has been conducted through the implementation of JACPoL in a policy engine operated in reTHINK testbed (reTHINK Project Testbed, 2016)). At last JACPoL is carefully positioned in comparison with existing policy languages.

The main contribution of this work is therefore the definition of JACPoL, which utilizes JSON to encode a novel access control policy specification language with well-defined syntax and semantics. The authors identify key requirements and technical trends for future policy languages. They incidentally propose the new notion of Implicit Logic Operators (ILO), which can greatly reduce the size and complexity of a policy set while providing fine-grained access control. Quantitative evaluations of JACPoL by comparison to XACML show that JACPoL systematically requires much less time and memory space than XACML. The authors also elaborate on the applicability of JACPoL on ABAC model, RBAC model and their combinations or their by-products. Last but not least, their implementation leads to a novel and performant policy engine adopting the PDP/PEP architecture (Yavatkar et al., 2000) and JACPoL policy language based on Node.js[1] and Redis[2].

The remainder of this chapter is structured as follows. In Section 2, the problematic is refined by delimiting precisely its perimeter. Section 3 provides an illustration in depth with representative policy examples of the design of the policy language in terms of the constructs, semantics and other important features like Implicit Logic Operators, combining algorithms and implementation. Section 4 further qualitatively evaluates JACPoL and compares it with other existing access control policy specification languages. In section 5 a detailed performance evaluation is given. The ABAC-native nature of JACPoL is detailed in section 6 along with a comprehensive discussion on other possible application of JACPoL to ARBAC (Attribute-centric RBAC) and RABAC (Role-centric ABAC) security models. In Section 7 the authors summarize their work and discuss future research directions.

PROBLEM STATEMENT

In the past decades, a lot of policy languages have been proposed for the specification of access control policies using XML, such as EPAL (Ashley et al., 2003), X-GTRBAC (Bhatti et al., 2005) and the standardized XACML (OASIS, 2013). Nevertheless, it is generally acknowledged that XACML suffers from providing poorly defined and counterintuitive semantics (Crampton & Morisset, 2012), which makes it not good in simplicity and flexibility. On the other hand, XML performs well in expressiveness and adaptability but sacrifices its efficiency and scalability, compared to which JSON is considered to be more well-proportioned with respect to these requirements, and even simpler, easier, more efficient and thus favoured by more and more nowadays' policy designers (Crockford, 2006; El-Aziz & Kannan, 2014; Griffin, 2012; W3schools).

To address the aforementioned inefficiency issues of the XML format, the XACML Technical Committee recently designed the JSON profile (Brossard, 2014) to be used in the exchange of XACML request and response messages between the PEP and PDP. However, the profile does not define the specification of XACML policies, which means, after the PDP parses the JSON-formatted XACML requests, it still needs to evaluate the parsed attributes with respect to the policies expressed in XML. Leigh Griffin and his colleagues (Griffin, 2012) have proposed JSONPL, a policy vocabulary encoded in JSON that semantically was identical to the original XML policy but stripped away the redundant meta data and cleaned up the array translation process. Their performance experiments showed that JSON could provide very similar expressiveness as XML but with much less verbosity. On the other hand, as much as it can be understood, JSONPL is merely aimed at implementing XACML policies in JSON and thus lacks its own formal schema and full specification as a policy specification language (Steven, 2013).

Major service providers such as Amazon Web Services (AWS) (Amazon Web Services) have a tendency to implement their own security languages in JSON, but such kind of approaches are normally for proprietary usage thus provide only self-sufficient features and support limited use cases, which are not suitable to be a common policy language. To the best of the authors' knowledge, there are very few proposals that combine a rich set of language features with well-defined syntax and semantics, and such kind of access control policy language based on JSON has not even been attempted before and as such JACPoL can be considered to be an original and innovative contribution.

JACPoL DETAILED DESIGN

This section presents JACPoL in depth. The foundations of JACPoL are first recalled, and then its structures is introduced with an overview of how an access request is evaluated with respect to JACPoL policies. After that, the syntax and semantics is described in detail along with policy examples.

Fundamental Design Choices

The goal is to design a simple but expressive access control policy language. To achieve this, the authors beforehand introduce the important design decisions for JACPoL as below.

First, JACPoL is JSON-formatted (ECMA).

Second, JACPoL is attribute-based by design but meanwhile supports RBAC (Ferraiolo & Kuhn, 2009). When integrating RBAC, user roles are considered as attributes (ARBAC) (Obrsta, 2012), or attributes are used to constrain user permissions (RABAC) (Jin et al., 2012), which obtains the advantages of RBAC while maintaining ABAC's flexibility and expressiveness.

Third, JACPoL adopts hierarchically nested structures similar to XACML. The layered architecture as shown in Figure 1 not only enables scalable and fine-grained access control, but also eases the work of policy definition and management for policy designers.

Forth, JACPoL supports Implicit Logic Operators which make use of JSON built-in data structures (Object and Array) to implicitly denote logic operations. This allows a policy designer to express complex operations without explicitly using logical operators, and makes JACPoL policies greatly reduced in size and easier to read and write by humans.

Fifth, JACPoL supports Obligations to offer a rich set of security and network management features.

Policy Structure

JACPoL uses hierarchical structures very similar to the XACML standard (Ferraiolo et al., 2016). As shown in Figure 1, JACPoL policies are structured as Policy Sets that consist of one or more child policy sets or policies, and a Policy is composed of a set of Rules.

Because not all Rules, Policies, or Policy Sets are relevant to a given request, JACPoL includes the notion of a Target. A Target determines whether a Rule/Policy/Policy Set is applicable to a request by setting constraints on attributes using simple Boolean expressions. A Policy Set is said to be Applicable if the access request satisfies the Target, and if so, then its child Policies are evaluated and the results returned by those child policies are combined using the policy-combining algorithm; otherwise, the Policy Set is skipped without further examining its child policies and returns a Not Applicable decision. Likewise, the Target of a Policy or a Rule has similar semantics.

The Rule is the fundamental unit that is evaluated eventually and can generate a conclusive decision (Permit or Deny specified in its Effect field). The Condition field in a rule is a simple or complex Boolean expression that refines the applicability of the rule beyond the predicates specified by its target, and is optional. If a request satisfies both the Target and Condition of a rule, then the rule is applicable to the request and its Effect is returned as its decision; otherwise, Not Applicable is returned.

For each Rule, Policy, or Policy Set, an id field is used to be uniquely identified, and an Obligation field is used to specify the operations which should be performed (typically by a PEP) before or after granting or denying an access request, while a Priority is specified for conflict resolution between different Rules, Policies, or Policy Sets.

Syntax and Conventions

JACPoL uses JSON syntax to construct and validate its policies. A policy must follow correct JSON syntax to take effect. In this subsection a list of fundamental characteristics of JSON is recalled; a more detailled treatment of JSON can be found in (EMA):

- JSON is built on two universal data structures: object and array.

Figure 1. JACPoL's hierarchical nested structure

Policy Set	Policy	Rule
id	id	id
target	target	target
policy sets/policies	rules	condition
policy combining algorithm	rule combining algorithm	effect
obligation	obligation	obligation
priority	priority	priority

- An object is denoted by braces ({ }) that can hold multiple name-value pairs. For each name-value pair, a colon (:) is used to separate the name and the value, whilst multiple name-value pairs are separated by comma (,) as in the following example: {"id": 1, "effect": "permit"}.
- An array is denoted by brackets ([ ]) that can hold multiple values separated by commas (,) as in the following example: ["Monday", "Friday", "Sunday"].
- A value can be a string in double quotes, or a number, or a Boolean value (true or false), or null, or an object or an array.
- Whitespace can be inserted between any pair of JSON tokens ({ } [ ] ",:).

In the subsequent subsections, the syntax and semantics for each policy element are elaborated. To illustrate better, the following conventions are used:

- The following characters are special characters used in the description of the grammar and are not included in the policy syntax: < > ... () |.
- If an element allows multiple values, it is indicated using the repeated values, commas, and an ellipsis (...). Example: [<rule_block>, <rule_block>, ...].
- A question mark (?) following an element indicates that this element is optional. Example: {"condition"?: <boolean_expression>}.
- A vertical line (|) between elements indicates alternatives. Parentheses define the scope of the alternatives. The default value is underlined if the field is optional. Example: {"algorithm"?: ("permitOverrides" | "firstApplicable")}.
- Elements that must be literal strings are enclosed in double quotation marks.

Policy Sets, Policies and Rules

This subsection describes the grammar of the Policy Set, the Policy and the Rule. In JACPoL, a policy set, a policy, or a rule always starts and ends with a brace, which denotes a policy set block, a policy block, or a rule block.

Policy set block. Figure 2 describes the grammar of the policy set block, which is composed of six name-value pairs that exactly correspond to the six elements of a policy set. As shown in the figure, the "id" field is a string which can be either numeric or descriptive to uniquely identify a policy set. The "target" specifies a Boolean expression indicating the resources, subjects, actions or the environment attributes to which the policy set is applied. The "policies" stores a list of policy blocks with each one corresponding to a policy. The "algorithm" field specifies the name of a decision-combining algorithm to compute the final decision according to the results returned by its child policies. The "obligation" specifies actions to take in case a particular conclusive decision (Permit or Deny) is reached. The "priority" provides a numeric value indicating the weight of the policy set when its decision conflicts with other policy sets under the highestPriority algorithm.

Note that elements like *target, algorithm, obligation* and *priority* are optional and, if omitted, the predefined default values would be taken (e.g., target: *true,* algorithm: *firstApplicable,* obligation: *null,* priority: 0.5).

- **Policy Block**: As shown in Figure 3, a policy block contains an id, a target, an algorithm, an obligation and a priority similar to a policy set. The difference concerns the fact that it has a "rules" list that holds one or more rule blocks instead of policy blocks.
- **Rule Block**: Figure n4 describes the grammar of the rule block. Unlike a policy set block or a policy block, a rule block does not contain leaf nodes like child policies or child rules and thus a decision-combining algorithm field is not needed either. Instead, it possesses a "condition" element that specifies the condition for applying the rule, and an "effect" element that, if the rule is applied, would be the returned decision of the rule as either *Permit* or *Deny*. In comparison to a target, a con-dition is typically more complex and often includes functions (e.g., "greater-than") for the comparison of attribute values, and logic operations (e.g., "and", "or") for the combination of multiple conditions. If either the target or the condition is not satisfied, a *Not Applicable* would be taken as the result instead of the specified effect. Note that the *Condition* is by default true if omitted.

Targets and Conditions

As aforementioned, a Target or a Condition is a Boolean expression specifying constraints on attributes such as the subject, the resource, the environment, and the action of requests. The Boolean expression

Figure 2. Grammar of the policy set block

```
{
    "id":          <string>,
    "target"?:     <boolean_expression>,
    "policies":    [<policy_block>, <policy_block>, ...],
    "algorithm"?:  ("permitOverrides"|"denyOverrides"|"firstApplicable"|"highestPriority"),
    "obligation"?: <obligation_statement>,
    "priority"?:   <number>
}
```

Figure 3. Grammar of the policy block

```
{
    "id":          <string>,
    "target"?:     <boolean_expression>,
    "rules":       [<rule_block>, <rule_block>, ...],
    "algorithm"?:  ("permitOverrides"|"denyOverrides"|"firstApplicable"|"highestPriority"),
    "obligation"?: <obligation_statement>,
    "priority"?:   <number>
}
```

Figure 4. Grammar of the rule block

```
{
    "id":          <string>,
    "target"?:     <boolean_expression>,
    "effect":      ("permit"|"deny"),
    "condition"?:  <boolean_expression>,
    "obligation"?: <obligation_statement>,
    "priority"?:   <number>
}
```

of a Target is often simple and very likely to be just a test of string equality, but that of a condition can be sometimes complex with constraints on multiple attributes (attribute conditions).

Attribute Condition is a simple Boolean expression that consists of a key-value pair as shown below:

```
{"<attribute_expression>": <condition_expression>}
```

The key is an attribute expression in string format that specifies an attribute or a particular computation between a set of attributes; the value is a condition expression, which is a JSON block composed of one or more operator-parameter pairs specifying specifically the requirements that the attribute expression needs to meet. The simplest format of an attribute condition is to verify the equality/inequality between the attribute (e.g., time) and the parameter (e.g., 10:00:00) using comparative operators (e.g., greater-than, less-than, equal-to, etc.):

```
{"<attribute>": {"<comparative_operator>": <parameter>}}
```

However, there are also cases where occur multiple constraints (operator-parameter pairs) on the same attribute, connected by logical relations like *AND, OR, NOT*, which are respectively denoted by the keywords *allOf, anyOf* and *not*.

- **Logical Operator:** JACPoL uses logical operators in a form of constructing key-value pairs. The logical operator is the key and, depending on the number of arguments, allOf and anyOf operators are to be followed by an array ([ ]) of multiple constraints, while the not operator is to be followed by an object ({ }). An allOf operation would be evaluated to true only if all subsequently included constraints are evaluated to true, but an anyOf operation would be true as long as there is at least one of the constraints which is true. An not operation would be true if the followed constraint is evaluated to false. Logical operators can be nested to construct logical relations such as not any of, not all of. For example, an attribute condition containing multiple constraints with nested logical operators as below:

```
{"sumOf x y": {"not": {"anyOf": [
                            {"between": "j k"},
                                    {"equals": "z"}]}}}
```

In addition, logical operators can also be used to combine multiple attribute conditions in order to express complex constraints on more than one attribute, easily and flexibly. As an example, the condition below expresses constraints on two attributes and would be evaluated to true only when both (allOf the two) constraints are met:

```
{"allOf": [<attribute_condition>, <attribute_condition>]}
```

- **Less is More: Implicit Logical Operators:** A complex condition might contain many logical operators which make the policy wordy and hard to read. To overcome this, the JSON's built-in data structures, *object* and *array*, allow to define following implicit logical operators as alternatives to *allOf* and *anyOf*:

An *object* is implicitly an *allOf* operator which would be evaluated to true only if all the included key-value pairs are evaluated to true.

An *array* is implicitly an *anyOf* operator which would be evaluated to true as long as at least one of its elements is evaluated to true.

For example, below is a condition statement using implicit logical operators to verify if it is working hour.

```
{
        "time":{"between": ["09:00 12:00", "14:00 18:00"]},
        "weekday": {"not": {"equals": ["saturday", "sunday"]}}
}
As a comparison, below is for the same verification with explicit logical op-
erators.
{
        "allOf": [{
                "time": {"anyOf": [
```

```
                      {"between": "09:00 12:00"},
                      {"between": "13:00 18:00"}]}
       },{
       "weekday": {"not": {"anyOf": [
               {"equals": "saturday"},
       {"equals": "sunday"}]}}}]
}
```

Apparently, implicit operators save a lot of space and make policies more readable, which has later turned out to be very useful in the policy engine implementation.

Combining Algorithms

In JACPoL, policies or rules may conflict and produce totally different decisions for the same request. JACPoL resolves this by adopting four kinds of decision-combining algorithms: *Permit-Overrides*, *Deny-Overrides*, *First-Applicable*, and *Highest-Priority*. Each algorithm represents a different way for combining multiple local decisions into a single global decision:

- *Permit-Overrides* returns *Permit* if any decision evaluates to *Permit*; and returns *Deny* if all decisions evaluate to *Deny*.
- *Deny-Overrides* returns *Deny* if any decision evaluates to *Deny*; returns *Permit* if all decisions evaluate to *Permit*.
- *First-Applicable* returns the first decision that evaluates to either of *Permit* or *Deny*. This is very useful to shortcut policy evaluation.
- *Highest-Priority* returns the highest priority decision that evaluates to either of *Permit* or *Deny*. If there are multiple equally highest priority decisions that conflict, then *deny-overrides* algorithm would be applied among those highest priority decisions.

Please note that for all of these combining algorithms, *Not Applicable* is returned if not any of the child rules (or policies) is applicable. Hence, the set of possible decisions is 3-valued.

Obligations

JACPoL includes the notion of obligation. An Obligation optionally specified in a Rule, a Policy or a PolicySet is an operation that should be performed by the PEP in conjunction with the enforcement of an authorization decision. It can be triggered on either Permit or Deny. The format below is introduced to express obligations in JACPoL:

```
{"<decision>": {"<operation>": [<parameter>, <parameter>, ...]}}
```

For example, the obligation below is for the access control of a document.

```
{
       "permit": {"watermark": ["DRAFT"]},
```

```
"deny": {
        "feedback": ["ACCESS DENIED"],
        "notify": ["admin@gmail.com", "hr@gmail.com"]
    }
}
```

It specifies that if an access request is denied, the user would be informed with an access denied message and the administrator and HR would also be notified; if an access request is approved, watermark the document "DRAFT" before delivery. It is worth mentioning that the referred obligations have an eminently locale nature in the sense that their execution is the exclusive prerogative of the PEP which can possibly rely on the information available in the PIP (Yavatkar et al., 2000). More general and distributed obligations deserve a dedicated investigation.

Implementation

An implementation of JACPoL has been done in a Javascript/Node.js/Redis based policy engine (re-THINK CSP Policy Engine, 2016) which is available on Github. As shown in Figure 5, the policy engine employs the classical PDP/PEP architecture (Yavatkar et al., 2000). The PDP retrieves policies from the PRP (Policy Retrieval Point), and evaluates authorization requests from the PEP by examining the finite relevant attributes against the policies. If more attributes are required to reach a decision, the PDP will request the PIP(Policy Information Point) as an external information source. The latter may also be requested in the case of obligations.

The non-blocking nature of Node.js allows the system to provide an efficient and scalable access control, and a Redis server was employed to enable flexible and high-performance data persistence and caching. In order to validate its functionality, this policy engine has been deployed on a messaging node

Figure 5. Policy engine architecture

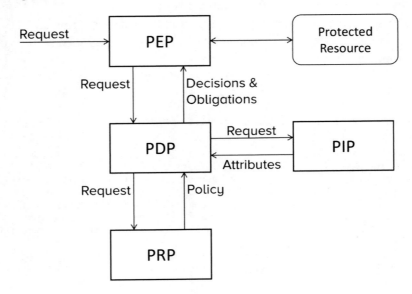

of reTHINK project (reTHINK Project, 2016). This reTHINK policy engine (reTHINK CSP Policy Engine, 2016) adopted the ABAC model and customized the vocabulary of JACPoL for the requirements of reTHINK framework. With JACPoL based lightweight policies, Node.js based non-blocking I/O, and Redis based fast caching, it provided a highly performant access control according to various tailored attributes in an expressive and flexible way (reTHINK Deliverable 6.4, 2016). In reTHINK, in addition to comparative operators greaterThan, lessThan, equalsTo, JACPoL is extended to support more operators as listed in Figure 6 with a rule example:

COMPARATIVE ANALYSIS

This section evaluates JACPoL with a comprehensive comparison to other pre- and post-XACML policy languages, which respectively are JSONPL (Steven, 2013), AWS IAM (Amazon Web Services), XACML (OASIS, 2013), Ponder (Damianou et al., 2001), Rei (Kagal et al., 2003), XACL (Hada & Kudo, 2000), KAoS (Uszok et al., 2004), EPAL (Ashley et al., 2003), and ASL (Jajodia et al., 1997), followed by a simple quantitative comparison with XACML in terms of processing delay. To begin with, the following requirements are identified for an access control policy language to meet the increasing needs of security management for today's ICT systems:

- *Expressiveness* to support wide range of policy needs and be able to specify various complex, advanced policies that a policy maker intend to express (He et al., 2013).
- *Extensibility* to cater for new features or concepts of policy in the future (Damianou et al., 2001).
- *Simplicity* to ease the policy definition and management tasks for the policy makers with different levels of expertise. This includes both conciseness and readability to avoid long learning curve and complex training.
- *Efficiency* to ensure the speed for machines to parse the policies defined by humans. This can be affected by policy structure, syntax, and data format.
- *Scalability* to ensure the performance as the network grows in size and complexity. This is important especially in large-scale or multi-domain networks.
- *Adaptability* to be compatible with any access control tasks derived from an ICT system. Any user could directly tailor the enforcement code and related tool set provided by the policy language to their authorization systems.

Figure 6. Other supported operators (left) and a rule example (right)

Other Operators
x **in** [a, b, c]
x **between** "a b"
x **contains** "c"
x **like** "/resources/*"
x **exists**

```
{
    "id": "dpt-01-ac-01",
    "target": {"type": {"equalsTo": "create"}},
    "condition": {
        "weekday": {"in": ["saturday", "sunday"]},
        "time": {"between": "18:00 07:00"},
        "url": {"like": "*/core/*/contactlist"}
    },
    "effect": "deny"
}
```

Table 1 shows the complete evaluation of these policy languages. In the table, '!' and '!!' respectively indicate 'support' and 'strongly support', while '+', '++', '+++' and '++++' mean 'poor', 'good', 'very good' and 'excellent'. The comparison mainly focuses on their design and implementation choices regarding *authorization*, *obligation*, *index*, *syntax* and *scheme*, and their performance with respect to the six previously defined criteria. Among these features, *index* refers to whether there exists a special item for policy engine to retrieve the required policies more efficiently.

Like many other languages, JACPoL provides support for authorization and obligation capabilities as previously introduced. In addition, it includes a concept of Target within each Policy Set, Policy and Rule to allow efficient policy index. In terms of expressiveness, JACPoL, Rei and KAoS extensively support the specification of constraints, which can be set on numerous attributes in a flexible expression (Neuhaus et al., 2011).

On the other hand, compared to XML-based languages, JSON-based JACPoL is simpler and more efficient, but meanwhile, there is a clear agreement that JSON is less sophisticated than XML, which accordingly may make JACPoL less extensible. JACPoL is scalable and the reasons are twofold: first, its efficient performance in policy index and evaluation allows it to deal with complex policies under a large-scale network environment; second, its concise semantics and lightweight data representation make it easily replicable and transferable for distributed systems. As for adaptability, compared to other languages, the application specific nature of AWS IAM makes it relatively harder to be adapted to other systems.

PRELIMINARY PERFORMANCE EVALUATION

This section presents the results of preliminary performance tests on JACPoL and XACML. The assessment is given of respectively how both languages' evaluation time and memory usage are affected with regards to the increase of nesting policies (policy depth) and the increase of sibling ones (policy scale). The values are ranged from 0 to 10000 with a step of 1000, as shown in Figure 7.

The two policy languages are used to express the same policy task and to compare their performances with different depth (number of nesting policies) and scale (number of sibling policies). Figure 8 provides XACML and JACPoL policy examples used for assessment. The two ellipses in each example indicate nesting (the upper and inner ellipsis) and sibling (the lower and outer ellipsis) child policies respectively. When processing a given request, the Boolean expression in the Target field of each policy is evaluated to verify the applicability of its child policies until the last child policy is evaluated. Note that the JSON profile of XACML defines XACML requests and responses but not policies, therefore it is not possible to compare JACPoL with JSON-formatted XACML.

As shown in Figure 9, the policy evaluation performance of the PDP is very related to the writing, loading and processing performance of a policy language. It is clear that the schemes and technologies used in requesting/responding operations would also influence the performance, which is however beyond the scope of current JACPoL's specification.

Therefore, four sets of tests are conducted in order to evaluate the writing, loading and processing speed and the memory consumption of the two policy languages. Respectively, the writing test measures the average time (in seconds) to write policies from the memory into a single file; the loading test measures the average time (in seconds) to load policies from a single file into the memory; the processing test measures the average time (in seconds) to process a request against policies that are already

Table 1. Evaluation and comparison between JACPoL and other policy languages

Policy Languages	Year	Authorization	Obligation	Index	Syntax	Scheme	Expressiveness	Extensibility	Simplicity	Efficiency	Scalability	Adaptability
JACPoL	2017	✓	!	✓	JSON-based	ABAC	++++	++	+++	+++	+++	+++
JSONPL	2012	✓		✓	JSON-based	ABAC	++	++	+++	+++	+++	++
AWS IAM	2010	✓			JSON-based	RBAC	++	++	+++	+++	++	+
XACML	2003	✓	!	✓	XML-based	ABAC	+++	+++	+	++	++	+++
Rei	2003	✓	✓		Logic-based	OBAC	++++	+++	+	++	+++	+++
EPAL	2003	✓	!	✓	XML-based	RBAC	+++	+++	+	++	++	+++
Ponder	2001	✓	✓		Specific	RBAC	+++	+	++	++	+++	+++
XACL	2000	✓			XML-based	RBAC	+	+	+	++	+	+
KAoS	1997	✓	✓		OWL-based	OBAC	++++	+++	+	++	+++	+++
ASL	1997	✓			Logic-based	RBAC	+	+	+	++	+	++

Figure 7. Examples of nesting policies (a) and sibling policies (b)

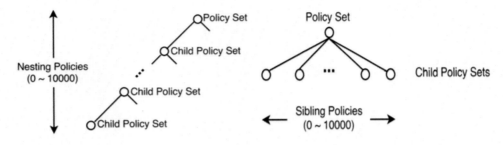

Figure 8a. Examples of XACML policies

```
<PolicySet Id="0" PolicyCombiningAlgorithm="firstApplicable" Update="2017-03-14 17:18:31" Version="1">
    <Target>
        <Subjects>
            <Subject>
                <SubjectMatch MatchId="...#string-equal">
                    <AttributeValue DataType="...#string">Sam</AttributeValue>
                    <SubjectAttributeDesignator AttributeId="...:subject:subject-id" DataType="...#string" />
                </SubjectMatch>
            </Subject>
        </Subjects>
    </Target>
    <PolicySet Id="1" PolicyCombiningAlgorithm="firstApplicable" Update="2017-03-14 17:18:31" Version="1">
        ...
    </PolicySet>
    ...
</PolicySet>
```

loaded in the memory; and the last test measures the space consumption (in Megabytes) of policies in the memory. Each test evaluates the two languages with different policy nesting depth and sibling scale, and was repeated 10000 times conducted using Python on a Windows 10 ASUS N552VW laptop with 16G memory and a 2.6GHz Intel core i7-6700HQ processor.

Figure 10 shows the writing time versus the number of policies. It can be observed that there are near linear correlations between the average writing time and number policies (both in depth and in scale) for both languages. Compared to XACML, JACPoL consumes only approximately half of the time taken by the former.

Figure 11 shows the average loading time versus the number of policies in depth and in scale. Similar to Figure 10, there is an almost linear correlation between the loading time and the number of policies. It can be seen that the loading time of JACPoL becomes much less than XACML as the number of policies increases.

Figure 12 shows the processing time versus the number of policies. Similar as the writing time and loading time, there is also an almost linear correlation between the processing time and the number of policies. On the other hand, unlike Figure 10 and Figure 11, it can be seen that the policy structure

Figure 8b. JACPoL policies

```json
{
    "Target": {"Subject": {"equals": "Sam"}},
    "Update": "2017-03-14 17:18:31",
    "PolicyCombiningAlgorithm": "firstApplicable",
    "Version": 1,
    "Id": 0,
    "Policies": [
        {
            "Target": {"Subject": {"equals": "Sam"}},
            "Update": "2017-03-14 17:18:31",
            "PolicyCombiningAlgorithm": "firstApplicable",
            "Version": 1,
            "Id": 1,
            "Policies": [...]
        },
        ...
    ]
}
```

Figure 9. Policy evaluation procedure

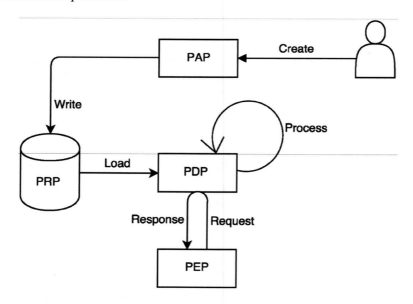

Figure 10. Comparing writing time consumption between JACPoL and XACML

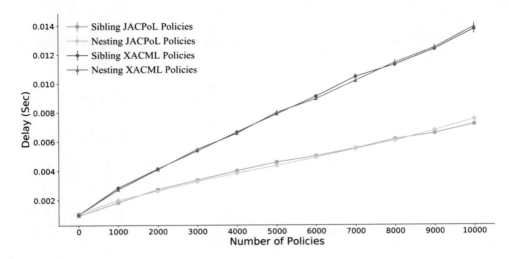

Figure 11. Comparing loading time consumption between JACPoL and XACML

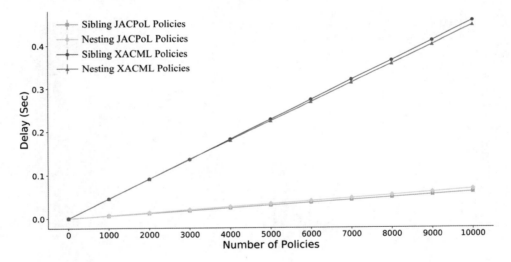

would influence the processing time given the same policy size. It can also be observed that JACPoL is processed faster than XACML policies.

Figure 13 shows the memory consumption versus the number of policies. Similar as all figures above, the memory consumption increases also almost linearly with the growth of the number of policies. Given the same policy size, the memory space used by JACPoL is nearly half of that used by XACML.

These figures demonstrate that JACPoL is highly scalable and efficient in comparison with XACML, with much faster writing, loading, processing speed and lower memory consumption. The involved evaluation is however preliminary in the sense that we used several assumptions which limit its scope.

Figure 12. Comparing processing time consumption between JACPoL and XACML

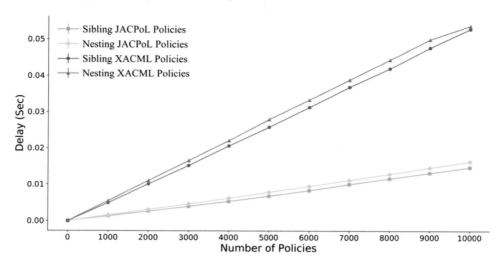

Figure 13. Comparing memory consumption between the JACPoL and XACML

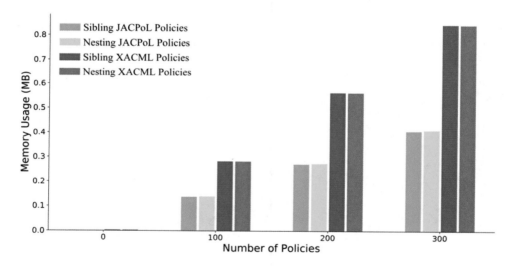

We indeed compared two generic and structurally identical families of policies without taking into account their corresponding application domain neither the algorithmic used to implement the different evaluted processes, neither its eventual optimisation which could be derived from the underlying language XML or JSON. If this evaluation demonstrates that JACPoL offers interesting and promising prospects in terms of results, it will however have to be validated by an extensive and in-depth analysis that is out the scope of this work.

APPLICATION OF JACPoL TO SECURITY MODELS

RBAC vs. ABAC

In policy-based access control systems, a request for access to protected resources is evaluated with respect to a policy that defines which requests are authorized. The policy itself conforms to a security model upstream chosen by the system security administrator because it elegantly copes with the constraints associated with the targeted information system. In the RBAC model, roles are pre-defined and permission sets for resources are pre-assigned to roles. Users are then granted one or more roles in order to receive access to resources (Empower ID, 2013). ABAC, on the other hand, relies on user attributes for access decisions. These include: subject attributes, which are attributes concerning the actor being evaluated; object attributes, which are attributes of the resource being affected; action attributes, which are attributes about the operation being executed; and environment attributes, which provides other contextual information such as time of the day, etc. (Hu et al., 2013). Generally speaking, RBAC is simple, static and auditable, but is not expressive nor context-aware, while ABAC, by contrast, provides fine-grained, flexible and dynamic access control in realtime but is complex and unauditable. Combining these two models judiciously to integrate their advantages thus becomes an essential work in recent research (Empower ID, 2013; Coyne & Weil, 2014; Jin et al., 2012; Kuhn et al., 2010).

Attribute-Centric RBAC Application

JACPoL can be implemented to express permission specification policies (PSP) in an attribute-centric RBAC model. For example, Figure 14 defines a policy set with each policy specifying permissions that are associated to the targeted role. When evaluating a request, the PDP first retrieves all the roles (e.g., from the PIP) that are pre-assigned to the requester, and then examines the permission policies that are associated to these roles to reach a decision. Unlike other traditional statically defined RBAC permissions, JACPoL allows its permissions to be expressed in a quite dynamic and flexible way similar to ABAC. Please note that the role attribute is suggested to be placed as the target for the topmost level of policies in order to allow an easier view of user permissions as shown in Figure 14.

Figure 14. An example ARBAC permission specification policy and its structure tree

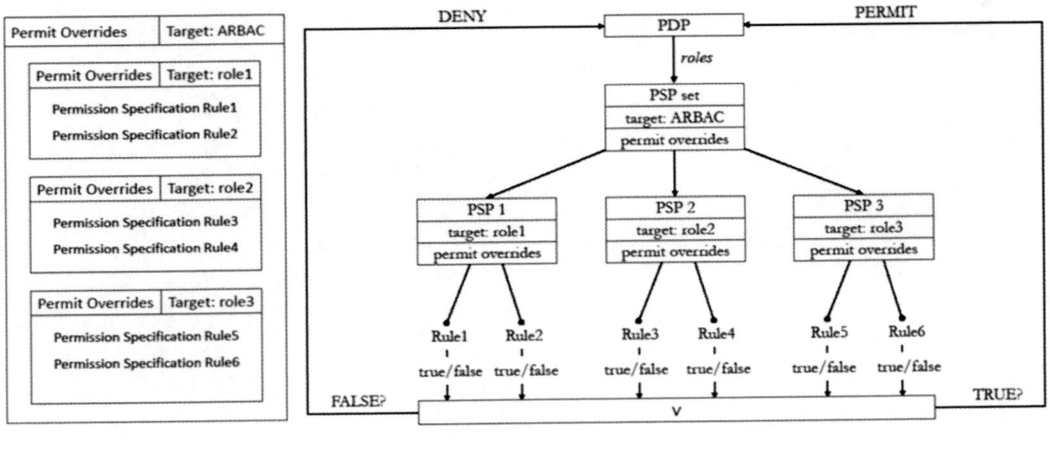

Role-Centric ABAC Application

JACPoL can also be used to implement a language for permission filtering policies (PFP) in a role-centric ABAC model (Jin et al., 2012). Similar to the ABAC model in Figure 5, but in addition to external attributes, the PDP also relies on the PIP to get role permission sets which, as defined by NIST RBAC model, specify the maximum set of available permissions that users can have. These permission sets can be further constrained by the filtering policies based on JACPoL, as shown in Figure 15. Note that this time the target of each PFP maps each object to a subset of the filtering rules. At the same time, the target and condition of each rule determine whether or not the rule is applicable. The applicable filtering rules are invoked one by one against each of the permissions in the permission set. If any of the rules return FALSE, the permission is then blocked and removed from the available permission set for the current session. At the end of this process, the final available permission set available to users therefore will be the intersection of P and R, where P is the set of permissions assigned to the subject's active roles and R is the set of permissions specified by the applicable JACPoL rules (Kuhn et al., 2010).

CONCLUSION

Traditionally, performance has not been a major focus in the design of access control systems. Applications are emerging, however, that require policies to be evaluated with a very low latency and high throughput. Under this background, JACPoL, a fast JSON-based, attribute-centric and light-weight access control policy language has been designed and implemented. JACPoL provides a good solution for policy specification and evaluation in such applications with low processing delay. The qualitative evaluation of this policy language is given with respect to a set of representative criteria in comparison with other existing policy languages. The evaluation showed that JACPoL can be as expressive as XACML but more simple, scalable and efficient.

Figure 15. An example RABAC permission filtering policy and its structure tree

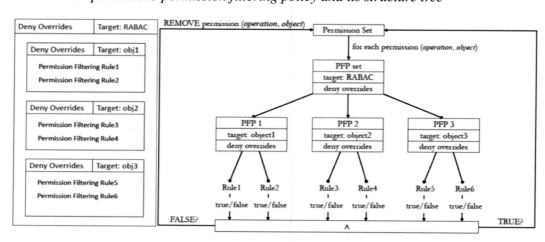

A preliminary quantitative evaluation is introduced focusing on the PDP performances by assessing the speed of writing, loading and processing generic families of policies expressed in JACPoL and XACML together with their relative memory consumption. The comparisons show that JACPoL systematically requires much less time and memory space and demonstrate that it offers interesting and promising prospects that should be validated by an extensive and in-depth analysis.

On the other hand, JACPoL leaves room for future improvements in many areas. For example, obligation capabilities can be further enhanced and delegation support can be formally introduced. It could also be considered to combine JACPoL and XACML to benefit, for example, from the good performance of the former and the high extensibility of the latter, by integrating them into a common framework. Actually JACPoL and XACML follows the same PEP/PDP model and Rule/Policy/PolicySet architecture, the integration would be supported (or almost supported with minor development required) by design, one possible solution could be for example to support inserting an XACML policy in a JACPoL policySet, or an XACML rule in a JACPoL policy.

REFERENCES

W3schools. (n.d.). *JSON vs XML*. Retrieved from www.w3schools.com/js/js_json_xml.asp

Amazon Web Services. (n.d.). *AWS Identity and Access Management(IAM) User Guide*. Retrieved from http://docs.aws.amazon.com/IAM/latest/UserGuide/introduction.html

Ashley, P., Hada, S., Karjoth, G., Powers, C., & Schunter, M. (2003). *Enterprise privacy authorization language (EPAL)*. IBM Research.

Bhatti, R., Ghafoor, A., Bertino, E., & Joshi, J. B. (2005). X-GTRBAC: An XML-based policy specification framework and architecture for enterprise-wide access control. *ACM Transactions on Information and System Security*, 8(2), 187–227.

Borders, K., Zhao, X., & Prakash, A. (2005). CPOL: High-performance policy evaluation. *The 12th ACM conference on Computer and communications security*.

Brossard, D. (2014). *JSON Profile of XACML 3.0 Version 1.0*. XACML Committee Specification 01. Retrieved from http://docs.oasis-open.org/xacml/xacml-json-http/v1.0/cs01/xacml-json-http-v1.0-cs01.pdf

Clarkson, M. R., & Schneider, F. B. (2010). Hyperproperties. *Journal of Computer Security*, 18(6), 1157–1210. doi:10.3233/JCS-2009-0393

Coyne, E., & Weil, T. R. (2014). ABAC and RBAC: Scalable, flexible, and auditable access management. *IT Professional*, 15(3), 14–16. doi:10.1109/MITP.2013.37

Crampton, J., & Morisset, C. (2012). PTaCL: A language for attribute-based access control in open systems. In *International Conference on Principles of Security and Trust* (pp. 390-409). Springer. 10.1007/978-3-642-28641-4_21

Crockford, D. (2006). *JSON — The fat-free alternative to XML*. Retrieved from http://www.json.org/fatfree.html

Damianou, N., Dulay, N., Lupu, E., & Sloman, M. (2001). *The ponder policy specification language.* doi:10.1109/WOCC.2013.6676386

ECMA International. (n.d.). *ECMA-404 The JSON Data Interchange Standard.* Retrieved from http://www.json.org/

El-Aziz, A. A., & Kannan, A. (2014). JSON encryption. In *Computer Communication and Informatics (ICCCI), 2014 International Conference on.* IEEE.

Empower, I. D. (2013). *Best practices in enterprise authorization: The RBAC/ABAC hybrid approach.* Empower ID, White paper.

Ferraiolo, D. (2016). Extensible Access Control Markup Language (XACML) and Next Generation Access Control (NGAC). *Proceedings of the 2016 ACM International Workshop on Attribute Based Access Control.* 10.1145/2875491.2875496

Ferraiolo, D. F., & Kuhn, D. R. (2009). *Role-based Access Controls.* arXiv preprint arXiv: 0903.2171

Griffin, L., Butler, B., de Leastar, E., Jennings, B., & Botvich, D. (2012). On the performance of access control policy evaluation. In *Policies for Distributed Systems and Networks (POLICY), 2012 IEEE International Symposium on* (pp. 25-32). IEEE. 10.1109/POLICY.2012.15

Hada, S., & Kudo, M. (2000). *XML Access Control Language: provisional authorization for XML documents.* Academic Press.

He, L., Qiu, X., Wang, Y., & Gao, T. (2013). Design of policy language expression in SIoT. In *Wireless and Optical Communication Conference* (pp. 321-326). IEEE.

Hu, V.C., Ferraiolo, D., & Kuhn, R. (2013). *Guide to attribute based access control (ABAC) definition and considerations.* NIST special publication 800.162.

Jajodia, S., Samarati, P., & Subrahmanian, V. S. (1997). A logical language for expressing authorizations. In *Proceedings of IEEE Symposium on Security and Privacy.* IEEE.

Jin, X., Sandhu, R., & Krishnan, R. (2012). RABAC: role-centric attribute-based access control. In *International Conference on Mathematical Methods, Models, and Architectures for Computer Network Security.* Springer.

Kagal, L., Finin, T., & Joshi, A. (2003). A policy language for a pervasive computing environment. In *Policies for Distributed Systems and Networks. Proceedings. POLICY 2003. IEEE 4th International Workshop on.* IEEE.

Kuhn, D. R., Coyne, E. J., & Weil, T. R. (2010). Adding attributes to role-based access control. *Computer, 43*(6), 79–81. doi:10.1109/MC.2010.155

Neuhaus, C., Polze, A., & Chowdhuryy, M. M. (2011). *Survey on healthcare IT systems: standards, regulations and security. No. 45.* Universitätsverlag Potsdam.

OASIS XACML Technical Committee. (2013). *eXtensible access control markup langage (XACML) Version 3.0. Oasis Standard, OASIS*. Retrieved from http://docs.oasis-open.org/xacml/3.0/xacml-3.0-core-spec-os-en.html

Obrsta, L., McCandlessb, D., & Ferrella, D. (2012). Fast semantic Attribute-Role-Based Access Control (ARBAC) in a collaborative environment. *8th International Conference on Collaborative Computing: Networking, Applications and Worksharing*.

reTHINK CSP Policy Engine. (2016). Retrieved from github.com/reTHINK-project/dev-msg-node-nodejs/tree/master/src/main/components/policyEngine

reTHINK Deliverable 6.4. (2016). *Assessment Report*. reTHINK H2020 Project.

reTHINK Project. (2016). Retrieved from github.com/reTHINK-project/

reTHINK Project Testbed. (2016). *Deliverable D6.1: Testbed Specification*. Retrieved from https://bscw.rethink-project.eu/pub/bscw.cgi/d35657/D6.1%20Testbed%20specification.pdf

Steven, D., Bernard, B. & Leigh, G. (2013). *JSON-encoded ABAC (XACML) policies. FAME project of Waterford Institute of Technology*. Presentation to OASIS XACML TC concerning JSON-encoded XACML policies.

Uszok, A., Bradshaw, J. M., & Jeffers, R. (2004). Kaos: A policy and domain services framework for grid computing and semantic web services. In *International Conference on Trust Management*. Springer. 10.1007/978-3-540-24747-0_2

Yavatkar, R., Pendarakis, D., & Guerin, R. (2000). *A Framework for Policy-based Admission Control*. IETF, RFC 2753.

ENDNOTES

[1]   nodejs.org
[2]   Redis.io

Chapter 5
A Survey on JSON Mapping With XML/RDF

Gbéboumé Crédo Charles Adjallah-Kondo
Nanjing University of Aeronautics and Astronautics, China

Zongmin Ma
Nanjing University of Aeronautics and Astronautics, China

ABSTRACT

As a data format, JSON is able to store and exchange data. It can be mapped with RDF (resource description framework), which is an ontology technology in the direction of web resources. This chapter replies to the question about which techniques or methods to utilize for mapping XML to JSON and RDF. However, a plethora of methods have been explored. Consequently, the goal of this survey is to give the whole presentation of the currents approaches to map JSON with XML and RDF by providing their differences.

INTRODUCTION

The conspicuous development in the semantic web has given birth to different data formats sanctioning exchange, management and storage of data. The challenge is to find a way for mapping a data format to another which has different structure, common (XML, JSON, RDF) and convenient dealing with different applications. First, researches stipulate that it is better to utilize JSON (JavaScript Object Notation) than XML (Extensible Markup Language derived from an older standard format called SGML). Also, XML and REST APIs can support JSON. Converting subsisting XML document to JSON became a consequential question. Albeit they have unique purport, XML has to be parsed by XML parser and JSON by a standard JavaScript function. On the other hand, verbalizing about another format, RDF (Resource Description Framework) is a standard promote mundane data format and exchange protocols on the Web. Since JSON cannot be used directly on the web of data due to certain consequential features like URIs and semantical links, the conversion from JSON to RDF is then primordial.

DOI: 10.4018/978-1-5225-8446-9.ch005

JSON designated in early 2000s (Resource Description Framework, n.d.) by Douglas Crockford, is a lightweight data-interchange format. It's a syntax sanctioning to store and exchange data. JSON is a text format predicated on Java Script programming language and is thoroughly independent language data format. It is elaborated as human-readable, "self-describing" and facile for computer to understand. It is nowadays an ideal data-interchange language on the web especially in web applications and used to supersede XML.

XML, (XML essentials, n.d.) derived from an older standard format called SGML (Standard Generalized Markup Language - ISO 8879), is text format and markup language much homogeneous to HTML. It was designed to store and convey structured data and additionally designed to be self-descriptive, simple and human-machine readable. XML was recommended by W3C (World Wide Web Consortium) in early February 1998. It is one of the most widely-used formats for sharing structured information today.

The RDF is a fundamental lower layer on top of which the semantic web is built. It is also a framework for representing information in the Web. RDF is a (Resource Description Framework, n.d.) standard model for data interchange on the Web and has features that facilitate data merging even if the underlying schemas differ, and it specifically supports the evolution of schemas over time without requiring all the data consumers to be changed. The RDF specification defines a data model and a syntax which is defined on top of the XML syntax. RDF data can be expressed with different notations like XML (for machine interchange), N3 and Turtle (human readable).

This paper elucidates the current methods that can be habituated to convert first XML to JSON and the mapping from JSON to RDF. For longtime, XML was the only option to sanction data storage and interchange. But with the apparition of JSON, it is now a popular alternative to XML for sundry reasons. The findings of this study will redound to benefit of developer dealing with APIs and users to share, exchange and store data without format issues on the web and applications.

The section one dedicatory to the conversion of XML to JSON, in particular, gives definitions, main differences and kindred attributes between them; explores methods for how this mapping can be done and conclusively explores the approach by (Falco & Thom, 2014) deeply in details. Moving on, the second part will verbalize mainly about mapping JSON to RDF. Afore this can be done, it provides definitions, the kindred attributes and convergences, analyses subsisting approaches. Furthermore, the current method to go about converting JSON to RDF is explored from the commencement to his implementation. This method emanates from Pasquale Lisena and Raphaël Troncy in Transforming the JSON Output of SPARQL Queries for Linked Data Clients. After all then comes the conclusion.

Background

This component introduces a formal data model for JSON, XML and RDF documents reflecting the comparison between these data formats. After introducing them, highlights the difference and the homogeneous attributes.

JSON Data Modeling

JSON exchanges data between browser and server. JSON is text so it can be converted in any JavaScript object and Vis versa without any complicated pursing or translation. It is built (Introducing JSON, n.d.)

on two structures which are collection of name/value pairs (e.g., object, record, struct, dictionary, hash table, keyed list, or associative array depending on the language) and ordered list of values (e.g., *array, vector, list, or sequence depending on various languages*).

JSON Document Structures

A JSON can have the following structures or forms:

- Object (an unordered set of name/value pairs.)
- Array (an ordered collection of values)
- Value (It can be string in double quotes, or a number, or true or false or null, or an object or an array.)
- String (sequence of zero or more Unicode characters, wrapped in double quotes, using backslash escapes.)
- Number (is very also like a C or Java number, a countable number of an ordered values. Here, the octal and hexadecimal formats are not used.)

The following example (Figure 1) describes all forms of JSON presented above. This JSON data gives information about a random student.

Figure 1. Simple example of JSON

```
{
  "Student": [
    {
      "name": "Credo Adjallah",
      "age": 24,
      "Nationality": "Togolese",
      "Birthday": "February 4, 1994",
      "wife": null,
      "weight": 67.5,
      "hasChildren": false,
      "hasBlackHair": true,
      "latestDiploma": [
        "Bachelor",
        "HighTechnicianDegree",
      ]
    }

  ]
}
```

JSON Schema

Earlier research (Pierre, Juan, Fernando, & Domagoj, 2016) stated that there is a lack of specification and also JSON schema has no proper schema. So, in their work, they proposed the first time the definition of JSON schema syntax by implementing with an efficient algorithm which worked successfully with the Wikidata database and second, defined JSON Schema as tree. JSON schema can be defined as a vocabulary that allows annotating and validating a JSON documents. Later, JSON schema work group released the current Internet-Drafts at the IETF are the draft-handrews-json-schema*-01 documents, which correspond to the draft-07 meta-schemas (JSON schema, n.d.). These were published on 2018-03-19 (Core and Validation) and 2018-01-19 (Hyper-Schema and Relative JSON Pointer). This draft mainly defines the basic foundation of JSON Schema, keywords, documentation hyperlink and interaction control of JSON. It is necessary to note that no fractional part is allowed in the term of mathematical integers.

XML Data Modeling

The XML data model provides an abstract representation of XML documents describes the logical structure of a set of data and follows the XPath 2.0 and the XQuery 1.0 data model. In order to define XML lexicon, data model becomes paramount (XML Data Model, n.d.).

As verbalized before, XML like JSON has its own structure and it can be compared to a tree and every node in the tree are character strings. The whole composing then the information content of XML.

XML Documents

XML documents can contain key constructs based on the document needs or purpose. Here is some of the key construct which can probably appear in XML documents.

- Element (logical document component that can contain markup, other elements and uses start-tag and end-tag)
- Character (String of characters)
- Processor and application (Processor which is referred to XML parser, analyses the markup and conducts the structured information to an application)
- Declaration (in most of cases, the XML declaration is present in the document expressing information about the version and encoding such as: "<?xml version="1.0" encoding="UTF-8"?>"
- Markup and content (characters marking up XML document)
- Tag (markup construct which has three types: start-tag, end-tag and empty-element tag)
- Attribute (single value and can only appears once on each element)

The following instructions (Figure 2) are an example of XML document given information about a student. This document shows some of the features listed above.

XML Schema

An XML Schema is a description of a type of XML document, typically expressed in terms of constraints on the structure and content of documents of that type, (XML Schema, n.d.) above and beyond

Figure 2. Simple example of XML

```
<?xml version="1.0" encoding="UTF-8"?>
<student>
   <infos>
      <name>Credo</name>
      <age>24</age>
      <nationality>Togolese</nationality>
   </infos>
</student>
```

the rudimental syntactical constraints imposed by XML itself. It defines also the foundation of XML document, the number of elements, data types (the greatest power of XML schema) and default values. Supporting data type, using XML syntax and secure in data communication, it allows document description, the manipulation of schema with XML DOM and their transformation in XSLT (XML schema tutorial, n.d.). Note that XSD is a valid XML document. Since XSD can also provide a primitive data types such as Boolean, data, double, duration, float, string time…, it allows first restriction on values specification, regular expressions and constraints; second list and union mechanism. XSD is based and elaborated on XML and has no data content, it is just a validation providing a proper use of XML document for different aims.

This example (Figure 3) is a corresponding XSD of the content of XML document (Figure 2)

JSON vs. XML

There are several differences and kindred attributes between JSON and XML. XML has been the industry standard, fortifies majority of API and has an abundance of fortifying frameworks and standards

Figure 3. Simple XSD Document

```
<xs:schema attributeFormDefault="unqualified" elementFormDefault="qualified"
xmlns:xs="http://www.w3.org/2001/XMLSchema">
   <xs:element name="student">
      <xs:complexType>
         <xs:sequence>
            <xs:element name="infos">
               <xs:complexType>
                  <xs:sequence>
                     <xs:element name="name" type="xs:string" />
                     <xs:element name="age" type="xs:int" />
                     <xs:element name="nationality" type="xs:int" />
                  </xs:sequence>
               </xs:complexType>
            </xs:element>
         </xs:sequence>
      </xs:complexType>
   </xs:element>
</xs:schema>
```

to govern the implementation but JSON has been engendered to supersede XML so it's incipient and does not have standards like Schematrons, XSDs, for implementation. With XML, metadata can be put into the tags in the form of attributes while with JSON it can only be by making the entity an object and integrating the attributes as members of the object. It has been proved by (Nurzhan, Michael, Randall, & Clemente, 2009) by comparing XML and JSON data interchange that: first, JSON is more expeditious and uses fewer resources than its XML, second JSON and XML provide unique strengths and additionally JSON used less total resources, more utilizer CPU, and less system CPU. Since they've used RedHat machines, it was shown that higher utilizer CPU utilization is propitious. All these mean, in performance term, JSON is the best.

Moving on, it is withal reported that XML and JSON both are Human Readable but JSON with the utilization of parentheses is highly cryptic. XML sanctions the storage of any data type but JSON can just store text and numbers. They are oriented but it's arduous to map it to objects in graph structure but JSON is more proximate to the graph structure of objects.

Furthermore, according to (Patt, 2017), XML and JSON are like cardboard. It was argued that they are flexible, dynamic, self-identifying, self-describing and the utilization are safe to store data. XML is a Markup language, it can contain facilely contain markup but JSON does not have such kind facile way to introduce markup naturally. Last but not least, (Guanhua, 2011) in his research found that in web applications JSON serialization is expeditious and convenient withal the XML serialization is puissant. The difference occurs depending on the situation of the application. The table (Table 1) below describes the variance between the two models.

RDF Data Model

An RDF data model (W3C, 2014) can be looked as a directed graph, in which subjects and objects are nodes and properties are arcs that can refer to any resources. The core structure of the abstract syntax is a set of triples, each consisting of a subject, a predicate and an object. An RDF graph is such triple of such nodes. Each triple is denoted by **<s, p, o>** and can be represented as an arc (Figure 4)

Predicate

Let consider a set of terms *v* composed by three disjoint sets:

Table 1. Comparison between JSON and XML

Description	XML	JSON
Data structure	Tree, tag, meta-data	Array, object, value, number, string; map
Supporting object	Attributes and elements expressions	Native
Data type	XML Schema, structured data	Scalar type and structured data
Display ability	Yes	No
Speed	AJAX	Web application
Safety	Web services	AJAX
Language type	Independent	Independent
Parsing	XML parser	JavaScript function

Figure 4. RDF graph with two nodes and triple connection

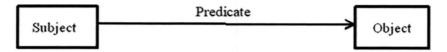

- A set μ of URI references (urirefs),
- A set β of blank nodes,
- And a set ι of literals.

The set ι is composed of two disjoint sets: the set ιP of plain literals and the set ιT of typed literals. Let V be a subset of *v*, then we denote the set of urirefs of V by μ(V), denote the set of blank nodes of V by β(V). The rest may be deduced by analogy. There are a lot of definitions for RDF and RDF graph according to researches.

An *RDF triple* consists of three components:

- The *subject*, which is an IRI or a blank node
- The *predicate*, which is an IRI
- The *object*, which is an IRI, a literal or a blank node

It is written in the order of subject, predicate, object. The set of *nodes* of an RDF graph is the set of subjects and objects of triples in the graph. It is possible for a predicate IRI to also occur as a node in the same graph.

JSON-LD (JavaScript Object Notation for Linked Data), is a lightweight (Processing Algorithms and API, 2018) Linked Data format withal a method of encoding Linked Data utilizing JSON. It is facile for humans to read and to indite. It is predicated on the already prosperous JSON format and provides a way to avail JSON data interoperate at Web-scale. JSON-LD is an ideal data format for programming environments, REST Web accommodations, and unstructured databases such as CouchDB and MongoDB. It is a method sanctioning to build a network of standards-predicated, machine-readable data across Web sites. It sanctions an application to commence at one piece of Linked Data, and follow embedded links to other pieces of Linked Data that are hosted on different sites across the Web. JSON-LD is designed around the concept of a "context" to provide supplemental mappings from JSON to an RDF model. The context links object properties in a JSON document to concepts in a given ontology.

In order to map the JSON-LD syntax to RDF, JSON-LD sanctions values to be coerced to a designated type or to be tagged with a language. A context can be embedded directly in a JSON-LD document or put into a separate file and referenced from different documents (from traditional JSON documents via an HTTP Link header). It was a goal to require as minuscule effort as possible from developers to transform their subsisting JSON to JSON-LD sanctioning data to be serialized in such way that satiates the homogeneous attribute to traditional JSON. JSON-LD syntax is engendered to be facilely implemented and to be used directly as JSON. Figure 5 shows an example of JSON-LD document. It is W3C recommendation additionally initially developed by the JSON for Linking Data Community Group for afore being transferred to the RDF Working Group for review, amendment, and standardization.

Figure 5. Example of JSON-LD document

```json
{
    "@context": {
      "name": "http://xmlns.com/foaf/0.1/name",
      "homepage": {
        "@id": "http://xmlns.com/foaf/0.1/workplaceHomepage",
        "@type": "@id"
      },
      "Person": "http://xmlns.com/foaf/0.1/Person"
    },
    "@id": "https://me.example.com",
    "@type": "Person",
    "name": "John Smith",
    "homepage": "https://www.example.com/"
}
```

MAPPING XML TO JSON

The conception of mapping XML to JSON is not incipient but it is genuinely conspicuous that researches regarding this are not numerous. Convert XML to JSON in PHP from IBM work group is part and there are many which are not officially published.

(Guanhua, 2011) published about the amelioration of data transmission by utilizing the translation between JSON and XML in the context of web application. In his paper, he first compared the two data formats already discussed in the previous paragraphs and presented two kinds of methods. However, they have the same function, they were deployed in two applications, first in web application and the secondly in AJAX (Asynchronous JavaScript and XML) application. The XML serialization is mostly utilized in the first one because of the security but according to the haste, the JSON serialization is preferred. From the third-party Web Accommodation, the date is translated into Local web accommodation and the JSON data to another data processing. For the second approach, here JSON is preferred because of it speed trough AJAX application but coming to security, XML is utilized in data transmission through third-party applications. Utilizing translator and third-party in this approach can amend data exchange on the web efficiently. The current approach uses XSD document through Prolog/CHR to get JSON data as output. However, this one, mainly analysis function XML and JSON features and abilities vis-à-vis of applications and web service.

Current Approach in Translating XML to JSON

Some researchers have worked to elucidate how to translating XML to JSON as verbalized in the prelude, we are a theater of approaches. In this section, we explicit the current one by (Falco Nogatz & Frühwirth, 2014) which is to translating XSD document to JSON predicated on Prolog programming logic language and CHR (Constraint Handling Rules). Their paper describes all steps from the translation process to the final result.

Work Description

The main purpose is to get an equivalent JSON to a given XML document. It is important to note that XSD is a valid instance of XML and this was done with existing XML document.

XML schema consists to define four components: elements (xs:element nodes), simple types (xs:simpleType nodes), complex types (xs:complexType nodes) and attributes (xs:attribute nodes). Here the XML version used it is 1.0 because the recommended version 1.1 with the introduction of XPATH expressions has no XPATH equivalent to JSON. This will of course be impossible for the translation. Draft 04 is the version of the specification used because it can support numerous of JSON validators in multiple languages. The equivalent JSON must follow this semantic: first, there is a list of values; second, the list contains at most five values and lastly, every value must be a nonnegative integer.

The use of Prolog and CHR provides a translation rules for XSD fragments and specify the translation in declaration way. A new CHR is generated for each XSD node so it makes possible to create the rules without having to implement the tree traversal of the XSD document. The following CHR constraints are introduced to keep given XSD information:

- *node(Namespace,Name,ID,Children IDs,Parent ID)*
- A new node/5 constraint is generated to hold namespace and tag name. To get a reference, a unique identifier is added as well as the list of its parent's and children's identifiers.
- *node attribute(ID,Key,Value,Source)*
- A new node attribute/4 constraint is generated to hold its name as Key, its Value and the identifier of the related node/5 constraint.
- *text node(ID,Text,Parent ID)*
- If an element's child is simply a text and no nested XML node, a text node/3 constraint is generated. It gets a unique identifier like a regular child node and holds the text as well as the identifier of its parent element.

All translated fragments are store in json (ID, JSON) constraints to hold the JSON Schema of the XSD node with the identifier. Because the entire JSON Schema is built step by step, the innermost fragments of the XSD propagate the first json/2 constraints. These will be picked up for the translation of their parent elements, resulting in a JSON Schema for the entire XSD. The next stage describes how the translation is done.

Translation Process

The translation process is subdivided in six different stages as showing the above figure (Figure 6). The main part here is the fourth one, the translation rules of XSD fragments. Let introduce now the example of new XML and the valid JSON.

Read in XML Schema into Prolog

Since SWI-Prolog is a support for working with XML, using it SGML/XML parser, an XSD document can be read in as a nested Prolog term. The term is generated by the built-in load structure/3 predicate for the XSD of Figure 9.

Figure 6. All steps of translation process

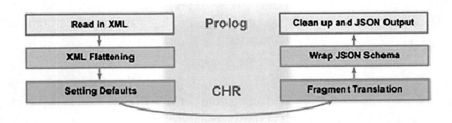

Figure 7. Example of XML

```
<?xml version="1.0" ?>
<percentages>
<value>99</value>
<value>42</value>
<value>0</value>
</percentages>
```

Figure 8. Valid JSON document against JSON Schema

```
{
"value": [ 99, 42, 0]
}
```

Figure 9. Possible XSD for XML of Figure 7

```
<?xml version="1.0" ?>
<xs:schema
xmlns:xs="http://www.w3.org/2001/XMLSchema">
<xs:element name="percentages">
<xs:complexType>
<xs:sequence>
<xs:element
name="value"
maxOccurs="5"
type="xs:nonNegativeInteger" />
</xs:sequence>
</xs:complexType>
</xs:element>
</xs:schema>
```

XML Flattening

This nested Prolog term can be traversed recursively to propagate the related node/5, node attribute/4 and text node/3 constraints. Their positions are retained by their unique identifiers and references to parent and child nodes.

Setting Defaults

Adding the default attribute reposes on the fact that the parser will only read in explicitly set attributes. The attributes like minOccurs and maxOccurs are optional so they can be omitted but to keep them always present, the node attribute/4 is generated with the Source set to default. In case it occurs an identical node attribute/4 constraint with its last component set to source, the default one is removed by a CHR.

Fragment Translation

In this stage, the authors described a library to serialize JSON and show that Prolog lists are the representation of JSON arrays.

The translation of XSD fragments to equivalent JSON schema can be done according to constraints generated in lasted stages. All translation rules follow the same form: They propagate a single json/2 constraint that holds the JSON Schema of this XSD fragment; the guard ensures that all node/5 and node attribute/4 constraints are of the XML Schema namespace.

Hereby the propagation rule to generate the JSON Schema for the innermostxs:element of Figure 9 is:

```
node(NS,element,ID,_C,_Parent), node_attribute(ID,type,With_NS,_)
==> xsd_namespace(NS), valid_xsd_type(With_NS,Type)
| convert_xsd_type(Type,JSON), json(ID,JSON).
```

This rule is applied if the xs:element node has an XSD namespace and is of a primitive XSD data type. Since XML Schema provides various predefined data types however the defined JSON data types are limited. There is a possibility to restrict them similarly to constraining facets in XSD and then define a convert xsd type/2 predicate by providing JSON's equivalents of all predefined XML data types like in Table 2 in excerpts. At the last part of the stage, the translation of nested XSD nodes is done.

Wrap JSON Schema

The globally defined type definitions are merged into the definitions object of the root's json/2 constraint.

Figure 10. Nested Prolog term of the XSD document of Figure 9

```
[ element(
'http://www.w3.org/2001/XMLSchema':schema,          % namespace and name
[ xmlns:xs='http://www.w3.org/2001/XMLSchema' ],     % attributes
[ element(                                           % nested elements
'http://www.w3.org/2001/XMLSchema':element,
[ name=percentages ],                                % attributes
[ ... ])                                             % the other nested
elements
])]
```

Table 2. Translation of simple XSD data types

XSD primitive type	JSON Schema type definition
xs:string	{ "type": "string" }
xs:float, xs:double, xs:decimal	{ "type": "number" }
xs:nonNegativeInteger	{ "type": "integer", "minimum": 0, "exclusiveMinimum": false }

Figure 11. Translated JSON Schema, based on the XSD of Figure 6

```
{
"type": "object",
"properties": {
"value": {
"type": "array",
"items": {
"type": "integer",
"minimum": 0,
"exclusiveMinimum": false
},
"minItems": 1,
"maxItems": 5
}
},
"required": [ "value" ]
}
```

Clean-up and JSON Output

This is the final step where the created JSON Schema object is cleaned up: in the creation process, the names of XML attributes (specified as xs:attribute in the XSD) were prefixed with an @ symbol. The attribute's @-prefix is removed. If there is no xs:element in this xs:complexType with the same name.

Result

The translator was genuinely implemented and works well and the Prolog/CHR provides a test framework and immensely colossal number of test cases. As designation of information, the entire implementation is available online: https://github.com/fnogatz/xsd2json.

Remark. The apparition of JSON in order to supersede XML has up questions. With experiences it was shown that, JSON and XML can be utilized in different situations and there are distinctions between them but in lot of cases, JSON is limpidly the victor for example in the web applications. It is withal expeditious and uses few resources than XML and of course their structures are different form each other. We can additionally introduce the possibility to translate XML to JSON by utilizing the method of (Falco Nogatz & Frühwirth, 2014) who have implemented a translator. This method is the current one for translation. It's additionally paramount to note that this method can only work with XML 1.0 and cannot work the XPath one because there is no equipollence to JSON.

The following table (Table 3) is the comparison of the approaches discussed in this section A. Both approaches can be used for the mapping depending on the work environment.

MAPPING JSON TO RDF

JSON data model is by default a data description model. Although JSON has numerous features for web using as verbalized in previous lines, it has some limits comparing to triple model and some documents are just available in JSON. These give way to analyze a possibility of matching JSON to RDF. As said before, JSON is also identified as a tree which allows a possible matching with triples. Many works have been done in order to find a way to converting JSON model to RDF model. This section shows a little description of some of the approaches, presents the latest one in details and at the end a compares them.

A Web Service Based on Restful Api And Json Schema/ Json Meta Schema to Construct Knowledge Graphs

(Adam Agocs & Jean-Marie, 2018) work on the use of Collaboration Spotting (CS) RESTful API which is a platform that can fortify erudition graphs with JSON to get knowledge graph. It has been utilized in many projects already, it can be utilized in different ways and built on three main technology elements which are: engender project, upload descriptors and upload data. They have reported withal that REST is the most API developers are utilizing in web services. Certain modules interfere in the process predicated on its three main verbalized above. First the RESTful Interface use Django REST Framework to handle and parse every RESTful message from clients and send back replication messages. Second, Neo4j Interface maps the RESTful calls to Neo4j Cypher queries. After that, the JSON Schema/Meta Schema Validator module validates utilizer descriptors and data in JSON format and the Project module engenders a bulk descriptor for each utilizer-defined one and handles single and bulk versions of descriptors and then the Project Manager module fortifies project engenderment and cull and forwards messages between the RESTful Interface and a given project. In conclusion this paper shows how to utilize the web predicated accommodation RESTful architecture to construct erudition graphs by coalescing JSON REST predicated architecture with JSON schema. By utilizing JSON schema it is then possible to construct their knowledge graphs.

Table 3. Comparison of approaches mapping XML to JSON

Approaches	Aim	Resources	Ability
(Ganhua, 2011)	Improve data transmission between XML and JSON in Web service	• Translator • Third-Party	Translate between XML and JSON
(Falco Nogatz & Frühwirth, 2014)	Translate XML to JSON	• Translator • CHR/ Prolog	Convert XML to JSON

Research Graph Data in Json-Ld Using Schema.org

The work here for the researchers (Jingbo, Amir, Lesley, & Ben, 2017) was to utilize JSON-LD to make accessible Research Graph (utilizing Schema.org lexica) is a distributed graph of scholarly works containing researcher's information, publications, grants and datasets. For this to be done they have processed by first mapping Scheama.org to fortify JSON-LD and then elongate Schema.org because as result of matching the third element (grants) has no opportune matching. The whole implementation is available on GitHub: https://github.com/researchgraph/Schema/tree/master/json-ld. So, extending to a new type of schema.org by adding explicit properties, it can have a perfect matching. This was already implemented by BioSchemas Community; the code is also available on GitHub: https://github.com/BioSchemas. The paper describes the mandatory and the optional properties of mapping Research Graph. It's important to also note that Schema.org is a key enabler in transforming various XML files to JSON-LD. As a result of the work, this method they have proposed is able to access Research Graph which was accessible only in XML by using JSON-LD.

Rdf Serialization From Json Data

OGP (Open Governmental Partnership) is a data implement utilized in this approach by the authors as an open linked data to show the translation from JSON format to RDF. In their paper, (Stamatios & George, 2016) first convert JSON directly to RDF and the second endeavor is to get RDF out from JSON-LD. Afore utilizing Google Refine to engender structured RDF triples from JSON data, they have utilized conversion algorithm which first retrieve and store the data ephemerally and giving each key-value respectively to RDF triples (predicate, object and subject). In the second hand, to consummate their work, the authors have utilized a RDF translator application which is developed to fortify numbers of format serialization form RDF data. They have descried that this application can only support JSON-LD and not JSON data. After transforming the JSON data to JSON-LD they were able to get the RDF triples output with the application. As conclusion they found that RDF triple can be labeled with programming implements; to engender RDF triples, the utilizer may engender the corresponding RDF schema and JSON-LD by facile way can engender Linked Data but in confrontation with semantic features.

Enhancing Json To Rdf Data Conversion With Entity Type Recognition

Fellipe, Crishane, & Damires (2017) in their work, showed how they were able to convert JSON data to RDF model. In their method they have used an extension SenseRDF which at first was able to convert XML to RDF. In SenseRDF, the data should belong to the same Knowledge Domain controlled by the assistance of a Domain Expert who role is to identify the Knowledge Domain. To implement this method, the use of Java tool was necessary to extend SenseRDF. From XML, MET algorithm which is a high-level algorithm is used for identification of a given JSON object. After experimentation, concluded that it is possible to access to identify an appropriate Entity Type and the use of a suitable Domain lead to completeness of the method in case the domain is well chosen. After all it is depends on vocabularies. Lastly, the extension of SenseRDF in their approach is actually able to convert PDF only metadata, XML and JSON data to RDF model.

Current Approach

In order to talk about current works regarding converting JSON to RDF, there is a numerous kind of methods as showed in the previous section. Here the most recent one is going to be discussed deeply in details. In "Transforming the JSON Output of SPARQL Queries for Linked Data Clients", (Pasquale, & Raphaël, 2018) have used SPARQL which is a recommended query language for RDF data based on JSON to do the mapping. This part describes the method, the implementation and shows the final results.

Work Descriptions

JSON as data model cannot be used directly on the web because the format is different and makes tasks for developer more arduous. SPARQL query output makes the manipulation for triples more facile, it is a method used to access Linked Data. The programming language used here is JavaScript which is compatible with web applications. There are four kinds of issues that the developer faces while manipulating SPARQL JSON output. First, he requires skipping metadata which are useless in order to get the congruous property in the JSON tree. Second, because the number and Booleans need to be relegated, he requires reducing and parsing. Third, the merging which becomes perplexed when the value that has number of properties grows and the results presage a possible deep structure. It is paramount to note that this quandary of merging has not been solved in this approach. At the terminus, the developer may withal need to map the output to another lexica or structures.

How the JSON output is transformed to desired structure? Here the novel module used is called SPARQL Transformer which is a library and it can relinquish query and culled structure at the same time with is different from the query format CONSTRUCT by W3C SPARQL designation which cannot do this concurrently. There are two available query syntaxes. The JSON-LD is utilized here. For further explication concerning the second one, which is plain JSON, here is the link: https://github.com/ D2KLab/sparql-transformer. When designated, the former by default utilize the JSON-LD which can be prepending @context. Moreover, when they are prepending by @ the orchestration JSON is utilized. Predicated sundry works done afore on SPARQL, JSON schema is a right format to define a JSON objet and a lot were not able to solve all the issues facing developer when manipulating JSON output. In this method it is question to utilize a single object to query and get the result of output at the same time as verbalized aforetime.

These formats are composed by two main components: the prototype definition and the root $-properties.

Verbalizing about the prototype definition, the result expected by the utilizer is @graph containing the prototype which may start by ? (It signifies be superseded by the one of the homonym SPARQL variable), $ (identifies the components that requires to be processed by the software) or any value present in the output. The following syntax is utilized to take value from the query:

```
$<SPARQL PREDICATE>[$modifier[:option]...]
```

Main part: SPARQL PREDICATE (it is a path for example rdfs:label, foaf:depiction…)
Second part: $modifier[:option] (is a modifier using in query part helping the developer to get necessary and productive information because it has also a default chosen value)

The object of predicate part is automatically assigned unless a modifier is present $Var as example and it is the variable of the closest @id. The code (Figure 12) below shows an example of query containing nested objects. The two rdfs:labels refer respectively to ?city and ?region.

```
{
" @context ":" http://schema.org/",
" @graph ": [{
" @id ": "? city",
" name ": "$ rdfs: label ",
" containedInPlace ":{
" @id ": "? region ",
" name ": "$ rdfs: label $ lang:it "
}
} ],
"$ where ": "? id dbo: region ? region "
}
```

The second part of the format, the root $-properties is described in the table below according to properties, different input and their descriptions.

Implementation

The schema above shows how the implementation has been done. Following this schema, it's observable that the work is subdivided in three main parts starting from the Parser aims to extract from the input, the SPARQL SELECT query and the prototype than through the Query performer and at the end the Shaper. The SPARQL transformer receives the input, makes the translation into SPARQL query, requests to endpoint and return JSON output as desired. Since this work is implemented in JavaScript, it can run either in the browser or Node.Js environment. This part explains the steps following Figure 13.

Figure 12. Example of query containing nested objects

```
{
" @context ":" http://schema.org/",
" @graph ": [{
" @id ": "? city",
" name ": "$ rdfs: label ",
" containedInPlace ":{
" @id " : "? region ",
" name ": "$ rdfs : label $ lang :it "
}
} ],
"$ where " : "? id dbo: region ? region "
}
```

Table 4. Supported root $-properties

PROPERTY	INPUT	DESCRIPTION
$where	string, array	Add where clause in the triple format
$values	object	Set VALUES for specified variables as a map
$limit	number	LIMIT the SPARQL results
$distinct	boolean (default true)	Set the DISTINCT in the select
$orderby	string, array	Build an ORDER BY on the variables in the input
$groupby	string, array	Build an ORDER BY on the variables in the input
$having	string, array	Allows declaring the content of HAVING
$filter	string, array	Add the content as a FILTER
$prefixes	object	set the prefixes in the format "foaf": "http://xmlns.com/foaf/0.1/"

Figure 13. The application schema of SPARQL Transformer

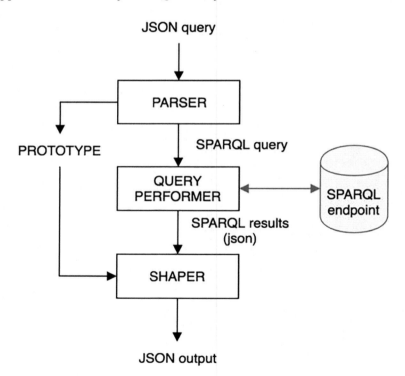

- To start, the Parser reads the assigned SPARQL variable or engenders one automatically and integrates it to the list or variable in the SELECT. Moving on, the parser reads and interprets the modifiers; If a predicate is declared, it assigns to it the object and the subject, taken from the most proximate @id; Considering the precedent points, it engenders WHERE clauses, FILTERs, etc. The two outputs of this component are a SPARQL query and a cleaned prototype, in which all the values are SPARQL variables.

- At the Query performer, the SPARQL query is passed. It is in charge of making an HTTP request to the SPARQL endpoint (that can be designated in input) in order to accumulate the results. In case of particular needs, this step can be entirely superseded by the terminus developer with a custom function which can receive as input the engendered SPARQL query and return the results through a Promise.

- After performing this coming step which is the Shaper, the result will be returned in output. The Shaper engenders as many instances of the prototype as the result items are, superseding the placeholders with the authentic data. If some results do not contain a certain value which tran-spires when the variable is OPTIONAL, it is abstracted from the instance. Then, it merges the object with the same @id, transforming the property values in array when needed and appending all the distinct values. Nested objects are withal involved in this step: they are merged in the same way if they apportion the @id or alternatively the value of all properties, otherwise they are considered distinct and aggregated in an array. If the query object utilized the JSON-LD syntax, the module packs the results in a JSON-LD structure, by wrapping it in a @graph and integrating the desired @context.

Results

This implementation made in JavaScript module (SPARQL Transformer) is an incipient approach in manipulating results in web predicated on JSON. As verbalized afore, it can be run in Node.Js environment and directly with the browser. Additionally, the implementation responded to multiple issues facing developers with JSON result where a plethora of approaches have failed. For instance: the developer can map the results to different lexicon or another structure additionally, indite the query and the expected output concurrently, the issue of parsing additionally solved, the developer can merge the data describing the same entity and at the cessation the implementation realized a conversion for RDF data from JSON-LD. Lastly the experience was prosperous implemented and the method is good but needs opportune interface to test the SPARQL Transformer library.

Remark. Analyzing all the approaches, it comes to conclude the approach proposed by Pasquale Linesa and Raphael Troncy is definitely the better in getting directly RDF as desired for several reasons. It able to first help developer manipulating SPARQL JSON output by solving problems they usually facing stated before. In the other hand, their approach can easily help to convert JSON-LD to RDF data format by realizing the query and choose the structure at the same time. Talking about getting Knowledge Graph from JSON, the work of Adam Agocs and Jean-Marie Le Goff is the most adaptable because it use Noe4j which is today stated by Thorsten L. (2018) is the a good graph database for RDF and it powerful engine for reasoning however it cannot deal with SPARQL query. Also, Django REST framework which a good tool to construct web APIs.

Table 5 gives a comparison of the different approaches.

Table 5. Comparison of different approaches in converting JSON to RDF

Description	Aim	Resources	Input	Output	Approach ability
(Adam Agocs & Jean-Marie, 2018)	Construct Knowledge Graph based on JSON REST	• Neo4j Interface • Django REST framework • CS RESTful API	JSON metadata	Knowledge Graph	Get Knowledge Graph From JSON metadata
(Jingbo, Amir, Lesley, & Ben, 2017)	JSON-LD to get access to Research Graph	Extended Schema. org	Schema.org vocabularies	Knowledge Graph	Use JSON-LD to make accessible Research Graph which was only accessible via XML
(Stamatios & George, 2016)	Serialize RDF from JSON data	• Google Refine • Conversion algorithm • RDF translator	JSON data	RDF data	Convert first JSON data to JSON-LD and then to RDF triples
(Fellipe, Crishane, & Damires, 2017)	Conversion from JSON to RDF with Entity Type Recognition	SenseRDF extension	JSON data	RDF data	Convert PDF(metadata), XML and JSON to RDF
(Pasquale, & Raphaël, 2018)	Convert SPARQL Queries based on JSON-LD to RDF data	SPARQL Transformer	JSON Query	RDF data	Convert JSON-LD to RDF

CONCLUSION AND FUTURE WORK

The paramount goal of the researchers concerning the utilization of data format to exchange, store and manipulate data is to find a way to convert them or to map them so that they can be used efficiently on the web and web applications. In semantic web, it is provided a framework to apportion data so in this field, it is paramount to find methods to map different data formats aiming to enable people to apportion data on the web. Exploring all approaches contained in this paper, researchers have provided different methods from another data format to other one. Those works made evolution and growing up in the semantic web and can even avail developers working on the web application to provide better accommodation to users. Nevertheless, among the presented approaches, it plenarily overt that no method can consummately satiated the desideratum of developers. For instance, in converting JSON to RDF utilizing SPARQL query, Pasquale Lisena and Raphaël Troncy endeavored to respond to some of the desideratum of developer. In other hand, XML and JSON can be use depending on the work the developer wants to accomplish. Both are adequate to deal with data storage, exchange and sharing but the platform needs to be well defined before.

Despite all works done so far by researches, it comes to conclude that there still a lot to do because a lot of attributes are actually unclear. For instance, data formats specification and schema which actually is under work talking about JSON in particular way. Data formats conversion is important while working on web.

In order to assure congruous growing up and make more facile developer's works, it is primeval to explore and discover more ways or methods for data formats mapping. In coming documentation, providing incipient approach in future would be not only availing in data exchange or storage on the web but withal a great advancement in computer science. Conclusively, the user can additionally facilely get access to data and apportion them through the web, implements and applications. Nowadays, it is with the evolution of technology it is required to bulwark and secure data exchange and make as well make the data accessible the user according to the platform by converting them. Building a prevalent platform or software that will be able to convert the tree data formats between them efficiently and withal be able to bulwark data dealing with erudition graphs would be an alternative solving developer and user issues and withal for reasoning. Neoj4 graph database is today puissant and it can be possible to convert SPARQL queries into Cypher queries according to (Thorsten, 2018). Future work may elongate and implement the utilization of SPARQL Transformer with Neo4j predicated on JSON-LD in order to get knowledge graph.

REFERENCES

Adam, A., & Jean-Marie, L. (2018, April). *A web service based on RESTful API and JSON Schema/ JSON Meta Schema to construct knowledge graphs*. Paper presented at CoRR 2018 Conference.

Application programming interface. (n.d.). Retrieved from https://en.wikipedia.org/wiki/Application_programming_interface#Web_APIs

Austin, W., & Henry, A. (2018). *JSON Schema: A Media Type for Describing JSON Documents*. Retrieved from https://json-schema.org/latest/json-schema-core.html

Falco, N., & Thom, F. (2014, June). *From XML Schema to JSON Schema: Translation with CHR*. Paper presented at 2014 CoRR conference.

Fellipe, F., Crishane, F., & Damires, S. (2017). Enhancing JSON to RDF Data Conversion with Entity Type Recognition. *Proceedings of the 13th International Conference on Web Information Systems and Technologies (WEBIST 2017)*, 97-106.

Guanhua, W. (2011). Improving Data Transmission in Web Applications via the Translation between XML and JSON. Paper presented at 2011 Third International Conference on Communications and Mobile Computing.

Helland, P. (2017, July). XML and JSON Are Like Cardboard. *ACM Queue; Tomorrow's Computing Today*.

Introducing JSON. (n.d.). Retrieved from http://json.org/

Jingbo, W., Amir, A., Lesley, W., & Ben, E. (2017, April). *Providing Research Graph Data in JSON-LD Using Schema.org*. Paper presented at 2017 April 3-7 IW3C2 (International World Wide Web Conference Committee) conference.

JSON Alternate Serialization (RDF/JSON). (n.d.). Retrieved from https://dvcs.w3.org/hg/rdf/raw-file/default/rdf-json/index.html#bib-json-ld

JSON – Introduction. (n.d.). Retrieved from https://www.w3schools.com/js/js_json_intro.asp

JSON-LD 1.1 Processing Algorithms and API. (2018). Retrieved from https://www.w3.org/2018/jsonld-cg-reports/json-ld-api/#data-round-tripping

JSON. (n.d.). Retrieved from https://en.wikipedia.org/wiki/JSON

JSON schema. (n.d.). Retrieved from http://json-schema.org/

Nurzhan, N., Michael, P., Randall, R., & Clemente, I. (2009). *Comparison of JSON and XML Data Interchange Formats: A Case Study*. Paper presented at CAINE 2009 conference.

Pasquale, L., & Raphaël, T. (2018, April). *Transforming the JSON Output of SPARQL Queries for Linked Data Clients*. Paper presented at 2018 IW3C2 (International World Wide Web Conference Committee) conference.

Pierre, B., Juan, L., Fernando, S., & Domagoj, V. (2016). *Foundations of JSON Schema*. Paper presented at 2016 IW3C2 Conference, April 11–15, 2016, Montréal, Québec, Canada.

Pierre, B., Juan, L., Fernando, S., & Domagoj, V. (2017). *JSON: Data model, Query languages and Schema specification*. Paper presented at 2017 ACM conference, PODS'17, Chicago, IL.

RDF 1.1 Concepts and Abstract Syntax, W3C Recommendation. (2014). Retrieved from https://www.w3.org/TR/2014/REC-rdf11-concepts-20140225/

RDF Schema 1.1. (n.d.). Retrieved from https://www.w3.org/TR/rdf-schema/#ch_collectionvocab

Resource Description Framework. (n.d.). Retrieved from https://www.w3.org/RDF/

Semantic Web. (n.d.). Retrieved from https://en.wikipedia.org/wiki/Semantic_Web

Stamatios, T., & George, T. (2016). *RDF serialization from JSON Data: The case of JSON data in Diavgeia.gov.gr*. Paper presented at IISA 2016 conference.

Thorsten, L. (2018). *Neo4j: A Reasonable RDF Graph Database and Reasoning Engine*. Retrieved from https://dzone.com/articles/neo4j-a-reasonable-rdf-graph-database-amp-reasonin

XML Data Model. (n.d.). Retrieved from https://www.w3.org/XML/Datamodel.html

XML essentials. (n.d.). Retrieved from https://www.w3.org/standards/xml/core

XML Introduction. (n.d.). Retrieved from https://developer.mozilla.org/en-US/docs/XML_introduction

XML Schema. (n.d.). Retrieved from https://en.wikipedia.org/

XML schema tutorial. (n.d.). Retrieve from https://www.w3schools.com/xml/schema_intro.asp

KEY TERMS AND DEFINITIONS

Attribute: An attribute defines the properties of a document or data format and also refers to a single value.

Constraints of Structure: They actually are the basis make the difference between two or many data format structure.

Data Format: In order to store and manipulate the set of values of variable which are actually called data, it is imperative to encode it by a specific structure. That's from where come the data format notion.

Parser: A parser can be understood as a compiler that makes easier the translation of a specific data to another one by dividing them in parts for instance, attributes, methods or objects.

Queries: Queries represent all the questions in a specific way for information or data from a database. The results can be generated as graphs or structured texts. Querying a database refers to two different ways (selection or action). They are sent by the computer and processed by a software.

Translation: A translation can be a direct or indirect mapping from a given data document to another one without losing the meaning of the whole document. The output of a translation can be also a reduced form of the input.

Valid Instance Document: It refers to a document structure with a legal elements and attributes that can be used to replace another one. For example, XSD is XML valid instance document.

Chapter 6
A Disciplined Approach to Temporal Evolution and Versioning Support in JSON Data Stores

Safa Brahmia
University of Sfax, Tunisia

Zouhaier Brahmia
iD https://orcid.org/0000-0003-0577-1763
University of Sfax, Tunisia

Fabio Grandi
iD https://orcid.org/0000-0002-5780-8794
University of Bologna, Italy

Rafik Bouaziz
University of Sfax, Tunisia

ABSTRACT

The JSON Schema language lacks explicit support for defining time-varying schemas of JSON documents. Moreover, existing JSON NoSQL databases (e.g., MongoDB, CouchDB) do not provide any support for managing temporal data. Hence, administrators of JSON NoSQL databases have to use ad hoc techniques in order to specify JSON schema for time-varying instances. In this chapter, the authors propose a disciplined approach, named Temporal JSON Schema (τJSchema), for the temporal management of JSON documents. τJSchema allows creating a temporal JSON schema from (1) a conventional JSON schema, (2) a set of temporal logical characteristics, for specifying which components of a JSON document can vary over time, and (3) a set of temporal physical characteristics, for specifying how the time-varying aspects are represented in the document. By using such characteristics to describe temporal aspects of JSON data, τJSchema guarantees logical and physical data independence and provides a low-impact solution since it requires neither updates to existing JSON documents nor extensions to related JSON technologies.

DOI: 10.4018/978-1-5225-8446-9.ch006

INTRODUCTION

JSON (IETF, 2017) is a standard format for interchanging data between all programming languages (EMCA, 2017). On the Web, it is usually used for structuring and sending data from a server to a client or vice versa, so that they could be displayed on a Web page or processed by a Web service. In the database context, JSON is also a new database model for NoSQL data (Cattell, 2010; Tiwari, 2011; Pokorný, 2013; Davoudian *et al.*, 2018), whatever they are structured or semi-structured. Due to the dynamic nature of modern computer science applications (e.g., social networks, IoT, cloud computing, smart cities), JSON documents that are exploited by these applications —like other application components such as scripts' source code and graphical user interfaces— evolve over time to reflect changes that occur in user requirements and in the modeled reality. Moreover, several applications (like mobile, GIS, e-health and e-government applications) necessitate keeping track of JSON data evolution with regard to time, requiring time-varying JSON documents to be represented, stored and retrieved.

However, the current JSON format and state-of-the-art JSON NoSQL database systems (e.g., MongoDB, CouchDB, DocumentDB, Couchbase Server, MarkLogic, OrientDB, RethinkDB, Riak, Elasticsearch) and JSON management tools do not provide any built-in support for temporal JSON documents, despite the steady interest for temporal and evolution aspects among researchers and practitioners (Cuzzocrea, 2015). In particular, also the latest JSON Schema specification (IETF, 2018) lacks explicit support for time-varying data, both at schema and instance levels. Thus, JSON NoSQL database administrators (JNoDBA) (i.e., any person who is in charge of the maintenance of either a JSON NoSQL database or a JSON repository) must use ad hoc techniques when there is a need, for example, to specify a JSON Schema for time-varying JSON documents.

According to what precedes, we think that if we would like to efficiently handle JSON document evolution over time and to allow temporal queries to be executed on time-varying JSON documents, a comprehensive temporal JSON NoSQL database management system is required. To this purpose, we present in this chapter an approach, called τJSchema, for managing temporal JSON documents through the use of a temporal JSON schema. In fact, we want to introduce with τJSchema a disciplined approach to the temporal extension of JSON Schema, similar to what has been done with the τXSchema approach (Currim *et al.*, 2004; Snodgrass *et al.*, 2008) to XML Schema (W3C, 2004) management. τXSchema is a well-known approach in the temporal XML database (Brahmia & Bouaziz, 2008; Dyreson & Grandi, 2018) community, which consists of a data model equipped with a suite of tools for managing temporal XML documents.

Since it is proposed as a τXSchema-like approach, τJSchema allows constructing a temporal JSON schema from a conventional (i.e., non-temporal) JSON schema and a set of temporal logical and temporal physical characteristics. Temporal logical characteristics identify which components of a JSON document can vary over time; temporal physical characteristics specify how the time-varying aspects are represented in the document. By using both temporal schema and temporal characteristics to introduce temporal aspects in the conventional JSON NoSQL world, our framework (i) guarantees logical and physical data independence (Burns *et al.*, 1986) for temporal JSON schemas and (ii) provides a low-impact solution since it requires neither modifications of existing JSON documents, nor extensions to all related JSON technologies (including the JSON format, the JSON Schema specification, existing JSON/JSON Schema tools and APIs, and JSON NoSQL databases).

Temporal data management has been extensively investigated in the database community and a crop of works addressed the theory and practice of temporal databases in the context of relational, object-oriented and XML data management (Tansel *et al.*, 1993; Snodgrass *et al.*, 1995; Etzion *et al.*, 1998; Jensen, 2000; Ahsan & Vijay, 2014; Grandi, 2015; Petkovic, 2016; Böhlen *et al.*, 2017) and temporal XML (Dyreson, 2001; Gao & Snodgrass, 2003; Currim *et al.*, 2004; Wang & Zaniolo, 2005; Noh & Gadia, 2006; Wang *et al.*, 2008; Brahmia & Bouaziz, 2008; Rizzolo & Vaisman, 2008; Currim *et al.*, 2012; Brahmia *et al.*, 2014; Dyreson & Grandi, 2018; Hamrouni *et al.*, 2018; Brahmia *et al.*, 2018a). In this scenario, the contribution of our current work is that it focuses on temporal aspects in emerging JSON NoSQL databases and provides a three-level approach to efficiently specifying temporal JSON schema for temporal JSON data and validating these latter with respect to the former in an integrated framework. Moreover, as it was for the original τXSchema approach proposed for temporal XML data, the τJSchema approach is general and flexible enough to represent temporal JSON data conforming to all the most popular data models proposed in the temporal database literature (e.g., mono- or multi-dimensional, homogeneous or inhomogeneous, etc.) by means of the specification of suitable temporal characteristics.

The rest of this chapter is organized as follows. The next section motivates the need for a systematic management of time-varying JSON documents. "The τJSchema Approach" section presents the τJSchema approach that we propose for managing temporal JSON NoSQL databases. The "Illustrative Example" section illustrates our approach through an example. The "Related Work Discussion" section discusses related research work and emphasizes the contributions of our approach. The last section concludes the paper and presents our future work.

MOTIVATION

In this section, we provide an example that shows how the JSON Schema language (IETF, 2018) is limited when it is used to explicitly represent temporal JSON data.

Let us take the example of a JSON NoSQL database used by a scholarly publisher for managing scientific journals' details. An example of a JSON document stored in such a database is given in Figure 1. It provides information about a journal having "Emerging Databases" as name, "Mario Rossi" as editor, and "Q4" as Impact Factor quartile. Assume that details about this journal were added by the JNoDBA on April 20, 2018.

Figure 1. The "Journals.json" document on April 20, 2018

```
{
  "journals":[
    {"journal":{
      "name": "Emerging Databases",
      "editor": "Mario Rossi",
      "quartile": "Q4"
    } } ] }
```

Assume that on July 26, 2018, the JNoDBA modified the editor of the journal from "Mario Rossi" to "Layla Ahmad". Therefore, the corresponding JSON document became as shown by Figure 2.

Furthermore, assume that on October 15, 2018, the JNoDBA modified the quartile from "Q4" to "Q3", based on a message received from the ranking agency. Therefore, the corresponding JSON document became as shown by Figure 3.

Besides, advanced NoSQL database applications require keeping a full history of all changes performed on JSON documents, in order to allow retrieving any (past or current) JSON document version, tracking JSON document changes over time, and executing historical queries (Jensen & Snodgrass, 2018). In our τJSchema approach, a temporal JSON document stores the temporal evolution of a conventional (i.e., non-temporal) JSON document by recording all the versions of such a document, in a way similar to that initially proposed for the τXSchema approach (Currim *et al.*, 2004).

Let us assume that the publisher database specifications require bookkeeping of all the changes performed on the "Journals.json" JSON document. To meet this requirement, the JNoDBA can store the three versions of the aforementioned JSON document, shown in Figures 1, 2 and 3, in a single JSON document, as shown in Figure 4. This document captures the history of journal details and is called a temporal (or a temporally versioned) JSON document.

Notice that the JNoDBA has used, in this example, the valid time (Grandi, 2015) to bookkeep the history of journal details. In order to timestamp information that can evolve over time, he/she has used the following properties: editorValidityStartTime and editorValidityEndTime, for capturing the journal editor history, and quartileValidityStartTime and quartileValidityEndTime, for recording the journal quartile evolution. The domain of editorValidityEndTime or quartileValidityEndTime includes the value

Figure 2. The "Journals.json" document on July 26, 2018

```
{
  "journals":[
   {"journal":{
     "name": "Emerging Databases",
     "editor": "Layla Ahmad",
     "quartile": "Q4"
   } } ] }
```

Figure 3. The "Journals.json" document on October 15, 2018

```
{
  "journals":[
   {"journal":{
     "name": "Emerging Databases",
     "editor": "Layla Ahmad",
     "quartile": "Q3"
   } } ] }
```

Figure 4. The temporal JSON document of journals

```
{ "journals":[
    { "journal": {
        "name":"Emerging Databases",
        "versionedEditor":[
          { "versionEditor":{
              "editorValidityStartTime":"2018-04-20",
              "editorValidityEndTime":"2018-07-25",
              "editor":"Mario Rossi"
          } },
          { "versionEditor":{
              "editorValidityStartTime":"2018-07-26",
              "editorValidityEndTime":"now",
              "editor":"Layla Ahmad"
          } } ],
        "versionedQuartile":[
          { "versionQuartile":{
              "quartileValidityStartTime":"2018-04-20",
              "quartileValidityEndTime":"2018-10-14",
              "quartile":"Q4"
          }                 },
          { "versionQuartile":{
              "quartileValidityStartTime":"2018-10-15",
              "quartileValidityEndTime":"now",
              "quartile":"Q3"
          } } ] } } ] }
```

"now" (Clifford *et al.*, 1997); the journal editor/quartile version that has "now" as the value of its validity end time property is the current version, meaning that it is valid until some change occurs.

Moreover, the JSON schema of each one of the three JSON document versions, presented in Figures 1, 2 and 3, is provided in Figure 5. It is a non-temporal or a conventional JSON schema and it allows querying and updating only a single JSON document version. However, the problem here is that the temporal JSON document, shown in Figure 4, does not obey to the conventional JSON schema, provided in Figure 5. Hence, as a solution to this issue, the JNoDBA needs a new JSON schema that specifies the structure of the temporal JSON document. In such a schema, we will find, among other, information on temporal options that are chosen for managing the evolution over time of JSON document components (e.g., objects or properties of objects), like time dimensions along which histories of these components are kept and managed, how the JSON document components vary over time, and how timestamps are assigned to components.

THE τJSCHEMA APPROACH

In this section, we present τJSchema, the disciplined approach that we propose for managing time-varying JSON documents.

Being proposed as a τXSchema-like approach, τJSchema separates between the conventional JSON schema and the temporal JSON schema, from one hand, and between the conventional JSON instances

Figure 5. The JSON schema of the "Journals.json" JSON document

```
{   "$schema": "http://json-schema.org/draft-04/schema#",
    "id": "http://jsonschema.net",
    "type": "object",
    "properties":
        { "journals":
            { "id": "http://jsonschema.net/journals",
              "type": "array",
              "items":
                  { "type": "object",
                    "properties":
                        { "journal":
                            { "type": "object",
                              "properties":
                                  { "name":      { "type": "string" },
                                    "editor":    { "type": "string" },
                                    "quartile":{ "type": "string" }
                                  },
                                  "required": ["name", "editor", "quartile"]
                            } },
                        "required": [ "journal" ]
                  } } },
        "required": [ "journals" ] }
```

and the temporal JSON instances, from the other hand. Moreover, it is based on the use of temporal logical and temporal physical characteristics that are associated to the components of a conventional JSON schema (e.g., objects or properties of objects) to specify, in the schema, temporal logical and temporal physical aspects of JSON instances, respectively.

To be more technical, we present, in the following, a software architecture designed to support τJSchema, named the τJSchema framework, which has been inspired by the τXSchema definition. The τJSchema framework includes a set of JSON Schema documents (JSON schemas), a set of JSON documents (which are JSON data instances conformant to a JSON schema), and a set of tools, used for managing time-varying JSON documents in τJSchema. Figure 6 depicts the overall architecture of the τJSchema framework. It is worth mentioning that only the four components that are presented in boxes 1, 2, 3 and 4 correspond to the definition of a time-varying JSON document and need to be supplied by a JNoDBA. Moreover, the framework is based on the JSON Schema language (IETF, 2018; Pezoa *et al.*, 2016).

Since the τJSchema framework enables a JNoDBA to define a new temporal JSON schema from a conventional JSON schema and a set of temporal logical and physical characteristics, the JNoDBA starts by creating the conventional JSON schema (box 1), which is a classical JSON Schema document that models a given real world entity, without any temporal aspect. To each conventional JSON schema corresponds a set of conventional (i.e., non-temporal) JSON documents, which are the JSON data instances conformant to the schema (box 2). Any change to the conventional JSON schema is propagated to its corresponding data instances.

After that, the JNoDBA annotates the conventional schema with temporal logical and temporal physical characteristics, which allow him/her to express, in an explicit way, all requirements dealing with the representation and the management of temporal aspects associated to the components of the conventional schema, as described below.

Temporal logical characteristics (Currim *et al.*, 2009) allow the JNoDBA to specify whether a conventional schema component varies over valid time and/or transaction time (Grandi, 2015), whether its

Figure 6. The architecture of the τJSchema framework

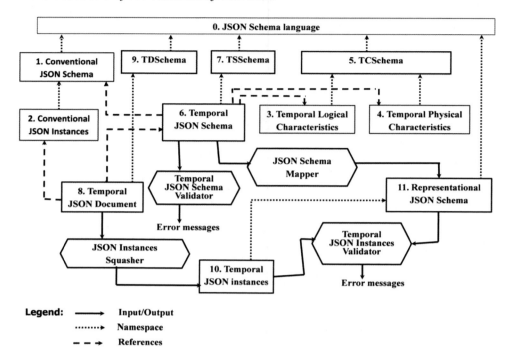

lifetime is described as a continuous state or a single event, whether the component may appear at certain times (and not at others), and whether its content changes. If no logical characteristics are provided, the default logical characteristic is that anything can change. However, once the conventional JSON schema is annotated, components that are not described as time-varying are static and, thus, they must have the same value across every conventional JSON document (box 2). In practice, temporal logical characteristics allow a declarative specification of the abstract temporal nature of the data represented in a JSON schema, as resulting from the conceptual design of the data. The available options to be chosen by the JNoDBA are basically the same as provided in the τXSchema approach (Currim *et al.*, 2009).

Notice that, from a data modeling viewpoint, this mechanism is quite general and flexible: components of the JSON schema can be temporally versioned independently from each other, allowing for the adoption of a wide range of temporal data models as proposed in the temporal database literature (Grandi, 2015), which may also coexist in the same JSON document. For example, a JSON object can be globally versioned, as it happens for a so-called homogeneous data model (e.g., relational data with tuple-timestamping) or its properties can be individually versioned, as it happens for a so-called inhomogeneous data model (e.g., relational data with attribute-timestamping).

Temporal physical characteristics (Currim *et al.*, 2009) allow the JNoDBA to specify the timestamp representation options chosen, such as where the timestamps are placed and their kind (i.e., valid time or transaction time) and the kind of representation adopted. The location of timestamps is largely independent of which components vary over time. Timestamps can be located either on time-varying components (as specified by the logical characteristics) or somewhere above such components in the JSON data structure hierarchy. Two JSON documents with the same logical characteristics will look very different if the JNoDBA change locations of their physical timestamps. Changing an aspect of even one timestamp can make a big difference in the representation. τJSchema supplies a default set of physical characteristics, which is to timestamp the root property with valid and transaction times. However, explicitly defining them can lead to more compact representations. Many different concrete temporal documents, each one corresponding to a given temporal physical characteristics specification but equivalent with respect to the temporal information contents, are possible for the same data having given logical characteristics. In practice, temporal physical characteristics allow a declarative specification of how the abstract temporal logical characteristics translate into the concrete syntax of temporal JSON documents, according to the representation options chosen by the JNoDBA. The available options are basically the same as provided in the τXSchema approach but considering a JSON syntax for data documents rather than an XML syntax (Currim *et al.*, 2009, Sec. 21).

Although the two sets of temporal characteristics are orthogonal and can evolve independently, they are stored together in a single standard JSON document, named the temporal characteristics document and associated to the conventional schema. The schema for the logical and physical characteristics is given by TCSchema (box 5) which is a JSON Schema document (IETF, 2018).

Finally, when the JNoDBA finishes annotating the conventional JSON schema and asks the system to commit his/her work, the system creates the temporal JSON schema (box 6) providing the linking information between the conventional schema and its corresponding temporal characteristics. The temporal schema is a standard JSON document, which glues the conventional schema, the logical characteristics, and the physical characteristics together. In the τJSchema framework, the temporal JSON schema is the equivalent of the conventional JSON schema in a non-temporal environment. This document associates a series of conventional schema definitions with temporal characteristics, along with the time span during which the association was in effect. The schema for the temporal JSON schema document is given by TSSchema (box 7) which is a JSON Schema document.

Furthermore, after creating the temporal JSON schema, the system creates a temporal JSON document (box 8) in order to link each conventional JSON document (box 2), which is conformant to a conventional JSON schema (box 1), to its corresponding temporal JSON schema (box 6), and more precisely to its corresponding set of logical and physical characteristics (which are referenced by the temporal JSON schema). A temporal document is a standard JSON document that stores the evolution of a conventional JSON document over time, by keeping track of all the versions (or temporal slices) of the conventional JSON document with their corresponding timestamps and by specifying the temporal JSON schema associated to these versions. This document associates a series of conventional JSON documents with logical and physical characteristics, along with the time span during which the association was in effect. Therefore, the temporal JSON document facilitates the support of historical queries involving past conventional JSON document versions or dealing with changes between conventional JSON document versions. The schema for the temporal document is the JSON Schema document TDSchema (box 9).

Notice that, whereas TCSchema (box 5), TSSchema (box 7), and TDSchema (box 9) have been developed in this work, JSON Schema (box 0) corresponds to the existing language endorsed by the Internet Engineering Task Force (IETF, 2018) for specifying the structure of conventional JSON documents.

For its functioning, the τJSchema framework includes four tools: the *Temporal JSON Schema Validator*, the *JSON Schema Mapper*, the *JSON Instances Squasher*, and the *Temporal JSON Instances Validator*, which are described in the following.

Similarly to what happens in the τXSchema framework, the temporal JSON schema (box 6) is processed by the *Temporal JSON Schema Validator* tool in order to ensure that the logical and physical characteristics are valid with respect to TCSchema, and consistent with the conventional JSON schema.

The *Temporal JSON Schema Validator* tool reports whether the temporal JSON schema document is valid or invalid.

Once all the characteristics are found to be consistent, the *JSON Schema Mapper* tool generates the representational JSON schema (box 11) from the temporal JSON schema (i.e., from the conventional JSON schema plus the logical and physical characteristics); it is the result of transforming the conventional schema according to the requirements expressed through the different temporal characteristics. The representational JSON schema becomes the schema for temporal JSON data instances (box 10). These temporal instances could be obtained in four ways: (i) automatically from the temporal JSON document (box 8) (i.e., from non-temporal JSON instances (box 2) and the temporal JSON schema (box 6)), using the *JSON Instances Squasher* tool (such an operation is called "squash" in the τXSchema approach); (ii) automatically from instances stored in a JSON-based NoSQL database, that is as the result of a "temporal query" or a "temporal view"; (iii) automatically from a third-party tool; (iv) manually: temporal JSON instances are directly added by the JNoDBA to the τJSchema repository.

Moreover, temporal JSON instances are validated against the representational JSON schema through the *Temporal JSON Instances Validator* tool, which reports whether the temporal JSON instances (box 10) are valid or invalid.

The four mentioned tools are currently under development. For example, the *Temporal JSON Instances Validator* tool is being implemented as a temporal extension of an existing conventional JSON instances validator (IETF, 2013), based on the source code of the corresponding τXSchema tool.

As far as the formal semantics of the proposed approach is concerned, we can say that there is basically nothing new under the sun. This can be easily seen by "unsquashing" a temporal JSON document, that is decomposing it via timeslicing into a collection of non-temporal document versions, each one of which is a standard JSON document. Such document versions conform to a conventional JSON schema, whose semantics has been formalized in (Pezoa *et al.*, 2016, Sec. 2) and against which they can be validated using the techniques proposed in (Pezoa *et al.*, 2016, Sec. 3). As to the semantics of the temporal infrastructure by means of which such component versions are assembled to make up the temporal JSON document, this corresponds to a generic data timestamping method. The precise resulting temporal data model to which they conform depends on the specific temporal characteristics chosen by the JNoDBA during the design phase. Validation of the resulting temporal JSON document against such a temporal data model is demanded to the execution of the *JSON Instance Validator* tool mentioned above, which is implemented according to the techniques developed in the τXSchema framework for the τXMLL$_{INT}$ tool as described in (Currim *et al.*, 2009, Sec. 9.3).

ILLUSTRATIVE EXAMPLE

To illustrate the functionalities of the τJSchema approach, we provide in this section an example that shows how time-varying JSON documents are explicitly managed.

Let us resume the example of the "Motivation" section. On April 20, 2018, the JNoDBA defined a conventional JSON schema (box 6), named "journals_ConventionalSchema.json" (as in Figure 5), and a conventional JSON document (box 2), named "journals_ConventionalDocument_V1.json" (as in Figure 1), which is conformant to this schema. Further, assume that the JNoDBA specified (on the same date) a set of temporal logical and physical characteristics (boxes 3 and 4), associated to that conventional

Figure 7. The temporal characteristic document ("journals_TemporalCharacteristics.json") on April 20, 2018

```
{ "temporalCharacteristicSet":{
    "logical":{
      "logicalItems":[
        { "target":"$.properties.journals..journal.properties.editor",
          "validTime":{
            "kind":"state",
            "content":"varying",
            "existence":"constant" } },
        { "target":"$.properties.journals..journal.properties.quartile",
          "validTime":{
            "kind":"state",
            "content":"varying",
            "existence":"constant" } } ] },
    "physical":{
      "stamps":[
        { "target":"$.properties.journals.items.properties.journal",
          "dataInclusion":"expandedVersion",
          "stampKind":{
            "timeDimension":"transactionTime",
            "stampBounds":"extent" } } ] }
} }
```

JSON schema; they are stored in a temporal characteristic document, named "journals_TemporalCharacteristics.json" (as shown in Figure 7).

As to temporal logical characteristics, he/she decided to make the content of the "editor" and of the "quartile" property varying in valid-time (in order to maintain the history along valid time of the changes the editor and the quartile of each journal undergo). As to temporal physical characteristics, he/she chose to add a transaction-time physical timestamp to the "journal" object, which means that whenever any property (i.e., "editor", or "quartile") of a "journal" object changes, the entire "journal" object is replicated to represent a new temporal "journal" version.

After that, when the JNoDBA asked the system to commit his/her work, the system performed the following tasks, within the same transaction:

- First, it created the temporal JSON schema (box 6), as shown in Figure 8, which ties "journals_ConventionalSchema.json" and "journals_TemporalCharacteristics.json" together; this schema is saved in a standard JSON file, named "journals_TemporalSchema.json".
- Then, it used the temporal JSON schema (see Figure 8) and the conventional JSON document (shown in Figure 1) to generate the temporal JSON document (box 8), named "journals_TemporalDocument.json" (as shown in Figure 9), which list the first version (i.e., temporal "slice") of the conventional JSON document ("journals_ConventionalDocument_V1.json", shown in Figure 1) with its associated timestamp. The squashed version (box 10) of the temporal JSON document, named "journals_SquashedDocument.json" (as shown in Figure 10), is also implicitly generated by the *JSON Instances Squasher*.

On July 26, 2018, the JNoDBA modified the conventional JSON document "journals_ConventionalDocument_V1.json" as presented in the "Motivation" section to produce a new conventional JSON document, named "journals_ConventionalDocument_V2.json" (as shown in Figure 2). Since the conventional JSON schema (i.e., "journals_ConventionalSchema.json") and the temporal characteristics

Figure 8. The temporal JSON schema ("journals_TemporalSchema.json") on April 20, 2018

```
{ "temporalJSONSchema":{
    "convetionalJSONSchema":{
        "sliceSequence":[
            { "slice":{
                "location":"journals_ConventionalSchema.json",
                "begin":"2018-04-20" } } ] },
    "temporalCharacteristicSet":{
        "sliceSequence":[
            { "slice":{
                "location":"journals_TemporalCharacteristics.json",

                "begin":"2018-04-20" } } ] } } }
```

Figure 9. The temporal JSON document ("journals_TemporalDocument.json") on April 20, 2018

```
{ "temporalRoot":{
    "temporalJSONSchema":{
        "location":"journals_TemporalSchema.json"},
    "sliceSequence": [
        { "slice":{
            "location":"journals_ConventionalDocument_V1.json",
            "begin":"2018-04-20" } }
    ] } }
```

Figure 10. The squashed document ("journals_SquashedDocument.json") on April 20, 2018

```
{ "journals":[
    { "journal":{
        "name":"Emerging Databases",
        "editor_RepItem":[
            { "editor_Version":{
                "timestamp_ValidExtent":{
                    "begin":"2018-04-20",
                    "end":"now"
                },
                "editor":"Mario Rossi"
            } } ],
        "quartile_RepItem":[
            { "quartile_Version":{
                "timestamp_ValidExtent":{
                    "begin":"2018-04-20",
                    "end":"now"
                },
                "quartile":"Q4"

            } } ] } } ] }
```

document (i.e., "journals_TemporalCharacteristics.json") were not changed, the temporal JSON schema (i.e., "journals_TemporalSchema.json") was consequently not changed. Nevertheless, the system updated the temporal JSON document, in order to include the new slice of the new conventional JSON document, as shown in Figure 11. The squashed version corresponding to the updated temporal JSON document is provided in Figure 12.

Finally, on October 15, 2018, the JNoDBA modified the conventional JSON document "journals_ConventionalDocument_V2.json" as presented in the "Motivation" section to produce a new conventional JSON document, named "journals_ConventionalDocument_V3.json" (as shown in Figure 3). Since the conventional JSON schema and the temporal characteristics document were not updated, the temporal JSON schema was consequently not changed. However, the system updated the temporal JSON document, in order to include the new slice of the new conventional JSON document, as shown in Figure 13. The squashed version associated to the updated temporal JSON document is provided in Figure 14.

Notice that the squashed document (shown in Figures 12 and 14) must be valid with respect to a schema, named the representational JSON schema (box 11), which is automatically created by the *JSON Schema Mapper* tool from the temporal JSON schema (shown in Figure 8).

In order to execute a timeslice query, for instance to find all journal data valid on September 10, 2018, the squashed document "journals_SquashedDocument.json" can be used, and its contents retrieved by replacing all the versioned parts with the only version whose valid timestamp include 2018-09-10 (i.e., having timestamp_ValidExtent with begin $\leq$ 2018-09-10 $\leq$ end), if any. Otherwise, the temporal JSON document "journals_TemporalDocument.json" can be used in order to identify in the slice sequence the qualifying conventional document that contains the desired data. The qualifying slice is the one with begin $\leq$ 2018-09-10 such that the next slice in the sequence has begun $>$ 2018-09-10, and contains the desired conventional document name (i.e., "journals_ConventionalDocument_V2.json") as location value. The resulting data would obviously be the same in both cases.

RELATED WORK DISCUSSION

In the literature, there are few works that have dealt with managing temporal aspects in NoSQL databases, as briefly surveyed in the following.

Figure 11. The temporal JSON document ("journals_TemporalDocument.json") on July 26, 2018

```
{ "temporalRoot":{
    "temporalJSONSchema":{
        "location":"journals_TemporalSchema.json"},
    "sliceSequence": [
        { "slice":{
            "location":"journals_ConventionalDocument_V1.json",
            "begin":"2018-04-20" } },
        { "slice":{
            "location":"journals_ConventionalDocument_V2.json",
            "begin":"2018-07-26" } } ] } }
```

Figure 12. The squashed document ("journals_SquashedDocument.json") on July 26, 2018

```
{ "journals":[
    { "journal":{
        "name":"Emerging Databases",
        "editor_RepItem":[
            { "editor_Version":{
                "timestamp_ValidExtent":{
                    "begin":"2018-04-20",
                    "end":"2018-07-25"
                },
                "editor":"Mario Rossi"
            } },
            { "editor_Version":{
                "timestamp_ValidExtent":{
                    "begin":"2018-07-26",
                    "end":"now"
                },
                "editor":"Layla Ahmad"
            } } ],
        "quartile_RepItem":[
            { "quartile_Version":{
                "timestamp_ValidExtent":{
                    "begin":"2018-04-20",
                    "end":"now"
                },
                "quartile":"Q4"

        } } ] } } ] }
```

Figure 13. The temporal JSON document ("journals_TemporalDocument.json") on October 15, 2018

```
{ "temporalRoot":{
    "temporalJSONSchema":{
        "location":"journals_TemporalSchema.json"},
    "sliceSequence": [
        { "slice":{
            "location":"journals_ConventionalDocument_V1.json",
            "begin":"2018-04-20" } },
        { "slice":{
            "location":"journals_ConventionalDocument_V2.json",
            "begin":"2018-07-26" } },
        { "slice":{
            "location":"journals_ConventionalDocument_V3.json",

            "begin":"2018-10-15" } } ] } }
```

Monger *et al.* (2012) deal with integrating temporal aspects into conventional JSON document-oriented NoSQL databases. They use four particular properties, i.e., StartTransactionTime, EndTransactionTime, StartValidTime, and EndValidTime, to represent and store bi-temporal data in a JSON document.

Castelltort and Laurent (2013) propose a versioning system for representing data history in a graph-oriented NoSQL database. Such a system is based on the following concepts: DataGraph (i.e., the current

Figure 14. The squashed document ("journals_SquashedDocument.json") on October 15, 2018

```
{ "journals":[
    { "journal":{
        "name":"Emerging Databases",
        "editor_RepItem":[
            { "editor_Version":{
                "timestamp_ValidExtent":{
                    "begin":"2018-04-20",
                    "end":"2018-07-25"
                },
                "editor":"Mario Rossi"
            } },
            { "editor_Version":{
                "timestamp_ValidExtent":{
                    "begin":"2018-07-26",
                    "end":"now"
                },
                "editor":"Layla Ahmad"
            } } ],
        "quartile_RepItem":[
            { "quartile_Version":{
                "timestamp_ValidExtent":{
                    "begin":"2018-04-20",
                    "end":"2018-10-14"
                },
                "quartile":"Q4"
            } },
            { "quartile_Version":{
                "timestamp_ValidExtent":{
                    "begin":"2018-10-15",
                    "end":"now"
                },
                "quartile":"Q3"
            } } ] } } ] }
```

version of a graph), Transaction (i.e., a sequence of operations performed on a DataGraph), Revision (i.e., the version of a graph produced by a Transaction), and VersionGraph (i.e., the history of all versions of a DataGraph).

In (Hu & Dessloch, 2014), the authors propose two alternative table representations for representing temporal data versions in conventional column-oriented NoSQL tables: explicit history representation (EHR) and tuple timestamping representation (TTR). Each data version is timestamped with an explicit temporal interval. The authors also propose two enhanced temporal relational algebras, named column-oriented temporal operator model (CTO) and TTR operator model (TTRO), for manipulating EHR tables and TTR tables, respectively. Each one of these algebras includes seven temporal data management operators, union, difference, intersection, projection, filter, Cartesian product, and theta-join, which extend the corresponding traditional temporal operators (Dey *et al.*, 1996).

Felber *et al.* (2014) have dealt with non-temporal versioning of instances in distributed key-value stores. More precisely, they study the design options that are available for implementing a versioned distributed key-value store on top of a conventional one. They also present their generic versioning system, ALEPH, which has been implemented on top of Infinispan (an industrial key-value store), and evaluate it against real access traces and datasets from Wikipedia. Based on experimental results, the authors conclude that adding versioning support to an existing key-value store is feasible, but the cost is considerably significant with regard to the following aspects: load balancing, latency, and storage overhead.

In his survey, Cuzzocrea (2015) studies the state of the art on temporal aspects of big data management (e.g., spatio-temporal modeling of big data, change detection in temporally-evolving network big data). He also presents several future research directions related to this topic (e.g., indexing temporal big data, in-memory processing engines for temporal big data management). Among these directions, the author mentions "integration with NoSQL platforms" and claims that NoSQL systems are the most suitable computational platforms for managing temporal big data.

As our τJSchema is a τXSchema-like approach, the works concerning τXSchema are also naturally related with it. These include the foundational works of the Snodgrass's team (Currim *et al.*, 2004), (Dyreson *et al.*, 2006), (Snodgrass *et al.*, 2008), and (Currim *et al.*, 2009), from one hand, and the further development works of our team (Brahmia *et al.*, 2011), (Brahmia *et al.*, 2012), and (Brahmia *et al.*, 2014), from the other hand.

Currim *et al.* (2004) proposed an initial version of τXSchema for the management of temporal XML documents but did not deal with schema versioning. Schema versioning (Brahmia *et al.*, 2014; Brahmia *et al.*, 2018b; Roddick, 2018), as required by advanced applications, prescribes that all the versions of evolving document schemas are maintained along with their underlying instance document versions. Hence, τXSchema has been extended to support the management of schema versioning in (Dyreson *et al.*, 2006) and (Snodgrass *et al.*, 2008). Dyreson *et al.* (2006) studied cross-schema change validation; Snodgrass *et al.* (2008) enhanced the work done in (Dyreson *et al.*, 2006) by addressing three important aspects: how to accommodate gaps in the existence time of an item, transaction semantics, and non-sequenced integrity constraints. In (Currim *et al.*, 2009), which is an expanded technical report, the authors provide more details on their approach by (i) showing how to construct a temporal document through the gluing of individual conventional documents (or snapshots) into an integrated history and the use of a temporal XML schema, (ii) dealing with both instance and schema versioning, and (iii) reviewing the entire τXSchema language. Notice that, since the focus of all these works was on the validation of temporal XML documents against temporal XML schemas in a τXSchema setting, they supposed that any schema change can be done and, therefore, they did not investigate what are the schema change operations that can be supported, or how these operations could be actually performed in an operational context.

As far as our previous works on τXSchema are concerned, first Brahmia *et al.* (2011) have dealt with versioning of annotations by proposing a complete and sound set of low-level operations for changing physical and logical annotations in τXSchema, and by defining their operational semantics. Then, Brahmia *et al.* (2012) have studied versioning of conventional schemas by providing another complete and sound set of low-level operations for evolving such schemas. After that, Brahmia *et al.* (2014) have completed the picture by introducing a global and integrated approach for schema versioning in τXSchema. Indeed, the authors have focused on versioning both conventional schemas and annotations, while implicitly propagating the effects of schema changes to temporal schemas, conventional documents and temporal documents. Thus, the completed approach supports an efficient management of all schema changes that could be done in a τXSchema repository, and provides a complete history of both evolving data and schemas in such an environment.

Moreover, application requirements for schema versioning are often experienced also in the Big Data and NoSQL domains (Cuzzocrea, 2015). In order to fulfill such requirements, as it was for τXSchema, we intend to extend our τJSchema approach to full support of schema versioning (Brahmia *et al.*, 2014; Brahmia *et al.*, 2018b; Roddick, 2018). The first results in this direction can be found in (Brahmia *et al.*, 2017; Brahmia *et al.*, 2018c).

Finally, a preliminary version of this work has also been published as (Brahmia *et al.*, 2016). With respect to that paper, in the present chapter, we also discuss semantics, syntax, validation and modeling issues related to our τJSchema framework (in "The τJSchema Approach" section), and compare our proposal with state-of-the-art and related works (in this section).

CONCLUSION

In this chapter, we presented our approach, named τJSchema, for managing time-varying JSON documents. It allows a JNoDBA to define a temporal JSON schema from a conventional JSON schema, and a set of temporal logical and physical characteristics that are associated to it. τJSchema has several advantages: it (i) guarantees logical and physical data independence for temporal JSON schemas, as it is a three-level schema approach that separates between the conventional structure of JSON data, their temporal characteristics and their physical representations, (ii) provides a low-impact solution since it requires neither modifications of already existing JSON documents, nor extensions to all related JSON technologies (the JSON language, the JSON Schema specification, existing JSON/JSON Schema tools and APIs, JSON NoSQL databases, etc.), (iii) facilitates the activity of JNoDBA when specifying temporal aspects of entities and their properties, (iv) supports both valid time and transaction time in JSON NoSQL databases, (v) proposes a large set of temporal logical options to satisfy temporal requirements of JNoDBAs, and (vi) offers several physical representations for temporal JSON documents.

In order to show the feasibility of our proposal, a system prototype is currently under development on top of MongoDB, as a JSON NoSQL temporal database system. It will support τJSchema and assist JNoDBAs in the definition and the maintenance of temporal JSON NoSQL databases. We plan to use such a prototype as a testbed to experimentally evaluate the performances of our framework, including the behavior of the validating and squashing tools in addition to query performance.

Finally, since the state of the art of NoSQL databases does not include any temporal NoSQL query language, we plan to propose a temporal extension to the (conventional) JSONiq language (Florescu & Fourny, 2013), which is a widely used and powerful language for querying (non-temporal) JSON data, in order to allow a user to query temporal JSON documents in a friendly and efficient manner.

REFERENCES

Ahsan, K., & Vijay, P. (2014). *Temporal Databases: Information Systems*. Bloomington, IN: Booktango.

Böhlen, M. H., Dignös, A., Gamper, J., & Jensen, C. S. (2017). Temporal Data Management - An Overview. *LNBIP*, *324*, 51–83.

Brahmia, S., Brahmia, Z., Grandi, F., & Bouaziz, R. (2016). τJSchema: A Framework for Managing Temporal JSON-Based NoSQL Databases. *Proceedings of the 27th International Conference on Database and Expert Systems Applications (DEXA'2016)*, 167-181. 10.1007/978-3-319-44406-2_13

Brahmia, S., Brahmia, Z., Grandi, F., & Bouaziz, R. (2017). Temporal JSON Schema Versioning in the τJSchema Framework. *Journal of Digital Information Management*, 15(4), 179–202.

Brahmia, S., Brahmia, Z., Grandi, F., & Bouaziz, R. (2018c). Managing Temporal and Versioning Aspects of JSON-based Big Data via the τJSchema Framework. *Proceedings of the International Conference on Big Data and Smart Digital Environment (ICBDSDE'2018)*. 27-39

Brahmia, Z., & Bouaziz, R. (2008). An Approach for Schema Versioning in Multi-Temporal XML Databases. *Proceedings of the 10th International Conference on Enterprise Information Systems (ICEIS 2008)*, 290-297.

Brahmia, Z., Bouaziz, R., Grandi, F., & Oliboni, B. (2011). Schema Versioning in τXSchema-Based Multitemporal XML Repositories. *Proceedings of the 5th IEEE International Conference on Research Challenges in Information Science (RCIS 2011)*, 1-12.

Brahmia, Z., Grandi, F., Oliboni, B., & Bouaziz, R. (2012). Versioning of Conventional Schema in the τXSchema Framework. *Proceedings of the 8th International Conference on Signal Image Technology & Internet Systems (SITIS'2012)*, 510-518.

Brahmia, Z., Grandi, F., Oliboni, B., & Bouaziz, R. (2014). Schema Change Operations for Full Support of Schema Versioning in the τXSchema Framework. *International Journal of Information Technology and Web Engineering*, 9(2), 20–46. doi:10.4018/ijitwe.2014040102

Brahmia, Z., Grandi, F., Oliboni, B., & Bouaziz, R. (2018a). Supporting Structural Evolution of Data in Web-Based Systems via Schema Versioning in the τXSchema Framework. In A. Elçi (Ed.), *Handbook of Research on Contemporary Perspectives on Web-Based Systems* (pp. 271–307). Hershey, PA: IGI Global. doi:10.4018/978-1-5225-5384-7.ch013

Brahmia, Z., Grandi, F., Oliboni, B., & Bouaziz, R. (2018b). Schema Versioning in Conventional and Emerging Databases. In M. Khosrow-Pour (Ed.), *Encyclopedia of Information Science and Technology* (4th ed.; pp. 2054–2063). Hershey, PA: IGI Global. doi:10.4018/978-1-5225-2255-3.ch178

Burns, T., Fong, E., Jefferson, D., Knox, R., Mark, L., Reedy, C., ... Truszkowski, W. (1986). Reference Model for DBMS Standardization, Database Architecture Framework Task Group (DAFTG) of the ANSI/X3/SPARC Database System Study Group. *SIGMOD Record*, 15(1), 19–58.

Castelltort, A., & Laurent, A. (2013). Representing history in graph-oriented NoSQL databases: A versioning system. *Proceedings of the 8th International Conference on Digital Information Management (ICDIM 2013)*, 228-234. 10.1109/ICDIM.2013.6694022

Cattell, R. (2010). Scalable SQL and NoSQL Data Stores. *SIGMOD Record*, 39(4), 2–27.

Clifford, J., Dyreson, C. E., Isakowitz, T., Jensen, C. S., & Snodgrass, R. T. (1997). On the Semantics of "Now" in Databases. *ACM Transactions on Database Systems*, 22(2), 171–214. doi:10.1145/249978.249980

Currim, F., Currim, S., Dyreson, C. E., Joshi, S., Snodgrass, R. T., Thomas, S. W., & Roeder, E. (2009). *τXSchema: Support for Data- and Schema-Versioned XML Documents*. TimeCenter, Technical Report TR-91. Retrieved January 31, 2019, from http://timecenter.cs.aau.dk/TimeCenterPublications/TR-91.pdf

Currim, F., Currim, S., Dyreson, C. E., & Snodgrass, R. T. (2004). A Tale of Two Schemas: Creating a Temporal XML Schema from a Snapshot Schema with τXSchema. *Proceedings of the 9th International Conference on Extending Database Technology (EDBT 2004)*, 348-365. 10.1007/978-3-540-24741-8_21

Currim, F., Currim, S., Dyreson, C. E., Snodgrass, R. T., Thomas, S. W., & Zhang, R. (2012). Adding Temporal Constraints to XML Schema. *IEEE Transactions on Knowledge and Data Engineering, 24*(8), 1361–1377. doi:10.1109/TKDE.2011.74

Cuzzocrea, A. (2015). Temporal Aspects of Big Data Management: State-of-the-Art Analysis and Future Research Directions. *Proceedings of the 22nd International Symposium on Temporal Representation and Reasoning (TIME 2015)*, 180-185. 10.1109/TIME.2015.31

Davoudian, A., Chen, L., & Liu, M. (2018). A Survey on NoSQL Stores. *ACM Computing Surveys, 51*(2), 40. doi:10.1145/3158661

Dey, D., Barron, T. M., & Storey, V. C. (1996). A complete temporal relational algebra. *The VLDB Journal, 5*(3), 167–180. doi:10.1007007780050022

Dyreson, C. E. (2001). Observing Transaction-time Semantics with TTXPath. *Proceedings of the 2nd International Conference on Web Information Systems Engineering (WISE 2001)*, 193-202.

Dyreson, C. E., & Grandi, F. (2018). Temporal XML. In L. Liu & M. T. Özsu (Eds.), *Encyclopedia of Database Systems* (2nd ed.). New York: Springer-Verlag; doi:10.1007/978-1-4614-8265-9_411

Dyreson, C. E., Snodgrass, R. T., Currim, F., Currim, S., & Joshi, S. (2006). Validating Quicksand: Schema Versioning in τXSchema. *Proceedings of the 22nd International Conference on Data Engineering Workshops (ICDE Workshops 2006)*, 82. 10.1109/ICDEW.2006.161

EMCA International. (2017). *The JSON Data Interchange Syntax, Standard ECMA-404* (2nd ed.). Retrieved January 31, 2019, from https://www.ecma-international.org/publications/files/ECMA-ST/ECMA-404.pdf

Etzion, O., Jajodia, S., & Sripada, S. (Eds.). (1998). *Temporal Databases: Research and Practice. LNCS* (Vol. 1399). Berlin, Germany: Springer-Verlag. doi:10.1007/BFb0053695

Felber, P., Pasin, M., Riviere, E., Schiavoni, V., Sutra, P., Coelho, F., ... Vilaça, R. M. P. (2014). On the Support of Versioning in Distributed Key-Value Stores. *Proceedings of the 33rd IEEE International Symposium on Reliable Distributed Systems (SRDS 2014)*, 95-104. 10.1109/SRDS.2014.35

Florescu, D., & Fourny, G. (2013). JSONiq: The History of a Query Language. *IEEE Internet Computing, 17*(5), 86–90. doi:10.1109/MIC.2013.97

Gao, D., & Snodgrass, R. T. (2003). Temporal Slicing in the Evaluation of XML Documents. *Proceedings of the 29th International Conference on Very Large Data Bases (VLDB 2003)*, 632-643.

Grandi, F. (2015). Temporal Databases. In M. Khosrow-Pour (Ed.), *Encyclopedia of Information Science and Technology* (3rd ed.; pp. 1914–1922). Hershey, PA: IGI Global. doi:10.4018/978-1-4666-5888-2.ch184

A Disciplined Approach to Temporal Evolution and Versioning Support in JSON Data Stores

Hamrouni, H., Brahmia, Z., & Bouaziz, R. (2018). A Systematic Approach to Efficiently Managing the Effects of Retroactive Updates of Time-varying Data in Multiversion XML Databases. *International Journal of Intelligent Information and Database Systems*, *11*(1), 1–26. doi:10.1504/IJIIDS.2018.091583

Hu, Y., & Dessloch, S. (2014). Defining Temporal Operators for Column Oriented NoSQL Databases. *Proceedings of the 18th East European Conference on Advances in Databases and Information Systems (ADBIS 2014)*, 39-55. 10.1007/978-3-319-10933-6_4

IETF (Internet Engineering Task Force). (2013). *JSON Schema: interactive and non interactive validation*. Retrieved January 31, 2019, from http://tools.ietf.org/html/draft-fge-json-schema-validation-00

IETF (Internet Engineering Task Force). (2017). *The JavaScript Object Notation (JSON) Data Interchange Format*. Retrieved January 31, 2019, from https://tools.ietf.org/html/rfc8259

IETF (Internet Engineering Task Force). (2018). *JSON Schema: A Media Type for Describing JSON Documents*. Retrieved January 31, 2019, from https://json-schema.org/latest/json-schema-core.html

Jensen, C. S. (2000). *Temporal Database Management* (PhD thesis). Department of Computer Science, Aalborg University, Aalborg, Denmark.

Jensen, C. S., & Snodgrass, R. T. (2018). Temporal Query Languages. In L. Liu & M. T. Özsu (Eds.), *Encyclopedia of Database Systems (2nd ed.)*. New York: Springer-Verlag. doi:10.1007/978-1-4614-8265-9_407

Monger, M. D., Mata-Toledo, R. A., & Gupta, P. (2012). Temporal Data Management in NoSQL Databases. *Journal of Information Systems & Operations Management*, *6*(2), 237–243.

Noh, S.-Y., & Gadia, S. K. (2006). A comparison of two approaches to utilizing XML in parametric databases for temporal data. *Information and Software Technology*, *48*(9), 807–819. doi:10.1016/j.infsof.2005.10.002

Petkovic, D. (2016). Temporal Data in Relational Database Systems: A Comparison. *Proceedings of the 4th World Conference on Information Systems and Technologies (WorldCIST'2016)*, 13-23. 10.1007/978-3-319-31232-3_2

Pezoa, F., Reutter, J. L., Suárez, F., Ugarte, M., & Vrgoč, D. (2016). Foundations of JSON Schema. *Proceedings of the 25th International Conference on World Wide Web (WWW'2016)*, 263-273. 10.1145/2872427.2883029

Pokorný, J. (2013). NoSQL databases: A step to database scalability in web environment. *International Journal of Web Information Systems*, *9*(1), 69–82. doi:10.1108/17440081311316398

Rizzolo, F., & Vaisman, A. A. (2008). Temporal XML: Modeling, Indexing, and Query Processing. *The VLDB Journal*, *17*(5), 1179–1212. doi:10.100700778-007-0058-x

Roddick, J. F. (2018). Schema Versioning. In L. Liu & M. T. Özsu (Eds.), *Encyclopedia of Database Systems* (2nd ed.). New York: Springer-Verlag. doi:10.1007/978-1-4614-8265-9_323

Snodgrass, R. T. (Ed.). (1995). The TSQL2 Temporal Query Language. Norwell, MA: Kluwer Academic Publishers.

Snodgrass, R. T., Dyreson, C. E., Currim, F., Currim, S., & Joshi, S. (2008). Validating Quicksand: Schema Versioning in τXSchema. *Data & Knowledge Engineering*, *65*(2), 223–242. doi:10.1016/j. datak.2007.09.003

Tansel, A. U., Clifford, J., Gadia, S. K., Jajodia, S., Segev, A., & Snodgrass, R. T. (Eds.). (1993). *Temporal Databases: Theory, Design and Implementation*. Redwood City, CA: Benjamin/Cummings Publishing Company.

Tiwari, S. (2011). *Professional NoSQL*. Indianapolis, IN: John Wiley & Sons, Inc.

Wang, F., & Zaniolo, C. (2005). An XML-Based Approach to Publishing and Querying the History of Databases. *World Wide Web: Internet and Web Information Systems*, *8*(3), 233–259. doi:10.100711280-005-1317-7

W3C (World Wide Web). (2004). *XML Schema Part 0: Primer Second Edition*. W3C Recommendation. Retrieved January 31, 2019, from http://www.w3.org/TR/2004/REC-xmlschema-0-20041028/

Wang, F., Zaniolo, C., & Zhou, X. (2008). ArchIS: An XML-based approach to transaction-time temporal database systems. *The VLDB Journal*, *17*(6), 1445–1463. doi:10.100700778-007-0086-6

KEY TERMS AND DEFINITIONS

τJSchema: A data model equipped with a suite of tools that allow the definition and validation of time-varying JSON documents through the use of a temporal JSON schema.

Conventional JSON Document: In the τJSchema framework, a standard JSON document that does not store data evolution over time. It keeps only the last version of any data without any temporal reference.

Conventional JSON Schema: In the τJSchema framework, a standard JSON schema document that describes the structure of one or several conventional JSON documents.

NoSQL Database: A nontraditional database that usually does not require a fixed schema, avoids join operations, and typically scales horizontally.

Temporal Database: A database with built-in support for managing time-varying data.

Temporal JSON Document: In the τJSchema framework, a standard JSON document that stores the evolution over time of a conventional JSON document, by keeping track of all the versions of this latter with their corresponding timestamps and by specifying the temporal JSON schema associated to these versions.

Temporal JSON Schema: In the τJSchema framework, a schema that is composed of a conventional JSON schema annotated with a set of temporal logical and temporal physical characteristics.

Temporal Logical Characteristics: In the τJSchema framework, specifications that identify which components of a conventional JSON schema can vary over time.

Temporal Physical Characteristics: In the τJSchema framework, specifications on how the time-varying aspects are physically represented in the time-varying JSON document.

Chapter 7

Modeling Temporal Information With JSON

Zhangbing Hu
Nanjing University of Aeronautics and Astronautics, China

Li Yan
Nanjing University of Aeronautics and Astronautics, China

ABSTRACT

As a ubiquitous form of data in human natural life, time has been widely used in military, finance, medical treatment, environment and other fields. Therefore, temporal data models used to express the dynamic development process of data have been proposed constantly. Currently, the main research achievements focus on temporal database and temporal XML. With the rapid development and popularization of network technology, the requirement of efficiency and security is getting higher and higher. JSON, a new generation of data exchange language, has been widely used because of its lightweight, fast parsing and high transmission efficiency. However, modeling temporal information with JSON has not been studied enough. The chapter proposes a temporal data model based on JSON. What is more, the temporal query language and the JSON Schema is also mentioned.

INTRODUCTION

With the popularity and development of the Internet, amount of data onto all domains is growing exponentially. According to the data volume growth report that released by China Cloud Computing Conference Website in 2018, the amount of Web data in 2020 will be 44 times that of today. Due to the increasing amount of data volume and the improvement in software and hardware computing capability, cloud computing, big data, data mining, machine learning, and other intelligent technologies has developed rapidly, therefore it is very valuable and necessary to use these technologies excavating the hidden trends and laws behind a large number of data (Han, 2005; Mitsa, 2010; Chen & Petrounias, 1998). Time as an omnipresent property of the realistic natural world, it has a great significance when studying the ceaseless application area. Meanwhile, mining the laws behind time dimension from a large number of data have received wide attention in academia and industry (Mitsa, 2010). As early as in 1998, A framework

DOI: 10.4018/978-1-5225-8446-9.ch007

for temporal data mining has raised (Chen & Petrounias, 1998). In the field of medicine,describes the temporal data mining aspects of a research project that deals with the definition of methods and tools for the assessment of the clinical performance of hemodialysis (HD) services (Chittaro, Combi, & Trapasso 2003; Bellazzi, et al. 2005). What is more, spatio-temporal data mining for typhoon image collection may forecast the typhoon trends (Kitamoto, 2002). Summarizing industry's work, the work in the paper shows how to mine the temporal laws behind temporal information about SOM, SVM, temporal periodic pattern algorithm and so on (Post & Jr, 2008). Furthermore, the intelligent technology of big data, Hadoop, spark, druid, has been widely applied in temporal field.

The JavaScript Object Notation (JSON) has presented by Dougalas Crockford to IETF RFC draft (Bray, 2014).

1. It is a lightweight data-interchange format based on the pro-type of the JavaScript programming language;
2. It is easy for human to read and write and easy for machine to parse and generate;
3. JSON is a text format that is completely language independent but uses conventions that are familiar to programmers of the C-family of languages.

These characteristics make JSON an ideal data-interchange language. In addition, JOSN has higher flexibility and scalability when compared with XML (Lin, et al. 2012). Therefore, JSON has been widely used. It is currently the predominant format for sending API requests and responses over the HTTP or HTTPS protocol for its high data transmission efficiency (Sheth, Henson & Sahoo, 2008). JSON data format obtains a wide application. Research on the applications of JSON data interchange format in heterogeneous system integration (Gu & Shen, 2012; Wang & Zhu, 2018). There is a way to realize Android efficiently and safely accessing from a remote database by using JSON format (Soewito, et.al, 2017). JSON was also applied in asynchronous distributed genetic algorithms (Merelo, et.al, 2008). What is more, the implementation of document database in non-relational database classification, MongoDB, CouchDB, are all based on JSON grammar format (Bellazzi, et.al 2016; Boicea, et.al,2012). But the real world is changing over time, non-temporal data model can not well reflect the development and change process of data.

In this paper, we propose a temporal data model based on JSON. First, we introduce a non-temporal data model based on JSON, then we obtain our temporal model by adding validity time to model that represents the history of a fact in the modeled reality. Finally, we make a formal definition of our temporal data model. The main contributions of this paper are summarized as follows:

1. We propose a temporal data model based on JSON that can reflect the change of the JSON document, the temporal model greatly reduces data redundancies.
2. On the basis of the temporal JSON data model proposed in this paper, we briefly discussed the query language upon the temporal model. To the best of our knowledge, it is the first effort to present query language for temporal JSON data model.

The remainder of this paper is organized as follows. The second section presents the related work in the temporal database and temporal XML. The third section simply explains the time domain, syntax and data types of the JSON model. The fourth section formally introduces a temporal JSON data model by extending a non-temporal JSON data model and proposes physical implements of our model. Query language about temporal JSON document and schema mentioned in the fifth section. The final section concludes this paper and makes a prospect of our future work.

RELATED WORK

The present work in this paper is closely related to a temporal database model and temporal model based on XML.

Temporal Databases

Along with the rapid development of database technology, the temporal database has always been a hot topic in database research. Since the 1980s one of the topics which interest several researchers of the temporal database community. The glossary of temporal database concepts that are well-defined, well understand, and widely used in the work, in addition to defined and named the concept, the glossary also explains the decisions made (Jensen, et.al, 1992). James Clifford first presented a history relational database model (HRDM) by adding time attribute to existing relational model (Clifford & Croker, 1987). It enables time to stamp data values when there is a need to track all changes from data and to have a complete history of the modeled reality. Relational temporal model is divided into two categories: grouped record (add validity start time and end time to record), and non-grouped (according to time grouping) (Gadia & Yeung, 1988), like Figure 1 and Figure 2. Owing to the constraint of temporal representation of unary temporal databases, bitemporal database System has been proposed that can manage the data onto transaction time (i.e., the time when a datum is, currently stored in the database) and valid time (i.e., the time when a datum was, is or will be valid in the real world) dimension (Knolmayer & Myrach, 2001; Wei & Elmasri, 2000). Combi has implemented an object-oriented database system that can explicitly deal with several temporal dimensions of data (Combi, 2009). Zheng and Zhou applied temporal semantics with graph database (Zheng, et.al, 2017).

Temporal XML

Modern computer applications (e.g., social network and collaborative web information system) are changing fast. And this requires high transmission efficiency for data exchanging format over the Internet. Extensible Markup Language (XML) has been playing a dominant role in the field of data exchanges with the high-speed development of web technology since drafted by W3C in the 80s of last century. For the sake of managing the version of the XML document by multiple client edits, a wide range of research of XML-based temporal models has been proposed (Wang, Zhou & Zaniolo, 2004). Amagasa

Figure 1. Ungrouped record

name	rank	start	end
tom	middle school	v1	e1
tom	high school	v2	e2
tom	university	v3	e3

Figure 2. Grouped record

v1	v1 middle school e2
tom	v2 high school e2
e3	v3 university e3

and Yoshikawa presented a temporal data model by extending the XPath data model (Amagasa, Yoshikawa & Uemura, 2000), it adds validity time for every edge represents the child node whether exist in the model. For convenient and efficient management of normative text in XML format, Grandi implemented a temporal data model based on XML in (Grandi, et.al, 2003), which encodes the hierarchical organization of normative texts (i.e. as in many other countries, also in Italy norms are based on a contents-section-article-paragraph hierarchy) in a tree-like inner structure by means of an XML schema. The model considers publication time, validity time, efficacy time and transaction time dimensions. A comparison of a various temporal data model based on XML was presented in (Ali & Pokorný, 2009). In order to guarantee the consistency of temporal date model and retrieve the desired information inside the XML document, methodology for indexing and querying the XML documents has attracted huge attention (Li, et.al, 2010; Chamberlin, Robie & Florescu, 2000; Mendelzon, Rizzolo & Vaisman, 2004). With the growing maturity of the unary temporal data model, query language and indexing structure, an XML-based bitemporal data model and its applications a for versions raised in (Wang & Zaniolo, 2004). Therefore, time is always highly concerned in many fields because of its unique characteristics. Usually, a time dimension is added to the XML model by using an additional attribute or a time tag as shown in Figure 3 and Figure 4.

PRELIMINARIES

Temporal Representation

The first step of our work is modeling time when process temporal information. In the field of temporal information processing, there are mainly two dimensions always inferred:

- **Validity Time:** It is the time of a fact that the fact is true in the modeled reality;
- **Transaction Time:** It is the time of a fact that the fact actually stored in the database;
- **User-Define Time:** It is the time that according to the user's or object's own needs.

In this paper, we just take validity time into consideration for sake of simplicity. But in our future work, we will take both validity time and transaction time into our temporal model. What is more, we adopt a discrete time model where time consists with of atomic chronons. Consecutive chronons may be grouped together into granules with different groupings yielding distinct granularities. The timeline

Figure 3. Add time to attribute

```
<student>
    <name vstart=v1, vend=e3>
      birkhoff
    </name>
    <grade vstart=v1, vend=e1>
      middle school
    </grade>
    <grade vstart=v2, vend=e2>
      high school
    </grade>
    <grade vstart=v3, vend=e3>
      university
    </grade>
</student>
```

Figure 4. Add time tag

```
<student>
  <name>
        <vstart>v1</vstart> <vend>e3</vend>
          tom
  </name>
  <grade >
        <vstart>v1</vstart> <vend>e3</vend>
          middle school
  </grade>
  <grade >
        <vstart>v1</vstart> <vend>e3</vend>
          high school
  </grade>
  <grade >
        <vstart>v1</vstart> <vend>e3</vend>
          university
  </grade>
</student>
```

is bounded by the relative beginning and the current time is represented by a special symbol "now". In addition, we take time instant which is a particular chronon on the timeline as our time data type. Let us, for instance, lookt at a time interval [*tstart*, *tend*](*tstart* < *tend*), which represents the fact is valid in modeled reality from *tstart* to *tend*.

JSON Specification

According to the JSON format definition, JSON documents are dictionaries consisting of key-value pairs, where the value can be a JSON document, thus allowing an arbitrary level of nesting. The process of using JSON document is mainly built on two data structures:

1. A collection of key-value pairs. In various languages, this is realized as an object, record, struct, dictionary, hash table, keyed list, or associative array, we call it an object in this paper. An object is an unordered set of key-value pairs, but the key of the object must be different, compared with the XML data model.
2. An ordered list of values. In most languages, this is realized as an array, vector, list, or sequence, we call it an array in this paper. An array is an ordered collection of values.

There are universal data structures. Virtually all modern programming a language support them in one form or another. It makes sense that a data format that is interchangeable with programming languages also be based on these structures. In JSON syntax that take on these forms as follows:

The full JSON specification defines seven types of values, including string, number, object, array, true, false and null, respectively. However, to abstract from encoding details, we assume that our JSON documents are only formed by object, array, string and natural number. Next, we explain these data types in turn.

An object is an unordered set of key-value pairs. An object begins with "{" and end with "}". Each name is following by ":", and the key-value pairs are separated by ",". For instance, if v1, v2, ..., vn are JSON values and s1, s2, ..., sn are pair-wise distinct string values, then {s1:v1, s2:v2, ..., sn:vn}is a JSON value, called an object. In this case, each si:vi is called a key-value pair of this object, and v1, v2, ..., vn can also be an array, object or atomic type.

Next, without loss of generality, to abstract from encoding details, we assume our JSON documents are only formed by object, array, string and natural number. Formally, $\sum$ denotes the set of all Unicode characters. JSON values are defined as follows. First, any natural number $n \geq 0$ is a JSON value, called a number. Furthermore, if s is a string in $\sum^*$, "s" is a JSON value, called a string.

Finally, if v1, v2, ..., vn are JSON values then [v1, v2, ..., vn] is a JSON value called an array. In this case v1, v2, ..., vn are called the elements of the array, and v1, v2, ..., vn can also be an array, object or atomic type like the elements of the object, but the difference is that v1, v2, ..., vn must be unifying type.

We present a simple example of a JSON document that comes from a forum website is given in Figure 5. As we can see here, apart from simple dictionaries, JSON also supports arrays and atomic types such as integers and strings. Arrays and dictionaries can again contain arbitrary JSON documents, thus making the format fully compositional.

The next part of this paper, we propose a new data model for capturing the history of the JSON document which is extended by a non-temporal JSON data model. Despite the popularity of JSON, the coverage of the specifics of JSON format in the research literature is very sparse. The non-temporal JSON data

Figure 5. An example of a JSON document

```
{
     "name" : {"firstname" : "Tom"  "lastname" : "Doe"},
     "age"  : 18,
     "hobbies" : ["fish","tennis"]
}
```

model mentioned earlier is proposed, which is called JSON Trees. We first modify the JSON trees data model and then propose a temporal JSON Trees data model built on modification of JSON Trees model.

The Temporal JSON Trees Data Model

In this section, we propose a temporal data model for dynamic JSON document. The goal is to reflect the history of the whole document contents. and that will be used later on the basis of our formalization of JSON query language. Firstly, we begin by introducing a non-temporal JSON data model, called JSON Trees, proposed by Pierre Bourhis. Afterward, we obtain our formal data model by making a slight modification of the JSON Trees model and propose a temporal JSON Trees model by adding valid time for the non-temporal model. Finally, we make a comparison between the temporal JSON model and temporal model based on XML.

JSON Trees Data Model

JSON Trees data model viewed JSON document as a JSON object, according to the JSON format syntax, JSON object is a set of key-value pairs, in which values can again be a JSON object. This naturally suggests to use a tree-shaped structure to model an JSON document. For this purpose, Pierre Bourhis has proposed JSON Trees data model (Bourhis et.al, 2017). For example, consider Figure 5 as the JSON document J, the whole document views as a JSON object according to JSON Trees model, there are total eight JSON value inside this document: the complete document itself, plus the liter,Tom", "Doe", 18, "fish", "tennis", "hobbies":["fish","tennis"]}, {"firstname":"Tom", "lastname":"Doe"}, {"hobbies":["fish","tennis"]}, {"age":18}. If we are to preserve the compositional structure of JSON, then the most natural representation is by using the following edge-labeled tree.

The root of the tree represents the entire document. The three edges labeled "name", "age", "hobbies" represents three keys inside this JSON object, and they lead to nodes that represent their respective values. In the case of the key "age", the value of that just a JSON atomic data type, and the value of key "hobbies" is an array, a compound data type of JSON format syntax, and there are two another atomic string type in the array, and the value of the "name" is also another compound type of JSON, JSON object, that is represented as a sub-tree of the entire tree. So, we have a formal definition of JSON trees data model as follows.

- **Labeled Edges**: The edges of JSON Trees data model are labeled by the keys forming the key-value pairs in a JSON object. JSON Tress data model implied that the keys of a JSON object are unique. they will emerge to an array if some keys of a JSON object are equal, as the value of the key "hobbies" in the above instance.

Figure 6. JSON Trees Data Model

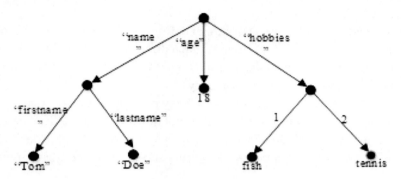

- **Nodes**: in the model of JSON Trees. a node represents the data type in JSON syntax. According to the above description, in JSON format syntax, there are two kinds of data types. One is an atomic type, such as string, integer and etc. In the JSON trees data model, the leaf nodes correspond to this data type, which can be also assigned a concrete value. The another is a compositional data type, including JSON object and array. JSON object represents the whole document or sub-document that is formed by the key-value pairs. Arrays are formed by atomic data type or JSON object, as arrays are ordered, so the model viewed the array as the node whose children are accessed by axes labeled with natural numbers reflecting their position in the array.

As JSON trees model is a tree-shaped, Pierre Bourhis used tree domain as its theoretical basis. A tree domain is a prefix-closed subset of N*. Without loss of generality assume that for all tree domain D, if D contains a node n·i, for n∈N*, then D contains all n·j with $0 \leq j < i$.

Let $\sum$ be an alphabet. Then a JSON tree over $\sum$ is a structure J = {D, Obj, Arr, Str, Int, A, O}, where D is a tree domain that is partitioned by Obj, Arr, Str and Int, O ⊆ Obj × $\sum$* × D is the object-child relation, A ⊆ Arr × N × D is the array child relation, val: Str∪Int→ $\sum$*∪N is the string and number value function, and where the following holds:

- For each node n∈Obj and child n·i of n, O contains one triple (n, w, n·i), for a word w∈$\sum$*.
- The first two components of O form a key: if (n, w, n·i) and (n, w, n·j) are in O, then i = j.
- For each node n∈Arr and child n·i of n, Acontains the triple (n, i, n·i).
- If n is in Str or Int then D can not contain nodes of form n·u.
- The value function assigns to each string node in Str a value in $\sum$* and to each number node in Int a natural number.

In the context of XML model, a tree model for XML document is proposed. For example, a representative of a tree model is an XPath model, which is widely discussed. In addition, a temporal model based on XML is commonly extended by the XPath model (Amagasa, Yoshikawa & Uemura, 2000). Although XML document and JSON document always tree-shaped, there are still several differences for each other.

1. XML tree mainly through parent tag contains some child labels, but JSON tree mainly through the key contains a JSON object or array;

2. In XML tree, the node represents a tag or attribute, but in JSON tree, the node usually represents their date type in JSON document;

3. Although XML tree and JSON tree has a similar definition of nodes that divide node to several kinds by their node type, the definition of Edge is much different: the edge in XML tree just represents the parent-child relation, and the edge in JSON tree the labeled edge may represent the key of the JSON object or the natural number of the array.

4. JSON trees are deterministic by design, as each key can appear at most once inside a dictionary.

5. Arrays are explicitly defined in JSON, which is not the case in the XML data model.

6. JSON values can also be a JSON object, thus making equality comparisons much more complex than in case of XML, since we are now comparing sub-trees and not just atomic values.

Temporal JSON Trees Data Model

However, with the requirements of system business, the structure and content of documents change over time. For Instance, at December 15, 2017, the user's firstname change to "Alen". And then, at December 31, 2017, the JSON document needs to add an attribute, named "vip", represent the user whether is the VIP user of the forum website, the user register as a member immediately, in addition, the user add yoga to their list of hobbies. And finally, the user removes tennis from their list of hobbies at January 5, 2018. Because non-temporal JSON model can not well reflect the change of document. So, we propose our temporal JSON Trees data model by extend the non-temporal JSON Trees model. Temporal models have state information that records documents in the past, present and even future,thus, it can well reflect the process of data change, what is more, It can better serve time-based data mining technology. In the next, the definitions and concepts related to the temporal JSON model are introduced.

We first make a slight modification on the JSON Trees model, we divide the node into a number of types by their data type, what is more, we introduce a virtual node, text to value node, which represents the value of the atomic data type. So, we obtained our non-temporal JSON data model that formal defined are below:

Definition 1 (Node): Let J be a JSON document, where $V(J)$ is a set of nodes of J. There are six kinds of nodes, including root, string, number, boolean, text, array, and object. Each of them is referred to as r, $Vs(J)$, $Vn(J)$, $Vb(J)$, $Vt(J)$, $Va(J)$ and $Vo(J)$, respectively. These set are pair-wise disjoint and $V(J) =\{r\}\cup Vs(J)\cup Vn(J)\cup Vb(J)\cup Vt(J)\cup Va(J)\cup Vo(J)$. For the sake of simplifying. It should be noted that we do not take the atomic type, null, into consideration.

Definition 2 (Edge): Being similar to the definition of that in the JSON trees model, a labeled edge represents the key in a JSON object or the nature number of an array. But the difference is that our model divides all nodes into several kinds and introduce the text node, which represents the value of the atomic node. This raises a question: how to represent the edge between the text node and the atomic node type. Learning from the XPath data model of XML, we omit the difference between this kind of edge and another edge. Let $E(J)$ be a set of edges (p, c) in a JSON document, where each pair is one of the followings: p represents the label of the labeled edge, so p has four kinds set. Including the set of the key in JSON document, defined Ek (J), the set of the natural number of an array, defined En(J), and the connection of atomic type nodes and text value nodes defined Et(J), finally is the edge that connected the root node and the whole document node, called Er. Therefore, $p\in Ek(J)\cup En(J)\cup Et(J)\cup Er$, $c\in V(J)$.c represents the value of the pair, thus $c\in V(J)- r$.

According to the definition of our basic non-temporal JSON data model, we obtain a representation of the above-extended content. As shown in Figure 7.

Next, we just add valid time to the extended data model for the sake of the simplicity of representation.

1. We add valid time label onto the edge;
2. We distinguish every node's value node as a virtual node that one node can have multiple edges shoot out representing the lifespan of the value. According to reflect versions of the user information, we give the formal definition of the temporal data model:
    a. **Definition 3 (Edge):** Due to our temporal JSON model is introducing time to the edge, thus we should determine the definition of the edge again. Let J be a temporal JSON document, E(J) is a set of labeled edges ((p, c), t), where (p, c) is same to the definition of the basic JSON model. t represents the valid time. In other words, the (p, c) is valid only in the valid time.
    b. **Definition 4 (Consistent Temporal JSON Document):** On the basis of the definition, a temporal JSON document J is consistent if the two conditions are satisfied:
        i. Let *l* belong to ((p, c), t) except for *Er*, the valid time of l must be the union of valid time that is forming by the children of l, such as ((p, c), t_1), ((p, c), t_2), ((p, c), t_3) …… ((p, c), t_n). Then,
        ii. $\cup_{1 \leq i < n} t_i \subseteq t$
        iii. 2. b. iii. Let *r* be the root of *J*, *di* and *dj* be the different nodes which represent the whole JSON document. Ei and Ej are the edges between the root node and the whole document node.ti and tj is the valid time of the Ei and Ej. if i ≠ j. Then,

$$t_i \cap t_j = \Phi$$

Because our temporal JSON Trees should reflect the history content of the whole document. Now we assumed that the valid start time of the document is 2017-12-01, we first modified the document on the value of the key "firstname", we modified the value "Tom" to "Alen" on 2017-12-15. The next modification on the document is the state of the key "vip" and adding "yoga" into the array that represents the key "hobbies" on 2018-01-01, and then we get rid of "tennis" from the hobbies array on 2018-01-05. Finally, the modification is the value of the "age" from 18 to 19 on 2018-01-22.

Figure 7. Non-Temporal JSON data model

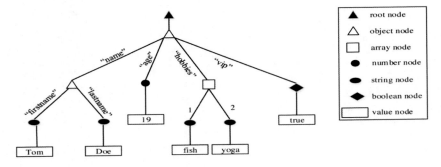

On the basis of the formal definition of our temporal JSON data model that by extended JSON Trees data model, it can reflect the histories of the document. According to the modification of the document, we obtain the representation of histories of the document by adding the valid time in Figure 8.

How we receive our temporal document from the temporal JSON data model. We designed a program algorithm that can translate the model to the JSON document. The input of the program algorithm is the root node of the temporal JSON data model, the algorithm will first find the child node that root can access, and then make every labeled edge's attribute to a key-value pair, the key is the labeled attribute, and the value is an array.

Next, the procedure checks if every node is an atomic node or compositional node if the node's type is an object, then recursive call the procedure, and the input are the sub-object. Else, the process generates an object by the labeled valid time, a labeled valid time will generate an object that contains two key-value pairs, the key of each object is labeled attribute, and the value is content of the text node. In addition, each node contains a key-value pair that the key is "validtime" and value is a time interval. We present the temporal model translation in Algorithm 1.

According to the algorithm above, we can obtain a temporal JSON document shown in Figure 9.

Temporal Query Language and JSON Schema

- **Query Language:** One of the motivations for proposing a temporal data model is to support query languages that make complex queries easy to express. Although there is no a standard for JSON query language, for non-temporal JSON document, there are already some query languages for retrieve information from the document, such as JSONPath, JSONiq, N1QL etc. JSONPath similar to XPath's location in XML documents. The path expression can accept the format of "dot-notation" or "bracket-notation", for instance, if we want search firsname of user from Figure 5, we can use JSONPath expression: $.name.firstname or $["name"]["firstname"], are both returns the correct result that we want. If we want to retrieve information from temporal JSON document, especially involves time operations, traditional JSONPath cannot handle it well. So, in this section, we firstly propose temporal JSONPath by extend JSONPath.

Figure 8. Temporal JSON data model

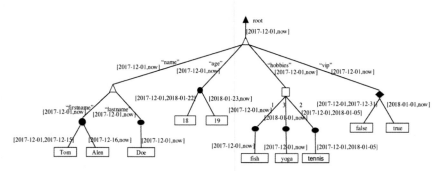

Algorithm 1. Temporal Model Translation

```
Input:  temporal model root node R
Output: temporal document
1.          D← getDocument (R)                    //receive document by parsing the
temporal model
2.          getDocumetn (N) {
3.            If(N is object):
4.              getDocument(N)                     // recursive call
5.            else:
6.             If(N is array):
7.               foreach edge:
8.                   p1 ← createKVpair(N.attribute,N.text) //create a key-
valur for each label
9.                   p2 ← createKVpair("validtime", time) //create a validtime
key-value pair
10.              else:
11.               Foreach edge:
12.                   p1 ← createKVpair(N.attribute,N.text) //create a key-
valur for each label
13.                   p2 ← createKVpair("validtime", time) //create a valid-
time key-value pair
14.           }
15.              createKVpair (key, value) {
16.          kv.set(key)
17.          kv.set(value)
18.          retrun kv
19.          }
```

Figure 9. Temporal JSON document

```
{
"name":[{"name":{"firstname":[{"firstname":"John","validtime": [2017-12-01,2017-12-15] } ,
                              {"firstname":"Alen","validtime" : [2017-12-16,now]}]
         "lasttime":[{"lastname":"Doe","validtime":[2017-12-01,now]}] }
                    "validtime" : [2017-12-01,now]
         }]
     "age":[{"age":18, "validtime": [2017-12-01,2018-01-22]},
            { "age":19, "validtime": [2018-01-23,now] }]

"hobbies":[{"hobbies":["fish", "tennis",], "validtime":[2017-12-01,2018-01-01] },
           {"hobbies":["fish", "tennis", " yoga"], "validtime":[2018-01-01,2018-01-05] },
           {"hobbies":["fish", "yoga"],"validtime" : [2018-01-06,now] }]
    "vip":[{ "vip":false, "validtime" : [2017-12-01,2017-12-31] },
              {"vip":true, "validtime" : [2018-01-01,now] }],
  "validtime": [2017-12-01,now]
}
```

According to the syntax specification of JSONPath path expression, and combining with the representation method of temporal JSON document. Two temporal filter assertions "@.from" and "@.to" are proposed to extend the temporal operation. The filter "@.from" denotes filtering the query results according to the effective start time and the filter "@.to" denotes filtering the query results according to the effective end time. Because of the limitation of JSONPath path expression, it can only locate data according to path navigation instructions, so the two temporal filter assertion extensions can be compatible with JSONPath and can satisfy the operation of JSONPath query language for temporal data processing. For example, if we want retrieve the user's hobbies at 2018-01-03. We can use the query expression as follows:

```
"$.hobbies[?(@.from >="2018-01-03" && @. to <="2018-01-03")]"
```

But with the representation of temporal JSON documents, The execution structure needs to be treated as follows:

1. Because temporal JSON document Using the form of double key-value pairs, so, the above query statement execute dual path navigation instruction location as follows:

    ```
    "$.hobbies[?(@.from >="2018-01-03" && @. to <="2018-01-03")].hobbies"
    ```

2. Then, because JSON grammar does not support time data types, in order to extend temporal operations, the proposed approach is to mark time types as string types. According to the definition of string, the comparison of time point can be based on the comparison of string itself. In addition, since temporal extension needs to satisfy the upward compatibility, i.e. compatibility with non-temporal query languages, this paper defines non-temporal semantics as the current query time of the system, i.e. query ()=query (now). Therefore, when the above query statements are not time-constrained, they should be converted to as follows:

```
"$.hobbies[?(@.from = ="now"&& @. to = ="now")]"
```

3. Finally, according to the representation of the temporal JSON document, when the result of executing the query statement is the atomic type or the array type, the query statement Returns the result of the path expression directly. But if the type of result is object, the query engine needs to restructure the result. We propose a method ObjRet(Object,time), the specific algorithmic process of object reorganization is described in Algorithm 2.

In order to fully demonstrate the temporal extension effect of JSONPath, the following will be classified according to the types of temporal JSONPath query statements. Because of the restriction of the grammatical structure of the temporal JSONPath query language, it can not complete the comparison operation between different state snapshots of the temporal JSON documents, so the temporal JSONPath query statements belong to the sequential query type. For the query statements of temporal JSONPath, there are three types of sequential query: non-temporal query, temporal query with atomic or array returned results, and temporal query with object returned results. In the next, we illustrate it with specific query examples.

Algorithm 2. Temporal Model Translation

```
Input:   Object and filter time
Output:  JSON document
1.          Result ← ObjRet(Object,interval)
2.          ObjRet (Object,interval) {
3.             Ret  // result
4.             attributes ← allAtttributes(Object)
5.             For attr in attributes
6.                 value ← $.attr[?(@.from >= start(interval) && @.to <=
end(interval))]
7.                 If (value is Object) do
8.                     Ret ← ObjRet(value,interval)  // recursive restructured
9.                 Else
10.                    Ret ← createKVpair(a,value.attr)
11.            return Ret
12.         }
13.         createKVpair(key,value) {
14.             pair ← key:value
15.         }
```

1.   **Non-Temporal Query**

For example, ones query the user's age at the March 4,2018. Then the query statement and result are shown as follows:

```
Query1: $.age
Execute: $.age[?(@.from=="now" && @. to = ="now")].age
Result: 19
```

2.   **Temporal Query with Atomic or Array Returned Results**

For example, ones query the user's hobbies at March 3,2018. Then the query statement and result are shown as follows:

```
Query2: $.hobbies
Execute: $.hobbies[?(@.from = = "2018-01-03" && @.to = = "2018-01-03")].hob-
bies
Result: ["fish", "tennis", " yoga"]
```

What is more, when the filter time is not a time point but a time interval, the result may be more than one, for instance, when the filter of above query statement is a time interval [2018-01-03,2018-01-11], the query statement and result as follows:

Table 1. Query response times

Query statement	Query response time(/ms)
Query1	190
Query2	210
Query3	220
Query4	410
Query5	721

```
Query3: $.hobbies[?(@.from >= "2018-01-03" && @.to <= "2018-01-11")]
Execute: $.hobbies[?(@.from >= "2018-01-03" && @.to <= "2018-01-11")].hobbies
Result: ["fish", "tennis", " yoga"], ["fish", "yoga"]
```

3.   Temporal Query With Object Returned Results

For example, ones query the user's name at December 12, 2017. Then the query statement and result are shown as follows:

```
Query4: $. name[?(@.from == "2017-12-02" && @. to == "2017-12-02")]
Execute: $. name[?(@.from == "2017-12-02" && @. to == "2017-12-02")].name
Result: {"firstname":"Tom", "lastname":"Doe"}
```

Similarly, when the filter time is not a time point but a time interval, the result returned is the Cartesian product based on the time interval. For Instance, when the filter of above query statement is a time interval [2017-12-02,2018-01-01], the query statement and result as follows:

```
Query5: $. name[?(@.from >= "2017-12-02" && @. to <= "2018-01-01")]
Execute: $. name[?(@.from >= "2017-12-02" && @. to <= "2018-01-01")].name
Result: {"firstname":"Tom", "lastname":"Doe"}, {"firstname":"Alen",
"lastname":"Doe"}
```

Because of the limitations of JSONPath's functional structure,we can not complete more complicated queries, like projection, join and etc. The query language JSONiq that can execute more complicated query will discuss in our future work.

According to the implement of temporal JSONPath, the query response time of above Query1 to Query5 are given in Table 1.

Because no related temporal query language has been put forward, it is impossible to make a comparative analysis.

- **JSON Schema:** In XML, there are DTD or XML Schema to define and verify the XML document that XML Schema is more commonly used now for its advantages compared with DTD as follows:

1. It is one of the most important features to support data types, and DTD is all characters.
2. Its format has XML format, which can meet the needs of future expansion.
3. XML Schema support for namespaces.

In the JSON document, there is similarly a corresponding mechanism called JSON Schema to constrain and verify JSON document that checks whether the value conforms to the definition of JSON scheme. According to the draft of specification about JSON Schema, we can obtain the schema of Figure 10.

Be similar to XML schema, JSON Schema's format is also itself-JSON document, thus we can use JSON Trees model to represent the JSON Schema document. In the above JSON Schema document, firstly, the attribute "$schema" represents a unique schema, it may be in our located file system, also may be on the Internet. Next, the "title" and "type" represent the information about JSON object, then the attribute of "properties" represents what attribute the document object has, and the key-value pairs in the value of "properties" represents the schema of the attribute of the value. Finally, the value of attribute "properties" that represents what attribute must require. However, not all specifications in JSON Schema we have mentioned. Like "patternProperties" that represents the regular expression of the value, "minimum" and "maximum" that represents the minimum and maximal number value, and etc. Figure 11 shows the form for all keywords in JSON Schema.

However, with the change of information, the schema may also need to change. Like Figure 7, we add an attribute, "vip". Thus, the schema must be transformed to keep consistency with the document. We can also regard the schema document as a temporal JSON document because of JSON schema format. Thus, we can obtain the temporal JSON Schema as follows by our translation algorithm.

CONCLUSION AND FUTURE WORK

In this paper, we proposed a temporal JSON data model that draw lessons from JSON Trees model and Temporal XML model, which allows us to receive the document at any time point. In addition, the temporal JSON document translated from a temporal model that can reflect changes of the document. Furthermore, we investigated several issues on implements of our model, such as array value translation, consistency of time and JSON schema. Finally, we discuss and resolve the issues above.

Figure 10. Non-Temporal JSON Schema

```
{
    "$schema": "http://json-schema.org/draft-04/schema#",
    "title" : "Member",
    "type": "object", {
        "properties": {
                "name" :{ "id":" http://jsonschema.com/name",
            "type" : "string"
                },
                "age": { "id":" http://jsonschema.com/age"
            "type": "number"
        },
                "hobbies" :{ "id":" "http://jsonschema.com/hobbies",
            "type" : "array",
            "items":{ "type" : "string"}
                }
    },
    "require" :[ "name", "age", "hobbies"]
}
```

Figure 11. JSON Schema keywords

string Schemas	"type" : "string', "pattern": exp
number	"type":"number", "multipeOf" : i "minimum" : i, "maximum" ; i
boolean Schema	"type":boolean,
array Schema	"type": array, "items" :[$J_1,J_2... J_n$], "uniqueItems" : true , "additionalItem" : J
object Schema	"type":object , "required":[k1,$k_2...k_n$] "minProperties": i, "maxProperties":i "properties":{k_1:J_1, k_2:J_2... k_n:J_n} "patternProperties":{"e_1":J_1, "e_2":J_2..."e_n":J_n} "additionalProperties": J

Figure 12. Temporal JSON Schema

```
{
    "$schema":[{ "$schema":"http://json-schema.org/draft-04/schema#", "validtime":[2017-12-01,now]],
    "title":[{ "title": "Member",  "validtime":[2017-12-01,now]}],
    "type":[{ "type": "object",  "validtime":[2017-12-01,now]} ],
    "properties":[{ "properties":{
        "name":[{ "name":[{ "id":{ "id":"http://jsonschema.com/name",  "validtime":[2017-12-01,now]
                            "type":{ "tpye": "string", "validtime":[2017-12-01,now]}
                          }],
                "age":[{ "age":[{ "id":{ "id":"http://jsonschema.com/age",
                                        "validtime":[2017-12-01,now]
                                "type":{ "type":"number", "validtime":[2017-12-01,now]}}
                              }]
        "hobbies":[{ "hobbies":[{ "id" : { "id":"http://jsonschema.com/hobbies",
                                            "validtime":[2017-12-01,now]
                                "type":{ "type":"array", "validtime":[2017-12-01,now]}}
                              }]
        "vip":[{ "vip":[{ "id":{ "id":"http://jsonschema.com/vip",
                                "validtime":[2017-12-31,now]
                        "type":{ "type":"Boolean", "validtime":[2017-12-31,now]}}
                      }]
        },
        "validtime":[2017-12-01,now]
    }]
    "required":[{ "required":["name","age","hobbies"], "validtime":[2017-12-01,2017-12-31]  },
      { "required":["name","age","hobbies","vip"],"validtime":[2018-01-01,now]  }]
}
```

For the reason of the length of the paper, we do not specifically discuss the query language of temporal JSON document and optimized method. Thus, in the future, we plan to develop a query language by proposing an extension of the JSONip query language for retrieving information, and then put forward some indexing method to improve query efficiency.

REFERENCES

Ali, K. A., & Pokorný, J. (2009). *A comparison of XML-based temporal models. Advanced Internet Based Systems and Applications* (pp. 339–350). Berlin, Germany: Springer. doi:10.1007/978-3-642-01350-8_31

Amagasa, T., Yoshikawa, M., & Uemura, S. (2000). A data model for temporal XML documents. In *Proceedings of the 2000 International Conference on Database and Expert Systems Applications* (pp. 334-344). Berlin, Germany: Springer. 10.1007/3-540-44469-6_31

Bellazzi, R., Larizza, C., Bellazzi, R., & Bellazzi, R. (2005). Temporal data mining for the quality assessment of hemodialysis services. *Artificial Intelligence in Medicine*, *34*(1), 25–39. doi:10.1016/j.artmed.2004.07.010 PMID:15885564

Bhardwaj, N. D., & Bhardwaj, N. D. (2016). Comparative study of couchdb and mongodb – nosql document oriented databases. *International Journal of Computers and Applications*, 136(3), 24-26.

Boicea, A., Radulescu, F., & Agapin, L. I. (2012). MongoDB vs Oracle -- Database Comparison. In *Proceedings of the 2012 Third International Conference on Emerging Intelligent Data and Web Technologies*. IEEE. 10.1109/EIDWT.2012.32

Bourhis, P., Reutter, J. L., Suárez, F., & Vrgoč, D. (2017). JSON: data model, query languages and schema specification. In *Proceedings of the 36th ACM SIGMOD-SIGACT-SIGAI Symposium on Principles of Database Systems* (pp. 123-135). ACM. 10.1145/3034786.3056120

Bray, T. (2014). IETF RFC7159, The JavaScript Object Notation (JSON) Data Interchange Format. Retrieved from https://www.ietf.org/rfc/rfc7159.txt

Chen, X., & Petrounias, I. (1998). A framework for temporal data mining. *Proceedings of the 1998 International Conference on Database and Expert Systems Applications* (pp. 796-805). Berlin, Germany: Springer.

Chittaro, L., Combi, C., & Trapasso, G. (2003). Data mining on temporal data: A visual approach and its clinical application to hemodialysis. *Journal of Visual Languages and Computing*, *14*(6), 591–620. doi:10.1016/j.jvlc.2003.06.003

Clifford, J., & Croker, A. (1987). The historical relational data model (HRDM) and algebra based on lifespans. In *1987 IEEE Third International Conference on Data Engineering* (pp. 528-537). IEEE.

Combi, C. (2009). *Temporal object-oriented databases. In Encyclopedia of Database Systems* (pp. 2998–3004). Boston, MA: Springer.

Gadia, S. K., & Yeung, C. S. (1988). A generalized model for a relational temporal database. *SIGMOD Record*, *17*(3), 251–259. doi:10.1145/971701.50233

Grandi, F., Mandreoli, F., Tiberio, P., & Bergonzini, M. (2003). A temporal data model and management system for normative texts in XML format. In *Proceedings of the 5th ACM International Workshop on Web Information and Data Management* (pp. 29-36). ACM. 10.1145/956699.956706

Gu, F. Z., & Shen, B. (2012). Application study on JSON data exchange format in integration of Heterogeneous System. *Railway Computer Application*, *21*(2), 1–4.

Han, J. (2005). *Data Mining: Concepts and Techniques*. Morgan Kaufmann Publishers Inc.

Jensen, C. S., Clifford, J., Gadia, S. K., Segev, A., & Snodgrass, R. T. (1992). A glossary of temporal database concepts. *SIGMOD Record*, *21*(3), 35–43. doi:10.1145/140979.140996

Kitamoto, A. (2002). Spatio-temporal data mining for typhoon image collection. *Journal of Intelligent Information Systems*, *19*(1), 25–41. doi:10.1023/A:1015560319636

Knolmayer, G. F., & Myrach, T. (2001). Concepts of bitemporal database theory and the evolution of web documents. In *Proceedings of the 34th Annual Hawaii International Conference on System Sciences* (p. 10). IEEE. 10.1109/HICSS.2001.927091

Li, X., Liu, M., Ghafoor, A., & Sheu, P. C. (2010). A pattern-based temporal XML query language. In *Proceedings of the 2010 International Conference on Web Information Systems Engineering* (pp. 428-441). Berlin, Germany: Springer.

Lin, B., Chen, Y., Chen, X., & Yu, Y. (2012). Comparison between JSON and XML in Applications Based on AJAX. In *Proceedings of the 2012 International Conference on Computer Science and Service System* (pp. 1174-1177). IEEE Computer Society. 10.1109/CSSS.2012.297

Mendelzon, A. O., Rizzolo, F., & Vaisman, A. (2004). Indexing temporal XML documents. In *Proceedings of the Thirtieth International Conference on Very Large Data Bases* (pp. 216-227). VLDB Endowment.

Merelo-Guervós, J. J., Castillo, P. A., Laredo, J. L. J., Garcia, A. M., & Prieto, A. (2008). Asynchronous distributed genetic algorithms with Javascript and JSON. In *Proceedings of the 2008 IEEE Congress on Evolutionary Computation* (pp. 1372-1379). IEEE. 10.1109/CEC.2008.4630973

Mitsa, T. (2010). *Temporal Data Mining*. Chapman & Hall/CRC. doi:10.1201/9781420089776

Post, A. R., & Jr, H. J. (2008). Temporal data mining. *Clinics in Laboratory Medicine*, 28(1), 83–100. doi:10.1016/j.cll.2007.10.005 PMID:18194720

Sheth, A., Henson, C., & Sahoo, S. S. (2008). Semantic sensor web. *IEEE Internet Computing*, 12(4), 78–83. doi:10.1109/MIC.2008.87

Soewito, B., Isa, S. M., Iskandar, K., Gaol, F. L., & Kosala, R. (2017, February). Server for SQLite database: Multithreaded HTTP server with synchronized database access and JSON data-interchange. In *Proceedings of the 19th International Conference on Advanced Communication Technology* (pp. 786-790). IEEE.

Wang, D., Zhu, Y., & University, L. T. (2018). *Application of geojson in heterogeneous geographic information data integration. Geomatics & Spatial Information Technology.*

Wang, F., & Zaniolo, C. (2004). XBiT: an XML-based bitemporal data model. In *Proceedings of the 2004 International Conference on Conceptual Modeling* (pp. 810-824). Berlin, Germany: Springer. 10.1007/978-3-540-30464-7_60

Wang, F., Zhou, X., & Zaniolo, C. (2004). Temporal information management using XML. In *Proceedings of the 2004 International Conference on Conceptual Modeling* (pp. 858-859). Berlin, Germany: Springer. 10.1007/978-3-540-30464-7_72

Wei, H. C., & Elmasri, R. (2000). Schema versioning and database conversion techniques for bi-temporal databases. *Annals of Mathematics and Artificial Intelligence*, 30(1-4), 23–52. doi:10.1023/A:1016622202755

Zheng, L., Zhou, L., Zhao, X., Liao, L., & Liu, W. (2017). The Spatio-Temporal Data Modeling and Application Based on Graph Database. In *Proceedings of the 4th International Conference on Information Science and Control Engineering* (pp. 741-746). IEEE. 10.1109/ICISCE.2017.159

KEY TERMS AND DEFINITIONS

Schema: Different from the definition in database domain, the schema of JSON or XML represent the constraints and validation rules of the document, which means the structure of the relation in database model.

Temporal Attribute: Intuitively, temporal attributes are time data in the real world. But after the temporal attribute has been modeled, it represents the time data in the temporal model.

Temporal Date Model: Add the temporal attribute to traditional data model, XML data model, relation database data model, etc., that can obtain the corresponding temporal data model.

Chapter 8
Prediction of Uncertain Spatiotemporal Data Based on XML Integrated With Markov Chain

Luyi Bai
Northeastern University, China

Nan Li
Northeastern University, China

Chengjia Sun
Northeastern University, China

Yuan Zhao
Northeastern University, China

ABSTRACT

Since XML could benefit data management greatly and Markov chains have an advantage in data prediction, the authors study the methodology of predicting uncertain spatiotemporal data based on XML integrated with Markov chain. To accomplish this, first, the researchers devise an uncertain spatiotemporal data model based on XML. Then, the researchers put forward the method based on Markov chains to predict spatiotemporal data, which has taken the uncertainty into consideration. Next, the researchers apply the prediction method to meteorological field. Finally, the experimental results demonstrate the advantages the authors approach. Such a method of prediction could broaden the research field of spatiotemporal data, and provide a significant reference in the study of forecasting uncertain spatiotemporal data.

DOI: 10.4018/978-1-5225-8446-9.ch008

INTRODUCTION

Spatiotemporal data is a kind of special data which can contain time information and spatial information simultaneously (Pfoser, Tryfona, & Jensen, 2005). Spatiotemporal data has the characteristics of multi-source, large scale and fast update. It can describe the information of the object more accurately because it contains the attributes of time and space. It also can look up the characteristic of the stage behavior of the object in real-time, and can observe and predict the probability of the occurrence of a specific stage behavior with reference to the spatiotemporal association constraint model. Spatiotemporal database is a complex system to store and process spatiotemporal data, and it is an important branch in the field of database querying. However, spatial database and temporal database are independent of each other and there is no intersection of both research fields before 1990s. With the development of temporal database and spatial database, researchers found the relationship between the two kinds of databases and combined the two to study gradually, resulting in a spatiotemporal database. The content of spatiotemporal database is very complex and huge, which can be used to manage spatiotemporal data. It can express the time and change, and can solve the problem of storage and management of spatiotemporal data in general database. Therefore, the spatiotemporal database has more research value than other forms of databases, and can be applied to a wider range of fields, such as the meteorological information management systems (Kurte, Durbha, King, Younan, & Potnis, 2017), environmental changes monitoring (Li et al., 2017), vehicle detection and tracking (Huang, Lee, & Lin., 2017; Ramanathan, & Chen, 2017), video surveillance (Hampapur et al., 2005), online estimation of temperature (Xu, Li, & Liu, 2018), even gesture recognition (Zhang, Zhu, Shen, & Song, 2017), spatiotemporal distribution of birds (Ferreira et al., 2011), and so on.

Unfortunately, the uncertainty of spatiotemporal data is widespread and cannot be avoided due to the existence of data distortion, loss or network delay in the transmission process (Tossebro, & Nygård, 2002). Therefore, a series of works on uncertain spatial-temporal data emerge. Such as modeling, querying and predicting uncertain spatiotemporal data and so on. As for modeling, Yazici et al. (2001) introduce a semantic data modeling approach for spatiotemporal database applications, which utilizes unified modeling language (UML) for handling spatiotemporal information, uncertainty and fuzziness, especially at the conceptual level of database design; Bai et al. (2018) propose an uncertain spatiotemporal data model based on XML, and present a series of algebraic operations based on the model they proposed to capture uncertain spatiotemporal information; Emrich et al. (2012) model the uncertain object by a homogeneous Markov chain with an initial probabilistic density function. As for querying, Emrich et al. (2012) reduce all queries on the uncertain spatiotemporal object model to simple matrix multiplications, and present two approaches towards efficient query processing as well. They are called object-based approach and query-based approach, and the latter is more efficient. Along with window queries (Emrich, Kriegel, Mamoulis, Renz, & Zufle, 2012; Tao, Papadias, Sun, 2003), there are also range queries (Trajcevski, Choudhary, Wolfson, Ye, & Li, 2010), similarity queries (Niedermayer et al., 2013a) and kNN queries (Niedermayer et al., 2013b; Trajcevski, Tamassia, Ding, Scheuermann, & Cruz, 2009) can be solved using both proposed solution approaches (i.e. equivalent worlds and monte-carlo sampling). There are also event queries on probabilistic data streams (Ré, Letchner, Balazinksa, & Suci, 2008). However, the research on the prediction of uncertain spatiotemporal data has not received too much attention. There is a system that models spatiotemporal events through the combination of kernel density estimation for event distribution and seasonal trend decomposition by loess smoothing for temporal predictions (Maciejewski et al., 2011). There is also a congestion prediction for urban areas (Wang,

Zhou, 2017). But they are not appropriate for the prediction of meteorological fields. Bai et al. (2017) investigate the prediction based on the spatiotemporal XML model integrated with the grey dynamic model and applied to tropical storm, but their work ignored the uncertainty. The prediction of uncertain spatiotemporal data still merits further attention. As a result, the authors will focus on the prediction of uncertain spatiotemporal data in this chaper, and apply it to predict the trajectory of typhoon to reduce unnecessary damage.

In the aspect of data prediction, some prediction models are proposed, such as grey model, time series prediction model and Markov prediction model and so on. Grey system refers to a system with fuzzy levels and structure of the relationship, random dynamic changes and uncertain index data. Meanwhile, Not only known information is included in the grey system, but also unknown information or unascertained information is included. In the grey system theory, there are some data with the characteristic of the grey system behavior, which can be used to create the model (Deng, 1989). This model can describe the continuous changes of the inner thing of the grey system, which is called grey model (i.e. GM model). Grey model is a process to use a small amount of incomplete information for grey differential prediction modeling, which can make a long-term fuzzy description of the law of development of things. Time series prediction is a statistical prediction method, which studies the relationship between the prediction target and the evolution of the time process (Solow, 1994). According to the statistical regularity, it constructs the best mathematical model to fit $X(t)$. The prediction concentrates the time series information, simplifies the time series representation, and predicts the future with the best mathematical model. Markov chain is a discrete-time stochastic process in mathematical expression, whose time discontinuity corresponds to its state and situation at each moment (Rabiner, 1989). In the process of Markov chain prediction, the past (i.e. the historical state before the current moment) is irrelevant to the prediction of the future (i.e. the future state after the current moment) when the information of current state is given. The Markov chain model can be represented as a 3-tuple { S, P, Q }, where S is a state set of all possible states, which is non-empty; P is the probability transition matrix of state, which represents the probability matrix of different state changes; Q is the initial probability distribution, which refers to the probability of the current state of the object. This chapter devotes to the prediction of uncertain spatiotemporal data based on Markov model because of its excellent prediction performance.

Before the prediction, the researchers need to model the uncertain spatiotemporal data. For the sake of improving the management and application of uncertain spatiotemporal data, this chaper models uncertain spatiotemporal data based on XML to reduce the shortcomings of spatiotemporal data in some respects. XML (Extensible Markup Language), as a subset of extensible markup language and standard universal markup language, is a kind of markup language used to tag electronic files to make them structured (Bray et al., 1997). As the next generation of Internet language, XML plays an important role increasingly. At the same time, XML has been gradually used as a medium for data exchange and fusion because of its simplicity, readability and portability. XML tree structure and semi-structured features make XML have great advantages in data management. For this reason, XML can not only describe the content of the data, but also highlight the description of the data structure. Therefore, XML provides a great opportunity to study the uncertain spatiotemporal data model. In this chaper, the uncertain spatiotemporal data is modeled based on XML, and the tree structure of XML is used to manage the uncertain spatiotemporal data in a more standard way, which is beneficial to the following prediction.

In this chapter, the authors propose an uncertain spatiotemporal data model for prediction, which is based on XML integrated with Markov chain. The main contributions of this chapter as follows:

1.   An uncertain spatiotemporal XML model for prediction in this chapter is proposed;
2.   A prediction method based on Markov chain for uncertain spatiotemporal data is put forward;

The rest of the chapter is organized as follows: Section 2 is the basic knowledge. The modeling of uncertain spatiotemporal data is proposed in Section 3. Section 4 investigates the prediction method of uncertain spatiotemporal XML data. Section 5 is the application and evaluation of the forecasting method and Section 6 summarizes the chapter.

PREREQUISITE KNOWLEDGE

Given a discrete random process as a state space, the state at time t_0 is known, and the state after t_0 is independent of that before t_0, which only depends on the state at time t_0, the characteristic of that is called no aftereffect. The main principle can be summed up into two steps simply: the first step is to discretize and transform the data into several types; the second one is to calculate the relevant probability distribution types and analyze their changes to approximate the real evolutionary process. In general, the researchers can use the probability vector to describe the probability distribution of the attribute type at time t. For example, the transition between different types can be represented as a Markov one-step transition matrix of $k \times k$, and transition between the time to be predicted and the current time can be expressed as an n-step transition matrix. The final prediction results can be obtained through calculating the probability vector of the current time and the n-step transition matrix. The following is a detailed introduction through mathematical methods.

Definition 1 (Markov Chain): Given a discrete random sequence $\{X(n), n = 0, 1, 2, 3 \dots \}$, where the state space I is discrete and the parameter is non-negative. $\{X_n\}$ is the Markov chain if

$$P\left\{X_{n+1} = j \middle| X_0 = i_0, X_1 = i_1, \dots, X_n = i \right\} = P\left\{X_{n+1} = j, X_n = i\right\}$$

In order to describe $n + 1$-dimensional probability distribution in detail, two concepts are introduced as follows: initial probability $P\{X_0 = i_0\}$ and conditional probability $P\{X_{k+1} = j| X_k = i\}$. The initial probability is the probability of each state at the current time and the conditional probability is the probability that the next moment occurs in the case of the probability at the current moment. The transition probability from the state i at the time $k + 1$ to the state j at the next time is $p_{ij}(k)$, which is a one-step transition probability. If the state space of a Markov chain is finite and the number of states is assumed to be N, then the matrix of state probabilities is described as follows:

$$P(k) = \left[P_1(k) \quad P_2(k) \quad \cdots \quad P_N(k)\right]^T$$

The initial matrix is:

$$P(n) = \begin{bmatrix} P_1(n) & P_2(n) & \cdots & P_N(n) \end{bmatrix}^T$$

The one-step transition matrix is:

$$\mathrm{P}^{(1)} = \begin{bmatrix} P_{00} & P_{01} & \cdots & P_{0N} \\ P_{10} & P_{12} & \cdots & P_{1N} \\ \cdots & \cdots & \cdots & \cdots \\ P_{N0} & P_{N1} & \cdots & P_{NN} \end{bmatrix}$$

The probability of the final prediction can be represented by

$$\mathrm{P}(n+k) = P(n) \times P^{(k)} = \begin{bmatrix} \mathrm{P}_1(\mathrm{n}) & \mathrm{P}_2(\mathrm{n}) & \cdots & \mathrm{P}_N(\mathrm{n}) \end{bmatrix} \times \begin{bmatrix} P_{00} & P_{01} & \cdots & P_{0N} \\ P_{10} & P_{11} & \cdots & P_{1N} \\ \cdots & \cdots & \cdots & \cdots \\ P_{N0} & P_{N1} & \cdots & P_{NN} \end{bmatrix}^{(k)}$$

MODELING OF UNCERTAIN SPATIOTEMPORAL DATA BASED ON XML

The structure of XML document is an ordered tree with root node. In order to express the uncertain spatial-temporal data model clearly, the nodes are classified as root node, element node, uncertainty node, attribute node, value node, probability node and temporal node, respectively. In the process of modeling uncertain spatiotemporal XML data, nodes are represented by different shapes to distinguish the various types, as shown in Figure 1.

The XML document consists of the tree structure, so the researchers can regard the uncertain spatiotemporal data as an empty XML document tree. According to the characteristics of the uncertain spatiotemporal data, the authors put forward the following definitions:

Definition 2 (U, Uncertain Spatiotemporal Data): Defining an Uncertain spatiotemporal XML Data U as a 4-tuple USP = {OID, ATTR, UP, UT}, where
- *OID* depicts the historical change of uncertain spatiotemporal data;
- *ATTR* represents the attributes of uncertain spatiotemporal data;
- *UP* describes the position of uncertain spatiotemporal data;
- *UT* records the time of uncertain spatiotemporal data;

Changes of *OID* describe spatiotemporal objects change into other spatiotemporal objects. It can not only represent changing types of objects (i.e. creation, splitting, mergence and elimination), but also what the object comes from (i.e. precursor), and what the object becomes (i.e. successor). *ATTR* describes the attributes of spatiotemporal data, which contains general attributes and spatial attributes. In fact,

Figure 1. Node types and descriptions

Node type	Description	Symbol
Root node	There is only one root node in an XML document, which is the parent of other elements.	
Element node	An element node can act as the parent of other nodes, but its parent must be a root node or an element node.	
Uncertainty node	As an element of the uncertain spatio-temporal data, the uncertainty of the data is represented by the probability in the uncertain spatio-temporal model.	
Attribute node	It is usually paired with its parent node.	
Value node	Leaf node, including the number or text.	
Probability node	The range of probabilities is [0, 1]. It is usually paired with uncertainty node.	
Temporal node	It is used to describe the temporal attribute of spatio-temporal object.	

it depicts the static attributes rather than the dynamic ones. There may be one or more attributes in a spatiotemporal object and the attributes may be uncertain. The position of the uncertain spatiotemporal data can be obtained from the *UP*, and *UT* records the time of the uncertain spatiotemporal data.

As shown in Figure 2, not only the object after changing but also the type of change needs to be proposed from one spatiotemporal object to another.

Definition 3 (OID, Changing Types of Uncertain Spatiotemporal XML data): Change types of uncertain spatiotemporal XML data is a 4-tuple CH(O) = {pre, sue, type, T}, where

- *Pre* is the spatiotemporal object before changing, that is, by whom the change occurs. If the current time is *t*, *Pre* is the state of the spatiotemporal object at *t* - 1.
- *Sue* is the spatiotemporal object after changing, which is the state of the spatiotemporal object that changed into at *t* + 1.
- *Type* is the type of change (i.e. creation, splitting, mergence, and elimination), represented by *c*, *s*, *m*, and *e* in Figure 2, respectively.
- *T* is the attribute of an object that represents the time point or time interval (i.e. start time: *Ts*, end time: *Te*)

Attributes of uncertain spatiotemporal XML objects (*ATTR*) are general attributes, which are composed of defined general attributes and uncertain general attributes. The general attributes include the time of the spatiotemporal objects and so on. Uncertain attributes refer to the uncertainty of spatiotemporal

Figure 2. The historical change structure of the uncertain spatiotemporal object

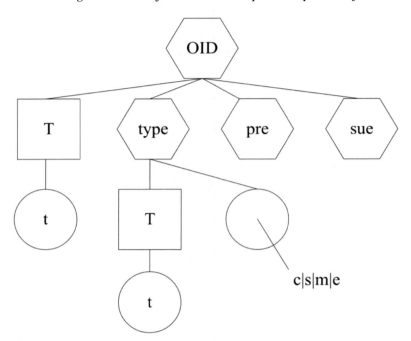

data, such as the distortion or loss of spatiotemporal data in the transmission process, the changes of spatiotemporal objects and so on. The nodes of the uncertain attributes are described in Figure 1. The overall description of the general attributes is shown in Figure 3, where *Patt* represents the value of the uncertain attribute (i.e. conjunction and disjunction); *Disjunctive* means to select one of them; *Conjunctive* takes their union. The general attribute is composed of the definite time attribute and the uncertain attribute. The time attribute includes the time node and the value of the time, while the uncertain attribute includes the value category of the uncertain attribute (i.e. conjunction and disjunction), the uncertain probability node and the value of it.

Definition 4 (UP, Position of Uncertain Spatiotemporal XML Data): Position of uncertain spatiotemporal XML data UP is a 5-tuple {T, P, X, Y, Q}, where
- *T* is the time of uncertain spatiotemporal XML data objects;
- *P* is the probability of uncertainty of spatiotemporal data;
- *X* and *Y* contribute to depict the coordinates of position of the object;
- *Q* records the probability of change in the formation of the model.

In this chapter, the vector data of points, lines and surfaces are represented by coordinate system. For a point, the authors use the coordinates of the point. For a line, the coordinates of the two endpoints are used to represent the line. For a surface, the shape of a spatial object is abstracted and approximated, then represented by a minimal boundary rectangle (MBR) approximately.

Definition 5 (Point): For a spatiotemporal object at the position of a point O, the coordinates of that position can be represented as (x_o, y_o).

Figure 3. The general attribute structure of uncertain spatiotemporal object

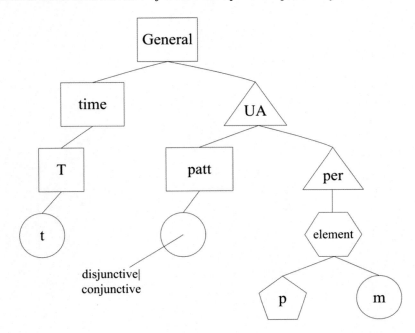

Definition 6 (Line): For a spatiotemporal object at the position of a line *AB*, it can be represented by the endpoint coordinates at both ends of the line. If the coordinates of the left endpoint *A* is (x_l, y_l) and the right endpoint *B* is (x_r, y_r), the position of the object can be represented as (x_l, y_l), (x_r, y_r).

Definition 7 (Region): For a spatiotemporal object at the position of a region α, if there are two points $L(x_a, y_a)$, $R(x_b, y_b)$ in α, where $x_a = \min\{x_1, x_2 \ldots x_n\}$, $y_a = \min\{y_1, y_2 \ldots y_n\}$, $x_b = \max\{x_1, x_2 \ldots x_n\}$ and $y_b = \max\{y_1, y_2 \ldots y_n\}$, then the position of the region can be represented as (x_a, y_a), (x_b, y_b).

As shown in Figure 4, the position structure of an uncertain spatiotemporal object is represented by a tree structure. The position is denoted by a defined time and other uncertain factors. Uncertain factors include changes in the abscissa and ordinate of different spatiotemporal objects, the minimum value of the abscissa and the ordinate of spatial position are *xstart* and *ystart*, respectively, and the maximum value of the abscissa and the ordinate are *xend* and *yend*, respectively. When the spatial position of the object is a straight line or a region, the method above mentioned can describe the position of the object better. If the spatial position of the object is a point, the position of *xstart* is the same as *xend* and *ystart* is the same as *yend*. In addition to the uncertainty of the position, there is the uncertainty of the data and changes. In order to describe the distortion and loss of the uncertain spatiotemporal data caused by the uncertain factors in the changing process, *P* is used to indicate the probability of the object appearing at this position.

Figure 4. The position structure of the uncertain Spatiotemporal object

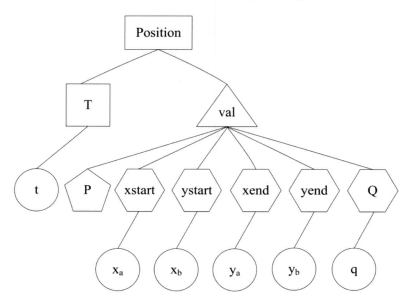

Figure 5 is the representation of the structure of XML data tree, in which: *OID* denotes the historical changes of uncertain spatiotemporal data, including the nodes before changing and after in addition to the types of changes; *ATTR* describes the attributes of uncertain spatiotemporal data, including general attributes and uncertain attributes of time and space, where spatial position is represented by (*xstart*, *ystart*), (*xend*, *yend*). *T* depicts the time of the uncertain spatiotemporal data; *P* represents the uncertain attributes.

Figure 5. The uncertain Spatiotemporal data model

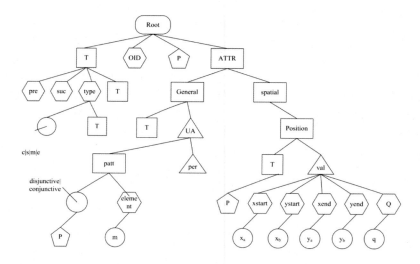

PREDICTION OF UNCERTAIN SPATIAL-TEMPORAL XML DATA BASED ON MARKOV MODEL

Markov Chain Prediction Based on Spatiotemporal XML Data

In the prediction process, Definition 4 is used to specify the position of the spatiotemporal object, where Q is an element added to the uncertain spatiotemporal XML data model, aims to represents the uncertainty when there are errors in the prediction process base on Markov chain.

The storage of data is very important because that Markov prediction needs a large amount of data. In this chapter, the position of spatiotemporal object is stored in the database in order by time T. As shown in Figure 6, the *FIFO* (first in first out) strategy is used when the data is being stored and fetched. The storage of each data called position, which consists of time, probability, the position of spatiotemporal object at certain time and the possibility of a change in the location of the spatiotemporal object. Using these data to predict, and finally the authors can get the predicted position of the spatiotemporal object, which can be applied to other aspects after improving the Definition 4.

The Method of Prediction

Because the form of the position of different objects at a certain time is different, its coordinate representation is also different, such as Definition 5 to Definition 7. The method of prediction is on the basis that the object's position is a point in this chapter, and the other cases are similar to this method. The process of predicting uncertain spatiotemporal data based on XML integrated with Markov chain is shown in Figure 7.

The method of prediction in detail as follows:

Integrating the Changes of the Position of Spatiotemporal Object

This is a numbered term. First of all, the data should be processed. The data extracted is a 5-tuple $\{T, P, X, Y, Q\}$, including time, probability, abscissa and ordinate of the object at the certain time (i.e. spatial position) and the probability of change, which can't be used for prediction directly. It can predict the moving trend of spatiotemporal objects in the future in virtue of the prediction process is based on the changes of the position of spatiotemporal object. The researchers should extract the abscissa and ordinate of the spatial positions of all the stored data and organize them in time order. It is noted that the researchers only need to organize the changes of the two adjacent moments, which is from time t_i to t_{i+1} (the abscissa and ordinate of the time t_i are x_i and y_i, respectively).

Figure 6. The access procedure of uncertain Spatiotemporal database

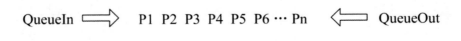

QueueIn $\implies$ P1   P2   P3   P4   P5   P6 $\cdots$ Pn $\impliedby$ QueueOut

Figure 7. The prediction process of the spatiotemporal data based on XML integrated with Markov chain

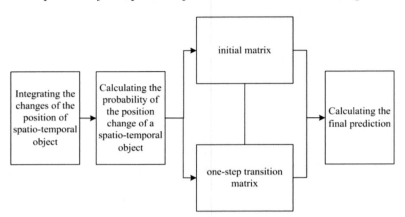

As shown in Table 1, where *A* represents the change of the abscissa *x* of the spatiotemporal object, a_1 depicts the number of changes of the abscissa *x* from position 1 to n, including a_{11}, a_{12}, a_{13}, ..., a_{1n}, which indicate the number of changes of abscissa *x* from position 1 to 1, from position 1 to 2, ..., from position 1 to n, respectively. a_2, a_3, ..., a_n are similar, too. B represents the change of the ordinate *y* of the spatiotemporal object, and b_1 represents the number of changes of the ordinate *y* from position 1 to n, including b_{11}, b_{12}, b_{13}, ..., b_{1n}, which depict the number of changes of ordinate *y* from position 1 to 1, from position 1 to 2, from position 1 to n, respectively. b_2, b_3, ..., b_n are similar, too.

Calculating the Probability of the Position Change of a Spatiotemporal Object

According to the change of the position of the spatiotemporal object in the previous step, the probability of each change in the abscissa and ordinate of the spatiotemporal object is calculated and put into a matrix, which is a one-step transition matrix. The one-step transition matrix is used to calculate the state of the spatiotemporal object at next time. When the difference between the calculated time and the current time are two time units, the two-step transition matrix is brought in, and so on. The probability is the ratio of each change number to all changes, which means to calculate the probability of n different changes of the abscissa and ordinate of the spatiotemporal object from time t_i to another time t_j.

As shown in Table 2, for the spatiotemporal object, *O* represents the probability of the change of abscissa *x*, o_1 represents the probability of the abscissa *x* from position 1 to n, and o_{11}, o_{12}, o_{13}, ..., o_{1n} indicate the probability of the abscissa *x* from position 1 to 1, from position 1 to 2, ..., from position 1 to n, respectively. o_2, o_3, ..., o_n are similar as well; P denotes the probability of the change of ordinate *y*,

Table 1. The position changes of spatiotemporal data

A	B
$a_{1:}$ $x_1 \rightarrow x_n$, n = 1.2......n	$b_{1:}$ $y_1 \rightarrow y_n$, n = 1.2......n
$a_{2:}$ $x_2 \rightarrow x_n$, n = 1.2......n	$b_{2:}$ $y_2 \rightarrow y_n$, n = 1.2......n
...	...
$a_{n:}$ $x_n \rightarrow x_n$, n = 1.2......n	$b_{n:}$ $y_n \rightarrow y_n$, n = 1.2......n

p_1 denotes the probability of the ordinate y from position 1 to n, and $p_{11}, p_{12}, p_{13}, \ldots, p_{1n}$ denote the probability of the ordinate y from position 1 to 1, from position 1 to 2, ..., from position 1 to n, respectively. $p_2, p_3, \ldots, p_n$ are similar, too.

Calculating the Final Prediction

Finally, for the spatiotemporal object, representing the abscissa and ordinate of the spatial position at the current time as an initial matrix, respectively; calculating the initial matrix and the one-step transition matrix as step (2), then the authors will get the final prediction of the spatial position. If the predicted object is the next moment of the current time, the predicted result is the product of the initial matrix and the one-step transition matrix. If the difference between the time to be predicted and the current time are two time units, the space position of the spatiotemporal object to be predicted is the product of the two-step transition matrix and the initial matrix. By analogy, the predicted result is the product of the initial matrix and the n-step transition matrix (where the n-step transition matrix is the nth-power of the one-step transition matrix) when the predicted spatiotemporal object is the nth time after the current time. After improving the 5-tuple of the predicted spatiotemporal object, it can be applied to other fields.

$$
P_x^{(1)} = \begin{bmatrix} m_{11} & m_{12} & \cdots & m_{1n} \\ m_{21} & m_{22} & \cdots & m_{2n} \\ \cdots & \cdots & \cdots & \cdots \\ m_{n1} & m_{n2} & \cdots & m_{nn} \end{bmatrix} \quad P_y^{(1)} = \begin{bmatrix} n_{11} & n_{12} & \cdots & n_{1n} \\ n_{21} & n_{22} & \cdots & n_{2n} \\ \cdots & \cdots & \cdots & \cdots \\ n_{n1} & n_{n2} & \cdots & n_{nn} \end{bmatrix}
$$

Result of calculation:

$$
P_n = \vec{P} \, P \left(t_n - t_m \right)
$$

Table 2. The probability of position change of the uncertain spatiotemporal data

O	$x_1 \rightarrow x_n, n = 1.2\ldots\ldots n, o_1 = \{z \vert z = a_n/a_1, n = 1.2\ldots\ldots n\}$
	$x_2 \rightarrow x_n, n = 1.2\ldots\ldots n, o_2 = \{z \vert z = a_n/a_2, n = 1.2\ldots\ldots n\}$
	$\ldots$
	$x_n \rightarrow x_n, n = 1.2\ldots\ldots n, o_n = \{z \vert z = a_n/a_n, n = 1.2\ldots\ldots n\}$
P	$y_1 \rightarrow y_n, n = 1.2\ldots\ldots n, p_1 = \{z \vert z = b_n/b_1, n = 1.2\ldots\ldots n\}$
	$y_2 \rightarrow y_n, n = 1.2\ldots\ldots n, p_2 = \{z \vert z = b_n/b_2, n = 1.2\ldots\ldots n\}$
	$\ldots$
	$y_n \rightarrow y_n, n = 1.2\ldots\ldots n, p_n = \{z \vert z = b_n/b_n, n = 1.2\ldots\ldots n\}$

Given the initial probability distribution $\vec{P}$, for the spatiotemporal position of the object, $P_x^{(1)}$ represents the one-step transition matrix of the change of the abscissa, and $P_y^{(1)}$ represents the one-step transition matrix of the change of the ordinate. Where t_n is the moment to predict, t_m is the current moment and $p(t_n - t_m)$ depicts the *m-n* step transition matrix from time t_m to t_n.

The general prediction process is described as following expression *FLWOR*:

```
<positions>
{
For $posi  at $posi/T:=ti  in doc (" positions,xml") /positions/position
Let $posi/val/xend-position/val/xstart:=xi
Let $posi/val/yend-position/val/ystart:=yi
For $posi  at $posi/T:=tj  in doc("positions,xml") /positions/position
Let $posi/val/xend-position/val/xstart:=xj
Let $posi/val/yend-position/val/ystart:=yj
Where xj=xi*q
Where yj=yi*q
Return
<position>  xj = "{posi/val/xend-posi/val/xstart}"
yj = "{posi/val/yend-posi/val/ystart}">
<position>
}
</positions>
```

Examples

The authors will explain the prediction process in detail with an example, and the spatiotemporal data is shown in Table 3.

Table 3. The uncertain spatiotemporal data

T	T_1	T_2	T_3	T_4	T_5	T_6
X	1	3	2	1	1	2
Y	2	2	3	2	4	3
P	0.80	0.70	0.90	0.80	0.80	0.70
T	T_7	T_8	T_9	T_{10}	T_{11}	
X	1	2	2	3	1	
Y	2	3	3	2	3	
P	0.90	0.80	0.80	0.70	0.90	

First, the X, Y, P and T in Table 3 are improvements of five-tuple $\{T, P, X, Y, Q\}$ in Definition 4, where X, Y are used to denote the spatial position of the spatiotemporal object, T is used to represent the time and P is used to record the uncertainty. The element in the XML document can be expressed as follows:

```xml
<?xml version = "1.0"?>
<positions>
<position T = "t1">
<val p = 0.80>
<x>1</x>
<y>2</y>
<position T = "t2">
<val p = 0.70>
<x>3</x>
<y>2</y>
 <position T = "t3">
<val p = 0.90>
<x>2</x>
<y>3</y>
<position T = "t4">
<val p = 0.80>
<x>1</x>
<y>2</y>
<position T = "t5">
<val = 0.80>
<x>1</x>
<y>4</y>
<position T = "t6">
<val = 0.70>    <x>2</x>
<y>3</y>
<position T = "t7">
<val = 0.90>
<x>1</x>
<y>2</y>
<position T = "t8">
<val = 0.80>
<x>2</x>
<y>3</y>
<position T = "t9">
<val p = 0.80>
<x>2</x>
<y>3</y>
<position T = "t10">
<val = 0.70>
<x>3</x>
```

```
<y>2</y>
<position T = "t₁₁">
<val = 0.90>
<x>1</x>
<y>3</y>
</position>
</positions>
```

Then, according to the method of prediction presented in Section 4.2, the data in Table 3 are calculated as follows:

1. Processing data x and y separately, the changes of x and y from the last time to the next time and the times of various changes are shown in Table 4.
2. Calculating the probabilities of changes in x and y, respectively, as shown in Table 5.
3. Representing the initial matrix and one-step transition matrix of x and y, respectively, and calculating the spatial position at time t_{12}.

The initial matrix of the abscissa x is:

$$\vec{P}_x = \begin{bmatrix} 1 & 0 & 0 \end{bmatrix}$$

The one-step transition matrix of the abscissa x is:

$$P_x^{(1)} = \begin{bmatrix} 0.1 & 0.2 & 0.1 \\ 0.2 & 0.1 & 0.1 \\ 0.1 & 0.1 & 0 \end{bmatrix}$$

Table 4. The position change of example

X	Y
x = 1→x = 1, 1 time; x = 1→x = 2, 2 times x = 1→x = 3, 1 time; x = 2→x = 1, 2 times x = 2→x = 2, 1 time; x = 2→x = 3, 1 time x = 3→x = 1, 1 time	y = 2→y = 2, 1 time; y = 2→y = 3, 3 times y = 2→y = 4, 1 time; y = 3→y = 2, 3 times y = 3→y = 3, 1 time; y = 4→y = 3, 1 times

Table 5. The probability of position change

P_X	P_Y
P(x = 1→x = 1) = 0.1 P(x = 1→x = 2) = 0.2 P(x = 1→x = 3) = 0.1 P(x = 2→x = 1) = 0.2 P(x = 2→x = 3) = 0.1 P(x = 3→x = 1) = 0.1 P(x = 3→x = 2) = 0.1	P(y = 2→y = 2) = 0.1 P(y = 2→y = 3) = 0.3 P(y = 2→y = 4) = 0.1 P(y = 3→y = 2) = 0.3 P(y = 3→y = 3) = 0.1 P(y = 4→y = 3) = 0.1

The probability matrix of abscissa x at time t_{12} is:

$$P_x^{12} = \vec{P}_x P_x^{(1)} = \begin{bmatrix} 1 & 0 & 0 \end{bmatrix} \times \begin{bmatrix} 0.1 & 0.2 & 0.1 \\ 0.2 & 0.1 & 0.1 \\ 0.1 & 0.1 & 0 \end{bmatrix} = \begin{bmatrix} 0.1 & 0.2 & 0.1 \end{bmatrix}$$

The probability of the abscissa $x = 1$ is 0.1, the probability of $x = 2$ is 0.2, and the probability of $x = 3$ is 0.1. Therefore, the abscissa of the spatial position is $x = 2$ at the time.

The initial matrix of ordinate y is:

$$\vec{P}_y = \begin{bmatrix} 0 & 1 & 0 \end{bmatrix}$$

The one-step transition matrix of the ordinate y is:

$$P_y^{(1)} = \begin{bmatrix} 0.1 & 0.333 & 0.1 \\ 0.333 & 0.1 & 0 \\ 0 & 0.1 & 0 \end{bmatrix}$$

The probability matrix of ordinate y at time t_{12} is:

$$P_y^{12} = \vec{P}_y P_y^{(1)} = \begin{bmatrix} 0 & 1 & 0 \end{bmatrix} \times \begin{bmatrix} 0.1 & 0.333 & 0.1 \\ 0.333 & 0.1 & 0 \\ 0 & 0.1 & 0 \end{bmatrix} = \begin{bmatrix} 0.333 & 0.1 & 0.1 \end{bmatrix}$$

The probability of the ordinate of $y = 2$ is 0.333, the probability of $y = 3$ is 0.1, and the probability of $y = 4$ is 0.1. Therefore, the ordinate of the spatial position is $y = 2$ at the time.

Finally, applying this example to the expression FLWOR proposed in Section 4.3, and the prediction process as follows:

```
<positions>
{
For $posi  at $posi/T:=t₁₁ in doc (" positions,xml") /positions/position
Let $posi/val/x:=x₁₁
Let $posi/val/y:=y₁₁
For $posi  at $posi/T:=t₁₂ in doc("positions,xml") /positions/position
Let $posi/val/x:=x₁₂
Let $posi/val/y:=y₁₂
Where x₁₂=x₁₁*pₓ⁽¹⁾
Where y₁₂=y₁₁*p_y⁽¹⁾
```

```
Return
<position>  x_12="{posi/val/x}"
Y_12="{posi/val/y}">
<position>
}
</positions>
```

EVALUATIONS

In this chapter, the authors use an example to verify the prediction of the uncertain spatiotemporal data model based on XML integrated with Markov chain proposed in Section 3. By using MATLAB software to express the prediction results with images, comparing the real value with the prediction value and analyzing the error. In the meantime, the accuracy of the prediction of Markov chain model in uncertain spatial-temporal XML data will be tested. Besides, the authors also verify the characteristic rules of the prediction.

Experimental Environment

Typhoon is the typical spatial-temporal data with two major attributes which are space and time. Its occurrence track has a certain rule, which is very suitable for the verification of this chapter. The real track of typhoon Nicole as Figure 8 shows [27].

Table 6 shows the data of typhoon monitoring.

Figure 8. The path of typhoon Nicole

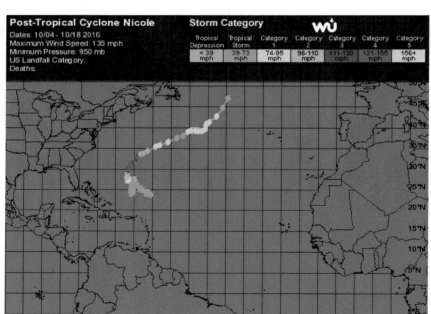

Table 6. The data of typhoon monitoring

Date	Time	Lat	Lon	Date	Time	Lat	Lon
Oct/04/2016	1500 GMT	23.8	-60.4	Oct/11/2016	1500 GMT	27.3	-65.9
Oct/04/2016	2100 GMT	24.1	-61.1	Oct/11/2016	2100 GMT	27.4	-66.4
Oct/05/2016	0300 GMT	24.2	-61.3	Oct/12/2016	0300 GMT	27.3	-66.6
Oct/05/2016	0900 GMT	24.3	-61.8	Oct/12/2016	0900 GMT	27.9	-67.0
Oct/05/2016	1500 GMT	25.0	-62.8	Oct/12/2016	1500 GMT	28.4	-66.9
Oct/05/2016	2100 GMT	25.3	-63.5	Oct/12/2016	2100 GMT	29.2	-66.6
Oct/06/2016	0300 GMT	26.0	-64.1	Oct/13/2016	0300 GMT	30.1	-66.4
Oct/06/2016	0900 GMT	26.5	-64.7	Oct/13/2016	0900 GMT	31.1	-65.8
Oct/06/2016	1500 GMT	26.8	-64.8	Oct/13/2016	1500 GMT	32.3	-64.6
Oct/06/2016	2100 GMT	27.5	-65.1	Oct/13/2016	2100 GMT	33.6	-63.2
Oct/07/2016	0300 GMT	27.4	-65.2	Oct/14/2016	0300 GMT	34.4	-61.2
Oct/07/2016	0900 GMT	27.3	-65.2	Oct/14/2016	0900 GMT	35.4	-59.2
Oct/07/2016	1500 GMT	27.5	-65.3	Oct/14/2016	1500 GMT	35.8	-58.0
Oct/07/2016	2100 GMT	27.0	-65.2	Oct/14/2016	2100 GMT	36.5	-55.7
Oct/08/2016	0300 GMT	26.3	-65.3	Oct/15/2016	0300 GMT	37.4	-53.3
Oct/08/2016	0900 GMT	25.9	-65.6	Oct/15/2016	0900 GMT	38.1	-51.6
Oct/08/2016	1500 GMT	25.2	-65.7	Oct/15/2016	1500 GMT	39.0	-50.3
Oct/08/2016	2100 GMT	24.8	-65.8	Oct/15/2016	2100 GMT	39.4	-49.4
Oct/09/2016	0300 GMT	24.4	-65.7	Oct/16/2016	0300 GMT	39.4	-48.3
Oct/09/2016	0900 GMT	24.3	-65.7	Oct/16/2016	0900 GMT	39.2	-47.7
Oct/09/2016	1500 GMT	24.0	-65.4	Oct/16/2016	1500 GMT	39.1	-46.6
Oct/09/2016	2100 GMT	24.2	-65.3	Oct/16/2016	2100 GMT	39.7	-45.6
Oct/10/2016	0300 GMT	24.4	-65.3	Oct/17/2016	0300 GMT	40.5	40.340
Oct/10/2016	0900 GMT	25.0	-65.2	Oct/17/2016	0900 GMT	41.0	-45.2
Oct/10/2016	1500 GMT	25.7	-65.2	Oct/17/2016	1500 GMT	41.4	-44.6
Oct/10/2016	2100 GMT	26.3	-65.4	Oct/17/2016	2100 GMT	42.7	-42.6
Oct/11/2016	0300 GMT	26.8	-65.5	Oct/18/2016	0300 GMT	44.8	-41.0
Oct/11/2016	0900 GMT	27.1	-65.9	Oct/18/2016	0900 GMT	47.1	-39.5

Experiments

The experiments in this section is composed of two parts, the first one is the test of the whole object, including error analysis and so on; the second one is to decompose the typhoon into parts and analyze the accuracy of prediction of uncertain spatiotemporal XML data based on the Markov chain in detail.

The First Part of Experiments

Inputting the code of the Markov chain into the MATLAB software through the data in Table 6, and the researchers will get Figure 9. The abscissa is the longitude of the track of typhoon, the ordinate is the latitude, the blue curve is the real track of the typhoon, and the red curve is the track predicted by the Markov chain. From Figure 9 to Figure10, they show some difference between the two curves in certain places, which need to be further analyzed.

Figure 10 (a) is the analysis of the latitude residual analysis in the spatial position of the typhoon, and Figure10 (b) is the longitude residual analysis, which show the error of the position of the typhoon in latitude and longitude, respectively. The circle indicates the difference between predicted value and real value. The green data is normal and more accurate, while the red ones indicate the abnormal data which shows that there are some errors in the prediction. The vertical lines in the image represent the confidence interval of the residuals. When the confidence interval is at both sides of the zero, the data is more accurate. Otherwise, the data accuracy is low and abnormal when the confidence interval is at one side of the zero.

The Second Part of Experiments

Because of the large amount of data to predict, it is hard to determine the relationship between the real path and the predicted path of a typhoon in an image accurately. In the meantime, there are some errors between the predicted path and the real one of typhoon in Figure 9. Therefore, the authors discuss data of the path of typhoon in groups. The parts with obvious errors and the parts with small errors are analyzed separately. The researchers divide the data into four groups, which are 1-35, 36-45, 46-51 and 52-57, respectively. Each group of data is reconstructed by MATLAB to compare the real track of typhoon with the forecast one, and generate the comparison and residual charts. Compared with Figure

Figure 9. The comparison between the real path and predictive path of the typhoon

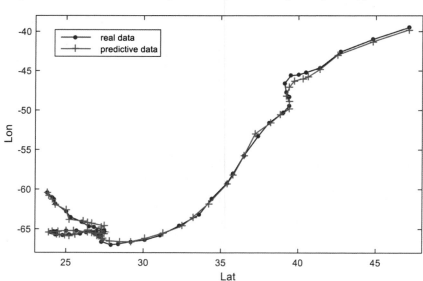

Figure 10. The residual analysis of prediction

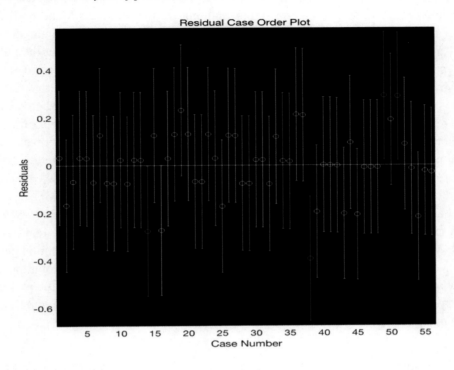

(a)

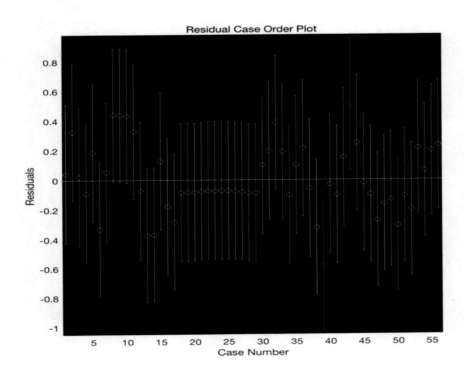

9, it is more clear and intuitionistic and each group can carry on analysis independently, which makes the experiment more credible. At last, the authors summarize the problems found in different groups, find the causes of the error and explore the accuracy of Markov chain prediction model.

Figure 11 and Figure12 are contrast graphs and residual analysis graphs about the predicted values and real of typhoon data in the first group. Comparing with the real typhoon track, the uncertain spatio-temporal XML data of typhoon track predicted by Markov chain have obvious error. The real track of this typhoon is more fluctuant, unstable and reiterative. The degree of coincidence between the predicted track and the real track of typhoon is lower. At the same time, the difference between some of the real data and the predicted data in the residual analysis chart is larger. Therefore, a conclusion can be drawn: The more the real path of typhoon fluctuates, the more unstable it is, and the worse the forecast accuracy is.

Then the researchers analyze the rest three groups of data and discuss whether the conclusions are universal and credible or not.

Figure 13 and Figure 14 are the images generated by the second group of data in MATLAB. From Figure 13, it can be seen that the predicted path of typhoon coincides with the real track of Markov chain model. Meanwhile, it is observed that the track of this group of the typhoon is gentle relatively and holding a stable upward trend. Figure 14 shows residual analysis maps of longitude and latitude, there are few abnormal points in the prediction and the residual value between the predicted data and the real is very small. So the authors can draw a conclusion: the more stable and regular the real path of typhoon, the more accurate the prediction.

Figure 11. The comparison of predicted values with real values of typhoon data in the first group

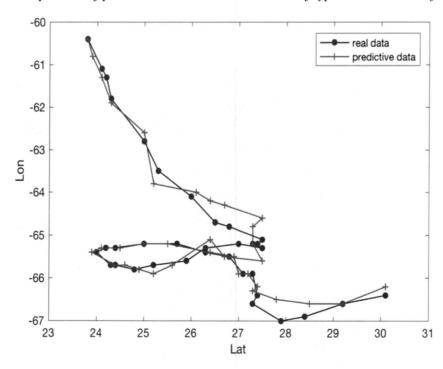

Figure 12. The residual analysis of typhoon data in the first group

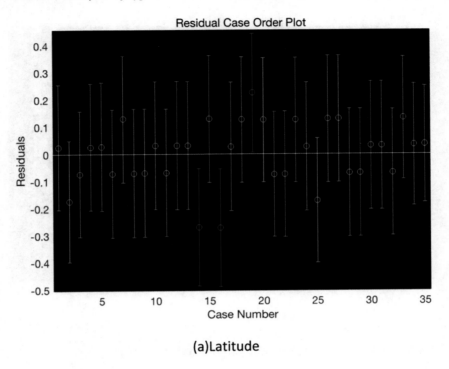

(a)Latitude

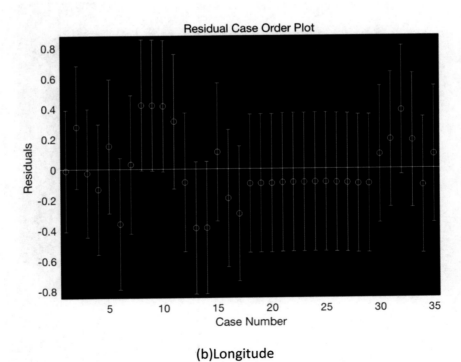

(b)Longitude

Figure 13. The comparison of predicted values with real values of typhoon data in the second group

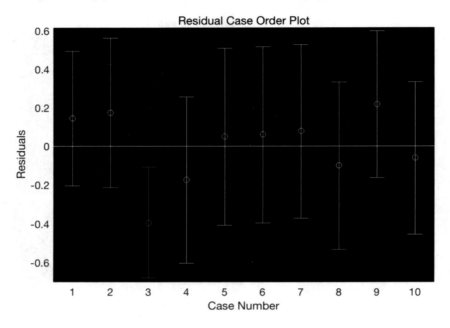

Figure 14. The residual analysis of typhoon data in the second group

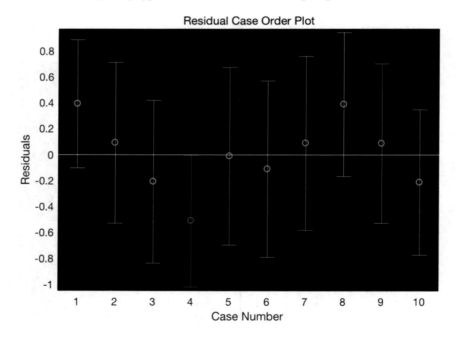

Figure 15 and Figure 16 are the images generated by data in the third group. Figure 15 shows a comparison between the predicted track of a typhoon and the real. There is a big gap between the two curves, and the residual value between the predicted value and the real of some data is also large. The path of this group is more fluctuant and unstable than the second one, and the accuracy of prediction is worse. Therefore, a conclusion can be drawn: the more the real path of typhoon fluctuates, the more unstable it is, and the worse the forecast accuracy is, which proves that the conclusion is universal.

Figure 17 and Figure 18 are the images generated by the last group of data in MATLAB. Figure 17 is a comparison of the data predicted by the Markov model with the real data. The two curves are highly similar, and the same with corresponding data on them. Figure 18 is the residual analysis of the last group, from which only one abnormal point has been found, and the residual value between the predicted data and the real data is very small. The track of this group is similar to the second one; both of them have steady upward trends without obvious fluctuation. Therefore, the fourth group has verified the conclusion: the more stable and regular the real path of typhoon, the more accurate the prediction.

ANALYSIS AND CONCLUSION

Through the Markov chain prediction model generated by four groups of data in MATLAB, the relationship between the data can be ascertained from the comparison of the predicted track with the real track and the graphs of the residual analysis, so the conclusion with more credibility can be drawn.

In Section 5.2, two hypotheses are proposed through error analysis of data in the first group and the in the second, then using the data in the third group and in the fourth to validate the hypotheses. The track of typhoon from the data in the first group is similar to that from the third. Both of them are fluctuant and unstable, especially in the first group. They are also reiterative, which has impact on the

Figure 15. The comparison of predicted values with real values of typhoon data in the third group

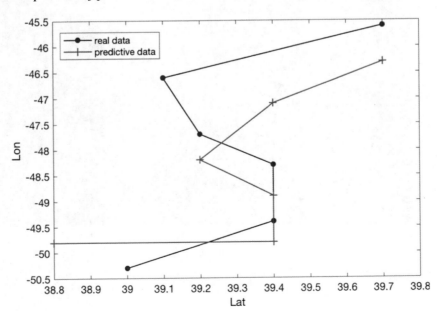

Figure 16. The residual analysis of typhoon data in the third group

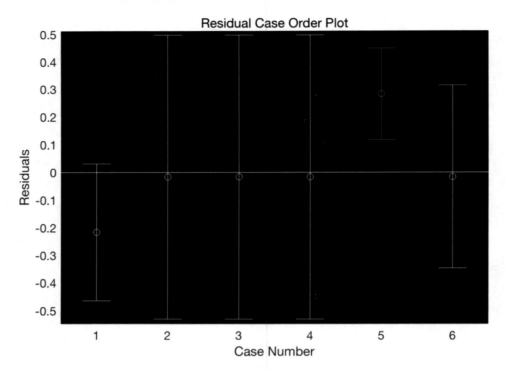

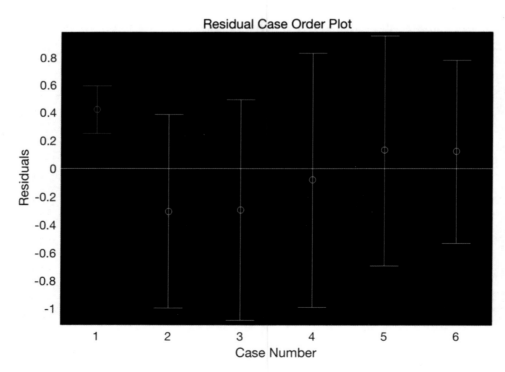

Figure 17. The comparison of predicted values with real values of typhoon data in the fourth group

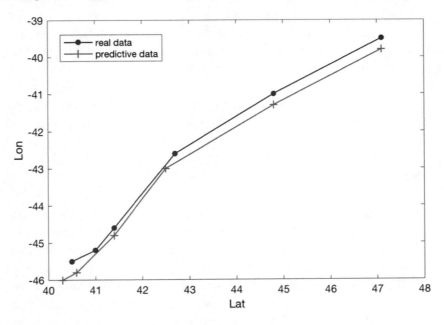

Figure 18. The residual analysis of typhoon data in the fourth group

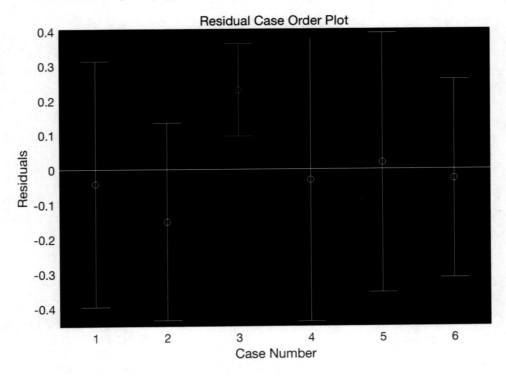

prediction of Markov chain model, so the predicted value of Markov chain model has large partial data errors compared with the real value. The track of typhoon of the second group and the fourth group are similar, which are stable and in steady upward trends. Meanwhile, the similarity between predicted value and the real is very high, the errors of the data are quite small and the prediction of the Markov chain model is more accurate. As a result, the following conclusions can be drawn:

Conclusion 1: The accuracy of prediction is worse when the real path of typhoon is fluctuant and unstable.
Conclusion 2: The accuracy of prediction is better when the real path of typhoon is stable and regular.

CONCLUSION

This chapter studies the prediction of uncertain spatial-temporal data mainly. In order to finish the work of this chapter, the authors put forward to model the uncertain spatiotemporal data base on XML, because the tree structure of XML document is conducive to manage the uncertain spatiotemporal data. At the same time, the speed of querying data is also improved, which benefits the prediction of spatiotemporal data. Then a prediction method based on Markov chain is proposed, it considers the uncertainty of spatiotemporal data and can predict the spatiotemporal data in future time by the original data. Finally, the authors apply this method of prediction to the meteorological field, and test the performance of this forecasting method. The proposed approach could contribution to the study of spatiotemporal data, especially in uncertain spatiotemporal data prediction.

In this chapter, there are still some shortcomings, such as large error and lack of accuracy in the case of large fluctuations in the original spatiotemporal data. The future work is to improve the modeling method of uncertain spatiotemporal data and optimize the prediction model of Markov chain. It is believed that the accuracy of the prediction value of uncertain spatiotemporal data will be improved obviously through the improvement. In addition, we will give comparisons between the proposed method and the state-of-the-art methods in effectiveness and performance aspects in the future.

ACKNOWLEDGMENT

This work was supported by the National Natural Science Foundation of China (61402087), the Natural Science Foundation of Hebei Province (F2019501030), and the Fundamental Research Funds for the Central Universities (N172304026).

REFERENCES

Bai, L., Cao, X., & Jia, W. (2018). Uncertain spatiotemporal data modeling and algebraic operations based on XML. *Earth Science Informatics*, *11*(1), 109–127. doi:10.100712145-017-0322-6

Bai, L., Yan, L., & Ma, Z. (2017). Interpolation and prediction of spatiotemporal data based on XML integrated with grey dynamic model. *ISPRS International Journal of Geo-Information*, *6*(4), 113. doi:10.3390/ijgi6040113

Bray, T., Paoli, J., Sperberg-McQueen, C. M., Maler, E., Yergeau, F., & Cowan, J. (1997). Extensible markup language (XML). *World Wide Web Journal, 2*(4), 27–66.

Deng, J. (1989). Introduction to grey system theory. *Journal of Grey System, 1*(1), 1–24.

Emrich, T., Kriegel, H. P., Mamoulis, N., Renz, M., & Zufle, A. (2012). Querying uncertain spatiotemporal data. In *Proceedings of International Conference on Data Engineering,* Washington, DC (pp. 354-365). Piscataway, NJ: IEEE.

Ferreira, N., Lins, L., Fink, D., Kelling, S., Wood, C., Freire, J., & Silva, C. (2011). Birdvis: Visualizing and understanding bird populations. *IEEE Transactions on Visualization and Computer Graphics, 17*(12), 2374–2383. doi:10.1109/TVCG.2011.176 PMID:22034358

Hampapur, A., Brown, L., Connell, J., Ekin, A., Haas, N., Lu, M., ... Pankanti, S. (2005). Smart video surveillance: Exploring the concept of multiscale spatiotemporal tracking. *IEEE Signal Processing Magazine, 22*(2), 38–51. doi:10.1109/MSP.2005.1406476

Huang, H., Lee, C., & Lin, H. (2017). Nighttime vehicle detection and tracking base on spatiotemporal analysis using RCCC sensor. In *Proceedings of 2017 IEEE 9th International Conference on Humanoid, Nanotechnology, Information Technology, Communication and Control, Environment and Management,* Manila, Philippines (pp. 1-5). Piscataway, NJ: IEEE. 10.1109/HNICEM.2017.8269548

Kurte, K. R., Durbha, S. S., King, R. L., Younan, N. H., & Potnis, A. V. (2017). A spatiotemporal ontological model for flood disaster monitoring. In *Proceedings of 2017 IEEE International Geoscience and Remote Sensing Symposium,* Fort Worth, TX (pp. 5213-5216). Piscataway, NJ: IEEE. 10.1109/IGARSS.2017.8128176

Li, Z., Hu, F., Schnase, J. L., Duffy, D. Q., Lee, T., Bowen, M. K., & Yang, C. (2017). A spatiotemporal indexing approach for efficient processing of big array-based climate data with MapReduce. *International Journal of Geographical Information Science, 31*(1), 17–35. doi:10.1080/13658816.2015.1131830

Maciejewski, R., Hafen, R., Rudolph, S., Larew, S. G., Mitchell, M. A., Cleveland, W. S., & Ebert, D. S. (2011). Forecasting hotspots—A predictive analytics approach. *IEEE Transactions on Visualization and Computer Graphics, 17*(4), 440–453. doi:10.1109/TVCG.2010.82 PMID:20498509

Niedermayer, J., Züfle, A., Emrich, T., Renz, M., Mamoulis, N., Chen, L., & Kriegel, H. P. (2013). Similarity search on uncertain spatiotemporal data. In *Proceedings of International Conference on Similarity Search and Applications* (pp. 43-49). Berlin, Germany: Springer. 10.1007/978-3-642-41062-8_5

Niedermayer, J., Züfle, A., Emrich, T., Renz, M., Mamoulis, N., Chen, L., & Kriegel, H. P. (2013). Probabilistic nearest neighbor queries on uncertain moving object trajectories. *Proceedings of the VLDB Endowment International Conference on Very Large Data Bases, 7*(3), 205–216. doi:10.14778/2732232.2732239

Pfoser, D., Tryfona, N., & Jensen, C. S. (2005). Indeterminacy and Spatiotemporal Data: Basic definitions and case study. *GeoInformatica, 9*(3), 211–236. doi:10.100710707-005-1282-4

Rabiner, L. R. (1989). A tutorial on hidden Markov models and selected applications in speech recognition. *Proceedings of the IEEE, 77*(2), 257–286. doi:10.1109/5.18626

Ramanathan, A., & Chen, M. (2017). Spatiotemporal vehicle tracking, counting and classification. In *Proceedings of 2017 IEEE Third International Conference on Multimedia Big Data,* Laguna Hills, CA (pp. 246-247). Piscataway, NJ: IEEE. 10.1109/BigMM.2017.85

Ré, C., Letchner, J., Balazinksa, M., & Suciu, D. (2008). Event queries on correlated probabilistic streams. In *Proceedings of the 2008 ACM SIGMOD international conference on Management of data,* Vancouver, Canada (pp. 715-728). 10.1145/1376616.1376688

Solow, A. R. (1994). Time series prediction: Forecasting the future and understanding the past. *Science, 265*(5179), 1745–1747. doi:10.1126cience.265.5179.1745 PMID:17770902

Tao, Y., Papadias, D., & Sun, J. (2003). The tpr*-tree: An optimized spatiotemporal access method for predictive queries. In *Proceedings of the 29th International Conference on Very Large Data Bases,* Berlin, Germany (pp. 790-801). .

Tossebro, E., & Nygård, M. (2002). Uncertainty in spatiotemporal databases. In *Proceedings of International Conference on Advances in Information Systems* (pp. 43-53). Berlin, Germany: Springer. 10.1007/3-540-36077-8_5

Trajcevski, G., Choudhary, A. N., Wolfson, O., Ye, L., & Li, G. (2010). Uncertain range queries for necklaces. In *Proceedings of 2010 Eleventh International Conference on Mobile Data Management,* Kansas City, MO (pp. 199-208). Piscataway, NJ: IEEE. 10.1109/MDM.2010.76

Trajcevski, G., Tamassia, R., Ding, H., Scheuermann, P., & Cruz, I. F. (2009). Continuous probabilistic nearest-neighbor queries for uncertain trajectories. In *Proceedings of the 12th International Conference on Extending Database Technology: Advances in Database Technology,* Saint Petersburg, Russian Federation (pp. 874-885). 10.1145/1516360.1516460

Wang, L., & Zhou, Z. (2017). Congestion prediction for urban areas by spatiotemporal data mining. In *Proceedings of 2017 International Conference on Cyber-Enabled Distributed Computing and Knowledge Discovery,* Nanjing, China (pp. 290-297). Piscataway, NJ: IEEE. 10.1109/CyberC.2017.61

Weather Underground. (2016). *Tracking Map and Storm Track Coordinates of Post-Tropical Cyclone Nicole.* Retrieved from https://www.wunderground.com/hurricane/atlantic/2016/Post-Tropical-Cyclone-Nicole?MR=1

Xu, K., Li, H., & Liu, Z. (2018). ISOMAP-based spatiotemporal modeling for lithium-ion battery thermal process. *IEEE Transactions on Industrial Informatics, 14*(2), 569–577. doi:10.1109/TII.2017.2743260

Yazici, A., Zhu, Q., & Sun, N. (2001). Semantic data modeling of spatiotemporal database applications. *International Journal of Intelligent Systems, 16*(7), 881–904. doi:10.1002/int.1040

Zhang, L., Zhu, G., Shen, P., & Song, J. (2017). Learning spatiotemporal features using 3DCNN and convolutional LSTM for gesture recognition. In *Proceedings of the IEEE Conference on Computer Vision and Pattern Recognition,* Venice, Italy (pp. 3120-3128). Piscataway, NJ: IEEE. 10.1109/ICCVW.2017.369

KEY TERMS AND DEFINITIONS

Markov Chain: A Markov chain is a random process that undergoes transitions from one state to another on a state space.

Residual: The difference between results obtained by observation and by computation from a formula or between the mean of several observations and any one of them.

Spatiotemporal Data: Spatiotemporal data is a kind of special data which can contain time information and spatial information simultaneously.

Transition Matrix: A Markov transition matrix is a square matrix describing the probabilities of moving from one state to another in a dynamic system. In each row are the probabilities of moving from the state represented by that row, to the other states. Thus, the rows of a Markov transition matrix each add to one.

Chapter 9
A Fuzzy RDF Graph-Matching Method Based on Neighborhood Similarity

Guanfeng Li
Ningxia University, China

Zongmin Ma
Nanjing University of Aeronautics and Astronautics, China

ABSTRACT

With the popularity of fuzzy RDF data, identifying correspondences among these data sources is an important task. Although there are some solutions addressing this problem in classical RDF datasets, existing methods do not consider fuzzy information which is an important property existing in fuzzy RDF graphs. In this article, we apply fuzzy graph to model the fuzzy RDF datasets and propose a novel similarity-oriented RDF graph matching approach, which makes full use of the 1-hop neighbor vertex and edge label information, and takes into account the fuzzy information of a fuzzy RDF graph. Based on the neighborhood similarity, we propose a breadth-first branch-and-bound method for fuzzy RDF graph matching, which uses a state space search method and uses truncation parameters to constrain the search. This algorithm can be used to identify the matched pairs.

INTRODUCTION

Resource description framework (RDF) (Klyne & Carroll, 2006) is a standard data model recommended by the World Wide Web Consortium (W3C) to capture resource information the context of the semantic web (Berners-Lee, Hendler, & Lassila, 2001). This model represents data as sets of triples where each triple consists of three elements that are referred to as the subject, the predicate, and the object of the triple. These triples allow users to describe arbitrary things in terms of their attributes and their relationships to other things. At the same time, information is often vague or imprecise in the real-world applications. Therefore, the study of fuzzy extension of RDF models has emerged (Ma, Li, & Yan, 2018;

DOI: 10.4018/978-1-5225-8446-9.ch009

Ma, & Yan, 2018; Mazzieri, & Dragoni, 2008; Straccia, 2009). Nowadays fuzzy RDF has been widely used in a variety of real scenarios (Pivert, Slama, & Thion, 2016; Zhang, 2017).

An increasing amount of data is becoming available in RDF format. Multiple datasets are effectively published according to the linked-data principles (Zhang, Song, He, Shi, & Dong, 2012). Integrating these datasets through interlink or fusion is needed in order to assure interoperability between the resources composing them. To do this, we need to automatically discover the correspondence between these data sources in different information stores. Data matching is the process of bringing data from different data sources together and comparing them in order to find out whether they represent the same real-world object in a given domain (Dorneles, Gonçalves, & dos Santos Mello, 2011). Efficient RDF data matching becomes the technical foundation of many tasks in Semantic Web (Li, & Ma, 2018; Zou, & Özsu, 2017).

Fuzzy RDF data have a natural representation in the form of a labeled directed graph in which the vertices present the resources and values (also called literals), and edges represent semantic relationships between resources. So, RDF data matching problem has been often addressed in terms of graph matching approach. Graph matching is usually based on the graph isomorphism or homomorphism, combining a specific application environment to find similar topology graph. Some works (Carroll, 2002) has been dedicated to the search for the best match between two graphs or subgraphs. Unfortunately, the traditional graph matching algorithms based on graph isomorphic have been proved that its complexity is NP-complete (Ullmann, 1976). For this reason, some works (Costabello, 2014; Dorneles, Gonçalves, & Mello, 2011) of approximate matching based on similarity or distance metrics use a specific index structure to reduce the complexity of RDF graph matching. However, these approximate matching approaches ignored many features of RDF graph. Firstly, these approaches only take the similarity of vertices and edges into account in RDF graph, do not concern structure among the vertices and edges. Secondly, vertices in RDF graphs have incomplete information or even anonymized information (blank vertices), and the partial neighborhood information available from a source graph will be helpful to identify entities in the target graph. More importantly, these methods cannot process fuzzy information in the matching process.

Clearly, there is a need to adopt approximate similarity matching techniques to solve the above problem. There is a kind of structural similarity approaches (Melnik, Garcia-Molina, & Rahm, 2002), in which an element in source graph G_S and an element in target graph G_T are considered similar if their respective neighborhoods within G_S and G_T are similar. This kind of approaches is particularly suitable for the lack of syntactical information (blank vertices in our case) in graphs. Note that this kind of approaches concerns only the pure structural similarity, while the utilization of other evaluation methods such as string similarities is not considered. Furthermore, it does not take edges similarities into consideration, which are key properties in RDF graph. In order to avoid anonymized information of blank vertices, improve the accuracy of vertex similarity, and fully consider the fuzzy information, we propose a 1-hop neighborhood-based similarity measure. This method combines the similarity of vertex and edge labels in the 1-hop neighborhood, and consider an edge fuzzy degree as a whole semantic unit to improve the matching accuracy.

Neighborhood-based similarity measure provides a large set of correspondences. To efficiently identify the matched pairs from the results of 1-hop neighborhood similarity measure, we need a method to solve the optimal solution of a complex combinatorial optimization problem. Branch and bound (Clausen, 1999) is an algorithm design paradigm for discrete and combinatorial optimization problems, as well as mathematical optimization. A branch-and-bound algorithm consists of a systematic enumeration of candidate solutions by means of state space search: the set of candidate solutions is thought of as forming a rooted tree with the full set at the root. Zhang (Zhang, 2000) has developed a truncated depth first branch-and-bound algorithm and shown that use of truncated branch-and-bound as a heuristic gives better results than most of the heuristics. To solve the graph matching problem, a basis truncated branch and bound algorithm is developed (Sambhoos, Nagi, Sudit, & Stotz, 2010). Based on the above two methods, an inexact graph matching based heuristic is being introduced, where a state space search approach is adapted, and truncation parameters are used to constrain the search. This algorithm can be used to identify the matched pairs.

In summary, we address fuzzy RDF graph matching problem in the chapter. We propose a neighborhood-based similarity measure that could avoid costly graph isomorphism and edit distance computation. Under this new measure, we propose a revision of the traditional branch and bound algorithm to reduce its complexity and to identify the matched pairs during the process of fuzzy RDF graphs matching.

The remainder of the chapter is organized as follows. Section 2 is a brief literature review on graph matching. Section 3 presents the definitions and the problem description. Section 4 presents fuzzy RDF graph matching method. Finally, the conclusions are presented in Section 5.

RELATED WORK

The present work in this chapter is closely related to the issues of classical RDF matching. There are a number of efforts in RDF data matching. Basically, we can identify three types of approaches for RDF data matching: schema-based mapping, instance-based matching and structure-based methods.

Schema-based methods rely on alignments or mapping rules to identify the same real- world object. Nikolov et al. (Nikolov, Uren, & Motta, 2009), for example, proposed a data fusion method based on mapping rules to resolve the semantic heterogeneity of datasets. Zhu et al. (Zhu, Zhong, Li, & Yu, 2002) introduced an approach for semantic search by matching RDF graphs and its similarity definition was based upon the ontology which consists of type hierarchies on vertices and edges.

Instance-based matching methods seek to identify the instances of a real-world object in two different datasets by using string similarities such as edit distance (Levenshtein, 1966), Jaro similarity (Jaro, 1989), and JaroWinkler similarity (Winkler, 1999). Castano et al. (Castano, Ferrara, Montanelli, & Varese, 2011) provided an overview of RDF instance-matching techniques, where most of the works stem from ontology matching strategies (Castano, Ferrara, Montanelli, & Varese, 2011). Costabello (Costabello, 2014) presented an optimal error-tolerant subgraph isomorphism algorithm between RDF graphs using the notion of graph edit distance to determine whether the sensed context is compatible with some context declarations. Araujo et al. (Araujo, Hidders, Schwabe, & Vries, 2012) proposed an approach, called SERIMI, for solving the RDF instance-matching problem automatically. SERIMI matched instances between a source and target datasets, without prior knowledge of the data, domain or schema of these datasets. It was done so by approximating the notion of similarity by pairing instances based on entity labels as well as structural context. Liu et al. (Liu, Scharffe, & Zhou, 2008) developed an RDF dataset fusion method based on the similarity of literal contents and the graph structure of the RDF dataset. Isele et al. (Isele, 2014) provided a linked data integration framework based on Silk-Link Specification Language (Isele, Jentzsch, & Bizer, 2010), which can identify the same real-world entity.

Structure-based methods usually employ the topological properties of an RDF graph. For testing RDF software, Carroll (Carroll, 2002) proposed an RDF graph matching algorithm based on vertices of classification and graph isomorphism. For the purpose of data dissemination, Wang et al. (Wang, Jin,

& Li, 2004) described an effective algorithm to match RDF graph pattern and RDF graph exactly and propose an ontology-based publish/subscribe system. Zhang et al. (Zhang, Song, He, Shi, & Dong, 2012) proposed a similarity-oriented RDF graph matching approach for ranking linked data, which considering the element-level and structure-level similarity of statements. Raimond et al. (Raimond, Sutton, & Sandler, 2008) proposed an algorithm that considers both the similarity of the resources and the similarity of their neighbors for matching music-related datasets on the web. Matching evidence was propagated through other resources via object properties, in a similar manner to the similarity flooding algorithm proposed in (Melnik, Garcia-Molina, & Rahm, 2002). Its basic idea was that the corresponding elements in a graph are similar when their adjacent elements are similar. Several application-oriented algorithms, such as behavioral similarity (Nejati, Sabetzadeh, Chechik, Easterbrook, & Zave, 2012) and heterogeneous events matching (Zhu, Song, Lian, Wang, & Zou, 2014), also utilized the idea of recursively computing vertex similarity degrees based on the degree of neighboring vertices.

However, all the aforementioned graph alignment algorithms do not consider fuzzy information in the matching process. A key problem is that formulas for computing similarity between elements from precise RDF graph can't be directly applied to those elements from fuzzy RDF graph. The matching algorithm proposed in the chapter uses a hybrid approach combining the semantic similarities of fuzzy RDF data and structural heuristics to generate the overall similarities.

PRELIMINARIES

In this section, we introduce some basic notions and definitions that are necessary for our discussions later. First, we recall the main features of the RDF data model briefly, and then we provide a brief introduction to fuzzy RDF graphs.

Resource Description Framework

RDF standard provides the basis for a core agreed-upon data model on the Semantic Web. It follows the W3C design principles of interoperability, extensibility, decentralization and evolution. Particularly, the RDF model was designed to have a simple and agreed-upon data model, with a formal semantics and provable inference, with an extensible URI-based vocabulary, and which allows anyone to make statements about any resource (Arenas, Gutierrez, & Pérez, 2009). Herein, we give a brief walkthrough of the core concepts of RDF from a database point of view. More definitions can refer to related literature (Klyne & Carroll, 2006).

The elemental constituents of the RDF data-model are RDF terms that can be used in reference to resources: anything with identity. We can now provide formal notation for referring to the different sets of RDF terms and the notion of an RDF triple as follows:

The set of RDF terms is decomposed into three pair-wise disjoints sets: the set of all Unique Resource Identifiers (U), the set of all blank nodes (B) and the set of all literals (L). The set of literals can be further broken down into the union of two disjoint sets: the set of plain literals (L_p) and the set of typed literals (L_t). Note that $U \cap B \cap L_p \cap L_t = \Phi$.

Formally, an RDF triple is a 3-tuple (s, p, o) from $(U \cup B) \times U \times (U \cup L \cup B)$, where s is the subject, p is the property (a.k.a. predicate) and o is the object of the triple. Informatively, the subject element refers to the primary resource being described by the triple, the property element identifies the relation between the subject and the object, and the object element fills the value of the relation. The interpretation of each triple (statement) is that subject *s* has property *p* with value *o*. Thus, an RDF triple can be seen as representing an atomic "fact" or a "claim."

As the name of RDF graph already hints at, the RDF data model can be seen as essentially a graph-based data model, albeit with special features such as vertexes that can act as edge labels and no fundamental distinction between schemas and instances, which can be represented in one and the same graph (Li, & Ma, 2018). In a finite set of RDF triples, any object from one triple can play the role of a subject in another triple which amounts to chain two labeled edges in a graph-based structure. As such, RDF triples datasets can be naturally represented as a directed labeled RDF graph, each vertex corresponding to a subject (or object), and the edge representing predicate.

A finite set of RDF triples *G* is called an RDF graph, in which each triple (s, p, o) describes a directed edge labeled with *p* from the vertex labeled with *s* to the vertex labeled with *o*.

In the following, we refer to an RDF term as any value of $U \cup L \cup B$ and to an RDF element as any among the subject, predicate, and object of an RDF triple. The elemental constituents of the RDF data model are RDF terms that can be used in reference to resources: anything with identity.

Fuzzy Set Theory and Fuzzy Graphs

Fuzzy set theory is originally introduced by Zadeh (Zadeh, 1999) for modeling sets whose boundaries are not clear-cut. In fuzzy set theory, an element belongs to a set with certain membership degree, which is measured by a membership function in the real unit interval [0, 1]. Let *S* be a universe of discourse, formally, a membership function $\mu_A: S \rightarrow [0, 1]$ is defined to describe the fuzzy set *A* where $\mu_A(u)$ for any $u \in S$ denotes the degree of membership of *u* in the fuzzy set *A*. Following the notations used in fuzzy set theory, we write $A = \{\mu(u_i) / u_i\}$ where $u_i \in S, 1 \leq i \leq n$.

A directed graph $G = (V, E)$ is defined by a finite set *V* of vertices and a set *E* of directed edges which connect certain pairs of vertices. The edge (u, v) is referred to as an out-edge of vertex *u* and an in-edge of vertex *v*. For any vertex $u \in V$, the indegree of *u* is the number of in-edges that connect to it, and the outdegree of *u* is the number of out-edges that connect to it.

A fuzzy graph (Rosenfeld, 1975) $FG = (\mu, \rho)$ is a pair of functions $\mu: V \rightarrow [0, 1]$, $\rho: V \times V \rightarrow [0, 1]$ which satisfies $\forall (u_1, u_2) \in V \times V, \rho(u_1, u_2) \leq \mu_1(u_1) \wedge \mu_2(u_2)$, where $\wedge$ denotes the minimum.

Data Model for Fuzzy RDF Graphs

In order to represent the fuzziness of three components of triples, Lv *et al.* (Lv, Ma, & Yan, 2008) propose a fuzzy extension of RDF, which annotates three components of triples (i.e., *subject*, *predicate*, and *object*) instead of whole triples with degrees in [0, 1]. This is a general fuzzy RDF graph model that considers the element-level fuzziness based on fuzzy graph theory. The element-level fuzzy RDF model is formally defined as follows.

Definition 1 (Fuzzy RDF Triple): A triple $(\mu_s/s, \mu_p/p, \mu_o/o)$ is called a element-level fuzzy RDF triple, where *s* is a fuzzy subject and $\mu_s \in [0, 1]$ denotes the degree of subject to the universe of an RDF dataset, *p* is a fuzzy predicate and $\mu_p \in [0, 1]$ expresses the fuzzy degree to the property or relationship being described, *o* is a fuzzy object and $\mu_o \in [0, 1]$ represents the fuzzy degree of the property value.

In the following, we give the formalization of fuzzy RDF data model, which is defined based on the data model of fuzzy RDF graph (Rosenfeld, 1975). A fuzzy RDF dataset can be naturally represented as a directed labeled fuzzy graph, each vertex corresponding to subject (or object), and the edge representing predicate. We refer to both edges and vertices as *graph elements*. There are two types of elements in fuzzy RDF graph: crisp elements and fuzzy elements. The former are the regular RDF elements and the fuzzy elements describe a possibility of these elements' labels, which mean the possibility that the labels exist in the universe of the RDF graph. In particular, if the vertex label of the fuzzy RDF graph is a URI representing a resource corresponding to a real-world entity, the fuzzy degree specifies the possibility that the resource exists in the graph. Another case, if the vertex label is literal that represents a property value of an entity, the fuzzy degree specifies the possibility that the property value is distributed in the graph. Furthermore, the edge between two vertices represents semantic relationship, and the degree of membership associated with each edge represents the possibility of the corresponding relationship between the two vertices.

Let U be a set of URI references, L a set of literals and P a set of properties, a fuzzy RDF graph is defined as follows.

Definition 2 (Fuzzy RDF Graph): (Ma, Li, & Yan, 2018). A fuzzy RDF graph G is *a* 6 element tuple $G = (V, E, \Sigma, L, \mu, \rho)$ where V is a finitude set of vertices, $E \subset V \times V$ is a set of directed edges, Σ is *the sets of vertices and edge labels*, $L: V \cup E \to \Sigma$ is a *labeling* function assigning labels to vertices and edges respectively, $\mu: V \to [0, 1]$ is a fuzzy subset, and $\rho: E \to [0, 1]$ is a fuzzy relation of on fuzzy subset μ. Note that $\rho(v_i, v_j) \leq \mu(v_i) \wedge \mu(v_j)$ $v_i, v_j \in V$.

In Definition 2, each vertex $v_i \in V$ of graph G has a label $L(v_i)$, which corresponds to the *subject* or *object* in RDF triples. Moreover, $(v_i, v_j) \in E$ is a directed edge from vertex v_i to vertex v_j, with an edge label $L(v_i, v_j)$ that corresponds to the predicate in RDF triples. The membership degree associated with each vertex indicates the possibility that vertex takes the label, and the membership degree associated with each edge represents the possibility on the corresponding relationship between vertices. Note that, a fuzzy RDF graph as defined above may contain both fuzzy vertices (or edges) and crisp vertices (or edges) as a fuzzy vertex (or edge) with a degree of 0 or 1 can be considered as crisp. Along the same line, a crisp RDF graph is simply a special case of fuzzy RDF data graph (where $\mu: V \to \{0, 1\}$ for all $v_i \in V$ and $\rho: V \times V \to \{0, 1\}$ for all $(v_i, v_j) \in E$), and the fuzzy RDF graph is a generalization of the crisp RDF graph.

Throughout this chapter, we only consider the simple case of a crisp set of vertices. In this case, ρ qualifies the intensity of the relationship involved in the RDF triple. Intuitively, ρ attaches fuzzy degrees to "edges" of the graph. Having a value of 0 for ρ is equivalent to not belonging to the graph. Having a value of 1 for ρ is equivalent to fully satisfy the associated concept.

For example, Figure 1 (a) and (b) illustrates two fragments of fuzzy RDF data graph with some fuzzy elements, and crisp ones (equivalent to a corresponding degree of 1). The fuzzy triple (pID2, has-address, addID2, 0.9) in Figure 1 (a) represents the fact that the person labeled pID2, whose address label is addID2. And the possibility of the fact is 0.9. In this example, the degree is based on a simple statistical notion, which can be made of subtler by fuzzy operations or the integration of expert knowledge. Note that opaque labels exist as shown in Fig. 1 (b). The resource "_:" is distinct from others, and it makes the resource name garbled. According to the RDF specification (Araujo, Hidders, Schwabe, & Vries, 2012), a blank vertex can be assigned an identifier prefixed with "_:".

Figure 1. The fuzzy RDF graphs

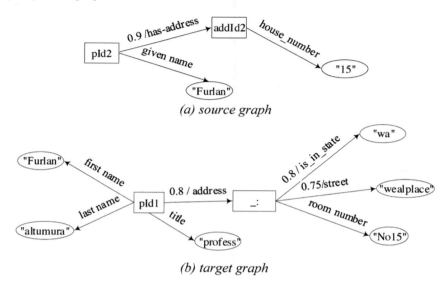

(a) source graph

(b) target graph

In order to solve the problem raised by the edge mismatch cost function, we define a novel neighborhood-based similarity measure by comparing the 1-hop neighbors of a vertex, defined as follows.

Definition 3 (1-Hop Neighbors): Given a fuzzy RDF graph G and a vertex $v \in V$, the 1-hop neighborhood of v is the set of vertices u whose distance from v is equal to 1.

To compare the neighborhoods of two vertices, we resort to an information propagation model (Melnik, Garcia-Molina, & Rahm, 2002) that is able to transform neighborhoods into vectors in a multidimensional space, where sophisticated indexing and fast similarity search algorithms are available.

FUZZY RDF GRAPH MATCHING

In this section, we first introduce the formal problem statement. Then, we focus on the neighborhood-based similarity measure in fuzzy RDF graph. The method makes full use of the vertex and edge label information, and take into account the structural characteristics of fuzzy RDF graph. Finally, we explore the application of this measure to graph matching.

Fuzzy RDF Graph Matching Semantics

RDF graph matching refers to the process of determining whether two descriptions refer to the same real-world entity in a given domain. For the purpose of describing our approach clearly, we distinguish the two fuzzy RDF graph involved in the matching process, source graph (also input graph) and target graph (also template graph), and denoted by G_s and G_t, respectively. For a fuzzy RDF graph matching, the objective is to investigate the syntactic and semantic occurrence of the target graph in the source graph.

Definition 4 (Fuzzy RDF Graph Matching): Given two fuzzy RDF graphs G_s and G_t from a given domain, the matching problem is to identify all correspondences between graphs G_s and G_t representing the same real-world object. The match result is typically represented by a set of correspondences, sometimes called a mapping. A correspondence $c = (id, C_s, C_t, m)$ interrelates two element C_s and C_t from graphs G_s and G_t. An optional similarity degree $m \in [0, 1]$ indicates the similarity or strength of the correspondence between the two elements.

An essential requirement for any graph matching algorithm is a method for calculating similarity between elements of the target and source graphs. What criteria should we use for calculating similarity? How can we quantify these criteria? To obtain a satisfactory correspondence relation, RDF graph matching process employs a similarity function to compare elements values.

Definition 5 (Similarity Function): Let G_s and G_t are two datasets, a similarity function is defined as: $F_s(s, t) \rightarrow [0, 1]$, where $(s, t) \in G_s \times G_t$, i.e., the function computers a normalized value for every pair (s, t). The higher the score value, the more similar s and t are. The advantage of using similarity functions is to deal with a finite interval for the score values.

The similarity function depends on the specific problem and semantics. More definitions of similarity function can be found in the work (Li, & Ma, 2018).

Definition 6 (Similarity Matrix): Consider fuzzy RDF graphs G_s and G_t. We assume a *similarity matrix* SM. For each vertex pair (v_s, v_t) of vertices in $V_s \times V_t$, $SM_V(L(v_s), L(v_t))$ is a similarity score matrix. Each entry $sim_v(L(v_s), L(v_t))$ in the matrix is calculated using the similarity function. Correspondingly, given $e_s \in E_s$ and $e_t \in E_t$, there is a similarity score matrix between these two edges, defined as $SM_E(L(e_s), L(e_t))$. Each entry in the matrix is the similarity $sim_e(L(e_s), L(e_t))$ of the edge pair (e_s, e_t).

Similarity Measure Based on the Adjacent Vertex

In many cases, two vertices are similar in distinct RDF graphs, the adjacent vertices of them are similar too (Melnik, Garcia-Molina, & Rahm, 2002). Based on this idea, the partial neighborhood information available from a source graph can also be helpful to identify entities in the target graph, when the vertices in graphs have incomplete information or even anonymized information (blank vertices). Our strategy is to develop a method that can utilize the adjacent vertices or edges scoring for atomic elements (vertices and edges) while increasing its topological accuracy during matching. These neighborhoods consist of a root vertex and all other vertices of edge distance 1 away. For a pair of source and target graph vertex, a linear assignment problem (Sambhoos, Nagi, Sudit, & Stotz, 2010) is solved over their neighborhood. The linear assignment problem takes the score matrix with individual elements as the aggregation of the neighboring vertex-to-vertex score and connecting edge-to-edge score. So, each neighborhood -based similarity score will be a unique score depending on its corresponding neighborhood.

Figure 2 illustrates the similarity measure procedure based on 1-Hop neighborhood. As input to the procedure, we take two RDF files containing all the information of the source graph and target, and then output an alignment results sets. Moreover, we define a similarity score threshold t to indicate the suitability of matches for different domains of data. The higher this threshold is set, the fewer 1-Hop

Figure 2. The framework of 1-hop neighborhood procedure

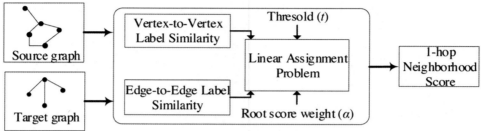

neighborhood assignments would be determined, which in turn leads to improved performance (but potential loss of optimality). The following steps are given to compute the 1-hop neighborhood procedure:

In the first phase, the procedure is to compute a vertex-to-vertex similarity score $sim_v(L(v_s), L(v_t))$ using different similarity functions (Li, & Ma, 2018) for each vertex in the target graph to each vertex in the source graph. For each vertex we then sort this list in descending order. Using the threshold t as the input to the algorithm, we can prune the amount of assignment we have to run for this source vertex. Even if there is a perfect neighborhood assignment score, the root vertex score below this value does not have the possibility of a total score above the threshold.

To get a more accurate ranking the vertex-to-vertex and edge-to-edge scores are needed. The edge-to-edge label similarity scores are calculated in the same way as the vertices. Those similarity functions assign a similarity degree $sim_e(L(e_s), L(e_t))$ to every edge pair (e_s, e_t). However, in the fuzzy RDF graph, it is not enough to calculate the basic similarity of the labels on the edges. In order to make good use of the fuzzy information between edges of two fuzzy RDF graphs, we further take edge fuzzy degree into consideration. For the fuzzy degree information of the edge, we use a measure of fuzzy degrees, which is based on the difference as well as the sum of corresponding grades of membership (Mazzieri, & Dragoni, 2008). Let ρ_s and ρ_t are the fuzzy degrees of edges e_s and e_t, respectively. The measure relationship of fuzzy values ρ_s and ρ_t is defined by

$$R(\rho_s, \rho_t) = 1 - \frac{(\rho_s \vee \rho_t) - (\rho_s \wedge \rho_t)}{\rho_s + \rho_t} \tag{1}$$

Here $(\rho_s \vee \rho_t) = \max(\rho_s, \rho_t), (\rho_s \wedge \rho_t) = \min(\rho_s, \rho_t)$.

Based on the above discussion, the total edge-to-edge similarity calculation requires the aggregate of edge label similarity and edge fuzzy degree relationship. In this way, the general formula for this combination task can be given as following:

$$sim_e(e_s, e_t) = sim_e(L(e_s), L(e_t)) \times R(\rho_s, \rho_t) \tag{2}$$

In the second stage, the procedure is to compute the scores for the 1-hop neighbors of each root vertex pair. This returns the optimal assignment of neighbors of the root vertex in the source graph to the neighbors of the root vertex in the target graph. The work deal with the pairing of vertices across two graphs and rely on domain-specific metadata (e.g., vertex and edge labels) as well as structural relationships.

The principle of the algorithm is that the similarity between two vertices must depend on the similarity between their adjacent vertices. For each vertex pair (v_s, v_t), the 1-hop neighborhood score is given by

$$sim\,(v_s, v_t) = (\alpha \times sim_v(v_s, v_t) + (1 - \alpha) \times sim_n(v_s, v_t)) \qquad (3)$$

Here $sim_v(v_s, v_t)$ is the score of the root vertex pair and $sim_n(v_s, v_t)$ is the score of the neighborhood assignment, which is given by Eq. (4). α characterizes the amount of weight to be given to the neighbors. a varies between [0, 1], and its value has inverse proportion with the neighborhood assignment.

$$sim_n\left(v_s, v_t\right) = \sum_{i=1}^{m} \frac{1}{2}\left(sim_v\left(v_{si}', v_{ti}'\right) + sim_e\left(e_{si}, e_{ti}\right)\right)\Big/m \qquad (4)$$

Here, $sim_n(v_s, v_t)$ is to calculate the similarity score of the 1-hop neighborhood. $v_s', v_t' \in V$ are the 1-hop adjacency vertices of root vertices v_s and v_t, respectively. m represents the number of neighbors to root template vertex. $sim_v\left(v_{si}', v_{ti}'\right)$ is the vertex similarity between the ith 1-hop vertex derived from root vertex v_s and its matching vertex derived from v_t. whereas $sim_e(e_{si}, e_{ti})$ is the edge similarity between the ith edge derived from v_s and its matching edge derived from v_t.

Although the neighbor vertices v_s' and v_t' of v_s and v_t, respectively, have high similarity degree, if the similarity of edge e_s is different from the similarity of e_t or the fuzzy degree ρ_s deviates far from the fuzzy degree ρ_t, the similarity degree of v_s' and v_t' will have less effect on the similarity degree of v_s and v_t.

1-hop neighborhood score is responsible for the vertex-to-vertex similarity scores and the edge-to-edge similarity scores. The score of the 1-hop neighborhood assignment is solved using the linear assignment problem between the root vertex and the adjacent vertices and forming the edges of the solution matrix. Using the results of 1-hop neighborhood score, a finding optimal solutions of difficult combinatorial optimization algorithm for matching is developed, which will be discussed in the next section.

Approximate Match Algorithm

The vertex scoring method presented in the previous section yields a matrix of similarity scores between vertices taken pairwise from each graph, which naturally suggests matching the vertices of two graphs by computing a maximum weight matching on this matrix of scores. The matching goal is identifying matched pairs from source data vertices to target graph vertices. It is difficult to identify the matched pairs by using the result of the 1-hop neighborhood score. Truncated branch-and-bound algorithm (Zhang, 2000) is a complete algorithm that is typically used to find optimal solutions of difficult combinatorial optimization problems. The algorithm explores a state space and finds many suboptimal solutions with increasingly better qualities. These solutions are approximations to the optimal solution if it is terminated prematurely. Sambhoos et al. (Sambhoos, Nagi, Sudit, & Stotz, 2010) gives the basis for a truncated branch and bound algorithm for solving the graph matching problem. Based on the algorithm, we propose a breadth-first branch-and-bound method for fuzzy RDF graph matching, which uses a state space search method and uses truncation parameters to constrain the search.

Breadth-first branch-and-bound is a truncated search tree algorithm that explores vertices or subproblems in a breadth first order. Like best-first search, it uses a fixed number b as space-bounded, and subproblems search only unfolds the first b most promising vertices at each depth. The search tree is dynamically generated during the search and initially contains only the root. Starting at the root vertex, this algorithm always processes all the vertices at one level of the search tree before any vertex at a deeper level. In each iteration of the algorithm, a subproblem is selected from the set of active subproblems using the scores of the current match. When a new source graph vertex is added, the score at that level is calculated using the average of the scores of all the vertex pairs and edge pairs connecting them, at that level. Each subproblem at level i ($i = 0, 1, 2, \ldots$) has exactly i pairs. In order to avoid the problem that the search tree to explode exponentially as it goes deeper, we use a parametric mechanism to control the state space growth. The parameter $k_i = l$ ($i = 0, 1, 2, \ldots$) denotes the l best child subproblems. The parameter b_i denotes the total number of sub-problems at each level i, i.e. it is the breadth of the search tree. The parameter h controls the depth of the search tree. By using the truncation parameter mechanism, we can control the growth of the state space. Now we give the approximate match algorithm as follows.

In Algorithm 1, the search tree is generated dynamically during the search and initially consists of only the root. The algorithm begins by initializing problem set and available mapping in lines 1-2. Starting at the root vertex, the algorithm always selects a recently generated vertex to examine next. At each iteration of this algorithm, a subproblem is selected for exploration from the pool of live subproblems using the scores of the current match in line 4. If the level of the search tree has reached the threshold h or the number of vertices of the source, the search progress stops and the result is outputs in lines 5-6. Otherwise, proceed to the next search. In what follows, the algorithm chooses at most l best subproblems (available mappings) from adjacent mappings and add them into parent problem set in lines

Algorithm 1. Approximate match algorithm

```
Input: Target graph G, source graph Q, 1-hop neighbor similarity matrix
Output: match set between V_t and V_s
1:   Initialize ParentVertexSet;
2:   Initialize and sort available mappings;
3:   GenTreeLevel (ParentVertexSet);
4:   for each ParentVertex ∈ ParentVertexSet
5:       if (TreeLevel >= h || TreeLevel > | V_t |)
6:           Output (ParentVertex
7:       else
8:           for (k best sub-problems in adjacent mappings)
9:               ChildVertex = ParentVertex + NewMapping;
10:                  If ChildVertex have identical match pairs
11:                      Prune (ChildVertex);
12:                  else
13:                      ChildVertex = AvailableMapping (ParentVertex);
14:                      FindAdjacentMappings (ChildVertex);
15:                      NewParentVertexSet += ChildVertex;
16:           SortDescending (NewParentVertexSet);
17:           If (|ChildVertexs | > b)
18:               NewParentVertexSet = subset (NewParentVertexSet, 0, b_i);
19:           GenTreeLevel (NewParentVertexSet);
```

8-15. Each available mapping is generated by adding one pair to its parent problem in line 9. The vertex pairs that are eligible to be added correspond to at least one source vertex and one target graph vertex respectively in the parent problem. If two or more available mappings at the same level have identical match pairs, this algorithm only keep one of them and prune the others in lines 10-11. The newly added source vertex must be connected to the existing source vertex in exactly the same way as the target graph vertices in the corresponding pair. When a new target graph vertex is added, the average of the pair of edges on that level and the pair of edges that connect them are used to calculate the score for that level. The new vertices are added in lines 13-15. At each level in the algorithm, the best b vertices are sorted in descending order. If the extension in level i has reached the upper bound, then the new level appears and loops into the next iteration in lines 16-19.

After running this algorithm, each branch produces a series of matched pairs. Then the target graph vertices in the matched pairs generate a subgraph, which is the final match of the source graph. There is a set of resulting subgraphs with various matching values and topologies. The worst-time complexity of full enumeration of the algorithm is $O(mn^m)$, where m and n are the vertices number of source and target graph, respectively. The problem of state space search is that it can become exponential, so we have used parameters to constrain the state space. Therefore, the time complexity is $O(k_i b_i h)$ in our algorithm.

CONCLUSION

RDF data matching in the context of fusion and interlink of RDF datasets are the key task of determining if two resources are referred to the same entity in the real world. In this chapter, we propose a neighborhood-based similarity measure that could avoid costly graph isomorphism and edit distance computation. We have defined 1-hop neighbor similarity of vertices based on labels and their neighborhood structure, in which we take fuzzy edge values and edge similarities and into consideration. Then, we have implemented a breadth-first branch-and-bound method for fuzzy RDF graph matching, which uses a state space search method and uses truncation parameters to constrain the search.

We have investigated the approximate graph matching methods for fuzzy RDF graphs. Without a loss of generality, the work can be extended as a general approach which may be applied to any directed and weighted labeled graphs. Since there are no RDF benchmarks for testing the performance of fuzzy RDF graph data matching at this point, this chapter does not present an experimental measure to demonstrate our proposed method. In the future work, we will implement and experimentally measure our approaches proposed in the chapter with fuzzy RDF datasets. Another research direction is to optimize and improve this algorithm so that it meets the requirements of handling large fuzzy RDF graphs.

ACKNOWLEDGMENT

The work was supported by the National Natural Science Foundation of China (61772219) and the Natural Science Foundation of Ningxia Province, China (2019AAC03033).

REFERENCES

Araujo, S., Hidders, J., Schwabe, D., & Vries, A. P. D. (2012). Serimi - resource description similarity, RDF instance matching and interlinking. In *Proceedings of the International Semantic Web Conference.* Aachen, Germany: CEUR-WS.org.

Arenas, M., Gutierrez, C., & Pérez, J. (2009, August). Foundations of RDF databases. In Reasoning Web International Summer School (pp. 158-204). Berlin, Germany: Springer. doi:10.1007/978-3-642-03754-2_4

Berners-Lee, T., Hendler, J., & Lassila, O. (2001). The semantic web. *Scientific American, 284*(5), 34–43. doi:10.1038cientificamerican0501-34 PMID:11396337

Carroll, J. J. (2002). Matching RDF graphs. *In International Semantic Web Conference*, pp. 5-15.

Castano, S., Ferrara, A., Montanelli, S., & Varese, G. (2011). Ontology and instance matching. In *Knowledge-driven multimedia information extraction and ontology evolution* (pp. 167–195). Berlin, Heidelberg: Springer. doi:10.1007/978-3-642-20795-2_7

Clausen, J. (1999). Branch and bound algorithms-principles and examples. Department of Computer Science, University of Copenhagen.

Costabello, L. (2014). *Error-Tolerant RDF Subgraph Matching for Adaptive Presentation of Linked Data on Mobile. In The Semantic Web: Trends and Challenges.* Springer International Publishing.

Dorneles, C. F., Gonçalves, R., & dos Santos Mello, R. (2011). Approximate data instance matching: A survey. *Knowledge and Information Systems, 27*(1), 1–21. doi:10.100710115-010-0285-0

Euzenat, J., & Shvaiko, P. (2013). *Ontology Matching.* Springer Berlin Heidelberg. doi:10.1007/978-3-642-38721-0

Isele, R. (2014). Methoden der Linked Data Integration. In T. Pellegrini, H. Sack, & S. Auer (Eds.), *Linked Enterprise Data* (pp. 103–120).

Isele, R., Jentzsch, A., & Bizer, C. (2010, November). Silk server-adding missing links while consuming linked data. In *Proceedings of the First International Conference on Consuming Linked Data-Volume 665* (pp. 85-96). Aachen, Germany: CEUR-WS.org.

Jaro, M. A. (1989). Advances in record-linkage methodology as applied to matching the 1985 census of Tampa, Florida. *Journal of the American Statistical Association, 84*(406), 414–420. doi:10.1080/01 621459.1989.10478785

Klyne, G., & Carroll, J. J. (2004). *Resource description framework (RDF): Concepts and Abstract Syntax.* W3C Recommendation. Retrieved from http://www.w3.org/TR/2004/REC-RDF-concepts-20040210/

Levenshtein, V. I. (1966, February). Binary codes capable of correcting deletions, insertions, and reversals. *Soviet Physics, 10*(8), 707–710.

Li, G., & Ma, Z. (2018). An efficient matching algorithm for fuzzy RDF graph. *Journal of Information Science and Engineering, 34*(2), 519–534.

Liu, Y., Scharffe, F., & Zhou, C. (2008, December). Towards practical RDF datasets fusion. In *Workshop on Data Integration through Semantic Technology (DIST2008)*.

Lv, Y., Ma, Z. M., & Yan, L. (2008). Fuzzy RDF: A data model to represent fuzzy metadata. In *IEEE International Conference on Fuzzy Systems*. Hong Kong, China (pp. 1439-1445).

Ma, Z., Li, G., & Yan, L. (2018). Fuzzy data modeling and algebraic operations in RDF. *Fuzzy Sets and Systems*, *351*, 41–63. doi:10.1016/j.fss.2017.11.013

Ma, Z., & Yan, L. (2018). Modeling fuzzy data with RDF and fuzzy relational database models. *International Journal of Intelligent Systems*, *3*(7), 1534–1554. doi:10.1002/int.21996

Mazzieri, M., & Dragoni, A. F. (2008). A fuzzy semantics for the resource description framework. In *Uncertainty Reasoning for the Semantic Web I* (pp. 244–261). Berlin, Germany: Springer. doi:10.1007/978-3-540-89765-1_15

Melnik, S., Garcia-Molina, H., & Rahm, E. (2002). Similarity Flooding: A Versatile Graph Matching Algorithm and Its Application to Schema Matching. In *Proceedings of the 18th IEEE Computer Society International Conference on Data Engineering* (pp. 117-128). IEEE. 10.1109/ICDE.2002.994702

Nejati, S., Sabetzadeh, M., Chechik, M., Easterbrook, S., & Zave, P. (2012). Matching and merging of variant feature specifications. *IEEE Transactions on Software Engineering*, *38*(6), 1355–1375. doi:10.1109/TSE.2011.112

Nikolov, A., Uren, V., & Motta, E. (2009). Towards data fusion in a multi-ontology environment. In *Proceedings of the www Workshop on Linked Data on the Web*.

Pivert, O., Slama, O., & Thion, V. (2016). An extension of SPARQL with fuzzy navigational capabilities for querying fuzzy RDF data. In *IEEE International Conference on Fuzzy Systems*, Vancouver, Canada (pp. 2409-2416). 10.1109/FUZZ-IEEE.2016.7737995

Raimond, Y., Sutton, C., & Sandler, M. B. (2008). Automatic interlinking of music datasets on the semantic web. In *Proceedings of the WWW2008 Workshop on Linked Data on the Web (LDOW 2008)* (pp. 137-145).

Rosenfeld, A. (1975). In L. A. Zadeh, K. S. Fu, K. Tanaka, & M. Shimura (Eds.), *Fuzzy Graphs, Fuzzy Sets and Their Applications to Cognitive and Decision Processes* (pp. 77–95). New York: Academic Press. doi:10.1016/B978-0-12-775260-0.50008-6

Sambhoos, K., Nagi, R., Sudit, M., & Stotz, A. (2010). Enhancements to high level data fusion using graph matching and state space search. *Information Fusion*, *11*(4), 351–364. doi:10.1016/j.inffus.2009.12.001

Straccia, U. (2009, October). A minimal deductive system for general fuzzy RDF. In *International Conference on Web Reasoning and Rule Systems* (pp. 166-181). Springer. 10.1007/978-3-642-05082-4_12

Ullmann, J. R. (1976). An algorithm for subgraph isomorphism. *Journal of the Association for Computing Machinery*, *23*(1), 31–42. doi:10.1145/321921.321925

Wang, J., Jin, B., & Li, J. (2004). An ontology-based publish/subscribe system. In *Proceedings of the 5th ACM/IFIP/USENIX international conference on Middleware* (pp. 232-253). Springer.

Winkler, W. E. (1999). *The state of record linkage and current research problems*. Statistical Research Division, US Census Bureau.

Zadeh, L. A. (1999). Fuzzy sets as a basis for a theory of possibility. *Fuzzy Sets and Systems*, *100*(1), 9–34. doi:10.1016/S0165-0114(99)80004-9

Zhang, D. (2017). High-speed Train Control System Big Data Analysis Based on Fuzzy RDF Model and Uncertain Reasoning. *International Journal of Computers, Communications & Control*, *12*(4), 577. doi:10.15837/ijccc.2017.4.2914

Zhang, D., Song, T., He, J., Shi, X., & Dong, Y. (2012). A Similarity-Oriented RDF Graph Matching Algorithm for Ranking Linked Data. In *IEEE 12th International Conference on Computer and Information Technology (CIT)* (pp.427-434). IEEE.

Zhang, W. (2000) Depth-first branch-and-bound versus local search: a case study. In *Proceedings of 17th National Conference on Artificial Intelligence* (pp. 930–935).

Zhu, H., Zhong, J., Li, J., & Yu, Y. (2002). An Approach for Semantic Search by Matching RDF Graphs. In *Proceedings of Fifteenth International Florida Artificial Intelligence Research Society Conference (FLAIRS-02)* (pp. 450-454).

Zhu, X., Song, S., Lian, X., Wang, J., & Zou, L. (2014). Matching heterogeneous event data. In *Proceedings of ACM SIGMOD International Conference on Management of Data* (pp. 1211-1222).

Zou, L., & Özsu, M. T. (2017). Graph-Based RDF Data Management. *Data Science and Engineering*, *2*(1), 56–70. doi:10.100741019-016-0029-6

KEY TERMS AND DEFINITIONS

Branch-and-Bound: Branch-and-bound is an algorithm design paradigm for discrete and combinatorial optimization problems. The algorithm depends on efficient estimation of the lower and upper bounds of regions/branches of the search space.

Graph Matching: Graph matching is the problem of finding a similarity between graphs. Matching methods are the ones based on identification of possible and impossible pairings of vertices between the two graphs.

Linear Assignment Problem: The linear assignment problem is one of the fundamental combinatorial optimization problems in the branch of optimization or operations research in mathematics.

Resource Description Framework (RDF): RDF is a family of World Wide Web Consortium (W3C) specifications originally designed as a metadata data model. It has come to be used as a general method for conceptual description or modeling of information that is implemented in web resources, using a variety of syntax notations and data serialization formats.

Similarity Measure: Similarity measure or similarity function is a real-valued function that quantifies the similarity between two objects.

Chapter 10
An Interactive Personalized Spatial Keyword Querying Approach

Xiangfu Meng
Liaoning Technical University, China

Lulu Zhao
Liaoning Technical University, China

Xiaoyan Zhang
Liaoning Technical University, China

Pan Li
Liaoning Technical University, China

Zeqi Zhao
Liaoning Technical University, China

Yue Mao
Liaoning Technical University, China

ABSTRACT

Existing spatial keyword query methods usually evaluate text relevancy according to the frequency of occurrence of query keywords in the text information associated to spatial objects, without considering the degree of preference of users to different query keywords, and without considering semantic relevancy. To deal with the above problems, this chapter proposes an interactive personalized spatial keyword querying approach which is divided into two stages. In the offline processing stage, Gibbs algorithm is adopted to estimate the thematic probability distribution of text information associated to spatial objects, and then an LDA model is used for semantic expansion of spatial data set.

DOI: 10.4018/978-1-5225-8446-9.ch010

INTRODUCTION

Information query refers to the activity and process of searching, identifying and obtaining relevant facts, data and text for solving various problems. As an inseparable part of human social activities, people are more and more concerned about how to quickly and accurately find the information they need from the massive size of information sources. With the advent of GPS and other location-based service technologies, it becomes easier to obtain geographic spatial dimension information. As a result, more and more spatial objects with location information emerged on the Web, such as hotels, cafes and tourist attractions. These spatial objects are often referred to as Point of Interests (POIs). A spatial object contains the geographic location (usually in the form of latitude and longitude) and a textual description (such as object name, facility, comment, and so on). Spatial keyword query takes geographical location and keyword as parameters and returns spatial object that meets the query condition. Specifically, each POI/spatial object in the spatial database contains spatial location information and text information. Assuming the geographic location of a given user and a set of query keywords, the location-based service system returns the POIs related to the query both in spatial and textual from the spatial database. Now there are a large number of online resources, which can obtain large-scale geographic text objects, such as Google Places, yahoo, Foursquare, and other social networks, trip advisory groups and public comments, etc., which need technology to support the effective processing of spatial keyword query.

Traditional spatial queries and keyword search using a different indexing technology and query algorithms. To effectively deal with spatial keyword query, it is need to combine spatial index and text index as the spatial-text index, and to propose the corresponding query algorithms. According to the spatial index and text index combined with the different methods, existing query processing techniques can be roughly divided into three categories: loose coupling, spatial and text preference. Loose combination, which is for spatial data to establish a spatial index (generally the R-tree or Quad-tree), for the text data-based text index (usually Inverted index), respectively. There is no or only loose connection between the two types of indexes. During query processing, starting from spatial index and text index respectively, the objects that satisfy spatial constraint and text constraint are found, and then they are integrated. Spatial priority: in this kind of query processing technology, spatial text index is obtained by enhancing spatial index and adding text information. Spatial index mainly uses R-tree, while a few works use grid index. In this scenario, a spatial-text index is an enhancement of a text index (such as an Inverted file) that maps each keyword to a data structure that contains spatial information. In this paper, IR-tree index in the spatial priority scheme is used, which is combined by R-tree and Inverted list to achieve rapid filtering and expeditiously find the spatial objects required by users.

A spatial object o mainly contains two parts of information: spatial information and text information. Spatial information is usually represented by longitude and latitude while text information is the text description of the spatial object. The form of a spatial keyword query q is: $q(loc, keywords, k, \alpha)$, where $q.loc$ stands for the query location, $q.keywords$ is the set of query keywords, k is the number of results returned, $\alpha \in [0, 1]$ is a weight coefficient. Currently, the commonly used scoring function for a spatial object o and a spatial keyword query q is as follows:

$$Score(o, q) = \alpha \cdot S_{spatial}(o.loc, q.loc) + (1 - \alpha) \cdot S_{text}(o.doc, q.keywords) \tag{1}$$

$S_{spatial}$ and S_{text} respectively represent the normalized location proximity and text similarity between object o and query q (Li, 2015; João et al., 2011; Zhang et al., 2014). However, this kind of method has two shortcomings: (1) only support the strict matching process between query keywords and text information, while ordinary users' query intention is usually not clear and some semantically related results may also be accepted by users, so semantic query matching is required; (2) the weight of query keywords is solely evaluated according to the frequency of occurrence of keywords in text information, without considering the preference degree of users to different query keywords, which may lead to a large deviation between the results and user's actual expectation. Therefore, user's implicit preferences should be discovered from their relevant feedback information and the weights of query keywords should be adjusted accordingly.

Example 1. Figure 1 shows a spatial keyword query and five spatial objects. The spatial keyword query is:*q*: (*q.location*, {beefsteak, music}).

The query expresses that the user would like to find a restaurant offering beefsteak and music near his/her location. The set of spatial objects $o_1 \sim o_5$ is a nearby restaurants and teahouses. Each object contains the normalized Euclidean distance to query q and as well as the text information associated to the object. If the scoring function showed in Equation (1) is adopted in this scenario, o_2, o_5, and o_1 would be the query results (assuming that $\alpha = 0.5$ and $k = 3$ in equation (1)). In fact, however, this result set cannot satisfactory to all users because the users' preferences are usually different from each other. For example, some users may prefer to choose o_3 for the convenience of not going further places, that is, o_3 may also be one of the top-3 choices of these users. In other words, the traditional scoring methods cannot reflect the user's personalized and semantic query requirements.

To deal with the problems mentioned above, this chapter proposes an interactive personalized spatial keyword querying approach. This approach is divided into two stages. In the first stage, the text information of the spatial object is extended semantically by using the Gibbs method and LDA topic model in the offline time, so that each spatial object in the database has added the semantic related text description on the basis of the original text information. In the second stage, for a given spatial keyword query, the

Figure 1. An example of a spatial keyword query and spatial objects

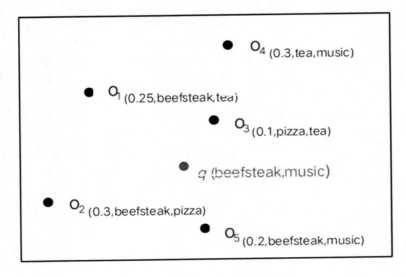

candidate result set containing k objects is first obtained by using the IR-tree index from the semantic extended spatial database, and users are required to label the spatial objects they are interested in (i.e. relevant feedback). And then, based on the user interactive information, the improved Rocchio algorithm is adopted to update the weight of query keywords and form a new query. Next, the updated query condition is used to retrieve the database and the process is repeated until the result is satisfactory to the user.

The rest of this chapter is arranged as follows. The related work is summarized in Section 2. Section 3 proposes the candidate set generation method. Section 4 proposes the query update method based on user feedback. Section 5 reports the experimental results and the chapter is concluded in Section 6.

RELATED WORK

In recent years, the massive increase of POIs on the Internet and the universal application of mobile devices, a large number of geographic location information and text description information of POI appeared on the Web, which needs the support of spatial keyword querying models. According to (Zheng et al., 2015), spatial keyword query can be divided into four categories: (i) Boolean Range Queries: this query retrieves all objects and returns the POIs whose text description contains all spatial keywords and whose geographical location is within the query region. (ii) Boolean kNN (k Nearest Neighbor) Queries (Lu et al., 2014; Ariel, Ouri & Naphtali, 2010): this kind of query model returns the first k POIs closest to the query location and the text description contains all the query keywords. (iii) Top-k Range Queries: this kind of query model is used to retrieve the top k POIs whose geographic location is within the query region and whose text description has the highest textual relevancy to the query keyword. (iv) Top-k kNN(k Nearest Neighbor) Queries (Chen et al., 2013; João B et al., 2011): this kind of query model takes into account the location proximity and text relevancy of POIs and query points, and carries out top-k retrieval. The four methods mentioned above are developed in a progressive manner and the latter is complementary to the former. The disadvantage of Boolean range query is that it cannot control the size of query results and the query results are not sorted. Boolean k-nearest neighbor query sorts query results according to the distance between POIs and query points. The closer the POI to the query point, the higher the ranking of POI. Both methods require that the text description of the point of interest contain all the query keywords, which is likely to result in either empty or a small number of query results or results that are far from the query point. To solve this problem, top-k range query and top-kk-nearest neighbor query do not require the description information of POIs to contain all query keywords, only partial query keywords can also be returned as query results. However, the sorting method of top-k range query only considers the text relevance of POIs without considering the location proximity, and top-kk-nearest neighbor query also considers the location proximity and text relevance of POIs and query. This is measured by the weighted combination of the spatial distance between POIs and query points and their text description and text similarity between query keywords.

The location similarity calculation method of a spatial object o and query q is as follows:

$$S_{spatial} = 1 - \frac{dist(o.loc, q.loc)}{MaxDist} \qquad (2)$$

where $dist(o.loc, q.loc)$ represents the Euclidean distance between o and q, and *MaxDist* represents the maximum distance between o and all spatial objects.

The basic idea of text similarity evaluation between a spatial object o and query q is as follows. First, spatial object text and query keyword are vectorized, respectively, represented by V_o and V_q (the dimension of vector is the total number of different keywords contained in all spatial object text information), and text similarity is calculated by using the Cosine similarity, which shows as follows:

$$S_{text} = \cos(o, q) = \frac{\sum_{i=1}^{n} V_o[i] * V_q[i]}{\sqrt{\sum_{i=1}^{n} V_o[i]^2} * \sqrt{\sum_{i=1}^{n} V_q[i]^2}} \tag{3}$$

It should be noted that existing spatial keyword queries only match keywords in form and only consider text similarity, while the semantic relevancy of query and text and the preference degree of users to different query keywords are neglected. Hu et al. proposed the fuzzy query problem of top-k keyword (Hu et al., 2012), allowing string input errors, providing a very flexible fault-tolerant way. However, it did not consider the semantic relevance of text information.

There has been a lot of work on the similarity measuring between texts, which mainly divided into two categories. The one is the cosine similarity, and the other is based on the topic model. The traditional text similarity model converts text information into text vectors, where feature term weight is calculated using tf-idf, and then cosine similarity is used to calculate the similarity between texts. For the topic model, Chen proposed the implicit semantic indexing (LSI) model (Chen, 2010), which mapped text vectors in high-dimensional vector space into low-dimensional latent semantic space, and then the similarity between texts is calculated. Based on LSI, Hofmann proposed a Probabilistic Latent Semantic Indexing (pLSI). pLSI model is seen as a true sense of the subject model. Since Blei puts forward Latent Dirichlet Allocation (LDA) to further improve the subject model. Blei, Ng, and Jordan use the LDA model for text modeling, which is to conduct "implicit semantic analysis" on the text. The purpose is to use the co-occurrence feature of term in the text to find the topic structure of the text. The implicit semantic representation of text can be used to model the linguistic phenomena of "polysemy" and "polysemy", which makes the results retrieved by the system match with the query of the user at the semantic level, rather than just the intersection at the lexical level. Compared with VSM and hamming distance methods, LDA focuses more on semantic mining with increased probability information.

Compared with the existing methods, in order to understand the semantic information reflected by the text information of spatial objects, this chapter proposes a special case of Gibbs Sampling algorithm of Markov Chain Monte Carlo algorithm (Sun et al., 2015), and meanwhile, in order to quickly and effectively obtain the spatial keyword query results, this requires the support of spatial data indexes, which are usually a combination of spatial index and text index structures. In this chapter, IR-tree, a mixed index structure integrated by R-tree spatial index and Inverted File text index, is used to retrieve spatial database, so that a set of spatial objects can be obtained quickly and efficiently. In addition, this chapter further studies the user interactive information to understand the user actual query intentions.

SEMANTIC EXTENSION AND CANDIDATE SET GENERATION

This section mainly describes the semantic extension method of spatial database based on LDA-Gibbs model and the generation method of candidate result set by using the IR-tree index.

Semantics Extending of Spatial Database

The basic idea of semantic extending to the spatial database is that, (i) integrates all the text information of the spatial object in the database into a document (assuming that the document contains K topics), (ii) the LDA model is used to generate the topic distribution of the document, and then the corresponding word distribution is generated for a topic. A word is randomly selected from the word distribution of a topic, and the process is repeated until several words are available under a specific topic; (iii) the text information of the spatial object o in the keywords of *o.doc* compared with the words in the generated theme-word distribution, if the same, the words under the corresponding theme ($\varphi_{k,t}$ of the word should be greater than the given threshold) are added into the *o.doc* to generate a new text information, so that the new text information reflects the semantics of the original information.

LDA Subject Distribution

LDA (Latent Dirichlet Allocation) is a kind of document theme generation model, also known as a three-tier Bayesian probability model. LDAmodel contains three layers: word, topic and document. Document to topic obeys polynomial distribution and topic to word obeys polynomial distribution. The LDA model clusters similar words into a topic by means of word clustering, bring up the semantic meaning between subject and topic, for terms in the same theme generally have the characteristics of synonyms, while the same word in different themes has the characteristics of polysemy. Thus, in the process of text similarity computer, the similarity between terms is eliminated, and the similarity between text items can be calculated by using the topic distribution of text. In addition, the computational results also have semantic effect when no external dictionary is needed, which is more robust than the algorithm based on external dictionary.

LDA adopts the method of "bag of words", which treats each document as a word frequency vector. However, the word bag method does not consider the order between words, which simplifies the complexity of the problem and provides an opportunity for the improvement of the model. This chapter uses LDA to identify the topic information in the text information associated to the spatial object.

Figure 2 shows the LDA probability model. In this model, α is the Dirichlet prior parameter of multiple distribution of subjects in the document; β is the Dirichlet prior parameter of the multiple distribution of words under the theme; z_n is the subject of the *n-th* word of the document; w_n is the *n-th* word of this document; K is the number of topics; N is the number of words in the document. Both θ and φ_k are unknown hidden variables to be solved, θ represents the subject distribution under the document. φ_k is the word distribution of the *k-th* topic.

Assuming that the text information of all spatial objects in the spatial database consist of a document D, w_n is a known variable that can be observed, α and β is a prior probability given by experience, we set $\alpha = 0.5$, $\beta = 0.1$, respectively. According to the probability model diagram of LDA in figure 2, the joint probability distribution of subject and word can be expressed as,

Figure 2. LDA probability model diagram

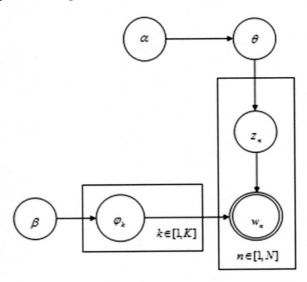

$$p(z, w, \theta, \Phi \mid \alpha, \beta) = \prod_{n=1}^{N} p(w_n \mid \phi_{z_n}) \cdot p(z_n \mid \theta) \cdot p(\theta \mid \alpha) \cdot p(\Phi \mid \beta) \qquad (4)$$

where $\Phi = \{\phi_k\}_{k=1}^{K}$.

LDA Learning Process Based on Gibbs Sampling

The unknown implicit variables in LDA model are θ and φ_k, and Gibbs Sampling algorithm is adopted to learn parameters. Gibbs sampling was proposed by Stuart and Donald Germain, brothers, in 1984. It is an algorithm used in statistics for Markov Monte Carlo (MCMC), which is used to approximately extract the sample sequence from a multi-variable probability distribution when it is difficult to directly sample. The sequence can be used to approximate joint distributions, marginal distributions of partial variables, or to compute integrals (such as the expected value of a variable). Gibbs sampling is a special case of Metropolis - Hastings algorithm. Gibbs Sampling operates by selecting one dimension of the probability vector each time and randomly selecting the value of the current dimension given the variable values of other dimensions. The process procedure mentioned above is repeated until the parameters are estimated. Figure 3 shows the LDA learning process based on Gibbs Sampling.

The process first initializes each word in document D, randomly assigning the topic, and then counts the number of words w appearing under each topic z and the number of keywords in topic z appearing under this document, namely $n(w|z)$ and $n(z|D)$. Each round calculates $p(z_i | z_{-i}, d, w)$, and estimates the probability that the subject of the current word belongs to each subject according to the subject assignment of other words. According to the probability distribution that the current word belongs to all topics z, a new topic is randomly selected for this word. Loop to update the subject of the next word, when θ and φ_k converge, the algorithm stops, output the estimated parameters θ and φ_k. Here, $p(z_i | z_{-i}, w)$ is the Gibbs updating rule, the calculation formula is as follows,

Figure 3. LDA learning process based on Gibbs sampling algorithm

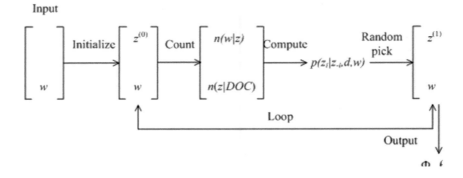

$$p(z_i = k \mid z_{-i}, w) = \frac{p(w, z)}{p(w, z_{-i})} = \frac{p(w \mid z)}{p(w_{-i} \mid z_{-i})p(w_i)} \cdot \frac{p(z)}{p(z_{-i})}$$

$$\propto \frac{n_{k,-i}^{(t)} + \beta_t}{\sum_{t=1}^{V} n_{k,-i}^{(t)} + \beta_t} (n_{DOC,-i}^{(k)} + \alpha_k)$$

(5)

where, w_n is initialized to obtain t, V is the number of words. $n_{k,-i}^{(t)}$ represents the number of times that the current word except t is assigned to the k-*th* topic, and $n_{D,-i}^{(k)}$ represents the number of times that the k-*th* topic is assigned to other words other than the current word in the document D.

When Gibbs sampling converges, calculate θ and φ_k according to the subject assignment of all words in document D as the implicit variable in the estimated probability graph model. The posterior distribution of topics on document D and the word posterior distribution under each topic are calculated as follows,

$$p(\theta \mid z, \alpha) = Dir(\theta \mid n_{DOC} + \alpha)$$

(6)

$$p(\phi_k \mid z, w, \beta) = Dir(\phi_k \mid n_k + \beta)$$

(7)

And then, we use the expected formula of the Dirichlet distribution, which shows as follows.

$$< Dir(a) > = a_i / \sum_i a_i$$

Two Multinomial distribution parameters are available on θ and φ_k,

$$\phi_{k,t} = \frac{n_k^{(t)} + \beta_t}{\sum_{t=}^{V} n_k^{(t)} + \beta_t}$$

(8)

$$\vartheta_k = \frac{n_{DOC}^{(k)} + \alpha_k}{\sum_{k=}^{K} n_{DOC}^{(k)} + \alpha_k} \tag{9}$$

Semantic Extension of Spatial Object Text Information

The text information of each spatial object in the spatial database is studied according to the LDA-Gibbs model to the theme-word distribution for implicit semantic analysis, and then the original spatial data set is expanded into a new spatial data set with semantics. The keyword in the text information *o.doc* of spatial object *o* is compared with that in the theme-word distribution. If the word is the same, the word under the theme ($\varphi_{k,t}$ of the word is greater than 0.07) is added into the *o.doc* to generate a new text information, so that the new text information can fully express the semantics of the original text information.

Figure 1 illustrates semantic extension of spatial object text using the Gibbs Sampling algorithm. The text information of POIs in figure 1 is integrated into a document, and the number of topics is assumed to be 2. Then the theme-word distribution can be obtained by LDA model and the result as follows:

Topic0: beefsteak 0.25, pizza 0.745454
Topic1: tea 0.598125, music 0.396975

At last, the keywords in $o_1 \sim o_5$ are matched with the words in theme-word distribution and the words with the same matching and the parameter value greater than 0.5 are added into $o_1 \sim o_5$, and extended into a new set of spatial objects:

o_1: (0.25, beefsteak, tea, pizza)
o_2: (0.3, beefsteak, pizza)
o_3: (0.1, pizza, tea)
o_4: (0.3, tea, music)
o_5: (0.2, beefsteak, music, pizza, tea)

Candidate Set Generation

In recent years, with the popularization of the Internet and the rapid development of geographic information system, a large amount of data emerges on the Web, making the spatial database too large. Therefore, the construction of mixed index structure of spatial database is required. There are many spatial objects in spatial database. Therefore, in the process of feedback, it is unrealistic to provide user feedback through the whole spatial database in each round. Therefore, the purpose of this stage is to generate a smaller candidate set and provide it to the user for feedback.

This section mainly studies the selection of candidate sets for spatial keyword query based on IR-tree index. IR-tree is a popular hybrid index structure for indexing the spatial objects with the text information. IR-tree is composed of R-tree spatial index and Inverted file. Each node of IR-tree contains two types information, namely the minimum boundary distance of the sub-tree and the inverted list containing keywords. Figure 4 and Figure 5 show the IR-tree constructed over the spatial objects appeared in figure 1, respectively.

Figure 4. Minimum boundary rectangle of spatial objects in Figure 1

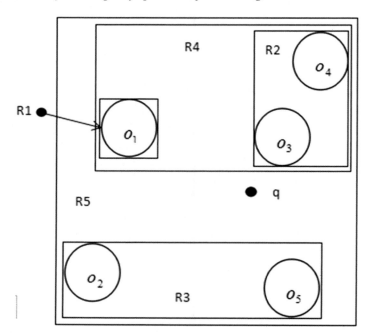

Figure 5. IR-tree structure

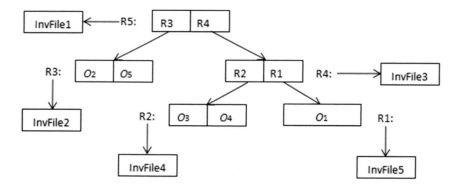

The process of candidate set generation by using the IR-tree index is as follows:

1. Initializes the priority queue U and a list V, which stores the entries already accessed in the IR-tree, and list V stores the candidate set, e is an entry which has an Inverted list and matrix with keyword set.

2. Given a query q, then iteratively deletes the top entry from U to e, and if e is a spatial object, adds it to V. If e is a non-leaf node, determines whether the minimum distance between query q and node rectangle is less than the distance between e and query, if less than that, determines whether the set of keywords in the text information of query q and the set of keywords in the sub-items of node e intersect, then e sub-entry are added to U. Otherwise, if e is a leaf node, the distance between

query q and spatial object is smaller than that between e and query point. If it is smaller, the set of keywords in the text information of query q and the set of keywords in the objects contained in node e are judged to be intersected. If there is intersection, the objects contained in e are added to U. If U is empty, the above process is terminated.

3. Lastly, according to the scoring function, the retrieved result set V is sorted by the scores, and the first k objects with the highest scores are obtained as candidate set for the given query.

The above process of spatial keyword query using IR-tree index is shown in algorithm 1.

In Algorithm 1, lines 1 and 2 are the initialization process, lines 3-19 are the initial retrieval of IR-tree, and line 20 is the selection of the first k spatial objects of the retrieval results as candidate sets using the score function.

Since there are many spatial objects in spatial database, it is not realistic to provide user feedback through the whole spatial database in each round in the process of feedback. The goal of this phase is to provide feedback to users by generating a smaller set of candidates. Algorithm 1 prepares the personalized query for relevant feedback in section 4.

Algorithm 1. Candidate set generation

Input: dataset D, query q, number k
Output: candidate set S
1. Initialize an empty list V
2. Initialize a priority queue U
3. Add root node of tr to U
4. **while** U is not empty **do**
5. $e \leftarrow$ top entry of U
6.   **if** e *is spatial object o* **then**
7.   Add e to V;
8.   break;
9.   else
10.   **if** e *is non-leaf entry* **then**
11.   **for** each *child* e_i *in* e **do**
12.   **if** (distance between e_i and query < distance between e and query **and** e_i contains query keywords)
13. e_i add to U;
14.   **else**
15.   **for** each *object* o_i *in* e **do**
16.   **if** (distance between o_i and query < distance between e and query **and** o_i contains query keywords)
17. o_i add to U;
18. $S \leftarrow$ Use score function to select the first k spatial objects from V

PERSONALIZED QUERY BASED ON USER INTERACTIVE FEEDBACK

User Interactive Feedback

Through the user's interactive feedback, the purpose is to enhance the weights of keywords appearing in the semantic relevant text information and reduce the weights of keywords appearing in the non-relevant text information, so that users can gradually approach their actual needs and finally get satisfactory results. The characteristic of relevant feedback is that the query operation is decomposed into a series of small query steps to gradually approach the target domain the user wants.

Given a query q, the IR-tree index is first used in the spatial database for query matching, returned to a group of spatial objects, and then the first k objects are obtained as candidate sets sorting by the scoring function. On this basis, the user marks out the relevant and irrelevant objects in the candidate set, that is, the interactive relevant feedback. After user feedback, near the query related objects, thus far from unrelated objects, using the related object and unrelated object Rocchio algorithm of key words in the text information extends the initial query to form new query. It finally returned to the user an improved more object set to satisfy user needs. Repeat the above process, the user is expected to get a more accurate query, and then use the index to retrieve a better result set. Each time the relevant user feedback is performed, the query is expanded and the weight is recalculated, and the "improved" query is executed, which is known as a "feedback query". The process repeats execution until the result is satisfactory to the user, and the feedback is terminated.

Evaluate Keyword Weights Based on Rocchio Algorithm

In query extension, the weight of the keyword reflects the importance of the keywords and should be recalculated. The existing methods usually use Equation (3) to measure the text similarity between query keywords and spatial object, in which V_o and V_q are vectors with the same dimension, making $V_o = \{d_1, d_2, ..., d_n\}$, $V_q = \{q_1, q_2, ..., q_n\}$. Where, d_i and q_i are the keyword weights contained in the spatial object and query, the vector space model values them at 0 or 1. Here, 0 for the presence of the keyword in the vector and 1 stands for a carte Blanche keyword. Now they are mostly at [0,1]. In this way, a vector space can be constructed and the matching process of spatial object and query condition can be transformed into the similarity calculation problem of V_o and V_q in the vector space. n represents the text information of the spatial object collection and the total number of different keywords contained in the query condition.

The weight of keyword is calculated using *tf-idf* function, and the Formula is as follows:

$$w_{t_i} = tf(t_i, o.doc) * idf(t_i, O) \tag{10}$$

where, the word frequency $tf(t_i, o.doc)$ is the frequency of the keyword t_i appearing in $o.doc$, the inverse document frequency $idf(t_i, O) = 1/f(t_i, O)$, and $f(t_i, O)$ is the number of objects containing the keyword t_i.

When extending a query based on user feedback, the weight of keyword in the query is recalculated using the Rocchio algorithm (Chen, Fu & John, 2005).

$$V_q = \{q'_1, q'_2, ..., q'_n\} \tag{11}$$

Specifically, q_i is the initial weight of the *i-th* keyword of query q. If the query keyword t_i is a keyword for expansion, then there is no q_i, then $q_i = 0$. Otherwise, q'_i is the new weight of the keyword t_i after recalculating the weight. $|rel|$ represents the number of objects that users judge to be related to user requirements, $|norrel|$ is the number of unrelated objects, and w_{ti} represents the weight of keyword in related and unrelated objects. α, β, and γ is the constant parameters of the adjustment formula, respectively. On this basis, Rocchio Formula can be defined as:

$$q_i' = \alpha * q_i + \beta * \frac{1}{|rel|}\sum_{rel} w_{t_i} - \gamma * \frac{1}{|norrel|}\sum_{norrel} w_{t_i} \tag{12}$$

where, β is positive feedback, γ is negative feedback, and the value of α, β, γ is used to adjust the relative importance of the text information between the original query, the relevant object and the irrelevant object. When query is extended, all the keywords are extracted from all the objects judged to be relevant. However, some query extension keywords may also appear in unrelated objects. While γ does not add any keywords to the query, its role is only to reduce the weight of some extended query keywords, because these keywords appear in irrelevant literature. Lton and Buckley's experiments found that when $\alpha = 1$, $\beta = 0.75$, and $\gamma = 0.25$, Rocchio method can get the best results (Xu, Zhang & Zhong, 2005), w_{ti} is calculated by using Formula (10).

In combination with figure 1, which is an example of spatial keyword query, for spatial keyword query q, it is assumed that o_1, o_2, and o_5 are related, while o_3 and o_4 are not. The expanded query Q' can be calculated by Rocchio Formula as follows.

$$Q' = 1 * (1,1,0,0) + 0.75 * \frac{1}{3} * (\frac{1}{9} + \frac{1}{6} + \frac{1}{12}, 0 + 0 + \frac{1}{8}, \frac{1}{12} + \frac{1}{8} + \frac{1}{16}, \frac{1}{12} + 0 + \frac{1}{16})$$
$$- 0.25 * \frac{1}{2} * (0 + 0, 0 + \frac{1}{4}, \frac{1}{8} + 0, \frac{1}{8} + \frac{1}{8})$$
$$= (1.09028, 1.00000, 0.05208, 0.00521)$$

Table 1. Keyword weight intext information of query and object

	beefsteak	music	pizza	tea
Q	1	1	0	0
o_1	0.1111	0	0.0833	0.0833
o_2	0.1667	0	0.125	0
o_3	0	0	0.125	0.125
o_4	0	0.25	0	0.125
o_5	0.0833	0.125	0.0625	0.0625
Q'	1.0911	1.0000	0.0521	0.0052

To determine which objects can meet the user query conditions, some similarity measurement methods are needed. In the vector space retrieval model, the degree of correlation between the text information of the spatial object and the text information of the query condition is determined by calculating the similarity between the two pairs of vectors. According to Table 1 and Equation (3), Table 2 can be obtained as follows.

As can be seen from Table 2, although the object o_3 is not related to the query, the new query after feedback has semantic relevance with object o_3, because the objects o_1, o_2, and o_5 are related to the query containing keywords in the text information associated to object o_3. The fewer query keywords appear during the query, the more likely this will occur. In general, the Rocchio algorithm based on relevant feedback improves the semantic relevance of related objects and increases user satisfaction with queries. The process of spatial keyword query based on user feedback is illustrated by Algorithm 2.

The time complexity of IR-tree retrieval based on Rocchio algorithm is $O(|q.\varphi|\cdot\log|O|)$. Where, $|q.\varphi|$ is the number of keywords in query q, and $|O|$ is the number of spatial objects in spatial database.

Table 2. Text similarity between queries and objects

	o_1	o_2	o_3	o_4	o_5
Q	0.14907	0.21822	0	0.28868	0.25516
Q'	0.16303	0.23782	0.00977	0.27931	0.25936

Algorithm 2. User feedback process based on Rocchio algorithm

```
Input: candidate set S, query q
Output: result set P
1. The text information d of the object in the candidateset S is vectorized
2. text information Q of query q is vectorized
3. Initialize the empty list P, rel, norrel
4. while true do
5.    Present objects in S to users;
6. rel ← user pick his/her favourite o_i from S;
7. norrel ← user pick his/her dislike o_i from S;
8. Q' ← Q based on the Rocchio formula
9. S ← Q' for IR-tree retrieval
10. if terminate is truethen
11. P ← S
12. break;
13. return P;
```

Termination of User Feedback

There are two ways to stop user feedback. The one is to judge whether the final result is satisfactory. The other one is the system automatically calculates the stop threshold. In this section, a method of automatic determination of stop threshold is presented.

Let f^m and f^{m-1} represent the results obtained by user feedback in m-*th* round and $(m$-$1)$-*th* round respectively. If the intersection reaches a certain number, user feedback will be terminated. The calculation method is as shown in equation (13).

$$terminate = \frac{\{f^m\} \cap \{f^{m-1}\}}{\{f^m\}} \tag{13}$$

EXPERIMENTS

Experimental Settings

Dataset: We used real POI datasets captured from Yelp's Comment Website for our experimental study. Yelp is a famous American merchant review website containing information about merchants in restaurants, shopping centers, hotels, tourism and other fields, as well as user evaluation and shopping experience. These real POI data are processed with 174567 POIs, and each POI has an ID, a location (expressed in longitude and latitude) and a user comment. We use location as spatial information and user reviews as text information.

- **Query Set:** We randomly select 10 objects in the data set as query conditions. The location information extracted from the 10 spatial objects is used as the location information of the query condition (expressed in the form of longitude and latitude). At the same time, a certain number of words are randomly selected from the text information in the data set and randomly combined as the text information of the query condition. The number of query keywords is controlled at 2~8. This experiment designed the number of keywords in the text information of query conditions, which are 2, 4, 6, and 8, respectively. Among them, there are 2 query objects with the number of keywords 2, 4, and 8, and 4 query objects with the number of keywords 6. In the process of spatial keyword query, the spatial object is excluded from the data set.

EXPERIMENTAL RESULTS AND ANALYSIS

User Satisfaction Survey

The purpose of this experiment is to test the difference in user satisfaction between the existing method of calculating location similarity and text similarity (namely, formula (1), and α=0.5) and our method proposed. The evaluation criterion is showed in Equation (14),

$$Accueacy = \frac{\{relevant\} \cap \{top-10\ retrieved\}}{10} \tag{14}$$

Here, *relevant* is a set of objects that users choose to get related to the query, and *Top-10 retrieved* is the first 10 objects obtained by the spatial keyword query method.

- **Experimental Setup:** We invited five users. For each test query, we can obtain a candidate set of 30 objects that contains relevant and irrelevant objects by collecting the top-10 results of RANDOM, our method, and text similarity method.

After this, we invited one user to mark the top 10 objects that he/she considers are most relevant to the given query in the candidate set composed of 30 objects corresponding to each query, and these 10 objects are treated as the criteria for the accuracy evaluation. Then, the text similarity method (Equation (1)) and our method were used to obtain the first 10 objects, and then the accuracy of the query was calculated by Equation (14) (that is, the overlapping degree of the standard 10 objects and the 10 objects retrieved by different methods). Figure 6 shows the accuracy of the query results obtained by the same user for the different queries.

We also invited 10 users (tutors, graduate students and some undergraduates) to select the top 10 objects that are most relevant to a specific query in the candidate set. Then, the text similarity method (Formula (1)) and our method are used to obtain the top 10 objects related to the query, and the user

Figure 6. The comparison of accuracy between text similarity method and our user feedback method for different queries

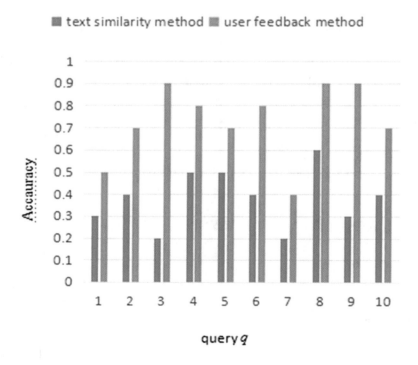

Figure 7. The comparison of accuracy between text similarity method and our method corresponding different users

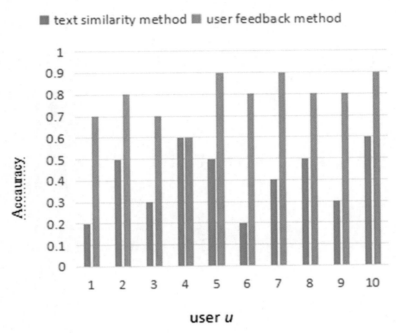

satisfaction can be checked. Figure 7 shows the comparison of satisfaction among different users under the same query.

According to Figure 6 and Figure 7, the average accuracy was calculated respectively. Under different queries, the accuracy of the result set obtained by the same user using the text similarity method is 0.38, and that of the user interactive feedback method (i.e., our method) is 0.73. The accuracy of the result set obtained by different users using the text similarity method is 0.41, and that of our method is 0.79. The user satisfaction of our method is relatively high, because through semantic extension of spatial object text information and user related feedback, the relevance feedback technique can improve the retrieval performance greatly, the result of this method can better meet users' semantic needs and preferences.

Feedback Termination

This experiment aims to evaluate the effect of termination threshold on the rate of convergence of user feedback based on the Rocchio algorithm. We limited the maximum round count to 10 to avoid difficult situations. Where, the number of candidate sets $k=\{10, 20\}$ and the number of keywords $n=8$, and the value of τ is 0.2, 0.4, 0.6, and 0.8, respectively.

From Figure 8, it can be seen that as the value k increases, the greater the intersection between the result set obtained in current round and the previous one, the slower the convergence speed, and the number of feedback rounds increases. When value τ is set too high, the user feedback process cannot even be terminated. Generally, users can get satisfactory results after 7 rounds of feedback.

Figure 8. The impact of the termination threshold

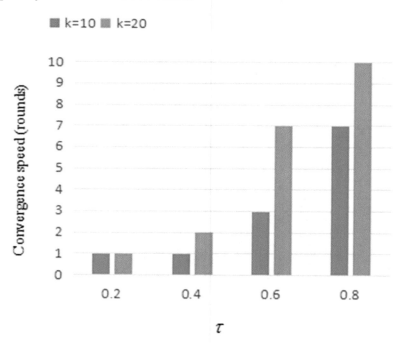

CONCLUSION

In order to better understand the user's query intention, this chapter proposes a user interactive feedback based personalized spatial keyword semantic query approach. The semantic extension of spatial data sets makes the newly generated text information reflect the semantics of the original information. The final result set, which is the closest to the user query and can meet the user's query demand closely, is obtained through interactive feedback. Through the experiment comparison, it can be seen that the accuracy rate by using our method is higher than that of text similarity measuring, indicating that the result set obtained by using the spatial keyword query based on user interactive feedback is closer to the query and more consistent with the user's query intention.

The difference between this paper and the existing method is that the spatial keyword query uses user feedback. The user expands the query through several rounds of independent selection of objects related to the query, making the new query closer to the real intention of the user and making the final retrieved result set more satisfying to the user. In the retrieval experiment of spatial keyword query, it is found that the method proposed in this paper is effective for improving user efficiency and meeting users' query requirements. However, in order to make more effective use of semantic information and better understand user intention, and improve the accuracy of result set, in future work, the author will study spatial keyword query based on relevant feedback in probabilistic latent semantic model. The difference between this paper and the existing methods is that it reflects the semantics of the original information and uses user feedback to reflect the personalized query. In the retrieval experiment of spatial keyword query, it is found that our method is effective for improving user efficiency and meeting users' query needs.

REFERENCES

Cao, X., Chen, L., Cong, G., & Jensen, C. (2012). Spatial keyword querying. In *Proceedings of the International Conference on Data Engineering (ICDE'12)* (pp. 16-29).

Cao, X., Cong, G., Jensen, C., & Ooi, B. (2011). Collective spatial keyword querying. In *Proceedings of the ACM SIGMOD International Conference on Management of Data (SIGMOD'11)* (pp. 373-384). 10.1145/1989323.1989363

Cary, A., Wolfson, O., & Rishe, N. (2010). Efficient and scalable method for processing top-k spatial boolean queries. In *Proceedings of the Scientific and Statistical Database Management (SSDBM'10)* (pp.87–95). 10.1007/978-3-642-13818-8_8

Chen, L., Cong, G., Jensen, C., & Wu, D. (2013). Spatial keyword query processing: an experimental evaluation. In *Proceedings of the International Conference on Very Large Data Bases (VLDB'13)* (pp. 217-228) 10.14778/2535569.2448955

Chen, Z., & Fu, B. (2005, August). A quadratic lower bound for Rocchio's similarity-based relevance feedback algorithm. In *International Computing and Combinatorics Conference* (pp. 955-964). Berlin, Germany: Springer.

Dabringer, C., & Eder, J. (2011). Efficient top-k retrieval for user preference queries. In *Proceedings of the ACM Symposium on Applied Computing* (SAC'11) (pp. 1045-1052). 10.1145/1982185.1982414

Felipe, I., Hristidis, V., & Rishe, N. (2008). Keyword search on spatial databases. In *Proceedings of the International Conference on Data Engineering (ICDE'08)* (pp.656–665)

Guo, L., Shao, J., Aung, H., & Tan, K. (2015). Efficient continuous top-k spatial keyword queries on road networks. *GeoInformatica*, *19*(1), 29–60. doi:10.100710707-014-0204-8

Hu, J., Fan, J., Li, G., & Chen, S. (2012). Top-k fuzzy spatial keyword search. *Chinese Journal of Computers*, *36*(2), 1930–1942.

Li, G., Feng, J., & Xu, J. (2012). Desks: direction-aware spatial keyword search. In *Proceedings of the International Conference on Data Engineering (ICDE'12)* (pp. 474-485).

Li, J., Liu, C., Zhou, R., & Wang, W. (2011). Top-k keyword search over probabilistic XML data. In *Proceedings of the International Conference on Data Engineering (ICDE'11)* (pp. 673-684). 10.1109/ICDE.2011.5767875

Li, W. (2015). *Research on the survey of spatial keyword query.*

Lihua, C. (2010). Comment on Latent Semantic Analysis of Retrieval Precision Rate Factors Based on the Impact of Natural Language. *Journal of Modern Information*, *3*, 26–31.

Liu, X. P., Wan, C. X., Liu, D. X., & Liao, G. Q. (2016). Survey on spatial keyword search. *Journal of Software*, *27*(2), 329–347.

Liu, Y., Liu, C., Liu, B., Qu, M., & Xiong, H. (2016). Unified Point-of-Interest recommendation with temporal interval assessment. In *Proceedings of the ACM SIGKDD International Conference on Knowledge Discovery & Data Mining (KDD'16)* (pp.121-130) 10.1145/2939672.2939773

Lu, Y., Lu, J., Cong, G., Wu, W., & Shahabi, C. (2014). Efficient algorithms and cost models for reverse spatial-keyword k-nearest neighbor search. ACM Transactions on Database Systems, 39(2), 573–598.

Qian, Z., Xu, J., Zheng, K., Zhao, P., & Zhou, X. (2017). Semantic-aware top-k spatial keyword queries. *World Wide Web*, 21(3), 573–594.

Rocha-Junior, J., Gkorgkas, O., Jonassen, S., & Nørvåg, K. (2011). Efficient processing of top-k spatial keyword queries. In *Proceedings of the International Symposium on Spatial and Temporal Databases* (pp. 93-104). 10.1007/978-3-642-22922-0_13

Roy, S., & Chakrabarti, K. (2010). Location-aware type ahead search on spatial databases: semantics and efficiency. In *Proceedings* of *the ACM SIGMOD International Conference on Management* of *Data (SIGMOD'10)* (pp. 361-372). New York: ACM.

Sun, C. N., Zheng, C., & Xia, Q. S. (2013). Chinese text similarity computing based on LDA. *Computer Technology and Development*, 23(1), 217–220.

Wang, X., Zhang, X., Zhang, W., Lin, X., & Huang, Z. (2016). Skype: top-k spatial-keyword publish/subscribe over sliding window. In *Proceedings of the International Conference on Very Large Data Bases (VLDB'16)* (pp.588-599). 10.14778/2904483.2904490

Wu, D., Yiu, M., Jensen, C., & Cong, G. (2011). Efficient continuously moving top-k spatial keyword query processing. In *Proceedings of the International Conference on Data Engineering (ICDE'11)* (pp. 541-552). 10.1109/ICDE.2011.5767861

Xu, X., Zhang, B., & Zhong, Q. (2005). Text categorization using SVMs with Rocchio ensemble for intemet information classification. In *Proceedings of the International Conference on Communications, Networking and Mobile Computing* (pp. 1022-1031).

Yu, A., Agarwal, P., & Yang, J. (2010). Processing a large number of continuous preference top-k queries. In *Proceedings* of *the ACM SIGMOD International Conference on Management* of *Data (SIGMOD'10)* (pp. 397-408). New York: ACM.

Zhang, D., Chan, C., & Tan, K. (2014). Processing spatial keyword query as a top-k aggregation query. In *Proceedings of the International ACM SIGIR Conference on Research and Development in Information Retrieval (SIGIR'14)* (pp. 355–364). New York: ACM. 10.1145/2600428.2609562

Zheng, K., Su, H., Zheng, B., Shang, S., Xu, J., Liu, J., & Zhou, X. (2015). Interactive top-k spatial keyword queries. In *Proceedings of the International Conference on Data Engineering (ICDE'15)*, (pp. 423-434).

KEY TERMS AND DEFINITIONS

IR-Tree: IR-tree is a spatial text index that combines R-tree with an inverted list.

LDA: LDA is a kind of unsupervised machine learning technology, which can be used to identify the hidden subject information in massive document collection or corpus.

Chapter 11
Voronoi–Based kNN Queries Using K–Means Clustering in MapReduce

Wei Yan
Liaoning University, China

ABSTRACT

The kNN queries are special type of queries for massive spatial big data. The k-nearest neighbor queries (kNN queries), designed to find k nearest neighbors from a dataset S for every point in another dataset R, are useful tools widely adopted by many applications including knowledge discovery, data mining, and spatial databases. In cloud computing environments, MapReduce programming model is a well-accepted framework for data-intensive application over clusters of computers. This chapter proposes a method of kNN queries based on Voronoi diagram-based partitioning using k-means clusters in MapReduce programming model. Firstly, this chapter proposes a Voronoi diagram-based partitioning approach for massive spatial big data. Then, this chapter presents a k-means clustering approach for the object points based on Voronoi diagram. Furthermore, this chapter proposes a parallel algorithm for processing massive spatial big data using kNN queries based on k-means clusters in MapReduce programming model. Finally, extensive experiments demonstrate the efficiency of the proposed approach.

INTRODUCTION

The k nearest neighbor query (kNN query) is a classical problem that has been extensively studied, due to its many important applications, such as knowledge discovery, data mining, and spatial databases. The k nearest neighbor query (kNN) is a special type of query that is k nearest neighbors from points in S for each query point r in dataset R. The kNN query typically serves as a primitive operation and is widely used in spatial databases. The basic idea of implementing kNN queries is to perform a pairwise computation of distance between each object point in S and each object point in R. The computational complexity of such pairwise calculation is $O(|R| \times |S|)$. Then, finding the k nearest neighbors in S for every r in R corresponds to sorting the computational distances, and easily leads to a complexity of $|S|$

DOI: 10.4018/978-1-5225-8446-9.ch011

× log|S|. Therefore, a lot of research works have been dedicated to improve the efficiency of the *k*NN queries and reduce the computational complexity of the *k*NN queries (Jagadish et al. 2005) (Bohm et al. 2004) (Ciaccia et al. 1997) (Yu et al. 2010). With the rapid growth of spatial data, the parallel *k*NN query has become a challenging task.

MapReduce is a parallel processing framework that uses parallel and distributed patterns to process massive data sets. The MapReduce programming model provides good scalability, flexibility and fault tolerance. MapReduce was first introduced by Google (Dean et al. 2008) and ran on the Hadoop clusters, which is an open source framework. MapReduce provides a programming model to process the large scale data sets, which can be distributed easily. The MapReduce programming framework can install on computational clusters and automatically distribute a work job on clusters of machines. Therefore, MapReduce programming model becomes an ideal framework of processing *k*NN queries over massive spatial datasets. This chapter proposes a method of parallel *k*NN queries based on k-means clusters using MapReduce programming model.

Now, lots of researches (Yao et al. 2010) have been devoted to improve the performance of *k*NN query algorithms. However, all these approaches are performed on a single, centralized server. In single machine, the computational capability and storage are limited, and its efficiency is low. How to perform the *k*NN query on parallel machines is an important issue in cloud computing environments. ALL the existing work has concentrated on the spatial databases based on the centralized paradigm. Xia et al. (2004) proposed a novel *k*NN-join algorithm, called the Gorder *k*NN join method. Gorder is a block nested loop join method that exploits sorting, join scheduling and distance computation filtering and reduction to reduce both I/O and CPU costs. It is simple and yet efficient, and handles high-dimensional data efficiently. However, the system of centralized server will eventually suffer from performance deterioration as the size of the dataset increases. A solution is to consider the parallel query processing in distributed cloud computing environment. However, an efficient parallel *k*NN queries in MapReduce programming framework are challenging tasks. Firstly, the classical query processing algorithms need to be redesigned in MapReduce programming framework. Second, the strategies of data partitioning and distribution need to be designed also in parallel programming model. For this purpose, we improve previous implementations of kNN queries in MapReduce programming framework, focusing on the different steps involved in Map and Reduce phases.

Parallel spatial query processing has been studied in parallel database, cluster systems as well as cloud computing platform. In cloud computing environments, a large part of data-processing using MapReduce (Dean et al. 2004) programming model runs extensively on Hadoop. The MapReduce programming model provides a powerful parallel and distributed computing paradigm. For such data intensive applications, the MapReduce programming framework has applied as a platform for big data processing. Cui et al. (2014) addressed the problems of processing large-scale data using *k*-means clustering algorithm and proposed a novel processing model in MapReduce to eliminate the iteration dependence and obtain high performance. A data structure that is extremely efficient in exploring a local neighborhood in a geometric space is Voronoi diagram (Okabe et al. 2000). Given a set of points, a general Voronoi diagram uniquely partitions the space into disjoint regions. The region corresponding to a point *p* covers the points in space that are closer to *p* than to any other point. Recently, the parallel *k*NN queries in MapReduce programming framework, such as H-zkNNJ (Zhang et al. 2012), H-BRJ (Zhang et al. 2012) and PGBJ (Lu et al. 2012), were proposed. The method PGBJ is shown to outperform H-zkNNJ and H-BRJ since PGBJ performs the early pruning of object points for non-*k*NN queries. However, the pruning power of method PGBJ is not effective when the size of datasets becomes very large.

This chapter investigates the problem of implementing kNN queries in MapReduce programming framework. To compute the *k*NN queries efficiently, this chapter presents a partitioning method using Voronoi diagram that is multi-dimensional spatial datasets partition into Voronoi cell. Moreover, this chapter uses *k*-means clustering algorithm to apply on the Voronoi cell. The *k*-means clustering algorithm is a well-known method for partitioning *n* points that lie in the *d*-dimensional space into *k* clusters. Then, this chapter proposes a method of pivot for the Voronoi diagram-based data partitioning, which uses the *k*-means clustering algorithm to choose as pivot. Furthermore, this chapter proposes an efficient algorithm for processing *k*NN queries based on *k*-means clustering algoritnm using MapReduce programming framework.

The objectives of the chapter are summarized as follows:

- This chapter proposes an implementation of kNN queries in MapReduce programming framework, especially for large scale of multi-dimensional spatial datasets. The implementation uses the mapper and reducer task jobs to improve the performance of the *k*NN queries.
- This chapter proposes a partitioning method using Voronoi diagram that partitions the multi-dimensional spatial datasets into Voronoi cell. The Voronoi diagram-based partitioning divides the object points into groups, each of which is executed by mappers to perform the *k*NN queries.
- This chapter proposes the *k*-means clustering algorithm to apply on the Voronoi cell. The center point for each cluster is chosen as pivots of Voronoi diagram.
- This chapter proposes an efficient algorithm for processing *k*NN queries based on *k*-means clustering algorithm using MapReduce programming framework.

BACKGROUND

Related Works

Performing *k*NN queries in spatial databases has been extensively studied in the research of Xia et al. (2004). Yao et al. (2010) proposed both the *k*NN query and the *k*NN join in the relational database, used the user-defined-function that a query optimizer cannot optimize. The authors designed algorithms that could be implemented by SQL operators using a small constant number of random shifts for databases, and guaranteed to find the approximate *k*NN. However, these works focus on the centralized, single-thread method that is not directly applicable in MapReduce programming model. Zhang et al. (2009) proposed a parallel spatial join algorithm in MapReduce, dealing with only spatial distance joins, which does not solve *k*NN joins. Zhang et al. (2012) proposed novel algorithms in MapReduce to perform efficient parallel *k*NN joins on large data. The authors proposed the exact H-BRJ algorithms and approximate H-zkNNJ algorithms, and the H-zkNNJ algorithms deliver performance which is orders of magnitude better than baseline methods, as evidenced from experiments on massive real datasets. Jiang et al. (2010) proposed the performance study of MapReduce (Hadoop) on a 100-node cluster of Amazon EC2 with various levels of parallelism. The authors identify five design factors that affect the performance of Hadoop, and investigate alternative but known methods for each factor. Their works show that by carefully tuning these factors, the overall performance of Hadoop can be improved by a factor of 2.5 to 3.5 for the same benchmark, and is thus more comparable to that of parallel database systems.

Recently, the methods of parallel kNN queries are proposed to deal with big datasets in cloud computing environment. Wu et al. (2014) presented a local search method FloS (Fast Local Search) for efficient and exact top-k proximity query in large graphs, which is based on the on local optimum property of proximity measures. The method introduces several simple operations on transition probabilities, which allow developing lower and upper bounds on the proximity. Ni et al. (2016) proposed a method of the location privacy protection under user privacy preferences for location-based kNN queries, which defines a location privacy model that facilitates query users a convenient way to express their location privacy preferences. Peng et al. (2017) proposed a reusable and single-interactive SANN paradigm in Euclidean high-dimensional space, which uses B^c-tree to quickly locate high-dimensional candiates in cloud. The method acquired approximate k-nearest neighbors by linearly scanning over the candidates. Song et al. (2015) proposed the existing systems to perform the kNN operation in the context of MapReduce, which follows three main steps to compute kNN over MapReduce, namely the pre-processing of data, the partitioning and the actual computation. Kim et al. (2016) proposed the efficient parallel algorithm kNN-MR to process the kNN join using MapReduce, and developed the novel vector projection pruning which identifies non-kNN points thar are guaranteed not to be included in the result of a kNN join.

Furthermore, Kim et al. (2012) investigated how the top-k similarity join algorithms can get benefits from the popular MapReduce framework. The authors first developed the divide-and-conquer and branch-and-bound algorithms. Next, the authors proposed the all pair partitioning and essential pair partitioning methods to minimized the amount of data transfers between map and reduce functions. Finally, the authors performed the experiments with not only synthetic but also real-life data sets. Okcan et al. (2011) proposed join model simplifies creation and reasoning about joins in MapReduce. Using this model, the authors derive a surprisingly simple randomized algorithm, called 1-Bucket-Theta, for implementing arbitrary joins (theta-joins) in a single MapReduce job.

Regarding the method of k-means clusters, Vattani (2011) presented how to construct a two-dimensional instance with k clusters for which the k-means algorithm requires $2^{\Omega(k)}$ iterations. Bahmani et al. (2012) proposed k-means++ initialization algorithm, which obtains an initial set of centers that is provably close to the optimum solution. About the work of parallel clustering algorithm, Ene et al. (2011) proposed clustering algorithms that can be used in MapReduce, which are the practical and popular clustering problems k-center and k-median. Ma et al. (2007) proposed a distributed k-median clustering algorithm for use in a distributed environment. Several approximate methods for computing the median in a distributed environment are proposed and analyzed in the context of the iterative k-median algorithm. Xu et al. (1999) presented PDBSCAN, a parallel version of the clustering algorithm. The authors uses the shared-nothing architecture with multiple computers interconnected through a network. A fundamental component of a shared-nothing system is its distributed data structure. The authors introduced a distributed spatial index structure in which the data is spread among multiple computers and the indexes of the data are replicated on every computer. Debatty et al. (2014). proposed a MapReduce implementation of G-means, a variant of k-means that is able to automatically determine k, the number of clusters. Other techniques that run a clustering algorithm with different values of k and choose the value of k that provides the best results have a computation cost that is proportional to nk^2. Zhao et al. (2009). proposed a fast parallel k-means clustering algorithm based on MapReduce, which has been widely embraced by both academia and industry. Akdogan et al. (2010) proposed the method of parallel geospatial query processing with the MapReduce programming model. The proposed approach creates a spatial index, Voronoi diagram, for given data points in two-dimensional space and enables efficient processing of a wide range of Geospatial queries. Vernica et al. (2010) proposed an efficient parallel set-similarity join in MapReduce. The authors propose a three-stage approach for end-to-end set-similarity joins, and take as input a set of records and output a set of joined records based on a set-similarity condition.

*k*NN Queries

In n-dimensional space D, given two points r and s, $|r, s|$ represents the distance between point r and s in space D. In this chapter, the Euclidean distance is used as the distance.

$$| r, s |= (\sum_{i=1}^{n} (r[i] - s[i])^2)^{1/2} \tag{1}$$

where, $r[i]$ (resp. $s[i]$) denotes the value of r (resp. s) along the ith dimension in space D.

Definition 1 [*k* nearest neighbors] Given a point r, a dataset S in space D and an integer k, the k nearest neighbors of r from S, denoted as $k\mathrm{NN}(r, s)$, is a set of k point from S that $\forall p \in k\mathrm{NN}(r, S)$, $\forall s \in S - k\mathrm{NN}(r, S)$, $|p, r| \leq |s, r|$.

Definition 2 [*k*NN queries] Given two dataset R and S in space D, and an integer k. kNN queries of R and S (denoted as $knnQ$), combine each point $r \in R$ with its k nearest neighbors from S.

$$knnQ(R, S) = \{(r, k\mathrm{NN}(r, S)) \mid \text{for all } r \in R\} \tag{2}$$

Voronoi Diagram

The Voronoi diagram of a given set $P = \{p_1, p_2, ..., p_n\}$ of n points in R^d partitions the space of R^d into n regions. Each region includes all points in R^d with a common closest point in the given set P using the distance metric $Dist()$, which is proposed by the authors Okabe et al. (2000). The region corresponding to the point $p \in P$ contains all the points $q \in R^d$.

$$\forall p' \in P, p' \neq p, Dist(q, p) \leq Dist(q, p') \tag{3}$$

The equality holds for the points on the borders of p's regions.

Figure 1 shows the Voronoi diagram of five points in two-dimensional space, where the distance metric is Euclidean. This chapter represents the region $V(p)$ containing the point p as its Voronoi cell. Using Euclidean distance in two-dimensional space, $V(p)$ is a convex polygon. Each edge of the convex polygon is a segment of the perpendicular bisector of the line segment connecting p to another point of the set P. Each of these edges represents as Voronoi edge and each of its end-points as a Voronoi vertex of the point p. For each Voronoi edge of the point p, this chapter refers to the corresponding point in the set P as a Voronoi neighbor of p. This chapter uses $VN(p)$ to denote the set of all Voronoi neighbors of p. The point p represents as the generator of Voronoi cell $V(p)$. Finally, the set given by $VD(P) = \{ V(p_1), V(p_2), ..., V(p_n)\}$ is called the Voronoi diagram generated by P with respect to the distance function $Dist()$.

Figure 1. Voronoi diagram

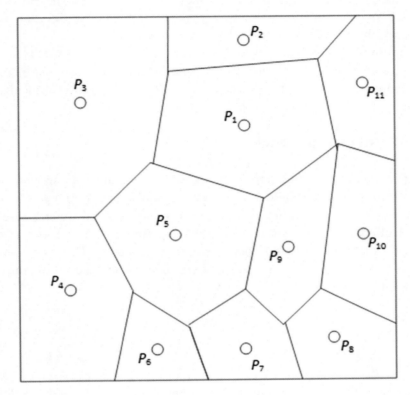

Definition 3 [Voronoi pivot] Given a Voronoi diagram $VD(P)$, select n objects as Voronoi pivots and then split the Voronoi diagram $VD(P)$ into n disjoint Voronoi cells where each Voronoi cell is assigned to the partition with its closest pivot.

Throughout this chapter, the Euclidean distance function is used in two-dimensional space. Also, this chapter simply uses Voronoi diagram to denote ordinary Voronoi diagram of a set of points in two-dimensional space.

K-Means Algorithm

K-means algorithm is the well-known and commonly used clustering method. The algorithm takes the input parameter k and partitions a set X of n data points D in R^d into k clusters. Given the initial set of k cluster centers in R^d, every data point is assigned to the cluster whose center is closest to it. *K*-means wish to choose the collection of k centers C, so as to minimize the potential function:

$$\varphi = \sum_{x \in D} \min_{c \in C} \| x - c \|^2 \tag{4}$$

The algorithm assigns each point to the cluster whose center is nearest. The center's coordinates are the arithmetic mean for each dimension separately over all the points in the cluster. Suppose *icb* is the convergent boundary, the *k*-means clustering algorithm as follows:

Firstly, the algorithm 1 randomly selects *k* objects from the whole points which represent initial cluster centers. Each remaining point is assigned to the cluster, which is most similar based on the distance between the points and the cluster center. The new mean of each cluster is then calculated. This process iterates until the criterion function converges.

MapReduce Programming Model

MapReduce is a popular programming framework to support data-intensive applications using shared-nothing clusters (Dean, 2004). A MapReduce program typically consists of a pair of user-defined map and reduce functions. The map function takes an input key-value pair and produces a set of intermediate key-value pairs. MapReduce runtime system then groups and sorts all the intermediate values associated with the same intermediate key, and sends them to the reduce function. The reduce function accepts an intermediate key and its corresponding values, applies the processing logic, and produces the final result which is typically a list of values.

$$\text{map } (k_1, v_1) \rightarrow \text{list } (k_2, v_2)$$

$$\text{reduce}(k_2, \text{list}(v_2)) \rightarrow \text{list } (k_3, v_3) \tag{5}$$

Figure 2 shows the framework of MapReduce programming model. Input data is loaded into HDFS (hoop distributed file system), where each file is partitioned into smaller data blocks, also called input splits. A file's splits are then distributed, and possibly replicated, to different machines in the cluster. A Map-Reduce computation begins with a Map phase where each input split is processed in parallel by as many map tasks as there are splits. Each input split is a list of key-value pairs. A map task applies the user-defined map function to each key-value pair to produce a list of output key-value pairs. To execute

Algorithm 1. K-means (D, k)

```
Input: integer k, a set X of n data points D
Output: k-means clustering
1.          Let i = Float.MAXVALUE; j = 1
2.          Choose k centers from D, let C^(0) = c_1^(j), c_2^(j), ..., c_k^(j)
3.          for i > icb do
4.            from k clusters by assigning each points in X to its nearest cen-
ter
5.            find new centers of the k clusters c_1^(++j), c_2^(++j), ..., c_k^(++j)
```

$$6. \qquad i \leftarrow \sum_{m=0}^{k} || c_m^j - c_m^{j-1} ||^2$$

```
7.          endfor
8.          output C^(j)
```

Figure 2. The framework of MapReduce programming model

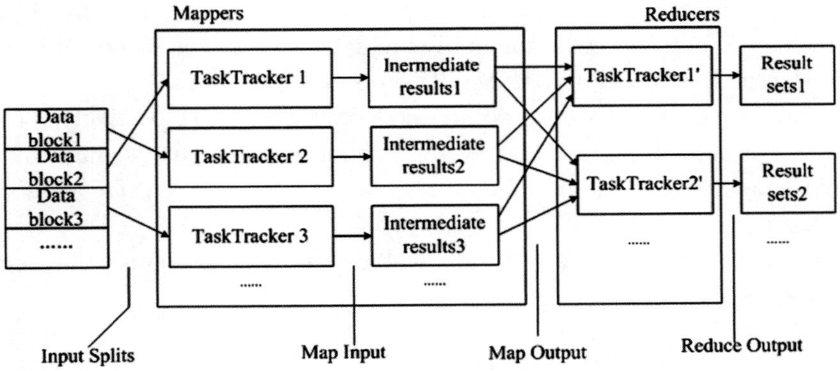

a MapReduce job, the users specify the input file, the number of desired map tasks m and reduce tasks r, and supply the map and reduce function.

The output key-value pairs from a map task are partitioned on the basis of their key k_2. Each partition is then sent across the cluster to a remote node in the shuffle phase. A shuffle and sort stage is commenced, during which the i'th reducer r_i copies records from $b_{i,j}$, the i'th bucket from each of the jth map task. Corresponding partitions from the map tasks are merged and sorted at their receiving nodes.

For each key, the associated values are grouped together to form a list. The key and the corresponding list are given to the user-specified reduce function. The reduce function is invoked once for each distinct k_2 and it processes a k_2's associated list of values $list(v_2)$, i.e. it is passed a $(k_2, list(v_2))$ pair per invocation. For every invocation, the reduce function emits 0 or more final key value pairs (k_3, v_3). The output of each reduce task ($list (k_3, v_3)$) is written into a separate distributed file residing in the HDFS.

The resulting key-value pairs are written back to the HDFS and form the final output. To reduce the network traffic caused by repetitions of the intermediate keys k_2 produced by each mapper, an optional combine function for merging output in map stage, combine $(k_2, list(v_2)) \rightarrow list (k_2, v_2)$, can be specified.

PARTITIONED METHOD BASED ON VORONOI DIAGRAM

This section partitions the two-dimensional data sets using Voronoi diagram.

Voronoi Diagram-Based Partitioned Method of Two-Dimensional Space

The Voronoi diagram decomposes two-dimensional space into disjoint polygons. Given a set of point set S in two-dimensional space, the Voronoi diagram associates all point in the two-dimensional space to their closest point. Each point s has a Voronoi polygon consisting of all points closer to s than to any other point. Hence, the nearest neighbor of a query point q is closed Voronoi polygons. The set of Voronoi polygons associated with all the points is called the Voronoi diagram (VD). The polygons are mutually exclusive except for their boundaries.

Definition 4 [Voronoi Polygon] Given set of points $P = \{p_1, p_2, ..., p_n\}$ where $2 < n < \infty$ and $p_i \neq p_j$ for $i \neq j$, i, j $= 1, 2, ..., n$, the Voronoi polygon of p_i is $VP(p_i) = \{p \mid d\,(p, p_i) \leq d\,(p, p_j)\}$ for $i \neq j$ and $p \in VP(p_i)$ where $d\,(p, p_i)$ specifies the minimum distance between p and p_i in Euclidean space.

Property 1: The Voronoi diagram for given set of points is unique.

Property 2: Let n and n_e be the number of points and Voronoi edges, respectively, then $n_e \leq 3n$-6.

Property 3: Every Voronoi edge is shared by two Voronoi polygons, the average number of Voronoi edges per Voronoi polygon is at most 6, i.e., $2*(3n\text{-}6)/n = 6n\text{-}12/n \leq 6$. This states that no average, each point has 6 adjacent points.

Property 4: The nearest points of p_i (e.g., p_j) is among the points whose Voronoi polygons share Voronoi edges with $VP(p_i)$.

Assume that the VD(P) is the Voronoi diagram of P. Figure 3 shows the Voronoi diagram of the space points. To bound the Voronoi polygons with infinite edges (e.g., $V(p_3)$), this section clips them using a large rectangle bounding the points in P (the dotted rectangle).

Constructing Voronoi Diagram With MapReduce

Construction of Voronoi diagram (VD) is suitable for MapReduce programming model, because Voronoi diagram can be obtained by merging multiple Voronoi polygons (VP). Specifically, each of Voronoi polygons (VP) can be created by the mappers using parallel method and the reducers using combining method in single Voronoi diagram (VD).

Figure 3. Voronoi diagram-based partition

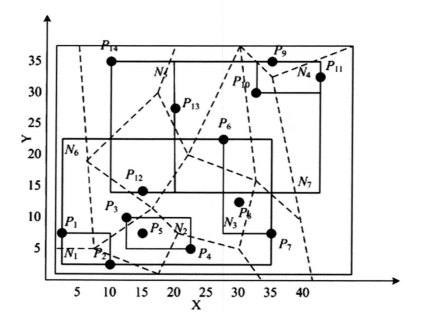

Given a set of data point $P = \{p_1, p_2, ..., p_n\}$ as input, firstly the point set is sorted in increasing order according to x coordinate. Secondly, the point set P is separated into several subsets of equal size. Finally, the Voronoi polygons (VP) are generated for the points of each subset, and then all of the Voronoi polygons (VP) are merged to obtain the final Voronoi diagram (VD) for the point set P.

- **Map Phase of MapReduce Programming Model:** Given a point set sorted by x coordinate, each mapper reads an input block using the format of <key, value>. Then each mapper generates a Voronoi polygons (VP) for the point set in its data block, marks the boundary polygons and emits the generated Voronoi polygons (VP) in the form of <key', value$_i$'> where i denotes the number of data block. The key' is common to all Voronoi polygons (VP), so that all Voronoi polygons (VP) can be grouped together and merged in the subsequent reduce phase.
- **Reduce Phase of MapReduce Programming Model:** The reducers aggregates all Voronoi polygons (VP) in the same group and combines them into a single Voronoi diagram (VD). In the reduce phase, the boundary polygons are detected with a sequential scan, and then new Voronoi edges and vertices are generated by delecting superfluous boundary portions from Voronoi polygons (VP). As the final output, the reducers emit each point and its Voronoi neighbors.

THE DISTANCE BETWEEN POINTS OF VORONOI DIAGRAM

In the Voronoi diagram, the most calculation of k-means algorithm is the calculation of the distances between points. The computation of the distance between points with the clustering centers is irrelevant to the computation of the distance between other points with the corresponding centers. Let P is the set of pivots of the Voronoi diagram. $\forall p_i \in P$, P_i^Q represents the set of points from Q that takes p_i as their closest pivot. For a point q, let p_q and P_q^Q be its closest pivot and the corresponding partition in Voronoi diagram respectively.

Definition 5 [Distance Threshold] Given a point set P and a point q, the distance threshold δ is all points (denoted as $\overline{P}$) of P, such that $\forall p' \in \overline{P}$, $|q, p'| \le \delta$.

By splitting the dataset into a set of partitions, Hjaltason *et al.* (2003) proposed following theorem:

Theorem 1: Given two pivots p_i, p_j, let $HP(p_i, p_j)$ be the generalized hyperplane, where any point q lying on $HP(p_i, p_j)$ has the equal distance to p_i and p_j. $\forall q \in P_j^Q$, the distance of q to $HP(p_i, p_j)$, denoted as $dist(q, HP(p_i, p_j))$ is:

$$dist(q, HP(p_i, p_j)) = \frac{|q, p_i|^2 - |q, p_j|^2}{2 \times |p_i, p_j|} \tag{6}$$

Figure 4 shows the distance $dist(q, HP(p_i, p_j))$.
According to the triangle inequality,

Figure 4. The distance dist (q, HP (p$_i$, p$_j$))

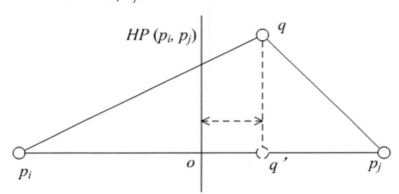

$$| q, p_i |^2 = | q, q' |^2 + | q', p_i |^2$$

Similarly,

$$| q, p_j |^2 = | q, q' |^2 + | q', p_j |^2$$

Hence,

$$| q, p_i |^2 - | q, p_j |^2 = | q', p_i |^2 - | q', p_j |^2$$

$$| q, p_i |^2 - | q, p_j |^2$$
$$= (\frac{1}{2} | p_i, p_j | + dist(q, HP(p_i, p_j)))^2 - (\frac{1}{2} | p_i, p_j | - dist(q, HP(p_i, p_j)))^2$$

$$| q, p_i |^2 - | q, p_j |^2 = 2 | p_i, p_j | \times dist(q, HP(p_i, p_j))$$

Clearly,

$$dist(q, HP(p_i, p_j)) = \frac{| q, p_i |^2 - | q, p_j |^2}{2 \times | p_i, p_j |}$$

Given point q, its belonging partition P_q^ϱ, and another partition P_i^ϱ, according to theorem 1, it is able to compute the distance from q to $HP(p_q, p_i)$. Hence, derive the following corollary.

Corollary 1: Given a partition P_i^ϱ and P_q^ϱ, if derive *dist* $(q, HP(p_q, p_i)) > \delta$, then $\forall q \in P_i^\varrho$, $|q, i| > \delta$.

PARALLEL K-MEANS ALGORITHM USING MAPREDUCE

The MapReduce programming model processes data according to (key, value) pairs and it expresses computation model in terms of two functions: map and reduce. The map function produces key-value pairs based on the input data and outputs a list of intermediate key-value pairs. All intermediate values corresponding to the same intermediate key are grouped together and passed to a reduce function. The reduce function performs a specific task on a group of pairs with same key and produces a list of key-value pairs that form the final output. This section introduces parallel kNN queries algorithm using MapReduce programming model.

First MapReduce Phase

The first MapReduce phase selects the pivots in point set R of two-dimensional space using k-means clustering algorithm for Voronoi diagram. Firstly, the master node assigns a key to each point $r \in R$, saves these keys to distributed file system (DFS), and adds the file to the distributed cache, which is communicated to all mappers during initialization.

Each mapper chooses k centers using k-means clustering method according to the Algorithm 1. Then, it assigns k centers in set R to k different groups.

From step 4 to step 6, the Map logic algorithm assigns center of each clusters C_m to the nearest group. Then, the algorithm 2 computes the center for each group. Furthermore, the algorithm 2 outputs key-value pairs. Meanwhile, the algorithm gets i-th center as key k_i. Then, the algorithm gets j-th group as g_j. Finally, the algorithm 2 outputs key-value pairs (k_i, g_j).

Algorithm 2. Map logic algorithm

```
Input: the multi-dimensional point set R and S,
Output: key-value pairs
1.        assign a key to each point r ∈ R
2.        choose k centers using k-means clustering according to the algorithm
1
3.        assign k centers in set R to k different groups
4.        for m =1 to k do
5.        assign center of C_m to the nearest group
6.        endfor
7.        compute the center for each group
8.        for i=1 to k do
9.            i-th center as key k_i
10.       endfor
11.       for j=1 to k do
12.           j-th group as g_j
13.       endfor
14.       output key-value pairs (k_i, g_j)
```

Algorithm 3. Reduce logic algorithm

```
Input: intermediate key-value pairs of Mappers
Output: key-value pairs of first MapReduce phase
1.          for each point r_i ∈ R do
2.                  choose k clustering centers using k-means algorithm
3.                  compute the distance between the point r_i and clustering center
according to formula (6)
4.                  assign input points to appropriate centers
5.          endfor
6.          let the clustering centers as the pivots
7.          for i=1 to k do
8.                  compute the central point p_i of the groups
9.          endfor
10.                 output key-value pairs  (p_i, G_i)
```

In the reduce stage, a reduce task is started to assign input point to appropriate clustering centers. The reduce function first chooses k clustering centers using k-means algorithm. From lines 1 to lines 6 of the algorithm 3, the reducer computes each point r_i, and computes the distance between the point r_i and clustering center according to formula (6). Then, the algorithm assigns input points to appropriate centers. From lines 7 to lines 9 of the algorithm 3, the reducer computes the central point p_i of the groups, and sets the clustering centers as the pivots. Finally, the algorithm outputs key-value pairs (p_i, G_i).

Second MapReduce Phase

The second MapReduce phase is to find the corresponding subset S_i for each R_i. Then, reducer performs the kNN join between a pair of S_i and R_i.

The second Map logic algorithm first constructs the Voronoi diagram to generate the Voronoi polygons in point set P_i^R. The pivots of the Voronoi diagram are the outputs of reducers in first MapReduce phase. Then, the master loads the file to the distributed cache, and starts mappers for each split of P_i^R and P_j^S and written to distributed file system (DFS). From step 1 to step 5 of the algorithm 4, the algorithm gets the ID *pid* of the partitions G_i. The Voronoi polygons (VP$_j$) contains the partitions G_i. Moreover, for each points s_i the algoritm 4 partitions the point set S_i to P_j^S. Furthermore, the algorithm computes the distance *dist* (P_i^R, P_j^S) less than δ. Finally, the algorithm output key-value pairs $(pid, (P_i^R, P_j^S))$.

The algorithm 5 computes P_j^S for each $r_i \in P_i^R$. In this way, points in each partition of R and their potential k nearest neighbors will be sent to the same reducer. A reducer first ranks the $P_{j1}^S, P_{j2}^S, ..., P_{jN}^S$ according to the ascending order of the distance $|p_i, p_j|$. Each reduce task then calls the reduce function only once, passing in all points for its (P_j^S, P_i^R) partition. From line 1 to line 8 of the algorithm 5, the algorithm finds P_j^S for P_i^R. Moreover, the algorithm computes the distance between p_i and p_j. When the distance between p_i and p_j less than threshold δ. Finally, the algorithm outputs the key-value pairs$(r, kNN(r, S))$.

Algorithm 4. Second Map logic algorithm

Input: the outputted key-value pairs of first Reduce logic algorithm
Output: key-value pairs
1.   for each pivot p_i do
2.   construct the Voronoi diagram to generate the Voronoi polygons in point set P_i^R
3.   the Voronoi polygons (VP_i) contains the partitions G_i
4.   get the ID pid of the partitions G_i
5.   endfor
6.   for each point $s_i \in S$ do
7.   partition the point set S_i to P_j^S
8.   endfor
9.   for each P_i^R do
10.   compute the distance $dist$ $(P_i^R, P_j^S) < \delta$
11.   output key-value pairs (pid, (P_i^R, P_j^S))
12.   endfor

Algorithm 5. Second Reduce logic algorithm

Input: the outputted intermediate key-value pairs of second Map logic algorithm
Output: key-value pairs
1.   for each partition P_i^R and P_j^S do
2.   rank the P_{j1}^S, P_{j2}^S, …, P_{jN}^S according to the ascending order of the distance $|p_i, p_j|$
3.   if $|p_i, p_j| < \delta$
4.   output $(r, kNN(r, S))$
5.   else
6.   updates $kNN(r, S)$ by s
7.   endif
8.   endfor
9.   output $(r, kNN(r, S))$

EXPERIMENTS

Experimental Setup

To evaluate the effectiveness of the method, this chapter used the OpenStreet dataset from the OpenStreetMap project for an empirical evaluation, and showed performance results of the parallel queries of k nearest neighbor based on k-means clustering in MapReduce (PKCM) method. The Openstreet dataset represents the road networks for a US state. The entire dataset has the road networks for 50 states, containing more than 160 million records in 8GB. All the experiments were implemented in JDK 6.0, and performed on a heterogeneous cluster consisting of 18 nodes with 2.9GHz Intel Pentium G2020 processor and 4GB of RAM. Each node is connected to a Gigabit Ethernet switch and runs hadoop 2.2.0.

This chapter generates a number of different datasets as R and S from the complete OpenStreet dataset. We extracted 40 million records from this dataset, where each record consists of 2 real values (longitude and latitude) and a description with variable length.

The experiment aims at evaluating the efficiency of different kNN queries methods: (1) The parallel queries of k nearest neighbor based on k-means clustering in MapReduce method, henceforth referred to as PKCM; (2) The Hadoop Block R-tree Join approach described in the work of Zhang et al. (2012), henceforth referred to as H-BRJ. The H-BRJ method is to build an index for the local S block in a bucket in the reducer, to help find kNNs of a record r from the local R block in the same bucket. For each block S_{bj} ($1 \leq j \leq n$), the H-BRJ method builds a reducer-local spatial index over S_{bj}, in particular the H-BRJ method used the R-tree, before proceeding to find the local kNNs for every record from the local R block in the same bucket with S_{bj}. Then, the chapter uses kNN functionality from R-tree to answer kNN(r, S_{bj}) in every bucket in the reducer. Bulk-loading a R-tree for S_{bj} is very efficient, and kNN search in R-tree is also efficient, hence this overhead is compensated by savings from not running a local nested loop in each bucket.

Query Performance Experiment

This section evaluates the execution time of PKCM and H-BRJ method with different dataset configurations. From the Figure 5, it can be seen that the overall execution time of the two approaches increases when we enlarge the data size. The PKCM method delivers much better running time performance than H-BRJ method. The trends in Figure 5 also indicate PKCM becomes increasingly more efficient than H-BRJ as the dataset sizes increase. In particular, when data size becomes larger, the running time of PKCM grows much slower than that of H-BRJ.

Figure 5. Execution times of PKCM and H-BRJ method

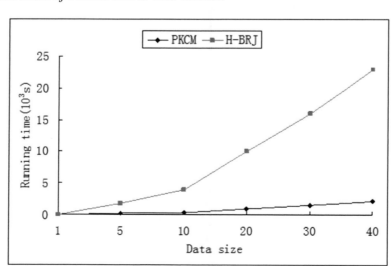

Precision and Recall of Different Queries Method

This section uses the formal precision and recall metrics to measure the retrieval quality. Precision is the ratio of the number of relevant query nodes retrieved to the total number of retrieved nodes:

$$Precision = \frac{|\, relevant \cap retrieved \,|}{|\, retrieved \,|} \tag{7}$$

Recall is the ratio of the number of relevant nodes retrieved to the total number of relevant nodes:

$$Recall = \frac{|\, relevant \cap retrieved \,|}{|\, relevant \,|} \tag{8}$$

This experiment measures the precision and recall of the results returned by PKCM and H-BRJ method. It can be seen that PKCM method outperforms H-BRJ method, and PKCM always achieves higher precision and recall than H-BRJ. The experiment uses the OpenStreet datasets and gradually increases datasets from 1 to 40. The average precision and recall of PKCM method are above 90% all the time. However, the average precision and recall of H-BRJ method are below 70%.

Speedup Experiment

The speedup for each algorithm is the ratio of the execution time on a given cluster configuration over the execution time on the smallest cluster configuration.

Figure 6. Precision of PKCM and H-BRJ method

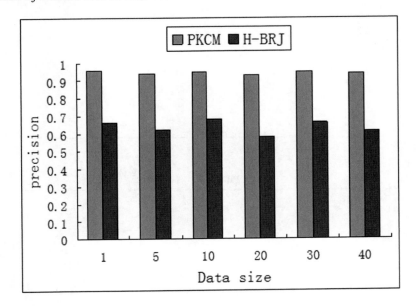

Figure 7. Recall of PKCM and H-BRJ method

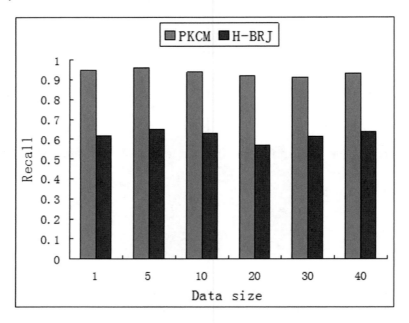

Figure 8. Speedup of PKCM and H-BRJ method

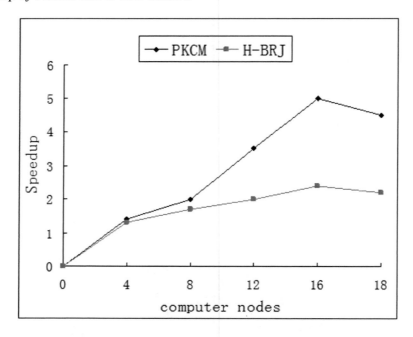

The Figure 8 shows that both PKCM and H-BRJ method achieve almost a linear speedup up to nodes 16. Both PKCM and H-BRJ method achieve the best performance when nodes n=16, and degrade when n>16. The PKCM method has a better speedup than H-BRJ when more physical slaves are becoming available in the cluster.

Effect of K

The Figure 9 shows the execution time for PKCM and H-BRJ method with different k. It can be seen that PKCM method performs consistently better than H-BRJ method. For small k values, kNN queries are the determining factors for performance. For large k values, communication overheads gradually become a more significant performance factor for PKCM and H-BRJ method.

H-BRJ requires each reducer to build a R-tree index for all the received points from S. To find the kNN for a point from R, the reducers will traverse the index and maintain candidate points as well as set of intermediate nodes in a priority queue. Both operations are costly for multi-dimensional space points, which result in the long running time. In PKCM, the parallel k-means method using MapReduce clusters the space points into groups only if the distances between them are restricted by a distance threshold. The PKCM method designs an efficient mapping method that divides points into groups, each of which is processed by a reducer to perform the kNN query.

CONCLUSION

This chapter proposes a method of kNN queries for big spatial data based on Voronoi diagram partitioning using k-means clustering algorithm in MapReduce programming model. Firstly, this chapter presents

Figure 9. Execution time of PKCM and H-BRJ method with different k

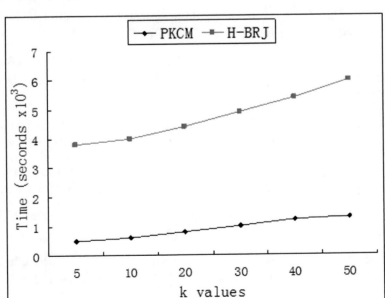

the problem of *k*NN queries for multi-dimensional space data. Then, this chapter introduces the k-means algorithm, which can cluster the space data and assign each point to the cluster whose center is nearest.

Secondly, this chapter proposes the partitioned method based on Voronoi diagram in two-dimensional space. The Voronoi diagram decomposes two-dimensional space into disjoint polygons. This chapter constructs Voronoi diagram using MapReduce programming model, because Voronoi diagram can be obtained by merging multiple Voronoi polygons.

Thirdly, this chapter proposes the method of computing the distance between points of Voronoi polygons. Moreover, this chapter proposes the definition of the distance threshold.

Fourthly, this chapter proposes the parallel *k*-means clustering algorithm in MapReduce programming model, which consists of two MapReduce phase. Moreover, this chapter presents the algorithm of parallel *k*NN queries using MapReduce programming model.

Finally, the extensive experimental results demonstrate that proposed method is better than existing works. The future research direction is the issue of parallel query for massive spatial data in MapReduce programming model which is a well-accepted framework for data-intensive applications over clusters of computers, and studies the problem of parallel geospatial query processing with MapReduce programming model further.

REFERENCES

Akdogan, A., Demiryurek, U., Banaei-Kashani, F., & Shahabi, C. (2010). Voronoi-based geospatial query processing with mapreduce. In *Proceedings of the International Conference Cloud Computing* (pp. 9-16). IEEE.

Bahmani, B., Moseley, B., Vattani, A., Kumar, R., & Vassilvitskii, S. (2012). Scalable k-means++. *Proceedings of the VLDB Endowment International Conference on Very Large Data Bases*, 5(7), 622–633. doi:10.14778/2180912.2180915

Bohm, C., & Krebs, F. (2004). The k-Nearest Neighbour Join: Turbo Charging the KDD Process. *Knowledge and Information Systems*, 6(6), 728–749. doi:10.100710115-003-0122-9

Ciaccia, P., Patella, M., & Zezula, P. (1997). M-tree: An Efficient Access Method for Similarity Search in Metric Spaces. In *Proceedings of the International Conference on Very Large Data Bases* (pp. 426-435). Morgan Kaufmann.

Cui, X., Zhu, P., Yang, X., Li, K., & Ji, C. (2014). Optimized big data k-means clustering using MapReduce. *The Journal of Supercomputing*, 70(3), 1249–1259. doi:10.100711227-014-1225-7

Dean, J., & Ghemawat, S. (2004). MapReduce: simplified data processing on large clusters. In *Proceedings of the Symposium on Operating System Design and Implementation* (pp. 137-150). USENIX Association.

Dean, J., & Ghemawat, S. (2008). MapReduce: Simplified data processing on large clusters. *Communications of the ACM*, 51(1), 107–113. doi:10.1145/1327452.1327492

Debatty, T., Michiardi, P., Mees, W., & Thonnard, O. (2014). Determining the k in k-means with MapReduce. In *Proceedings of the Workshops of the EDBT/ICDT 2014 Joint Conference* (pp. 19-28). CEUR-WS.org.

Ene, A., Im, S., & Moseley, B. (2011). Fast clustering using MapReduce. In *Proceedings of the 17th ACM SIGKDD International Conference on Knowledge Discovery and Data Mining* (pp. 681-689). ACM.

Hjaltason, G. R., & Samet, H. (2003). Index-driven similarity search in metric spaces. *ACM Transactions on Database Systems*, *28*(4), 517–580. doi:10.1145/958942.958948

Jagadish, H. V., Ooi, B. C., Tan, K. L., Yu, C., & Zhang, R. (2005). iDistance: An adaptive B+-tree based indexing method for nearest neighbor search. *ACM Transactions on Database Systems*, *30*(2), 364–397. doi:10.1145/1071610.1071612

Jiang, D., Ooi, B. C., Shi, L., & Wu, S. (2010). The performance of MapReduce: An in-depth study. *Proceedings of the VLDB Endowment International Conference on Very Large Data Bases*, *3*(1), 472–483. doi:10.14778/1920841.1920903

Kim, W., Kim, Y., & Shim, K. (2016). Parallel computation of k-nearest neighbor joins using MapReduce. In *Proceedings of the IEEE International Conference on Big Data* (pp. 696-705). Washington, DC: IEEE. 10.1109/BigData.2016.7840662

Kim, Y., & Shim, K. (2012). Parallel top-k similarity join algorithms using MapReduce. In *Proceedings of the International Conference on Data Engineering* (pp. 510-521). IEEE Computer Society. 10.1109/ICDE.2012.87

Lu, W., Shen, Y., Chen, S., & Ooi, B. C. (2012). Efficient Processing of k Nearest Neighbor Joins using MapReduce. *Proceedings of the VLDB Endowment International Conference on Very Large Data Bases*, *5*(10), 1016–1027. doi:10.14778/2336664.2336674

Ma, A., & Sethi, I. K. (2007). Distributed k-median clustering with application to image clustering. In *Proceedings of the 7th International Workshop on Pattern Recognition in Information System* (pp. 215-220). Funchal, Portugal: INSTICC.

Ni, W., Gu, M., & Chen, X. (2016). Location privacy-preserving k nearest neighbor query under user's preference. *Knowledge-Based Systems*, *103*, 19–27. doi:10.1016/j.knosys.2016.03.016

Okabe, A., Boots, B., Sugihara, K., & Chiu, S. N. (2000). *Spatial tessellations, concepts and applications of Voronoi diagrams* (2nd ed.). John Wiley and Sons Ltd. doi:10.1002/9780470317013

Okcan, A., & Riedewald, M. (2011). Processing theta-joins using MapReduce. In *Proceedings of the ACM SIGMOD International Conference on Management of Data* (pp. 949-960). Athens, Greece: ACM.

Peng, Y., Cui, J., Li, H., & Ma, J. (2017). A reusable and single-interactive model for secure approximate k-nearest neighbor query in cloud. *Information Sciences*, *387*, 146–164. doi:10.1016/j.ins.2016.07.069

Song, G., Rochas, J., Huet, F., & Magoules, F. (2015). Solutions for Processing K Nearest Neighbor Joins for Massive Data on MapReduce. In *Proceedings of the 23rd Euromicro International Conference on Parallel, Distributed, and Network-Based Processing* (pp. 279-287). Turku, Finland: IEEE Computer Society. 10.1109/PDP.2015.79

Vattani, A. (2011). K-means requires exponentially many iterations even in the plane. *Discrete & Computational Geometry*, *45*(4), 596–616. doi:10.100700454-011-9340-1

Vernica, R., Carey, M. J., & Li, C. (2010). Efficient parallel set-similarity joins using mapreduce. In *Proceedings of the ACM SIGMOD International Conference on Management of Data* (pp. 495-506). Indianapolis, IN: ACM.

Wu, Y., Jin, R., & Zhang, X. (2014). Fast and unified local search for random walk based k-nearest-neighbor query in large graphs. In *Proceedings of the ACM SIGMOD International Conference on Management of Data* (pp. 1139-1150). Snowbird, UT: ACM. 10.1145/2588555.2610500

Xia, C., Lu, H., Ooi, B. C., & Hu, J. (2004). Gorder: an efficient method for knn join processing. In *Proceedings of the International Conference on Very Large Data Bases* (pp. 756-767). Toronto, Canada: Morgan Kaufmann.

Xu, X., Jager, J., & Kriegel, H. (1999). A fast parallel clustering algorithm for large spatial databases. *Data Mining and Knowledge Discovery*, *3*(3), 263–290. doi:10.1023/A:1009884809343

Yao, B., Li, F., & Kumar, P. (2010). K nearest neighbor queries and kNN-joins in large relational databases (almost) for free. In *Proceedings of the International Conference on Data Engineering* (pp. 4-15). Long Beach, CA: IEEE. 10.1109/ICDE.2010.5447837

Yu, C., Zhang, R., Huang, Y., & Xiong, H. (2010). High-dimensional kNN joins with incremental updates. *GeoInformatica*, *14*(1), 55–82. doi:10.100710707-009-0076-5

Zhang, C., Li, F., & Jestes, J. (2012). Efficient parallel kNN joins for large data in MapReduce. In *Proceedings of the International Conference on Extending Database Technology* (pp. 38-49). Berlin, Germany: ACM. 10.1145/2247596.2247602

Zhang, S., Han, J., Liu, Z., Wang, K., & Xu, Z. (2009). SJMR: Parallelizing spacial join with MapReduce on clusters. In *Proceedings of the IEEE International Conference on Cluster Computing* (pp. 1-8). New Orleans, LA: IEEE Computer Society. 10.1109/CLUSTR.2009.5289178

Zhao, W., Ma, H., & He, Q. (2009). Parallel k-means clustering based on MapReduce. In *Proceedings of the First International Conference CloudCom* (pp. 674-679). Beijing, China: Springer.

KEY TERMS AND DEFINITIONS

Distance Between Points r **and** s**:** In n-dimensional space D, given two points r and s, $|r, s|$ represents the distance between point r and s in space D. In this chapter, the Euclidean distance is used as the distance. $|r, s| = (\sum_{i=1}^{n} (r[i] - s[i])^2)^{1/2}$ where, $r[i]$ (resp. $s[i]$) denotes the value of r (resp. s) along the ith dimension in space D.

k**-Means Algorithm:** k-means algorithm is the well-known and commonly used clustering method. The algorithm takes the input parameter k and partitions a set X of n data points D in R^d into k clusters.

k**-Nearest Neighbors:** Given a point r, a dataset S in space D and an integer k, the k nearest neighbors of r from S, denoted as $kNN(r, s)$, is a set of k point from S that $\forall p \in kNN(r, S)$, $\forall s \in S - kNN(r, S)$, $|p, r| \leq |s, r|$.

kNN Queries: Given two dataset R and S in space D, and an integer k. kNN queries of R and S (denoted as $k$nnQ), combine each point $r \in R$ with its k nearest neighbors from S: $knnQ(R, S) = \{(r, kNN(r, S)) \mid$ for all $r \in R\}$.

MapReduce Programming Model: MapReduce is a popular programming framework to support data-intensive applications using shared-nothing clusters.

Voronoi Diagram: The Voronoi diagram of a given set $P = \{p_1, p_2, ..., p_n\}$ of n points in R^d partitions the space of R^d into n regions. Each region includes all points in R^d with a common closest point in the given set P using the distance metric $Dist()$. The region corresponding to the point $p \in P$ contains all the points $q \in R^d$: $\forall p' \in P, p' \neq p, Dist(q, p) \leq Dist(q, p')$.

Voronoi Polygon: Given set of points $P = \{p_1, p_2, ..., p_n\}$ where $2 < n < \infty$ and $p_i \neq p_j$ for $i \neq j$, i, j = 1, 2, ..., n, the Voronoi polygon of p_i is $VP(p_i) = \{p \mid d(p, p_i) \leq d(p, p_j)\}$ for $i \neq j$ and $p \in VP(p_i)$ where $d(p, p_i)$ specifies the minimum distance between p and p_i in Euclidean space.

Chapter 12
Efficient Storage and Parallel Query of Massive XML Data in Hadoop

Wei Yan
Liaoning University, China

ABSTRACT

In order to solve the problem of storage and query for massive XML data, a method of efficient storage and parallel query for a massive volume of XML data with Hadoop is proposed. This method can store massive XML data in Hadoop and the massive XML data is divided into many XML data blocks and loaded on HDFS. The parallel query method of massive XML data is proposed, which uses parallel XPath queries based on multiple predicate selection, and the results of parallel query can satisfy the requirement of query given by the user. In this chapter, the map logic algorithm and the reduce logic algorithm based on parallel XPath queries based using MapReduce programming model are proposed, and the parallel query processing of massive XML data is realized. In addition, the method of MapReduce query optimization based on multiple predicate selection is proposed to reduce the data transfer volume of the system and improve the performance of the system. Finally, the effectiveness of the proposed method is verified by experiment.

INTRODUCTION

In recent years, with the rapid growth of data on the Internet, XML has become the de-facto standard for data representation, data storage and data exchange on the World Wide Web (Bray *et al.* 1997). As a semi-structured data format, XML has many advantages such as simplicity, scalability and cross-platform. Many data have been produced and transformed into XML data format. With the rapid development of data generation and collection technology, the volume of XML data has become enormous and also grows very quickly. Traditional query processing model of XML data is difficult to deal with the problem, which is query processing for massive XML data. In this way, how to store massive XML data effectively and how to query massive XML data has become a hot issue in the current academic community.

DOI: 10.4018/978-1-5225-8446-9.ch012

In the real world, scientific data and log messages are often kept in the form of XML, and the scale of data is becoming very large. For example, UniprotKB provides the data set of global protein resource (Bairoch *et al.* 2005). It is the most comprehensive resource for protein information, providing protein sequences and functional information. For the time being, the size of an XML dataset in the UniprotKB dataset exceeds 260GB, and new XML elements and attributes are continually added to this dataset. Wikipedia provides a knowledge base as the XML data format with a size of over 40 GB. At present, the query processing techniques of massive XML data have attracted attention of the academic community. This chapter adopts the MapReduce programming framework to design the query system of massive XML data on the Hadoop platform, and proposes a parallel query method for processing massive XML data.

Currently, the widespread use of XML data led to an increasing interest in searching and query XML data. XML provides a natural model for tree-structured heterogeneous sources, and that XPath and XQuery are the most commonly used XML query languages (Eisenberg *et al.* 2013). The XPath query language plays an important role in XML query processing: it is widely used in almost every XML technology, starting from query languages such as XQuery and XSLT, to access control languages such as XACML, to JavaScript engine of popular web browsers. The traditional mechanism of XML query processing usually represents user's query request in the form of the predicate in XPath query statement and returns the query result that matches query expression of the predicate exactly. With the continuous growth of XML data volume, the time-consuming and efficiency of storing and querying massive XML data exceeds the ability of traditional XML query processing techniques. How to store and query massive XML data is an important issue in cloud computing environments.

Because XML data has the characteristics of structure and content, the MapReduce programming model is proposed to process the XML file through a pipeline, which is a series of processing steps that receive XML structured data (Zinn *et al.* 2010). The XML data are then updated by the black box function, resulting in the output of the modifying XML structures. Emoto *et al.* (2012) proposes an effective algorithm to deal with the XPath query of tree structure in parallel with the MapReduce programming model. Linear acceleration is realized for tree reduction computations of large-scale XML data, which implements various tree computations such as XPath queries. The above literatures used MapReduce programming model to process massive XML data. However, they did not propose an effective method for partitioning XML data blocks, which were distributed in the XML parallel query system and increased the workload of the system. Under the MapReduce programming model, Bidoit *et al.* (2013) showed a prototype system for querying and updating data on large XML documents, which can statically and dynamically partition the inputted XML documents, so to distribute the computing load among the machines of MapReduce clusters. Choi *et al.* (2012) showed a prototype system HadoopXML, which simultaneously processes many twig pattern queries for a massive volume of XML data in parallel on the Hadoop platform using MapReduce programming model. Specifically, HadoopXML provides an efficient way to process a single large XML file in parallel, and processes multiple twig pattern queries simultaneously with a shared input scan.

However, the existing method of querying massive XML data based on MapReduce programming model does not propose effective storing strategies and clear parallel querying algorithm. For this reason, this chapter proposes a storing and querying method of massive XML data on the Hadoop platform using MapReduce framework. First of all, this chapter proposes the system architecture of processing massive XML data on the Hadoop platform, in which massive XML data are split into data blocks and store in HDFS. The system represents the user's query in the form of the query predicate, which uses the parallel XPath query to process the query predicate. To further send numerous query predicate to the data blocks of massive XML, the system uses the MapReduce programming model to parallel query partitioning XML data blocks. Finally, this chapter proposes the parallel query algorithm to obtain the final query processing results. In this way, this chapter proposes the parallel XPath query method based on multiple predicate selection to process massive XML data, and effectively improves the efficiency of massive XML data query processing. The proposed method satisfies the user's query processing requirements for the massive XML data.

The rest of this chapter is organized as follows. Section 2 presents background of XML database and XPath query, Hadoop distributed file system, and MapReduce programming model. Section 3 provides the system architecture of processing massive XML on Hadoop. Section 4 provides the storage of massive XML data in HDFS. Section 5 provides parallel XPath queries of massive XML data using MapReduce. Section 6 provides the experiments. Section 7 concludes the chapter.

BACKGROUND

Related Works

The large-scale XML data processing has been extensively researched in database community. Some existed works focus on querying distributed XML data on Hadoop platform. Fan *et al.* (2018) proposed an efficient distributed XML query processing method using MapReduce, which simultaneously processes several queries on large volumes of XML data. Song *et al.* (2016) proposed an approach to exploit data parallelisms in XML processing using MapReduce in Hadoop. The approach introduced an SDN labeling algorithm and a distributed hierarchical index using DHTs, which designed a two-phase MapReduce solution that is able to efficiently address the issues of labeling, indexing, and query processing on big XML data. Fan *et al.* (2016) presented a method TwigStack-MR, which simultaneously processes several twig pattern queries for a massive volume of XML data based on MapReduce framework. Fan *et al.* (2016) proposed an efficient distributed XPath query processing using MapReduce, which simultaneously processes queries for a massive volume of XML data. Antonellis *et al.* (2015) proposed three different approaches for distributed XML filtering using the Hadoop framework. The method of XML partitioning and storage strategy is proposed, in which twig queries can be efficiently processed in a single-round MapReduce job with good scalability (Bi *et al.* 2015).

It is worth noting that parallel processing methods have proposed, which include parallel labelling, indexing, and parallel query processing for massive XML data. Ahn *et al.* (2017) proposed a dynamic and parallel approach of XML labeling algorithm with MapReduce for the repetitive prime number labeling scheme. Two optimization techniques are devised: the label assignment order adjustment to further reduce the label size and the upper tree compressing technique to reduce the memory requirements during the labeling process. Song *et al.* (2016) proposed an approach to exploit data parallelisms in XML processing using MapReduce in Hadoop, which designed an advanced two phase MapReduce solution that is able to efficiently address the issues of labeling, indexing, and query processing on big XML data. Ahn *et al.* (2016) proposed a cluster-based technique wherein all parent nodes for a node are aggregated to compute its label by two-step MapReduce jobs. Song *et al.* (2016) proposed a solution that integrates data storage, labelling, indexing, and parallel queries to process a massive amount of XML data. Camacho-Rodriguez *et al.* (2015) demonstrated a novel system PAXQuery that parallelizes the execution of XQuery queries over large collections of XML documents, which compiles a rich subset of XQuery into plans expressed in the PArallelization ConTracts (PACT) programming model. Wu *et al.* (2017) proposed a novel technique to use MapReduce to distribute labels in inverted lists in a computing cluster, so that structural joins can be parallelly performed to process queries. The author also proposed an optimization technique to reduce the computing space in their framework, to improve the performance of query processing. Ogden *et al.* (2013) described a data-parallel approach for the processing of streaming XPath queries based on pushdown transducers, which permits XML data to be split into arbitrarilysized chunks, with each chunk processed by a parallel automaton instance. Choi *et al.* (2014) devised parallel tree labeling algorithms for massive XML data, which focus on how to efficiently label a single large XML file in parallel. The authors first propose parallel versions of two prominent tree labeling schemes based on the MapReduce framework, and then present techniques for runtime workload balancing and data repartition to solve performance issues caused by data skewness and MapReduce's inherited limitation. Feng *et al.* (2010) proposed an efficient parallel PathStack algorithm, named P-PathStack, for processing XML twig queries, which first efficiently partitions input element lists into multiple buckets, and then processes data in each bucket in parallel. Fadika *et al.* (2009) presented both a parallel and distributed approach to analyze how the scalability and performance requirements of large-scale XML-based data, which uses Piximal toolkit for processing large-scale XML datasets that utilizes the capabilities for parallelism that are available in the emerging multi-core architectures.

Different researchers proposed the methods of parallel Xpath query processing. Regarding the parallel XPath query processing of massive XML data, a method of parallelizing XPath queries is implemented in two ways on top of a state-of-the-art XML database engine (Sato *et al.* 2018). Afrati *et al.* (2015) presented two algorithms, each depending on a different data fragmentation of the XML tree, which compute XPath queries in MapReduce, by first computing subqueries and then combining their results. Huang *et al.* (2014) used dynamic mapping to improve XPath query performance, which can achieve better load balance no matter what XML document is queried. Slavov *et al.* (2014) addressed the problem of cardinality estimation of XPath queries over XML data stored in a distributed, Internet-scale environment, and presented a novel gossip algorithm called XGossip, which given an XPath query estimates the number of XML documents in the network that contain a match for the query. Senk *et al.* (2014) proposed a system that enables to query XML data with XPath, which evaluates the queries in parallel using the MR framework. Slavov *et al.* (2014) presented a novel tool called XGossip for Internet-scale cardinality estimation of XPath queries over distributed XML data. Damigos *et al.* (2014) proposed a technique for integrating large amount of XML data and use the MapReduce framework to efficiently query the integrated data, and proposed a single-step, MapReduce algorithm which takes advantage of virtual structure and computes efficiently the answer of a given XPath queries in a distributed manner. Damigos *et al.* (2013) investigated the problem of efficiently evaluating XPath queries over large XML data stored in a distributed manner, and propose a MapReduce algorithm based on a query decomposition which computes all expected answers in one MapReduce step, which can be applied over large XML data which is given either as a single distributed document or as a collection of small XML documents. Damigos *et al.* (2012) proposed algorithms for evaluating XPath queries over an XML tree that is partitioned horizontally and vertically, and is distributed across a number of sites, also presented a MapReduce algorithm for evaluating Boolean XPath queries based on partial evaluation which evaluates XPath queries on very large XML trees in a centralized setting.

XML Database and XPath Query

An XML database is a collection of XML documents. XML represents data using tags, which are identifiers enclosed in angle brackets. XML has strict rules about opening and closing tags. It means that once a tag is opened (for example <section>), it has to be closed (using </section>). For example, Figure 1 shows a simple example of an XML document concerning book.

Although XML documents can have complex internal structures, they can generally be modeled as trees, where tree nodes represent document elements, attributes, and character data and edges represent the element-subelement relationship. Such a tree model can be represented as an XML document tree.

Definition 1 [XML document tree] XML document is a semi-structured data format with hierarchical relationship and nested structure, which can be represented by the tree structure $T = (N, E, r)$. N represents the set of all nodes in the data tree, E represents the set of edges between nodes in the data tree, and r represents the root node of the data tree.

Definition 2 [The node of XML document tree] The node of an XML document tree can be defined as a triple (*id*, *label*, <*text*>), in which *id* is an identifier that uniquely identifies a node, *label* is the corresponding element or the attribute name, and *text* is the text content or attribute value of the corresponding element.

Figure 2 shows the tree representation of an XML document, which has rather complex internal structures.

XPath is an expression language, which is a general language for addressing, searching, and processing pieces of an XML document. XPath allows to specify the name of nodes (i.e., tags) and attributes in the

Figure 1. An example of XML document

```
<book>
   <title> XML query processing </title>
   <chapter>
     <section>
        <title> introduction </title>
        <text>" An XML document starts with a prolog markup ..."
        </text>
     </section>
     <section>
        <title> XML tree pattern processing </title>
     </section>
     <section>
        <title> ordered and generalized XML tree pattern processing </title>
        <text>" Ordered XML twig query means ..."
        </text>
     </section>
   </chapter>
   <author> Lu </author>
   <year> 2013 </year>
   <publisher> Springer </publisher>
</book>
```

Figure 2. Tree representation of an XML document

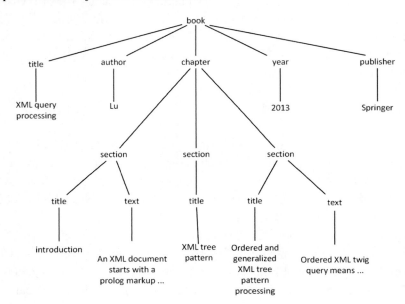

XML document tree. XPath querying mechanism is based on a boolean logic: the nodes retrieved from an XPath expression are those matching the path of the XML tree. The result of an XPath expression may be a selection of nodes from the input XML documents.

XPath uses a path expression to navigate in the hierarchy of an XML document. The XPath expression uses the symbol / to represent absolute path, which starts from the root node of the XML document. The XPath expression also uses the symbol // to represent relative path, which starts from any nodes of the XML document.

The XPath expression consists of multiple location steps. A location step has three parts:

1. An axis, which specifies the tree relationship between the nodes selected by the location step and the context node,
2. A node test, which specifies the node type and expanded-name of the nodes selected by the location step,
3. Zero or more predicates, which use arbitrary expressions to further refine the set of nodes selected by the location step.

Definition 3 [XML predicate query] The predicate query on XML document can be expressed as: $path_1$ [$predicate_1$] // $path_2$ [$predicate_2$] //...// $path_n$ [$predicate_n$], where $path_1$, $path_2$, ..., $path_n$ is the query path expression in the XPath query language. $predicate_i$ is the query predicate with a selection condition of the form $A_i\ \theta\ a_i$, where $i \in (1, ..., n)$, A_i represents the attribute nodes of an XML document, a_i represents the attribute values, and $\theta \in \{=, >, <, \text{and, or, not, contains}\}$.

For example, query predicate is of the form year = 2013, price > 35, pages < 50, price >45 and price < 75, year >2013 or year <2016, not (price >58), text.contains(XML).

The users use the query predicate in XPath query language to specify the query condition, and they can obtain the query results that meet the query needs. Thus, the traditional XML query processing methods return the query results that exactly match the query predicate. How to extend the traditional XML query processing method to satisfy the requirements of massive XML data query processing has become a hot topic in the academic community.

Hadoop Distributed File System

At present, the amount of data on the Internet is growing rapidly from the TB level to the PB level. The storage requirement of massive data brings new challenges to traditional data processing technology. The Hadoop distributed file system (HDFS) is an open source distributed storage system inspired by the design of Google File System (GFS) (Ghemawat *et al.* 2003). HDFS is a distributed file system that divides large-scale data files into smaller data blocks to store massive data.

HDFS is a block structured distributed file system, which uses a method of data partition to store large scale data files. This data file is split into multiple fixed-size data blocks, which is distributed among the computing nodes of the system. It avoids the limitation of the size of the hard disk in any computing node of the system. HDFS stores metadata of large-scale files and application data separately. HDFS stores metadata of large-scale files on a dedicated server, called the NameNode. Application data are stored on other all servers called DataNode. All servers are fully connected and communicate with each other using TCP-based protocols. In this way, HDFS can effectively store large-scale data files and reduce the cost of storing massive data. For example, it is difficult to store 100 TB data on a computing node, but it is easy to divide this large-scale data file into blocks and distribute them across each computing node of the system. On the other hand, the HDFS simplifies the storage system by partitioning the massive data into blocks. The Hadoop system sets the size of each block to 64MB, which is easy to manage the storage system of computing node.

In order to avoid the problem that the data stored by a single computing node in the system cannot be used normally due to the failure, HDFS adopts the replication strategy of data blocks, which stores the copies of data blocks on different computing node of the system. In general, HDFS sets the number of copies of the data block to 3. When one of the computing node failed or the stored data block damaged in the HDFS system, the HDFS system can find a replication of the data block at other computing node. Furthermore, the replication strategy of data blocks improves the fault tolerance and the scalability of Hadoop system.

MapReduce Programming Model

MapReduce is a popular programming framework to support data-intensive applications using shared-nothing clusters (Dean *et al.* 2004). Hadoop consists of two layers: a data storage layer is called HDFS, and a data processing layer is called MapReduce. HDFS is a block-structured distributed file system. A MapReduce-based program, referred to as a job, performs in two phases: the map and the reduce stages.

The map function takes an input key-value pair and produces a set of intermediate key-value pairs. MapReduce runtime system then groups and sorts all the intermediate values associated with the same intermediate key, and sends them to the reduce function. The reduce function accepts an intermediate key and its corresponding values, applies the processing logic, and produces the final result which is typically a list of values.

map $(k_1, v_1) \rightarrow$ list (k_2, v_2)

reduce$(k_2,$ list$(v_2)) \rightarrow$ list (k_3, v_3) (1)

For each key, the associated values are grouped together to form a list. The key and the corresponding list are given to the user-specified reduce function. The reduce function is invoked once for each distinct k_2 and it processes a k_2's associated list of values $list(v_2)$, i.e. it is passed a $(k_2, list(v_2))$ pair per invocation. For every invocation, the reduce function emits 0 or more final key value pairs (k_3, v_3). The output of each reduce task $(list (k_3, v_3))$ is written into a separate distributed file residing in the HDFS.

The resulting key-value pairs are written back to the HDFS and form the final output. To reduce the network traffic caused by repetitions of the intermediate keys k_2 produced by each mapper, an optional combine function for merging output in map stage, combine $(k_2, list(v_2)) \rightarrow$ list (k_2, v_2), can be specified. The combine () function is optionally applied to perform pre-aggregation to minimize the communication cost taken to transfer intermediate outputs to reducers.

Figure 3 shows the framework of MapReduce programming model. Hadoop provides distributed computing environment through HDFS. The computers have two roles on Hadoop: one is JobTracker, which is used to schedule system tasks; the other is TaskTracker, which maintains communication with JobTracker and performs Map or Reduce tasks on assigned data blocks. The Hadoop uses JobClient to configure and submit tasks. First, the Hadoop system divides the massive data into data blocks with the same size and loads them into the HDFS. Then, the JobClient submits the job request to the JobTracker, and JobTracker accepts the request, then the data block is transferred into the Mappers separately, and then the TaskTracker executes the Map function to process the request.

Inputted data are loaded into HDFS (hoop distributed file system), where each file is partitioned into smaller data blocks, also called input splits. The splits are distributed, and possibly replicated, to different machines in the cluster. A Map-Reduce computation begins with a Map phase where each input split is processed in parallel by as many map tasks as there are splits. Each input split is a list of key-value pairs. A map task applies the user-defined map function to each key-value pair to produce a list of output key-value pairs. To execute a MapReduce job, the users specify the input file, the number of desired map tasks m and reduce tasks r, and supply the map and reduce function.

Figure 3. The framework of MapReduce programming model

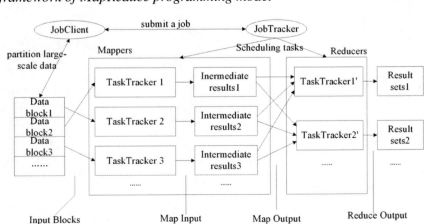

THE SYSTEM ARCHITECTURE OF PROCESSING MASSIVE XML ON HADOOP

Figure 4 shows the system architecture of processing massive XML on Hadoop. The system processes massive XML data in two steps: the storage of massive XML data and querying of massive XML data. In storage step, massive XML documents are partitioned into equal-sized XML data blocks and then loaded into HDFS. At the loading time, a large XML document is split into many HDFS blocks. The partitioning method of massive XML data avoids the loss of XML tags and maintains semantic consistency of massive XML data.

In query processing step, the system processes the massive XML data blocks based on MapReduce programming model. Each map task processes XML data in an InputSplit. By processing an XML document in blocks, the system executes multiple map tasks on a single XML document in parallel. However, map tasks can not process all XML data completely for two reasons. First, each map task does not have any information about XML blocks located in the other InputSplit since each map task works only on its InputSplit. Second, a start-tag and its corresponding end-tag may not be placed together in an InputSplit. To solve this problem, our system uses the method of parallel XPath queries based on multiple predicate selection, which assigns the query predicate to different map task trackers. Furthermore, our system uses the partitioning method of massive XML data to avoid the loss of XML tags semantic. Finally, each reducer merges the partial query results into a set of complete results at the reduce stage.

THE STORAGE OF MASSIVE XML DATA IN HDFS

In practical application, with the rapid growth of XML data on the Internet, traditional XML data storage methods cannot effectively manage massive XML data. HDFS is a distributed file system of Hadoop platform, which is used to store large-scale data files. On the Hadoop platform, massive XML data are partitioned into equal-sized data blocks, which are loaded into HDFS and different computers.

Figure 4. The system architecture

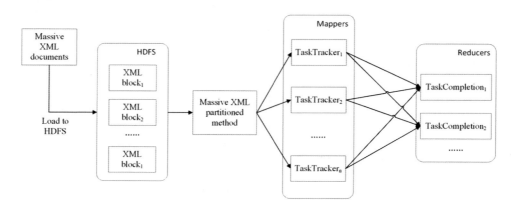

The Storage Architecture of Massive XML Data in HDFS

The HDFS uses the Master/Slave architecture to manage the data files, in which the NameNode is the Master node. The NameNode is responsible for management of the namespace and maintains the metadata information of massive XML data. The DataNode is the Slave node, which is responsible for storing massive XML data. The massive XML data stored in HDFS, which are usually splatted into numerous data blocks. This data blocks store on different DataNode in the form of replication. The DataNode sends the list information of data blocks to the NameNode periodically, so that users can obtain the information of the DataNode through the NameNode to directly access the data resources of the DataNode. The storage architecture of massive XML data is shown in Figure 5.

In this storage architecture, XMLMetaData is a metadata manager for processing massive XML data. Metadata mainly includes IP address and location information of each DataNode, directory information of the file system, the information of file name, and the number of replicas. The metadata manager XMLMetaData is equivalent to the NameNode of HDFS. It is mainly responsible for managing the underlying DataNode and distributed XML data blocks. The HDFS first searches the metadata manager XMLMetaData to determine DataNode, which stores XML data blocks. In addition, the size of the partitioning XML data blocks is approximately equal, so as to balance the workload of the system. After XML data blocks are stored, the system automatically updates the metadata manager XMLMetaData to facilitate the management of the DataNode.

Figure 5. The storage architecture of massive XML data in HDFS

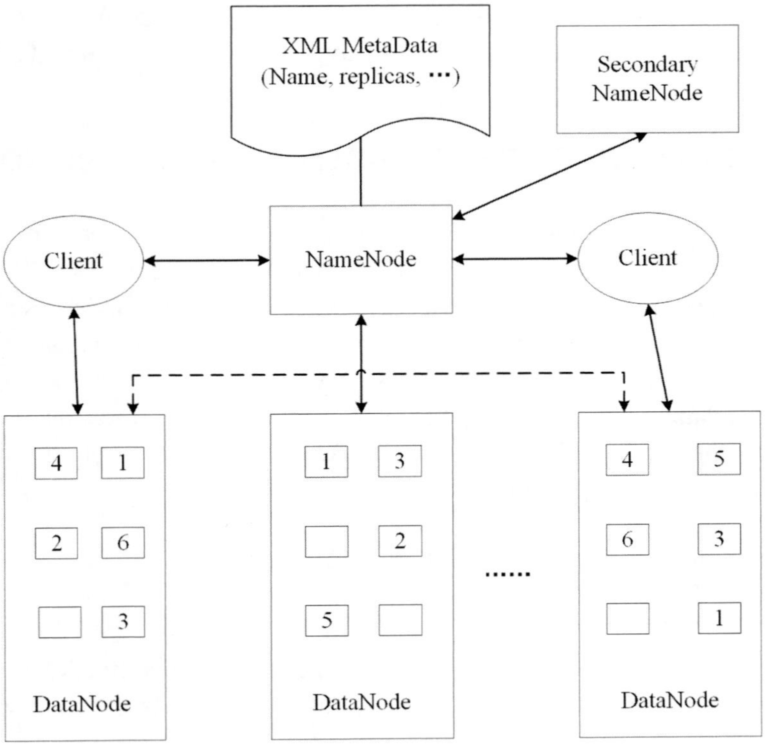

The Client of HDFS can read and write the XML data blocks, which are stored in the DataNode. First, the Client retrieves the metadata information of the XML data blocks from the NameNode and determines the location information of the DataNode. Then, the Client updates the information of the XML data blocks, which are stored on the corresponding DataNode. Finally, the Client sends updated information of the XML data blocks to the NameNode and saves it to the metadata manager XMLMetaData.

The Partitioning Method of Massive XML Data

The massive XML data are splatted into equal-sized XML data blocks and stored in the DataNode through data partitioning. The metadata manager XMLMetaData is responsible for splitting an inputted large-scale XML file into multiple XML data blocks, each of which is fixed in 64MB in size. Moreover, the metadata manager XMLMetaData determines the location information of each XML data block in the DataNode and the number of replicas, so that the system can manage these XML data blocks.

Since the system lacks the semantic information of XML and the size of each XML data block is fixed at 64MB, this may result in an inappropriate partition of an XML document. For example, an XML document contains the tag of publisher information <publisher> Springer </publisher>. The XML document is partitioned into two XML data blocks, which are the XML data block$_1$ and the XML data block$_2$. Two XML data blocks respectively store the tags of publisher information <publisher> Springer </ and publisher>. This partitioning method violates the rules of XML syntax, because the end tag of an XML element is of the form </tagname>.

In order to solve this problem, the partitioning method increases the mechanism of XML semantic analysis to the metadata manager XMLMetaData. The metadata manager XMLMetaData adjusts the label boundaries of each XML data block, in which the labels of each XML element cannot be partitioned into two XML data blocks. The metadata manager XMLMetaData extends the information of tag boundary in the XML data block, so that the XML data blocks contains the complete tag of XML element.

THE PARALLEL XPATH QUERIES OF MASSIVE XML DATA USING MAPREDUCE

Aiming at massive XML data, traditional query processing techniques cannot resolve the resource consumption and the requirements of response time, and need to be further expanded. This chapter proposes the method of the parallel XPath queries for massive XML data using the MapReduce programming model. Firstly, the Client of HDFS retrieves the metadata manager XMLMetaData to determine the location information of the XML data blocks. These XML data blocks store on DataNode. Then, the HDFS searches XML data nodes that satisfy the query conditions and stores them to the intermediate results. The users use the query predicate to query the XML attribute node on the corresponding XML data blocks using parallel XPath querying, which can satisfy the query request.

Map Logic Algorithm Using Parallel XPath Queries Based on Multiple Predicate Selection

The MapReduce programming model uses parallel XPath queries for massive XML data based on multiple predicate selection, which retrieves the query results that satisfies the use's query request. Map logic algorithm and Reduce logic algorithm can be implemented by using algorithm 1 and algorithm 2 respectively:

In the Map logic algorithm, for each Mappers task, the system uses the different query predicate *predicate*$_i$ as the key to generate the output results. When the number of intermediate results generated by the TaskTracker$_i$ of the Mappers task is less than the number k of query results expected by the user, the Map function evaluates the predicate *predicate*$_i$ for the value part of the key-value pairs set <key, value>. If the value satisfies the query constraint of the predicate *predicate*$_i$, the result of the predicate evaluation is true. The Map function outputs the key-value pairs set <key$_{predicatei}$, list (value')> as the intermediate query result, waiting for the call of the Reducers task to continue processing. Since each XML data block is processed in an isolated parallel manner in TaskTracker$_i$, each Mappers task attempts to output a set of k key-value pairs. Assuming that the total number of TaskTracker$_i$ in the Mappers task is m, then the maximum number of the intermediate results is $m * k$.

Reduce Logic Algorithm Using Parallel XPath Queries Based on Multiple Predicate Selection

The algorithm 2 proposes the reduce logic algorithm, which uses paralell Xpath queries for massive XML data based on multiple predicates selectivity.

In the Reduce logic algorithm, for each Reducers task, the system combines the values with the same key$_{predicate\ i}$ value according to the query predicate *predicate*$_i$ in the intermediate query results, and then transmits it to the Reduce function, so that the Reduce function receives a inputted set of the form of <key$_{predicate\ i}$, (list of values)>. Then, the Reduce function processes the value set and outputs a collection of final query results. If the number of final query results is less than or equal to the number of query results k expected by the users, the set of value is directly output as the final output results; otherwise, the system merges the value with the same key$_{predicate\ i}$, and outputs the first k query results as the final results. The outputted results can satisfy the user's query requirements.

Algorithm 1. Map logic algorithm for multiple predicate selection under MapReduce

Input: The number k of query results, inputted key-value pairs <key, value>, and the query predicate *predicate*$_i$.
Output: The collection of key-value pairs of intermediate results
1.   for the set of all key-value pairs   do
2.   if the number of intermediate query results generated by Task-Tracker$_i$ <k then
3.   if the value satisfies predicate *predicate*$_i$ then
4.   the number of intermediate query results ++
5.   output a collection of key-value pairs
6.   endif
7.   endif
8.   endfor

Algorithm 2. Reduce logic algorithm for multiple predicate selection under MapReduce

```
Input: The number k of query results, the intermediate results of the Map
phase < key_predicate i, list (value')>
Output: A collection of key-value pairs of the final results
1.        the collection of the form list (value') ⇒ final query result
2.        if  the number of final query results ≤ k  then
3.            output a collection of final query results
4.        else
5.            merge the same value with key_predicate i and output the first k query
results
6.        endif
```

The Optimization Method Under MapReduce Based on Multiple Predicate Selection

Under the MapReduce programming model, the system uses the parallel XPath querying method for massive XML data based on multi-predicate selection. Because of the large scale of massive XML data, the amount of data transmitted between Mappers and Reducers is increasing, and the time cost of the system is also increasing. Accordingly, the performance of the system continues to decline, so this paper further designs the MapReduce optimization method of query processing for massive XML data to reduce the amount of data transmission of the system, which can effectively improve the performance of the system.

In the Map phase, the system uses the query predicate $predicate_i$ to perform query evaluation on the XML data blocks. If the query fragment satisfies the constraint of the query predicate $predicate_i$ on the partitioned XML data blocks, the Map function outputs the intermediate query results. Assuming that the number of query results is k, which is expected by the users. If the number of intermediate query results is greater than k, then the system stops inputting the XML data; otherwise, the system continues to input the XML data and continuously evaluates the query predicate $predicate_i$. In this way, there are m TaskTracker$_i$ in the Mappers task, the intermediate query results are at most $m*k$, and then the intermediate query results are transmitted to the Reducers task, which effectively reduces the number of intermediate query results, and improves the system performance.

EXPERIMENTS

Experimental Setup

The experimental environment of this chapter is composed of 8 computer clusters connected by high-speed network. Each computer is configured as Intel Pentium G2020 2.9GHz CPU, 8G memory and 1TB hard disk. One computer is used as JobTracker node, and the other computers are used as TaskTracker node. The system uses Hadoop 2.7.7, JDK 6.0 environment development software.

- **Dataset**: the standard XMark dataset 120GB and TreeBank dataset 85GB. The XMark dataset stores data in a large-scale XML document and simulates an online auction site that evaluates the query processing capabilities of XML data in real-world applications. The TreeBank dataset contains the syntactic analysis and annotation information of the linguistic texts of linguistic research. Its characteristic is that the structure of the data is deeply nested and has not regularity, in which the text information is encrypted.

- **Comparison algorithm**: In (Emoto *et al.* 2012), an effective MapReduce algorithm is proposed, which queries large-scale XML data trees in parallel and achieves the better speedup. The method is representative and has comparable with the proposed method. The method (Emoto *et al.* 2012) is recorded as PTRM (Parallel Tree Reduction on MapReduce). The PTRM method is based on the MapReduce programming model. It uses two Map and Reduce loops to calculate the large-scale XML data tree in parallel BSP model. In this chapter the PXQMS (Parallel XPath Query based on Multi-predicate Selection) method is proposed, which uses the parallel XPath based on multi-predicate selection method to query massive XML data under the MapReduce programming model. This chapter proposes the corresponding Map logic algorithm and Reduce logic algorithm to process massive XML data at one time.

The experiments use the query predicate to parallel query the massive XML data, and the XPath expression contains the predicate. The query predicate is of the form $A_i \theta a_i$, where $i \in (1, …, n)$, A_i represents the attribute nodes of an XML document, a_i represents the attribute values, and $\theta \in \{=, >, <, and, or, not, contains\}$. Due to the large number of predicates in the Hadoop distributed environment, so specific predicate is not described.

System Speed-Up Experiment

The speed-up is used to indicate that how much faster a computer cluster can execute than a single computing node. It is an important performance test indicator of a computer cluster. The speed-up of the PXQMS method proposed in this chapter and the PTRM method (Emoto *et al.* 2012) in XMark data sets and TreeBank datasets are compared respectively. The experimental results are shown in Figures 6 and Figure 7.

It can be seen from the Figure 6 and 7 that the PXQMS method runs stably on the two datasets of XMark and TreeBank, which is slightly higher than the speed-up of the PTRM method, indicating that the PXQMS method achieves better speed-up on large-scale XML datasets. On the XMark dataset, the system execution performance of 8 compute nodes is faster than the performance of a single computing node. The PXQMS method has a speed-up of 6.9 and the PTRM method has a speed-up of 6.2. On the TreeBank dataset, the PXQMS method has a speed-up of 6.6 and the PTRM method has a speed-up of 6.

Query Throughput Experiment

Query throughput is the number of system queries processing per second. It is an important indicator for measuring system query performance. When testing the query throughput, the user submits the query request to the system, then the computing node sends it to the system. After obtaining the information of the last query, the system sends the query again. Since the user's query is represented as the query predicate, the experiment compares the ability of the PXQMS method and the PTRM method, which

Figure 6. Speed-up of PXQMS and PTRM method over XMark

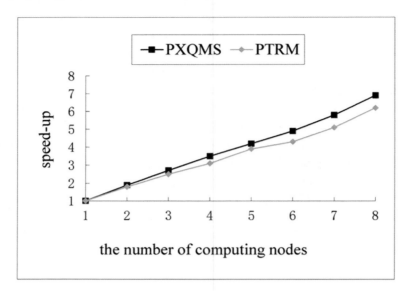

Figure 7. Speed-up of PXQMS and PTRM method over TreeBank

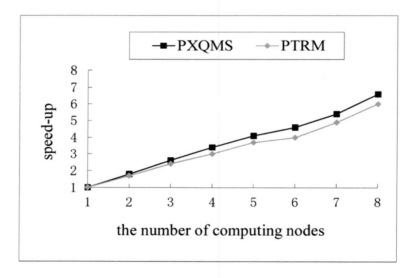

process the number of query predicate on the XMark and TreeBank data sets. The test time of each experiment is 180 seconds, and the number of query predicate is collected every 10 seconds, and the number of query predicate is counted. Finally, the average throughput of the query predicate in each experimental test is used as the final experimental results. Duo to the large number of predicates in the MapReduce programming frameworks, so the number of query predicate greater than 500 in Figures 8 and 9. The results of the experimental tests are shown in Figure 8 and Figure 9.

It can be seen from the Figure 8 and 9 that the number of query predicates gradually increases with the increasing computing node. This query predicate can be processed by the PXQMS method and the

PTRM method, and the query throughput of the PXQMS method is always higher than the query throughput of the PTRM method. This is because the MSPQ method sets replicas of XML data blocks, and the XML data blocks with higher operation frequency sets a higher number of replicas, thus improving the query throughput of the system.

Query Performance Experiment

In the two datasets XMark and TreeBank, this experiment compares the query performance of the PXQMS method and the PTRM method. The PTRM method uses two loops of Map function and Reduce function to process the large-scale XML data in parallel. In the first loop, Map function outputs local data

Figure 8. Throughput of PXQMS and PTRM method over XMark

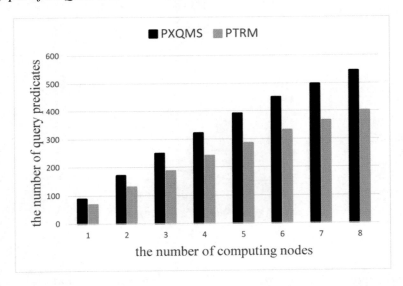

Figure 9. Throughput of PXQMS and PTRM method over TreeBank

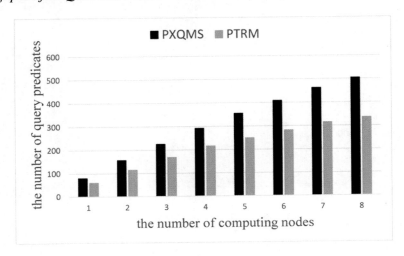

to the distributed file system. In the second loop, Map function reads from the distributed file system. In different MapReduce loops, two loops of Map function cannot share the same local data, which results in wasted system resources and reduced system performance.

As can be seen from the Figure 10 and 11, when the scale of the XMark dataset and TreeBank dataset is very small, such as the size of the dataset is 100MB, the query time performance of the PXQMS method and the PTRM method is similar, because the size of the dataset is relatively small. Some computing nodes of Mappers in the MapReduce programming model do not allocate data blocks. These comput-

Figure 10. Comparison of query performance of PXQMS and PTRM method over XMark

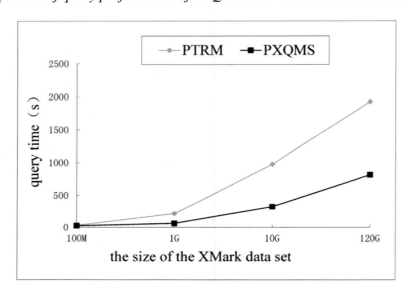

Figure 11. Comparison of query performance of PXQMS and PTRM method over TreeBank

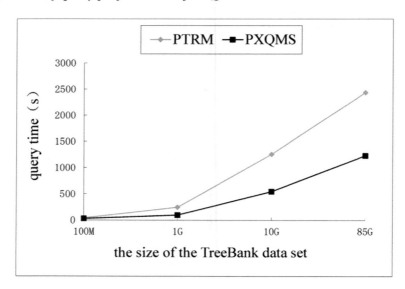

ing nodes are not fully working, so the query time performance of the PXQMS method and the PTRM method is relatively close. When the data size of the XMark dataset and the TreeBank dataset is large enough, each computing node of the parallel query processing system allocates data blocks, and the query time performance of the PXQMS method is significantly higher than the query time performance of the PTRM method.

CONCLUSION

With the rapid growth of XML data, the existing XML query processing method cannot adapt to the query processing requirements of massive XML data. In order to solve this problem, this chapter proposes a parallel query processing method for massive XML data based on multi-predicate selection. This chapter proposes the system architecture of processing massive XML data on the Hadoop platform. The user's query request is presented in the form of the query predicate, and then the multi-predicate selection is used in the MapReduce programming model to process massive XML data in a parallel query. The Map logic algorithm and the Reduce logic algorithm are designed to realize the parallel query processing of massive XML data. Finally, the effectiveness of the proposed method is verified by experiments, which can meet the user's query requirements for massive XML data. The future research direction is the issue of parallel twig query for massive XML data using MapReduce programming model on the Hadoop platform, and studies the problem of parallel XQuery query processing with MapReduce programming model further.

REFERENCES

Afrati, F. N., Damigos, M., & Gergatsoulis, M. (2015). Lower bounds on the communication of XPath queries in MapReduce. In *Proceedings of the Workshops of the EDBT/ICDT Joint Conference* (pp. 38-41). Brussels, Belgium: CEUR-WS.

Ahn, J., Im, D. H., Lee, T., & Kim, H. G. (2016). Parallel prime number labeling of large XML data using MapReduce. In *Proceedings of the International Conference on IT Convergence and Security*, (pp. 1-2). Prague, Czech Republic: IEEE Computer Society. 10.1109/ICITCS.2016.7740360

Ahn, J., Im, D. H., Lee, T., & Kim, H. G. (2017). A dynamic and parallel approach for repetitive prime labeling of XML with MapReduce. *The Journal of Supercomputing*, *73*(2), 810–836. doi:10.100711227-016-1803-y

Antonellis, P., Makris, C., & Pispirigos, G. (2015). Distributed XML filtering using Hadoop framework. In *Proceedings of the Algorithmic Aspects of Cloud Computing First International Workshop*, (pp. 75-83). Patras, Greece: Springer.

Bairoch, A., Apweiler, R., Wu, C. H., Barker, W. C., Boeckmann, B., Ferro, S., ... Yeh, L. L. (2005). The universal protein resource (UniProt). *Nucleic Acids Research*, *33*, 154-159.

Bi, X., Wang, G., Zhao, X., Zhang, Z., & Chen, S. (2015). Distributed XML twig query processing using MapReduce. In *Proceedings of the Web Technologies and Applications 17th Asia-PacificWeb Conference*, (pp. 203-214). Guangzhou, China: Springer. 10.1007/978-3-319-25255-1_17

Bidoit, N., Colazzo, D., Malla, N., Ulliana, F., Nole, M., & Sartiani, C. (2013). Processing XML queries and updates on map/reduce clusters. In *Proceedings of the International Conference on Extending Database Technology*, (pp. 745-748). Genoa, Italy: ACM. 10.1145/2452376.2452470

Bray, T., Paoli, J., & Sperberg-McQueen, C. M. (1997). Extensible markup language (XML). *World Wide Web Journal, 2*(4), 27–66.

Camacho-Rodriguez, J., Colazzo, D., Manolescu, I., & Naranjo, A. M., J. (2015). PAXQuery: Parallel analytical XML processing. In *Proceedings of the ACM SIGMOD International Conference on Management of Data*, (pp. 1117-1122). Melbourne, Victoria, Australia: ACM.

Choi, H., Lee, K., Kim, S. H., Lee, Y. J., & Moon, B. (2012). HadoopXML: a suite for parallel processing of massive XML data with multiple twig pattern queries. In *Proceedings of the ACM International Conference on Information and Knowledge Management*, (pp. 2737-2739). Maui, HI: ACM. 10.1145/2396761.2398745

Choi, H., Lee, K. H., & Lee, Y. J. (2014). Parallel labeling of massive XML data with MapReduce. *The Journal of Supercomputing, 67*(2), 408–437. doi:10.100711227-013-1008-6

Cong, G., Fan, W., Kementsietsidis, A., Li, J., & Liu, X. (2012). Partial evaluation for distributed XPath query processing and beyond. *ACM Transactions on Database Systems, 37*(4), 32:1-32:43.

Damigos, M., Gergatsoulis, M., & Kalogeros, E. (2014). Distributed evaluation of XPath queries over large integrated XML data. In *Proceedings of the 18th Panhellenic Conference on Informatics*, (pp. 61:1-61:6). Athens, Greece: ACM. 10.1145/2645791.2645804

Damigos, M., Gergatsoulis, M., & Plitsos, S. (2013). Distributed processing of XPath queries using MapReduce. In *Proceedings of the New Trends in Databases and Information Systems, 17th East European Conference on Advances in Databases and Information Systems*, (pp. 69-77). Genoa, Italy: Springer.

Dean, J., & Ghemawat, S. (2004). MapReduce: Simplified data processing on large clusters. In *Proceedings of the 6th Symposium on Operating System Design and Implementation*, (pp. 137-150). San Francisco, CA: USENIX Association.

Eisenberg, A. (2013). XQuery 3.0 is nearing completion. *SIGMOD Record, 42*(3), 34–41. doi:10.1145/2536669.2536675

Emoto, K., & Imachi, H. (2012). Parallel tree reduction on MapReduce. In *Proceedings of the International Conference on Computational Science*, (pp. 1827-1836). Omaha, NE: Elsevier.

Fadika, Z., Head, M. R., & Govindaraju, M. (2009). Parallel and distributed approach for processing large-scale XML datasets. In *Proceedings of the 10th IEEE/ACM International Conference on Grid Computing*, (pp. 105-112). Banff, Alberta, Canada: IEEE Computer Society. 10.1109/GRID.2009.5353070

Fan, H., Ma, Z., Wang, D., & Liu, J. (2018). Handling distributed XML queries over large XML data based on MapReduce framework. *Information Sciences, 453*, 1–20. doi:10.1016/j.ins.2018.04.028

Fan, H., Wang, D., & Liu, J. (2016). Distributed XPath query processing over large XML data based on MapReduce framework. In *Proceedings of the International Conference on Natural Computation, Fuzzy Systems and Knowledge Discovery*, (pp. 1447-1453). Changsha, China: IEEE. 10.1109/FSKD.2016.7603390

Fan, H., Yang, H., Ma, Z., & Liu, J. (2016). TwigStack-MR: An approach to distributed XML twig query using MapReduce. In *Proceedings of the IEEE International Congress on Big Data*, (pp. 133-140). San Francisco, CA: IEEE Computer Society. 10.1109/BigDataCongress.2016.79

Feng, J., Liu, L., Li, G., Li, J., & Sun, Y. (2010). An efficient parallel pathStack algorithm for processing XML twig queries on multi-core systems. In *Proceedings of the Database Systems for Advanced Applications, 15th International Conference*, (pp. 277-291). Tsukuba, Japan: Springer. 10.1007/978-3-642-12026-8_22

Ghemawat, S., Gobioff, H., & Leung, S. T. (2003). The google file system. In *Proceedings of the 19th ACM Symposium on Operating Systems Principles*, (pp. 29-43). Bolton Landing, NY: ACM.

Huang, X., Si, X., Yuan, X., & Wang, C. (2014). A dynamic load-balancing scheme for XPath queries parallelization in shared memory multi-core systems. *Journal of Computers, 9*(6), 1436–1445. doi:10.4304/jcp.9.6.1436-1445

Ogden, P., Thomas, D. B., & Pietzuch, P. R. (2013). Scalable XML query processing using parallel pushdown transducers. *Proceedings of the VLDB Endowment International Conference on Very Large Data Bases, 6*(14), 1738–1749. doi:10.14778/2556549.2556558

Sato, S., Hao, W., & Matsuzaki, K. (2018). Parallelization of XPath queries using modern XQuery processors. In *Proceedings of the New Trends in Databases and Information Systems - ADBIS Short Papers and Workshops*, (pp. 54-62). Budapest, Hungary: Springer. 10.1007/978-3-030-00063-9_7

Senk, A., Valenta, M., & Benn, W. (2014). Distributed evaluation of XPath axes queries over large XML documents stored in MapReduce clusters. In *Proceedings of the 25th International Workshop on Database and Expert Systems Applications*, (pp. 253-257). Munich, Germany: IEEE.

Slavov, V., Katib, A., & Rao, P. R. (2014). A tool for internet-scale cardinality estimation of XPath queries over distributed semistructured data. In *Proceedings of the IEEE 30th International Conference on Data Engineering*, (pp. 1270-1273). IEEE Computer Society. 10.1109/ICDE.2014.6816758

Slavov, V., & Rao, P. R. (2014). A gossip-based approach for internet-scale cardinality estimation of XPath queries over distributed semistructured data. *The VLDB Journal, 23*(1), 51–76. doi:10.100700778-013-0314-1

Song, K., & Lu, H. (2016). Efficient querying distributed big-XML data using MapReduce. *International Journal of Grid and High Performance Computing, 8*(3), 70–79. doi:10.4018/IJGHPC.2016070105

Song, K., & Lu, H. (2016). High-performance XML modeling of parallel queries based on MapReduce framework. *Cluster Computing, 19*(4), 1975–1986. doi:10.100710586-016-0628-z

Song, K., Lu, H., & Qin, X. (2016). An efficient parallel approach of parsing and indexing for large-scale XML datasets. In *Proceedings of the International Conference on IT Convergence and Security*, (pp. 1-2). Prague, Czech Republic: IEEE Computer Society. 10.1109/ICPADS.2016.0033

Wu, H. (2014). Parallelizing structural joins to process queries over big XML data using MapReduce. In *Proceedings of the Database and Expert Systems Applications - 25th International Conference*, (pp. 183-190). Munich, Germany: Springer. 10.1007/978-3-319-10085-2_16

Zinn, D., Bowers, S., Kohler, S., & Ludascher, B. (2010). Parallelizing XML data-streaming workflows via MapReduce. *Journal of Computer and System Sciences*, 76(6), 447–463. doi:10.1016/j.jcss.2009.11.006

KEY TERMS AND DEFINITIONS

HDFS: Hadoop distributed file system is an open source distributed storage system, which is a distributed file system that divides large-scale data files into smaller data blocks to store massive data.

MapReduce Programming Model: MapReduce is a popular programming framework to support data-intensive applications using shared-nothing clusters.

Node of XML Document Tree: The node of an XML document tree can be defined as a triple (*id*, *label*, *<text>*), in which *id* is an identifier that uniquely identifies a node, *label* is the corresponding element or the attribute name, and *text* is the text content or attribute value of the corresponding element.

XML Document Tree: XML document is a semi-structured data format with hierarchical relationship and nested structure, which can be represented by the tree structure $T = (N, E, r)$. N represents the set of all nodes in the data tree, E represents the set of edges between nodes in the data tree, and r represents the root node of the data tree.

XML Predicate Query: The predicate query on XML document can be expressed as: $path_1$ [$predicate_1$] // $path_2$ [$predicate_2$] //...// $path_n$ [$predicate_n$], where $path_1$, $path_2$, ..., $path_n$ is the query path expression in the XPath query language. $predicate_i$ is the query predicate with a selection condition of the form $A_i\, \theta\, a_i$, where $i \in (1, ..., n)$, A_i represents the attribute nodes of an XML document, a_i represents the attribute values, and $\theta \in \{=, >, <,$ and, or, not, contains$\}$.

Chapter 13
Towards Massive RDF Storage in NoSQL Databases:
A Survey

Zongmin Ma
https://orcid.org/0000-0001-7780-6473
Nanjing University of Aeronautics and Astronautics, China

Li Yan
Nanjing University of Aeronautics and Astronautics, China

ABSTRACT

The resource description framework (RDF) is a model for representing information resources on the web. With the widespread acceptance of RDF as the de-facto standard recommended by W3C (World Wide Web Consortium) for the representation and exchange of information on the web, a huge amount of RDF data is being proliferated and becoming available. So, RDF data management is of increasing importance and has attracted attention in the database community as well as the Semantic Web community. Currently, much work has been devoted to propose different solutions to store large-scale RDF data efficiently. In order to manage massive RDF data, NoSQL (not only SQL) databases have been used for scalable RDF data store. This chapter focuses on using various NoSQL databases to store massive RDF data. An up-to-date overview of the current state of the art in RDF data storage in NoSQL databases is provided. The chapter aims at suggestions for future research.

INTRODUCTION

The Resource Description Framework (RDF) is a framework for representing information resources on the Web, which is proposed by W3C (World Wide Web Consortium) as a recommendation (Manola and Miller, 2004). RDF can represent structured and unstructured data (Duan, Kementsietsidis, Srinivas and Udrea, 2011), and more important, metadata of resources on the Web represented by RDF can be shared and exchanged among application programming without semantic missing. Here metadata mean

DOI: 10.4018/978-1-5225-8446-9.ch013

the data that specify semantic information about data. Currently RDF has been widely accepted and has rapidly gained popularity. And many organizations, companies and enterprises have started using RDF for representing and processing their data. We can find some application examples such as the United States[1], the United Kingdom[2], New York Times[3], BBC[4], and Best Buy[5]. RDF is finding increasing use in a wide range of Web data-management scenarios.

With the widespread usage of RDF in diverse application domains, a huge amount of RDF data is being proliferated and becoming available. As a result, efficient and scalable management of large-scale RDF data is of increasing importance, and has attracted attentions in the database community as well as the Semantic Web community. Currently, much work is being done in RDF data management. Some RDF data-management systems have started to emerge such as *Sesame* (Broekstra, Kampman and van Harmelen, 2002), *Jena-TDB* (Wilkinson, Sayers, Kuno and Reynolds, 2003), *Virtuoso* (Erling and Mikhailov, 2007 & 2009), *4Store* (Harris, Lamb and Shadbolt, 2009)), *BigOWLIM* (Bishop *et al.*, 2011) and *Oracle Spatial and Graph with Oracle Database 12c*[6]. Here BigOWLIM is renamed to OWLIM-SE and further to GraphDB. Also some research prototypes have been developed (e.g., RDF-3X (Neumann and Weikum, 2008 & 2010), SW-Store (Abadi, Marcus, Madden and Hollenbach, 2007 & 2009) and RDFox[7]).

RDF data management mainly involves scalable storage and efficient queries of RDF data, in which RDF data storage provides the infrastructure for RDF data management and efficient querying of RDF data is enabled based on RDF storage. In addition, to serve a given query more effectively, it is necessary to index RDF data. Indexing of RDF data is enabled based on RDF storage also. Currently many efforts have been made to propose different solutions to store large-scale RDF data efficiently. Traditionally relational databases are applied to store RDF data and various storage structures based on relational databases have been developed. Based on the relational perspective, Sakr and Al-Naymat (2009) present an overview of relational techniques for storing and querying RDF data. It should be noted that the relational RDF stores are a kind of centralized RDF stores, which are a single-machine solution with limited scalability. The scalability of RDF data stores is essential for massive RDF data management. NoSQL (for "not only SQL") databases have recently emerged as a commonly used infrastructure for handling Big Data because of their high scalability and efficiency. Identifying that massive RDF data management merits the use of NoSQL databases, currently NoSQL databases are increasingly used in massive RDF data management (Cudre-Mauroux *et al.*, 2013).

This chapter provides an up-to-date overview of the current state of the art in massive RDF data stores in NoSQL databases. We present the survey from three main perspectives, which are key value stores of RDF data in NoSQL databases, document stores of RDF data in NoSQL databases and RDF data stores in graph databases. Note that, due to the large number of RDF data-management solutions, this chapter does not include all of them. In addition to provide a generic overview of the approaches that have been proposed to store RDF data in NoSQL databases, this chapter presents some suggestions for future research in the area of massive RDF data management with NoSQL databases.

The rest of this chapter is organized as follows. The second section presents preliminaries of RDF data model. It also introduces the main approaches for storing RDF data. The third section introduces NoSQL databases and their database models. The fourth section provides the details of the different techniques in several NoSQL-based RDF data stores. The final section concludes the chapter and provides some suggestions for possible research directions on the subject.

RDF Model and RDF Data Storage

Being a W3C recommendation, RDF (Resource Description Framework) provides a means to represent and exchange semantic metadata. With RDF, metadata about information sources are represented and processed. Furthermore, RDF defines a model for describing relationships among resources in terms of uniquely identified attributes and values.

The RDF data model is applied to model resources. A resource is anything which has a universal resource identifier (URI) and is described using a set of RDF statements in the form of (*subject, predicate, object*) triples. Here *subject* is the resource being described, *predicate* is the property being described with respect to the resource, and *object* is the value for the property.

Formally, an RDF triple is defined as (s, p, o), in which s is called the subject, p the predicate (or property), and o the object. Triple (s, p, o) means that the subject s has the property p whose value is the object o. The abstract syntax of RDF data model is a set of triples. Among these triples, it is possible that an object in one triple (e.g., o_i in (s_i, p_i, o_i)) can be a subject in other triples (e.g., (o_i, p_j, o_j)). Then RDF data model is a directed, labelled graph model for representing Web resources (Huang, Abadi and Ren, 2011). A key concept for RDF is that of URIs (Unique Resource Identifiers), which can be applied in either of the s, p and o positions to uniquely refer to entity, relationship or concept (Kaoudi and Manolescu, 2015). In addition, literals are allowed in the o position. Let I, B, and L denote infinite sets of *IRI*s, blank nodes, and literals, respectively. Then we have $(s, p, o) \in (I \cup B) \times I \times (I \cup B \cup L)$. Concerning the syntaxes for RDF, we have RDF/XML, N-Triple and Turtle. Among them, N-Triple is the most basic one and it contains one triple per line.

In (Bornea *et al.*, 2013), a sample of DBpedia RDF data is presented and it contains 21 tuples and 13 predicates. Let us look at a fragment of the sample, which contains 6 triples {(Google, industry, Software), (Google, industry, Internet), (Google, employees, 54,604), (Android, developer, Google), (Android, version, 4.1), (Android, kernel, Linux)} and 5 predicates {industry, employees, developer, version, kernel}. For a triple, say (Google, industry, Internet), its resource is *Google*, this resource has the property *industry*, and the value for the property is *Internet*. With the set of triples, we have an RDF graph shown in Figure 1.

As we know, in the context of common data management, data are stored early in file systems and late in databases (such as relational databases and object-oriented databases). Similarly, RDF data management relies on RDF data storage also. It is especially true for managing large-scale RDF data in the real-world applications. Nowadays many approaches of RDF data storages have been developed. Given the large number of RDF data-management solutions, there is a richness of perspectives and approaches to RDF data storages. But few classifications of RDF data-storage approaches have been reported in the

Figure 1. An RDF graph

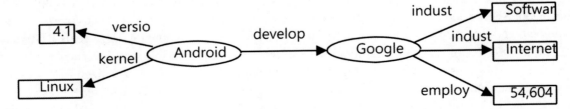

literature. Basically, proposals for RDF data storage are classified into two major categories in (Sakr and Al-Naymat, 2009; Bornea *et al.*, 2013), which are *native stores* and *relational stores*, respectively. Here the native stores use customized binary RDF data representation and the relational stores distribute RDF data to appropriate relational databases. Viewed from three basic perspectives of the relational, entity and graph-based perspectives, proposals for RDF data storage are classified into three major categories in (Luo *et al.*, 2012), which are *relational stores*, *entity stores* and *graph-based stores*, respectively.

RDF data stores can be classified relying on the underlying infrastructure. First, for the native stores, we can identify *main-memory-based RDF native store* and *disk-based RDF native store*. The major difference between these two native stores is that the former works on RDF data stored completely in main memory and the latter works on RDF data stored in disk. The disk-based RDF native store is built directly on the file system. It is not difficult to see that the native stores can only deal with small-scale RDF data. At this point, traditional relational databases are hereby applied to store RDF data. In the relational stores of RDF data, different relational schemas can be designed, depending on how to distribute RDF triples to an appropriate relational schema. This has results in three major categories of RDF relational stores (Sakr and Al-Naymat, 2009; Bornea *et al.*, 2013; Luo *et al.*, 2012), which are *triple stores*, *vertical stores* and *property (type) stores*. In the tripe stores, all RDF triples are directly stored in a single relational table over relational schema (*subject, predicate, object*), and each RDF triple becomes a tuple of the relational database. In the vertical stores, a subject-object relation is directly represented for each predicate of RDF triples and a relational table contains only one predicate as a column name. As a result, we have a set of binary relational tables over relational schema (*subject, object*), each relational table corresponds to a different predicate, and this predicate can be the name of the corresponding relational table. In the type stores, one relational table is created for each RDF data type, in which an RDF data type generally corresponds to several predicates, and a relational table contains the properties as *n*-ary table columns for the same subject.

The reason why there are three major approaches for storing RDF data in relational databases is that each approach has its advantages and disadvantages simultaneously. First, the triple stores use a fixed relational schema and can hereby handle dynamic schema of RDF data, but the triple stores involve a number of self-join operations for querying. Second, the vertical stores using a set of relational tables generally involve many table join operations for querying and cannot handle dynamic schema of RDF data because new predicates of new inserted triples result in new relational tables. Finally the type stores involve fewer table join operations than the vertical stores using multiple relational tables and, compared with the triple stores using a single relational table, no self-join operations, but the type stores generally contain null values and multi-valued attributes, and cannot handle dynamic schema of RDF data because new predicates of new inserted triples result in changes to relational schema.

Several representative relational RDF data stores and their major features are summarized in Table 1.

It can be seen from Table 1 that any one of the approaches for relational RDF data stores presented above cannot deal with RDF data stores well. So, some efforts have been made to store RDF data by using two or more of three major store approaches together or revising three major store approaches (Kim, 2006; Sperka and Smrz, 2012; Bornea *et al.*, 2013). Such an approach is called *hybrid stores*. It should be noted that the hybrid stores cannot still satisfy the need of managing large-scale RDF data.

The native RDF stores and the relational RDF stores (including the triple stores, vertical stores, type stores and hybrid stores) are actually categorized as *centralized RDF stores*. Centralized RDF stores are single-machine solutions with limited scalability. To process large-scale RDF data, recent research has devoted considerable effort to the study of managing massive RDF data in distributed environments.

Table 1. Representative relational RDF data stores and their major features

	Typical store systems	Advantages	Disadvantages
Triple stores	*Sesame* (Broekstra, Kampman and van Harmelen, 2002); Hexastore (Weiss, Karras and Bernste, 2008)	*no null values; no multi-valued attributes; fixed relational schema*	*too many self-joins*
Vertical stores	*SW-Store* (Abadi, Marcus, Madden and Hollenbach, 2007 & 2009)	*no null values; no multi-valued attributes*	*too many table joins; dynamic relational schema*
Type stores	*Jena* (McBride, 2002); *FlexTable* (Wang, Du, Lu and Wang, 2010); *RDFBroker* (Sintek and Kiesel, 2006)	*few table joins*	*null values; multi-valued attributes; dynamic relational schema*

Distributed RDF stores can hash partition triples across multiple machines and parallelize query processing. NoSQL databases have recently emerged as a commonly used infrastructure for handling Big Data (Pokorny, 2011). Massive RDF data management merits the use of NoSQL databases and currently NoSQL databases are increasingly used in RDF data management (Cudre-Mauroux *et al.*, 2013). Typically, NoSQL database stores of RDF data are distributed RDF stores. Depending on concrete data models adopted, the NoSQL database stores of RDF data are categorized into *key-value stores*, *column-family stores*, *document stores* and *graph databases stores*.

Summarily, we can classify current RDF data stores into the centralized RDF stores and the NoSQL database stores of RDF data (Papailiou *et al.*, 2013). The centralized RDF stores can be further classified into the native RDF stores and the relational RDF stores, in which the native RDF stores contain main-memory-based native RDF store and disk-based native RDF store, and the relational RDF stores include triple stores, vertical stores and type stores. The NoSQL database stores of RDF data are further classified into key-value stores, column-family stores, document stores and graph databases stores. Figure 2 illustrates this classification for RDF data stores.

The native RDF stores and the relational RDF stores have been reviewed in (Sakr and Al-Naymat, 2009). The focus of this chapter is to investigate NoSQL database stores of RDF data. Before that, we first sketch NoSQL databases in the following section.

NoSQL Databases for Big Data

We use the term of Big Data to refer to massive and complex datasets that are made up of a variety of data structures. Big Data can be found in diverse application domains such as web clicks, social media,

Figure 2. Classification of RDF data stores

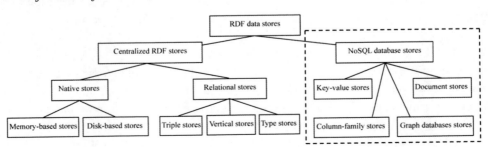

scientific experiments, datacenter monitoring and so on. Actually, there is not a common definition of Big Data so far (Stuart and Barker, 2013). But Big Data are generally characterized by three basic *V*s: *Volume*, *Variety* and *Velocity* (Laney, 2001).

- **Volume:** Volume means that Big Data have big data scale in the range of TB to PB and even more.
- **Variety:** Variety means Big Data have rich data types with many formats such as structured data, unstructured data, semistructured data, text, multimedia, and so on.
- **Velocity:** Velocity means that Big Data must be processed speedily. Also, Velocity means that Big Data are being produced speedily.

Then Big Data is high-volume, high-velocity and high-variety information assets that demand cost-effective, innovative forms of information processing for enhanced insight and decision making. In addition to the three *V*s above, a *V* associated with *Veracity* has been introduced to Big Data in (Snow, 2012) and a *V* associated with *Value* has been introduced to Big Data in (Gamble and Goble, 2011).

- **Veracity:** Veracity means that inherent imprecision and uncertainty in data should be explicitly considered so that the reliability and predictability of imprecise and uncertain Big Data can be managed.
- **Value:** Value means that Big Data must be worthwhile and has value for business.

The Veracity of data is a basis of Big Data processing because the data with volume and variety may contain errors, noises or imperfection. Actually, the Veracity of data is a precondition and guarantee of Big Data management, which can increase the robustness and accuracy of Big Data processing. Regarding to the Value of data, Value sets a basic criterion in the choice and processing of Big Data, which is especially true in the context of the data with volume, variety and velocity.

Also, there are several other *V*s that are applied to describe the properties of Big Data in literature (e.g., *Visualization*, *Visualization* and *Volatility*). Among them, Volatility means that Big Data that we are interested in are temporally valid. It is possible that, at one point, specific data are no longer relevant to the current processing and analysis of Big Data. It should be noted that the several *V*s mentioned above only characterize some properties of Big Data partially. So, some other characteristics rather than the *V*s presented above are assigned to Big Data.

Being similar with common data (not Big Data) management, Big Data management needs database systems. As we know, the relational databases are very powerful and have been widely applied for structured, semi-structured and even unstructured data. However, the relational databases are unable to manage Big Data. The reason is that the relational databases must meet ACID according to relational databases theory but Big Data management need CAP Theorem. ACID means the type of transaction processing done by relational database management system (RDBMS) as follows.

- **(A)tomcity:** If a part of operation fails, whole operation fails
- **(C)onsistency:** Information is always consistent, avoid read/write errors at all costs
- **(I)solation:** Multiple transactions at the same time do not impact each other
- **(D)urability:** Information has to be stored into database, not queued in memory

CAP Theorem is described by consistency, availability and partition as follows.

- **(C)onsistency:** Whenever data is written, everyone who reads the DB will see the latest version.
- **(A)vailability:** We can always expect each operation terminates in an intended response.
- **(P)artition Tolerance:** Database can still be read from/written to when parts of it are offline; afterwards, when offline nodes are back online, they are updated accordingly.

It is clear that the relational databases are not solutions in Big Data management. A new type of databases called NoSQL is hereby proposed, which means "not only SQL" or "no SQL at all".

NoSQL database systems have emerged as a commonly used infrastructure for handling Big Data. Comparing to traditional relational databases, NoSQL solutions provide simpler scalability and improved performance (Hecht and Jablonski, 2011; Pokorny, 2011; Moniruzzaman and Hossain, 2013; Gudivada, Rao and Raghavan, 2014) and generally have some characteristics as follows (Tauro, Aravindh and Shreeharsha, 2012).

- Distributed processing
- High availability
- High scalability and reliability
- Scheme-less
- Replication support
- Handle structured and unstructured data
- Data access via API
- Less strict adherence to consistency
- Improvements in performance

It should be noted that NoSQL databases are very diverse and there are more than one hundred NoSQL databases[8]. According to their data model, the various NoSQL databases are classified into four major categories as follows (Hecht and Jablonski, 2011; Grolinger *et al.*, 2013; Bach and Werner, 2014).

- Key-value NoSQL databases (e.g., DynamoDB, Riak, Redis)
- Column-oriented NoSQL databases (e.g., HBase, Cassandra, Hypertable)
- Document-oriented NoSQL databases (e.g., MongoDB, Couchbase Sever, Elasticsearch)
- Graph-oriented NoSQL databases (e.g., Neo4j, InfoGrid, HyperGraphDB)

Key-value stores have a simple data model based on key-value pairs, which contain a set of couples (key, value). A value is addressed by a single key. Here a value may be a string, a pointer (where the value is stored) or even a collection of couples (name, value) (e.g., in Redis[9]). Note that values are isolated and independent from others, in which the relationship is handled by the application logic.

Most column-family stores are derived from Google BigTable (Chang *et al.*, 2008), in which the data are stored in a column-oriented way. In BigTable, the dataset consists of several rows. Each row is addressed by a primary key and is composed of a set of column families. Note that different rows can have different column families. Representative column-family stores include Apache HBase[10], which directly implements the Google BigTable concepts. In addition, Cassandra (Lakshman and Malik, 2010) provides the additional functionality of super-columns, in which a column contains nested (sub)columns and super-columns are formed by grouping various columns together. According to (Grolinger *et al.*, 2013), there is one type of column-family store, say Amazon SimpleDB and DynamoDB (DeCandia *et al.*, 2007), in which only a set of column name-value pairs is contained in each row, without having column families. So SimpleDB and DynamoDB are generally categorized as key-value stores as well.

Document stores provide another derivative of the key-value store data model that uses keys to locate documents inside the data store. Most document stores represent documents using *JSON* (JavaScript Object Notation) or some format derived from it (e.g., *BSON* (Binary JSON)). JSON is a binary and typed data model which supports the data types list, map, date, Boolean as well as numbers of different precisions. Typically, CouchDB[11] and the Couchbase server[12] use the JSON format for data storage, whereas MongoDB[13] stores data in *BSON*.

Graph databases, a special category of NoSQL databases, use graphs as their data model. A graph is used to represent a set of objects, known as vertices or nodes, and the links (or edges) that interconnect these vertices. Representative graph databases include GraphDB (Güting, 1994) and Neo4j[14]. Neo4j is an open-source, highly scalable, robust native graph database that stores data in a graph. Note that graph databases actually are developed originally for managing data with complex structures and relationships such as data with recursive structure and data with network structure rather than Big Data management. Generally, graph databases run in single server (e.g., GraphDB and Neo4j). Recently few efforts have been made to develop distributed graph databases (Nicoara, Kamali, Daudjee and Chen, 2015). Typically, Titan[15] is a scalable graph database optimized for storing and querying graphs containing hundreds of billions of vertices and edges distributed across a multi-machine cluster.

Illustrative representations of four kinds of NoSQL models are shown in Figure 3, which are presented by Grolinger *et al.* (2013).

Following the four major categories of NoSQL models, some NoSQL databases have been developed and applied. Table 2 lists several representative NoSQL databases.

In the NoSQL data models presented above, column-family store and document store can be regarded as a kind of extended key value stores, in which document store is regarded that the key values are set to be the documents, and column-family store is regarded that a key value is a combination of ID of row, column number and timestamp. So sometimes column-family stores of NoSQL databases such as HBase and Cassandra are generally called key value stores of NoSQL databases. The true key value store model is too simple for many application domains such RDF data management.

NoSQL databases are designed especially for storing and processing datasets of Big Data. In the context of RDF datasets, NoSQL databases are applied for massive RDF data. In the following, we provide a survey on how massive RDF data management merits the use of NoSQL databases.

MASSIVE RDF DATA STORAGE IN NOSQL DATABASES

Being a commonly used infrastructure, NoSQL databases have been extensively applied for dealing with common Big Data. Note that, although NoSQL databases are not designed especially for RDF data management, massive RDF data management merits the use of NoSQL databases for Big Data infrastructure because of the scalability and high performance of NoSQL databases for Big Data management.

Depending on the concrete database models of NoSQL, we can identify four major kinds of RDF data stores in NoSQL databases, which are *storing RDF data in column-family stores of NoSQL databases*, *storing RDF data in document stores of NoSQL databases*, and *storing RDF data in graph databases*.

Figure 3. Different types of NoSQL data model

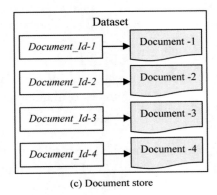

Key_1	Value_1
Key_2	Value_2
Key_3	Value_1
Key_4	Value_3
Key_5	Value_2
Key_6	Value_1
Key_7	Value_4
Key_8	Value_3

(a) Key value store

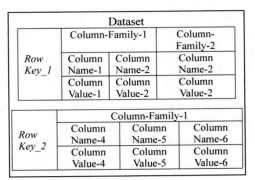

(b) Column-family store

(c) Document store

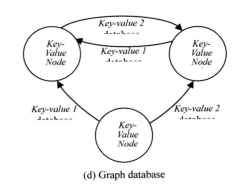

(d) Graph database

Table 2. Representative NoSQL databases

	Representative NoSQL Databases	**Remarks**
Key value store	Redis; SimpleDB; DynamoDB	In SimpleDB and DynamoDB, a set of column name-value pairs is contained in each row.
Column-family store	BigTable; HBase; Cassandra; Hypertable[16]	Cassandra provides the additional functionality of super-columns.
Document store	CouchDB; Couchbase server; MongoDB	CouchDB and Couchbase server use the JSON format for data storage. MongoDB stores data in BSON (Binary JSON)
Graph database	GraphDB; Neo4j; Titan	GraphDB and Neo4j run in single server. Titan is a distributed graph databases

Storing RDF Data in Column-Family Stores of NoSQL Databases

Among the NoSQL database systems available, HBase is typically a kind of *column-family stores of NoSQL databases* and has been the most widely applied NoSQL database. Apache HBase uses HDFS (Hadoop Distributed File System) as its storage back-end (Hua, Wu, Li and Ren, 2014), and supports MapReduce computing framework (Dean and Ghemawat, 2008). Being similar to the relational databases,

HBase uses data table named *HTable*, in which each row is uniquely identified by a row key. HBase generally creates indexing on the row keys.

We know that RDF triples can be stored in relational databases (Ma, Capretz and Yan, 2016). Similarly, RDF triples can be stored in HTable of HBase also. Here we identify several major storage structures for HTable-based RDF store as follows.

- First, based on the idea of Hexastore schema developed in (Weiss, Karras and Bernstein, 2008), scalable RDF store based on HBase is proposed in (Sun and Jin, 2010). They store RDF triples into six HBase tables (S_PO, P_SO, O_SP, PS_O, SO_P and PO_S), which covers all combinations of RDF triple patterns. And they index RDF triples with HBase provided index structure on row key.
- Second, based on HBase, two distributed triple stores H_2RDF and H_2RDF+ are developed in (Papailiou, Konstantinou, Tsoumakos and Koziris, 2012) and (Papailiou *et al.*, 2013), respectively. The main difference between H_2RDF and H_2RDF+ is the number of maintained indices (three versus six).

In addition, to manage distributed RDF data, HBase is sometimes applied by combining others together. HBase and MySQL Cluster, for example, are used in (Franke *et al.*, 2011). Combining the Jena framework with the storage provided by HBase, Khadilkar *et al.* (2012) developed several versions of a triple store. Figure 4 presents an overview of the architecture typically used by Jena-HBase (Khadilkar *et al.*, 2012).

Here six types layout are design, which are *simple layout, vertically partitioned (VP) layout, indexed layout, VP and indexed layout, hybrid layout,* and *hash layout.* In the simple layout, three HTable tables are created and each is indexed by subjects, predicates and objects (i.e., row key), and other two components are combined together as a column name. In the vertically partitioned (VP) layout, every unique

Figure 4. Architectural overview of Jena-HBase

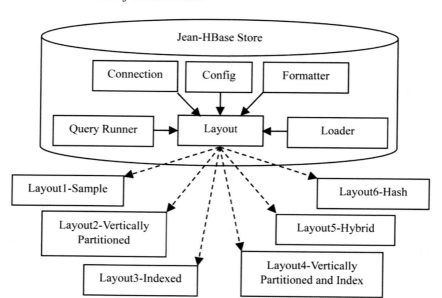

predicate creates two HTable tables and each is indexed by subjects and objects. In the indexed layout, six HTable tables are created for representing the six possible combinations of a triple, namely, SPO, SOP, PSO, POS, OSP and OPS. In the VP and indexed layout, the vertically partitioned (VP) layout and the indexed layout are combined together. As a result, the VP and indexed layout contains the all HTable tables in the vertically partitioned layout as well as three additional HTable tables for SPO, OSP and OS. In the hybrid layout, the simple layout and the vertically partitioned layout are combined together. So, the hybrid layout contains the three HTable tables in the simple layout as well as the all HTable tables in the vertically partitioned layout. The hash layout is a kind of hybrid layout with hash values for nodes and a separate table containing hash-to-node mappings. Khadilkar *et al.* (2012) compare with experiments these six layouts on features of data loading speed and querying efficiency and finally reveal that the hybrid layout has better performances. But the hybrid layout is complicated in design and implementation.

Storing RDF Data in Document Stores of NoSQL Databases

Document stores of NoSQL databases look like relational databases, in which each row is associated with a document instead of a tuple. It is clear that such a structure is suitable for storing semi-structure data. As mentioned above, documents in the document stores of NoSQL Databases are represented by using *JSON* (JavaScript Object Notation) or *BSON* (Binary JSON). Being a kind of data exchange format, JSON adopts text format and can be easily edited by persons and processed by machines simultaneously. As a result, it is convenient that JSON can be shared and exchanged among different systems.

In order to store massive RDF data in document stores of NoSQL databases, RDF data should be represented with JSON format. As we know, RDF triples contain three components, which are subjects, predicates and objects and meanwhile the structure of JSON only contains two components, which are keys and values. It is clear that they are not consistent. So it is necessary to establish a mapping to transform RDF to JSON. Basically, we can identify several basic mappings from RDF to JSON as follows.

1. Triple-centered mapping
2. Subject-centered mapping
3. JSON-LD approach

In the triple-centered mapping, all triples in an RDF graph can be stored in a rooted document object. The value of this document object is an array, and each element of the array corresponds to a triple of RDF. In the subject-centered mapping, each subject of RDF data is treated as the *"Key"* of an JSON object, and the corresponding *"Value"* is some embedded objects (Alexander, 2008). The *"Key"* of these embedded objects is the predicate of the present subject. JSON-LD[17], developed by W3C as a recommendation, is a data serialization and messaging format for Linked Data. It is primarily intended to be a way to use Linked Data in Web-based programming environments, to build interoperable Web services, and to store Linked Data in JSON-based storage engines. With JSON-LD, Linked Data which are represented by RDF can be easily stored in JSON-based document stores of NoSQL databases such as CouchDB. An JSON-LD document is an instance of RDF data model. JSON-LD can serialize a generic RDF data set after RDF data model is extended. Also a reverse serialization can be made with JSON-LD. API specifications in JSON-LD provide supports to obverse and reverse serializations between RDF and JSON-LD.

A simple example of JSON-LD from http://json-ld.org/ is shown in Figure 5. This fragment contains information about a person: his name is John Lennon, he was born on 1940-10-09, and his spouse is described in the website of http://dbpedia.org/resource/Cynthia_Lennon. For terms like "name", "born" and "spouse", their semantics are defined with IRIs (International Resource Identifiers). In addition, @ context is used to define the short-hand names that are used throughout a JSON-LD document, and @ id is used to uniquely identify things that are being described in the document with IRIs or blank node identifiers.

Storing RDF Data in Graph Database

Compared to relational database model which uses flat relational table, graph databases adopt graph model with vertices, edges and property, and are hereby very suitable to handle the data with network structure (Angles and Gutierrez, 2008). Many techniques and algorithms proposed in the context of Graph Theory (GT) can be applied in graph databases. Neo4j is a popular graph database, in which the data model it uses to express its data is a graph, storing nodes and relationships that connect them, supporting user defined properties on both constructs. Basically, Neo4j can traverse the vertices and edges of graph at the same speed and the traversing speed is not influenced by the amount of data constituting the graph. So Neo4j can support scalable store of big graph well.

RDF data model can be regarded as a kind of graph model. It is advocated in (Angles and Gutiérrez, 2005) to store RDF data in graph databases. So, it is a natural way to store massive RDF data in Neo4j. But the standard graph-database model is different from the triple-based RDF model. In order to manage massive RDF data with Neo4j, two basic approaches can be adopted. First, Neo4j can be extended and provided with an interface of processing RDF data and at this point, RDF data are actually stored with native or relational stores. Second, massive RDF data can be directly stored in Neo4j. Following the second approach, DBpedia data are stored in Neo4j in the project of Dbpedia4neo[18], and SPARQL (Simple Protocol and RDF Query Language) querying and some graph algorithms are then investigated.

As we know, SPARQL is a vendor-independent standard query language for the RDF triple data model (Prud'hommeaux and Seaborne, 2008), which is developed by W3C (World Wide Web Consortium). It should be noted that, although it is shown that graph databases can model RDF data in a natural way very well, some primary and useful querying operations for graph databases are not supported by current

Figure 5. A simple example of JSON-LD

```
{

   "@context": "http://json-ld.org/contexts/person.jsonld",

   "@id": "http://dbpedia.org/resource/John_Lennon",

   "name": "John Lennon",

   "born": "1940-10-09",

   "spouse": "http://dbpedia.org/resource/Cynthia_Lennon"
```

SPARQL query language. In this context, in order to manipulate RDF data, SPARQL query language should be extended to incorporate graph database query language primitives (Angles and Gutiérrez, 2005).

Storage of Special RDF Data in NoSQL Databases

With the wide application of RDF in concrete domains, some additional semantics specialized in the domains need to be accommodated into RDF data model. And this has resulted that special massive RDF data are emerging. Here we only illustrate several special types of massive RDF data and investigate their store in NoSQL databases.

Things in the real world may change as time goes on. Here we concentrate on temporal data modeling. As we know, big data have the well-known "3V" properties, which are *volume*, *velocity* and *variety*. Among them, velocity actually implies that big data are inherently temporal data. Traditionally, temporal data are managed in the relational databases. With the popularity of NoSQL for scalability and storage of big data, to manage big data that change over time, many research efforts have been invested in temporal big data management in NoSQL databases (Monger, Mata-Toledo and Gupta, 2012; Cuzzocrea, 2015). For the purpose of storing temporal big data, two major categories of NoSQL databases, which are column-oriented NoSQL databases (Hu and Dessloch, 2014 & 2015) and graph-oriented NoSQL databases (Castelltort and Laurent, 2013), respectively. In addition, in (Brahmia, Brahmia, Grandi and Bouaziz, 2016), a framework called temporal JSON Schema (τJSchema) is proposed to define a temporal JSON schema. On the basis, temporal JSON-based (document-oriented) NoSQL databases can be managed.

Temporal data have been dealt with in the context of NoSQL databases. But traditional RDF data model is unable to deal with temporal data. Data from real-world applications may be temporal. A temporal RDF model is proposed in (Gutierrez, Hurtado and Vaisman, 2007; Hurtado and Vaisman, 2006), which contains temporal RDF triples. A temporal triple is shaped as $(s, p, o):[ts, te]$, where (s, p, o) is an RDF triple and $[ts, te]$ is a time interval. Here, $(s, p, o):[t_1, t_2]$ denotes such a fact that triple (s, p, o) is valid at time interval $[ts, te]$. In (Pugliese, Udrea and Subrahmanian, 2008), a concept of a normalized *t*RDF database is proposed, in which a temporal RDF database consists of a set of temporally annotated RDF triples with a form of (*subject*, *property*:*annotation*, *object*). Then, we have three forms of temporal RDF triples: $(s, p:\{T\}, o)$, $(s, p:<n:T>, o)$ and $(s, p:[n:T], o)$, where $p:\{T\}$ means a *t*RDF triple is valid in a time points $\{T\}$, $p:<n:T>$ means a *t*RDF triple is valid at least at n distinct time points in T and $p:[n:T]$ means a tRDF triple is valid at most at n distinct time points in T. It is believed that massive RDF data management and massive temporal data management can work together and create a new issue of massive temporal RDF data management. How to deal with large scale temporal RDF triples on a cloud environment is receiving a recent attention (Ahn *et al.*, 2017).

In addition to temporal characteristics, things in the real world generally hold spatial characteristics, which may further change as time goes on. It means that we do need to manage spatial data and spatio-temporal data also. Some efforts have devoted to dealing with large spatio-temporal data with NoSQL databases (e.g., (Tear, 2014), (Orrù *et al.*, 2017) and (Detti *et al.*, 2017)). In the context of RDF data, spatial RDF data has been proposed and investigated in (Liagouris, Mamoulis, Bouros and Terrovitis, 2014; Shi, Wu and Mamoulis, 2016); both spatial and temporal (i.e., spatiotemporal) information are modeled with RDF in (Hoffart, Suchanek, Berberich and Weikum, 2013; Kyzirakos *et al.*, 2013; Wang, Zou and Zhao, 2014; Smeros and Koubarakis, 2016). Spatiotemporal data naturally have the properties of Big Data. To manage large spatiotemporal data in RDF, there is an increasing interest in storing large spatiotemporal RDF data with NoSQL databases.

The temporal/spatial/spatiotemporal RDF data can be viewed as a kind of annotated RDF (Udrea, Recupero and Subrahmanian, 2010). The annotations connected to RDF triples can be interpreted as various different meanings in the real world such as uncertainty, trust, provenance and so on. One of possible semantics for the annotations is uncertainty, which extensively exists in knowledge representation and reasoning. In this direction, two major categories of uncertain RDF data models can be identified, which are probabilistic RDF for objective uncertainty (e.g., (Lian and Chen, 2011), (Lian, Chen and Huang, 2015) and (Fang and Zhang, 2016)) and fuzzy RDF for subjective uncertainty (e.g., (Rubiera, Polo, Berrueta and Ghali, 2012) and (Ma, Li and Yan, 2018)), respectively. Here, let us look at the fuzzy RDF as the example of uncertain RDF.

Fuzzy RDF actually means fuzzy triples. Two levels of fuzziness can be identified in fuzzy triples, which are triple-level fuzziness and element-level fuzziness, respectively. The triple-level fuzzy RDF model is formally a 4-tuple (s, p, o) $[\mu]$, where n is a numeric value between 0 and 1. As we know, a triple (s, p, o) contains three components (elements). So, the element-level fuzziness of triples can be further identified as the fuzziness in whole three elements and the fuzziness in part of three elements. In (Ma, Li and Yan, 2018), the fuzzy RDF triple is formally a fuzzy triple $(\mu_s/s, \mu_p/p, \mu_o/o)$, where s is a fuzzy subject and $\mu_s \in [0, 1]$ denotes the degree of subject to the universe of an RDF dataset, p is a fuzzy predicate and $\mu_p \in [0, 1]$ expresses the fuzzy degree to the property or relationship being described, o is a fuzzy object and $\mu_o \in [0, 1]$ represents the fuzzy degree of the property value. In (Ma and Yan, 2018), the fuzzy RDF triple is formally a fuzzy triple $(s, p, (o, \mu))$, which means that subject s has property p and p further has value o with membership degree μ. More importantly, the issue of formally mapping fuzzy RDF data to relational databases is investigated in (Ma and Yan, 2018). It is believed that storing large fuzzy RDF data in NoSQL databases is essential for massive fuzzy RDF data management, but there are no report so far on this topic.

SUMMARY AND FUTURE WORK

With the increasing amount of RDF data which is becoming available, efficient and scalable management of massive RDF data is of increasing important. NoSQL databases are designed for storing and processing Big Data datasets, and massive RDF data management merits the use of Big Data infrastructure because of the scalability and high performance of cloud data management. In this chapter, we provide an up-to-date overview of the current state of the art in massive RDF data stores in NoSQL databases. RDF data management is a very active area of research, and there are a lot of research efforts in this area. The chapter presents the survey from three main perspectives, which are key value stores of RDF data in NoSQL databases, document stores of RDF data in NoSQL databases and RDF data stores in graph databases. Note that this chapter only concentrates on massive RDF data stores in NoSQL databases, and does not discuss issues of indexing and querying massive RDF data in NoSQL databases.

RDF data management typically involves the scalable storage and efficient queries of RDF data. In addition, to better serve a given query, it is needed to index RDF data, which is especially true for massive RDF data. RDF data stores in NoSQL databases provide an infrastructure for massive RDF data management. Currently, some efforts are concentrating on massive RDF data querying based on cloud computing (e.g., Garcia and Wang, 2013; Husain *et al.*, 2010 & 2011; Kim, Ravindra and Anyanwu, 2013, Li *et al.*, 2013). It should be noted that RDF data management based on NoSQL databases has only recently been gaining momentum, and the research in this direction is in its infancy. There are many research challenges and many interesting research opportunities for both the data management community and the Semantic Web community. Here we emphasize several major directions for future research.

1. First, following the success of NoSQL approaches for Big Data outside the RDF space in cloud environment, a major direction for research is the study and development of richer structural indexing techniques and related query processing strategies for RDF data in NoSQL databases.
2. Second, in addition to SELECT type of querying in SPARQL (Simple Protocol and RDF Query Language), a standard RDF querying language, how NoSQL databases can well support other types SPARQL querying such as CONSTRUCT, ASK and DESCRIBE should be investigated.
3. Finally, for massive RDF data management in the context of the diversity in RDF application domains (e.g., computing biology (Anguita *et al.*, 2013) and geological information systems (Garbis *et al.*, 2013)), novel RDF data store structures and querying strategies need to be developed on the basis of NoSQL databases.

ACKNOWLEDGMENT

The work was supported in part by the *National Natural Science Foundation of China* (61772269 and 61370075).

REFERENCES

Abadi, D. J., Marcus, A., Madden, S., & Hollenbach, K. 2007, Scalable semantic Web data management using vertical partitioning, *Proceedings of the 33th International Conference on Very Large Data Bases*, 411-422.

Abadi, D. J., Marcus, A., Madden, S., & Hollenbach, K. (2009). SW-Store: A vertically partitioned DBMS for Semantic Web data management. *The VLDB Journal*, *18*(2), 385–406. doi:10.100700778-008-0125-y

Ahn, J. H., Eom, J.-H., Nam, S., Zong, N., Im, D.-H., & Kim, H.-G. (2017). xStore: Federated temporal query processing for large scale RDF triples on a cloud environment. *Neurocomputing*, *256*, 5–12. doi:10.1016/j.neucom.2016.03.116

Alexander, K. (2008). *RDF in JSON: A specification for serialising RDF in JSON*. Retrieved from http://www.semanticscripting.org/SFSW2008

Angles, R., & Gutiérrez, C. (2005). Querying RDF data from a graph database perspective. *Proceedings of the 2005 European Semantic Web Conference*, 346-360. 10.1007/11431053_24

Angles, R., & Gutierrez, C. (2008). Survey of graph database models. *ACM Computing Surveys*, *40*, 1:1-1:39.

Anguita, A., Martin, L., Garcia-Remesal, M., & Maojo, V. (2013). RDFBuilder A tool to automatically build RDF-based interfaces for MAGE-OM microarray data sources. *Computer Methods and Programs in Biomedicine*, *3*, 220-227.

Bach, M., & Werner, A. 2014, Standardization of NoSQL database languages: Beyond databases, architectures, and structure. In *Proceedings 10th International Conference*. Ustron, Poland: Springer.

Bishop, B., Kiryakov, A., Ognyanoff, D., Peikov, I., Tashev, Z., & Velkov, R. (2011). Owlim: A family of scalable semantic repositories. *Semantic Web*, *2*(1), 1–10.

Bornea, M. A., Dolby, J., Kementsietsidis, A., Srinivas, K., Dantressangle, P., Udrea, O., & Bhattacharjee, B. (2013). Building an efficient RDF store over a relational database. *Proceedings of the 2013 ACM International Conference on Management of Data*, 121-132. 10.1145/2463676.2463718

Brahmia, S., Brahmia, Z., Grandi, F., & Bouaziz, R. (2016). τJSchema: A Framework for Managing Temporal JSON-Based NoSQL Databases. *Proceedings of the 27th International Conference on Database and Expert Systems Applications*, 167-181. 10.1007/978-3-319-44406-2_13

Broekstra, J., Kampman, A., & van Harmelen, F. (2002). Sesame: A generic architecture for storing and querying RDF and RDF schema. *Proceedings of the 2002 International Semantic Web Conference*, 54-68. 10.1007/3-540-48005-6_7

Castelltort, A., & Laurent, A. (2013). Representing history in graph-oriented NoSQL databases: A versioning system. *Proceedings of the Eighth International Conference on Digital Information Management*, 228-234. 10.1109/ICDIM.2013.6694022

Chang, F., Dean, J., Ghemawat, S., Hsieh, W. C., Wallach, D. A., Burrows, M., … Gruber, R. E. (2008). BigTable: A distributed storage system for structured data. *ACM Transactions on Computer Systems*, *26*(2), 4:1-4:26.

Cudre-Mauroux, P., Enchev, I., Fundatureanu, S., Groth, P., Haque, A., Harth, A., ... Wylot, M. (2013). NoSQL databases for RDF: An empirical evaluation. *Proceedings of the 12th International Semantic Web Conference*, 310-325. 10.1007/978-3-642-41338-4_20

Cuzzocrea, A. (2015). Temporal aspects of big data management--state-of-the-art analysis and future research directions. *Proceedings of the 22nd International Symposium on Temporal Representation and Reasoning*, 180-185 10.1109/TIME.2015.31

Dean, J., & Ghemawat, S. (2008). MapReduce: Simplified data processing on large clusters. *Communications of the ACM*, *51*(1), 107–113. doi:10.1145/1327452.1327492

DeCandia, G., Hastorun, D., Jampani, M., Kakulapati, G., Lakshman, A., Pilchin, A., ... Vogels, W. (2007). Dynamo: Amazon's highly available key-value store. *Proceedings of the 21st ACM Symposium on Operating Systems Principles*, 205-220.

Detti, A. (2017). Application of Information Centric Networking to NoSQL databases: The spatio-temporal use case. *Proceedings of the 2017 IEEE International Symposium on Local and Metropolitan Area Networks*, 1-6. 10.1109/LANMAN.2017.7972131

Duan, S., Kementsietsidis, A., Srinivas, K., & Udrea, O. (2011). Apples and oranges: a comparison of RDF benchmarks and real RDF datasets. *Proceedings of the 2011 ACM SIGMOD International Conference on Management of Data*, 145-156. 10.1145/1989323.1989340

Erling, O., & Mikhailov, I. (2007). RDF support in the virtuoso DBMS. *Proceedings of the 1st Conference on Social Semantic Web*, 59-68.

Erling, O., & Mikhailov, I. (2009). *Virtuoso: RDF support in a native RDBMS. In Semantic Web Information Management* (pp. 501–519). Springer-Verlag.

Fang, H., & Zhang, X. W. (2016). pSPARQL: A Querying Language for Probabilistic RDF (Extended Abstract). *Proceedings of the ISWC 2016 Posters & Demonstrations Track.*

Franke, C., Morin, S., Chebotko, A., Abraham, J., & Brazier, P. (2011). Distributed semantic web data management in HBase and MySQL Cluster. *Proceedings of the 2011 IEEE International Conference on Cloud Computing*, 105-112. 10.1109/CLOUD.2011.19

Gamble, M., & Goble, C. (2011). Quality, Trust and Utility of Scientific Data on the Web: Toward a Joint model. *Proceedings of the 2011 International Conference on Web Science*, 15:1-15:8. 10.1145/2527031.2527048

Garbis, G., Kyzirakos, K., & Koubarakis, M. (2013). Geographica: A benchmark for geospatial RDF stores. *Proceedings of the 12th International Semantic Web Conference*, 343-359.

Garcia, T., & Wang, T. (2013). Analysis of Big Data technologies and method - Query large Web public RDF datasets on Amazon cloud using Hadoop and Open Source Parsers. *Proceedings of the 2013 IEEE International Conference on Semantic Computing*, 244-251. 10.1109/ICSC.2013.49

Grolinger, K., Higashino, W. A., Tiwari, A., & Capretz, M. A. M. (2013). Data management in cloud environments: NoSQL and NewSQL data stores. *Journal of Cloud Computing: Advances, Systems and Applications*, 2(22).

Gudivada, V. N., Rao, D., & Raghavan, V. V. (2014). NoSQL Systems for Big Data Management, *2014 IEEE World Congress on Services*, 190-197. 10.1109/SERVICES.2014.42

Gutierrez, C., Hurtado, C. A., & Vaisman, A. (2007). Introducing time into RDF. *IEEE Transactions on Knowledge and Data Engineering*, 19(2), 207–218. doi:10.1109/TKDE.2007.34

Güting, R. H. (1994). GraphDB: Modeling and querying graphs in databases. *Proceedings of 20th International Conference on Very Large Data Bases*, 297-308.

Harris, S., Lamb, N., & Shadbolt, N. (2009). 4store: The design and implementation of a clustered RDF store. *Proceedings of the 5th International Workshop on Scalable Semantic Web Knowledge Base Systems*, 94-109.

Hecht, R., & Jablonski, S. (2011). NoSQL evaluation: A use case oriented survey. In *Proceedings of the 2011 International Conference on Cloud and Service Computing*. Hong Kong, China: IEEE. 10.1109/CSC.2011.6138544

Hoffart, J., Suchanek, F. M., Berberich, K., & Weikum, G. (2013). YAGO2: A spatially and temporally enhanced knowledge base from Wikipedia. *Artificial Intelligence*, 194, 28–61. doi:10.1016/j.artint.2012.06.001

Hu, Y., & Dessloch, S. (2014). Defining Temporal Operators for Column Oriented NoSQL Databases. *Proceedings of the 18th East European Conference on Advances in Databases and Information Systems*, 39-55. 10.1007/978-3-319-10933-6_4

Hu, Y., & Dessloch, S. (2015). Temporal Data Management and Processing with Column Oriented NoSQL Databases. *Journal of Database Management*, *26*(3), 41–70. doi:10.4018/JDM.2015070103

Hua, X. Y., Wu, H., Li, Z., & Ren, S. P. (2014). Enhancing throughput of the Hadoop Distributed File System for interaction-intensive tasks. *Journal of Parallel and Distributed Computing*, *74*(8), 2770–2779. doi:10.1016/j.jpdc.2014.03.010

Huang, J., Abadi, D. J., & Ren, K. (2011). Scalable SPARQL querying of large RDF graphs. *Proceedings of the VLDB Endowment International Conference on Very Large Data Bases*, *4*(11), 1123–1134.

Hurtado, C., & Vaisman, A. (2006). Reasoning with temporal constraints in RDF. *Proceedings of the 2006 International Conference on Principles and Practice of Semantic Web Reasoning*, 164-178. 10.1007/11853107_12

Husain, M. F., Khan, L., Kantarcioglu, M., & Thuraisingham, B. M. (2010). Data intensive query processing for large RDF graphs using cloud computing tools. *Proceedings of the 2010 IEEE International Conference on Cloud Computing*, 1-10. 10.1109/CLOUD.2010.36

Husain, M. F., McGlothlin, J. P., Masud, M. M., Khan, L. R., & Thuraisingham, B. M. (2011). Heuristics-based query processing for large RDF graphs using cloud computing. *IEEE Transactions on Knowledge and Data Engineering*, *23*(9), 1312–1327. doi:10.1109/TKDE.2011.103

Kaoudi, Z., & Manolescu, I. (2015). RDF in the clouds: A survey. *The VLDB Journal*, *24*(1), 67–91. doi:10.100700778-014-0364-z

Khadilkar, V., Kantarcioglu, M., Thuraisingham, B. M., & Castagna, P. (2012). Jena-HBase: A distributed, scalable and efficient RDF triple store. *Proceedings of the 2012 International Semantic Web Conference*.

Kim, H. S., Ravindra, P., & Anyanwu, K. (2013). Optimizing RDF(S) queries on cloud platforms, *Proceedings of the 2013 International World Wide Web Conference*, 261-264. 10.1145/2487788.2487917

Kim, S. W. (2006). Hybrid storage scheme for RDF data management in Semantic Web. *Journal of Digital Information Management*, *4*(1), 32–36.

Kyzirakos, K. (2013). The Spatiotemporal RDF Store Strabon. *Proceedings of the 13th International Symposium on Advances in Spatial and Temporal Databases*, 496-500. 10.1007/978-3-642-40235-7_35

Lakshman, A., & Malik, P. (2010). Cassandra: A decentralized structured storage system. *ACM SIGOPS Operating System Review*, *44*(2), 35–40. doi:10.1145/1773912.1773922

Laney, D. (2001). *3D data management: Controlling data volume, velocity and variety*. Meta Group, Gartner. Retrieved from http://blogs.gartner.com/doug-laney/files/2012/01/ad949-3D-Data-Management-Controlling-Data-Volume-Velocity-and-Variety.pdf

Li, R., Yang, D., Hu, H. B., Xie, J., & Fu, L. (2013). Scalable RDF graph querying using cloud computing. *Journal of Web Engineering*, *12*(1 & 2), 159–180.

Liagouris, J., Mamoulis, N., Bouros, P., & Terrovitis, M. (2014). An Effective Encoding Scheme for Spatial RDF Data. *Proceedings of the VLDB Endowment International Conference on Very Large Data Bases, 7*(12), 1271–1282. doi:10.14778/2732977.2733000

Lian, X., & Chen, L. (2011). Efficient query answering in probabilistic RDF graphs. *Proceedings of the ACM SIGMOD International Conference on Management of Data,* 157-168. 10.1145/1989323.1989341

Lian, X., Chen, L., & Huang, Z. (2015). Keyword Search Over Probabilistic RDF Graphs. *IEEE Transactions on Knowledge and Data Engineering, 27*(5), 1246–1260. doi:10.1109/TKDE.2014.2365791

Luo, Y., Picalausa, F., Fletcher, G. H. L., Hidders, J., & Vansummeren, S. (2012). *Storing and indexing massive RDF datasets. In Semantic Search over the Web* (pp. 31–60). Springer-Verlag Berlin Heidelberg. doi:10.1007/978-3-642-25008-8_2

Ma, Z., Capretz, M. A. M., & Yan, L. (2016). Storing massive Resource Description Framework (RDF) data: A survey. *The Knowledge Engineering Review, 31*(4), 391–413. doi:10.1017/S0269888916000217

Ma, Z., Li, G., & Yan, L. (2018). Fuzzy data modeling and algebraic operations in RDF. *Fuzzy Sets and Systems, 351*, 41–63. doi:10.1016/j.fss.2017.11.013

Ma, Z., & Yan, L. (2018). Modeling fuzzy data with RDF and fuzzy relational database models. *International Journal of Intelligent Systems, 33*(7), 1534–1554. doi:10.1002/int.21996

Manola, F., & Miller, E. (2004). *RDF Primer.* W3C Recommendation. Retrieved from http://www.w3.org/TR/2004/REC-rdf-primer-20040210/

McBride, B. (2002). Jena: A Semantic Web toolkit. *IEEE Internet Computing, 6*(6), 55–59. doi:10.1109/MIC.2002.1067737

Monger, M. D., Mata-Toledo, R. A., & Gupta, P. (2012). Temporal Data Management in NoSQL Databases. *Romanian Economic Business Review, 6*(2), 237–243.

Moniruzzaman, A. B. M., & Hossain, S. A. (2013). NoSQL Database: New Era of Databases for Big data Analytics - Classification, Characteristics and Comparison. *International Journal of Database Theory and Application, 6*(4), 1–14.

Neumann, T., & Weikum, G. (2008). RDF-3X: A RISC-style engine for RDF. *Proceedings of the VLDB Endowment International Conference on Very Large Data Bases, 1*(1), 647–659. doi:10.14778/1453856.1453927

Neumann, T., & Weikum, G. (2010). The RDF-3X engine for scalable management of RDF data. *The VLDB Journal, 19*(1), 91–113. doi:10.100700778-009-0165-y

Nicoara, D., Kamali, S., Daudjee, K., & Chen, L. (2015). Hermes: Dynamic partitioning for distributed social network graph databases. *Proceedings of the 18th International Conference on Extending Database Technology,* 25-36.

Orrù, M. (2017). Demonstration of OpenGeoBase: The ICN NoSQL spatio-temporal database. *Proceedings of the 2017 IEEE International Symposium on Local and Metropolitan Area Networks,* 1-2. 10.1109/LANMAN.2017.7972184

Papailiou, N., Konstantinou, I., Tsoumakos, D., Karras, P., & Koziris, N. (2013). H2RDF+: High-performance distributed joins over large-scale RDF graphs. *Proceedings of the 2013 IEEE International Conference on Big Data*, 255-263. 10.1109/BigData.2013.6691582

Papailiou, N., Konstantinou, I., Tsoumakos, D., & Koziris, N. (2012). H2RDF: Adaptive query processing on RDF data in the cloud. *Proceedings of the 21st World Wide Web Conference*, 397-400. 10.1145/2187980.2188058

Pokorny, J. (2011). NoSQL databases: A step to database scalability in web environment. *Proceedings of the 2011 International Conference on Information Integration and Web-based Applications and Services*, 278-283. 10.1145/2095536.2095583

Pokorny, J. (2011). NoSQL Databases: A step to database scalability in Web environment. *International Journal of Web Information Systems*, *9*(1), 69–82. doi:10.1108/17440081311316398

Prud'hommeaux, E., & Seaborne, A. (2008). *SPARQL Query Language for RDF*. W3C Recommendation. Retrieved from http://www.w3.org/TR/2008/REC-rdf-sparql-query-20080115/

Pugliese, A., Udrea, O., & Subrahmanian, V. S. (2008). Scaling RDF with time. *Proceedings of the 2008 International Conference on World Wide Web*, 605-614.

Rubiera, E., Polo, L., Berrueta, D., & Ghali, A. E. (2012). TELIX: An RDF-Based Model for Linguistic Annotation. *Proceedings of the 9th Extended Semantic Web Conference*, 195-209. 10.1007/978-3-642-30284-8_20

Sakr, S., & Al-Naymat, G. (2009). Relational processing of RDF queries: A survey. *SIGMOD Record*, *38*(4), 23–28. doi:10.1145/1815948.1815953

Shi, J. M., Wu, D. M., & Mamoulis, N. (2016). Top-k Relevant Semantic Place Retrieval on Spatial RDF Data. *Proceedings of the 2016 International Conference on Management of Data*, 1977-1990. 10.1145/2882903.2882941

Sintek, M., & Kiesel, M. (2006). RDFBroker: A signature-based high-performance RDF store. *Proceedings of the 3rd European Semantic Web Conference*, 363-377.

Smeros, P., & Koubarakis, M. (2016). Discovering Spatial and Temporal Links among RDF Data, *Proceedings of the 2016 Workshop on Linked Data on the Web*.

Snow, D. (2012). *Dwaine Snow's Thoughts on Databases and Data Management*. Retrieved from http://dsnowondb2.blogspot.cz/2012/07/adding-4th-v-to-big-data-veracity.html

Sperka, S., & Smrz, P. (2012). Towards adaptive and semantic database model for RDF data stores. *Proceedings of the Sixth International Conference on Complex, Intelligent, and Software Intensive Systems*, 810-815.

Stuart, J., & Barker, A. (2013). *Undefined By Data: A Survey of Big Data Definitions*. CoRR, abs/1309.5821

Sun, J. L., & Jin, Q. (2010). Scalable RDF store based on HBase and MapReduce. *Proceedings of the 3rd International Conference Advanced Computer Theory and Engineering*, V1-633-V1-636.

Tauro, C., Aravindh, S., & Shreeharsha, A. B. (2012). Comparative Study of the New Generation, Agile, Scalable, High Performance NOSQL Databases. *International Journal of Computer Applications, 48*(20).

Tear, A. (2014). SQL or NoSQL? Contrasting Approaches to the Storage, Manipulation and Analysis of Spatio-temporal Online Social Network Data. *Proceedings of the 14th International Conference on Computational Science and Its Applications*, 221-236.

Udrea, O., Recupero, D. R., & Subrahmanian, V. S. (2010). Annotated RDF. *ACM Transactions on Computational Logic, 11*(2), 10:1-10:41.

Wang, D., Zou, L., & Zhao, D. Y. (2014). gst-Store: An Engine for Large RDF Graph Integrating Spatiotemporal Information. *Proceedings of the 17th International Conference on Extending Database Technology*, 652-655.

Wang, Y., Du, X. Y., Lu, J. H., & Wang, X. F. (2010). FlexTable: Using a dynamic relation model to store RDF data. *Proceedings of the 15th International Conference on Database Systems for Advanced Applications*, 580-594. 10.1007/978-3-642-12026-8_44

Weiss, C., Karras, P., & Bernstein, A. (2008). Hexastore: Sextuple indexing for semantic web data management. *Proceedings of the VLDB Endowment International Conference on Very Large Data Bases, 1*(1), 1008–1019. doi:10.14778/1453856.1453965

Wilkinson, K., Sayers, C., Kuno, H. A., & Reynolds, D. (2003). Efficient RDF storage and retrieval in Jena2. *Semantic Web and Databases Workshop*, 131-150.

ADDITIONAL READING

Aluc, G., Özsu, M. T., & Daudjee, K. (2014). Workload matters: Why RDF databases need a new design. *Proceedings of the VLDB Endowment International Conference on Very Large Data Bases, 7*(10), 837–840. doi:10.14778/2732951.2732957

Cardoso, J. (2007). The Semantic Web vision: Where are We? *IEEE Intelligent Systems, 22*(5), 84–88. doi:10.1109/MIS.2007.4338499

Cattell, R. (2011). Scalable SQL and NoSQL data stores. *SIGMOD Record, 39*(4), 12–27. doi:10.1145/1978915.1978919

Kelly, J. (2012, August). Accumulo, 2012, Why the world needs another NoSQL database. *Big Data*.

Schindler, J. (2012). I/O characteristics of NoSQL databases. *Proceedings of the VLDB Endowment International Conference on Very Large Data Bases, 5*(12), 2020–2021. doi:10.14778/2367502.2367565

Shadbolt, N., Berners-Lee, T., & Hall, W. (2006). The Semantic Web revisited. *IEEE Intelligent Systems, 21*(3), 96–101. doi:10.1109/MIS.2006.62

Stonebraker, M. (2010). SQL databases v. NoSQL databases. *Communications of the ACM, 53*(4), 10–11. doi:10.1145/1721654.1721659

KEY TERMS AND DEFINITIONS

ACID: ACID means four properties, which are (A)tomcity, (C)onsistency, (I)solation and (D)urability. ACID is the type of transaction processing done by relational database management system (RDBMS).

Big Data: Big data is a broad term for data sets so large or complex that traditional data processing applications are inadequate. There is not a common definition of big data, and big data are generally characterized by some properties such as volume, velocity, variety, and so on.

CAP: CAP theorem means three properties, which are consistency, availability, and partition tolerance.

JSON: JSON (JavaScript Object Notation) is a binary and typed data model which is applied to represent data like list, map, date, Boolean as well as different precision numbers.

NoSQL Databases: NoSQL means "not only SQL" or "no SQL at all." Being a new type of non-relational databases, NoSQL databases are developed for efficient and scalable management of big data.

RDF: Resource description framework (RDF) is a W3C (World Wide Web Consortium) recommendation which provides a generic mechanism for representing information about resources on the web.

SPARQL: SPARQL (Simple Protocol and RDF Query Language) is an RDF query language which is a W3C recommendation. SPARQL contains capabilities for querying required and optional graph patterns along with their conjunctions and disjunctions.

ENDNOTES

[1] http://www.data.gov/

[2] http://www.data.gov.uk/

[3] http://data.nytimes.com/

[4] http://www.bbc.co.uk/blogs/bbcinternet/2010/07/bbc_world_cup_2010_dynamic_sem.html

[5] http://www.chiefmartec.com/2009/12/best-buy-jump-starts-data-web-marketing.html

[6] http://www.oracle.com/us/products/database/options/spatial/overview/index.html

[7] http://www.cs.ox.ac.uk/isg/tools/RDFox/

[8] http://nosql-databases.org

[9] http://redis.io/

[10] http://hbase.apache.org/

[11] http://couchdb.apache.org/

[12] http://www.couchbase.com/couchbase-server/overview

[13] http://www.mongodb.org/

[14] http://neo4j.com/

[15] http://thinkaurelius.github.io/titan/

[16] http://hypertable.org

[17] https://github.com/claudiomartella/dbpedia4neo

[18] http://www.w3.org/TR/json-ld/

Chapter 14
Big Data Processing and Big Analytics

Jaroslav Pokorny
Charles University, Czech Republic

Bela Stantic
Griffith University, Australia

ABSTRACT

Development and wide acceptance of data-driven applications in many aspects of our daily lives is generating waste volume of diverse data, which can be collected and analyzed to support various valuable decisions. Management and processing of this big data is a challenge. The development and extensive use of highly distributed and scalable systems to process big data have been widely considered. New data management architectures (e.g., distributed file systems and NoSQL databases) are used in this context. However, features of big data like their complexity and data analytics demands indicate that these concepts solve big data problems only partially. A development of so called NewSQL databases is highly relevant and even special category of big data management systems is considered. In this chapter, the authors discuss these trends and evaluate some current approaches to big data processing and analytics, identify the current challenges, and suggest possible research directions.

INTRODUCTION

One of the main characteristics of Big Data is its volume, which exceeds the normal range of databases in practice. For example, web clicks, social media, scientific experiments, and datacentre monitoring belong among data sources that generate vast amounts of raw data every day. To enable management of such volume of data there is need to have appropriate processing, i.e. Big Data computing, therefore, Big Data processing is an issue of the highest importance, generally referred in literature as *Big Analytics*. Big Analytics is another buzzword denoting a combination of Big Data and Advanced Analytics. J. L. Leidner (R&D at Thomson Reuters) in the interview with R. V. Zicari (ODMS.org, 2013) emphasizes that buzzwords like "Big Data" do not by themselves solve any problem – they are not magic bullets. He gives an advice how to tackle and solve any problem. There is need to look at the input data, specify

DOI: 10.4018/978-1-5225-8446-9.ch014

the desired output, and think hard about whether and how you can compute the desired result, which is basically nothing but "good old" computer science.

The recent advances in new hardware platforms, methods, algorithms as well as new software systems enables efficient Big Data processing and Big Analytics. Big Data and Big Analysis are decision making drivers in a 21st century world driven by web, mobile and IoT technologies.

Effective use of systems incorporating Big Data in many application scenarios requires adequate tools for storage and processing such data at low-level and analytical tools on higher levels. Moreover, applications working with Big Data are both transactional and analytical. However, they require usually different architectures.

Big Analytics is the most important aspect of Big Data computing mainly from a user's point of view. Unfortunately, large datasets are expressed in different formats, e.g., relational, XML, textual, multimedia or RDF, which may cause difficulties in their processing by data mining algorithms. Also, increasing either data volume in a repository or the number of users of this repository requires more feasible solution of scaling in such dynamic environments than it is offered by traditional database architectures.

Clearly, Big Analytics is done also on big amounts of transaction data as extension of methods used usually in technology of *data warehouses* (DW). Generally DW technology is focused on structured data in comparison to much richer variability of Big Data as it is understood today. Therefore, analytical processing of Big Data Analytics requires not only new database architectures but also new methods for integrating and analyzing heterogeneous data.

Big Data storage and processing are essential for cloud services. This reinforces requirements on the availability and scalability of computational resources offered by cloud services.

Users have a number of options associated with above mentioned issues. For storing and processing large datasets they can use:

- Traditional DBMS - relational (SQL), OO, OR,
- Traditional relational parallel database systems (shared nothing architectures),
- Distributed file systems and Hadoop technologies,
- Key-value datastores (so called NoSQL databases),
- New database architectures (e.g., NewSQL databases).

In particular, three last categories are not mutually exclusive and can and they should co-exist in many enterprises. Another adept to coexistence is, of course, a relational database management system (RDBMS) that ensures transactional data processing in the enterprise.

The NoSQL and NewSQL databases present themselves as data processing alternatives that can handle huge volumes of data and provide the required scalability. NoSQL databases are a type of databases which were initiated by Web companies in early 2000s. NewSQL databases are aiming to provide the scale-out advantages of NoSQL databases often on commodity hardware and maintain the transactional data consistency guarantees of traditional relational DBMS. They are also compatible with SQL. Especially, *massively parallel analytic databases* play an important role here. Algorithms supporting Big Analytics are presented on the top of these systems or they are a native part of their implementation.

The chapter is an attempt to cover principles and core features of these systems and to associate them to main application areas of Big Data processing and management in practice, particularly in relation to Big Analytics. We also focus in more extent on challenges and opportunities associated with Big Data. The text follows the work of Pokorny & Stantic (2016).

BACKGROUND

The fundamental concept of generating data has changed recently, in the past, several main sources have been generating data and all others have been consuming data. However, today all of us are both generating data and also consumers of this shared data. Usually we talk about the Big Data when the dataset size is beyond the ability of the current system to collect, process, retrieve and manage the data. (Manyika et al., 2011) describes Big Data as large pools of unstructured and structured data that can be captured, communicated, aggregated, stored, and analyzed. Big Data are now becoming part of every sector and function of the global economy. Data created both inside corporations and outside the firewall via the Web, mobile devices, IT infrastructure and other sources increases exponentially each year (Kelly, 2014).

Web plays a prominent role towards shifting to the Big Data paradigm. The textual Web content is a source that people want to easily consult and search. Challenges in this area include primarily document summarization, personalized search, sentiment analysis, and recommender systems. The social structures formed over the Web, mainly represented by the online social networking applications such as Facebook, LinkedIn and Twitter, contribute intensively to Big Data. Typically, the interactions of the users within a social networking platform form large and dynamic graph structures. Use cases identified for Big Data in enterprises include risk modelling, fraud detection, customer analysis, effectiveness of marketing campaigns, etc.

In general, Big Data come mainly from these contexts:

- Large data collections in traditional DWs or databases,
- Enterprise data of large, non-Web-based companies working with internet transactions,
- Data from large Web companies providing social networking and media,
- Data generated and/or transferred through mobile devices,
- Data streams generated by remote sensors and other IT hardware,
- Data archives from e-science (computational biology, bioinformatics, genomics, and astronomy).

A typical feature of Big Data is the absence of a schema characterization, which makes difficulties when we want to integrate heterogeneous datasets.

Big Data Characteristics

Big Data are most often characterized by several V's:

- **Volume:** Data scale in the range of TB to PB and even more. The big volume is not onl storage issue but also influences a Big Analytics. Not only data samples, but often all data are captured for analysis.
- **Velocity:** Both how quickly data is being produced and how quickly the data must be processed to meet demand (e.g., streaming data).
- **Variety:** Data is in many format types – structured, unstructured, semistructured, text, media, etc. Data does not come only from business transactions, but also from machines, sensors and other sources, making it much more complex to manage.
- **Veracity:** Managing the reliability and predictability of inherently imprecise data.

The first three V's have been introduced by Gartner in (Laney, 2001), the V associated with Veracity has been added by D. Snow in his blog (Snow, 2012). Both Variety and Velocity are actually working against the Veracity of the data. They decrease the ability to cleanse the data before analyzing it and making decisions.

The fifth V was introduced by Gamble and Goble (2011):

- **Value:** Indicates if the data is worthwhile and has value for business.

Data value vision includes creating social and economic added value based on the intelligent use, management and re-uses of data sources with a view to increase business intelligence (BI).

Several other V's have been mentioned in literature:

- **Visualization:** Visual representations and insights for decision making,
- **Variability:** The different meanings/contexts associated with a given piece of data,
- **Volatility:** How long the data is valid and how long should it be stored (at what point specific data is no longer relevant to the current analysis).
- **Validity:** The data are correct and accurate for the intended use. Clearly valid data is key to making the right decisions.

Sometimes also other characteristics (not only V's) are assigned to Big Data, associated not only to logic complexity and transactions complexity. Often a quality is accentuated (Nasser & Tariq, 2015).

- **Quality:** Quality characteristic measures how the data is reliable to be used for making decisions. Saying that the quality of data is high or low is basically de-pendent on four parameters: a) Complete: all relevant data are available, for example all details of vendors like name, address, bank account etc. exist b) Accurate: data is free of misspelling, typos, wrong terms and abbreviations c) Available: data is available when requested and easy to find d) Timely: data is up to date and ready to support decision.

Some come companies, e.g. SAS Institute, Inc. (2018), consider additional dimensions, e.g.

- **Complexity:** Today's data comes from multiple sources, which makes it difficult to link, match, cleanse and transform data across systems. However, it's necessary to connect and correlate relationships, hierarchies and multiple data linkages or your data can quickly spiral out of control.

These characteristics are not independent (Pokorný, 2017). For example, veracity (confidence or trust in the data) drops when volume, velocity, variety and variability increase. Some-times, a validity (additional V) is considered. Similar to veracity, validity refers to how accurate and correct the data is for its intended use.

An actual question is whether some V's are really definitional and not only confusing. For example, veracity expresses a quality of any data; it is not a definitional property of Big Data. When we use the Gartner´s definition "Big data is high-volume, -velocity and -variety information assets that demand cost-effective, innovative forms of information processing for enhanced insight and decision making", we simply see that the 3 V's are only 1/3 of the definition! The second part of the definition addresses the challenges we face to take the best of infrastructure and technology capabilities.

Big Data Processing and Big Analytics

Big Analytics is a genuine leap forward and a clear opportunity to realize enormous gains in efficiency, productivity, revenue, and profitability. It is process of analyzing large amounts of different types of data to uncover hidden patterns, correlations and other useful information. Big Analytics could accomplish much more than what can be done with smaller datasets. For example, Big Analytics allows move beyond linear approximation models towards complex models of greater sophistication because small datasets often limit our ability to make accurate predictions and assessments. Additionally, Big Data significantly improves the ability to locate and analyze the impact of rare events that might escape detection in smaller data sets. Access to larger datasets, affordable high-performance hardware, and new powerful analytical tools provide means for better accuracy in predictions. One source of valuable data is also social media, which can help in identifying sentiment and provide very high accuracy in demand and opinions (Alaei, Becken & Stantic, 2017). As data is becoming more and more complex its analysis is also becoming increasingly complex. To exploit this new resource, we need to scale both infrastructures and standard data management techniques.

Now the problem with data volume is its speed (velocity) not only size. Big Data processing involves interactive processing and decision support processing of *data at rest*, and real-time processing of *data in motion*. The former can be warehoused in a relatively traditional way or stored and processed by inexpensive systems, e.g., NoSQL databases. The latter is usually performed by Data Stream Management Systems. Time is an integral dimension of data in a stream which influences it's processing, i.e., the analyst cannot reanalyze the data after it is streamed. A velocity also can be a problem, since the value of the analysis (and often of the data) decreases with time. If several passes are required, the data has to be put into a DW where additional analysis can be performed.

Big Analytics is about turning information into knowledge using a combination of existing and new approaches. Related technologies include:

- Data management (uncertainty, query processing under near real-time constraints, information extraction, explicitly managed time dimension),
- New programming models,
- Machine learning and statistical methods,
- Complex systems architectures, and
- Information visualization.

Big Data is often mentioned only in context with BI; however, not only BI developers but also e-scientists analyze large collections of data. A challenge for computer specialists or data scientists is to provide these people with tools that can efficiently perform complex analytics considering the special nature of Big Data. It is important to emphasize that Big Analytics does not involve only the analysis and modelling phase because noisy context, heterogeneity, and interpretation of results are also necessary to be taken into account. All these aspects influence scalable strategies and algorithms, therefore, more effective preprocessing steps (filtering and integration) and advanced parallel computing environments are needed.

Besides these rather classical themes of mining Big Data, other interesting issues have appeared in last years, e.g., entity resolution and subjectivity analysis. The latter includes sentiment analysis and opinion mining as topics using information retrieval and Web data analysis. A particular problem is finding sentiment-based contradictions at a large scale and to characterize them. Graph pattern matching is commonly used in social network analysis, where the graph can involve billions of users and hundreds billions links. In any case the main problems of current data mining techniques applied on Big Data are related to their inadequate scalability and parallelization. Newer approaches include machine learning as a branch of artificial intelligence that focuses on allowing computers to learn new things without being explicitly programmed. Closely related to machine learning is predictive analytics enabling to predict what will happen in the future.

Concerning components of a complex Big Data architecture, Microsoft Azure (2018) offers its universal schema. The architecture contains the following components depicted in Figure 1.

Data for batch processing operations is typically stored in a distributed file store that can hold high volumes of large files in various formats. This kind of store is often called a *data lake*. To capture and store real-time messages for stream processing, a real-time message ingestion is necessary. This portion of a streaming architecture is often referred to as stream buffering. Most Big Data solutions consist of repeated data processing operations, encapsulated in workflows, which transform source data, move data between multiple sources and sinks, etc. To automate these workflows, an orchestration technology is used.

MAIN FOCUS OF THE CHAPTER

First we describe two types of database architectures in this context: the traditional universal one and Hadoop-like implementing MapReduce framework. Then we present a short overview of NoSQL technology, particularly data models, architectures, and some representatives of NoSQL databases. We also focus on some issues connected with transaction processing with these tools. Then we discuss issues related to Big Data storage and processing with NoSQL and Hadoop, particularly with respect to Big Analytics. The next section presents recent architectures usable for Big Data: Big Data Management Systems, NewSQL databases, and NoSQL databases with ACID transactions. In last two sections, we identify open problems associated with Big Data that represent a challenge for software engineering methods development and a research in the Big Data storage and processing area. Several conclusions finalize the chapter.

Figure 1. Components of a big data architecture

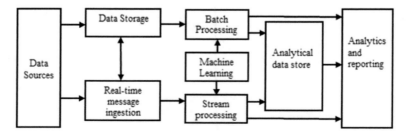

From the Universal DBMS Architecture to Hadoop

In Table 1 we show the well-known *universal DBMS architecture* (Härder, 2005) based on a mapping model consisting from five abstraction layers. In the most general version the architecture is encapsulated together with use of the SQL language in L5. Same model can be used in the case of distributed databases for every node of a network together with a *connection layer* responsible for communication, adaptation, or mediation services. Also, a typical shared nothing parallel relational DBMS can be described by this architecture. Layers L1-L4 are present usually at each machine in a cluster. A typical property of the universal architecture is that users can see only the outermost (SQL) layer.

The number of layers in the universal architecture is often reduced to the usual three-layer model.

In any case, associated database technologies both centralized and distributed were found not well suited for Web-scale data management of sources generating Big Data. Perhaps the most important problem is a hard scalability of traditional DBMSs in Web environment. A *vertical scaling* (called also *scale-up*), i.e. adding more CPU and more memory to each node or even new expensive big servers, was replaced by database partitioning across multiple cheap machines added dynamically to a network. In vertical scaling the data resides on a single node and scaling is done through the use of multi-cores, etc., i.e. spreading the load between the CPU and RAM resources of that single machine.

So-called *horizontal scaling* (also *scale-out*) can apparently ensure scalability in a more effective and cheaper way. Data is distributed horizontally in the network into groups of rows via consistent hashing or range partitioning based on ranges of a partition key in the case of tabular data. These groups stored into different segments may be located on different servers. A vertical data partitioning or combinations of both styles are being used as well. *Sharding* is just another name for horizontal partitioning. Horizontal data distribution enables to divide the computation into concurrently processed tasks. The advantage of this approach is the effective processing of range queries, because adjacent keys often reside in the same node.

To place multiple partitions on different machines is easier for NoSQL to implement because there is no enforcement of integrity except in the application. A sharding uses the shared nothing model, i.e., each server has its own data and processor. However, "database sharding" cannot provide high scalability at large scale due to the inherent complexity of the interface and ACID guarantees mechanisms. Multiple databases are unified even at application layer in this case. On the other hand, MPP (Massively Parallel Processing) can be used, i.e. a single DBMS with distributed storage.

Table 1. The five-layered DBMS mapping hierarchy

	Level of abstraction	Objects	Auxiliary mapping data
L5	non-procedural access or algebraic access	tables, views, rows	logical schema description
L4	record-oriented, navigational approach	records, sets, hierarchies, networks	logical and physical schema description
L3	records and access path management	physical records, access paths	free space tables, DB-key translation tables
L2	propagation control	segments, pages	buffers, page tables
L1	file management	files, blocks	directories

Sharding scales well for both reads and write, but it has not to be transparent, i.e. application needs to be partition-aware. Thus, it is necessary to manage parallel access in the application.

A typical layered architecture of open source software Hadoop (The Apache Software Foundation, 2018a) often used in NoSQL environment has also a three-layer model but it looks a little differently. The distributed file system considered here, i.e. *Hadoop Distributed File System* (HDFS) (Shvachko, Kuang, Radia, & Chansler, 2010), distinguishes from traditional network file systems (e.g., in UNIX). It uses file partitioning into big *data blocks* and replications. In additions to HDFS, Hadoop uses the highly scalable data-intensive MapReduce platform (Dean & Ghemawat, 2008). On the top of HDFS there is, e.g., the NoSQL database HBase (The Apache Software Foundation, 2018b). Complexity of tasks for data processing in such architectures is minimized using programming languages, like MapReduce. Obviously the approach is not easily realizable for arbitrary algorithm and arbitrary programming language. MapReduce, inspired by functional programming, enables to implement, e.g., multiplication of sparse matrices by a vector in a natural way. On the other hand, an effective implementation of the relational operation join in MapReduce requires special approach both in data distribution and indexing (Rajaman & Ullman, 2011). Also, the execution techniques used by MapReduce systems are suboptimal for analysis tasks such as iterative machine learning, and graph processing. Figure 2, based on the work of Borkar, Carey, & Li (2012), documents this architecture.

One remarkable difference of the Hadoop software stack from the universal DBMS architecture is that we can access data by three different sets of tools in particular layers. The middle layer Hadoop MapReduce system serves for batch analytics with Hadoop M/R jobs. HBase is available as a key-value layer (see the next section) with get/put operations as input. Finally, high-level languages HiveQL (Thusoo et al., 2009), PigLatin (Gates et al., 2009), and Jaql (Beyer et al., 2011) are for some users at disposal at the outermost layer.

The SQL-like language HiveQL enables non-procedural data analytics (with constructs select-from-group-by) without detailed programming. Queries in HiveQL are compiled into MapReduce jobs. Jaql is a declarative scripting language for analyzing large semistructured datasets. The use of declarative languages reduces code size by orders of magnitude and enables distributed or parallel execution. A high-level script language PigLatin is not declarative; programs are series of assignments similar to an execution plan of a relational database.

A relatively new category of application tools - *SQL-on-Hadoop* - refers to various implementations of SQL for the Hadoop platform. With SQL-on-Hadoop technologies, it is possible to access Big Data stored in Hadoop by using the SQL language. Apache Hive software was the first SQL-on-Hadoop engine. Now many new ones have been released, e.g., MemSQL (MemSQL Inc., 2018). There are three

Figure 2. The three-layered Hadoop software stack

	Level of abstraction	Data processing		
L5	non-procedural access	HiveQL/PigLatin/Jaql		
L2-L4	record-oriented navigational approach	Hadoop MapReduce Dataflow Leyer		M/R jobs
	records and access path management			Get/Put Ops
	propagation control		Hbase Key-Value Store	
L1	file management	Hadoop Distributed File System		

main classes of SQL-on-Hadoop tools available – ETL and Data Preparation Tools, Analytic Databases, and Data Engineering Tools. Hive belongs to the first class.

NOSQL DATABASES

For storing and processing some Big Data datasets NoSQL databases are often used. NoSQL means "not only SQL" or "no SQL at all", that makes this category of databases very diverse. NoSQL solutions starting in development from late 90s provide simpler scalability and improved performance comparing to traditional relational databases, see, e.g., (Hecht & Jablonski, 2011; Pokorný, 2011; Moniruzzaman & Hossain, 2013; Gudivada, Rao, & Raghavan, 2014). We shortly elaborate their data models, identify abilities of transaction processing, and index techniques used in their implementations.

Data Models Used in NoSQL Databases

What is principal in classical approaches to databases – a (logical) data model – is in NoSQL databases described rather intuitively, without any formal fundamentals. The NoSQL terminology is also very diverse and a difference between conceptual and database view of data is mostly blurred.

The simplest NoSQL databases called *key-value stores* (or *big hash tables*) contain a set of couples (key, value). A key uniquely identifies a value (typically string, but also a pointer, where the value is stored), JSON, BLOB (binary large object) etc. Even, a value can be a collection of couples (name, value), e.g., in Redis (Redis, 2018). This means that the data access operations, typically get and put, have only a key as the address argument. Though very efficient and scalable, the disadvantage of such too simple data model can be essential for such databases. On the other hand, NULL values are not necessary, since in all cases these databases are schema-less.

In a more complex case, NoSQL database stores combinations of couples (name, value) collected into collections, i.e. rows addressed by a key. Then we talk about *column NoSQL databases* whose column-oriented data structure accommodates multiple attributes per key. For example, in CASSANDRA (The Apache Software Foundation, 2016) new columns can be added to these collections. Each key identifies a row and each row has a variable number of elements. This ability to have rows with different elements means that we can store many different types of data. There is even further level of structure, called *super-columns*, where a column contains nested (sub)columns. Data access is improved by using column names in operations get, insert and delete.

The most general data models belong to *document-oriented NoSQL databases*. They are same as key-value stores but pair each key with an arbitrarily complex data structure reminding as a document. The JSON (JavaScript Object Notation) format is usually used for presentation of such data structures. JSON is a binary and typed data model which supports the data types list, map, date, Boolean as well as numbers of different precisions. JSON is similar to XML but it is smaller, faster and easier to parse than XML. CouchDB (The Apache Software Foundation, 2018c) is based on JSON. MongoDB (MongoDB, Inc., 2018) uses BSON (Binary JSON). Its types are a superset of JSON types. So the document-oriented DBs handle semistructured data. Querying document data is possible by other means than just a key (selection and projection over results are possible). Unlike simple key-value stores, both keys and values are fully searchable in document databases.

We can observe that all the data models are in principle key-valued. The three categories considered distinguish mainly in possibilities of aggregation of (key, value) couples and accessing the values. In general NoSQL databases can be classified in the categories contained in Table 2.

Graph databases are considered as a special category of NoSQL databases (see, e.g., the overview by Pokorný (2015)). They are based on undirected or directed graphs, multigraphs and hypergraphs, labelled or weighted graphs and their variants. The most used variant of graph databases are labelled and directed attributed multigraphs. They carry further information in the properties (attributes). Graph databases offer graph-partitioning strategies for large data, graph query languages designed for particular types of graph data, and efficient evaluation of queries (graph traversals, sub-graph and super-graph queries, and graph similarity evaluation). Although the graphs have properties, these DBMSs are optimized for relationships, i.e. traversing and not for querying. Some of them are also usable for storage and processing of Big Graphs. Neo4j is an open-source, highly scalable, robust native graph database that stores data in a graph. InfoGrid is primarily focused on social network analysis.

A special attention needs to be focused on operational part of NoSQL databases. A typical NoSQL API for a key-value database enables only a reduced access given by CRUD operations – create, read, update, delete, e.g.,

- get(key): extract the value given a key
- put(key, value): create or update the value given its key
- delete(key): remove the key and its associated value
- execute(key, operation, parameters): invoke an operation to the value (given its key) which is a special data structure (e.g., List, Set, Map, ..., etc.).
- multi-get(key1, key2, .., keyN): returns the list of values associated with the list of keys.

Particular NoSQL databases use some syntactical variants of these operation, e.g., CouchDB exposes a RESTful HTTP API to perform basic CRUD operations on all stored items and it uses the HTTP methods POST, GET, PUT, and DELETE. MongoDB has a rich query language that supports CRUD operations as well as data aggregation, text search, and geo-spatial queries.

NoSQL databases described in the list of well-maintained Web site (Edlich, 2018) include currently more than 225 products including multimodel, object-oriented, XML, grid & cloud database solutions, multidimensional databases, multivalue databases, event sourcing, time series/streaming database and others.

Table 2. Basic categories of NoSQL databases

Category	Representatives
key-value stores	SimpleDB (Amazon Web Services, 2018a), Redis, Memcached (Memcached, 2018), Dynamo (Amazon Web Services, 2018b), Voldemort (GitHub, Inc., 2018)
column-oriented	BigTable (Chang et al., 2008), HBase, Hypertable (Hypertable Inc., 2014), CASSANDRA, PNUTS (Cooper, 2008)
document-oriented	MongoDB, CouchDB
graph databases	Neo4j (Neo Technology, Inc., 2018), InfoGrid (Netmesh Inc., 2018)

Querying NoSQL Databases

In many cases the NoSQL API offers access to low-level data manipulation and selections methods (CRUD operations). Queries capabilities are often limited so queries can be expresses in a simple way. The same holds for some restricted variants of SQL used in NoSQL databases. NoSQL database systems are often highly optimized for retrieval and appending operations and mostly offer little functionality beyond record storage (e.g., key–value stores). The simplicity of CRUD operations in API of NoSQL databases implies that a functionality requiring more complex structures and dealing with these structures must be implemented in the client application interacting with the database, particularly in a key-value store.

On the other hand, there are some exclusions in querying in document-oriented and column-oriented categories. MongoDB offers SQL-like query language; similarly Cassandra uses a high-level language CQL. Cassandra supports range queries and Cassandra 2.2 introduced JSON support for SELECT and INSERT statements. In MongoDB, the db.collection.find() method retrieves documents from a collection. It is possible to specify equality conditions, IN operator, logical connectives AND, OR, matching array elements, and more complex combinations of these criteria. Find queries can be combined with some aggregation functions, like, e.g., count(). MongoDB does not support joins.

Some possibilities of querying are provided by MapReduce using map and reduce functions. For example, supposing a collection of documents, then the map is applied on each document to filter out irrelevant documents and to emit data for all documents of interest. Emitted data is sorted in groups to reduce for aggregation, or is the final result. This approach is procedural, i.e. it is a programming and not writing queries.

Transaction Processing

A special attention in NoSQL database community is devoted to data consistency. Transaction processing in traditional relational DBMS is based on ACID properties, i.e., *Atomicity*, *Consistency*, *Isolation*, and *Durability*. ACID properties mean that once a transaction is complete, its data is consistent and stable on disk. We call consistency in such databases *strong consistency*. In practice, ACID properties are hard to achieve, moreover, they are not always required, particularly *C*. In context of NoSQL databases ACID properties are not implemented fully, databases can be only *eventually consistent* or *weakly consistent*.

In distributed architectures we consider the triple of requirements including consistency (*C*), availability (*A*) and partitioning tolerance (*P*), shortly CAP.

- *Consistency* means that whenever data is written, everyone who reads from the database will always see the latest version of the data. The notion is different from one used in ACID.
- *Availability* means that we can always expect that each operation terminates in an intended response. High availability is usually accomplished through large numbers of physical servers acting as a single database through data sharing between various database nodes and replications. Traditionally, the requirement to have a server/process available 99.999% of time. For a large-scale node system, there is a high probability that a node is either down or that there is a network partitioning.
- *Partition tolerance* means that the database still can be read from and written to when parts of it are completely inaccessible, i.e. in the case of a network partition. That is write and read operations are redirected to available replicas when segments of the network become disconnected.

If we look on the CAP theorem formulated by Brewer (2000) and formally proved by Gilbert & Lynch (2002), then we see that for any system sharing the data it is impossible to guarantee simultaneously all of these three properties. Particularly, in Web applications based on horizontal scaling it is necessary to decide between *C* and *A*, i.e. two basic situations can occur:

1. Strong consistency is a core property and *A* is maximized. The advantage of strong consistency, which reminds ACID transactions, means to develop applications and to manage data services in more simple way. On the other hand, complex application logic has to be implemented, which detects and resolves inconsistency.
2. *A* is prioritized and *C* is maximized. Priority of *A* has rather economic justification. Unavailability of a service can imply financial losses. In an unreliable system, based on the CAP theorem, *A* cannot be guaranteed. For any *A* increasing it is necessary to relax *C*. Corporate cloud databases prefer *C* over *A* and *P*.

Table 3 shows how different NoSQL databases solve these problems.

By design, most graph databases are ACID compliant.

A recent transactional model used in Web distributed replicated databases uses properties *BASE* (*Basically Available, Soft state, Eventually consistent*) (Pritchett, 2008). The availability in BASE corresponds to availability in CAP theorem. An application works basically all the time (basically available), does not have to be consistent all the time (soft state) but the storage system guarantees that if no new updates are made to the object eventually (after the inconsistency window closes) all accesses will return the last updated value. When no updates occur for a long period of time, eventually all updates will propagate through the system and all the nodes will be consistent. For a given accepted update and a given node, eventually either the update reaches the node or the node is removed from service. For example, SimpleDB acknowledges a client's write before the write has propagated to all replicas. It offers even a range of consistency options.

In principle, if we abandon strong consistency we can reach better availability, which will highly improve database scalability. It can be in accordance to database practice where ACID transactions are also required only in certain use cases, however, not all data need to be treated at the same level of consistency. For example if we consider automated teller machines, in their design, *A* has a priority to *C*, but of course with a certain risk. Also, MongoDB provides strong consistency and guarantees ACID operations at the document level, which tends to be sufficient for most applications. Similarly, in online social networking services a certain amount of data errors is tolerable.

If we analyze NoSQL databases, we identify more sophisticated approaches to consistency:

Table 3. Consistency and availability preferences

Preferences	Representatives
CP	Redis, BigTable, HBase, Hypertable, MongoDB
AP	Dynamo, Voldemort, CASSANDRA, Memcached, PNUTS, CouchDB, SimpleDB

- *Tunable consistency* (e.g., in CASSANDRA),
- *Configurable consistency* (e.g., CP or AP in Oracle NoSQL database (Oracle, 2018)).

A tunable consistency means that the application developer can influence its degree. For any given read or write operation, the client application decides how consistent the requested data should be. This allows the developer to trade performance for consistency, and durability and enables to use CASSANDRA in applications with real time transaction processing.

By taking into account evaluations of the CAP theorem we can observe that a design of a distributed system requires a deeper approach dependent on the application and technical conditions. For Big Data computing with, e.g., of datacenter networking, failures in the network are minimized. Then we can reach both high *C* and *P* with a high probability. On the other hand, the practice has shown that discussed problems have not to be so critical. Brewer (2012) wrote that the CAP theorem has been widely misunderstood. CAP prohibits only a tiny part of the design space: perfect availability and consistency in the presence of partitions, which are rare. Bailis et al. (2013) introduce so called *Highly Available Transactions* (HAT), i.e. guarantees that do not suffer unavailability during system partitions or incur high network latency. They demonstrate that many weak replica consistency models from distributed systems are both HAT-compliant and simultaneously achievable with several ACID properties.

Basically NoSQL can be used for non-relational, distributed systems that do not attempt to provide ACID guarantees.

Indexing

NoSQL databases are generally based on the key-value store model which efficiently supports the single-key index and can respond to queries in milliseconds. To achieve this performance, different NoSQL databases utilize different indexing methods. For example, CouchDB has a B-tree index which is a bit different to the original. While it maintains all of the important properties, it adds Multi-Version Concurrency Control and an append-only design. B-trees are used to store the main database file as well as view indexes. One database is one B-tree, and one view index is one B-tree. MongoDB provides different types of indexes for different purposes and different types of content. *Single field indexes* only include data from a single field of the documents in a collection. They are applicable on fields at the top level of a document and on fields in sub-documents. A *compound index* includes more than one field of the documents in a collection. Also supported are *multikey indexes*, which support efficient queries against array fields. To improve efficiency, an index can be created as sparse and in this case the indexes will not include documents that do not have the indexed field.

However, numerous applications require multi-dimensional queries, which NoSQL databases do not support efficiently. Some solutions of NoSQL database that respond to multi-dimensional query are MapReduce and Table-Scan but they are inefficient and costly, especially when the selectivity of the query request is low. Multi-dimensional index technology has been extensively studied in traditional DBMSs. However, they cannot meet the increasingly requirements of scalability, high I/O throughput in the context of Big Data, therefore distributed *multi-dimensional index* for Big Data management on cloud platform management has been introduced. Indexes can be generally grouped into two categories according to the associated distributed storage architecture:

- **Peer-to-Peer System:** Several methods have been proposed in the literature including (Wu et al., 2009) who proposed a general index framework with global and local indexes. The local index is built on local data while the index framework selects nodes from local indexes by a respective cost model and organizes them together to form the global index. There is the RT-CAN proposal which employs R-trees for local indexes (Wang et al., 2010) and is based on CAN (Ratnasamy et al., 2001) protocol, while QT-Chord has a local index based on a quad tree (Ding et al., 2011).

- **Master-Slave Style:** EMINC is a two-layered index with R-Tree for a global index which is stored in master node, while slave nodes local data are indexed with K-d tree (Zhang et al., 2009). MD-HBase utilizes Z-order curve and K-d tree or Quad-Tree (Nishimura et al., 2011). EDMI in the global layer employs K-d tree to partition entire space into many subspaces and the local layer contains a group of Z-order prefix R-trees related to one subspace (Wang et al., 2010).

Some NoSQL databases are *in-memory databases*, which means that the data is stored in computer's memory to achieve faster access. The fastest NoSQL data stores such as Redis and Memcached entirely serve from memory. This trend is supported by hardware achievements in last years. Modern servers nowadays can possess large main memory capability that can size up to 2 Terabytes (TB) and more. As memory accesses are at least 100 times faster than disk, keeping data in main memory becomes an interesting design principle to increase the performance of data management systems. On the other hand, Redis and Memcached do not implement any partitioning strategy and leave it to the client to devise one. For completeness, let's add that MemcacheDB is a persistence enabled variant of Memcached.

Precomputing Architecture

Huge volume of data, along with its complexity poses big challenges to data analytic applications. Techniques proposed in data warehousing and online analytical processing, such as precomputed multidimensional cubes, dramatically improve the response time of analytic queries based on relational databases. There are some works extending similar concepts into NoSQL such as constructing cubes from NoSQL stores and converting existing cubes into NoSQL stores (Scriney et al., 2016) and attention was also given to precomputing structure within the NoSQL databases (Franciscus et al., 2016). Concept is based on architecture for answering temporal analytic queries over big data by precomputing the results of granulated chunks of collections which are decomposed from the original large collection. In extensive experimental evaluations on drill-down and roll-up temporal queries over large amount of data authors demonstrated the effectiveness and efficiency under different settings.

Spatial-Temporal Data Integration

The increasing use of GPS sources large amount of spatial-temporal trajectory data formats are emerging. Therefore, spatial-temporal trajectory data integration is significant to combine data from different sources into a unified format and platform for trajectory data-based applications. A novel system, shown in Figure 3. to represent and integrate spatial-temporal trajectory data from different sources and formats has been proposed (Peixoto et al., 2018). This system stores the formatted data into any of the provided primary storage platforms, i.e., MongoDB, HBase, VoltDB, or Local directory. This allows any trajectory-based system to process data from multiple heterogeneous datasets in a user-provided storage platform, without the need of re-implementation.

Figure 3. System workflow

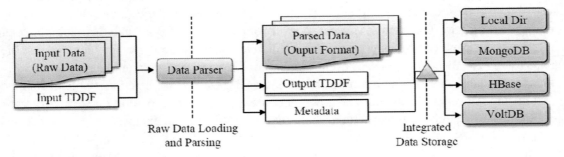

BIG DATA WITH NOSQL AND HADOOP

In this section we analyze pros and cons of tools discussed in the previous two sections and show possibilities of some current approaches. A lot of NoSQL databases are built on top of the Hadoop core, i.e. their performance depends on M/R jobs. It means these sections are not independent.

Usability of NoSQL Databases

Usability of NoSQL databases is closely related to unusual and often inappropriate phenomena of these tools:

- Have little or no use for data modelling, i.e., developers generally do not create a logical model,
- Database design is rather query driven,
- Data is unconstrained,
- Have only few facilities for ad-hoc query and analysis and even a simple query requires significant programming expertise.
- There is no standard query language,
- Some of them are more mature than others, but each of them is trying to solve similar problems,
- Migration from one such system to another is complicated.

Although belonging to one category, two NoSQL tools can be very different. For example, CouchDB uses a low-level query language, and scalability through replications. MongoDB owns a rich, declarative query language, and its scalability is achieved through sharding.

There are two types of NoSQL databases: OLAP-like and OLTP- like. The former are useful for complex analytical processing on relatively large amount of data with read/throughput optimization. This includes applications which do not require transactional semantics, e.g., address books, blogs, serving pages on high-traffic websites, delivering streaming media or managing data as typically occurs in social networking applications. Content management systems also fall to this category. NoSQL are appropriate here also for indexing a large number of documents. The latter uses not only reads but also updates/writes and needs transaction support mostly on relatively small amount of data.

Key-value stores are ideally suited to lightning-fast, highly-scalable retrieval of the values needed for application tasks like managing user profiles or sessions or retrieving product names.

Column-oriented databases provide distributed data storage appropriate especially for versioned data because of their time-stamping functions. Then they are appropriate for large-scale, batch-oriented data processing including sorting, parsing, and data conversion. In context of Big Analytics, Column-oriented NoSQL databases can perform exploratory and predictive analytics, however, they are not suitable for the majority of DW/BI applications, or even for many traditional web-based applications.

Document databases are good for storing and managing Big Data-size collections of literal documents, like text documents, email messages, and XML documents. They are also good for storing sparse data in general, that is irregular (semistructured) data that would require an extensive use of NULL values in a relational DBMS.

Graph databases are very good for storing information about the relationships between objects in cases when relationship between two objects in the database is at least as important as the objects themselves.

NoSQL are inadvisable for applications requiring enterprise-level functionality (ACID, security, and other features of relational DBMS technology). In turn they provide a good platform for Big Analytics, e.g., for analyzing high-volume, real time data. For example, Web log analysis and Web-site click streams analysis belong to high parallelizable problems which can be addressed with NoSQL databases. There are a number of reasons to justify this possibility:

- Enforcing schemas and row-level locking as in relational DBMS unnecessarily over-complicate these applications,
- Mobile computing makes transactions at large scale technically infeasible,
- Absence of ACID properties allows significant acceleration and decentralization of NoSQL databases.

For example, HBase enables fast analytical queries, but on column level only. Also commonly used BI tools do not provide connectivity to NoSQL.

An interesting question is how important are NoSQL DBMSs in the database world. An answer can be found on the DB-Engines ranking server (solid IT, 2018) where, e.g., in November 2018, 346 systems are ranked. The top ten popular DBMSs include well-known relational systems like Oracle, MySQL, etc., but also three NoSQL MongoDB, Redis, Cassandra on the 5th, 8th, and 10th place, respectively.

Big Data is often associated with a cloud computing. But cloud computing means only computing resources that are delivered as a service, typically over the Internet. A significant feature of cloud computing is the capability to deliver both software and hardware resources as services in a scalable way. NoSQL databases used in such environments are mostly sufficient for storage and processing of Big Data used there. However, as we consider more complex cloud architectures, NoSQL should not be the only option in the cloud. In consequence, it increases requirements on a general architecture of cloud computational environment, i.e. on ability to run on commodity heterogeneous servers, as most cloud environments are based on them.

Usability of Hadoop

MapReduce is still very simple technique compared to those used in the area of distributed databases. MapReduce is well suited for applications that analyze elements of a large dataset independently; however, applications whose data access patterns are more complex must be built using several invocations of the Map and Reduce steps. The performance of such design is dependent on the overall strategy as well as the nature and quality of the intermediate data representation and storage. For example, e-science applications involve complex computations, which pose new challenges to MapReduce systems. As scientific data is often skewed and the runtime complexity of the reducer task is typically high, the resulted data processing M/R jobs may be not too effective. MapReduce is also not appropriate for ad hoc analyses but rather for organized data processing.

There are many other reasons against MapReduce. For example, big velocity is one of many cases where MapReduce and Hadoop cannot fit to the "on-line" speed requirements. Often it is not possible to wait for a batch job on Hadoop to complete because the input data would change before we get any result from the processing process. The first-generation Big Analytics platforms like Hadoop lack an essential feature for Big Graph Analytics - iteration (or equivalently, recursion). Iteration is hardly achieved in NoSQL based on Hadoop MapReduce. The MapReduce programming model is not ideal for expressing many graph algorithms. Consequently, some modifications like HaLoop framework (Bu, Howe, Balazinska, & Ernstm, 2012) occur now which support iteration.

A more radical solution offers a flexible dataflow-based execution model that can express a wide range of data access and communication. An example is Pregel system (Malewicz et al., 2010) viewing its data as a graph and supporting large-scale iterative processing. Each node of the graph corresponds roughly to a task.

Problems with NoSQL concern their whole architecture. Stonebraker (2013) points out, that the Hadoop stack has a poor performance except where the application is "trivially parallel". Also, it has no indexing and it has very inefficient joins in Hadoop layer, additionally, it is "sending the data to the query" and not "sending the query to the data". Another example is Couchbase (Couchbase, 2018) which replicates the whole document if only its small part is changed.

Despite NoSQL are becoming dominant for Big Analytics they still have a lot disadvantages, e.g., a heavy computational model, low-level information about data processed, etc. There are exceptions, e.g., the Apache's library Mahout (The Apache Software Foundation, 2018d) which is implemented on top of Hadoop, brings very effective automated machine learning and data mining algorithms to find hidden trends and otherwise unthought-of or unconsidered ideas. In the Big Data world NoSQL databases dominate rather for operational capabilities, i.e. interactive workloads where data is primarily captured and stored. Analytical Big Data workloads, on the other hand, tend to be addressed by parallel database systems and MapReduce.

TOWARDS NEW ARCHITECTURES FOR BIG DATA PROCESSING

To address *Big Analytics* challenges, a new generation of scalable data management technologies has emerged in the last years. We describe so called Big Data Management Systems, NewSQL DBMSs, and NoSQL databases with transactions.

Big Data Management Systems

Managing Big Data requires a different approach to DBMSs because of the wide variation in data structure which does not lend itself to traditional DBMSs. Some authors use a term *Big Data Management System* (BDMS) specified informally is a highly scalable platform which supports requirements of Big Data processing.

A representative of BDMS is ASTERIX system (Alsubaiee et al, 2014).). It is fully parallel, able to store, access, index, query, analyze, and publish very large quantities of semistructured data. It has its own declarative query language (AQL) and semistructured NoSQL style data model (ADM). ADM is a "super-set" of JSON, with additional data types. AsterixDB supports its own native storage (hash-partitioned LSM B+ Trees) along with external storage (currently HDFS). It has support for different types of indices such as B+ Trees, spatial indices, and text indices. Its architecture shown in Figure 4 is similar to one presented in Figure 2, but with own Hyracks layer in the bottom to which manages parallel data computations, the Algebrics algebra layer in the middle, and the topmost ASTERIX system layer – a parallel information management system. Hyracks is a parallel runtime query execution engine. AQL (ASTERIX Query Language) is composable language reminding of XQuery and using fuzzy selections and joins appropriate for analytical purposes. The Asterix software stack includes also a Hadoop compatibility layer, Pregelix software for graph analytics, and other useful facilities.

Oracle Big Data Appliance (Oracle, 2017) classified also among BDBSs. Oracle Big Data Appliance is designed to integrate all enterprise data, whether it is structured or unstructured.

The major components of Oracle Big Data Appliance are Oracle Exadata, Oracle Exalytics, Oracle Cloudera Enterprise and, starting in version X4-2, Oracle Big Data Connectors for simplifying data integration and analytics of data from Hadoop. Oracle Big Data SQL is a new architecture for SQL-on-Hadoop, combining data from Oracle DB, Hadoop and NoSQL in a single SQL query; enables to query and analyze data in Hadoop and NoSQL.

The third representative of BDMS is Lily (NGDATA, 2018) integrating Apache Hadoop, HBase, Apache Solr (The Apache Software Foundation, 2014f) - enterprise search platform based on the popular full-text search engine Lucene), and machine learning (see Figure 5). Providing distributed search and index replication, Solr is highly scalable.

NewSQL Databases

A category of parallel DBMSs called *NewSQL databases* (Aslett, 2011) is characterized by the following properties:

- Are RDBMSs that combine OLTP, high performance, and scalability of NoSQL,
- Are designed to scale out horizontally on shared nothing machines,
- Partitioning is transparent,

Figure 4. The Asterix software stack

	Level of abstraction	Data processing				
L5	non-procedural access	AQL HiveQL XQuery				
L2-L4	algebraic approach	ASTERIX DB	Other HLL compilers	M/R jobs	Pregel jobs	
		Algebricks Algebra Layer		Hadoop M/R layer	Pregelix	Hyr. jobs
L1	file management	Hyrack Data-parallel Platform				

Figure 5. The three-layered Lily software stack

	Level of abstraction	Data processing		
L5	non-procedural access	Lily		
		M/R jobs	HiveQL	
L2-L4	record-oriented navigational approach	Hadoop Map Reduce	HBase Key-Value Store	Solr
	records and access path management			
	propagation control			
L1	file management	Hadoop Distributed File System		

- Still provide ACID guarantees,
- Applications interact with the database primarily using SQL (with joins),
- Employ a lock-free concurrency control,
- Provide higher performance than available from the traditional systems.

NewSQL databases aim to achieve the scalability same as NoSQL while preserving the complex functionality of relational databases. They can be categorized in the following way:

- General purpose pure relational DBMS: ClustrixDB (Clustrix, 2018), NuoDB (NuoDB, Inc., 2018), VoltDB (VoltDB, Inc., 2018),
- Google's hybrids: Spanner (Corbett et al., 2012) and F1 (Shute et al., 2012),
- Hadoop-relational hybrids: HadoopDB (Abouzeid at al, 2009) – a parallel database with Hadoop connectors, Vertica (MicroFocus Int., 2018),
- Supporting more data models: FoundationDB (FoundationDB, 2018), OrientDB (Orient Technologies LTD, 2018), Postgres NoSQL (EnterpriseDB Corporation, 2018) .

VoltDB and Clustrix use a traditional approach in which each table is partitioned using a single key and rows are distributed among servers by an appropriate hashing algorithm. Particularly NuoDB is appropriate for clouds. It is interesting that NuoDB stores its data into a key-value store. Spanner uses *semirelations*, i.e. each row has a name (i.e. always there is a primary key), versions, and hierarchies of tables. F1 is built on Spanner which provides synchronous cross-datacenter replication and strong consistency. Its authors characterize F1 as a fault-tolerant globally-distributed OLTP OLAP database. F1 includes a fully functional distributed SQL query engine. OrientDB has a document, key-value, and graph databases functionality. Postgres NoSQL owns native data types JSON and HSTORE in SQL. Remind that data type HSTORE enables to store key/value pairs within a single column. In FoundationDB, the core database exposes an ordered key-value store with transactions. Transactions are used to implement a variety of data models via layers.

Very different is also the approach of these DBMS to SQL. For example, VoltDB has a larger number of restrictions of SQL. It is not possible to use the HAVING clause, self-joins are not allowed, all joined tables must be partitioned over the same value. A special NewSQL tool is ScalArc iDB (ScaleArc, 2018) - a high performance SQL Accelerator appropriate for both for cloud and datacenters. Some NewSQL databases, e.g., MySQL Cluster and ClustrixDB use transparent sharding.

NewSQL provides performance and scalability not comparable with traditional DBMS and with Hadoop as well. For example, a comparison of Hadoop and Vertica shown that query times for Hadoop were a lot slower (1–2 orders of magnitude) (Pavlo et al., 2009).

A lot of success of some NewSQL solutions lies in new database architectures based on MPP (e.g., ClustrixDB and Vertica), but often even on massively parallel analytic databases. Technologies like columnar storage are often used there (e.g., Vertica). In memory data processing approach is used, e.g., in the MySQL-like database MemSQL and VoltDB. For example, MemSQL belongs to the fastest NewSQL tools in data loading and query execution times.

Most representatives of NewSQL are suitable for real-time analytics. But in general, their performance is still a problem (Stantic & Pokorný, 2014). New alternatives for Big Analytics with NewSQL include:

- HadoopDB (combines parallel database with Map Reduce),
- MemSQL, VoltDB (automatic cross-partition joins),
- ClustrixDB (for transaction processing and real-time analytics).

There are attempts of shipping to No Hadoop DBMSs in which the MapReduce layer is eliminated. Details of their comparison with NewSQL databases can be found in the more recent paper (Grolinger, Higashino, Tiwari, & Capretz, 2013).

NoSQL Databases With ACID Transactions

The last new generation of NoSQL databases we mention are NoSQL databases with ACID transactions. Many NoSQL designers are therefore exploring a return to transactions with ACID properties as the preferred means of managing concurrency for a broad range of applications. Using tailored optimizations, designers are finding that implementation of ACID transactions need not sacrifice scalability, fault-tolerance, or performance.

These DBMSs

- Maintain distributed design, fault tolerance, easy scaling, and a simple, flexible base data model,
- Extend the base data models of NoSQL,
- Are CP systems with global transactions.

A good example of such DBMS is a key-value FoundationDB with scalability and fault tolerance (and an SQL layer). Oracle NoSQL Database provides ACID complaint transactions for full CRUD operations, with adjustable durability and consistency transactional guarantees. Spanner is also NoSQL which can be considered as NewSQL as well. MarkLogic (MarkLogic Corp., 2018) is a NoSQL document database with JSON storage, HDFS, and optimistic locking. The distributed graph database OrientDB guarantees also ACID properties.

SQL and NoSQL: Towards Integrated Architectures

In practice, ITC and business professionals need to determine whether NoSQL technologies are better suited than RDBMS for a particular system. The choice of technology is critical for applications that can be both transactional and analytical. They typically require different software and hardware architectures (e.g., Pokorný, 2018).

Meijer & Bierman (2011) argue that the NoSQL databases are rather complementary to traditional transactional DBMSs. Complementary differences are given by properties given in Table 4.

This complementarity negatively influences integration possibilities of these datastores both at the data model and data processing level.

Particularly, normalization allows single object data in a relational database to be spread over multiple relations. For example, customer data is in one table, data about the banks where the account is in the second table. The interconnection is realized via foreign keys. In NoSQL database, this can be done in such a way that each bank "row" can contain data and account numbers for each customer. The basic feature of NoSQL is that they are denormalized, that is, they store copies of an object instead of the object. This, of course, leads to worse data update options.

In ICT history, different DBMSs were designed to solve different problems, considering still new and new data types. In addition to centralized RDBMSs, specialized servers, universal servers, relational DW, etc. appeared in the past. These tools were based on a fixed database schema and an associated query language (mostly SQL). OR SQL and its other extensions supported this strategy for a long time.

Concerning an integration of distributed data from different databases, two approaches based on a database schema management were at disposal:

- **Top-Down:** Starting with a global schema to design schemas for data in sites,
- **Bottom-Up:** Through middleware, i.e. to use schema mapping for schemas in sites into a middleware (e.g., OLE DB, JDBC) and then use a query transformation. Data is loosely integrated and managed by multiple servers.

We remind that the former concerns rather homogenous databases models, while the letter supports heterogeneous database models and consequently DBMSs.

Table 4. Complementary differences between RDBMS and NoSQL

Property	RDBMS	NoSQL
1 data model	data is strongly typed;	data is potentially dynamically typed;
2	data of dependent tables points to its parents (via foreign keys);	parent's data points to children data;
3	associated entities have an identity (primary key);	environment determines identity;
4	not compositional;	Compositional;
5	referential integrity based on values;	weak referential integrity based on computation or only "over" partition segments;
6 data processing	synchronous (ACID) updates over more rows;	asynchronous (BASE) updates within single values;
7	environment coordinates changes (transactions);	entities responsible to react to changes (eventual consistency);
8	query optimizer – responsibility by DBMS;	developer/pattern – responsibility by application;

In context of RDBMSs and NoSQL databases, it is not possible to use simply traditional approaches to data integration. The reason is the complementarity of these database types. Moreover, the problem of analysts is that the lack of data schemas (semantics) prevents them from understanding their structure and thus generating serious analyses. Now, the tendency is to create multilevel modelling approaches involving both relational and NoSQL architectures including their integration (Abbelo, 2015). Several approaches are under a development:

Polyglot persistence. We approach particular data stores with their original data access methods (Sadalage, & Fowler, 2013). The truth is that polyglot persistence is a method for data modelling problems, not a solution to them. Developers need to customize data models each one with their own particular objectives for an application and often need more than one, but they should not have to adopt different DBMS to get them. "Polyglot" means "able to speak many languages", not integration. As an integration architecture, polyglot persistence is its weakest form.

Multi-model approach. Maybe, it presents a more user-friendly solution of heterogeneous database integration. Multi-model represents an intersection of multiple models in one product. For example, OrientDB is a multi-model DBMS including geospatial, graph, fulltext and key-valued data models. OO concepts are used for user domain modelling in OrientDB. Similarly, ArangoDB is designed as a native multi-model database, supporting key-value, document and graph models. MarkLogic enables to store and search JSON and XML documents and RDF triples.

NoSQL relationally. The multi-model solution by (Curé et al, 2013) considers source document and column-oriented database integrated through a middleware into a virtual SQL database.

Multilevel modelling. Despite of the fact that database schemas are mostly not used in the NoSQL world, some variations on multilevel modelling approaches exist. In relation to solution of an alternative for data processing with relational and NoSQL data in one infrastructure, common design methods for such DBs are based on the modification of the traditional 3-level ANSI/SPARC approach (Herrero et al, 2013). The approach involves not only heterogeneous data sources but also the development of a data-base schema in the overall infrastructure, i.e., its variability. A strong motivation for this approach is the fact that when designing a database for Big Analytics, we must consider DM/ML patterns, clustering of some attributes, etc., to ensure adequate system performance. However, the conceptual design assumes the correctness of the current knowledge of the application domain. The following examples document activities in this area:

- **Special Abstract Model**: A database design methodology for NoSQL systems based on NoAM (NoSQL Abstract Model), a novel abstract data model for NoSQL databases, is presented in (Bugiotti et al, 2014). The associated design methodology starts with an UML class diagram, a designer identifies so called aggregates ("chunks" of related data) and maps the aggregates into NoAM blocks. These blocks are simply transformed into constructs of a particular NoSQL data model. (Oracle, 2016) uses the notion of unified query in this context. A single SQL statement can be executed seamlessly across more data stores: relational databases, Hadoop clusters, and NoSQL databases. A functional approach approaching graph databases and relational database is introduced in (Pokorný, 2018).
- **NoSQL-on-RDBMS.** A coexistence of RDBMS and a NoSQL databases includes, e.g., storing and querying JSON data in a RDBMS (see, ARGO/SQL (Chasseur, Li, Y, & Patel, 2013)).

- **Ontology Integration:** Ontology based semantic integration systems for RDBMSs already exist. A more advanced integrating architecture including several NoSQL databases is proposed in (Curé. Lamole, & Duc, 2013). MongoDB as a document database and Cassandra as a column family store are involved into a prototype architecture. The databases are described by several ontologies and a generated global ontology. Global SPARQL queries are transformed into query languages of sources.

Schema and data conversion. In practice, there are other options, such as the schema conversion model, in which the schema from the SQL database is converted to the NoSQL database schema (Zhao et al, 2014). Then, even a double-sided data migration between a RDBMS and a NoSQL databases can be performed. Authors of mention 7 major approaches for data migration from relational to NoSQL databases.

FUTURE RESEARCH DIRECTIONS

Key issues for building Big Data processing infrastructure are in decisions concerning NoSQL and NewSQL databases:

- Choosing the right (correct) product,
- Designing a suitable database architecture for a given application class.

Considering BI as Analytics 1.0 and methods used by online companies like Google, Yahoo, and Facebook as Analytics 2.0, the development comes on towards a new wave of complex Big Analytics - Analytics 3.0, which are able to predict future not just provide valuable information from data. Traditional data mining techniques, already widely applied in the layer (3) to extract frequent correlations of values from both structured and semistructured datasets in BI, are interesting solutions for Big Analytics, too, but they have to be extended and accommodated. Today's main challenges for research in Big Data and Big Analytics area include:

- Improving the quality and scalability of data mining methods. Indeed, the processes of query composition - especially in the absence of a schema - and the presentation and interpretation of the obtained answers may be non-trivial.
- Transforming the content into a structured format for later analysis as much data today is not natively in structured format.
- Improving performance of related applications and shipping to NoHadoop DBMSs, where MapReduce layer will be eliminated.

The second challenge means not only the integration step but also it concerns filtering and more effective representation of Big Data. For example, in a Big Data project working with digital sky surveys we can move with data transformations from TB data to dozens GB (Yaghob, Bednárek, Kruliš, & Zavoral, 2014).

The last but not least challenge concerns role of man in Big Analytics. So far the mining process is guided by the analyst or the data scientist, where depending on the application scenario he/she determines the portion of data where/from the useful patterns can be extracted. A better approach would be the automatic mining process and to extract approximate, synthetic information on both the structure and the contents of large datasets. This seems to be the biggest challenge in Big Data.

CONCLUSION

Efficient data storage and processing in a database style is only first assumption for Big Analytics. We have seen that NoSQL databases partially contribute to this goal. But their diversity and different properties contribute to key problems with application of them in practice:

- Choosing the right product, design of appropriate architecture for a given class of applications,
- Ensuring skilled developers of applications to be at disposal.

Edlich (2012) even suggests choosing a NoSQL database after answering about 70 questions in 6 categories, and building a prototype. Similarly, Grolinger, Higashino, Tiwari, & Capretz (2013) emphasize that although NoSQL and NewSQL data stores deliver powerful capabilities, the large number and immense diversity of available solutions make choosing the appropriate solution for the problem at hand especially difficult.

Despite of the fact that some companies offer reference models for Big Data, no common one is at disposal now. Such a model should contain layers for:

1. Data,
2. Integration,
3. Analytics, and
4. A layer for predictive and prescriptive analysis on the top.

In this chapter we discussed layers (1), (2), and (3) and their strong mutual correlation. The problem increases for more complex architectures. Hadoop, NoSQL and massively parallel analytic databases are not mutually exclusive. Kelly (2014) believes the three approaches are complementary to each other and can and should co-exist in many enterprises. The evolution of information architectures to include Big Data will likely provide the foundation for a new generation of enterprise infrastructure (Manoj, 2013).

ACKNOWLEDGMENT

This work was partially supported by the Charles University project Q48.

REFERENCES

Abelló, A. (2015): Big Data Design. In *Proc. of 11the Int. Workshop on Data Warehousing and OLAP*. ACM. 10.1145/2811222.2811235

Abouzeid, A., Bajda-Pawlikowski, K., Abadi, D., Silberschatz, A., & Rasin, A. (2009). HadoopDB - An Architectural Hybrid of MapReduce and DBMS Technologies for Analytical Workloads. *Proc. of VLDB '09*, 922-933.

Alaei, A. R., Becken, S., & Stantic, B. (2017). Sentiment Analysis in Tourism: Capitalizing on Big Data. *Journal of Travel Research.*

Alsubaiee, S., Altowim, Y., Altwaijry, H., Behm, A., Borkar, V., Bu, Y., … Westman, T. (2014). AsterixDB: A Scalable, Open Source BDMS. *Proceedings of the VLDB Endowment*, 7(14), 1905-1916. 10.14778/2733085.2733096

Amazon Web Services. (2018a). *Amazon SimpleDB*. Retrieved November 10, 2018, from http://aws.amazon.com/simpledb/

Amazon Web Services. (2018b). *Amazon DynamoDB*. Retrieved November 10, 2018, from http://aws.amazon.com/dynamodb/

ArangoDB Inc. (2018). *ArangoDB*. Retrieved November 10, 2018, from https://www.arangodb.com/

Aslett, M. (2011). NoSQL, NewSQL and Beyond: The drivers and use cases for database alternatives. *451 Research*. Retrieved November 10, 2018, from https://451research.com/report-long?icid=1389

Bailis, P., Davidson, A., Fekete, A., Ghodsi, A., Hellerstein, J. M., & Stoica, I. (2013). Highly Available Transactions: Virtues and Limitations (Extended Version). *PVLDB*, 7(3), 181–192.

Beyer, K., Ercegovac, V., Gemulla, R., Balmin, A., Eltabakh, M., Kanne, C.-Ch., … Shekita, E. J. (2011). Jaql: A scripting language for large scale semistructured data analysis. *PVLDB*, 4(12), 1272–1283.

Borkar, V., Carey, M.-J., & Li, Ch. (2012). Inside "Big Data management": ogres, onions, or parfaits? *Proceedings of EDBT Conference*, 3-14. 10.1145/2247596.2247598

Brewer, E. A. (2000). *Towards robust distributed systems*. Paper presented at PODC 2000, Portland, OR.

Brewer, E. A. (2012). CAP twelve years later: How the 'rules' have changed. *Computer*, 45(2), 22–29. doi:10.1109/MC.2012.37 PMID:24976642

Bu, Y., Howe, Y., Balazinska, M., & Ernstm, M. D. (2012). The HaLoop approach to large-scale iterative data analysis. *The VLDB Journal*, 21(2), 169–190. doi:10.100700778-012-0269-7

Bugiotti, F., Cabibbo, L., Atzeni, P., & Torlone, R. (2014). Database Design for NoSQL Systems. In *Proc. of ER Conf.*, LNCS 8824, 223-231.

Chang, F., Dean, J., Ghemavat, S., Hsieh, W. C., Wallach, D. A., Burrows, M., … Gruber, R. E. (2008). Bigtable: A Distributed Storage System for Structured Data. *Journal ACM Transactions on Computer Systems*, 26(2), 4.

Chasseur, C., Li, Y., & Patel, J. M. (2013). Enabling JSON Document Stores in Relational Systems. *Proceedings of 16th Int. Workshop on the Web and Databases (WebDB 2013)*, 1-6.

Clustrix. (2018). *Clustrix.* Retrieved November 10, 2018, from http://www.clustrix.com/

Cooper, B.F., Ramakrishnan, R., Srivastava, U., Silberstein, A., Bohannon, P., Jacobsen, H.A., … Zemeni, R. (2008). PNUTS: Yahoo!'s hosted data serving platform. *Journal PVLDB, 1*(2), 1277-1288.

Corbett, J. C., Dean, J. C., Epstein, M., Fikes, A., Frost, Ch., & Furman, J. J., …Woodford, D. (2012). Spanner: Google's Globally-Distributed Database. *Proceedings of 10th USENIX Symposium on Operation Systems Design and Implementation (OSDI 2012).*

Couchbase. (2018). *Couchbase.* Retrieved November 10, 2018, from http://www.couchbase.com/

Curé, O., Hecht, R., Duc, Ch. L., & Lamole, M. (2011). Data Integration over NoSQL Stores Using Access Path Based Mappings. *Proceedings of DEXA 2011, Part I, LNCS 6860*, 481–495. 10.1007/978-3-642-23088-2_36

Curé, O., Lamole, M., & Duc, C. L. (2013). *Ontology Based Data Integration over Document and Column Family Oriented NOSQL.* CoRR, arXiv:1307.2603.

Dean, D., & Ghemawat, S. (2008). MapReduce: Simplified Data Processing on Large Clusters. *Communications of the ACM, 51*(1), 107–113. doi:10.1145/1327452.1327492

Ding, L., Qiao, B., Wang, G., & Chen, C. (2011). An efficient quad-tree based index structure for cloud data management. *Proceedings of WAIM 2011, LNCS, 6897*, 238–250. 10.1007/978-3-642-23535-1_22

Edlich, S. (2012). *Choose the "Right" Database and NewSQL: NoSQL Under Attack.* Retrieved from http://www.infoq.com/presentations/Choosing-NoSQL-NewSQL

Edlich, S. (2018). *List of NoSQL databases.* Retrieved November 10, 2018, from http://nosql-database.org/

EnterpriseDB Corporation. (2018). *NoSQL Overview.* Retrieved November 10, 2018, from http://www.enterprisedb.com/nosql-for-enterprise

Foundation, D. B. (2018). *FoundationDB gives you the power of ACID transactions in a distributed database.* Retrieved November 10, 2018, from https://foundationdb.com/

Franciscus, N., Ren, X., & Stantic, B. (2017). Precomputing architecture for flexible and efficient big data analytics. *Vietnam Journal of Computer Science, 5*(2), 133–142. doi:10.100740595-018-0109-9

Gamble, M., & Goble, C. (2011). Quality, Trust and Utility of Scientific Data on the Web: Toward a Joint model. *Proceedings of WebSci'11 Conference.* 10.1145/2527031.2527048

Gaspar, D., & Coric, I. (2017). *Bridging Relational and NoSQL Databases.* IGI Global.

Gates, A., Natkovich, O., Chopra, S., Kamath,P., Narayanamurthy, S.M., Olston, C., …Sristava, U. (2009). Building a high level dataflow system on top of MapReduce: The pig experience. *PVLDB, 2*(2), 1414–1425.

Ghotiya, S., Mandal, J., & Kandasamy, S. (2017). Migration from relational to NoSQL database. In *Proceedings of 14th ICSET Conf.* IOP Publishing.

Gilbert, S., & Lynch, N. (2002). Brewer's conjecture and the feasibility consistent, available, partition-tolerant web services. *ACM SIGACT News*, *33*(2), 51–59. doi:10.1145/564585.564601

GitHub, Inc. (2018). *Project Voldemort - a distributed database*. Retrieved November 10, 2018, from http://www.project-voldemort.com/voldemort/

Grolinger, K., Higashino, W.A., Tiwari, A., & Capretz, M.A.M. (2013). Data management in cloud environments: NoSQL and NewSQL data stores. *Journal of Cloud Computing: Advances, Systems and Applications*, *2*(22).

Gudivada, V. N., Rao, D., & Raghavan, V. V. (2014). NoSQL Systems for Big Data Management. (SERVICES). *2014 IEEE World Congress on Services*, 190 – 197. 10.1109/SERVICES.2014.42

Härder, T. (2005). DBMS Architecture – the Layer Model and its Evolution. *Datenbank-Spektrum*, *13*, 45–57.

Hecht, R., & Jablonski, S. (2011). NoSQL evaluation: A use case oriented survey. *Proceedings 2011 Int Conf Cloud Serv Computing*, 336–341. 10.1109/CSC.2011.6138544

Herrero, V., Abelló, A., & Romero, O. (2016). NOSQL Design for Analytical Workloads: Variability Matters. *Proceedings of ER Conf.*, *LNCS 9974*, 50-64. 10.1007/978-3-319-46397-1_4

Hypertable Inc. (2014). *Hypertable*. Retrieved November 10, 2018, from http://hypertable.org/

Kelly, J. (2014). *Big Data: Hadoop, Business Analytics and Beyond*. Wikibon. Retrieved November 20, 2018 from http://wikibon.org/wiki/v/Big_Data:_Hadoop,_Business_Analytics_and_Beyond

Laney, D. (2001). *3D data management: Controlling data volume, velocity and variety*. Meta Group, Gartner. Retrieved November 6, 2018 from http://blogs.gartner.com/doug-laney/files/2012/01/ad949-3D-Data-Management-Controlling-Data-Volume-Velocity-and-Variety.pdf

Malewicz, G., Austern, M. H., Bik, A. J. C., Dehnert, J. C., Horn, I., Leiser, N., & Czajkowski, G. (2010). Pregel: A System for Large-scale Graph Processing. *Proceedings of the PODS*. 10.1145/1807167.1807184

Manoj, P. (2013). Emerging Database Models and Related Technologies. *International Journal of Advanced Research in Computer Science and Software Engineering*, *3*(2), 264–269.

Manyika, J., Chui, M., Brown, B., Bughin, J., Dobbs, R., Roxburgh, C., & Byers, A. H. (2011). *Big data: the next frontier for innovation, competition, and productivity*. McKinsey Global Inst. Retrieved November 6, 2018 from http://www.mckinsey.com/insights/business_technology/big_data_the_next_frontier_for_innovation

MarkLogic Corp. (2018). *MarkLogic*. Retrieved November 10, 2018, from http://www.marklogic.com/

Meijer, E., & Bierman, G. M. (2011). A co-relational model of data for large shared data banks. *Communications of the ACM*, *54*(4), 49–58. doi:10.1145/1924421.1924436

Memcached. (2018). Retrieved November 10, 2018, from http://memcached.org/

MemSQL Inc. (2018). *MemSQL*. Retrieved November 10, 2018, from http://www.memsql.com/

MicroFocus International. (2018). *Vertica Analytic Database*. Retrieved November 10, 2018, from http://www.vertica.com/

Microsoft. (2018). *Microsoft Azure*. Retrieved November 10, 2018, from https://docs.microsoft.com/en-us/azure/

MongoDB Inc. (2018). *MongoDB*. Retrieved November 10, 2018, from https://www.mongodb.org/

Moniruzzaman, A. B. M., & Hossain, S. A. (2013). NoSQL Database: New Era of Databases for Big data Analytics - Classification, Characteristics and Comparison. *International Journal of Database Theory and Application*, *6*(4), 1–14.

Nasser, T. & Tariq, R.S. (2015). Big Data Challenges. Journal of Computer Engineering & In-formation Technology. *SciTechnol, 4*(3).

Neo Technology, Inc. (2018). *Neo4j*. Retrieved November 10, 2018, from http://www.neo4j.org/

Netmesh Inc. (2018). *InfoGrid – the Web Graph Database*. Retrieved November 10, 2018, from http://infogrid.org/trac/

NGDATA. (2018). *Lily*. Retrieved November 10, 2018, from https://www.ngdata.com/platform/

Nishimura, S., Das, S., Agrawal, D., & Abbadi, A. E. (2011). MD-HBase: A scalable multidimensional data infrastructure for location aware services. In *Proceedings of the 2011 IEEE 12th Int. Conf. on Mobile Data Management*. IEEE Computer Society. 10.1109/MDM.2011.41

NuoDB Inc. (2018). *NuoDB*. Retrieved November 10, 2018, from http://www.nuodb.com/

ODMS.org. (2013). *Big Data Analytics at Thomson Reuters. Interview with Jochen L. Leidner*. Retrieved November 10, 2018, http://www.odbms.org/blog/2013/11/big-data-analytics-at-thomson-reuters-inter-view-with-jochen-l-leidner/

Oracle. (2016). *Unified Query for Big Data Management Systems Integrating Big Data Systems with Enterprise Data Warehouses*. Oracle White Paper.

Oracle. (2017). *Big Data Appliance*. Retrieved November 10, 2018, from https://www.oracle.com/tech-network/database/bigdata-appliance/overview/bigdataappliance-datasheet-1883358.pdf

Oracle. (2018). *Oracle NoSQL Database*. Retrieved November 10, 2018, from http://www.oracle.com/technetwork/database/database-technologies/nosqldb/overview/index.html

Orient Technologies, Ltd. (2018). *OrientDB*. Retrieved November 10, 2018, from http://www.orien-technologies.com/orientdb/

Pavlo, A., & Aslett, M. (2016). What's Really New with NewSQL? *SIGMOD Record*, *45*(2), 45–55. doi:10.1145/3003665.3003674

Pavlo, A., Paulson, E., Rasin, A., Abadi, D., DeWitt, D. J., Madden, S., & Stonebraker, M. (2009). A Comparison of Approaches to Large-Scale Data Analysis. *Proceedings of SIGMOD/PODS'09*. 10.1145/1559845.1559865

Peixoto, D. A., Zhou, X., Hung, N. Q. V., He, D., & Stantic, B. (2018). A System for Spatial-Temporal Trajectory Data Integration and Representation. *International Conference on Database Systems for Advanced Applications*, 807-812. 10.1007/978-3-319-91458-9_53

Pokorný, J. (2011). NoSQL Databases: A step to database scalability in Web environment. *Int J Web Info Syst*, *9*(1), 69–82. doi:10.1108/17440081311316398

Pokorný, J. (2015). Graph Databases: Their Power and Limitations. *Proc. of 14th Int. Conf. on Computer Information Systems and Industrial Management Applications (CISIM 2015)*, 58-69. 10.1007/978-3-319-24369-6_5

Pokorný, J. (2017). Big Data Storage and Management: Challenges and Opportunities. In J. Hřebíček, R. Denzer, G. Schimak, & T. Pitner (Eds.), *Environmental Software Systems. Computer Science for Environmental Protection. ISESS 2017. IFIP Advances in Information and Communication Technology* (Vol. 507, pp. 28–38). Cham: Springer. doi:10.1007/978-3-319-89935-0_3

Pokorný, J. (2018) Integration of Relational and NoSQL Databases. Intelligent Information and Database Systems, ACIIDS 2018, Part II, LNCS 10752, 35-45. doi:10.1007/978-3-319-75420-8_4

Pokorný, J., & Stantic, B. (2016). Challenges and Opportunities in Big Data Processing. In Managing Big Data in Cloud Computing Environments. IGI Global.

Pritchett, D. (2008). BASE: An ACID alternative. *ACM Queue; Tomorrow's Computing Today*, *6*(3), 48–55. doi:10.1145/1394127.1394128

Rajaman, A., & Ullman, J. D. (2011). *Mining of Massive Datasets*. Cambridge University Press. doi:10.1017/CBO9781139058452

Ratnasamy, S., Francis, P., Handley, M., Karp, R. M., & Shenker, S. (2001). A scalable content addressable network. In *Proceedings of SIGCOMM*. ACM.

Redis. (2018). Retrieved November 10, 2018, from http://redis.io/

Sadalage, P. J., & Fowler, M. (2013). *NoSQL Distilled: A Brief Guide to the Emerging World of Polyglot Persistence*. Pearson Education, Inc.

SAS Institute, Inc. (2018). *Big Data. What it is and why it matters*. Retrieved November 10, 2018, from https://www.sas.com/en_us/insights/big-data/what-is-big-data.html

ScaleArc. (2018). *ScaleArc*. Retrieved November 10, 2018, from http://scalearc.com/

Scriney, M., & Roantree, M. (2016). Efficient cube construction for smart city data. *Proceedings of the Workshops of the EDBT/ICDT 2016 Joint Conference*.

Shute, J., Vingralek, R., Samwel, B., Handy, B., Whipkey, Ch., Rollins, E.,... Apte, H. (2013). F1 A Distributed SQL Database That Scales. *PVLDB*, *6*(11), 1068-1079.

Shvachko, K., Kuang, H., Radia, S., & Chansler, R. (2010). The Hadoop Distributed File System, In *Proceedings of 2010 IEEE 26th Symposium on Mass Storage Systems and Technologies (MSST)*, Lake Tahoe, NV: IEEE. 10.1109/MSST.2010.5496972

Snow, D. (2012). *Dwaine Snow's Thoughts on Databases and Data Management*. Retrieved November 10, 2018, from http://dsnowondb2.blogspot.cz/2012/07/adding-4th-v-to-big-data-veracity.html

solid IT. (2018). *DB-engines*. Retrieved November 10, 2018, from http://db-engines.com/en/ranking

Stantic, B., & Pokorný, J. (2014). Opportunities in Big Data Management and Processing. *Frontiers in Artificial Intelligence and Applications*, *270*, 15–26.

Stonebraker, M. (2013). *No Hadoop: The Future of the Hadoop/HDFS Stack*. Retrieved November 10, 2018, from http://istc-bigdata.org/index.php/no-hadoop-the-future-of-the-hadoophdfs-stack/

The Apache Software Foundation. (2016). *Cassandra*. Retrieved November 10, 2018, from http://cassandra.apache.org/

The Apache Software Foundation. (2017). *Apache Solr™ 4.10*. Retrieved November 10, 2018, from http://lucene.apache.org/solr/

The Apache Software Foundation. (2018a). *Hadoop*. Retrieved November 10, 2018, from http://hadoop.apache.org/

The Apache Software Foundation. (2018b). *Apache HBase*. Retrieved November 10, 2018, from https://hbase.apache.org/

The Apache Software Foundation. (2018c). *Apache CouchDB™*. Retrieved November 10, 2018, from http://couchdb.apache.org/

The Apache Software Foundation. (2018d). *Mahout*. Retrieved November 10, 2018, from http://mahout.apache.org/

Thusoo, A., Sarma, J. S., Jain, N., Shao, Z., Chakka, P., Anthony, S., ... Murthy, R. (2009). Hive - a warehousing solution over a map-reduce framework. *PVLDB*, *2*(2), 1626–1629.

VoltDB Inc. (2018). *VoltDB*. Retrieved November 10, 2018, from http://voltdb.com/

Wang, J., Wu, S., Gao, H., Li, J., & Ooi, B. C. (2010). Indexing multi-dimensional data in a cloud system. In *Proceedings of SIGMOD*. ACM. 10.1145/1807167.1807232

Wu, S. & Wu, K. (2009). An indexing framework for efficient retrieval on the cloud. *IEEE Data Engineering Bulletin*, *1*(32), 75-82.

Yaghob, J., Bednárek, D., Kruliš, M., & Zavoral, F. (2014). Column-oriented Data Store for Astrophysical Data. In *Proceedings of 25th International Workshop on Database and Expert Systems Applications*. Munich, Germany: IEEE Computer Society.

Zhang, X., Ai, J., Wang, Z., Lu, J., & Meng, X. (2009). An efficient multi-dimensional index for cloud data management. In *Proceedings of CloudDB* (pp. 17–24). ACM. doi:10.1145/1651263.1651267

Zhao, G., Lin, Q., Li, L., & Li, Z. (2014). Schema Conversion Model of SQL Database to NoSQL. In *Proceedings of the 9th Int. Conf. on P2P, Parallel, Grid, Cloud and Internet Computing*. IEEE. 10.1109/3PGCIC.2014.137

Zhou, X., Zhang, X., Wang, Y., Li, R., & Wang, S. (2013). Efficient Distributed Multi-dimensional Index for Big Data Management. *Proceedings of WAIM 2013, LNCS 7923*, 130–141. 10.1007/978-3-642-38562-9_14

KEY TERMS AND DEFINITIONS

Big Analytics: A set of methods, algorithms, and tools to analyze a mix of structured, semi-structured and unstructured data in search of valuable business information and insights.

Big Data: Any collection of data sets so large and complex that it becomes difficult to process them using traditional data processing applications.

Hadoop: An open source software project that enables the distributed processing of large data sets across clusters of commodity servers.

NoSQL Databases: Databases mostly addressing some of the points: being non-relational, distributed, open-source and horizontally scalable.

Scalability: The ability of a system, network, or process to handle a growing amount of work in a capable manner or its ability to be enlarged to accommodate that growth.

Transaction Processing: Is a style of computing that divides work into individual, indivisible operations, called transactions.

Universal DBMS Architecture: An architecture based on a mapping model consisting from five abstraction layers.

Chapter 15
New Model for Geospatial Coverages in JSON:
Coverage Implementation Schema and Its Implementation With JavaScript

Joan Maso
CREAF, Spain

Alaitz Zabala Torres
Universitat Autonoma de Barcelona, Spain

Peter Baumann
Jacobs University, Germany

ABSTRACT

Map browsers currently in place present maps and geospatial information using common image formats such as JPEG or PNG, usually created from a service on demand. This is a clear approach for a simple visualization map browser but prevents the browser from modifying the visualization since the content of the image file represents the intensity of colors of each pixel. In a desktop GIS, a coverage dataset is an array of values quantifying a certain property in each pixel of a subdomain of the space. The standard used to describe and distribute coverages is called web coverage service (WCS). Traditionally, encoding of coverages was too complex for map browsers implemented in JavaScript, relegating the WCS to a data download, a process that creates a file that will be later used in a desktop GIS. The combination of a coverage implementation schema in JSON, binary arrays, and HTML5 canvas makes it possible that web map browsers can be directly implemented in JavaScript.

DOI: 10.4018/978-1-5225-8446-9.ch015

INTRODUCTION

In geospatial computer science geospatial information is mainly divided into two data models feature data (covering mainly vector data) and coverage data (covering mainly raster data). Feature data in JSON has been covered by the IETF RFC 7946 GeoJSON Format. This Chapter focuses on coverage data. Traditionally, aerial photographs, land cover maps, digital elevation models, etc have been encoded as a sequence of values in binary files, such as GeoTIFF. Geospatial Information Systems (GIS) required a better description for the spatio-temporal domain where these multidimensional arrays were situated (georeferenced) and about the exact meaning and restrictions of its values. The term "coverage" is defined in [ISO19123] as a family of data models based on a "feature that acts as a function to return values from its range for any direct position within its spatial, temporal or spatiotemporal domain" – in practice, spatio-temporal regular and irregular grids, point clouds, and general meshes. In other words, a coverage maps a distribution of space positions and time instants to a set of data values. For example, an UAV photograph can be modeled as a coverage that maps positions on the ground to the colors of the surface of the earth. A climate model maps a multidimensional grid (horizontal space coordinates, elevation, and time) to values of temperature, wind speed, humidity, etc.

Traditionally, encoding of coverages was too complex for web map browsers implemented in JavaScript, relegating the Open Geospatial Consortium (OGC) Web Coverage Service (WCS) standard to a data download; a process that creates a file that will be later used in a desktop GIS. To remedy this, the Chapter on hand presents an implementation that uses a combination of the Coverage Implementation Schema (CIS) in JSON, binary arrays, HTML5 canvas, and JSON styling rules, which makes possible that web map browsers can directly implement support to coverage visualization and analysis using only JavaScript code.

Based on the modern capabilities of the Web standards such as HTML5 and JavaScript, this Chapter describes the CIS standardized by the OGC which comes with a JSON encoding and compares it to a different recent initiative called CoverageJSON. Our modeling of JSON coverages, which is a main topic of this paper, is part of the OGC CIS version 1.1 standard.

BACKGROUND

Coverages represent homogeneous collections of values located in space/time, such as spatio-temporal sensor, image, simulation, and statistics data. Common examples include measures by a static sensor of a variable over time (1-D time series), optical satellite imagery (2-D imagery), series of geometrically corrected satellite images (3-D x/y/t time series), a interpolation representing the temperature distribution of the atmosphere (x/y/z geophysical voxel models), and a simulation representing the evolution of the temperature of the atmosphere over time (4-D x/y/z/t models). Coverages encompass multi-dimensional regular and irregular grids, point clouds, and general meshes. [Baumann et al, 2017]

Often the word "coverage" is used a synonymous of "gridded data", "raster data" or "imagery". Even if the three expressions are examples of coverages, this is not the whole picture. For example, non-gridded data (like a river gauge time series) can also be modeled as a coverage. Generally, the concept of *coverages* encompasses spatio-temporal regular and irregular grids (both discrete and continuous), point clouds, and general meshes.

The OGC Geography Markup Language (GML) (Portele, 2007) mainly focuses on feature data but also provides foundational elements to describe coverages in XML. Following literally the common practices for feature data, it requires the creation of a GML Application Schema (and specialized form of XML Schema) for each coverage type. The definition of Application Schemas has some degrees of freedom and, if we combine this with the lack of easy to find GML Application Schemas catalogues, the risk is that descriptions of the same kind of information done by different organizations result in different data structures, preventing interoperability. It also makes the implementation of applications more difficult because software programmers need to anticipate all possible variations of the Application Schemas.

The Coverage Implementation Schema (CIS) (Baumann, et al. 2017) is an Open Geospatial Consortium (OGC) standard where a coverage model by establishing as a concrete, interoperable, conformance-testable single coverage structure. CIS is interoperable in the sense that coverages can be conformance tested, regardless of their data format encoding, down to the level of single "pixels" or "voxels".

CIS allows for creating coverage descriptions of grid information encoded in common binary formats such as GeoTIFF, JPEG200 or NetCDF or in ASCII formats such as GML or JSON (Bray T., 2014). A coverage can be partitioned in more than one file. Coverages can be accessed through a variety of OGC services types, such as the Web Coverage Service (WCS) Standard suite (Baumann, 2017).

The services providing coverages were designed as downloading and server-side processing and analytics services capable of providing excerpts from coverages for analysis in your favorite GIS, RS or modeling tool. They were not originally designed for visualization and fast analysis in a web browser. In the last part of this Chapter we discuss how to use CIS encoded in JSON, combined with new functionalities of HTML5 such as raw binary arrays to communicate data in ways that can be consumed by modern web browsers directly (Maso et al 2018).

COVERAGE IMPLEMENTATION SCHEMA

The CIS defines a coverage as the combination of different *elements* that together from the data model. For example, in a grid coverage, the most common elements are: domainSet, rangeSet, rangeType and metadata. A coverage is defined by the existence of one or more axes in space/time or with "abstract" axes such as spectral range. In a *Grid Coverage*, on top of these axes, we define a multidimensional grid by specifying a set of points (or cells) in this grid that defines a *domainSet* in multidimensional space. Some *Discrete Coverage* specialization has no grid but a list of geometrical objects presenting positions in a multidimensional space. In a *Grid Coverage,* each grid cell will receive a value, and in a generalized Discrete Coverage each geometric object will receive a value which can be atomic or a composite record. All values share some common characteristics and limitations that are documented in a *rangeType*; for example, one of the most useful characteristic is the data type (e.g. floating point numbers), possibly with limits on the interval of values occurring in the coverage. Finally, the actual list of values that populates the grid or the geometrical objects is defined in the *rangeSet*. Additional *metadata* might complete the set, holding arbitrary ancillary information. *DomainSet* and *rangeType* are commonly present in a CIS document (that might be encoded in XML or in JSON), while the rangeSet list of values can be stored within this encoding, or alternatively can be referenced by the CIS "root" document and stored in some other format, such as a well known binary file format such as a NetCDF, a GeoTIFF or a JPEG2000 or can be simply stored in a RAW format as a sequence of binary values of a fixed size. If that is the case, the CIS "root" document is normally a short text document while the binary file containing the *rangeSet* is commonly a big file. Following the CIS standard, these files are combined through some "container format" such as MIME attachments (CIS 1.0) or any other suitable format like ZIP, SAFE (http://earth. esa.int/SAFE), etc. (CIS 1.1).

In this Chapter we will detail some examples of coverages and the corresponding JSON encoding. An XML and RDF encoding have also been defined by the OGC CIS 1.1 standard but its description will not be part of this book Chapter – see Bauman (2017b) for more details. The reader can refer to the OGC Schema repository (in http://schemas.opengis.net/cis/json/examples-1.1) to find the examples as JSON files (as well as the same examples in XML encoding in http://schemas.opengis.net/cis/gml/ examples-1.1).

UML Models Used in This Chapter

The CIS model is defined independently from the final encoding in UML class and object diagrams (Benson, 2016). Class diagrams are useful to describe the data types and relations among them and object diagrams are useful to show concrete examples. We limit to a set of characteristics in class and object diagrams exemplified in Figure 1.

Objects are instantiated from classes and values are assigned to their attributes. A class can be extended into another class by specifying new attributes. The extended class is related to the previous one by a *generalization* relation, represented by a continuous line with a triangle in the more general class extreme (see Class1 and AbstractClass1 in the diagram). Attribute types are specified as simple types or as complex types. Complex types can be defined as an independent class with *Data Type* stereotype and reused as many times as needed (see *Class4* and *attribute4* in the diagram). Complex types can also

Figure 1. Class, object and relation UML diagram

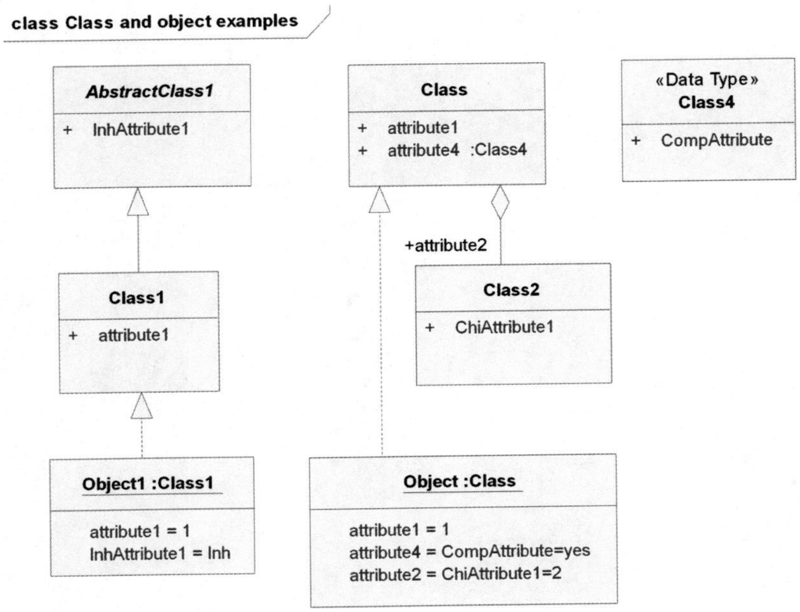

be defined on the fly by an *association* or a *composition* relation where an attribute name is used as the source name of the association or the composition (see *attribute2* associated to *Class* and defined as *Class2* in the diagram). There is no practical difference between the two approaches but the later is uses as much as possible for clarity (see how the *Object* has both complex type approaches in the diagram).

These diagrams follow the ISO TC211 Best Practices for UML diagram design (Jetlund K, 2015). The only exception is the *realization* relation. Realization is used between classes of different levels of abstraction or between a class and interfaces. In this chapter we are using the *realization* with a slightly different semantics to relate classes and their instantiation in objects (see *Object1* and *Class1* in the figure 1). We find this informative in diagrams showing concrete objects with attribute values that are implementing the related class.

A coverage can have several attributes including an id, an envelope, a domainSet, a rangeSet a rangeType an 0 or more metadata (Figure 2). In the following subsections we will review these and other options that the CIS model can offer.

Rules for Generating JSON Encoding From UML Based on the CIS Schema

A set of generic rules to transform UML class models into JSON Schemas and encodings was proposed the OGC Testbed 12 (Maso, 2017). One of the innovations presented in this Chapter is to apply them to generate JSON encodings and JSON Schemas based on the UML class model for the CIS. This work has become the JSON encoding part of CIS 1.1 standard recently approved by the OGC. A coverage is the root of the JSON files presented in this chapter. In JSON there is no name for the root element but the first attribute of the root object is the type of object: "CoverageByDomainAndRangeType". The general rules for transforming UML Class diagrams into JSON Schemas and objects can be summarized as follows: Each attribute in the UML model becomes an extra attribute of a JSON object. Each *association* or *composition* in the UML model becomes an attribute in the JSON model (that will be of

Figure 2. AbstractCoverage structure in CIS
Source: OGC 09-146r6

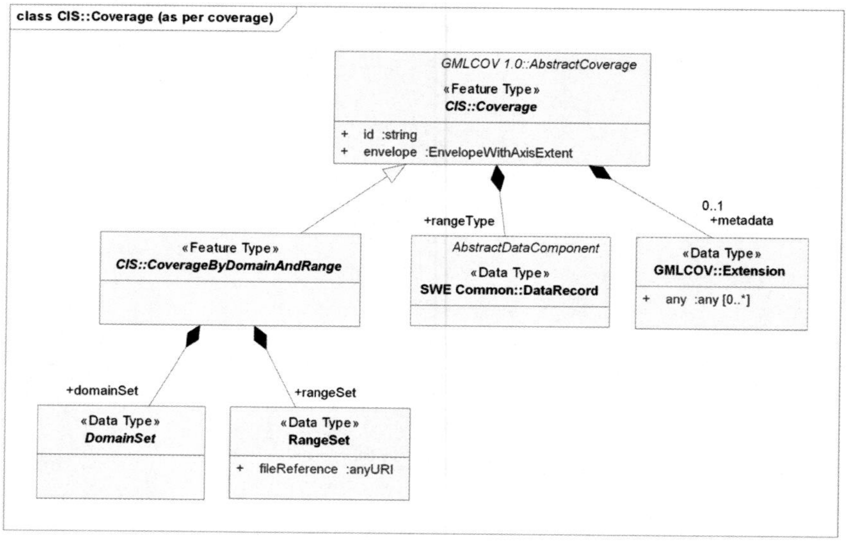

JSON "object" type). Simple attributes types in the model are mapped to the closest simple type in JSON (e.g. a *floating point* is encoded as a *number*). An element with multiplicity more than one becomes a JSON array. Attributes in the UML classes that are complex classes are also encoded as objects with the name of the class as a value of the "type" attribute. In case a class is a generalization of another, the most concrete one is used as "type" attribute value. For convenience, each object receives a unique identifier. The inclusion of id and type as properties of all JSON objects rules where designed to ensure proper compatibility with JSON-LD (Sporny, et al. 2014). This book Chapter presents these rules into practice in the examples for the CIS 1.1 developed in the next subsections. It is worth mentioning that other authors have made efforts to go in the opposite direction: the creation UML models for JSON documents (Izquierdo, 2016).

Grid Coverages

One of the most common coverages is the gridded coverage type. Gridded coverages have a grid as their domain set describing the direct positions in multi-dimensional coordinate space. The geometrical distribution of the values in a coverage encoded in a domainSet can have a regular or an irregular distribution. A raw image that has been captured from a satellite (sometimes called "swath data") is described by an irregular grid, because the values recorded are subjected to geometrical deformations of the optical system and to the effects of the variations on the elevation of the terrain. By executing a process called geometrical correction, deformations in the structure of the irregular grid can be determined and it can be compensated and data can be remapped into a regular grid. Spatial agencies and cartographic institutes distributing imagery provide regular grids that have already been rectified.

Regular Grid

Gridded coverages have a grid as their domain set describing the direct positions in multi-dimensional coordinate space, depending on the type of the grid. Here we describe the regular grids described by the axes they are composed of. Positions are defined by the interactions of the spaces defined in each axis. Axes can be defined as index axes or regular axes. An index axis allows only integer coordinates with spacing ("resolution") of 1. In contrast, regular axes can express a sampling common distance, i.e.: resolution, as a part of the axis definition (Figure 3).

In figure 4 we see a representation of a regular grid formed by indexAxis defining 9 cells by the intersection of 3 spaces in each axis.

Figure 5 illustrates the case of an image that is defined in a domain of 2 index axes both setting 3 steps, configuring grid of 3x3=9 cells. The use of index axes makes sense in an image has no associated any Coordinate Reference System (CRS) that places the image in the Earth, and cells are addressed by counting cells in the grid in both dimensions.

JSON is not a class based encoding because it does not natively incorporate the definition of concrete complex data *types*. Nevertheless, it permits construction of complex *objects* on-the-fly. This means that only the lower part of the model in figure 5 can be directly encoded in JSON. We defined objects that contain a property "type" that reproduces the class name they are based on. The following code is the transcription in JSON of the Figure 4. The rangeType part is included for completeness but its content is not reproduced because it will be described later in this chapter.

Figure 3. GeneralGridCoverage structure as per grid-regular
Source: OGC 09-146r6

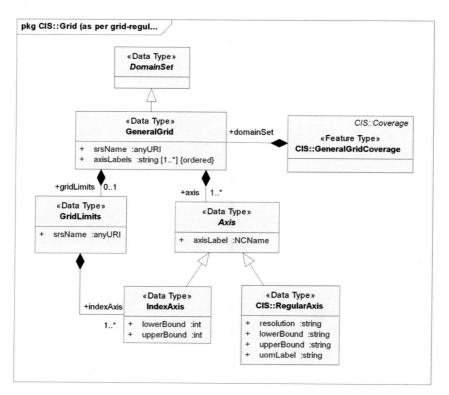

Figure 4. Representation of a 2D coverage with IndexAxis

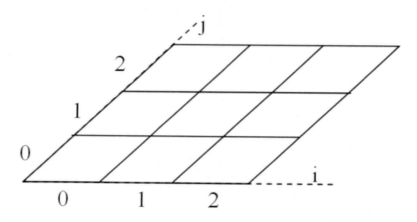

```
{
        "type": "CoverageByDomainAndRangeType",
        "id": "examples:CIS_05_2D",
        "domainSet":{
                "type": "GeneralGridType",
```

Figure 5. Description of a coverage with IndexAxis

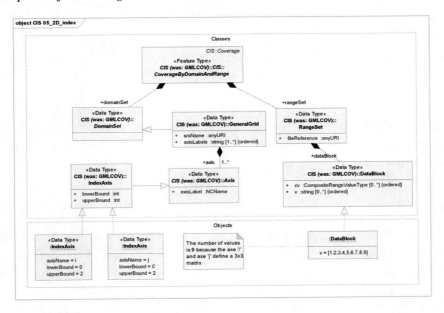

```
        "id": "examples:CIS_DS_05_2D",
        "srsName": "http://www.opengis.net/def/crs/OGC/0/Index2D",
        "axisLabels": ["i", "j"],
        "axis": [{
                "type": "IndexAxisType",
                "id": "examples:CIS_DS_GG_I_05_2D",
                "axisLabel": "i",
                "lowerBound": 0,
                "upperBound": 2
        },{
                "type": "IndexAxisType",
                "id": "examples:CIS_DS_GG_J_05_2D",
                "axisLabel": "j",
                "lowerBound": 0,
                "upperBound": 2
        }]
},
"rangeSet": {
        "type": "RangeSetType",
        "id": "examples:CIS_RS_05_2D",
        "dataBlock": {
                "id": "examples:CIS_RS_DB_05_2D",
                "type": "VDataBlockType",
                "values": [1,2,3,4,5,6,7,8,9]
```

```
                }
        },
        "rangeType": {
                ...
        }
}
```

Regular grids can also be described by regular axis where cells are defined as regularly spaced by a common distance, called resolution. In practice, this means that by specifying the start value, the end value and the resolution, all positions on the axes are defined.

Irregular Grids

An irregular grid can be defined through other types of axes. We will start by introducing the irregular axis that abandons the equidistant spacing of a regular axis. Therefore, all direct positions along such an axis must be enumerated explicitly which is achieved by replacing the lower bound / resolution / upper bound scheme by an ordered list of direct positions (h axis in figure 6).

Figure 7 illustrates an image that is defined in a domain of 3 dimension represented by 2 regular axes and one irregular axis, configuring grid of 3x3x3=27 cells. The domain is associated to a CRS that places the "cube" in the Earth. To map the actual cells with the domain set, a grid limits 3D data structured of index axes is also defined. The 27 values are provided in the rangeSet.

The following code is the transcription in JSON of the Figure 7.

Figure 6. A 3D coverage with 2 regularAxis defining cells in latitude and longitude and 1 irregularAxis representing 3 levels of elevation.

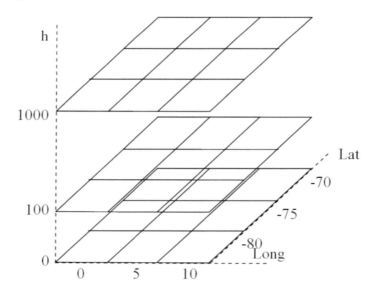

Figure 7. Description of a 3D coverage with two RegurlaAxis and one IrregularAxis

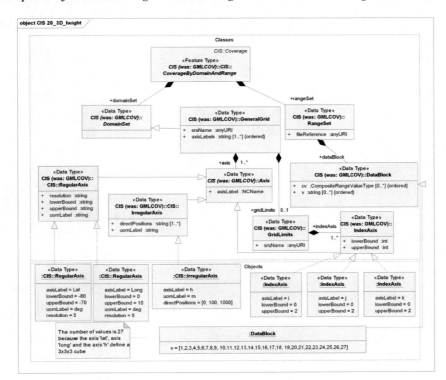

```
{           "type": "CoverageByDomainAndRangeType",           "id":
"examples:CIS_20_3D",           "domainSet":{                "type":
"GeneralGridType",           "id": "examples:CIS_
DS_20_3D",           "srsName": "http://www.opengis.net/def/
crs/EPSG/0/4979",           "axisLabels": ["Lat", "Long",
"h"],           "axis": [{                "type":
"RegularAxisType",           "id":
"examples:CIS_DS_GG_LAT_20_3D",           "ax-
isLabel": "Lat",           "lowerBound":
-80,           "upperBound": -70,           "uom-
Label": "deg",           "resolution":
5           },{           "type": "Regu-
larAxisType",           "id": "examples:CIS_
DS_GG_LONG_20_3D",           "axisLa-
bel": "Long",           "lowerBound":
0,           "upperBound": 10,           "uom-
Label": "deg",           "resolu-
tion": 5           },{           "t
ype": "IrregularAxisType",           "id":
"examples:CIS_DS_GG_H_20_3D",           "axisLabel":
```

```
"h",                          "uomLabel": "m",                          "co-
ordinate": [0, 100, 1000]                    }],                    "grid-
Limits": {                          "type":
"GridLimitsType",                          "id": "examples:CIS_
DS_GG_GL_20_3D",                          "srsName": "http://www.
opengis.net/def/crs/OGC/0/Index3D",                    "ax-
isLabels": ["i", "j", "k"],                    "in-
dexAxis": [{                          "type": "In-
dexAxisType",                          "id":
"examples:CIS_DS_GG_GL_I_20_3D",                          "ax-
isLabel": "i",                          "lower-
Bound": 0,                          "upperBound":
2                          },{
"type": "IndexAxisType",                          "id":
"examples:CIS_DS_GG_GL_J_20_3D",                          "ax-
isLabel": "j",                          "lower-
Bound": 0,                          "upperBound":
2                          },{
"type": "IndexAxisType",                          "id":
"examples:CIS_DS_GG_GL_K_20_3D",                          "ax-
isLabel": "k",                          "lower-
Bound": 0,                          "upperBound":
2                          }]                    }          },          "rang-
eSet": {                    "type": "RangeSetType",                    "id":
"examples:CIS_RS_20_3D",                    "data-
Block": {                          "id": "examples:CIS_RS_DB
_20_3D",                          "type": "VDataBlock-
Type",                          "values": [1,2,3,4,5,6,7,8,9,
10,11,12,13,14,15,16,
                                        17,18,
19,20,21,22,23,24,25,26,27]                    }          },          "rangeType":
{                    ...                    }  }
```

Displaced Grids

A displaced grid consists of building axis groups, informally called "nests", within which the coordinates of direct positions are not tied to the crossing points of "straight" grid lines. Instead, coordinates can vary freely; however, the topological neighbourhood relationship is retained. can be defined as by some other types of axis (Figure 8).

Figure 9 illustrates the case of an image that is defined in a domain of 3 dimension represented by a displaced nest, configuring grid of 9 cells defined by direct positions in the space. This nest is mapped to a 2D grid. The 3D grid is mapped into the cells of grid of 2D index axes with 3 positions each. The 9 values are provided in the rangeSet.

Figure 8. Representation of a 2D coverage defining a displaced grids of 2 axes.

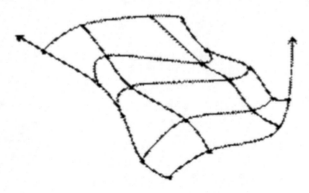

Figure 9. Description a 3D coverage in a displaced grid nest

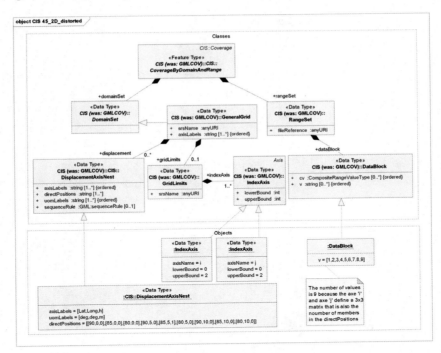

The following code is the transcription in JSON of the Figure 9.

```
{
        "type": "CoverageByDomainAndRangeType",
        "id": "examples:CIS_45_2D",
        "domainSet":{
                "type": "GeneralGridType",
                "id": "examples:CIS_DS_45_2D",
                "srsName": "http://www.opengis.net/def/crs/EPSG/0/4979",
```

```
                "axisLabels": ["Lat", "Long", "h"],
                "displacement": {
                        "type": "DisplacementAxisNestType",
                        "id": "examples:CIS_DS_GG_D_45_2D",
                        "axisLabels": ["Lat", "Long", "h"],
                        "uomLabels": ["deg", "deg", "m"],
                        "coordinates": [[90, 0, 0], [85, 0, 0], [80, 0, 0],
[90, 5, 0], [85, 5, 1], [80, 5, 0], [90, 10, 0], [85, 10, 0], [80, 10, 0]]
                },
                "gridLimits": {
                        "type": "GridLimitsType",
                        "id": "examples:CIS_DS_GG_GL_45_2D",
                        "srsName": "http://www.opengis.net/def/crs/OGC/0/In-
dex1D",
                        "axisLabels": ["i", "j"],
                        "axis": [{
                                "type": "IndexAxisType",
                                "id": "examples:CIS_DS_GG_GL_I_45_2D",
                                "axisLabel": "i",
                                "lowerBound": 0,
                                "upperBound": 2
                        },{
                                "type": "IndexAxisType",
                                "id": "examples:CIS_DS_GG_GL_J_45_2D",
                                "axisLabel": "j",
                                "lowerBound": 0,
                                "upperBound": 2
                        }]
                }
        },
        "rangeSet": {
                "type": "RangeSetType",
                "id": "examples:CIS_RS_45_2D",
                "dataBlock": {
                        "id": "examples:CIS_RS_DB_45_2D",
                        "type": "VDataBlockType",
                        "values": [1,2,3,4,5,6,7,8,9]
                }
        },
        "rangeType": {
                ...
        }
}
```

RangeSet

The range set contains the actual values associated with one direct position as defined in the domainSet. There are as many values as direct positions in the domainSet and in the same order that they have been defined. In the examples provided so far, the values in the rangeSet are included directly in the JSON encoding as an array of values in the dataBlock object but this is not a common in practice. Coverages that describe a certain area of the space at a reasonable level of detail require a large array in the rangeSet. If we take the example of the Shuttle Radar Topographical Mission (SRTM), the elevations of the Earth were measured every 3 seconds of arc (approximately every 100m) almost for the entire planet. Considering that there are 20 values every minute of arc, to cover the Earth 77760000 values as needed. Having this list of values as a text array will make it too long. Commonly you would like to use only a part of it but in text encoding low numbers are encoded in less characters that large numbers, making random access to a part of the data impossible without sequentially having to read all previous values (Witayangkurn, 2012). For these reasons, coverages are traditionally stored in binary files that are more compact and can be randomly addressed. In addition, these files have powerful compression algorithms that make them even more compact. The CIS encoding provide an alternative way to link to external binary files.

Figure 10 reproduces the same example illustrated in Figure 5 but replacing the list of values in the rangeSet by a reference to a external file; in this case in tiff format.

Figure 10. RangeSet as a reference to a file.

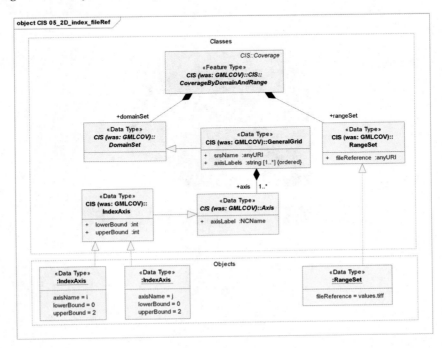

Coverage by Partitioning

Sometimes, to distribute or maintain the coverage in a single file is impractical. Examples are coverages that are tiled into smaller pieces (figure 11 shows one 1x1 degree fragment of the SRTM) or coverages representing temporal series where each time slide is stored in an independent file.

CIS provides a way to encode coverages that has its values arranged in more than one piece (more than one file) called coverageByPartitioning. Each partition is a fragment of a coverage that has the definition of the domainSet (the axes) replicated for each partition (Figure 12).

Figure 13 illustrates the case of an image that is defined in a domain of 3 dimension represented by 2 regular axes and one irregular axis. Each tile slide is defined by a partition that is stored in a different file.

The following code is the transcription in JSON of the Figure 13.

```
{
        "type": "CoverageByPartitioningType",
        "id": "examples:CIS_50_3D",
        "partitionSet":{
                "type": "PartitionSetType",
                "id": "examples:CIS_PS_50_3D",
                "partition":[{
                        "type": "PartitionRefType",
                        "id": "examples:CIS_PS_P1_50_3D",
```

Figure 11. Example of a 1x1 degree fragment of a SRTM v3 over Spain distributed as a single file
Source: https://earthexplorer.usgs.gov/

Data Set Attribute	Attribute Value
Entity ID	SRTM1N40W004V3
Acquisition Date	11-FEB-00
Publication Date	23-SEP-14
Resolution	1-ARC
Date Updated	
NW Corner Lat	41°00'00.00"N
NW Corner Long	4°00'00.00"W
NE Corner Lat	41°00'00.00"N
NE Corner Long	3°00'00.00"W
SE Corner Lat	40°00'00.00"N

Figure 12. Representation of a 3D coverage with 2 regularAxis defining cells in latitude and longitude and 1 irregularAxis representing 2 levels of time. Each time slide is defined in a different file

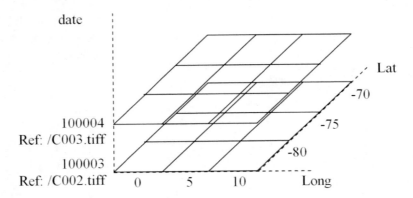

Figure 13. Description of a 3D coverage that is partitioned in 2 partitions stored in different files each one representing a different instant in time.

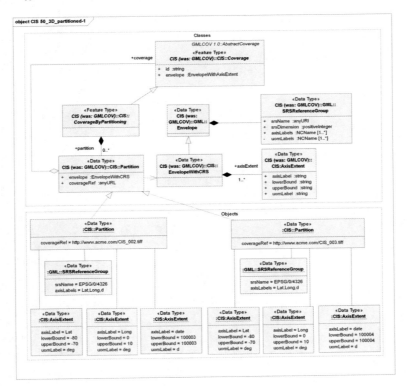

```
"envelope":{
        "type": "EnvelopeByAxisType",
        "id": "examples:CIS_PS_P1_E_50_3D",
        "srsName": "http://www.opengis.net/def/crs/
EPSG/0/4326",
```

```
                        "axisLabels": ["Lat", "Long", "d"],
                        "axis": [{
                                "type": "AxisExtentType",
                                "id": "examples:CIS_PS_P1_LAT_50_3D",
                                "axisLabel": "Lat",
                                "lowerBound": -80,
                                "upperBound": -70,
                                "uomLabel": "deg"
                        }, {
                                "type": "AxisExtentType",
                                "id": "examples:CIS_PS_P1_

LONG_50_3D",

                                "axisLabel": "Long",
                                "lowerBound": 0,
                                "upperBound": 10,
                                "uomLabel": "deg"
                        }, {
                                "type": "AxisExtentType",
                                "id": "examples:CIS_PS_P1_D_50_3D",
                                "axisLabel": "date",
                                "lowerBound": 100003,
                                "upperBound": 100003,
                                "uomLabel": "d"
                        }]
                },
                "coverageRef": "http://www.acme.com/CIS_002.tiff"
        }, {
                "type": "PartitionRefType",
                "id": "examples:CIS_PS_P2_50_3D",
                "envelope":{
                        "type": "EnvelopeByAxisType",
                        "id": "examples:CIS_PS_P2_E_50_3D",
                        "srsName": "http://www.opengis.net/def/crs/

EPSG/0/4326",

                        "axisLabels": ["Lat", "Long", "d"],
                        "axis": [{
                                "type": "AxisExtentType",
                                "id": "examples:CIS_PS_P2_LAT_50_3D",
                                "axisLabel": "Lat",
                                "lowerBound": -80,
                                "upperBound": -70,
                                "uomLabel": "deg"
                        }, {
                                "type": "AxisExtentType",
```

```
                                        "id": "examples:CIS_PS_P2_
LONG_50_3D",

                                        "axisLabel": "Long",
                                        "lowerBound": 0,
                                        "upperBound": 10,
                                        "uomLabel": "deg"
                        },{
                                        "type": "AxisExtentType",
                                        "id": "examples:CIS_PS_P2_D_50_3D",
                                        "axisLabel": "date",
                                        "lowerBound": 100004,
                                        "upperBound": 100004,
                                        "uomLabel": "d"
                        }]
                },
                "coverageRef": "http://www.acme.com/CIS_003.tiff"
            }]
        },
        "rangeType": {
                ...
        }
}
```

Discrete Coverages

The OGC coverage concept recognizes that beyond grids there are further kinds of coverages. The coverages that are not described by a grid are called *discrete coverages*; instead of containing points sitting on some grid they are composed of a bundle of some common vector geographical primitive of a specific dimension. In order of increasing dimensions, the domainSet can consist of a set of points (MultiPointCoverage), of curves (MultiCurveCoverage), of surfaces (MultiSurfaceCoverage), or of solids (MultiSolidCoverage). One recent application of this type of coverages that has become popular in recent years is the representation of a LIDAR campaign as a point cloud (Figure 14). While point clouds consist of a set of points like gridded data, the former do not have to be aligned to some grid as the latter do.

Figure 15 illustrates the case of a point cloud that is defined by a direct multi point of 3 dimensions. Each point has 3 values associated in the rangeSet.

The following code is the transcription in JSON of the Figure 15.

```
{
        "type": "MultiPointCoverageType",
        "id": "examples:CIS_90",
        "domainSet":{
                "type": "DirectMultiPointType",
                "id": "examples:CIS_DS_DMP_90",
```

Figure 14. Representation of a 3D coverage with a point cloud. The points are not arranged in a grid.

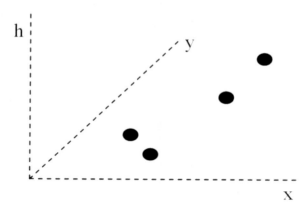

Figure 15. Description of a 3D point cloud that is defined by a direct multi point of 3 dimensions. Each point has 3 values associated in the rangeSet.

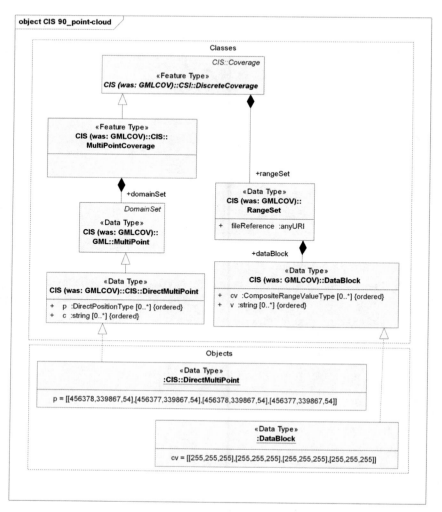

```
            "coordinates": [[456377.56, 339867.25, 53.95],
                                            [456377.50, 339867.22,
53.96],
                                            [456377.56, 339867.22,
53.95],
                                            [456377.50, 339867.22,
53.96]]
        },
        "rangeSet": {
                "type": "RangeSetType",
                "id": "examples:CIS_RS_90",
                "dataBlock": {
                        "id": "examples:CIS_RS_DB_90",
                        "type": "VDataBlockType",
                        "values": [[255,255,255],[255,255,255],[255,255,255],
[255,255,255]]
                }
        },
        "rangeType": {
                ...
        }
}
```

RangeType

Continuing with the example of satellite imagery, the values associated with each cell of the grid are related to the intensity of light received by the satellite at different frequencies. They do not directly represent any magnitude of the Earth surface or the atmosphere because reflections and absorptions of the light in its path has distorted them. Fortunately, there are ways to compensate for does effects. In the part, this compensation was done by the final user but now remote sensing agencies are doing the correction by themselves distributing what is called "analysis ready data". Whatever the process the new values gain semantics and this semantics needs to be recorded in the CIS model. The rangeType element of a coverage describes the semantics and type restrictions of the coverage's range set data structure. In the case of imagery, one expected information included is the "pixel data type"). Such a type often consists of one or more *fields* (also referred to as *bands* or *channels* or *variables*), however, much more general definitions are possible. The rangeType structure is based on the SWE Common DataRecord (Robin, 2011) allowing mapping sensor observations to coverages without loss of semantics. Figure 16 describes the values associated to the grid or the features. This way we expect that all cells of the grid or features to be of the same data type and have the same restrictions. The descriptions include the name of the properties, the null values (also called nilValues; that are values reserved to represented cells that were not measured or had a out of range value), the allowed values (allowedValues), the data quality and the value units (uom). The original data types (e.g. SWE Common Quantity), as imported from the SWE Common standard, also contain an attribute for specifying a constant *value. This value*

Figure 16. Description of the rangeType part of the CIS model.

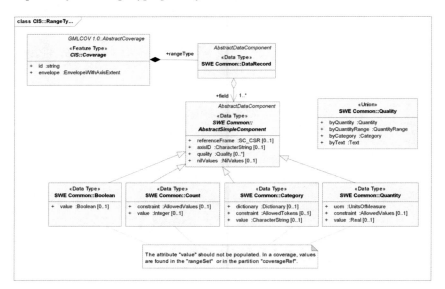

is not going to be used by the CIS; as we have reiteratively explained, values are expected to be found in the coverage rangeSet.

Figure 17 illustrates the case of a coverage where each grid cell or discrete coverage feature receives 3 values. The coverage is defining read, green and blue intensities in *digital numbers* that has a depth of 256 possibilities of brightness.

The following code is the transcription in JSON of the Figure 17. The rangeSet part was already exemplified previously and it is included only for completeness.

```
{
        "domainSet":{
                ...
        },
        "rangeSet": {
                "type": "RangeSetType",
                "dataBlock": {
                        "type": "VDataBlockType",
                        "values": [[255,255,255],[255,255,255],[255,255,255],
[255,255,255]]
                }
        },
        "rangeType": {
                "type": "DataRecordType",
                "field": [{
                        "type": "QuantityType",
                        "label": "red",
```

Figure 17. Description of the rangeType formed by 3 channels labelled red, green and blue.

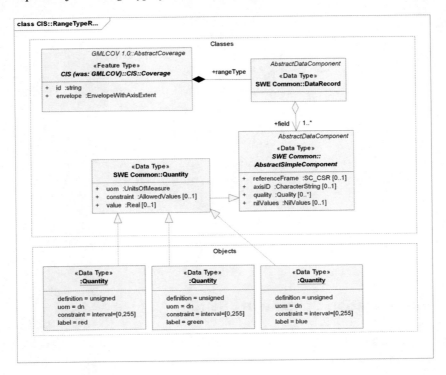

```
        "definition": "ogcType:unsigned",
        "uom": {
                "type": "UnitReference",
                "code": "dn"
        },
        "constraint": {
                "type": "AllowedValues",
                "interval": [0, 255]
        }
}, {
        "type": "QuantityType",
        "label": "green",
        "definition": "ogcType:unsigned",
        "uom": {
                "type": "UnitReference",
                "code": "dn"
        },
        "constraint": {
                "type": "AllowedValues",
                "interval": [0, 255]
        }
```

```
        },{
                "type": "QuantityType",
                "label": "blue",
                "definition": "ogcType:unsigned",
                "uom": {
                        "type": "UnitReference",
                        "code": "dn"
                },
                "constraint": {
                        "type": "AllowedValues",
                        "interval": [0, 255]
                }
        }]
    }
}
```

Coverage Implementation Schema in JSON

We have seen several examples of coverages encoded in JSON using CIS. JSON was defined as an object based encoding, as opposed to defining classes. CIS provides a JSON Schema validation designed to ensure that. All examples shown here can be validated against the JSON Schema that can be found in http://schemas.opengis.net/cis/1.1/json.

To understand the basics of the presented JSON Schema, we include a UML diagram (Figure 18) not showing anything new but is summarizing the different arrangements of the CIS model.

The equivalent JSON Schema describes the main structure of the JSON document. One of the characteristics that we immediately see is the number of times we are using a "oneOf" property to show different possibilities that a coverage has. Actually, each generalization forces a "oneOf" in the JSON Schema. This way, we can see that a coverage can be described by domainSet, rangeSet and rangeType (in the CoverageByDomainAndRange and in DiscreteCoverage) or by a envelop, partionSet and rangeType (in the CoverageByPartitioning). To be able to recycle the definitions of these elements, they are referenced to the definitions part of the Schema. Again, in the definition of a rangeSet we see another "oneOf" that present a choice between a dataBlock or a fileReference.

```
{
        "$schema": "http://json-schema.org/draft-04/schema#",
        "title": "Coverage object",
        "description": "Component of OGC Coverage Implementation Schema 1.1.
Last updated: 2016-may-18. Copyright (c) 2016 Open Geospatial Consortium, Inc.
All Rights Reserved. To obtain additional rights of use, visit http://www.
opengeospatial.org/legal/.",
        "type": "object",
        "oneOf": [{
                "required": [ "type", "domainSet", "rangeSet", "rangeType"],
```

Figure 18. Summary of all classes used in the previous examples.

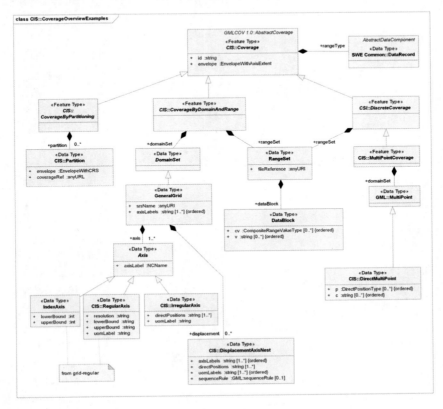

```
          "properties": {
                  "id": { "type": "string"},
                  "type": { "enum": [ "CoverageByDomainAndRangeType",
"MultiPointCoverageType" ] },
                  "envelope": { "$ref": "#/definitions/envelope" },
                  "domainSet": { "$ref": "#/definitions/domainSet" },
                  "rangeSet": { "$ref": "#/definitions/rangeSet" },
                  "rangeType": { "$ref": "#/definitions/rangeType" },
                  "metadata": { "$ref": "#/definitions/metadata" }
          }
     },{
          "required": [ "type", "partitionSet", "rangeType"],
          "properties": {
                  "id": { "type": "string"},
                  "type": { "enum": [ "CoverageByPartitioningType" ] },
                  "envelope": { "$ref": "#/definitions/envelope" },
                  "partitionSet": { "$ref": "#/definitions/partition-
Set" },
                  "rangeType": { "$ref": "#/definitions/rangeType" },
```

```
                  "metadata": { "$ref": "#/definitions/metadata" }
            }
      }],
      "definitions": {
            "envelope": {
                  ...
            },
            "domainSet": {
                  "title": "domainSet",
                  "description": "The domainSet describes the *direct
positions* of the coverage, i.e., the locations for which values are avail-
able.",
                  "oneOf": [
                  {
                        "description": "A general n-D grid is defined
through a sequence of axes, each of which can be of a particular axis type.
Use only if the parent object is type: 'CoverageByDomainAndRangeType'.",
                        ...
                  },{
                        "title": "domainSetMultiPoint",
                        "description": "The domainSet describes the
*direct positions* of the coverage, i.e., the locations for which values are
available. Use only if the parent object is type: 'MultiPointCoverageType'.",
                        "oneOf": [
                        {
                              "required": [ "type", "coordinates"
],
                              ...
                        },{
                              "required": [ "type", "fileReference"],
                              ...
                        }]
            },
            "rangeSet": {
                  "title": "rangeSet",
                  "description": "The rangeSet lists a value ",
                  "type": "object",
                  "oneOf": [{
                        "required": [ "type", "dataBlock"],
                        ...
                  },
                  {
                        "required": [ "type", "fileReference"],
                        "properties": {
```

```
                                                    "type": { "enum": [ "RangeSetRe-
fType"] },
                                                    "fileReference": { "type": "string",
"format": "uri" }
                                       }
                             }]
                    },
                    "partitionSet": {
                             "title": "Partitioning Set",
                             "type": "object",
                             ...
                    },
                    "rangeType": {
                             "title": "rangeType",
                             "description": "The rangeType element describes the
structure and semantics of a coverage's range values, including (optionally)
restrictions on the interpolation allowed on such values.",
                             "type": "object",
                             "oneOf": [{
                                      "required": [ "type", "field"],
                                      "properties": {
                                               "type": { "enum": [ "DataRecordType"]
},
                                               ...
                                      }
                             }
                    },{
                                      "required": [ "type", "fileReference" ],
                                      ...
                                      }
                             }]
                    },
                    "metadata": {
                             "title": "Metadata",
                             "type": "object"
                    }
          }
}
```

In addition to the Schema, in the OGC Schemas repository we can also find JSON Context documents that are used in CIS instances to describe the JSON files in a way that a JSON-LD engine can automatically transform the JSON CIS documents to a RDF encoding.

CoverageJSON

CoverageJSON is an alternative initiative for expressing coverages in JSON developed in a joint W3C-OGC effort that takes the work within the MELODIES project as a starting point. The objective is to develop a well-structured, consistent and easy-to-use JSON format for coverages that is able to encode many different kinds of coverage, including multidimensional grids, time series, vertical profiles, polygon-based coverages, point clouds and more. (Blower, et al. 2016).

In CoverageJSON, a Coverage consists of the following objects:

- One *domain* which encodes the set of points in space and time for which we have data values (a grid or a discrete series of geometrical features); equivalent to the domainSet in CIS.
- An array of *ranges* (one per scalar quantity or field), holding an array of actual data values; one per grid cell or geometrical feature; equivalent to the rangeSet in CIS.
- An array of *parameters* objects (one per scalar quantity), describing the data value type; equivalent to the rangeType in CIS.
- An optional array of *parameterGroup* objects, which describe the semantic associations between *parameters*.

The following example encodes a 4 dimensional gridded coverage with two fields (Sea Ice concentration and Land Cover) To elaborate it we have merged of two examples in the CoverageJSON playground: https://covjson.org/playground/)

```
{
  "type": "Coverage",
  "domain": {
    "type": "Domain",
    "domainType": "Grid",
    "axes": {
      "x": { "values": [-10,-5,0] },
      "y": { "values": [40,50] },
      "z": { "values": [ 5] },
      "t": { "values": ["2010-01-01T00:12:20Z"] }
    },
  },
  "parameters": [{
    "ICEC": {
      "type": "Parameter",
      "description": {
              "en": "Sea Ice concentration (ice=1;no ice=0)"
      },
      "unit": {
        "label": {
          "en": "Ratio"
        },
```

```json
      "symbol": {
        "value": "1",
        "type": "http://www.opengis.net/def/uom/UCUM/"
      }
    },
    "observedProperty": {
      "id": "http://vocab.nerc.ac.uk/standard_name/sea_ice_area_fraction/",
      "label": {
        "en": "Sea Ice Concentration"
      }
    }
  }
},{
  "LC": {
    "type": "Parameter",
    "description": {
      "en": "Land Cover according to xyz classification"
    },
    "observedProperty": {
      "id": "http://example.com/landcover",
      "label": {
        "en": "XYZ Land Cover"
      },
      "categories": [{
        "id": "http://example.com/landcover/categories/grass",
        "label": {
          "en": "Grass"
        },
        "description": {
          "en": "Very green grass."
        },
        "preferredColor": "#01A611"
      }, {
        "id": "http://example.com/landcover/categories/rocks",
        "label": {
          "en": "Rock"
        },
        "description": {
          "en": "Just rocks."
        },
        "preferredColor": "#A0A0A0"
      }]
    },
    "categoryEncoding": {
      "http://example.com/landcover/categories/grass": 1,
```

```
          "http://example.com/landcover/categories/rocks": 2
        }
      }
  }],
  "ranges": [{
    "ICEC": {
      "type": "NdArray",
      "dataType": "float",
      "axisNames": ["t","z","y","x"],
      "shape": [1, 1, 2, 3],
      "values": [ 0.5, 0.6, 0.4, 0.6, 0.2, null ]
    }
  },{
    "LC": {
      "type": "NdArray",
      "dataType": "integer",
      "axisNames": ["t","y","x"],
      "shape": [1, 2, 3],
      "values": [ 1, 1, null, 2, 1, 2 ]
    }
  }]
}
```

Comparing CIS JSON With CoverageJSON

The W3C Spatial Data on the Web Working Group has established CoverageJSON is an alternative JSON encoding of a concept named coverages, although it is structurally incompatible with the one accepted by the OGC coverages group; both should not be confused. We briefly discuss CoverageJSON in the sequel.

Both encodings look similar in the concepts and in the structure of the root element. Many differences are only superficial consisting in a different naming and grouping of properties. Nevertheless there are some fundamental difference between CIS JSON and CoverageJSON that are worth mentioning.

- CIS model uses a different object for grid coverages and discrete coverages (non-gridded coverages), whereas CoverageJSON uses the same object with internal differences.
- CIS allows each coverage to have exactly one CRS, whereas CoverageJSON allows different CRSs to be applied to different sets of coordinates in the domain (e.g. one CRS for x and y, and another CRS for z). The CIS approach is to define a composite CRS which encompasses all axes in a uniform manner, both they space or time.
- Version 1.1 of CIS defines a JSON encoding that uses a near-literal translation of the UML model that has its origins in GML structures (that were originally inspired by ISO 19123). CoverageJSON does not use GML as starting point and does not define any conceptual model. Instead it takes ISO 19123 as starting point and directly suggests a JSON encoding.

- CIS uses SWE Common to encode value types directly allowing for documenting data quality at the coverage field level and indirectly grid cell level quality. CoverageJSON focus on including grid cell statistical uncertainties.

- CoverageJSON includes default symbolization and category descriptions (for example for a land cover map classes) that are not available in the CIS encoding in JSON. CIS is engineered more specific and expects domain specific items to be added through extensions or application profiles (such as EO-WCS for satellite imagery and MetOcean-WCS for atmospheric data).

VISUALIZING AND ANALYZING COVERAGES ON THE WEB

The CIS coverage encoding and coverage services can be used to build a smart geospatial visualization web client replacing the traditional way of using a WMS service to send pictorial representations of maps to the client. This innovative approach is used in the H2020 ECOPotential web map browser, Protected Areas from Space: http://maps.ecopotential-project.eu/ (Figure 19) but it is also offered as a generic open source project in the GitHub (https://github.com/joanma747/MiraMonMapBrowser).

This web map client requests several coverage datasets from a server as arrays of gridded values for each coverage in the client. In the client side, the user can interact with a JavaScript based interface generating a on the fly visual representations based on CIS rangeSet data values. The advantage is that once the client has the CIS rangeSet data values it can do much more than simple data visualization, for example statistical calculations on what is in the screen or performing pixel based operations among coverages from different sources (Maso et al 2018). The generic web map browser software can be adapted to a particular application (e.g. ECOPotential) by encoding a configuration file config.json. The config specifies generic properties of the map browser as well as the list of geospatial layers to be seen, the server to retrieve the data and the symbolization information needed to represent each layer on the screen.

Figure 19. Protected Areas from Space Map Browser, general overview.

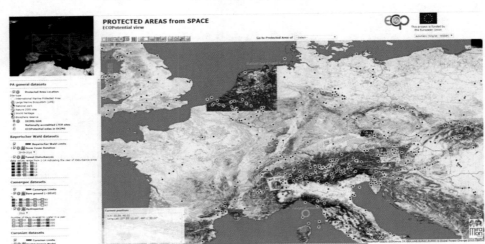

The web map client deals with several coverage types, such as quantitative, multiband and categorical coverages. In the area of Har Ha Negev Protected Area, an example of quantitative coverage is the Digital Terrain Model (DTM): a dataset that has values recording the elevation of each pixel. On the other hand, an example of multiband (as well as multitemporal) coverage is an image obtained by the Sentinel 2 satellite (from the ESA Copernicus program) which shows values for several available bands, covering different regions of the electromagnetic spectrum (13 bands for OLI sensor). An example of categorical coverage is the Land Use where each integer numerical value corresponds to a land use class (e.g. Natural Surface) (Figure 20).

Coverage Request and Storage

A map in the screen area has a stack of several overlaying transparent canvases of the exact same size, each one representing data coming from a coverage from a server. The JavaScript code uses the domain-Set information (mainly the bounding box coordinates and the fixed number of columns and rows of the canvas) to elaborate a request to a service that responses with a rangeSet with values corresponding one-to-one to the pixels of a map area in the screen. Web service response is sent in an asynchronous mode using the XMLHttpRequest() function configured for binary array responses:

Figure 20. Several coverage types and their legends for the Har Ha Negev Protected Area. Left: DTM (quantitative coverage); Center: Sentinel 2 image (multiband - coverage); Right: Land use (categorical coverage).

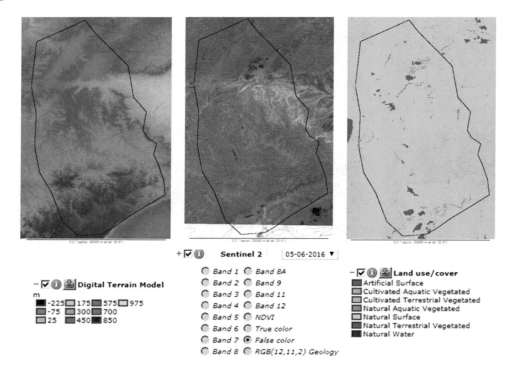

```
var xhr = new XMLHttpRequest();
xhr.onreadystatechange = function(){
if (xhr.readyState ===
        XMLHttpRequest.DONE &&
        xhr.status === 200)
        {
                // xhr.response contains the
                // binary array
        }
}
xhr.open("GET", path, true);
xhr.responseType = "arraybuffer";
xhr.send();
```

The web server generates a raw format with no headers but just values as a little-endian binary sequence. We avoid using a GeoTIFF file or similar because it will require considerably more work in the client side. Using the new JavaScript array buffer object, the data can be stored in a variable and accessed by creating a new DataView() object. Then, depending on the data type (contained in the CIS rangeType) of the binary values, values are extracted:

```
var dv=DataView(arrayBuffer);
var i_byte=(ncol*ifil+icol)
if (datatype=="uint16")
        getUint16(i_byte*2, true);
else if (datatype=="float32")
        getFloat32(i_byte*4, true);
else if ...
```

Next step is to represent the data in the map area of the screen. The binary arrays returned cannot be send directly to the canvas and are adapted to the appropriate format required by createImageData() function.

Coverage Encoding in the Client

Coverage Values Description

Each coverage in the client is described as an entry in the config.json file. For the sake of brevity we limit its description to the parameters needed to understand how to convert the rangeSet into RGB colors for the canvas. The information on the full composition of this file can be found in the config-schema. json document that is used not only for validation purposes but also as documentation.

When the image format is set to *application/x-img*, the client is aware that a coverage will be used and that certain other information (such as color palettes) will be described in the client. A *values* array contains a simplification of the information extracted from the rangeType information, consisting on the *data type*, *nodata* values and the compression format (currently limited to *none* or simple Run-Length-Encoding; RLE). See a DTM example:

```
"ImageFormat": "application/x-img",
"values": [{
        "compression": "RLE",
        "datatype": "int16",
        "nodata": [-9999]
}]
```

For multiband coverages (Sentinel 2 example) the *values* arrays has some extra parameters that describe the dimensions of the domainSet (in this example only one extra dimension with the bands of the coverage as an index axis).

```
"ImageFormat": "application/x-img",
"values": [{
        "param": [{"key": {"name": "DIM_BAND", "descr": "Band"}, "val-
ue": {"name": "B01", "descr": "1 Coastal aerosol (0.443µm)"}}],
        "compression": "RLE",
        "datatype": "uint16",
        "nodata": [65535, 0]
},
{
        "param": [{"key": {"name": "DIM_BAND", "descr": "Band"}, "val-
ue": {"name": "B02", "descr": "2 Blue (0.490µm)"}}],
        "compression": "RLE",
        "datatype": "uint16",
        "nodata": [65535, 0]
}, {
        "param": [{"key": {"name": "DIM_BAND", "descr": "Band"}, "val-
ue": {"name": "B03", "descr": "3 Green (0.560µm)"}}],
        "compression": "RLE",
        "datatype": "uint16",
        "nodata": [65535, 0]
}]
```

Each index axis is described in a key (the axis name) and value (the index) structure. This short example only describes the first three bands of the OLI sensor in the Sentinel 2 satellite, i.e. "1 Coastal aerosol (0.443µm)", "2 Blue (0.490µm)" and "3 Green (0.560µm)".

Styles Description

Styles are a set of rules that should be implemented in the JavaScript client to transform the rangeSet into the proper RGBA values compatible with the canvas. There are two main ways of doing that: using color palettes or creating RGB compositions.

In the first mode a single rangeSet of values is used to generate the visualization by mapping the values to a color map consisting on a predefined list of RGB values. If the value is described by a category text, the value of the cell is interpreted as a numerical index into the list of RGB values. In case that the value represents a continuous value, a linear transformation is applied to map the minimum possible value in the rangeSet to the first color of the color map list and the maximum possible value in the rangeSet to the last color of the color map list.

The second mode requires that 3 bands are requested to the server (The client does that in three separated asynchronous request). The first returned rangeSet is rescaled to represent the R color channel intensity between 0 and 255; the second will be rescaled to represent the G color channel and the third to represent the B color channel. This mode is useful to represent band combinations of satellite imagery (e.g. obtaining a natural color composition from a Sentinel 2 image by requesting the bands B04, B03 and B02).

For the first mode a single component is described and the minimum and maximum values to rescale the rangeSet to a color palette indices, as well as the units for the value are given.

```
"style": [{
        "descr":            "DTM",
        "ItemsDescr": "m",
        "component": [{
                "i_value": 0,
                "PaletteRescale": {
                        "maxValue": 1050,
                        "minValue": -300
                }
        }],
```

In the second mode, for an RGB composition, an array with three elements is used in the *component* property of the style to describe each of the three bands used for the RGB composition.

```
"style": [{
        "descr":            "False color",
        "component": [{
                "i_value": 7,
                "PaletteRescale": {
                        "maxValue": 8191,
                        "minValue": 0
                }
        }, {
                "i_value": 3,
```

```
            "PaletteRescale": {
                    "maxValue": 8191,
                    "minValue": 0
            }
    },{
            "i_value": 2,
            "PaletteRescale": {
                    "maxValue": 8191,
                    "minValue": 0
            }
    }],
```

Palette Encoding and Usage

When a color palette is needed, an extra property *palette* is included in the symbolization description. It contains a single property called *colors* which is an array containing a list of colors. The colors are encoded using hexadecimal notation. For example, for the Land Use coverage, the following JSON fragment is used:

```
    "style": [{
            "descr":        "LULC",
            (...)
            "palette": {
                    "colors": [null "#FF00FF", "#00FFFF", "#C0FF00",
"#00C07A", "#FFC0A0", "#008000", "#0000FF"]
            }
    }]
```

This simple example for land use a few colors are used, as shown in the encoding above and in Table 1.

The color palette is created in a way that the number of colors matches the rank of the rangeSet (starting from the lowest value). In this example a cell in the rangeSet with a value "2" will be colored with Cyan.

Usually quantitative coverages (such as DTM) are equipped with a color palette that defines a higher number of colors to give an impression of some continuous gradient. A common approach is to use a 256 color list to portray the coverage (even if in the client legend only a selection of them is shown for simplicity). As explained before, in the "component" property of the style description, the minimum and maximum values to rescale the color palette are included.

The encoding of the component and the color palette for the DTM example is (some encoded properties and some values in the colors' palette array are omitted and substituted by "*(...)*"):

```
    "style": [{
            "descr":        "DTM",
            "ItemsDescr": "m",
            "component": [{
```

Table 1. Land Use colors used adapt the data to the requirements of the canvas

HEX color	RGB color	Value	Textual color
null	null	0	*Not in the legend*
#FF00FF	rgb(255, 0, 255)	1	Pink ▪
#00FFFF	rgb(0, 255, 255)	2	Cyan ▫
#C0FF00	rgb(192, 255, 0)	3	Light green ▫
#00C07A	rgb(0, 192, 122)	4	Medium green ▪
#FFC0A0	rgb(255, 192, 160)	5	Salmon ▫
#008000	rgb(0, 128, 0)	6	Dark green ▪
#0000FF	rgb(0, 0, 255)	7	Blue ▪

```
        "i_value": 0,
        "PaletteRescale": {
                "maxValue": 1050,
                "minValue": -300

        }
    }],
    (...),
    "palette": {
            "colors": ["#000000", (...),"#003300", (...),
"#00CC00", (...), "#CCFF00", (...), "#FFCC00", (...), "#FF9900", (...),
"#FF6600", (...), "#CC6600", (...), "#999900", (...), "#663300", (...), "#FFC-
CFF", (...),"#FFB6FF"]
            }
        }]
```

In this example, 256 colors are described but only a few are selected and shown in the legend as represented in Table 2.

Categories Description Encoding

The rangeTypes of coverages should be numerical even if for coverage representing textual categories. This is encoded in the style description by adding an *attributes* and a *categories* properties:

```
        "style": [{
                "descr":            "LULC",
                "categories": [            null,
                        {"COVER": "Artificial Surface"},
                        {"COVER": "Cultivated Aquatic Vegetated"},
```

Table 2. Some representative colors used in the Digital Terrain Model color map

HEX color	RGB color	Values rank	Textual color
#000000	rgb(0, 0, 0)	[-300,-295]	Black *(not in the legend)*
#003300	rgb(0, 51, 0)	[-225,-221]	Dark green ■
#00CC00	rgb(0, 204, 0)	[-77,-73]	Medium green ▭
#CCFF00	rgb(204, 255, 0)	[23,28]	Light green ▭
#FFCC00	rgb(255, 204, 0)	[172,176]	Light orange ▭
#FF9900	rgb(255, 153, 0)	[299,303]	Medium orange ▭
#FF6600	rgb(255, 102, 0)	[447,451]	Dark orange ▭
#CC6600	rgb(204, 102, 0)	[574,578]	Light brown ▭
#999900	rgb(153, 153, 0)	[696,700]	Olive ▭
#663300	rgb(102, 51, 0)	[849,854]	Dark brown ■
#FFCCFF	rgb(255, 204, 255)	[971,975]	Pink ▭
#FFB6FF	rgb(255, 182, 255)	[1045,1050]	Dark pink *(not in the legend)*

```
        {"COVER": "Cultivated Terrestrial Vegetated"},
        {"COVER": "Natural Aquatic Vegetated"},
        {"COVER": "Natural Surface"},
        {"COVER": "Natural Terrestrial Vegetated"},
        {"COVER": "Natural Water"}],
    "attributes": [{
        "name": "COVER",
        "descr": "Land use/cover",
        "visible": true
    }],
```

In the *attributes* property, several rangeType fields can be defined for each coverage. In this case, only one attribute is described, as only one numerical field is available on this coverage. The *categories* array is linked to the range in the rangeSet; thus, here value 0 is linked to a null description (no pixel is having this value), value 1 is linked to "Artificial Surface", and so on.

Taking this into consideration, the table summarizing Land Use rangeSet values in the previous section can be extended with a new column including the category description as shown in Table 3.

The use of those textual descriptors instead of numerical values is extended not only in the client legend but in query results and statistical pie charts that show textual descriptors of coverages. As shown in Figure 21 and 22 below, for a quantitative coverage such as the DTM, the numeric values of the coverage (and its units of measure, if available) are shown and for a categorical coverage, the numerical value of the coverage is hidden and category descriptions are shown instead.

Table 3. Land Use color meaning used in the legend, data queries and statistical summaries

HEX color	RGB color	Value	Textual color	Category description
null	null	0	Black *(not in the legend)*	*null (no pixel has this value)*
#FF00FF	rgb(255, 0, 255)	1	Pink	Artificial Surface
#00FFFF	rgb(0, 255, 255)	2	Cyan	Cultivated Aquatic Vegetated
#C0FF00	rgb(192, 255, 0)	3	Light green	Cultivated Terrestrial Vegetated
#00C07A	rgb(0, 192, 122)	4	Medium green	Natural Aquatic Vegetated
#FFC0A0	rgb(255, 192, 160)	5	Salmon	Natural Surface
#008000	rgb(0, 128, 0)	6	Dark green	Natural Terrestrial Vegetated
#0000FF	rgb(0, 0, 255)	7	Blue	Natural Water

Figure 21. Quantitative and categorical coverages in queries for the Har Ha Negev Protected Area.

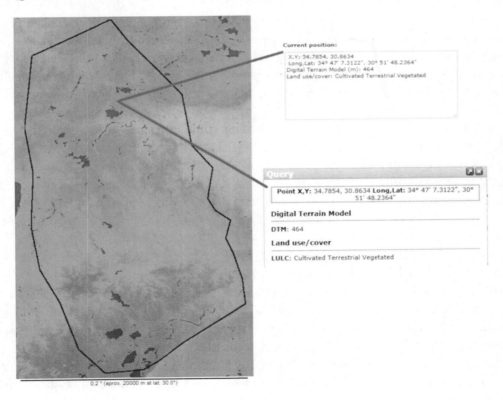

FUTURE RESEARCH DIRECTIONS

We have shown the similarities and the differences of the CIS encoding in JSON and the CoverageJSON. CoverageJSON proponents claim that some CIS structures are too complex and that CoverageJSON provides some extra functionalities missing in CIS. However, there are two points to be made from

Figure 22. Quantitative and categorical coverages in histograms and pie charts for the Har Ha Negev Protected Area.

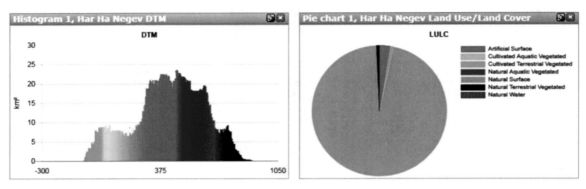

the OGC coverage standards perspective, on technical and interoperability aspects. Technically, OGC coverages form a piece of a complete ecosystem of data and service models, with a rich landscape of encoding formats, simple access formats, modular service model components, up to declarative datacube analytics; therefore facets appear in the coverage definition which CoverageJSON, due to its narrower fous, does not need to consider. From an interoperability perspective, it is disadvantageous that the W3C model has chosen to piggyback on the name "coverages", although incompatible with the OGC coverage standards established since many years. A different naming would allow proper distinction and, thereby, reduce confusion in the communities.

That said, it is desirable to achieve a harmonization. Similarities need to be exploited and lessons need to be learned from both models (in particular, the Petascale experience gained with OGC coverages and WCS) and a single harmonized model should emerge. One option under discussion is to establish CoverageJSON as an additional JSON encoding of OGC coverages, following the CoverageJSON adjustments required for this. Another option could be to define a simple profile for CIS that satisfies the needs of CoverageJSON community. OGC should take the lead in this process to avoid duplication of efforts and confusing implementers.

We have illustrated that, with a set of rules, the CIS UML class model can be converted in conformant JSON instances and JSON Schemas. It seems possible to generalize these practices to many other UML class model in the geospatial domain developed by OGC and ISO. In this respect, the Sensor Web Enablement family of standards should advance in the definition of JSON encodings using this approach. The JSON encoding might not result in the most compact possible but the advantage of having several encodings derived from the common UML model needs to be emphasized as a better good.

The encoding of coverages in JSON lowers the bar for implementing web map browsers and, at the same time, opens interactive possibilities for the user interfaces where users are able to play with the data. The possibilities and limitations opened by the presented implementation need to be exploited further. The application of canvas has demonstrated fast and easy to use but it is limited to 2D visualization. Presenting multidimensional information in a 2D computer screen is still a challenge that needs to be overcome.

The capability to have binary arrays at screen resolution has proved effective to do analytical calculations among datasets and present virtually computed layers that can be browsed because they are calculated on-the-fly. Statistical summaries of these visualizations can be calculated and shown but users have to take into account the implications of doing statistical assessments at screen resolution. More work needs to be done to assess the uncertainties introduced. Real time visual inspection needs to be complemented with slower but precise calculations done in the server side using for example the WCPS standard.

The client presented has revealed the feasibility of the approach. The initial set of tools (e.g. layer calculator, histogram, animation of time series, filter capabilities) has to be extended with a complete set of analytical capabilities.

CONCLUSION

The fundaments of what a coverage is and the data model behind it were defined many years ago in ISO19123. One of the first implementations was done in GML but it required an GML Application Schema to be created for each type of coverage. This level of abstraction if difficult to master what restricted the usability of the approach. The Coverage Implementation Schema elaborated by the OGC coverages group provides a generic coverage model in UML and a fixed schema that can be reused in all coverages and across all encodings. In parallel, in an OGC testbed generic rules to transform UML models into JSON instances and JSON schemas.

The work presented in this Chapter demonstrates how JSON can be used to represent and transmit coverage information in standard way. The Chapter presents and extends the work done in the elaboration of the version 1.1 of the CIS that was released as a conceptual model and three encodings, one of them in JSON. For the first time a JSON encoding was standardized by the OGC for describing coverages. The authors of this Chapter presents a successful stress test that demonstrates the applicability of the generic rules for directly derive JSON from UML class diagrams proposed in the Testbed. The JSON encoding for CIS is able to represent gridded and discrete as well as continuous coverages as defined by CIS. The data model covers the definition of the array of values (rangeSet) together with the description of the rules to generate the domainSet from axes or directly to individual geometries, and the semantics of the values (rangeType), plus any additional metadata. The JSON objects are instances of the class model.

Due to the flexibility of JSON, other alternative encodings for coverages can emerge that are perfectly valid from the JSON structure and validation point view such as the CoverageJSON done by a group in W3C, They produce different alternatives that are based on similar conceptual schemas that generate other JSON objects that are incompatible with the one presented in this chapter and represent a risk for interoperability, forcing implementations to include extra parser efforts to, in the end, achieve very similar functionalities. Even if they are correct JSON encodings, they are not embedded in the OGC and ISO standards ecosystem; and may be incomplete. For example, in the case of CoverageJSON they lack a service model such as OGC WCS.

The incorporation of JSON will easy the implementation of OGC standards in map browsers. The current web browsers that implement the new HTM5 and the enhanced JavaScript engines make possible to use coverages directly in the web browser. In HTML5 it is possible to create rich map representations that go beyond the mass marked approach of having only imagery and road maps. In the past, map browsers were only able to present JPEG images at screen resolution needing constant web service communication that results in delays and limited user experience. The client presented in this Chapter uses internal binary arrays embedded in JSON encoded coverage descriptions. For example and in addition to personalized visualization as interactive maps, the information can be presented to the user with statistics, graphics, dynamic time series, and all this increasing user experience. Expert users can combine OGC coverage data to do geospatial analysis directly in the web browser that will present virtual layer results. In the end, the server-side fusion capabilities of the OGC WCPS language will provide full access to the analytical results. This opens up additional degrees of freedom in system design.

ACKNOWLEDGMENT

This research was supported by the European Union's Horizon 2020 Programme [ECOPotential (641762-2)]; This work has been partially funded by the Spanish MCIU Ministry through the NEWFORESTS research project (RTI2018-099397-B-C21/C22 MCIU/AEI/FEDER, UE).

REFERENCES

Baumann, P. (2017). *OGC Web Coverage Service (WCS) 2.1 Interface Standard – Core v.2.1*. Open Geospatial Consortium (OGC 17-089r1). Retrieved from: http://docs.opengeospatial.org/is/17-089r1/17-089r1.html

Baumann, P., Hirschorn, E., & Maso, J. (2017). *OGC Coverage Implementation Schema v.1.1*. Open Geospatial Consortium (OGC 09-146r6). Retrieved from: http://docs.opengeospatial.org/is/09-146r6/09-146r6.html

Baumann, P., Hirschorn, E., Maso, J., Merticariu, V., & Misev, D. (2017). All in One: Encoding Spatio-Temporal Big Data in XML, JSON, and RDF without Information Loss. *Proceedings: IEEE International Conference on Big Data*, 3406-3415.

Benson, T., & Grieve, G. (2016). UML, BPMN, XML and JSON. In *Principles of Health Interoperability* (pp. 55–81). Cham: Springer. doi:10.1007/978-3-319-30370-3_4

Blower, J., & Riechert, M. (2016). *Coverages, JSONLD and RDF data cubes*. In Workshop on Spatial Data on the Web (SDW 2016), Montreal, Canada. Retrieved from: http://centaur.reading.ac.uk/74395/1/paper2.pdf

Bray, T. (2014). *IETF RFC7159, The JavaScript Object Notation (JSON) Data Interchange Format*. Retrieved from: https://www.ietf.org/rfc/rfc7159.txt

Izquierdo, J. L. C., & Cabot, J. (2016). JSONDiscoverer: Visualizing the schema lurking behind JSON documents. *Knowledge-Based Systems*, *103*, 52–55. doi:10.1016/j.knosys.2016.03.020

Jetlund, K. (2015). *Best practices for diagram design*. Retrieved from: https://github.com/ISO-TC211/UML-Best-Practices/wiki/Best-practices-for-diagram-design

Maso, J. (2017). *Testbed-12 JavaScript-JSON-JSON-LD Engineering Report (OGC 16-051)*. Retrieved from: http://docs.opengeospatial.org/per/16-051.html

Maso, J., Zabala, A., Serral, I., & Pons, X. (2018). Remote Sensing Analytical Geospatial Operations Directly in the Web Browser. *The International Archives of the Photogrammetry, Remote Sensing and Spatial Information Sciences, 42*(4), 403–410. doi:10.5194/isprs-archives-XLII-4-403-2018

OGC 07-011. (2015). *Abstract Specification Topic 6: Schema for coverage geometry and functions, version 7.0*. Retrieved from: http://portal.opengeospatial.org/files/?artifact_id=19820

Portele, C. (2007). *OpenGIS Geography Markup Language (GML) Encoding Standard. Ver 3.2.1, (OGC 07-036)*. Retrieved from: http://portal.opengeospatial.org/files/?artifact_id=20509

Robin, A. (2011). *OGC 08-094, OGC® SWE Common Data Model Encoding Standard, version 2.0*. Retrieved from: http://portal.opengeospatial.org/files/?artifact_id=41157

Sporny, M., Kellogg, G., & Lanthaler, M. (2014). *W3C JSON-LD 1.0, A JSON-based Serialization for Linked Data*. Retrieved from: http://www.w3.org/TR/json-ld/

Witayangkurn, A., Horanont, T., & Shibasaki, R. (2012). Performance comparisons of spatial data processing techniques for a large scale mobile phone dataset. In *Proceedings of the 3rd International Conference on Computing for Geospatial Research and Applications* (p. 25). ACM. 10.1145/2345316.2345346

KEY TERMS AND DEFINITIONS

Client: Software component that can invoke an operation from a server.

Coordinate Reference System: Coordinate system that is related to the real world by a datum.

Coordinate System: Set of mathematical rules for specifying how coordinates are to be assigned to points.

Coverage: A feature that acts as a function to return values from its range for any direct position within its spatiotemporal domain.

Displaced Grid: A grid whose direct positions are topologically aligned to a grid, but whose geometric positions can vary arbitrarily.

Geographic Information: Information concerning phenomena implicitly or explicitly associated with a location relative to the Earth.

Irregular Grid: A grid whose grid lines have individual distances along each grid axis.

Mesh: A coverage consisting of a collection of curves, surfaces, or solids, respectively.

Partition (of a Coverage): A separately stored coverage acting, by being referenced in the coverage on hand, as one of its components.

Regular Grid: A grid whose grid lines have a constant distance along each grid axis.

Service: Distinct part of the functionality that is provided by an entity through interfaces.

Chapter 16
Green Cloud Architecture to E-Learning Solutions

Palanivel Kuppusamy
Pondicherry University, India

ABSTRACT

Electronic learning or e-learning is the use of technology to enable learners to learn from anywhere and anytime. The delivery involves the use of electronic devices in some way to make available learning contents. Today, e-learning has drastically changed the educational environment. The e-learning methodology is a good example of green computing. Green computing refers to the study and practice of using computing resources in an eco-friendly manner. It is the practice of using computing resources in an energy efficient and environmentally friendly manner. In order to reduce costs, education services can be provided using cloud technology. The green cloud computing solutions save energy, reduce operational costs, and reduce carbon footprints on the environment. Hence, the objective is to provide a green cloud architecture to e-learning solutions. This architecture is addressing the issues such as improving resource use and reducing power consumption.

INTRODUCTION

Higher education institutions (HEIs) have been looking for new ways to respond to the changing professional field (Mircea, M. & Andreescu, A. I. 2011). The traditional teaching will be substituted by individual project-orientated and self-organized learning. The modern educational methods enable self-paced and self-directed learning with flexibility on time and site. The existing concept of self-contained study courses will be replaced by the concept of continuing professional development.

In an age determined to generate new paths to quality education, Information and Communications Technology (ICT) brings forward countless benefits, enabling learners with the right skill. ICT makes many ordinary tasks uncomplicated and facilitates communications from virtually any part of the globe. ICT in education has been linked with a shift in the quality of people's lives by improving teaching and learning. This is why a number of educational institutions are increasingly integrating ICT in their education system. Through this unique teaching method, learners gain a genuine learning experience, collaboratively constructing their own knowledge and applying their learning's in a real-world context.

DOI: 10.4018/978-1-5225-8446-9.ch016

The use of ICT techniques in teaching and learning has a very positive influence on a student's learning capabilities as well. It is established that students reflect in a very positive manner towards work and education when they are using computers to complete tasks given to them, encouraging and motivating them to soak in the knowledge. Students or learners who used technology to learn in educational institutions have self-esteem and self-confidence. Education with the help of technology has crossed borders and has opened up a world of opportunities for learners. From easy sharing of information to collaboration with the help of e-Mail and cloud applications to instant access to learning programmes anytime, anywhere. The technologies that alter the education sector are virtual reality, gamification, data analytics, cloud computing, machine learning, artificial intelligence, etc.

Cloud computing platform enables enterprises or educational institutions to consolidate computing resources, reduce management complexity and speed the response to business dynamics. Improving resource utilization and reduce power consumption are key challenges to the success of operating a cloud computing environment. To address such challenges, it is designed the Green cloud architecture to e-Learning systems. Green cloud [Kaur, G. & Kumar, P, (2013)] computing is envisioned to achieve not only efficient processing and utilization of computing infrastructure, but also minimize energy consumption. It is essential for ensuring that the future growth of Cloud computing is sustainable.

Hence, the objective of this chapter is to design a Green cloud architecture to e-Learning solutions. The proposed Green cloud architecture to e-Learning solutions helps to decrease the energy consumption of Clouds without affecting the service providers' objectives. This architecture is designed in a way to provide incentives to both e-Learning users and providers in order to utilize and deliver the greenest services respectively. The Green cloud architecture provides the security and quality of service to the clients. This architecture includes emission directory, which measures the best suitable service, which gives less carbon emission so straight away it indicates that energy will also decrease energy consumption. Therefore, Green cloud architecture reduces unnecessary power consumption in an e-Learning environment.

This chapter is sorted out as takes after: Section 2 presents about different specialized points of interest that required composing this chapter. Section 3 studied different designs, for example, benefit arranged, cloud-situated and Green-oriented. The proposed architecture is portrayed in section 4 and finally, section 5 concludes this chapter with future enhancements.

BACKGROUND

This section introduces state of art required to write this chapter. This includes cloud computing, e-Learning, the impact of e-learning in cloud computing, cloud computing, and energy usage, various energy efficiency models, features of clouds enabling green computing, and finally green computing in e-Learning applications.

Electronic Learning (or E-Learning)

The world has entered into the digital age, and technology has touched every part of human life, whether it is business, communication, travel, health, or education. The global education system has taken it hands-on and the implications of advanced technology have created wonders in this field. The increasing influence of technology in education is offering us a glimpse into a gradually evolving realm of unconstrained learning. Education with the help of technology has crossed borders and has opened up a world of opportunities for learners. From easy sharing of information to collaboration with the help of email and cloud applications to instant access to learning programmes anytime and anywhere.

Intentional use of electronic media and Information and Communication Technologies (ICT) in teaching and learning process is referred to as electronic learning or e-learning. It can also be described by many other terms including online learning, virtual learning, distributed learning, network, and web-based learning. e-Learning includes all educational activities carried out by individuals/groups working online/offline and synchronously/asynchronously through network/standalone computers and electronic devices. The components of e-Learning can include the content of multiple formats, management of the learning experience, and an online community of learners, content developers, and experts. The main advantages of e-Learning are flexibility, convenience, easy accessibility, consistency, and its repeatability. With Information Technologies (IT), there is a growing trend regarding the research and exploitation of this kind of e-Learning platforms.

As the development of technology grows, e-Learning helps students in their studies in an easy manner, anytime and anywhere. e-Learning has become a popular and acceptable way to study due to its flexibility and better innovativeness regarding the introduction of new/contemporary programs as compared to traditional faculty.

In e-Learning platforms (Fernandez, A. Peralta, D. Herrera, F. & Benítez, J. M. 2012), the demand of the teaching resources usually vary in a dynamic and very quick way and presents high peaks of activity. To attend requests during these periods without other system services to be resented, it will be necessary to prepare a quite superior infrastructure than that required for the regular working of the learning institution. An alternative would be to provide those services depending on the demand and only paying for the resources that are actually used. The solution to these necessities is the Cloud Computing environment. Additionally, the e-learning platforms of the large dimensions that we mentioned above generate extensive registers of interaction among students-platform-teachers.

Cloud Computing in Education

Cloud Computing may promote a new era of learning taking the advantage of hosting the e-Learning applications (Karim, F. & Goodwin, R. 2013) on a cloud and following its virtualization features of the hardware, it reduces the construction and maintenance cost of the learning resources. Improved IT capabilities and enterprise infrastructure at HEIs are needed to create a successful digital learning experience. The biggest advantage of cloud technologies is that they create a centralized repository of knowledge for students and teachers to access. This is taking the student-teacher collaboration beyond traditional classroom interaction.

Cloud-based technology in education has become such a phenomenon since it ensures sustained academic learning irrespective of the student's geographical positioning. Moreover, it ensures that the desired data is centrally available for processing and deriving deeper insights for a more effective learning experience. Cloud-based technology also enables educators to boost their reach without making any significant infrastructural spends. This, in turn, benefits end-users by reducing the cost of services, while simultaneously adding value to their education.

Cloud computing is an evolving paradigm which is enabling outsourcing of all IT needs such as storage, computation, and software through the Internet. Cloud computing is also called "Cloud" since a

Cloud server can have any configuration and can be located anywhere in the world. These Cloud services are made accessible and delivered to the end user. It is defined Cloud computing (Buyya, R. Yeo, C.S. & Venugopal, S. 2008) as follows:

A Cloud is a market-oriented distributed computing system consisting of a collection of interconnected and virtualized computers that are dynamically provisioned and presented as one or more unified computing resource(s) based on service-level agreements established through negotiation between the service provider and consumers.

The National Institute of Standards and Technology (NIST) defines Cloud computing (Mell, P. & Grance, T. 2009; Mell, P. Grance, T. 2011) as follows:

Cloud computing is a model for enabling convenient, on-demand network access to a shared pool of configurable computing resources (e.g., networks, servers, storage, applications, and services) that can be rapidly provisioned and released with minimal management effort or service provider interaction.

This Cloud model promotes high availability and is composed of characteristics, service models, and deployment models. The characteristics of Clouds include on-demand self-service, broad network access, resource pooling, rapid elasticity, and measured service. The key characteristics exhibited by Clouds are *autonomic, dynamic and distributed, elastic, pay as you go, service-oriented, shared or multi-tenant and virtualized.*

Cloud Computing Models

Cloud computing is mainly composed of three layers which cover all the computing stack of a system. Each of these layers offers a different set of services – Software-as-a-Service (SaaS), Platform as a Service (PaaS) and Infrastructure-as-a-Service (IaaS) to end users (Xhafa, F. & Bessis, N. 2014).

Software-as-a-Service (SaaS) is a software delivery model providing on-demand access to applications. SaaS providers maintain the customer data and configure the applications according to customer need. Examples are scientific applications, social networking, gaming, CRM and ERP applications. Multi-tenancy is another feature of SaaS, allowing providers to outsource the effort of managing large hardware infrastructure, maintaining and upgrading applications, and optimizing resources by sharing the costs among the large user base.

Platform as a Service (PaaS) offers Cloud users a development platform to build their applications. PaaS offers only the user-level middleware, which allows the development and deployment of applications on Cloud infrastructure. PaaS offerings provide developers and architects with services and APIs helping them to simplify delivering of elastically scalable and highly available Cloud applications. Examples are Google AppEngine (Google App Engine. 2010), Aneka (Vecchiola, C, Chu, X. & Buyya, R. 2009), and Microsoft Azure (Microsoft Azure. 2011).

Infrastructure-as-a-Service (IaaS) consists of virtual machines or physical machines, storage, and clusters. The IaaS guarantees runtime environment customization, application isolation, accounting and quality of service. Depending on the end user needs, the virtualized infrastructure is pre-configured with storage and programming environment, what saves time for users who do not need to build their system from scratch. The cloud physical resources are storage, virtualized, clusters, servers, network, etc.

The above models provide a different level of manageability and customization for your solution.

Cloud Computing Deployment Models

Cloud computing is deployed on physical infrastructure where Cloud middleware is implemented for delivering service to customers. Therefore, the Cloud deployments are classified mainly into three types: *public cloud*, *private cloud*, and *hybrid cloud,* as shown in Figure 1. Figure 1 illustrates the essential characteristics, the delivery, and deployment models of cloud computing.

Public Cloud is available to the end users (customers) on the Internet. It offers very good solutions to the customers having small enterprise or with infrequent infrastructure usage since these Clouds provide a very good option to handle peak loads on the local infrastructure and for an effective capacity planning. A public Cloud can offer IaaS, PaaS, and SaaS services. Examples of public Clouds are Amazon Web Services, Google AppEngine, and Microsoft Azure.

Private Cloud is deployed within the premise of an organization to provide IT services to its internal users. It offers greater control over the infrastructure, improving security and service resilience because its access is restricted to one or few organizations. Such private deployment poses an inherent limitation to end-user applications i.e. inability to scale elastically on demand, as can be done using public Cloud services.

Hybrid Cloud is the deployment, which emerged due to diffusion of both public and private clouds. In this model, organizations outsource non-critical information and processing to the public Cloud, while keeping critical services and data in their control. These services are temporarily leased in peak load times and then released. The hybrid Cloud applies to services related to IT infrastructure rather than software services.

The above model is opted to facilitate the choice of the appropriate deployment models of cloud computing for the ones with the most business-critical features.

Figure 1. Architecture model and the core components of cloud computing.

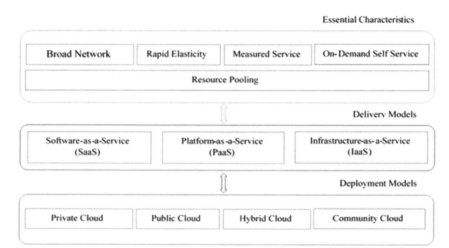

Cloud-Based E-Learning

Cloud-based e-Learning (A. Peralta, D. Herrera, F. & Benitez, J. M. 2012), can be viewed as education SaaS and IaaS. It lessens the burden of maintenance and support from the educational institution to the vendor. It is allowing them to focus on their core business, also obtaining the latest updates of the system without charges and sharing key resources. From the SaaS perspective, the cloud-based e-Learning offers the following:

- The learner's registration application provides to register their applications.
- The learning application deploys the subscribed learning contents to the learners.
- It allows centralized learners account management for the authorized learners.
- It provides the subscribed learning contents and manages the subscription of the learning contents.

From the IaaS perspective, the cloud-based e-Learning offers the following:

- It manages the learning contents storage for the learning system and the users.
- It balance load for all e-Learning systems in a distributed environment.
- It backup and restore for the e-Learning applications.

Nowadays, e-Learning is broadly used on unlike educational levels: constant education, training, educational courses, etc. There are different e-learning solutions (Pocatilu, P. 2010; Pocatilu, P. Alecu, F. & Vetrici, M. 2009) from an open source to business. With the huge growth of the number of students, education contents, services that can be offered and resources made available, e-Learning solutions dimensions grow at an exponential rate. The challenges are optimizing resource computation, content storage, communication requirements, dealing scalable demands and cost control.

Cloud-based e-Learning promotes a new era of learning taking the advantage of hosting the e-Learning applications on a Cloud, virtualization features of the hardware, reducing the construction and maintenance cost of the learning resources. Cloud-based e-Learning offers several benefits - the reduced costs, anytime and anywhere for the convenience of the learners. The learning content is easy to keep updated and the teacher or content creators may incorporate multimedia content to provide a friendly framework and to ease the understanding of the concepts. However, currently, Cloud-based e-Learning solutions are still weak on scalability at the infrastructure level. Several HEIs do not include the resources and infrastructure required to run the top e-learning solution.

Cloud Computing Model to E-Learning Solutions

Figure 2 illustrates the cloud computing model to e-Learning solutions. Each component is encapsulated and only connected to the middleware, which, in turn, exchanges contents and metadata in standardized formats via standardized interfaces. The Components and standards are described in turn.

The Learning App plays a key role in the e-Learning infrastructure. It is the entry point for learners to access courses, learning objects and lecture dates as well as to get recommendations for the next best contents to be learned and tracks all relevant learners interactions. It is a responsive Web application capable of being displayed on regular modern desktop Web environments, smartphones, and tablets. The application gives everywhere and every time access to all learning objects offered in the taken courses.

Figure 2. Cloud computing model to e-Learning solutions.

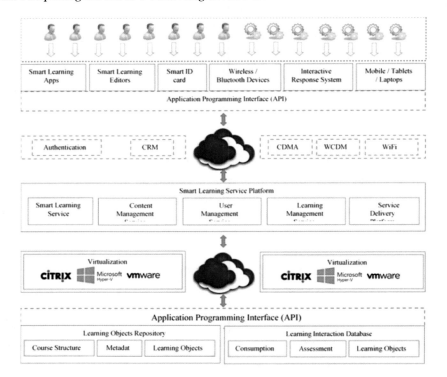

The layered architecture provides flexibility in managing functionalities at individual layers. However, managing the complexity of various layers and integrating outputs from one layer to other requires rigorous management of tasks at various layers.

Accessing learning object from different distributed repositories is required but usually, these distributed learning object sources may have different technological infrastructures including proprietary systems, desktop-based systems, web services, grids, clouds, and non-standardized data models, which make this task more challenging and requires rigorous analysis for data (learning object) accessibility, harmonization and transformation and compliance to policy requirements. To enable various stakeholders to visually design workflows, to compose and bind services for execution, to identify data sources and to execute these workflows in a cloud environment.

Cloud Architecture to E-Learning Solutions

The cloud environment underpins the making of a new era of e-Learning frameworks. In conventional electronic learning model, instructive establishments contribute a tremendous measure of cash on equipment and programming applications, foundation, support and the fitting preparing of staff to empower them to utilize innovation successfully. In cloud computing e-Learning model, instructive foundations with no base speculations can get capable programming with lower or no in advance expenses and fewer administration migraines in the classroom. Cloud registering significantly affects educating and learning environment (Fern. 2012). It is very reasonable in instruction for both understudies and instructors. The advancement of e-Learning administrations empowers clients to get to assorted programming applications, share information, work together more effectively, and keep their information securely in the framework. Besides, it can bring down costs, diminish vitality utilization, and assist associations with restricted IT assets with deploying and keep up required programming in an auspicious way.

The e-Learning architecture using cloud computing is shown in Figure 3. This e-Learning architecture can be divided into learning software layer, learning infrastructure layer and learning infrastructure layer.

Learning software (SaaS) layer provides with learning content production, learning content delivery, virtual laboratory, collaborative learning, assessment, and management features. The learning software layer is the specific learning applications of integration the teaching resources in the cloud computing model, including interactive courses and sharing the teaching resources. This layer mainly consists of learning content production, educational objectives, content delivery technology, assessment, and management component.

Learning platform layer (PaaS) layer mainly is composed of the operating system and middleware. Through middleware technology, a variety of software resources are integrated to provide a unified interface for software developers, so they can easily develop a lot of applications based on software resources and embed them in the cloud, making them available for cloud computing users.

Learning infrastructure layer (IaaS) layer is composed of information infrastructure and teaching resources. Information infrastructure contains Internet (public cloud)/ Intranet (private cloud), system software, information management system and some common software and hardware. The teaching resources are accumulated mainly in the traditional teaching model and distributed in different departments and domain. This layer is located in the lowest level of cloud service middleware (learning platform layer). The basic computing power like physical memory, CPU, memory is provided by the layer. With virtualization technology, physical server, storage and network form virtualization group for being called by an upper software platform. The physical host pool is dynamic and scalable, the new physical host can be added in order to enhance physical computing power for cloud middleware services.

The intended advantages derived from the cloud computing e-Learning architecture are powerful computing and storage capacity, high availability, high security and virtualization. The major advantage of the proposal is that it aims at providing easy access to costly e-Learning software running on high-performance processors to rural students at institutions, which lack considerable facilities. This smart learning environment (Jeong, J.S. Kim, M. & Yoo, K.H. 2013) is to provide a reusable generic

Figure 3. The cloud computing architecture to e-Learning solutions

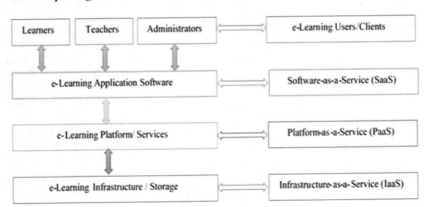

infrastructure for various users with different client devices, for different courses covering several topics without any restrictions. While users are still managed in the LMS, learning objects are stored only once in a repository and can be shared by and accessed from various LMSs.

Learning Data Centers

A cloud data center could contain numerous hundreds or a huge number of organized PCs with their relating stockpiling and systems administration subsystems, control dissemination and moulding gear, and cooling bases. These data centers can devour monstrous vitality utilization and discharge huge measure of carbon (Saurabh, K G. & Rajkumar, B. 2011). Consequently, to accomplish the extreme productivity in power utilization and CO_2 emanations, each of these gadgets should be outlined and utilized effectively while guaranteeing that their carbon impression is diminished. Figure 4 demonstrates an end client getting to Cloud administrations, for example, SaaS, PaaS, or IaaS over the Internet.

Client information goes from his own gadget through an Internet administration suppliers' switch, which thusly associates with a Gateway switch inside a Cloud datacenter. Inside datacenters, information experiences a neighborhood and are handled on virtual machines, facilitating Cloud administrations, which may get to capacity servers. Each of the figuring and system gadgets that are specifically gotten to serve Cloud clients add to vitality utilization. What's more, inside a Cloud datacenter, numerous different gadgets, for example, cooling and electrical gadgets devour control. The gadgets despite the fact that does not specifically help in giving Cloud administration are the real givers to the power utilization of a Cloud datacenter.

An energy-efficient datacenter exploits hardware heterogeneity and employs dynamic adaptation. We can develop algorithms to globally manage to compute, storage, and cyber-physical resources with the objective of minimizing the total energy dissipation.

Challenges in Cloud-Based E-Learning

As discussed in "advantages of Cloud Computing to e-Learning", the challenges regarding this topic about optimizing learning resource computation, learning content storage and communication requirements, energy efficiency and dealing with dynamic concurrency requests highlight the necessity of the use of a platform that meets scalable demands and cost control.

Figure 4. Learning data center usage model

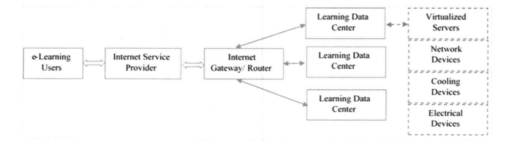

From the above study of current efforts in making Cloud computing energy efficient, it shows that even though researchers have made various components of Cloud efficient in terms of power and performance, still they lack a unified picture. Cloud providers, being profit oriented, are looking for solutions, which can reduce the power consumption and thus, carbon emission without hurting their market. Therefore, it provides a unified solution to enable e-Learning using Green Cloud Computing (Maskare, P. R. & Sulke, S. R. 2014).

Energy Efficiency of Cloud Computing

In recent years, power consumption has become one of the hottest research trends in computer science and industry. Most of the reasons are related to the operational budget and environmental issues. Cloud applications are deployed in remote data centers where high capacity servers and storage systems are located. The fast growth of demand for cloud-based services results into an establishment of enormous data centers consuming a high amount of electrical power. Energy efficient model is required for complete infrastructure to reduce functional costs while maintaining the vital quality of service (QoS). Energy optimization can be achieved by combining resources as per the current utilization, efficient virtual network topologies and thermal status of computing hardware and nodes.

The following investigates (Sindhu S. Pandya, 2014) the areas of a typical cloud setup that is responsible for a considerable amount of power dissipation and it will consolidate the possible approaches to fix the issues considering energy consumption as a part of the cost functions to be applied.

- **User Applications:** SaaS model has changed the way applications and software are distributed and used. More and more companies are switching to SaaS Clouds to minimize their IT cost. Thus, it has become very important to address the energy efficiency at the application level itself. In the development of commercial and enterprise applications, which are designed for a PC environment, generally, energy efficiency is neglected.

- **Cloud Software:** Virtualization and Provisioning plays an important role in power consumption. VM migration and the advancement in virtualization technology have led to a significant reduction in VM overhead which improves the energy efficiency of Cloud infrastructure. In addition, there are works on improving the energy efficiency of storage systems. The servers are then switched to inactive states for energy saving. Since power is dissipated in Cloud datacenter due to heat generated by the servers, several works also have been proposed for dynamic scheduling of VMs and applications, which take into account the thermal states or the heat dissipation in a data center. The consideration of the thermal factor in scheduling also improves the reliability of underline infrastructure.

- **Datacenter:** To build an energy efficient data center, several best practices have been proposed to improve the efficiency of each device from electrical systems to processor level. The datacenters may be constructed in such a way that electricity can be generated using renewable sources such as the sun and wind. In datacenter cooling, it is necessary that they directly cool the hot equipment rather than an entire room area. The Storage Area Networks (SAN) allows the building of an efficient storage network that consolidates all storage. The use of energy efficient disks such as tiered storage allows better energy efficiency.

- **Monitoring:** The monitoring (or metering) services measures at a higher level rather than attempting to measure each individual device's power consumption. These services take into account controller caching and algorithms, including protection schemes, and adjusts the workload accordingly. These services provide a uniform way to access the power monitoring sensors available on recent servers.

- **Network Infrastructure:** At the network level, the energy efficiency is achieved either at the node level (i.e. network interface card) or at the infrastructure level (i.e. switches and routers). The energy efficiency issues in networking are usually referred to as "green networking", which relates to embedding energy-awareness in the design, in the devices and in the protocols of networks.

The above has investigated the need for power consumption and energy efficiency in the cloud computing model. There are few major components of cloud architecture, which are responsible for a high amount of power dissipation in the cloud. Therefore, there is a necessity to study for designing an energy efficiency model to cloud-based e-Learning.

FEATURES OF CLOUDS ENABLING GREEN COMPUTING

Even though there is a great concern in the community that Cloud computing can result in higher energy usage by the datacenters, Cloud computing has a green lining. The key driver technology for energy efficient Clouds is *virtualization*. Virtualization allows significant improvement in energy efficiency of Cloud providers by leveraging the economies of scale associated with a large number of organizations sharing the same infrastructure. By consolidation of underutilized servers in the form of multiple virtual machines (Smith, J. & Nair, R. 2003) sharing same physical server at higher utilization, companies can gain high savings in the form of space, management and energy. The key factors (Saurabh. K G & Rajkumar. B. 2011), that have enabled Cloud computing to lower energy usage and carbon emissions from ICT are dynamic provisioning, multi-tenancy, server efficiency and data center efficiency.

- **Dynamic Provisioning:** In the traditional setting, datacenters and private infrastructure used to be maintained to fulfil worst-case demand. Thus, IT companies end up deploying far more infrastructure than needed. For example, the e-Learning Web Server receives a significant spike in traffic during the admission and examination period. This can increase in traffic into a certain level. Such scenarios can be readily managed by Cloud infrastructure. The datacenters always maintain the active servers according to current demand, which results in low energy consumption than the conservative approach of over-provisioning.
- **Multi-Tenancy**: Using multi-tenancy approach, Cloud computing infrastructure reduces overall energy usage and associated carbon emissions. The SaaS providers serve multiple companies on the same infrastructure and software. This approach is obviously more energy efficient than multiple copies of software installed on different infrastructure.
- **Server Utilization:** Using virtualization technologies, multiple applications can be hosted and executed on the same server in isolation. Thus, it dramatically reduces the number of active servers. Even though high utilization of servers results in more power consumption, the server running at higher utilization can process more workload with similar power usage.
- **Datacenter Efficiency:** The power efficiency of data centers has a major impact on the total energy usage of Cloud computing. Cloud computing allows services to be moved between multiple

datacenters which are running with better PUE values. This is achieved by using the high-speed network, virtualized services and measurement, and monitoring and accounting of datacenter.

Due to the above Cloud features, educational institutions can reduce carbon emissions by moving their applications to the Cloud. These savings are driven by the high efficiency of large-scale Cloud data centers.

Green Computing

Green computing (Kaur, A. 2014) aims to attain economic viability and improve the way computing devices are used. Green IT practices include the development of environmentally sustainable production practices, energy-efficient computers and improved disposal and recycling procedures. To promote green computing concepts at all possible levels, the following four approaches are employed:

- **Green Use:** Minimizing the electricity consumption of computers and their peripheral devices and using them in an eco-friendly manner
- **Green Disposal:** Repurposing existing equipment or appropriately disposing of, or recycling, unwanted electronic equipment
- **Green Design:** Designing energy-efficient computers, servers, printers, projectors and other digital devices
- **Green Manufacturing:** Minimizing waste during the manufacturing of computers and other subsystems to reduce the environmental impact of these activities

Green computing, also called green technology, is the environmentally responsible use of computers and related resources. Such practices include the implementation of energy-efficient central processing units (CPUs), servers and peripherals as well as reduced resource consumption and proper disposal of electronic waste (e-waste).

The goal of green computing is to attain economic viability and improve the way computing devices are used. Green computing practices include the development of environmentally sustainable production practices, energy efficient computers and improved disposal and recycling procedures. These energy-efficient devices produce less carbon during their operation and can be efficiently embedded in solar-powered devices. Also, many companies use virtualization software, a technique that enables Intel to combine several physical systems into a virtual machine that runs on a single, powerful base system, thus significantly reducing power consumption. There are other goals of green information technology, most notably at the design and manufacturing stages.

Green Storage

To reduce the carbon footprints and costs of data centers, energy-efficient products and storage methods are widely in practice. This practice is called *green storage*, which adds to carbon negativity. Carbon negativity reduces the carbon footprints below neutral levels so that the net effect becomes removing carbon dioxide from the atmosphere. The real goal of green storage is not just being environment-friendly, but also lowering costs, improving the efficiency of resources, and preserving energy. A various number of systems are capable of serving the purpose of green storage. The data centers can choose customization of solutions by analyzing the specific needs so that it leaves a positive impact on your environment.

Some other activities also exist and you can follow green storage practices like removing any unwanted data, installing only the necessary software and applications, etc. By using these green computing and green storage techniques, data centers can reduce carbon emission and footprints by using less electricity; also, they can be more efficient on energy and save costs on expensive hardware and repair costs.

Green Cloud Architecture

From the above study, Cloud computing makes energy efficient. Various components of Cloud make efficient in terms of power and performance. Most of the efforts for sustainability of Cloud computing have missed the network contribution, VM consolidation, redistribution of workload to support energy efficient cooling without considering the effect of virtualization. Hence, it is proposed a unified solution to enable Green cloud computing. Green cloud computing (Kamble, R. S. & Nikam, D. A. 2013), provides the energy consumption of Clouds. The high-level view of green Cloud architecture is given in Figure 5.

The goal of Green cloud architecture is to make Cloud green from both user and provider's perspective. The Green cloud architecture is designed to keep track of overall energy usage of serving a user request. From the user side, the Green Broker plays a crucial role in monitoring and selecting the Cloud services based on the user QoS requirements, and ensuring minimum carbon emission for serving a user. In general, a user can use Cloud to access any of these three types of services (SaaS, PaaS, and IaaS), and therefore the process of serving them should be energy efficient. In other words, from the Cloud provider side, each Cloud layer needs to be "Green" conscious.

Figure 5. Green cloud architecture

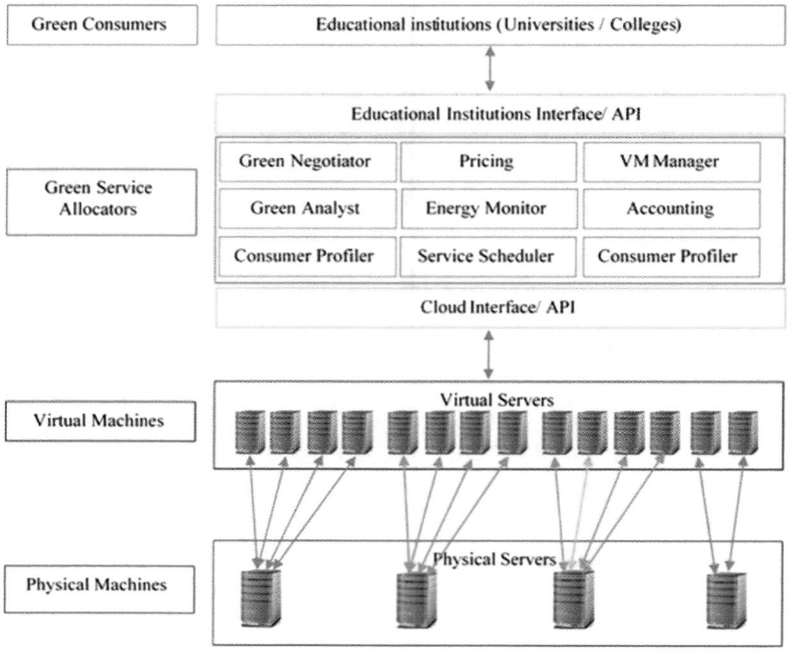

Since software (SaaS) providers mainly offer e-Learning software installed on their learning data-centers or resources from IaaS providers, the learning software providers need to model and measure the energy efficiency of their software design, implementation and deployment. For serving e-Learning users, learning software provider chooses the learning datacenters, which are not only energy efficient but also near to users. The minimum number of replicas of user's confidential data should be maintained using energy-efficient storage.

In the green cloud, the framework enables the end user to access to all three types of cloud services through one of the deployment models: private cloud, public cloud or hybrid cloud (Yeboah-Boateng & Cudjoe-Seshie, 2013).

SURVEY AND RELATED WORKS

Reviewing the literature is important for creating a reliable foundation for advancing knowledge. In order to obtain a sense of the current state of green cloud computing studies, it surveyed the literature. The target of this paper is to outline a Green cloud architecture to e-Learning solutions. Henceforth, it is proposed to survey existing works in the zone of engineering of Cloud Computing, Green Computing and both. This section review existing works in the area of Cloud Computing and Green Computing architecture and energy efficiency.

It is explored the concept of green computing (Shalabh, A. & Asoke, N. 2011) from the viewpoint of business and IT, implemented Green IT in order to ensure cost savings in an eco-friendly manner and also identified several approaches of implementing green computing in the ICT sector. It is described the benefits and challenging issues (Vinay, P, V. Chintan, M, B. & Hardik, S, J. 2014) of the cloud concept that motivate the adoption of a newly developed and an improved version of cloud technology i.e. green cloud computing. It is presented the Service-oriented cloud computing architecture (Lohmosavi, V. Nejad, A. F. & Hosseini, E. M. 2013), which is used to transfer e-learning into the cloud. These architectures cover challenges of e-learning such as scalability, application development, efficient use of resources, saving expense, and security. It is presented some possible cloud solutions (Engi, 2013) in e-learning environments by emphasizing its pros and cons. It is of paramount importance to choose the most suitable cloud model for an e-learning application or an educational organization in terms of scalability, portability and security. It distinguishes various deployment alternatives to cloud computing and discuss their benefits against typical e-learning requirements. Developments in computing are influencing many aspects of education. The purpose (Faten, 2013) is to assess the potential value of cloud computing as a platform for e-Learning. It discussed how cloud computing is different from other forms of computing and what makes it unique. As well as this, the potential advantages and disadvantages of using cloud computing as a platform for e-Learning will be outlined. Finally, the requirements of implementing cloud computing will be discussed, along with an assessment of the challenges to implementation and some potential ways to overcome them.

Cloud computing has attracted a great deal of attention in the education sector as a way of delivering more economical, securable, and reliable education services. It is proposed and introduced a cloud-based smart education system (Jeong, J.S. Kim, M. & Yoo, K.H. 2013) for e-learning content services with a view to delivering and sharing various enhanced forms of educational content, including text, pictures, images, videos, 3-dimensional (3D) objects, and scenes of virtual reality (VR) and augmented reality (AR).

The real-time virtualized Cloud infrastructure (Tomm, 2012) was developed in the context of the IRMOS European Project. It showed how different concepts, such as real-time scheduling, QoS-aware network protocols, and methodologies for stochastic modelling and run-time provisioning were practically combined to provide strong performance guarantees to soft real-time interactive applications in a Virtualized environment. The characteristics (Anwar, 2012) introduced in the current e-Learning and then analyzed the concept of cloud computing and describes the architecture of cloud computing platform by combining the features of e-Learning. They tried to introduce cloud computing to e-Learning, build an e-learning cloud, and make active research and exploration for it from the following aspects: architecture, construction method and external interface with the model.

With rising energy cost and growing environmental concerns, green computing is receiving more and more attention. Software and system architectures play a crucial role in both computing and telecommunication systems, and they have been analyzed for performance, reliability, maintainability, and security. Since most communication systems have to run 24/7 (e.g., most server farms, servers in a cloud computing infrastructure), the energy consumption of a system based on specific software architecture is of great importance.

A model proposed to analyze the energy consumption (Benjamin Z. 2010) of software architecture, given the CPU/processor that will be used. Thus, this model gives one an additional dimension to compare competing software architectures. It is investigated all possible areas in a typical cloud infrastructure (Arindam, B. Prateek, A. & N. Ch. S. N. Iyengar. 2013) that are responsible for the substantial amount of energy consumption and they addressed the methodologies by which power utilization can be decreased without compromising Quality of Services (QoS) and overall performance. It is stated that energy efficiency (Backialakshmi, M. & Hemavathi, N. 2015) was the major challenge of a cloud datacenter. In current trends, the users demand a wide range of services within optimal resource usage and cost. Therefore, to maintain energy usage of the datacenters we use various types of algorithms in terms of both hardware and software.

Green Computing or Green IT refers to the study and practice of using computing resources in an eco-friendly manner in order to tone down the environmental impacts of computing. It is the practice of using computing resources in an energy efficient and environmentally friendly manner. It discussed how Green Computing can be incorporated into different institutions (Shalabh, A. & Asoke, N. 2011), corporate/business sectors or may be in various IT companies. To reduce unnecessary energy consumption due to hazardous materials has become a major topic of concern today.

Software optimization and deployment can be a good means of implementing green computing. This can be achieved via efficiency in algorithms, proper allocation of resources, and virtualization. Current methods of saving energy include *algorithmic efficiency, virtualization, power management, hardware usage and cloud computing*. From the above study, the criteria for eco-efficient building blocks are as follows:

1. HEIs are in need of a cost-effective solution to their existing computing challenges, therefore, focusing on free and open source software (FOSS) is an important criterion in selecting cloud software. The cloud model may consider its operation costs and challenges relative to an existing computing system.
2. Huge power consumption and environmental pollution by current cloud data centers have been a challenge to data center operators. Thus focusing on energy consumption technologies is an important criterion.

3. Efficiency and flexibility of computing solution are very important for its acceptance. Thus, cloud computing building blocks should guarantee the quality of service. Accordingly, network connections must ensure reliability and availability of cloud computing services to end users. Moreover, virtual machine consolidation should not impact the performance of cloud services.

It has identified building blocks needed for designing eco-efficient cloud computing that aligns with the guidelines and issues related to green power utilization.

PROPOSED ARCHITECTURE

Recently, *smart learning* is to provide a reusable generic infrastructure for various users with different client devices, for different courses covering several topics without any restrictions. While users are still managed in the LMS, learning objects are stored only once in a repository and can be shared by and accessed from various LMSs.

As discussed earlier, it is clear to consider energy efficiency to manage the cloud services from requirements to run-time through construction, deployment, operation, and their adaptive evolution over time. Their availability will result in the implementation of a software stack for energy efficient-aware Clouds. Thus, an architecture supporting energy efficiency is proposed. Design principles that guide the selection of specific eco-efficient building blocks are characterized by features, which consider the economic, technological and environmental challenges that exist in the designated environment for cloud computing services.

Requirements of Proposed System

The most significant requirements to support Green cloud e-Learning solution are summarized below:

- **Many More Connections:** As e-Learning continues to grow and the number of connected 'things' increases, the network will need to handle a surge in connected devices.
- **Low Power Usage:** Traditional SIM-based connections, using the current mobile network infrastructure have access to a reliable power source or limited lifetimes. In order to support simple, cheap devices, such as basic sensors, that can operate for years (indeed decades) on standard batteries, new technologies need to be deployed, and/or current networks upgraded.
- **High Data Rates:** e-learning streaming applications will need to ensure data is transmitted at high rates in order to deliver full functionality. For example, video conferencing deployment, many cameras may be installed across the campus; when these cameras recognize an incident, they will stream the footage and large amounts of data will be stored and analyzed in the cloud.
- **Advanced Data Analytics:** For e-Learning applications, collecting and reporting data is the precursor to analyzing the data to automate decision-making. This will include aggregating data from a variety of sources to trigger an actuator. Real-time analytics can then control traffic signals and notify drivers of any changes to their route in order to reduce congestion.
- **Security and Data Management:** As the physical world becomes more closely linked to the virtual world, the potential for a security breach increases. Security and privacy issues arise around

control of things/devices and access to confidential information, whether it be a medical device and data, an industrial machine or a car.

- **Resilience and Local Autonomy:** As the HEIs becomes more dependent on e-Learning applications, the network will be relied upon to provide very high-reliability connectivity, which is resilient to outages.

The proposed Green cloud architecture to e-Learning solutions supports both functional and non-functional requirements. The functional key requirements are given below:

- Various e-learning, big data and analytical application types, including the batch and real-time analytics
- Industry-standard interfaces, so that existing e-learning, big data and analytical application applications can work for real-time streaming and processing of data
- Various data types and databases and interfaces
- Large volumes of e-Learning data in different formats

The non-functional requirements are simplified, reliable, fast and scalable, and secure. The issues addressed by perspectives are the non-functional requirements of the architecture. The stakeholder requirements clearly show a need for addressing non-functional requirements. Some perspectives are *evolution & interoperability, performance & scalability and availability & resilience.*

- **Evolution and Interoperability:** The ability of the system to be flexible in the face of the inevitable change that all systems experience after deployment, balanced against the costs of providing such flexibility
- **Performance and Scalability:** The concerns are processing volume, response time, responsiveness, throughput, predictability.
- **Availability and Resilience:** The ability of the system to be fully or partly operational as and when required and to effectively handle failures that could affect system availability.

Attributes of GCALS

The attributes of proposed Green cloud architecture to e-Learning solutions are awareness, analysis and auditability.

- **Awareness:** New technologies for pervasive interactions such as radio frequency identification (RFID), sensors, video cameras, a global positioning system (GPS), smart cards, and other tools will capture data on the identity, status, condition, and/or location of people and physical assets. Unified communications technologies such as 3G and 4G wireless networks will transport this data from these client devices back to central servers for analysis.
- **Analysis:** Business intelligence and specialized analytical software such as data mining and predictive analytics, video image analysis, pattern recognition, and artificial intelligence algorithms will determine whether businesses or governments should act on or ignore a pattern or an anomaly. Analyzing and storing the massive amounts of learning data that will be received is only possible with the more flexible and adaptable servers and storage devices enabled by server virtualization,

data center automation, and storage life-cycle management - as well as the potential for more flexible processing expansion and storage capacity through cloud computing.

- **Auditability:** Tracking all steps in the learning process to aid in regulatory compliance, compliance with company policies and goals, and improvement opportunities are critical. It includes elements of monitoring activity and learning how to do it better. Technology needs to capture, track, and analyze information on each stage of this cycle to make sure that the right actions were taken and to learn how to improve the analysis and identify better alternatives.

Features of GCALS

The attributes of proposed Green cloud architecture to e-Learning solutions are digital identity, learning apps, learning dashboards, load balancing, etc.

- **Digital Identity:** Digital identity is related to managing the relationship between individuals (teachers and students) and the objects that they use. Digital identity management enables centralized storage of all e-Learning user accounts in the centralized server, as well as centralized authentication, authorization and single sign-on/single sign out features. Using this identity features, e-Learning users of the platform should enter their authentication credentials only once, afterwards, they can have access to all pages they are authorized.

- The *Learning App* plays a key role in the infrastructure. It is the entry point for learners to access courses, learning objects and lecture dates as well as to get recommendations for the next best contents to be learnt and tracks all relevant user interactions. It is a responsive Web application capable of being displayed on regular modern desktop Web environments to enable learning. The Learning App gives everywhere and every time access to all learning objects offered in the taken courses.

- *Learning dashboards* to support teachers in different teaching contexts have been proposed by different authors. All dashboards provide some form of a visual summary of the use of learning contents by learners. Based on students' performance, the learning dashboard provides instructors with an overview of all learning objectives, represented by a bar each. Learning dashboards are being developed that adapt elements of the overview proposed to the bigger variety of learning objects present in e-Learning solutions.

- The *Load balancing* is to distribute the workload across the computing cloud to achieve optimal resource utilization, minimize the response time, and avoid overload of the system. As the result, some nodes in the system can be switched to the standby mode or just switched off. Although the energy can be saved at low power mode or inactive nodes, the overall system performance can be adversely impacted, which may be a reason for increasing the system energy utilization.

Goals of Proposed Architecture

The goal of GCALS architecture is to make green cloud from both user and provider's perspective. In the proposed Green Cloud architecture.

1. The end users (teachers, learners, administrators, etc.,) submit their cloud service requests through a new middleware Green Broker that manages the selection of the Green cloud provider to serve the user's request. A user service request can be of three types i.e., software, platform or infrastructure.

2. The Green cloud providers can register their services in the form of 'green offers' to a public directory which is accessed by Green Broker. The green offers consist of green services, pricing and time when it should be accessed for least carbon emission.

3. Green broker gets the status of energy parameters for using various Cloud services from carbon emission directory. The carbon emission directory maintains all the data related to energy efficiency of cloud service. This data may include PUE and cooling efficiency of Cloud datacenter which is providing the service, the network cost and carbon emission rate of electricity.

4. Green Broker calculates the carbon emission of all the Green Cloud Providers who are offering the requested cloud service. Then, it selects the set of services that will result in the least carbon emission and buy these services on behalf of users.

The proposed architecture is designed to keep track of overall energy usage of serving a user request. From the user side, the Green Broker plays a crucial role in monitoring and selecting the Cloud services based on the user QoS requirements, and ensuring minimum carbon emission for serving a user. In general, a user can use Cloud to access any of these three types of services (SaaS, PaaS, and IaaS), and therefore the process of serving them should be energy efficient.

Proposed Green Cloud Model

Figure 6 shows end users accessing Cloud services such as SaaS, PaaS or IaaS over the Internet. End-user data pass from his own device through an Internet service provider's router, which in turn connects to a Gateway router within a Cloud datacenter. Within data centers, data goes through a local area network and are processed on virtual machines, hosting Cloud services, which may access storage servers. Each of the computing and network devices that are directly accessed to serve Cloud users contribute to energy consumption. In addition, within a Cloud datacenter, there are many other devices, such as cooling and electrical devices, that consume power. These devices even though do not directly help in providing Cloud service, are the major contributors to the power consumption of a Cloud datacenter.

From the above typical Cloud usage scenario, it is analyzed various elements of Clouds and their energy efficiency. The energy consumption of the above devices and applications is detailed below.

- **User Applications:** The Cloud computing can be used for running applications owned by individual users or offered by the Cloud provider using SaaS. In both cases, the energy consumption depends on the application itself. If the application is long running with high CPU and memory requirements, then its execution will result in high-energy consumption. However, energy efficiency factor is not considered during the design of an application in most of the e-Learning domains.

- **Cloud Software:** The Cloud software stack leads to extra overhead in the execution of learner applications. For instance, it is well known that a physical server has higher performance efficiency than a virtual machine and IaaS providers offer general access to a virtual machine to its end users. The Cloud provider for meeting a certain level of service quality and availability, provision extra resources than generally required. Therefore, it is important to explore the relationships between Cloud components and the tradeoffs between QoS and energy consumption.

Figure 6. Green cloud usage model.

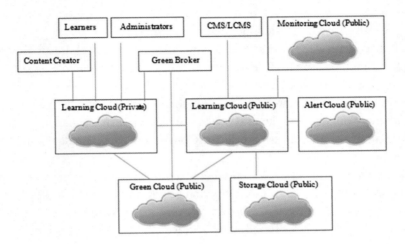

- **Network Infrastructure:** The network system is also consumed a non-negligible fraction of the total power consumption. In Cloud computing, since resources are accessed through the Internet, both applications and data are needed to be transferred to the computing the node. The user data travels through many devices before it reaches a datacenter, Therefore, with the growth of Cloud computing usage, it is expected that energy efficiency of switches and routers will play a very significant role in what since they need to provide the capacity of bandwidth. In the network infrastructure, the energy consumption depends especially on the power efficiency and awareness of the wired network, namely the network equipment or system design, topology design, and network protocol design.

- **Learning Data Center:** A learning data center could comprise many hundreds or thousands of networked computers with their corresponding storage and networking subsystems, power distribution and conditioning equipment, and cooling infrastructures. Due to a large number of equipment, data centers can consume massive energy consumption and emit a large amount of carbon. The servers and storage systems are not the only infrastructures that consume energy in the data center but also the cooling equipment consumes an equivalent amount of energy as the IT systems themselves.

Further energy consumption occurs due to lighting, loss in the power distribution, and other electrical equipment such as UPS. Thus, to achieve the maximum efficiency in power consumption and CO2 emissions, each of these devices needs to be designed and used efficiently while ensuring that their carbon footprint is reduced.

Proposed Green Cloud Architecture

Green cloud architecture (GCA) is a data center architecture (Rawson, A. Pfleuger, J. & Cader, T. 2008)] that aims to reduce data-center power consumption. The advantage of this architecture is that it guarantees real-time performance while saving in the total energy consumption of the data center. The GCA also helps consolidate the workload and achieves significant energy savings for the cloud-computing environment. This architecture was created to address the issues in the cloud-computing environment, such as improving resource use and reducing power consumption.

Figure 7 provide an overview of the proposed architecture - the green cloud architecture to e-Learning solutions (GCALS). It includes the high-level interactions of all components, is separated into distinct layers and follows the standard Cloud deployment model (Leloglu, E. Ayav, T. & Galip Aslan, B. 2013). Next, details on the interactions of the architectural components are discussed. Each component in GCALS is encapsulated and only connected to the middleware, which, in turn, exchanges contents and metadata in standardized formats via standardized interfaces. Components and standards are described in turn.

- The *user layer* is the one that end users interact in a direct manner. It mainly comprises of software systems delivered as service. Configurability and scalability are the two key features of this layer. Customers can easily customize their software system using Metadata. These layers allow users to use cloud-computing services optimally and achieve the kind of results they are looking for from the system.
- The *SaaS layer* has a set of components that interact to facilitate the design and construction of a Cloud-based e-Learning application. These components aid in evaluating energy consumption during its construction. This layer provides a number of plug-ins for a frontend integrated development environment (IDE) as a means for developers to interact with components within this layer. The IDE is intended to be the main entry point to the infrastructure for service designers and developers. The IDE integrates the graphical interfaces to the different tools available in the SaaS layer, thus offering a unified and integrated view to e-Learning users.
- The *PaaS layer* provides middleware functionality for a Cloud-based e-Learning application and facilitates the deployment and operation of the application as a whole. Components within this layer are responsible for selecting the most energy appropriate provider for a given set of energy requirements and tailoring the application to the selected provider's hardware environment. Application level monitoring is also accommodated for here, in addition, to support for service level agreement (SLA) negotiation.
- In the *IaaS layer*, the admission, allocation and management of virtual resource are performed through the orchestration of a number of components. Energy consumption is monitored, estimated and optimized using translated PaaS level metrics. These metrics are gathered via a monitoring infrastructure and a number of software probes.

As new distributed computing technologies like Clouds become increasingly popular, the dependence on power also increases. The majority of the energy used in today's society is generated from fossil fuels, which produce harmful CO2 emissions. Therefore, it is imperative to enhance the efficiency and potential sustainability of large data centers. Therefore, there is a need to create an efficient Cloud computing system that utilizes the strengths of the Cloud while minimizing its energy and environmental footprint.

The HEIs request consists of an application, its estimated length in time and number of resources required. These applications are submitted to the Green broker who acts as an interface to the Cloud infrastructure and schedules applications on behalf of HEIs. The Green Broker interprets and analyzes the service requirements of a submitted application and decides where to execute it. Green Broker schedule applications such that the CO_2 emissions are reduced and the profit is increased, while the Quality of Service (QoS) requirements of the applications are met. As Cloud data centers are located in different

Figure 7. Green cloud architecture to e-Learning solutions

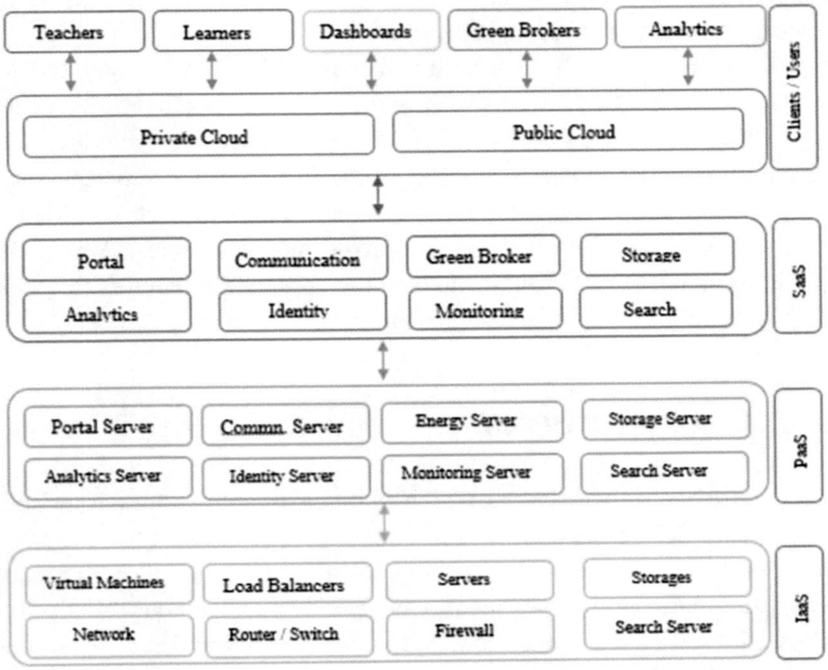

geographical regions, they have different CO_2 emission rates and energy costs depending on regional constraints. Each data center is responsible for updating this information to Carbon Emission Directory for facilitating the energy-efficient scheduling.

Analysis and Evaluation

The proposed architecture is evaluated by various metrics, namely, storage architecture, computing distribution, storage technology, analytics technology, and user experience.

A detailed and high-level view of Green cloud architecture to e-Learning solutions was designed inductively based on published material of the Cloud computing use cases. The proposed Green cloud architecture to e-Learning solutions is comprised of semi-detailed functional components and data storage, and data flows between them. The presented design contained a description of the architectural elements. The architecture was created inductively based on the published Green cloud functional architectures. Thus, only the observed functional components and data stores are present in the architecture. If the model is extended in the future based on other big data use cases, the model may need to be updated with new functional components or data stores.

The use case (Cucinotta, T. Checconi, F. Kousiouris, G. Konstanteli. et. al. 2012), is to adopt an existing data-intensive software and make it suitable for an energy-aware cloud environment (Srikantaiah, S. Kansal, A, & Zhao, F. 2009). This software has been built to assist news agencies in creating, managing and distributing breaking news quickly and efficiently to various customers through a variety of delivery methods. Its core functionality includes newsgathering, editing, archiving, managing the production process and delivering services through multiple channels.

The energy metrics at various levels (host, virtual machine, tasks) will be targeted in order to measure the energy consumed by applications events, operations or components defined at development time. These metrics have different contexts: software, platform, infrastructure, and architectural component level. Energy consumption at host physical systems is monitored, and the energy consumption of guest virtual systems is estimated. Power consumption at a given sampling frequency is monitored, as well as other metrics at a similar sampling frequency to avoid inconsistencies. Applications are generally interested in specific measurements that indicate how the application behaves (e.g. response time, user served, number of times an operation has been performed).

FUTURE RESEARCH DIRECTIONS

The proposed architecture has been presented, which includes the architectural roles and the components. This architecture complies with a standard Cloud architecture, considers the classical SaaS, PaaS and IaaS layers and supports components such as energy consumption, the infrastructure monitor, etc. The design of the proposed architecture support energy efficiency management. In this architecture, energy efficiency is addressed at all layers of the cloud software stack and during the complete lifecycle of a cloud application. Even though the proposed GCALS embeds various features to make Cloud computing much more Green, there are still many technological solutions are required to make it a reality. The challenges of the proposed architecture are customized analytics, real-time reporting during mobility and big data management in the Cloud environment and they will be the future challenges.

CONCLUSION

High operational costs and reduced cloud system reliability resulting from excessive heat are the major barriers to sustainable growth in computing power. The present economic situation will force different educational institutions and organizations to consider adopting a cloud solution. The energy efficiency of cloud computing has become one of the most pressing issues. Energy consumption of job execution on a private cloud, public cloud and localhost are pre-determined based on modelling scenario. The components of Clouds contribute carbon emission and the features of Clouds that make it "Green." The Cloud Computing platform is quite appropriate for the migration of this learning system so that it can fully exploit the possibilities offered by the creation of an effective learning environment that offers personalized contents and easy adaptation to the current education model. Green cloud computing initiatives will be vital when it comes to offloading the workload to clouds (public/private) while providing the best energy performance value.

REFERENCES

Backialakshmi, M., & Hemavathi, N. (2015). Survey on Energy Efficiency in Cloud Computing. *Journal of Information Technology & Software Engineering, 6*, 1.

Banerjee, & Agrawal & Iyengar. (2013). Energy Efficiency Model for Cloud Computing, *International Journal of Energy. Information and Communications, 4*(6), 29–42.

Benjamin, Z., Ming, F., & Chung-Horng, L. (2010). A Green Computing Based Architecture Comparison and Analysis. *IEEE/ACM International Conf. on Green Computing and Communications.*

Buyya, R., Beloglazov, A., & Abawajy, J. (2010). Energy-Efficient management of data center resources for cloud computing: A vision, architectural elements, and open challenges. *Proc. of the 2010 International Conference on Parallel and Distributed Processing Techniques and Applications (PDPTA 2010).*

Cucinotta, T., Checconi, F., Kousiouris, G., Konstanteli, K., Gogouvitis, S., Kyriazis, D., ... Stein, M. (2012). Virtualized e-Learning on the IRMOS Real-Time Cloud. *Service Oriented Computing and Applications, 6*(2), 151–166. doi:10.100711761-011-0089-4

Fernandez, A., Peralta, D., Herrera, F., & Benıtez, J. M. (2012). An Overview of e-learning in Cloud Computing. *Workshop on LTEC, AISC, 173,* 35–46. 10.1007/978-3-642-30859-8_4

Google App Engine. (2010). Retrieved from http://code.google.com/appengine/

Jain, A., & Pandey, U.S. (2013). Role of Cloud Computing in Higher Education. *International Journal of Advanced Research in Computer Science and Software Engineering, 3*(7), 966-972.

Jeong, J. S., Kim, M., & Yoo, K. H. (2013). A Content-Oriented Smart Education System based on Cloud Computing. *International Journal of Multimedia and Ubiquitous Engineering, 8*(6), 313–328. doi:10.14257/ijmue.2013.8.6.31

Kamble, R. S., & Nikam, D. A. (2013). Green cloud computing new approach of energy consumption. *International Journal of Latest Trends in Engineering and Technology, 3*(2), 124–131.

Karim, F., & Goodwin, R. (2013). Using Cloud Computing in e-learning Systems. *International Journal of Advanced Research in Computer Science & Technology, 1*(1), 65–69.

Kaur, A. (2014). Green computing: Emerging Trends in Information and Communication Technology. *International Journal of Engineering Inventions, 3*(9), 42–46.

Kaur, G., & Kumar, P. (2013). Compositional Framework of Green Cloud, *Intel. Journal of Emerging Trends in Engineering and Development, 1*(3).

Leloglu, E., Ayav, T., & Galip Aslan, B. (2013). A review of cloud deployment models for e-learning systems. *43rd Annual IEEE/IFIP International Conference on Dependable Systems and Networks (DSN),* 1-2. 10.1109/DSN.2013.6575331

Lohmosavi, V., Nejad, A. F., & Hosseini, E. M. (2013). E-learning ecosystem based on service-oriented cloud computing architecture. *International Conference on Information and Knowledge Technology (IKT),* 24-29. 10.1109/IKT.2013.6620032

Maskare, P. R., & Sulke, S. R. (2014). E-learning using cloud computing. *International Journal of Computer Science and Mobile Computing, 3*(5), 1281–1287.

Masud, M. A. H., & Huang, X. (2012). An e-Learning System Architecture based on Cloud Computing. *World Academy of Science, Engineering and Technology, 62,* 74–78.

Mell, P., & Grance, T. (2009). *Definition: Cloud computing.* NIST Special Publication 800-145.

Mell, P., & Grance, T. (2011). *The NIST definition of cloud computing.* NIST Special Publication 800-145.

Microsoft Azure. (2011). Retrieved from www.microsoft.com/windowsazure/

Mircea, M., & Andreescu, A. I. (2011). Using cloud computing in higher education: A Strategy to Improve Agility in the Current Financial Crisis. *Communications of the IBIMA, 20*(11), 1–15. doi:10.5171/2011.875547

Murugesan, S. (2008). Harnessing Green IT: Principles and Practices. *IT Professional, 10*(1), 24–33. doi:10.1109/MITP.2008.10

Palanivel, K., & Kuppuswami, S. (2014). Towards Service-Oriented Reference Model and Architecture to e-Learning Systems. *International Journal of Emerging Trends & Technology in Computer Science, 3*(4), 146–155.

Phankokkruad, M. (2012). Implement of cloud computing for e-learning system. *International Conference on Computer & Information Science (ICCIS).* 10.1109/ICCISci.2012.6297204

Pocatilu, P. (2010). Cloud Computing Benefits for e-Learning Solutions. *Economics of Knowledge, 2*(1), 9–14.

Pocatilu, P., Alecu, F., & Vetrici, M. (2009). Using cloud computing for e-Learning systems. *Proc. of the 8th WSEAS International Conference on Data networks, communications, computers,* 54-59.

Rawson, A., Pfleuger, J. & Cader, T. (2008). Green Grid Data Center Power Efficiency Metrics. Consortium green grid. *International Journal on Recent and Innovation Trends in Computing and Communication.*

Saurabh, K. G., & Rajkumar, B. (2011). *Green Cloud computing and Environmental Sustainability, Cloud computing and Distributed Systems (CLOUDS).* Laboratory Dept. of Computer Science and Software Engineering, The University of Melbourne.

Shalabh, A., & Asoke, N. (2011). Green Computing - a new Horizon of Energy Efficiency and Electronic waste minimization: a Global Perspective. *International Conference on Communication Systems and Network Technologies,* 688-693.

Sindhu, S. (2014). Green Cloud Computing. *International Journal of Information and Computation Technology, 4*(4), 431–436.

Smith, J., & Nair, R. (2003). *Virtual machines: Versatile Platforms for Systems and Processes.* Los Altos, CA: Morgan Kaufmann.

Srikantaiah, S., Kansal, A., & Zhao, F. (2009). Energy-aware Consolidation for Cloud Computing. *Cluster Computing, 12,* 1–15.

Vecchiola, C., Chu, X., & Buyya, R. (2009). Aneka: A Software Platform for. NET-based Cloud Computing. In High Performance & Large Scale Computing, Advances in Parallel Computing. IOS Press.

Vinay, P. V., Chintan, M. B., & Hardik, S. J. (2014). Green Cloud: Implementation and Adoption of Green Data Center. *International Conference on Emerging Research in Computing, Information, Communication and Applications*, 163-167.

Xhafa, F., & Bessis, N. (2014). *Inter-cooperative Collective Intelligence: Techniques and Applications. In Studies in Computational Intelligence, 495* (pp. 39–67). Berlin, Germany: Springer-Verlag.

Yeboah-Boateng, E. O., & Cudjoe-Seshie, S. (2013). Cloud Computing: The Emergence of Application Service providers (ASPs) in Developing Economies. *International Journal of Emerging Technology and Advanced Engineering*, *3*(5), 703–712.

KEY TERMS AND DEFINITIONS

Cloud Architecture: Cloud architecture refers to the various components in terms of databases, software capabilities, applications, etc. engineered to leverage the power of cloud resources to solve business problems.

Cloud Computing: Cloud computing is a general term for anything that involves delivering hosted services over the Internet. These services are broadly divided into three infrastructure-as-a-service (IaaS), platform-as-a-service (PaaS), and software-as-a-service (SaaS).

Data Center: A data center (or datacenter) is a facility composed of networked computers and storage that businesses or other organizations use to organize, process, store and disseminate large amounts of data. A business typically relies heavily upon the applications, services and data contained within a data center, making it a focal point and critical asset for everyday operations.

E-Learning: E-learning is all about intelligent learning and that which also makes the student interact with the course content.

Efficient Energy: Efficient energy use, sometimes simply called energy efficiency, is the goal to reduce the amount of energy required to provide products and services.

Energy Efficiency: Energy efficiency simply means using less energy to perform the same task – that is, eliminating energy waste. It brings a variety of benefits: reducing greenhouse gas emissions, reducing demand for energy imports, and lowering our costs on a household and economy-wide level.

Energy Usage: Energy usage data, especially when added to other data and processed, enables utilities to deliver actionable information to consumers to achieve energy efficiency's true potential.

Green Cloud: Green cloud refers to the potential environmental benefits that information technology (IT) services delivered over the Internet can offer society.

Green Cloud Architecture: Green cloud architecture (GCA) is an IDC architecture that aims to reduce data-center power consumption. The advantage of this architecture is that it guarantees real-time performance, while saving in the total energy consumption of the IDC.

Green Computing: Green computing is the environmentally responsible and eco-friendly use of computers and their resources. In broader terms, it is also defined as the study of designing, manufacturing/engineering, using and disposing of computing devices in a way that reduces their environmental impact.

Green Storage: Green storage is the practice of using a variety of "clean energy" storage methods and products to cut down on a data center's carbon footprint, as well as cost. With green storage, the goal goes beyond being environmentally friendly.

Reference Architecture: A reference architecture in the field of software architecture or enterprise architecture provides a template solution for an architecture for a particular domain. It also provides a common vocabulary with which to discuss implementations, often with the aim to stress commonality.

Reference Model: A reference model is a model representing a class of domains (e.g., a reference model for production planning and control systems). It is a conceptual framework or blueprint for system's development.

Chapter 17
Smart Education Using Internet of Things Technology

Palanivel Kuppusamy
Pondicherry University, India

ABSTRACT

Smart education is now a typical feature in education emerging from information communications technologies (ICT) and the constant introduction of new technologies into institutional learning. The smart classroom aims users to develop skills, adapt, and use technologies in a learning context that produces elevated learning outcomes which leads to big data. The internet of things (IoT) is a new technology in which objects equipped with sensors, actuators, and processors communicate with each other to serve a meaningful purpose. The technologies are rapidly changing, and designing for these situations can be complex. Designing the IoT applications is a challenging issue. The existing standardization activities are often redundant IoT development. The reference architecture provides a solution to smart education for redundant design activities. The purpose of this chapter is to look at the requirements and architectures required for smart education. It is proposed to design a scalable and flexible IoT architecture tor smart education (IoTASE).

INTRODUCTION

Technology has recently changed the educational landscape. The increase in human knowledge and steady technology advances higher educational institutions (HEI) make the best use of the resources available and keep learning up-to-date. In an age determined to generate new paths to quality education, Information and Communications Technology (ICT) brings forward countless benefits. ICT makes many ordinary tasks uncomplicated and facilitates communications from virtually any part of the globe. ICT in education has been linked with an upward shift in the quality of people's lives by improving teaching and learning.

DOI: 10.4018/978-1-5225-8446-9.ch017

The use of ICT techniques in learning/teaching has a very positive influence on a student's learning capabilities as well. It is established that students reflect in a very positive manner towards work and education when they are using computers to complete tasks given to them, encouraging and motivating them to soak in the knowledge. Students who used technology to learn in educational institutions have increased self-esteem and self-confidence. This is why a number of educational institutions are increasingly integrating ICT in their education system. With the advent of technologies, HEIs can now keep track of resources, create smarter lesson plans, design safer campuses and improve access to information. From the use of mobiles and tablets in the classroom, education looks very different today.

IoT and Education

Electronic learning or e-Learning is the use of ICT to enable learners to learn from anywhere and anytime. The delivery involves the use of electronic devices such as a smartphone and tablets in some way to make available learning contents. It makes the learning process more efficient for learners as well as teachers. By now, an e-Learning has been limited to virtual classrooms, video lectures and animations, online tutorials and study materials. In the age of information technology, developing with modern technology means to grow and achieve the benefits of the birth of new technology. Cloud computing, big data computing, Internet of Technology (IoT), etc. are some of the recent technologies, which have been introduced recently for the infrastructure level(s) of e-learning systems in the world of information technology.

The IoT and big data technology change everything including e-Learning platforms. It is important to identify a sophisticated strategy to combine different types of data in a way that they provide the best result to the learner, the user of the e-learning platform. In this context, big data learning integrates the mix of structured and unstructured data in one data repository to facilitate access in addition to an optimal relevance of search with adequate and consistent results according to the expectations of the learner. The big data learning system performs the capture of all types of data (text, image, video, audio, etc.) related to the subject of the theme and groups them in its raw data repository. It then includes data of any type, such as posts, pictures, videos, audio tracks, etc. IoT is a technology that capture data from the IoT enabled devices installed in the learning environment.

The introduction of the IoT in e-Learning can really help to transform education. The huge data created by the IoT is measured for high commercial value, and data mining algorithms can be applied to IoT to extract hidden information from data. It enables the collection, exchange, and analysis of generating information. The IoT has the potential to impact every aspect of learning processes. IoT continues to revolutionize e-Learning and is expected to bring in more 'connectedness' and smart classrooms in the future. They take the advantages of new capabilities by developing pedagogical approaches that leverage the technologies emerging in the environments around us (Watson, *et al.*, 2013).

Most e-Learning platform delivers video tutorials using smart devices. Video content is easily integrated into small IoT-enabled devices and can be more effective than the text content. This includes learning applications, which require managing huge and mixed volumes of information coming from IoT devices. HEIs have to adapt their technologies to be able to handle the large amounts of learning content generated by IoT devices. Once data has been received then it is to find big data technology platform for storing IoT data. The devices that will make up the IoT, as well as the kinds of data they generate, will vary by nature.

Introducing the big data and IoT with an ordinary classroom can be transformed into a smart education. They enable e-Learning professionals to customize the e-Learning experience to provide learners with more informative, engaging, and engaging e-Learning courses. They actively listen and analyzes voices, conversations, movements, behaviour, etc., in order to reach a conclusion about the teachers' presentation and learners' satisfaction. This enables teachers to consistently deliver better presentations and make a better impact, while the audience benefits from interesting learning contents. The IoT in e-Learning bring incredible challenges such as standards, reusability, interoperability, adaptation, etc. and opportunities to educational institutions. Thus, IoT architecture is needed to support big data e-Learning and overcome these challenges.

Motivation

The present education system has changed drastically in the past few years and will continue to transform. Technology is rapidly being used as a tool to deliver new and better ways of engagement among students and teachers. Digital books, MOOCs, personalized and Mobile learning are nowadays making waves, The future of technology in the education industry will broadly be influenced by virtual reality, wearables, location-based services and sensor technologies. The motivation behind to propose this work is shown in Fig. 1.

Figure 1. A scenario of smart education

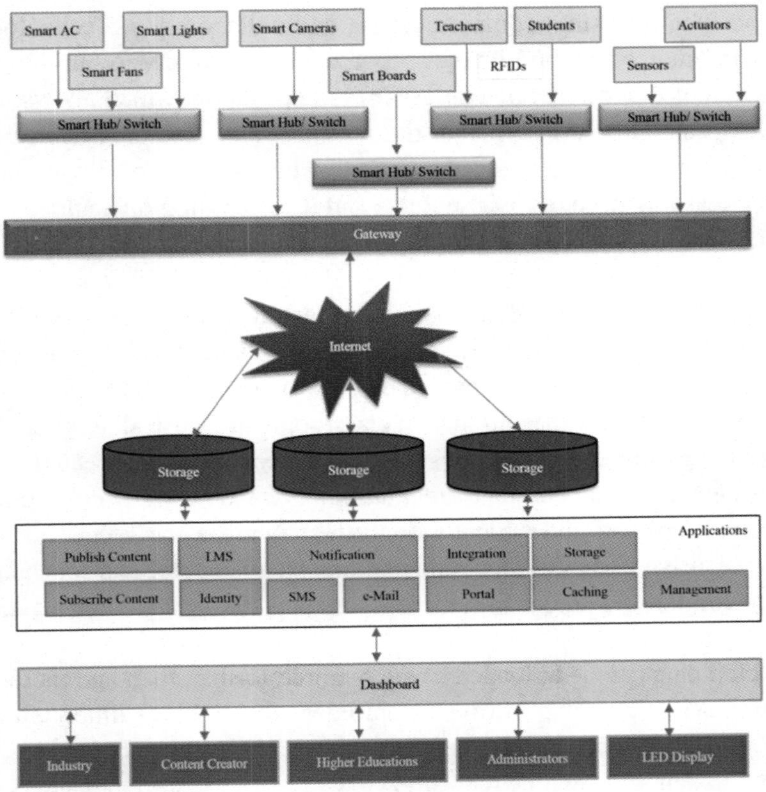

Traditional classrooms using blackboard, projector connected with the desktop system do not record their activity in any form. However, it can do the recording of teaching and learning activity can be collected through any enhanced devices. These recorded classroom activities help in many ways to all learners, even those who do not know those subjects, topics whereas teaching using IoT and mobile devices reaches out any corner of the world.

Issues and Challenges

There are a number of challenges and issues for utilizing ICT technology in an e-Learning environment. Some of the challenges and issues are given below:

1. Integration of physical objects with smart learning objects and activities
2. Design of scalable architecture that supports reliable devices for smart learning environment
3. Design of huge amount of storing and analyses of learning data

There is a big need to design a generic model and architecture in the e-learning industry to overcome the above challenges and issues. This generic model and architecture aim to facilitate scalability, interoperability, simplify development, and ease implementation.

IoT in Education

In order for students to be prepared for a more complex learning environment, a smart classroom must promote creativity, critical thinking, communication, and collaboration. Technology tools that allow students to create with audio, text, and images provide an opportunity to build higher-order thinking skills. The introduction of the Internet of Things (IoT) in education, which allows Internet-based communications, has changed higher educational institutions massively. IoT provides a more engaging learning environment for students and more data about the learning process to help teachers to enhance their knowledge about the learning pace of their students and their learning difficulties.

Higher education institutions begin to leverage solutions across an IoT platform, they are able to capture, manage and analyze big data (Palanivel K & Chithralekha T, 2017). The IoT does a collection of data from the smart classroom and store as big data for future use. For example, the IoT education system uses sensor-enabled devices mounted in classroom doorways and they attached to teachers and students identity card holders. The sensor-enabled devices tag to be teachers and student's identity cards and the sensor reader installed near the entrance of classrooms. Because all teachers and students would arrive at institutions at the same time in the morning and everyone needs to read their student card, then everyone must spend few minutes' complete attendances every day. Many educational institutions use sensor devices tags as the teachers and student's identity card and may be integrated with many functions into the card such as security, library, motorcycle parking, payment, etc. The conceptual working model by sensor devices or IoT devices to confirm all teachers and students attendance and total attendance number in this classroom.

The above-collected data can be uploaded in the required format, then and thereby using a learning management system (LMS). This application synchronizes those things timely duration to reach outsiders of the classroom. Therefore, learners can learn those lessons even being outside that classroom. This insight provides stakeholders with a real-time view of learners, staff and assets. It enables HEIs to make decisions that are more informed in an effort to improve student learning experiences, operational efficiency and campus security.

Proposed System

This chapter focuses on introducing the IoT in higher education, in order to demonstrate the new way of interaction among students and teachers and the movements produced in a smart academic environment. It is proposed to devise a generic IoT architecture to smart education that addresses the above challenges and issues presented above section. The IoT architecture will provide maximum reusability, interoperability, scalability, etc. Some of the common characteristics that the proposed IoT architecture should embrace including loosely coupled, modular, platform independent and based on open standards. The proposed architecture handles the requirements and forms a superset of functionalities, information structures, and mechanisms. The architecture must also be flexible so that it can be modified to change according to future needs. A qualitative survey was taken on the proposed IoT reference architecture solution, validating usability and acceptability of the referenced system among stakeholders in a tertiary educational environment.

Section 2 describes the background details that required to write this chapter. Section 3 reviews various research papers on IoT architectures on e-Learning domain. Section 4 describes the proposal that consists of requirements, IoT smart education model and IoT architectures to e-Learning domain. Finally, section 5 concludes and outline future works.

BACKGROUND

This section presents the background details that required to write this chapter. This includes smart education, Internet of Things and software architecture.

The Evolution of Technologies in Education

Today, technology can be as media or tools for accessing learning content, inquiry, communication and collaboration and evaluation of teaching and learning. The technology can be implemented and utilized in helping learners learn. This is described as technology-enhanced learning (TEL). TEL is used to provide flexibility in the mode of learning. Technologies, such as mobile computing, seamless learning, cloud computing, learning analytics, big data, Internet of things (IoT), wearable technology and etc., promote the emergence of smart education (Zhu, ZT. Yu, MH. & Riezebos, P. 2016).

With the development of the above technologies, learning has become a major TEL paradigm. Using mobile learning, ubiquitous learning (Hwang, 2008) and seamless learning, the learners can learn across time and locations, and they can convert the learning from one scenario to another conveniently encompassing formal and informal learning, individual and social learning through the smart personal device (Chan, T.W. Roschelle, J. His, S. et al. 2006). Technologies like cloud computing, learning analytics and big data focus on how learning data can be captured, analyzed and directed towards improving learning and teaching, support the development of the personalized and adaptive learning (Schönberger, M.V. & Cukier, K. (2013). With these adaptive learning technologies, learning platform reacts to individual learner data and adapts instructional resource (NMC, 2015). Wearable technology can integrate the location information, exercise log, social media interaction and visual reality tools into the learning.

As a new educational paradigm, smart learning bases its foundations on smart devices and technologies. For educational technology, 'smart' refers to accomplish its purpose effectively and efficiently (Spector J.M. 2014). The technology includes hardware and software. For hardware, 'smart' refers to the smart device much smaller, more portable and affordable. It is effective to support learner take place the learning anytime and anywhere with smart devices (e.g., smartphones, laptop, Google glass, etc.). For software, 'smart' refers to adaptive and flexible. It is efficient to carry out personalized learning for learner according to their personal difference, with adaptive learning technologies (e.g. Cloud computing, big data, learning analytics, Internet of Things, adaptive engine, etc.).

Smart Education

Smart education, a concept that describes learning in the digital age, has gained increased attention. It enables leading-edge technologies into educational institutions. The goal is to foster engaging learning experience to meet the diverse needs of learners, through the innovative use of information and communications technology (Education, 2007). Zhu, ZT. Yu, MH. & Riezebos, P. (2016) stated that "the essence of smart education is to create intelligent environments by using smart technologies, so that smart pedagogies can be facilitated as to provide personalized learning services and empower learners, and thus talents of wisdom who have a better value orientation, higher thinking quality, and stronger conduct ability could be fostered". The smart education proposed the keys for achieving - embracing and expanding online learning, utilizing transformative technologies, high-speed network connectivity, extending connectivity to the classroom, providing high-quality and continuous professional development (Smart, 2014).

Tikhomirov, V. Dneprovskaya, N. & Yankovskaya, E. (2015) stressed that nowadays progress of e-Learning that contribute to the formation of a new educational trend called smart education. This trend provided outstanding opportunities to acquire different professional skills, competencies and knowledge through active use ICT. Zhu, ZT. Yu, MH. & Riezebos, P. (2016) said that the goal of smart education. Intelligent technology plays an important role in the construction of smart educational environments. The smart educational framework is to describe the essential elements in a technology-facilitated environment that on the one hand helps learners to achieve higher thinking quality and leads to innovation and creativity and on the other hand enables teachers to personalize learning. The three essential elements in a smart education environment are taught, technology, and learner. Figure 2. shows the proposed framework for smart education.

This framework describes the essential elements in smart education: *smart environments*, *smart pedagogy*, and *smart learner*. Smart education emphasizes the ideology for pursuing a better education and thus had better be renamed as smarter education, which addresses the needs for smart pedagogies as a methodological issue and smart learning environments as a technological issue, and advances the educational goals to cultivate smart learners as results. Smart environments could be significantly influenced by smart pedagogy. Smart pedagogies and smart environments support the development of smart learners.

Figure 2. A framework of smart education.

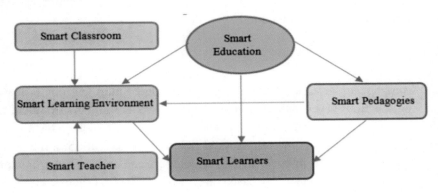

Smart Classroom

The smart classroom strategy is a learning initiative that assists educators to make ICT integral to learning as part of the education. A smart classroom is a transformative strategy to transition from traditional ways of working to a digital way of working that is meaningful, engaging and connected (Uskov, V. Howlett, R & Jain, L. 2015). Learner activities should be connected to both the content of the respective subject and the real world, however, the future classrooms (Kankaanranta, M. & Mäkelä, T. 2014) should not become a high-tech entertainment park. The smart classroom will be characterized as a classroom with IoT solutions that provide learning analytics solutions, learner-centred teaching, the digital revolution and related paradigm shift in education towards more personalized, collaborative and creative learning.

Smart Classroom (Shi, 2010) aims to build a real-time interactive classroom with tele-education experience by bringing pervasive computing technologies into traditional distance learning. The goal of the smart classroom is to narrow the gap between the teacher's experience in tele-education and that in the traditional classroom educating, by means of integrating these two currently separated education environments together. The smart classrooms' strategy for e-Learning is comprised of interrelated and co-dependent components (Byte, 2016) and they are digital or smart pedagogy, digital content and e-Learning spaces. These components co-exist to create the conditions for a new generation of digital learners. If one component is missing the approach is unbalanced and less effective. For successful integration of devices in a classroom environment, an education provider may have to face many difficulties (Gul, S. et al. 2017).

Smart classroom enables learners to digital resources and interact with the learning systems in any place and at any time, but also actively provides them with the necessary learning guidance, supportive tools or learning suggestions in the right place, at the right time, and in the right form.

Smart Teaching

Smart teaching largely involves the organization of teaching and learning activities with the help of software tools. In broader terms, smart teaching is a way of professionalizing the teaching and learning experience. Smart teaching can have classrooms with technology that goes beyond a set of teacher-centric tools and allows students to use the power of the internet to take part. Smart teaching is considered very controversial. It is described as a bunch of different teaching methods and strategies for teaching and from the other side how to use smart technology in the classroom. Smart teaching addresses the above issues common in traditional teaching in a number of ways.

Smart Learning

Smart learning is a broad term for education in today's digital age. Smart learning (s-learning) means a new learning paradigm which serves learners to have an effective learning environment that offers personalized mobile contents and easily adapting to the current education model. And it also allows learners to have a convenient communication environment and rich resources (Kim, S. Song, S. M. & Yoon, Y I. 2011). The concept of smart learning is (i) focuses on learners and content more than on devices, and (ii) it is effective, intelligent, tailored learning based on advanced IT infrastructure. Smart-learning plays an important role in the creation of an effective learning environment that offers personalized content and easy adaptation to the current educational model. The characteristics (Yang, S.J.H., Okamoto, T. & Tseng S.S. (2008) of context-aware and ubiquitous learning and the detailed descriptions of these aspects are shown in Table 1.

Smart learning combines the advantages of social learning and ubiquitous learning. The potential of ubiquitous learning results from the enhanced possibilities of accessing learning content and computer-supported collaborative learning environments at the right time, at the right place, and in the right form.

IoT in Education

The IoT solutions have started to reach into the education sector, as it is very conservative. The growth of the IoT has been a positive influence on education, and how technology is being used is slowly changing, from static applications to interactive classrooms. IoT in special education is only one example of many possibilities where the IoT has been utilized in the form of teaching aid. The possibilities of use of IoT in e-Learning are numerous (Charmonman, S. et al. 2015) as shown in Figure 3.

IoT can be used to reduce costs, improve performance, generate new revenue streams, enhance the student experience and provide differentiated services. The applications of IoT in the higher education sector are *campus energy management and ecosystem monitoring*, *security campus and classroom access control*, *student's health monitoring*, and *improving teaching and learning*. It has introduced changes in

Table 1. Aspects of smart learning

S.No.	Aspect	Description
1	Adaptability	The adjustability of learning contents and services
2	Interoperability	The interoperable operation between different standards of learning resources, services, and platforms.
3	Location awareness	The identification of learners' locations.
4	Mobility	The continuousness of computing while learners move from one place to another.
5	Pervasiveness	A transparent way of accessing learning materials and services and predicting
6	Seamlessness	The provision of everlasting service sessions
7	Situation awareness	The detection of learners' various situated scenarios
8	Social awareness	The awareness of learners' social relationship

Figure 3. Use of IoT in e-Learning

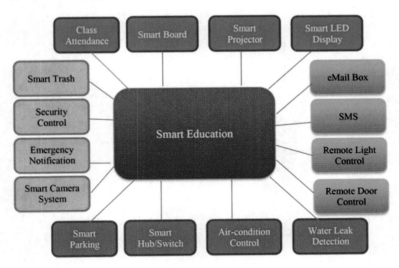

many parts of the canvas education, business model (Selinger, M. Sepulveda, A. & Buchan, J. (2013) and it can provide many benefits for educational organizations.

The term IoT in education is considered as a technological tool to enhance academic infrastructure and as a subject or course to teach fundamental concepts of Computer Science (Elyamany, H.F. & Alkhairi, A. H. 2015). It has not only changed the traditional teaching practices but has also brought changes in the infrastructure of educational institutions (Mohanapriya, M. 2016). IoT refers to the stringent connectedness between the digital and physical world (Atzori, 2010). It is defined by the ITU as:

A global infrastructure for the information society, enabling advanced services by interconnecting (physical and virtual) things based on, existing and evolving, interoperable information and communication technologies. (IoT, 2015)

The IoT system is comprised of a number of functional blocks to facilitate various utilities to the system such as sensing, identification, actuation, communication, and management. These functional blocks are a *device, communication, services, management, security and application.* Figure 4 shows the typical example of an IoT application.

The key features of IoT systems that represent important considerations for tomorrow's IoT (IEC, 2016) are data correlation and information retrieval, communication, integration and interoperation, and security, privacy and trust. As IoT is a dynamic system of systems, measures to attest the trustworthiness of IoT components throughout their lifetime are required.

Various IoT technologies such as *hardware* platforms and *wireless communication* protocols are used in different applications. These communication protocols allow devices to exchange data over the network. These communication protocols form the backbone of IoT systems and enable network connectivity and coupling to applications.

Figure 4. A typical example of an IoT application

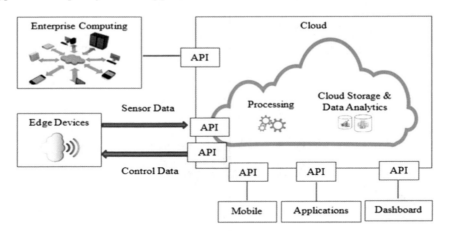

IoT Connectivity Models

Various IoT connectivity models are device-to-device, device-to-cloud, device-to-gateway and backend data sharing. Figure 5(a) – 5(d) shows the IoT connectivity models.

Device-to-device model represents two or more devices that directly connect and communicate with one another. They can communicate over many types of networks, including IP networks or the Internet, using protocols like Bluetooth, Z-Wave, and ZigBee. This model is commonly used in home automation systems to transfer small data packets of information between devices at a relatively low data rate.

Device-to-Cloud model communication involves an IoT device connecting directly to an Internet cloud service like an application service provider to exchange data and control message traffic. It often uses traditional wired Ethernet or Wi-Fi connections, but can also use cellular technology.

Device-to-Gateway model connects to an intermediary device to access a cloud service. This involves application software, operating on a local gateway device (like a smartphone or a "hub") that acts as an intermediary between an IoT device and a cloud service.

Back-end data-sharing model essentially extends the single device-to-cloud communication model so that IoT devices and sensor data can be accessed by authorized third parties. Under this model, users can export and analyze smart object data from a cloud service in combination with data from other sources, and send it to other services for aggregation and analysis.

The IoT connectivity model presented above with a model for data flow, which can simply be modelled by three stages: data creation, transmission, and consumption. This can be through simple systems that involve the user directly interacting with the device, for example, interacting with a wearable through an application on a mobile device or tablet.

Bilal, M., 2017 stated that IoT components cover a variety of the latest technologies used in the present era. Some of the major technologies are radio frequency technology (RFID), near field communication (NFC) and Bluetooth.

- The RFID is integrating a radio frequency (RF) technology via the electromagnetic spectrum to identify unique IoT devices. After all, RFID tags the devices that are readable at a certain distance in an efficient way.

Figure 5. (a). Device-to-device connectivity model, (b) device-to-cloud connectivity model, 5(c) device-to-gateway connectivity model, (d) back-end data-sharing model

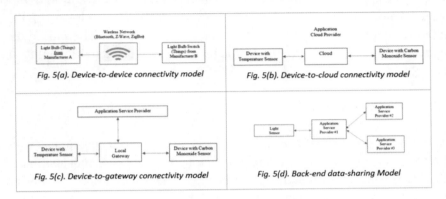

- NFC is a set of the communication-based protocol used for communication between two IoT devices in the short range. In NFC, the devices must be portable for the purpose of finding a suitable location. The most used applications are smartphones, parking meters, e-ticket booking etc.
- Bluetooth, a short-range communication technology designed for low consumption of power. The most commonly used applications are home automation, communication with peripherals etc. The collected data from data acquisition components will be transferred to the network.

The network is consumed and processed via different applications. The network is supported by a variety of communication-based technologies such as RFID, Wireless Fidelity (WiFi), Worldwide Interoperability for Microwave Access (WiMAX), NFC, x Digital Subscriber Line (xDSL), Bluetooth, Ethernet, Power Line Communication (PLC) and cellular-based networks.

IoT Applications

IoT is a revolutionary concept and it finds its applications in almost every field - healthcare, business, transportation, smart parking, air pollution, potable water monitoring, agriculture and management, etc. From the Figure 6, it is evident there are similar approaches and challenges when implementing an IoT project.

Figure 6. Various IoT application areas

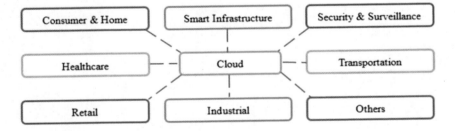

It shall find that, in all these application areas, IoT technologies have been able to significantly reduce human effort and improve the quality of life. There is a need to move from traditional education to smart education (Giovannella, C. Iosue, A. & Tancredi, A. 2012). With the IoT Platform, a broad spectrum of interoperable, cross-ecosystem IoT solutions can be built and optimized data management and analytics support (Intel, 2016). IoT systems/ applications have unique flexibility and ability to be suitable in any environment.

Design of Smart Classroom

The design of smart classroom should enable the control of audiovisual equipment's, projectors, interactive whiteboards, in order to facilitate interaction among teachers and students. In addition, it shows how the stored data are accessed through standard devices like smartphones, tablets, and laptops. The smart campus system (Amare, B. & Sengupta, J. (2017) has three parts as shown in Figure 7. The three parts are IoT hardware and software, IoT gateway and Network and Cloud. All of them combined to form an IoT-based system.

The things or hardware and software utilized in IoT systems include devices for a remote dashboard, devices for control, servers, actuators, a routing device, actuators and sensors. The main function of the IoT hardware is like system activation, action specification, security, communication and detection to support smart education. The software addresses its key areas of networking and action through platforms. The software is responsible for data collection and device integration within the youth network. IoT Gateway controls the system. The major function of the IoT gateway is device connectivity, protocol translation, data filtering and processing, security, management and more. It is a combination of sensor data, decipher between sensors protocol, process sensors, and data before sending it onward. To collect and store data from the wireless sensor network through their IoT gateway there must a server, which is

Figure 7. Design perspective smart classroom

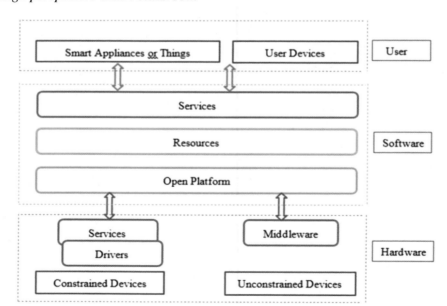

connected to the internet. On this server, a website used to access and control the sensors through the IoT gateway.

Software Architecture

Software architecture (Bass, L. Clements, P. & Kazman, R. 2003) is a flexible and hierarchical reusable architecture based on domain-specific and software product lines. IEEE Standard defined as

Architecture is the fundamental organization of a system embodied in its components, their relationships to each other and to the environment and the principles guiding its design and evolution. (IEEE, 2000)

It is also defined as the

Software architecture of a system is the set of structures needed to reason about the system, which comprise software elements, relations among them, and properties of both. (Bass, L. Clements, P. & Kazman, R. 2012)

The above definitions describe an architecture to be about structure and that this structure is formed by components or elements and the relations or connectors between them.

IoT Architecture

IoT architecture may be treated as a system which can be physical, virtual, or a hybrid, consisting of a collection of numerous active physical things, sensors, actuators, cloud services, specific IoT protocols, communication layers, users, developers, and enterprise layer. The IoT architecture is currently available for knowledge purpose:

A dynamic global network infrastructure with self-configuring capabilities based on standard and interoperable communication protocols where physical and virtual 'Things' have identities, physical attributes, and virtual personalities and use intelligent interfaces, and are seamlessly integrated into the information network. (Ray, P. P. 2018)

The most basic architecture is a *three-layer architecture*. It has three layers, namely, the perception, network, and application layer. It defines various applications in which the IoT can be deployed, for example, smart homes, smart cities, and smart health. The three-layer architecture defines the main idea of the IoT, but it is not sufficient for research on research because it often focuses on the finer aspects of the IoT. Figure 8 shows a simplified architecture of the IoT domain.

There is another architecture called *five-layer architecture*, which additionally includes the processing and business layers. There are some strategies that applied when planning data-driven IoT architectures. These strategies help the designer simplify development, manage complexity, and ensure that IoT solutions remain scalable, flexible, and robust. These strategies are adopting *a layered architecture, security by design, automate operations, design for interoperability and follow a reference architecture*. There are many initiatives currently working towards standardizing IoT architectures to improve interoperability. IoT platform vendors and research partners collaborate through these initiatives to define IoT

Figure 8. The simplified architecture of the IoT domain

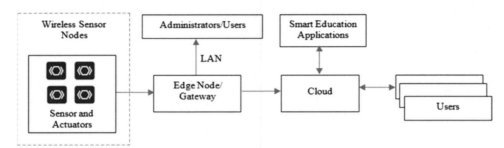

reference architectures. Some widely referenced IoT reference architectures include IoT-A (Bauer, M. 2007), IEEE P2413 and Industrial Internet Reference Architecture (IIRA). Reference architectures can be used as a template for developing IoT solutions. This approach helps to manage the complexity of IoT enabled smart education.

IoT Reference Model

A reference model is an abstract framework for understanding significant relationships among the entities of some environment (Armstrong, C., 2014). The IoT reference model provides the highest abstraction level for the definition of the IoT-A (Bauer, M. 2007). It is considered that current architecture models under development, such as the ITU-T model (ITU, 2014), the NIST model, the machine-to-machine (M2M) model or the architectural reference model.

The IoTRM aims at establishing a common grounding and a common language for IoT architectures and IoT systems. The IoT reference model introduces the main concepts of the IoT like devices, IoT services and virtual entities, and it also introduces the relations between these concepts. The IoTRM consists of a set of models, namely the domain, information and functionality. IoT reference models provide a description that is more abstract than what is inherent to actual systems and applications.

IoT Reference Architecture

A reference architecture maps onto software elements that implement the functionality defined in the reference model. It tries to show the most complete picture of what is involved in realizing the modelled entities. In the field of IoT, reference architecture handles requirements and forms a superset of functionalities, information structures, mechanisms and protocols (Weyrich, M. & Ebert, C. 2016). The key to enabling communication between all of these diverse "Things" is standardization. Reference architectures are of great help for standardization, as they define guidelines that can be used when planning the implementation of an IoT system. In order to achieve standardization, it is necessary to create high-level reference architectures like IoT-A.

The IoT reference architecture consists of a set of views and perspectives (Rozanski, N. & Woods, E. 2011) that actually define the IoT architecture. The set of views is functional, information and deployment. The functional view focuses on the decomposition into functional components. The information view describes the information flows, the interaction between components and the structure of information, in compliance with the information model. The deployment view comes later on and shows how the "logical" component part of the functional view is deployed within the developed concrete software modules. The IoT reference architecture is providing a language for everyone involved and an abstract, but a rich view of the domain.

MAIN FOCUS OF THIS CHAPTER

The focus of this chapter is to design a generic IoT architecture for smart education. To design an IoT architecture, it has to study the building methodology, literature review, quality attributes with some earlier works, architectural mythology, etc.

Building IoT Architecture

Building the IoT reference architecture (Maier, M. 2013 & Maier, M. 2007) consist of the following four steps.

Step 1: To conduct a qualitative literature study to define and describe the space of 'IoT in smart education' and related work and to gather typical requirements.

Step 2: To design the reference architecture, it will develop and describe a methodology from literature about designing software architectures, especially reference architectures. Based on the gathered requirements, it describes the methodology and design principles for IoT Smart education.

Step 3: To gather an overview of existing technologies available for handling and processing large volumes of heterogeneous data in a reasonable time.

Step 4: To verify and refine the resulting reference architecture by applying it to case studies and mapping it against existing IoT architectures from academic and industry literature.

Following a design method (Galster, M. & Avgeriou, P, 2011), it is decided to loosely follow the proposed development process, which consists of the following six steps.

Step 1: Decide on the reference architecture type

Step 2: Select the design strategy

Step 3: Empirical acquisition of data

Step 4: Construction of the reference architecture

Step 5: Enabling reference architecture with variability

Step 6: Valuation of the reference architecture

While developing a generic IoT architecture, the result should be relevant to a specific domain, i.e. IoT in smart education, that is incorporate domain knowledge and fulfil domain requirements, while still being general enough to be applicable in different contexts.

Literature Study

The availability of newer and newer technology reflects on how the relevant processes should be performed in the current fast-changing digital era. This leads to the adoption of a variety of smart solutions in HEIs to enhance the quality of life and to improve the performances of both teachers and students.

Rehman, A.U. Abbasi, A.Z. & Shaikh, Z.A. (2008) presented the sensing with RFID technology that should benefit students and faculty with identification, tracking, smart lecture room, smart lab, room security, smart attendance taking, etc. Lane, J. & Finsel, A. (2014) emphasized the importance of big data movement and how it could help to build Smarter Universities. They examined how the Big Data movement could help build smarter Universities. Al Shimmary, M.K, Al Nayar & Kubba M.M. (2015) analyzed the advantages of using RFID and wireless sensor networks (WSN) technology in the development of smart universities. Yu, Z. (2011) argued that the development of wireless communication and pervasive computing technology, smarter campuses are built to benefit the faculty and students, manage the available resources and enhance user experience with proactive services.

From the review, RFID, WSN as well as IoT are expected to be significant parts of smart Universities and strongly support sending characteristics of smart universities. Technology-based teaching gives for better communication between learner and teacher. It also gives affordable education with satisfying learners and recruiter expectations for learners.

Vharkute, M. & Wagh, S. (2015) proposed a system combining the different applications of e-Learning with the help of IoT. This system gives a standard design framework for the educational system. It proposed the reference model to improve the learning outcomes of learners. According to Ahmed, E. et al, (2017), "IoT might serve as the backbone for the ubiquitous learning environment, and enable smart environments to recognize and identify objects, and retrieve information from the internet to facilitate their adaptation functionality".

In research by Hameed, S. Badii, A. & Cullen, A J. (2008), two groups' 25 learners each were enrolled in a similar course. Nevertheless, one group was taught using traditional methods and others using an interactive system of the Internet of things. After conducting various tests and analysis, they concluded, "IoT applied as a tool to support the teaching process, improves student academic performance." AjazMoharkan, Z. et al. (2017) gave a model of smart learning using the IoT and the gamification technique of e-Learning. This model was proposed to use both smart and engaging. Charmonman, S. et al. (2015) discussed IoT in e-Learning on IoT technology, IoT potentials to transform education, and IoT to improve student performance.

From the literature, it is reviewed that there are many IoT models are available but no IoT architecture is available to smart education, and hence, the objective is to design a generic IoT architecture to smart education. The proposed architecture is like the backbone of IoT if it is not robust and flexible, deploying IoT will take more time than required. The proposed architecture includes solutions to various issues such as interoperability, performance and security issues.

Challenges

The IoT domain will encompass an extremely wide range of technologies, from stateless to stateful, from extremely constrained to unconstrained, from hard real-time to soft real time. Therefore, single reference architecture cannot be used as a blueprint for all possible concrete implementations. While a reference model can probably be identified, it is likely that several reference architectures will co-exist in the IoT.

This will also encompass several types of communications models such as Thing to Application Server, Thing to Human and Thing to Thing communication.

Architectural Methodology

The ISO/IEC/IEEE 2010 standard (IEEE, 2010) specifies how architectures should be designed. This standard motivates the terms and concepts used in describing the architecture and provides guidance on how architecture descriptions are captured and organized. It expresses architecture in terms of multiple views or more architecture models as shown in Figure 9.

As previously said, instead of developing an IoT architecture from scratch, this chapter uses existing IoT architectures as the basis such as the high-level architecture or architectural reference model among others. Both architectures are conceptually based on the (IEEE, 2010) approach. The architecture analysis and design process for IoT systems need to consider all possible things and services for IoT smart education.

SOLUTIONS AND RECOMMENDATIONS

IoT Architecture to Smart Education

This section presents the proposed IoT architecture to smart education (IoTASE) to design scenario description, goals, requirements, functional view, and the IoT reference architecture.

Scenario Description

Let assume teachers are interested in technology. They attempt to create a smart learning environment by automating teaching and learning operations using the cloud, mobile and ubiquitous learning aspects. They propose to their learners an environment for learning a course/subject, including with technology, a puzzle where learners could interact with each other to acquire skills related to those course/subject, their components and functioning modes. In the beginning, the teacher introduces the course. Then, the teacher proposes a collaborative activity where learners could interact with a subject the use of near field communication technology. Learners are equipped with near field communication enabled active devices to store information about the learning content. This collaborative activity aims to test the learn-

Figure 9. Architectural model

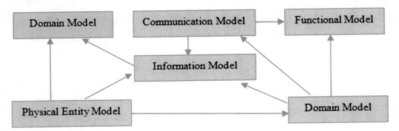

ers' comprehension level. The scenario provides a diversity of connected objects and several interactions' possibilities with the physical environment.

The main challenges here are to integrate physical learning objects with e-Learning objects and activities and to provide a flexible and scalable model/architecture for the learning environment.

Quality Attributes

It is important to select a minimum set of quality attributes that can be eligible for consideration while designing IoT architecture. The absence of quality in things or service can negatively affect the quality of the whole system. The quality attributes can be related to design-time and run-time quality of the things and services, quality of deployment infrastructure and quality of communication infrastructure. The key quality attributes for IoT are *security, availability, scalability and elasticity, reliability, multitenancy, interoperability, etc.*

Design Goals

The design goals for the proposed IoT architecture are efficiency, manageability, mobility, security and privacy.

1. *Efficiency* in terms of power management of the different devices connected to the architecture.
2. *Manageability* includes centralized and distributed based control.
3. *Mobility* is considered when users move from one place to another.
4. *Quality of Service (QoS)* is for the prioritization of different data traffic from devices.
5. *Security and privacy* deal with various issues such as authentication, encryption, etc.

Requirements

To meet the above design goals, it identifies the requirements of the proposed architecture. According to (ITU, 2014), the requirements are divided into functional and non-functional requirements. The *non-functional* requirements refer to the requirements related to the implementation and operation of the IoT itself. The non-functional requirements for reference architecture include interoperability, scalability, reliability and availability. The *functional requirement* refers to the requirements related to the IoT actors, i.e., entities which are external to the IoT and that interacts with the IoT. The IoT functional requirements are application support, service, communication, device management, data management, security, confidentiality and privacy (IoT Series, 2014).

As smart things collect a huge amount of sensor data, compute and storage resources are required to analyze store, and process this data. Most of the things are mobile. It is very difficult to communicate to their changing location in the cloud data centre because of changing network conditions across different locations. There should be a reliable communication between the things and the cloud data centre.

IoT Functional View

The functional view in Figure 10 defines the roles and the associated duties that the actors involved with it. The roles of actors dealing with IoT e-Learning platform are learning data producers, knowledge producers, virtualizes and learning service providers.

The proposed IoTASE considered various functional components and they are management, service, organization, IoT process, virtual entities, IoT communication service, and security. The management is user and configuration. The service organization is dedicated to components that are used as tools for modelling, creating and supporting to access and make use of data available at the IoT platform. The IoT process component allows for modelling either through graphical interface or scripting. The IoT communication service provides the IoT eco-system with a communication channel following the publish/subscribe paradigm. The security introduces various the functional components used for dealing with IoT e-Learning system. They are authentication and access control policies.

The IoTASE endows the new features required by classroom-based e-learning system. IoTASE is a roadmap to integrate IoT in e-Learning platform in a *scalable* manner. Here, learners can use these features easily on strong bound of IoT in the smart classroom with enhanced device's data collection and sharing subjects, e-notes to everyone. IoT communication model to IoTASE with IoT requisite of the perfect network to observe, sense, collect data related to classroom activities and transferred to the learners. It is used to enhance feature in the current education system.

IoT Functional Model

Figure 11, which is derived from Figure 10, illustrates the IoT model to smart education and its levels. It is important to note that in the IoT, data flows in both directions. The proposed IoT reference model starts with the device layer. Physical devices, actuators, things and controllers that might control multiple devices. Communications and connectivity are also concentrated in this layer. The most important function is reliable, timely information transmission. This includes transmissions between devices and the network, across networks and between the networks.

Figure 10. A functional model of IoT smart education

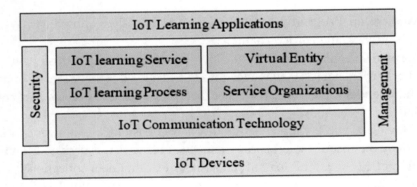

Figure 11. IoT model for smart education

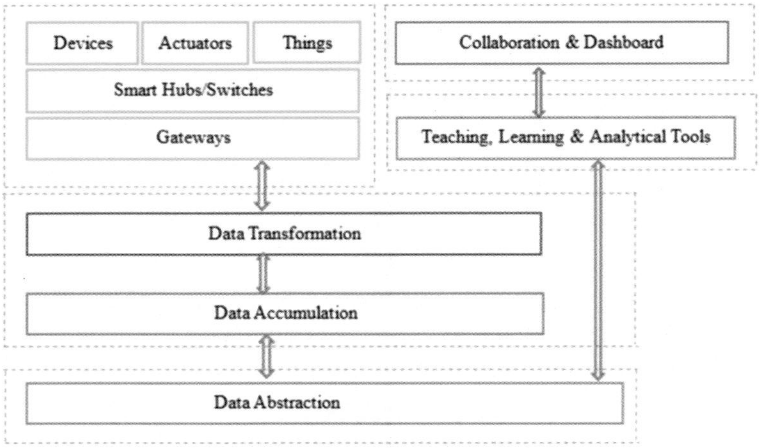

In data accumulation, data in motion is converted to data at rest. It captures data and puts it at rest; it is now usable by educational applications on a non-real-time basis. Applications access the data when necessary. It converts event-based data to query-based processing. The learning data abstraction requires multiple storage systems to accommodate IoT device data.

IoT Architecture

From a high-level perspective, IoTASE architecture follows a layered approach. The motivation behind the layered architecture view is the observation that typically different enablers have been designed to support the respective functionalities on the respective abstraction layers. In IoTASE, the aim is to choose standardized enablers that are best suited for the particular task and connecting them in a suitable way to combine the particular strengths while mitigating possible weaknesses. The characteristics of the proposed IoTASE includes the following:

- **Open Standards:** The communication between the layers is based on open standards to ensure interoperability.
- **Defined Application Programming Interfaces (APIs):** They allow for easy integration with existing applications and other IoT solutions.
- **Loosely Coupled:** It is important that each layer can be used independently with other layers.
- **Modular:** Each layer should allow the features to be sourced from different suppliers.
- **Platform-Independent**: Each layer should be independent of the host hardware and infrastructure.

The IoTASE provides flexibility for composability and extensibility to allow for a variety of technology choices driven by the specific solution requirements. Fig.12. that is derived from Fig.10 shows the general architecture of IoTASE. The IoTASE consists of learning data collection layer, learning data integration layer, learning information access layer and learning application layer.

The *learning data collection layer* provides a connection to the physical world. It can utilize a large number of different device and communication technologies. Key technologies are sensors and actuators for sensing and controlling relevant aspects of the physical world. These sensors may be part of specific, often resource-constraint sensor nodes or be attached to sensor platforms running on more powerful devices, e.g. mobile phones, gateways or dedicated servers.

The *learning data integration layer* integrates and homogenizes the access to the data and services provided by the *learning data collection layer*. The components in higher layers do not have to deal with heterogeneous access and communication technologies. However, the data may still be in its raw form, i.e. there may not be any common abstraction with respect to the data provided by different devices and technologies. In addition to providing access to the data, the *learning data integration layer* may also enable the management of devices in the *learning data collection layer* and configuring and controlling the connectivity and communication.

The *learning information access layer* provides access to information on a higher, common abstraction level. Applications and components of the *learning knowledge processing layer* can request information, specifying what information they need, and they get back exactly the requested information. The learning information access layer may provide different interaction styles, e.g. request-response or subscribe-notify. It integrates information from different sources in the learning data integration layer.

The *learning knowledge processing layer* process information and data, primarily information provided by the learning information access layer, to elicit higher-level knowledge, implicitly contained in the information. Smart applications may be supported through recommendations derived from the information while taking into account the application goals.

The *learning application layer* is the place for end-user applications. The applications primarily access learning knowledge processing layer and *learning information access layer* components to have a good basis for optimally supporting the users in their respective tasks. Applications directly interact with the users to find out about their goals, which are then the basis for interacting with the *learning information access layer* and the *learning knowledge processing layer* to retrieve the required information and knowledge.

Figure 12. IoT Reference Architecture to smart education

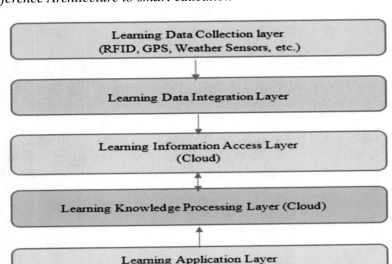

With the IoT Platform, a broad spectrum of interoperable, cross-ecosystem IoT architecture can be built and optimized—with the added advantages of scalable compute, security from device to cloud, and data management and analytics support.

Performance Improvement and Evaluation

Smart education enjoys better operational efficiency and improved learning experiences for students. IoT technology can help cut costs for budget constrained campuses and drastically improve public safety. Furthermore, implementing these new technologies allows learners to engage with science and technology. IoT will continue to grow, so it's imperative that schools begin to implement this technology in order to provide students with an enhanced learning environment that is adaptable to technological advancements. IoT devices provide substantial near real-time feedback, which can make resource management easier and more immediate. With location tracking capabilities and asset monitoring, an educational institution could audit the use of vehicles to survey driver behaviour and implement preventative maintenance features.

Evaluation of the software architectures plays a critical role to verify the quality of a software system. To validate the work, it evaluates the system and user comprehension respectively.

- The IoTASE is based on Web service technology that use mobile devices to access more easily.
- The architecture is designed using back-end data-sharing model for aggregation and analysis.
- The IoTASE achieved interoperability between various IoT enabled systems through the cloud.
- It achieved scalability by connecting more devices to the cloud, thereby increasing the latency.
- It adopted a layered architecture.
- It followed a reference architecture that standardizing IoT architectures to improve interoperability.

The IoTASE includes solutions to performance and security issues. Based on the above-mentioned requirements and features, the IoTASE evaluated and listed in Table 2. For evaluation, it has 25 different decision criteria that may or may not be fulfilled by the proposed IoT platform. The weighted sum model (Guzman, L. 2001) is used for evaluation. Table 3 lists the architecture and design patterns used in IoTASE.

Table 2 and Table 3 shows commonly reported quality requirements, reusability and some improvements suggested in the IoT model and architecture.

The IoT is rich in approaches, concepts, and structures. Various initiatives have already delivered IoT models, architectures, and tools. However, Weyrich, M. & Ebert, C. (2016) stated that a convergence of approaches and standards is required for simplification. This raises the following issues.

- Many technologies exist to implement communication as efficient and secure communication.
- It is questionable whether device-oriented, real-time or the diversity of real-time will continue.
- Big-data analytics and the human-machine interface are close to the education business.

FUTURE RESEARCH DIRECTIONS

Future work is proposed to incorporate blockchain technology and big data analysis to provide a secure framework for interconnectivity, accelerates the initiative of integrating emerging technologies and offers

Table 2. Evaluation of IoTASE

Sl. No.	Requirements/Features	Rating	Sl. No.	Requirements/Features	Rating
1	Architectural patterns used	M	14	Range of the physical area	M
2	Compatibility with ZigBee, Wi-Fi, LPWAN	H	15	Scalability	Y
3	Context awareness	N	16	Security, Privacy and Integrity	Y
4	Cost range	M	17	Size of hardware	M
5	Data reliability	Y	18	Support SOA approach	H
6	Data storage	Y	19	Support the heterogeneity	H
7	Data visualization	Y	20	Big data support	H
8	Device management	Y	21	Analytical tools	L
9	Dynamic adaptation	N	22	Open source technology	Y
10	Flexibility of Cloud architecture	H	23	Followed any reference architecture	Y
11	Interoperability	Y	24	Hardware / software availability	Y
12	Management of large volumes of data	M	25	Power consumption	Y
13	Number of connected devices	H	-	-	-

Note - H – High, M – Medium, L – Low, Y – Yes, N - No

Table 3. Design Patterns used in IoTASE

Sl. No.	Quality Attributes	Design Tactics
1	Performance	Distributed Components, Pipes and Filters, Prioritized Message Queues
2	Security	Proxy, Authentication, Authorization, and Session Tokens
3	Modifiability	Layered, Services-Oriented, Model View Controller (MVC) Pattern
4	Availability	Components' Redundancy
5	Reliability	Redundancy of Components and Data, Cloud Infrastructure
6	Scalability	Data Input Queues and Load Balancing
7	Auditing	Event Logs
8	Multi-tenancy	Publisher/Subscriber Architecture
9	Interoperability	Broker Pattern

a development platform for researchers. They reduce attack surface and uncertainty in e-Learning business models. Blockchain and data analysis have challenges such as high computational costs of manufacturing nodes and verifying transactions. These technologies are in their early years of development and have promising indicators for overcoming these hurdles. They can collaboratively work to address the balance between privacy, utility and affordability for a safeguarded cognitive IoT world.

CONCLUSION

IoT is going to expand at a very rapid rate and with it, there are going to be huge advancements in every field. In the field of education, IoT will take e-Learning to the next level. It can leverage the power of IoT to implement a smart learning environment that facilitates better learning and greater retention rates. This advancement in education to produce better individuals in terms of skills and knowledge. This chapter explains the need and significance of IoT, its applications with a specific focus on smart education. This chapter has also presented finally an education model which is both smart and engaging has been proposed. This chapter aimed to use e-Learning architecture with smart objects to design complex learning scenarios and keep track of the learner's learning experience. This architecture grants interoperability between standards and to provide context-aware activities to learners. However, IoT in smart learning is progressing very fast and so. A next-generation learning management system and experience application programming interfaces or APIs may enable real IoT integration and propel business training to the next level. LMS is part of e-Learning technology in future E-learning will be enabled with IoT.

REFERENCES

Ahmed, E. (2017). Internet of Things Architecture: Recent Advances, Taxonomy, Requirements, and Open Challenges. *IEEE Wireless Communications*, 24(3).

AjazMoharkan, Z. (2017). Internet of Things and its applications in E-learning. IEEE Intel. Conf. on Computational Intelligence and Communication Technology, 1-5.

Al Shimmary, M.K., Al Nayar, & Kubba, M.M. (2015). Designing Smart University using RFID and WSN. *International Journal of Computers and Applications*, *112*(15), 34–39.

Amare, B., & Sengupta, J. (2017). IoT Driven Design and Implementation of Smart Campus, *Intel. Journal of Computer Science Trends and Technology*, 5(4).

Armstrong, C. (2014). *Understanding Reference Models and Reference Architectures*. SATURN.

Bass, L., Clements, P., & Kazman, R. (2003). *Software Architecture in Practice. SEI Series in Software Engineering* (2nd ed.). Addison-Wesley.

Bass, L., Clements, P., & Kazman, R. (2012). *Software Architecture in Practice. SEI Series in Software Engineering* (3rd ed.). Addison-Wesley.

Bilal, M. (2017). *A Review of the Internet of Things Architecture, Technologies and Analysis Smartphone-based Attacks Against 3D printers*. Dept. of Computer Science Zhejiang University Hangzhou.

Byte. (2016). *eLearning for smart classrooms*. Bytes.

Chan, T. W., Roschelle, J., & His, S. (2006). One-to-One Technology-Enhanced Learning: An opportunity for global research collaboration. *Res. Pract. Technol. Enhance. Learn*, *1*(1), 3–29. doi:10.1142/S1793206806000032

Charmonman, S. (2015). Applications of the Internet of Things in E-Learning. *International Journal of the Computer, the Internet and Management*, 23(3), 1-4.

Elyamany, H. F., & Alkhairi, A. H. (2015). IoT-Academia Architecture: A Profound Approach. *2015 IEEE/ACIS 16th International Conference Software Engineering.*

Galster, M., & Avgeriou, P. (2011). Empirically-grounded Reference Architectures: a proposal. *Joint ACM SIGSOFT Conference on Quality of Software Architectures and Conference on Quality of Software Architectures and Symposium on Architecting Critical Systems*, 20–24.

Giovannella, C., Iosue, A., & Tancredi, A. (2012). Scenarios for active learning in smart territories. *Interaction Design and Architecture(s) Journal, 16*, 7–16.

Gul, S. (2017). A Survey on Role of the Internet of Things in Education. *International Journal of Computer Science and Network Security, 17*(5).

Guzman, L. (2001). Multi-Criteria Decision Making Methods: A Comparative Study, Applied optimization. *Journal of Multi-Criteria Decision Analysis, 10*(3), 175–175. doi:10.1002/mcda.300

Hameed, S., Badii, A., & Cullen, A. J. (2008). Effective E-Learning Integration with Traditional Learning in a Blended Learning Environment. *European and Mediterranean Conf, on Information Systems*, 1-16.

Hwang, G.J. (2014). *Definition, Framework and Research Issues of Smart Learning Environments - A Context-Aware Ubiquitous Learning Perspective.* Academic Press.

IEC. (2016). *IoT 2020: Smart & Secure IoT platform.* International Electro-technical Commission.

IEEE. (2000). *Recommended Practice for Architectural Description of Software-Intensive Systems. Standard Specification IEEE 1471-2000.* IEEE Computer Society.

IEEE. (2010). *ISO/IEC/IEEE 2010:2011, Systems and software engineering — Architecture description, the latest edition of the original IEEE Std 1471:2000.* Recommended Practice for Architectural Description of Software-intensive Systems.

Intel. (2016). *Solution Brief, Intel IoT Platform, End-to-End IoT Reference Model and Products.* Author.

IoT Series. (2014). *Common requirements of the Internet of things, Series Y.2066: Global Information Infrastructure.* Internet Protocol Aspects and Next-Generation Networks – Frameworks and Functional Architecture Models.

ITU. (2014). *Study Report on IoT Reference Architectures/Frameworks.* ISO.

Kankaanranta, M., & Makela, T. (2014). Valuation of Emerging Learning Solutions. *World Conf. on Educational Multimedia, Hypermedia and Telecommunications*, Tampere, Finland.

Kim, S., Song, S. M., & Yoon, Y. I. (2011). Smart Learning Services based on Smart Cloud Computing. *Sensors (Basel), 11*(8), 7835–7850. doi:10.3390110807835 PMID:22164048

Lane, J., & Finsel, A. (2014). *Fostering Smarter Colleges and Universities Data, Big Data, and Analytics.* State University of New York Press.

Maier, M. (2007). Internet of Things – Architecture (reference model for IoT). *European Commission within the Seventh Framework Programme.*

Maier, M. (2013). *Towards a Big Data Reference Architecture* (Master's Thesis). Eindhoven University of Technology, Department of Mathematics and Computer Science.

Mohanapriya, M. (2016). IoT Enabled Futures Smart Campus with effective e-Learning. *i-Campus, 3*(4), 81–87.

NMC. (2015). New Media Consortium, Horizon Report: 2015. *Higher Education Edition*, 1–50.

Palanivel, K., & Chithralekha, T. (2017). Big Data Reference Architecture for e-learning Analytical Systems. *International Journal on Recent and Innovation Trends in Computing and Communication, 6*(1), 55–61.

Ray, P. P. (2018). A survey on Internet of Things architectures. *Journal of King Saud University - Computer and Information Sciences, 30*(3), 291-319.

Rehman, A. U., Abbasi, A. Z., & Shaikh, Z. A. (2008). Building a Smart University using RFID technology. *International Conference on Computer Science and Software Engineering*.

Schonberger, V. S., & Cukier, K. (2013). *Big Data: A revolution that will transform how we live, work, and think*. Boston: Houghton Mifflin Harcourt.

Selinger, M., Sepulveda, A., & Buchan, J. (2013). *Education and the internet of Everything*. Cisco Consulting Services and Cisco EMEAR Education Team.

Smart. (2014). *New York Smart Schools Commission Report*. Retrieved from http://www.governor.ny.gov/ sites/ governor.ny.gov/ files/ archive/governor_files/SmartSchoolsReport.pdf

Spector, J. M. (2014). Conceptualizing the Emerging Field of Smart Learning Environments. *Smart Learning Environments, 1*(1), 1–10. doi:10.118640561-014-0002-7

Tikhomirov, V., Dneprovskaya, N., & Yankovskaya, E. (2015). *Three Dimensions of Smart Education*. Academic Press.

Uskov, V., Howlett, R., & Jain, L. (2015). *Smart Education and Smart e-Learning. In Smart Innovation, Systems and Technologies, 41*. Cham: Springer. doi:10.1007/978-3-319-19875-0

Vharkute, M., & Wagh, S. (2015). An architectural approach of the internet of things in E-Learning. In *International Conference on Communications and Signal Processing (ICCSP)*. IEEE. 10.1109/ ICCSP.2015.7322827

Weyrich, M., & Ebert, C. (2016). Reference Architectures for the Internet of Things. *IEEE Computers & Society*.

Yang, S. J. H., Okamoto, T., & Tseng, S. S. (2008). Context-Aware and Ubiquitous Learning (Guest Editorial). *Journal of Educational Technology & Society, 11*(2), 1–2.

Yu, Z. (2011). Towards a Smart Campus with Mobile Social Networking. *Proceedings of International Conference on Cyber, Physical and Social Computing*, 162–169. 10.1109/iThings/CPSCom.2011.55

Zhu, Z. T., Yu, M. H., & Riezebos, P. (2016). A Research Framework of Smart Education, Springer Open Online. *Learning Environment, 3*(1), 4. doi:10.118640561-016-0026-2

KEY TERMS AND DEFINITIONS

Bluetooth: Bluetooth is a telecommunications industry specification that describes how mobile devices, computers, and other devices can easily communicate with each other using a short-range wireless connection.

Device: A sensor, actuator, or tag. Usually the device is part of a thing. The thing processes the devices' context information and communicates selected information to other things. Furthermore, the thing can pass actions to actuators.

E-Book: An electronic book (also known as an e-book or eBook), is a book publication made available in digital form, consisting of text, images, or both, readable on the flat-panel display of computers or other electronic devices.

Function Model: A function model or functional model in systems engineering and software engineering is a structured representation of the functions (activities, actions, processes, operations) within the modeled system or subject area.

Functional View: The functional view of a system defines the architectural elements that deliver the system's functionality. The view documents the system's functional structure-including the key functional elements, their responsibilities, the interfaces they expose, and the interactions between them.

IoT Architecture: IoT architecture is the system of numerous elements: sensors, protocols, actuators, cloud services, and layers.

IoT Reference Architecture: IoT reference architectures are of great help for standardization, as they define guidelines that can be used when planning the implementation of an IoT system.

Learning Environment: A virtual learning environment (VLE) in educational technology is a Web-based platform for the digital aspects of courses of study, usually within educational institutions. They present resources, activities and interactions within a course structure and provide for the different stages of assessment.

Learning Platform: Learning platform is an integrated set of interactive online services that provides the teachers, learners, parents and others involved in education with information, tools and resources to support and enhance educational delivery and management.

Mobile Learning: Mobile learning (*m-learning*) is education via the Internet or network using personal mobile devices, such as tablets and smartphones to obtain learning materials through mobile apps, social interactions and online educational hubs. It is flexible, allowing students access to education anywhere, anytime.

MOOCs: MOOCs (massive open online courses) are free online courses available for anyone to enroll. MOOCs provide an affordable and flexible way to learn new skills, advance your career and deliver quality educational experiences at scale.

Near Field Communication: Near Field Communication (NFC) is a short-range wireless connectivity standard (Ecma-340, ISO/IEC 18092) that uses magnetic field induction to enable communication between devices when they are touched together, or brought within a few centimeters of each other.

Personalized Learning: Personalized learning is an educational approach that aims to customize learning for each student's strengths, needs, skills and interests. Each student gets a learning plan that is based on what he knows and how he learns best.

Reference Architecture: A reference architecture in the field of software architecture or enterprise architecture provides a template solution for an architecture for a particular domain. It also provides a common vocabulary with which to discuss implementations, often with the aim to stress commonality.

Reference Model: A reference model is a model representing a class of domains (e.g., a reference model for production planning and control systems). It is a conceptual framework or blueprint for system's development.

RFID: RFID (radio frequency identification) is a form of wireless communication that incorporates the use of electromagnetic or electrostatic coupling in the radio frequency portion of the electromagnetic spectrum to uniquely identify an object, animal, or person.

Smart Classroom: Smart classroom is technology-enhanced classrooms that foster opportunities for teaching and learning by integrating learning technology, such as computers, specialized software, audience response technology, assistive listening devices, networking, and audio/visual capabilities.

Smart Education: Smart education is a term used to describe learning in the digital age, has gained the attention of many researchers. The goal of smart education is to foster smart learners to meet the needs of the work and life in the 21st century.

Smart Learning: Smart learning environments are IoT-based learning solutions, which are seamlessly integrated into our working and learning environment. Smart learning environments are therefore physical environments enriched with context-aware digital devices to improve and accelerate learning.

Smart Teaching: Smart teaching largely involves the organization of teaching and learning activities with the help of software tools. In broader terms, smart teaching is a way of professionalizing the teaching and learning experience.

Software Architecture: Software architecture refers to the high-level structures of a software system and the discipline of creating such structures and systems. Each structure comprises software elements, relations among them, and properties of both elements and relations.

Thing: An object of our everyday life placed in our everyday environment. A thing can be a car, fridge, but can also be abstracted to a complete house or city depending on the use case.

Compilation of References

Abadi, D. J., Marcus, A., Madden, S., & Hollenbach, K. (2009). SW-Store: A vertically partitioned DBMS for Semantic Web data management. *The VLDB Journal, 18*(2), 385–406. doi:10.100700778-008-0125-y

Abadi, D. J., Marcus, A., Madden, S., & Hollenbach, K. 2007, Scalable semantic Web data management using vertical partitioning, *Proceedings of the 33th International Conference on Very Large Data Bases*, 411-422.

Abdullah Alger. (2017). *MySQL for JSON: Generated Columns and Indexes*. Retrieved from https://www.compose.com/articles/mysql-for-json-generated-columns-and-indexing/

Abelló, A. (2015): Big Data Design. In *Proc. of 11the Int. Workshop on Data Warehousing and OLAP*. ACM. 10.1145/2811222.2811235

Abouzeid, A., Bajda-Pawlikowski, K., Abadi, D., Silberschatz, A., & Rasin, A. (2009). HadoopDB - An Architectural Hybrid of MapReduce and DBMS Technologies for Analytical Workloads. *Proc. of VLDB '09*, 922-933.

Adam, A., & Jean-Marie, L. (2018, April). *A web service based on RESTful API and JSON Schema/JSON Meta Schema to construct knowledge graphs*. Paper presented at CoRR 2018 Conference.

Afrati, F. N., Damigos, M., & Gergatsoulis, M. (2015). Lower bounds on the communication of XPath queries in MapReduce. In *Proceedings of the Workshops of the EDBT/ICDT Joint Conference* (pp. 38-41). Brussels, Belgium: CEUR-WS.

Ahmed, E. (2017). Internet of Things Architecture: Recent Advances, Taxonomy, Requirements, and Open Challenges. *IEEE Wireless Communications, 24*(3).

Ahn, J. H., Eom, J.-H., Nam, S., Zong, N., Im, D.-H., & Kim, H.-G. (2017). xStore: Federated temporal query processing for large scale RDF triples on a cloud environment. *Neurocomputing, 256*, 5–12. doi:10.1016/j.neucom.2016.03.116

Ahn, J., Im, D. H., Lee, T., & Kim, H. G. (2016). Parallel prime number labeling of large XML data using MapReduce. In *Proceedings of the International Conference on IT Convergence and Security*, (pp. 1-2). Prague, Czech Republic: IEEE Computer Society. 10.1109/ICITCS.2016.7740360

Ahn, J., Im, D. H., Lee, T., & Kim, H. G. (2017). A dynamic and parallel approach for repetitive prime labeling of XML with MapReduce. *The Journal of Supercomputing, 73*(2), 810–836. doi:10.100711227-016-1803-y

Ahsan, K., & Vijay, P. (2014). *Temporal Databases: Information Systems*. Bloomington, IN: Booktango.

AjazMoharkan, Z. (2017). Internet of Things and its applications in E-learning. IEEE Intel. Conf. on Computational Intelligence and Communication Technology, 1-5.

Akdogan, A., Demiryurek, U., Banaei-Kashani, F., & Shahabi, C. (2010). Voronoi-based geospatial query processing with mapreduce. In *Proceedings of the International Conference Cloud Computing* (pp. 9-16). IEEE.

Al Shimmary, M.K., Al Nayar, & Kubba, M.M. (2015). Designing Smart University using RFID and WSN. *International Journal of Computers and Applications*, *112*(15), 34–39.

Alaei, A. R., Becken, S., & Stantic, B. (2017). Sentiment Analysis in Tourism: Capitalizing on Big Data. *Journal of Travel Research*.

Alexander, K. (2008). *RDF in JSON: A specification for serialising RDF in JSON*. Retrieved from http://www.semanticscripting.org/SFSW2008

Ali, K. A., & Pokorný, J. (2009). *A comparison of XML-based temporal models. Advanced Internet Based Systems and Applications* (pp. 339–350). Berlin, Germany: Springer. doi:10.1007/978-3-642-01350-8_31

Alsubaiee, S., Altowim, Y., Altwaijry, H., Behm, A., Borkar, V., Bu, Y., … Westman, T. (2014). AsterixDB: A Scalable, Open Source BDMS. *Proceedings of the VLDB Endowment*, 7(14), 1905-1916. 10.14778/2733085.2733096

Amagasa, T., Yoshikawa, M., & Uemura, S. (2000). A data model for temporal XML documents. In *Proceedings of the 2000 International Conference on Database and Expert Systems Applications* (pp. 334-344). Berlin, Germany: Springer. 10.1007/3-540-44469-6_31

Amare, B., & Sengupta, J. (2017). IoT Driven Design and Implementation of Smart Campus, *Intel. Journal of Computer Science Trends and Technology*, *5*(4).

Amazon Web Services. (2018a). *Amazon SimpleDB*. Retrieved November 10, 2018, from http://aws.amazon.com/simpledb/

Amazon Web Services. (2018b). *Amazon DynamoDB*. Retrieved November 10, 2018, from http://aws.amazon.com/dynamodb/

Amazon Web Services. (n.d.). *AWS Identity and Access Management(IAM) User Guide*. Retrieved from http://docs.aws.amazon.com/IAM/latest/UserGuide/introduction.html

Angles, R., & Gutierrez, C. (2008). Survey of graph database models. *ACM Computing Surveys*, *40*, 1:1-1:39.

Angles, R., & Gutiérrez, C. (2005). Querying RDF data from a graph database perspective. *Proceedings of the 2005 European Semantic Web Conference*, 346-360. 10.1007/11431053_24

Anguita, A., Martin, L., Garcia-Remesal, M., & Maojo, V. (2013). RDFBuilder A tool to automatically build RDF-based interfaces for MAGE-OM microarray data sources. *Computer Methods and Programs in Biomedicine*, *3*, 220-227.

Antonellis, P., Makris, C., & Pispirigos, G. (2015). Distributed XML filtering using Hadoop framework. In *Proceedings of the Algorithmic Aspects of Cloud Computing First International Workshop*, (pp. 75-83). Patras, Greece: Springer.

Apache Software Foundation. (n.d.). *Apache CouchDB*. Retrieved from http://couchdb.apache.org

Application programming interface. (n.d.). Retrieved from https://en.wikipedia.org/wiki/Application_programming_interface#Web_APIs

ArangoDB Inc. (2018). *ArangoDB*. Retrieved November 10, 2018, from https://www.arangodb.com/

Araujo, S., Hidders, J., Schwabe, D., & Vries, A. P. D. (2012). Serimi - resource description similarity, RDF instance matching and interlinking. In *Proceedings of the International Semantic Web Conference*. Aachen, Germany: CEUR-WS.org.

Arenas, M., Gutierrez, C., & Pérez, J. (2009, August). Foundations of RDF databases. In Reasoning Web International Summer School (pp. 158-204). Berlin, Germany: Springer. doi:10.1007/978-3-642-03754-2_4

Armstrong, C. (2014). *Understanding Reference Models and Reference Architectures*. SATURN.

Ashley, P., Hada, S., Karjoth, G., Powers, C., & Schunter, M. (2003). *Enterprise privacy authorization language (EPAL).* IBM Research.

Aslett, M. (2011). NoSQL, NewSQL and Beyond: The drivers and use cases for database alternatives. *451 Research.* Retrieved November 10, 2018, from https://451research.com/report-long?icid=1389

Austin, W., & Henry, A. (2018). *JSON Schema: A Media Type for Describing JSON Documents.* Retrieved from https://json-schema.org/latest/json-schema-core.html

Bach, M., & Werner, A. 2014, Standardization of NoSQL database languages: Beyond databases, architectures, and structure. In *Proceedings 10th International Conference.* Ustron, Poland: Springer.

Backialakshmi, M., & Hemavathi, N. (2015). Survey on Energy Efficiency in Cloud Computing. *Journal of Information Technology & Software Engineering, 6,* 1.

Bahmani, B., Moseley, B., Vattani, A., Kumar, R., & Vassilvitskii, S. (2012). Scalable k-means++. *Proceedings of the VLDB Endowment International Conference on Very Large Data Bases, 5*(7), 622–633. doi:10.14778/2180912.2180915

Bai, L., Cao, X., & Jia, W. (2018). Uncertain spatiotemporal data modeling and algebraic operations based on XML. *Earth Science Informatics, 11*(1), 109–127. doi:10.100712145-017-0322-6

Bai, L., Yan, L., & Ma, Z. (2017). Interpolation and prediction of spatiotemporal data based on XML integrated with grey dynamic model. *ISPRS International Journal of Geo-Information, 6*(4), 113. doi:10.3390/ijgi6040113

Bailis, P., Davidson, A., Fekete, A., Ghodsi, A., Hellerstein, J. M., & Stoica, I. (2013). Highly Available Transactions: Virtues and Limitations (Extended Version). *PVLDB, 7*(3), 181–192.

Bairoch, A., Apweiler, R., Wu, C. H., Barker, W. C., Boeckmann, B., Ferro, S., … Yeh, L. L. (2005). The universal protein resource (UniProt). *Nucleic Acids Research, 33,* 154-159.

Bamford, R., Nasoi, S., Zacharioudakis, M., Borkar, V., Brantner, M., Fischer, P. M., … Muresan, D. (2009). XQuery Reloaded. *Proceedings of the VLDB Endowment International Conference on Very Large Data Bases, 2*(2), 1342–1353. doi:10.14778/1687553.1687560

Banerjee, & Agrawal & Iyengar. (2013). Energy Efficiency Model for Cloud Computing, *International Journal of Energy. Information and Communications, 4*(6), 29–42.

Bass, L., Clements, P., & Kazman, R. (2003). *Software Architecture in Practice. SEI Series in Software Engineering* (2nd ed.). Addison-Wesley.

Baumann, P. (2017). *OGC Web Coverage Service (WCS) 2.1 Interface Standard – Core v.2.1.* Open Geospatial Consortium (OGC 17-089r1). Retrieved from: http://docs.opengeospatial.org/is/17-089r1/17-089r1.html

Baumann, P., Hirschorn, E., & Maso, J. (2017). *OGC Coverage Implementation Schema v.1.1.* Open Geospatial Consortium (OGC 09-146r6). Retrieved from: http://docs.opengeospatial.org/is/09-146r6/09-146r6.html

Baumann, P., Hirschorn, E., Maso, J., Merticariu, V., & Misev, D. (2017). All in One: Encoding Spatio-Temporal Big Data in XML, JSON, and RDF without Information Loss. *Proceedings: IEEE International Conference on Big Data,* 3406-3415.

Bellazzi, R., Larizza, C., Bellazzi, R., & Bellazzi, R. (2005). Temporal data mining for the quality assessment of hemodialysis services. *Artificial Intelligence in Medicine, 34*(1), 25–39. doi:10.1016/j.artmed.2004.07.010 PMID:15885564

Benjamin, Z., Ming, F., & Chung-Horng, L. (2010). A Green Computing Based Architecture Comparison and Analysis. *IEEE/ACM International Conf. on Green Computing and Communications.*

Benson, T., & Grieve, G. (2016). UML, BPMN, XML and JSON. In *Principles of Health Interoperability* (pp. 55–81). Cham: Springer. doi:10.1007/978-3-319-30370-3_4

Berndt, D. J., & Clifford, J. (1994, July). Using dynamic time warping to find patterns in time series. In KDD workshop (Vol. 10, No. 16, pp. 359-370). Academic Press.

Berners-Lee, T., Hendler, J., & Lassila, O. (2001). The semantic web. *Scientific American, 284*(5), 34–43. doi:10.1038 cientificamerican0501-34 PMID:11396337

Beyer, K. (2005). System RX: One Part Relational, One Part XML. In *Proceedings of the 2005 ACM SIGMOD International Conference on Management of Data* (pp. 347–358). ACM. 10.1145/1066157.1066197

Beyer, K., Ercegovac, V., Gemulla, R., Balmin, A., Eltabakh, M., Kanne, C.-Ch., ... Shekita, E. J. (2011). Jaql: A scripting language for large scale semistructured data analysis. *PVLDB, 4*(12), 1272–1283.

Bhardwaj, N. D., & Bhardwaj, N. D. (2016). Comparative study of couchdb and mongodb – nosql document oriented databases. *International Journal of Computers and Applications, 136*(3), 24-26.

Bhatti, R., Ghafoor, A., Bertino, E., & Joshi, J. B. (2005). X-GTRBAC: An XML-based policy specification framework and architecture for enterprise-wide access control. *ACM Transactions on Information and System Security, 8*(2), 187–227.

Biba, M., & Xhafa, F. (Eds.). (2011). *Learning Structure and Schemas from Documents* (Vol. 375). Springer. doi:10.1007/978-3-642-22913-8_1

Bidoit, N., Colazzo, D., Malla, N., Ulliana, F., Nole, M., & Sartiani, C. (2013). Processing XML queries and updates on map/reduce clusters. In *Proceedings of the International Conference on Extending Database Technology*, (pp. 745-748). Genoa, Italy: ACM. 10.1145/2452376.2452470

Bilal, M. (2017). *A Review of the Internet of Things Architecture, Technologies and Analysis Smartphone-based Attacks Against 3D printers*. Dept. of Computer Science Zhejiang University Hangzhou.

Bishop, B., Kiryakov, A., Ognyanoff, D., Peikov, I., Tashev, Z., & Velkov, R. (2011). Owlim: A family of scalable semantic repositories. *Semantic Web, 2*(1), 1–10.

Bi, X., Wang, G., Zhao, X., Zhang, Z., & Chen, S. (2015). Distributed XML twig query processing using MapReduce. In *Proceedings of the Web Technologies and Applications 17th Asia-PacificWeb Conference*, (pp. 203-214). Guangzhou, China: Springer. 10.1007/978-3-319-25255-1_17

Blower, J., & Riechert, M. (2016). *Coverages, JSONLD and RDF data cubes*. In Workshop on Spatial Data on the Web (SDW 2016), Montreal, Canada. Retrieved from: http://centaur.reading.ac.uk/74395/1/paper2.pdf

Böhlen, M. H., Dignös, A., Gamper, J., & Jensen, C. S. (2017). Temporal Data Management - An Overview. *LNBIP, 324*, 51–83.

Bohm, C., & Krebs, F. (2004). The k-Nearest Neighbour Join: Turbo Charging the KDD Process. *Knowledge and Information Systems, 6*(6), 728–749. doi:10.100710115-003-0122-9

Boicea, A., Radulescu, F., & Agapin, L. I. (2012). MongoDB vs Oracle -- Database Comparison. In *Proceedings of the 2012 Third International Conference on Emerging Intelligent Data and Web Technologies*. IEEE. 10.1109/EIDWT.2012.32

Borders, K., Zhao, X., & Prakash, A. (2005). CPOL: High-performance policy evaluation. *The 12th ACM conference on Computer and communications security*.

Borkar, V., Carey, M.-J., & Li, Ch. (2012). Inside "Big Data management": ogres, onions, or parfaits? *Proceedings of EDBT Conference*, 3-14. 10.1145/2247596.2247598

Bornea, M. A., Dolby, J., Kementsietsidis, A., Srinivas, K., Dantressangle, P., Udrea, O., & Bhattacharjee, B. (2013). Building an efficient RDF store over a relational database. *Proceedings of the 2013 ACM International Conference on Management of Data*, 121-132. 10.1145/2463676.2463718

Bourhis, P., Reutter, J. L., Su'arez, F., & Vrgoc, D. (2017). JSON: Data Model, Query Languages and Schema Specification. In *Proceedings of the 36th ACM SIGMOD-SIGACT-SIGAI Symposium on Principles of Database Systems* (pp. 123–135). ACM. 10.1145/3034786.3056120

Brahmia, S., Brahmia, Z., Grandi, F., & Bouaziz, R. (2016). τJSchema: A Framework for Managing Temporal JSON-Based NoSQL Databases. *Proceedings of the 27th International Conference on Database and Expert Systems Applications (DEXA'2016)*, 167-181. 10.1007/978-3-319-44406-2_13

Brahmia, S., Brahmia, Z., Grandi, F., & Bouaziz, R. (2017). Temporal JSON Schema Versioning in the τJSchema Framework. *Journal of Digital Information Management*, *15*(4), 179–202.

Brahmia, S., Brahmia, Z., Grandi, F., & Bouaziz, R. (2018c). Managing Temporal and Versioning Aspects of JSON-based Big Data via the τJSchema Framework. *Proceedings of the International Conference on Big Data and Smart Digital Environment (ICBDSDE'2018)*. 27-39

Brahmia, Z., & Bouaziz, R. (2008). An Approach for Schema Versioning in Multi-Temporal XML Databases. *Proceedings of the 10th International Conference on Enterprise Information Systems (ICEIS 2008)*, 290-297.

Brahmia, Z., Bouaziz, R., Grandi, F., & Oliboni, B. (2011). Schema Versioning in τXSchema-Based Multitemporal XML Repositories. *Proceedings of the 5th IEEE International Conference on Research Challenges in Information Science (RCIS 2011)*, 1-12.

Brahmia, Z., Grandi, F., Oliboni, B., & Bouaziz, R. (2012). Versioning of Conventional Schema in the τXSchema Framework. *Proceedings of the 8th International Conference on Signal Image Technology & Internet Systems (SITIS'2012)*, 510-518.

Brahmia, Z., Grandi, F., Oliboni, B., & Bouaziz, R. (2014). Schema Change Operations for Full Support of Schema Versioning in the τXSchema Framework. *International Journal of Information Technology and Web Engineering*, *9*(2), 20–46. doi:10.4018/ijitwe.2014040102

Brahmia, Z., Grandi, F., Oliboni, B., & Bouaziz, R. (2018a). Supporting Structural Evolution of Data in Web-Based Systems via Schema Versioning in the τXSchema Framework. In A. Elçi (Ed.), *Handbook of Research on Contemporary Perspectives on Web-Based Systems* (pp. 271–307). Hershey, PA: IGI Global. doi:10.4018/978-1-5225-5384-7.ch013

Brahmia, Z., Grandi, F., Oliboni, B., & Bouaziz, R. (2018b). Schema Versioning in Conventional and Emerging Databases. In M. Khosrow-Pour (Ed.), *Encyclopedia of Information Science and Technology* (4th ed.; pp. 2054–2063). Hershey, PA: IGI Global. doi:10.4018/978-1-5225-2255-3.ch178

Bray, T. (2014). IETF RFC7159, The JavaScript Object Notation (JSON) Data Interchange Format. Retrieved from https://www.ietf.org/rfc/rfc7159.txt

Bray, T. (2014). *IETF RFC7159, The JavaScript Object Notation (JSON) Data Interchange Format*. Retrieved from: https://www.ietf.org/rfc/rfc7159.txt

Bray, T., Paoli, J., Sperberg-McQueen, C. M., Maler, E., Yergeau, F., & Cowan, J. (1997). Extensible markup language (XML). *World Wide Web Journal*, *2*(4), 27–66.

Brewer, E. A. (2000). *Towards robust distributed systems*. Paper presented at PODC 2000, Portland, OR.

Brewer, E. A. (2012). CAP twelve years later: How the 'rules' have changed. *Computer, 45*(2), 22–29. doi:10.1109/MC.2012.37 PMID:24976642

Broekstra, J., Kampman, A., & van Harmelen, F. (2002). Sesame: A generic architecture for storing and querying RDF and RDF schema. *Proceedings of the 2002 International Semantic Web Conference*, 54-68. 10.1007/3-540-48005-6_7

Brossard, D. (2014). *JSON Profile of XACML 3.0 Version 1.0*. XACML Committee Specification 01. Retrieved from http://docs.oasis-open.org/xacml/xacml-json-http/v1.0/cs01/xacml-json-http-v1.0-cs01.pdf

Bugiotti, F., Cabibbo, L., Atzeni, P., & Torlone, R. (2014). Database Design for NoSQL Systems. In *Proc. of ER Conf.*, *LNCS 8824*, 223-231.

Burns, T., Fong, E., Jefferson, D., Knox, R., Mark, L., Reedy, C., ... Truszkowski, W. (1986). Reference Model for DBMS Standardization, Database Architecture Framework Task Group (DAFTG) of the ANSI/X3/SPARC Database System Study Group. *SIGMOD Record, 15*(1), 19–58.

Bu, Y., Howe, Y., Balazinska, M., & Ernstm, M. D. (2012). The HaLoop approach to large-scale iterative data analysis. *The VLDB Journal, 21*(2), 169–190. doi:10.100700778-012-0269-7

Buyya, R., Beloglazov, A., & Abawajy, J. (2010). Energy-Efficient management of data center resources for cloud computing: A vision, architectural elements, and open challenges. *Proc. of the 2010 International Conference on Parallel and Distributed Processing Techniques and Applications (PDPTA 2010)*.

Byte. (2016). *eLearning for smart classrooms*. Bytes.

Camacho-Rodriguez, J., Colazzo, D., Manolescu, I., & Naranjo, A. M., J. (2015). PAXQuery: Parallel analytical XML processing. In *Proceedings of the ACM SIGMOD International Conference on Management of Data*, (pp. 1117-1122). Melbourne, Victoria, Australia: ACM.

Cánovas Izquierdo, J. L., & Cabot, J. (2013). Discovering implicit schemas in JSON data. *Proceedings of ICWE, 2013*, 68–83.

Cao, X., Chen, L., Cong, G., & Jensen, C. (2012). Spatial keyword querying. In *Proceedings of the International Conference on Data Engineering (ICDE'12)* (pp. 16-29).

Cao, X., Cong, G., Jensen, C., & Ooi, B. (2011). Collective spatial keyword querying. In *Proceedings of the ACM SIGMOD International Conference on Management of Data (SIGMOD'11)* (pp. 373-384). 10.1145/1989323.1989363

Carroll, J. J. (2002). Matching RDF graphs. *In International Semantic Web Conference*, pp. 5-15.

Cary, A., Wolfson, O., & Rishe, N. (2010). Efficient and scalable method for processing top-k spatial boolean queries. In *Proceedings of the Scientific and Statistical Database Management (SSDBM'10)* (pp.87–95). 10.1007/978-3-642-13818-8_8

Castano, S., Ferrara, A., Montanelli, S., & Varese, G. (2011). Ontology and instance matching. In *Knowledge-driven multimedia information extraction and ontology evolution* (pp. 167–195). Berlin, Heidelberg: Springer. doi:10.1007/978-3-642-20795-2_7

Castelltort, A., & Laurent, A. (2013). Representing history in graph-oriented NoSQL databases: A versioning system. *Proceedings of the 8th International Conference on Digital Information Management (ICDIM 2013)*, 228-234. 10.1109/ICDIM.2013.6694022

Cattell, R. (2011). Scalable SQL and NoSQL Data Stores. *SIGMOD Record, 39*(4), 12–27. doi:10.1145/1978915.1978919

Chandra, D. G. (2015). BASE Analysis of NoSQL Database. *Future Generation Computer Systems*, *52*, 13–21. doi:10.1016/j.future.2015.05.003

Chang, F., Dean, J., Ghemawat, S., Hsieh, W. C., Wallach, D. A., Burrows, M., … Gruber, R. E. (2008). BigTable: A distributed storage system for structured data. *ACM Transactions on Computer Systems*, *26*(2), 4:1-4:26.

Chang, F., Dean, J., Ghemavat, S., Hsieh, W. C., Wallach, D. A., Burrows, M., ... Gruber, R. E. (2008). Bigtable: A Distributed Storage System for Structured Data. *Journal ACM Transactions on Computer Systems*, *26*(2), 4.

Chan, T. W., Roschelle, J., & His, S. (2006). One-to-One Technology-Enhanced Learning: An opportunity for global research collaboration. *Res. Pract. Technol. Enhance. Learn*, *1*(1), 3–29. doi:10.1142/S1793206806000032

Charmonman, S. (2015). Applications of the Internet of Things in E-Learning. *International Journal of the Computer, the Internet and Management*, *23*(3), 1-4.

Chasseur, C., Li, Y., & Patel, J. M. (2013a). Enabling JSON Document Stores in Relational Systems. In *Proceedings of the 16th International Workshop on the Web and Databases 2013, WebDB 2013*, (*Vol. 13*, pp. 14–15). Academic Press.

Chasseur, C., Li, Y., & Patel, J. M. (2013). Enabling JSON Document Stores in Relational Systems. *Proceedings of 16th Int. Workshop on the Web and Databases (WebDB 2013)*, 1-6.

Chasseur, C., Li, Y., & Patel, J. M. (2013). Enabling JSON Document Stores in Relational Systems. *Proceedings of WebDB*, *2013*, 1–6.

Chen, L., Cong, G., Jensen, C., & Wu, D. (2013). Spatial keyword query processing: an experimental evaluation. In *Proceedings of the International Conference on Very Large Data Bases (VLDB'13)* (pp. 217-228) 10.14778/2535569.2448955

Chen, X., & Petrounias, I. (1998). A framework for temporal data mining. *Proceedings of the 1998 International Conference on Database and Expert Systems Applications* (pp. 796-805). Berlin, Germany: Springer.

Chen, Y., Keogh, E., Hu, B., Begum, N., Bagnall, A., Mueen, A., & Batista, G. (2015, July). *The ucr time series classification archive*. Retrieved from www.cs.ucr.edu/~eamonn/time_ series_data/

Chen. (1977). The entity-relationship model: a basis for the enterprise view of data. *AFIPS '77 Proceedings*, 77-84.

Chen, P. P.-S. (2002). Entity Relationship Model—Toward a Unified View of Data. In *Software Pioneers* (pp. 311–339). Springer. doi:10.1007/978-3-642-59412-0_18

Chen, Z., & Fu, B. (2005, August). A quadratic lower bound for Rocchio's similarity-based relevance feedback algorithm. In *International Computing and Combinatorics Conference* (pp. 955-964). Berlin, Germany: Springer.

Chittaro, L., Combi, C., & Trapasso, G. (2003). Data mining on temporal data: A visual approach and its clinical application to hemodialysis. *Journal of Visual Languages and Computing*, *14*(6), 591–620. doi:10.1016/j.jvlc.2003.06.003

Choi, H., Lee, K. H., & Lee, Y. J. (2014). Parallel labeling of massive XML data with MapReduce. *The Journal of Supercomputing*, *67*(2), 408–437. doi:10.100711227-013-1008-6

Choi, H., Lee, K., Kim, S. H., Lee, Y. J., & Moon, B. (2012). HadoopXML: a suite for parallel processing of massive XML data with multiple twig pattern queries. In *Proceedings of the ACM International Conference on Information and Knowledge Management*, (pp. 2737-2739). Maui, HI: ACM. 10.1145/2396761.2398745

Ciaccia, P., Patella, M., & Zezula, P. (1997). M-tree: An Efficient Access Method for Similarity Search in Metric Spaces. In *Proceedings of the International Conference on Very Large Data Bases* (pp. 426-435). Morgan Kaufmann.

Clarkson, M. R., & Schneider, F. B. (2010). Hyperproperties. *Journal of Computer Security, 18*(6), 1157–1210. doi:10.3233/JCS-2009-0393

Clausen, J. (1999). Branch and bound algorithms-principles and examples. Department of Computer Science, University of Copenhagen.

Clifford, J., & Croker, A. (1987). The historical relational data model (HRDM) and algebra based on lifespans. In *1987 IEEE Third International Conference on Data Engineering* (pp. 528-537). IEEE.

Clifford, J., Dyreson, C. E., Isakowitz, T., Jensen, C. S., & Snodgrass, R. T. (1997). On the Semantics of "Now" in Databases. *ACM Transactions on Database Systems, 22*(2), 171–214. doi:10.1145/249978.249980

Clustrix. (2018). *Clustrix*. Retrieved November 10, 2018, from http://www.clustrix.com/

Codd, E. F. (1970). A Relational Model of Data for Large Shared Data Banks. *Communications of the ACM, 13*(6), 377–387. doi:10.1145/362384.362685

Combi, C. (2009). *Temporal object-oriented databases. In Encyclopedia of Database Systems* (pp. 2998–3004). Boston, MA: Springer.

Cong, G., Fan, W., Kementsietsidis, A., Li, J., & Liu, X. (2012). Partial evaluation for distributed XPath query processing and beyond. *ACM Transactions on Database Systems, 37*(4), 32:1-32:43.

Cooper, B.F., Ramakrishnan, R., Srivastava, U., Silberstein, A., Bohannon, P., Jacobsen, H.A., … Zemeni, R. (2008). PNUTS: Yahoo!'s hosted data serving platform. *Journal PVLDB, 1*(2), 1277-1288.

Corbett, J. C., Dean, J. C., Epstein, M., Fikes, A., Frost, Ch., & Furman, J. J., …Woodford, D. (2012). Spanner: Google's Globally-Distributed Database. *Proceedings of 10th USENIX Symposium on Operation Systems Design and Implementation (OSDI 2012)*.

Costabello, L. (2014). *Error-Tolerant RDF Subgraph Matching for Adaptive Presentation of Linked Data on Mobile. In The Semantic Web: Trends and Challenges*. Springer International Publishing.

Couchbase. (2018). *Couchbase*. Retrieved November 10, 2018, from http://www.couchbase.com/

Coyne, E., & Weil, T. R. (2014). ABAC and RBAC: Scalable, flexible, and auditable access management. *IT Professional, 15*(3), 14–16. doi:10.1109/MITP.2013.37

Crampton, J., & Morisset, C. (2012). PTaCL: A language for attribute-based access control in open systems. In *International Conference on Principles of Security and Trust* (pp. 390-409). Springer. 10.1007/978-3-642-28641-4_21

Crockford, D. (2006). *JSON — The fat-free alternative to XML*. Retrieved from http://www.json.org/fatfree.html

Cucinotta, T., Checconi, F., Kousiouris, G., Konstanteli, K., Gogouvitis, S., Kyriazis, D., ... Stein, M. (2012). Virtualized e-Learning on the IRMOS Real-Time Cloud. *Service Oriented Computing and Applications, 6*(2), 151–166. doi:10.100711761-011-0089-4

Cudre-Mauroux, P., Enchev, I., Fundatureanu, S., Groth, P., Haque, A., Harth, A., ... Wylot, M. (2013). NoSQL databases for RDF: An empirical evaluation. *Proceedings of the 12th International Semantic Web Conference*, 310-325. 10.1007/978-3-642-41338-4_20

Cui, X., Zhu, P., Yang, X., Li, K., & Ji, C. (2014). Optimized big data k-means clustering using MapReduce. *The Journal of Supercomputing, 70*(3), 1249–1259. doi:10.100711227-014-1225-7

Curé, O., Hecht, R., Duc, Ch. L., & Lamole, M. (2011). Data Integration over NoSQL Stores Using Access Path Based Mappings. *Proceedings of DEXA 2011, Part I, LNCS 6860*, 481–495. 10.1007/978-3-642-23088-2_36

Curé, O., Lamole, M., & Duc, C. L. (2013). *Ontology Based Data Integration over Document and Column Family Oriented NOSQL*. CoRR, arXiv:1307.2603.

Currim, F., Currim, S., Dyreson, C. E., Joshi, S., Snodgrass, R. T., Thomas, S. W., & Roeder, E. (2009). *τXSchema: Support for Data- and Schema-Versioned XML Documents*. TimeCenter, Technical Report TR-91. Retrieved January 31, 2019, from http://timecenter.cs.aau.dk/TimeCenterPublications/TR-91.pdf

Currim, F., Currim, S., Dyreson, C. E., & Snodgrass, R. T. (2004). A Tale of Two Schemas: Creating a Temporal XML Schema from a Snapshot Schema with τXSchema. *Proceedings of the 9th International Conference on Extending Database Technology (EDBT 2004)*, 348-365. 10.1007/978-3-540-24741-8_21

Currim, F., Currim, S., Dyreson, C. E., Snodgrass, R. T., Thomas, S. W., & Zhang, R. (2012). Adding Temporal Constraints to XML Schema. *IEEE Transactions on Knowledge and Data Engineering, 24*(8), 1361–1377. doi:10.1109/TKDE.2011.74

Cuzzocrea, A. (2015). Temporal Aspects of Big Data Management: State-of-the-Art Analysis and Future Research Directions. *Proceedings of the 22nd International Symposium on Temporal Representation and Reasoning (TIME 2015)*, 180-185. 10.1109/TIME.2015.31

Dabringer, C., & Eder, J. (2011). Efficient top-k retrieval for user preference queries. In *Proceedings of the ACM Symposium on Applied Computing* (SAC'11) (pp. 1045-1052). 10.1145/1982185.1982414

Damianou, N., Dulay, N., Lupu, E., & Sloman, M. (2001). *The ponder policy specification language*. doi:10.1109/WOCC.2013.6676386

Damigos, M., Gergatsoulis, M., & Plitsos, S. (2013). Distributed processing of XPath queries using MapReduce. In *Proceedings of the New Trends in Databases and Information Systems, 17th East European Conference on Advances in Databases and Information Systems*, (pp. 69-77). Genoa, Italy: Springer.

Damigos, M., Gergatsoulis, M., & Kalogeros, E. (2014). Distributed evaluation of XPath queries over large integrated XML data. In *Proceedings of the 18th Panhellenic Conference on Informatics*, (pp. 61:1-61:6). Athens, Greece: ACM. 10.1145/2645791.2645804

Davoudian, A., Chen, L., & Liu, M. (2018). A Survey on NoSQL Stores. *ACM Computing Surveys, 51*(2), 40. doi:10.1145/3158661

Dean, J., & Ghemawat, S. (2004). MapReduce: Simplified data processing on large clusters. In *Proceedings of the 6th Symposium on Operating System Design and Implementation*, (pp. 137-150). San Francisco, CA: USENIX Association.

Dean, J., & Ghemawat, S. (2004). MapReduce: simplified data processing on large clusters. In *Proceedings of the Symposium on Operating System Design and Implementation* (pp. 137-150). USENIX Association.

Dean, J., & Ghemawat, S. (2008). MapReduce: Simplified data processing on large clusters. *Communications of the ACM, 51*(1), 107–113. doi:10.1145/1327452.1327492

Debatty, T., Michiardi, P., Mees, W., & Thonnard, O. (2014). Determining the k in k-means with MapReduce. In *Proceedings of the Workshops of the EDBT/ICDT 2014 Joint Conference* (pp. 19-28). CEUR-WS.org.

DeCandia, G., Hastorun, D., Jampani, M., Kakulapati, G., Lakshman, A., Pilchin, A., ... Vogels, W. (2007). Dynamo: Amazon's highly available key-value store. *Proceedings of the 21st ACM Symposium on Operating Systems Principles*, 205-220.

Deng, J. (1989). Introduction to grey system theory. *Journal of Grey System, 1*(1), 1–24.

Detti, A. (2017). Application of Information Centric Networking to NoSQL databases: The spatio-temporal use case. *Proceedings of the 2017 IEEE International Symposium on Local and Metropolitan Area Networks*, 1-6. 10.1109/LAN-MAN.2017.7972131

Dey, D., Barron, T. M., & Storey, V. C. (1996). A complete temporal relational algebra. *The VLDB Journal, 5*(3), 167–180. doi:10.1007007780050022

Ding, L., Qiao, B., Wang, G., & Chen, C. (2011). An efficient quad-tree based index structure for cloud data management. *Proceedings of WAIM 2011, LNCS, 6897*, 238–250. 10.1007/978-3-642-23535-1_22

Dorneles, C. F., Gonçalves, R., & dos Santos Mello, R. (2011). Approximate data instance matching: A survey. *Knowledge and Information Systems, 27*(1), 1–21. doi:10.100710115-010-0285-0

Droettboom, M. (2015). *Understanding JSON Schema*. Available on: http://spacetelescope. github.io/understandingjsonschema/UnderstandingJSONSchema. pdf

Duan, S., Kementsietsidis, A., Srinivas, K., & Udrea, O. (2011). Apples and oranges: a comparison of RDF benchmarks and real RDF datasets. *Proceedings of the 2011 ACM SIGMOD International Conference on Management of Data*, 145-156. 10.1145/1989323.1989340

Dyreson, C. E. (2001). Observing Transaction-time Semantics with TTXPath. *Proceedings of the 2nd International Conference on Web Information Systems Engineering (WISE 2001)*, 193-202.

Dyreson, C. E., & Grandi, F. (2018). Temporal XML. In L. Liu & M. T. Özsu (Eds.), *Encyclopedia of Database Systems* (2nd ed.). New York: Springer-Verlag; doi:10.1007/978-1-4614-8265-9_411

Dyreson, C. E., Snodgrass, R. T., Currim, F., Currim, S., & Joshi, S. (2006). Validating Quicksand: Schema Versioning in τXSchema. *Proceedings of the 22nd International Conference on Data Engineering Workshops (ICDE Workshops 2006)*, 82. 10.1109/ICDEW.2006.161

ECMA International. (n.d.). *ECMA-404 The JSON Data Interchange Standard*. Retrieved from http://www.json.org/

Edlich, S. (2012). *Choose the "Right" Database and NewSQL: NoSQL Under Attack*. Retrieved from http://www.infoq.com/presentations/Choosing-NoSQL-NewSQL

Edlich, S. (2018). *List of NoSQL databases*. Retrieved November 10, 2018, from http://nosql-database.org/

Eisenberg, A. (2013). XQuery 3.0 is nearing completion. *SIGMOD Record, 42*(3), 34–41. doi:10.1145/2536669.2536675

El-Aziz, A. A., & Kannan, A. (2014). JSON encryption. In *Computer Communication and Informatics (ICCCI), 2014 International Conference on*. IEEE.

Elyamany, H. F., & Alkhairi, A. H. (2015). IoT-Academia Architecture: A Profound Approach. *2015 IEEE/ACIS 16th International Conference Software Engineering*.

EMCA International. (2017). *The JSON Data Interchange Syntax, Standard ECMA-404* (2nd ed.). Retrieved January 31, 2019, from https://www.ecma-international.org/publications/files/ECMA-ST/ECMA-404.pdf

Emoto, K., & Imachi, H. (2012). Parallel tree reduction on MapReduce. In *Proceedings of the International Conference on Computational Science*, (pp. 1827-1836). Omaha, NE: Elsevier.

Empower, I. D. (2013). *Best practices in enterprise authorization: The RBAC/ABAC hybrid approach*. Empower ID, White paper.

Emrich, T., Kriegel, H. P., Mamoulis, N., Renz, M., & Zufle, A. (2012). Querying uncertain spatiotemporal data. In *Proceedings of International Conference on Data Engineering,* Washington, DC (pp. 354-365). Piscataway, NJ: IEEE.

Ene, A., Im, S., & Moseley, B. (2011). Fast clustering using MapReduce. In *Proceedings of the 17th ACM SIGKDD International Conference on Knowledge Discovery and Data Mining* (pp. 681-689). ACM.

EnterpriseDB Corporation. (2018). *NoSQL Overview*. Retrieved November 10, 2018, from http://www.enterprisedb.com/nosql-for-enterprise

Erling, O., & Mikhailov, I. (2007). RDF support in the virtuoso DBMS. *Proceedings of the 1st Conference on Social Semantic Web*, 59-68.

Erling, O., & Mikhailov, I. (2009). *Virtuoso: RDF support in a native RDBMS. In Semantic Web Information Management* (pp. 501–519). Springer-Verlag.

Etzion, O., Jajodia, S., & Sripada, S. (Eds.). (1998). *Temporal Databases: Research and Practice. LNCS* (Vol. 1399). Berlin, Germany: Springer-Verlag. doi:10.1007/BFb0053695

Euzenat, J., & Shvaiko, P. (2013). *Ontology Matching*. Springer Berlin Heidelberg. doi:10.1007/978-3-642-38721-0

Fadika, Z., Head, M. R., & Govindaraju, M. (2009). Parallel and distributed approach for processing large-scale XML datasets. In *Proceedings of the 10th IEEE/ACM International Conference on Grid Computing*, (pp. 105-112). Banff, Alberta, Canada: IEEE Computer Society. 10.1109/GRID.2009.5353070

Fagin, R. (1979). Normal Forms and Relational Database Operators. *ACM SIGMOD International Conference on Management of Data.*

Falco, N., & Thom, F. (2014, June). *From XML Schema to JSON Schema: Translation with CHR*. Paper presented at 2014 CoRR conference.

Fang, H., & Zhang, X. W. (2016). pSPARQL: A Querying Language for Probabilistic RDF (Extended Abstract). *Proceedings of the ISWC 2016 Posters & Demonstrations Track.*

Fan, H., Ma, Z., Wang, D., & Liu, J. (2018). Handling distributed XML queries over large XML data based on MapReduce framework. *Information Sciences, 453*, 1–20. doi:10.1016/j.ins.2018.04.028

Fan, H., Wang, D., & Liu, J. (2016). Distributed XPath query processing over large XML data based on MapReduce framework. In *Proceedings of the International Conference on Natural Computation, Fuzzy Systems and Knowledge Discovery*, (pp. 1447-1453). Changsha, China: IEEE. 10.1109/FSKD.2016.7603390

Fan, H., Yang, H., Ma, Z., & Liu, J. (2016). TwigStack-MR: An approach to distributed XML twig query using MapReduce. In *Proceedings of the IEEE International Congress on Big Data*, (pp. 133-140). San Francisco, CA: IEEE Computer Society. 10.1109/BigDataCongress.2016.79

Felber, P., Pasin, M., Riviere, E., Schiavoni, V., Sutra, P., Coelho, F., ... Vilaça, R. M. P. (2014). On the Support of Versioning in Distributed Key-Value Stores. *Proceedings of the 33rd IEEE International Symposium on Reliable Distributed Systems (SRDS 2014)*, 95-104. 10.1109/SRDS.2014.35

Felipe, I., Hristidis, V., & Rishe, N. (2008). Keyword search on spatial databases. In *Proceedings of the International Conference on Data Engineering (ICDE'08)* (pp.656–665)

Fellipe, F., Crishane, F., & Damires, S. (2017). Enhancing JSON to RDF Data Conversion with Entity Type Recognition. *Proceedings of the 13th International Conference on Web Information Systems and Technologies (WEBIST 2017)*, 97-106.

Feng, J., Liu, L., Li, G., Li, J., & Sun, Y. (2010). An efficient parallel pathStack algorithm for processing XML twig queries on multi-core systems. In *Proceedings of the Database Systems for Advanced Applications, 15th International Conference*, (pp. 277-291). Tsukuba, Japan: Springer. 10.1007/978-3-642-12026-8_22

Fernandez, A., Peralta, D., Herrera, F., & Benıtez, J. M. (2012). An Overview of e-learning in Cloud Computing. *Workshop on LTEC, AISC, 173*, 35–46. 10.1007/978-3-642-30859-8_4

Ferraiolo, D. F., & Kuhn, D. R. (2009). *Role-based Access Controls*. arXiv preprint arXiv: 0903.2171

Ferraiolo, D. (2016). Extensible Access Control Markup Language (XACML) and Next Generation Access Control (NGAC). *Proceedings of the 2016 ACM International Workshop on Attribute Based Access Control*. 10.1145/2875491.2875496

Ferreira, N., Lins, L., Fink, D., Kelling, S., Wood, C., Freire, J., & Silva, C. (2011). Birdvis: Visualizing and understanding bird populations. *IEEE Transactions on Visualization and Computer Graphics, 17*(12), 2374–2383. doi:10.1109/TVCG.2011.176 PMID:22034358

Florescu, D., & Fourny, G. (2013). JSONiq: The History of a Query Language. *IEEE Internet Computing, 17*(5), 86–90. doi:10.1109/MIC.2013.97

Foundation, D. B. (2018). *FoundationDB gives you the power of ACID transactions in a distributed database*. Retrieved November 10, 2018, from https://foundationdb.com/

Fowler, M., & Sadalage, P. (2012). *NoSQL Database and Polyglot Persistence*. Retrieved from http://martinfowler.com/articles/nosql-intro-original.pdf

Franciscus, N., Ren, X., & Stantic, B. (2017). Precomputing architecture for flexible and efficient big data analytics. *Vietnam Journal of Computer Science, 5*(2), 133–142. doi:10.100740595-018-0109-9

Franke, C., Morin, S., Chebotko, A., Abraham, J., & Brazier, P. (2011). Distributed semantic web data management in HBase and MySQL Cluster. *Proceedings of the 2011 IEEE International Conference on Cloud Computing*, 105-112. 10.1109/CLOUD.2011.19

Gadia, S. K., & Yeung, C. S. (1988). A generalized model for a relational temporal database. *SIGMOD Record, 17*(3), 251–259. doi:10.1145/971701.50233

Galster, M., & Avgeriou, P. (2011). Empirically-grounded Reference Architectures: a proposal. *Joint ACM SIGSOFT Conference on Quality of Software Architectures and Conference on Quality of Software Architectures and Symposium on Architecting Critical Systems*, 20–24.

Gamble, M., & Goble, C. (2011). Quality, Trust and Utility of Scientific Data on the Web: Toward a Joint model. *Proceedings of the 2011 International Conference on Web Science*, 15:1-15:8. 10.1145/2527031.2527048

Gao, D., & Snodgrass, R. T. (2003). Temporal Slicing in the Evaluation of XML Documents. *Proceedings of the 29th International Conference on Very Large Data Bases (VLDB 2003)*, 632-643.

Garbis, G., Kyzirakos, K., & Koubarakis, M. (2013). Geographica: A benchmark for geospatial RDF stores. *Proceedings of the 12th International Semantic Web Conference*, 343-359.

Garcia, T., & Wang, T. (2013). Analysis of Big Data technologies and method - Query large Web public RDF datasets on Amazon cloud using Hadoop and Open Source Parsers. *Proceedings of the 2013 IEEE International Conference on Semantic Computing*, 244-251. 10.1109/ICSC.2013.49

Gaspar, D., & Coric, I. (2017). *Bridging Relational and NoSQL Databases*. IGI Global.

Gates, A., Natkovich, O., Chopra, S., Kamath, P., Narayanamurthy, S.M., Olston, C., …Sristava, U. (2009). Building a high level dataflow system on top of MapReduce: The pig experience. *PVLDB, 2*(2), 1414–1425.

Ghemawat, S., Gobioff, H., & Leung, S. T. (2003). The google file system. In *Proceedings of the 19th ACM Symposium on Operating Systems Principles*, (pp. 29-43). Bolton Landing, NY: ACM.

Ghotiya, S., Mandal, J., & Kandasamy, S. (2017). Migration from relational to NoSQL database. In *Proceedings of 14th ICSET Conf.* IOP Publishing.

Gilbert, S., & Lynch, N. (2002). Brewer's conjecture and the feasibility consistent, available, partition-tolerant web services. *ACM SIGACT News, 33*(2), 51–59. doi:10.1145/564585.564601

Giovannella, C., Iosue, A., & Tancredi, A. (2012). Scenarios for active learning in smart territories. *Interaction Design and Architecture(s) Journal, 16*, 7–16.

GitHub, Inc. (2018). *Project Voldemort - a distributed database.* Retrieved November 10, 2018, from http://www.project-voldemort.com/voldemort/

Google App Engine. (2010). Retrieved from http://code.google.com/appengine/

Grandi, F. (2015). Temporal Databases. In M. Khosrow-Pour (Ed.), *Encyclopedia of Information Science and Technology* (3rd ed.; pp. 1914–1922). Hershey, PA: IGI Global. doi:10.4018/978-1-4666-5888-2.ch184

Grandi, F., Mandreoli, F., Tiberio, P., & Bergonzini, M. (2003). A temporal data model and management system for normative texts in XML format. In *Proceedings of the 5th ACM International Workshop on Web Information and Data Management* (pp. 29-36). ACM. 10.1145/956699.956706

Griffin, L., Butler, B., de Leastar, E., Jennings, B., & Botvich, D. (2012). On the performance of access control policy evaluation. In *Policies for Distributed Systems and Networks (POLICY), 2012 IEEE International Symposium on* (pp. 25-32). IEEE. 10.1109/POLICY.2012.15

Grolinger, K., Higashino, W. A., Tiwari, A., & Capretz, M. A. M. (2013). Data management in cloud environments: NoSQL and NewSQL data stores. *Journal of Cloud Computing: Advances, Systems and Applications, 2*(22).

Grolinger, K., Higashino, W.A., Tiwari, A., & Capretz, M.A.M. (2013). Data management in cloud environments: NoSQL and NewSQL data stores. *Journal of Cloud Computing: Advances, Systems and Applications, 2*(22).

Guanhua, W. (2011). Improving Data Transmission in Web Applications via the Translation between XML and JSON. Paper presented at 2011 Third International Conference on Communications and Mobile Computing.

Gudivada, V. N., Rao, D., & Raghavan, V. V. (2014). NoSQL Systems for Big Data Management, *2014 IEEE World Congress on Services*, 190-197. 10.1109/SERVICES.2014.42

Gu, F. Z., & Shen, B. (2012). Application study on JSON data exchange format in integration of Heterogeneous System. *Railway Computer Application, 21*(2), 1–4.

Gul, S. (2017). A Survey on Role of the Internet of Things in Education. *International Journal of Computer Science and Network Security, 17*(5).

Guo, L., Shao, J., Aung, H., & Tan, K. (2015). Efficient continuous top-k spatial keyword queries on road networks. *GeoInformatica, 19*(1), 29–60. doi:10.100710707-014-0204-8

Gutierrez, C., Hurtado, C. A., & Vaisman, A. (2007). Introducing time into RDF. *IEEE Transactions on Knowledge and Data Engineering, 19*(2), 207–218. doi:10.1109/TKDE.2007.34

Güting, R. H. (1994). GraphDB: Modeling and querying graphs in databases. *Proceedings of 20th International Conference on Very Large Data Bases*, 297-308.

Guzman, L. (2001). Multi-Criteria Decision Making Methods: A Comparative Study, Applied optimization. *Journal of Multi-Criteria Decision Analysis*, *10*(3), 175–175. doi:10.1002/mcda.300

Hada, S., & Kudo, M. (2000). *XML Access Control Language: provisional authorization for XML documents*. Academic Press.

Halliday, L. (2018). *Unleash the Power of Storing JSON in Postgres*. Retrieved from https://blog.codeship.com/unleash-the-power-of-storing-json-in-postgres

Hameed, S., Badii, A., & Cullen, A. J. (2008). Effective E-Learning Integration with Traditional Learning in a Blended Learning Environment. *European and Mediterranean Conf, on Information Systems*, 1-16.

Hammerschmidt. (2015). *New SQL/JSON Query Operators (Part 2: JSON_QUERY)*. Retrieved from https://blogs.oracle.com/jsondb/the-new-sqljson-query-operators-part2:-jsonquery

Hampapur, A., Brown, L., Connell, J., Ekin, A., Haas, N., Lu, M., ... Pankanti, S. (2005). Smart video surveillance: Exploring the concept of multiscale spatiotemporal tracking. *IEEE Signal Processing Magazine*, *22*(2), 38–51. doi:10.1109/MSP.2005.1406476

Hamrouni, H., Brahmia, Z., & Bouaziz, R. (2018). A Systematic Approach to Efficiently Managing the Effects of Retroactive Updates of Time-varying Data in Multiversion XML Databases. *International Journal of Intelligent Information and Database Systems*, *11*(1), 1–26. doi:10.1504/IJIIDS.2018.091583

Han, J. (2005). *Data Mining: Concepts and Techniques*. Morgan Kaufmann Publishers Inc.

Haq, Z. U., Khan, G. F., & Hussain, T. (2015). A Comprehensive Analysis of XML and JSON Web Technologies. *New Developments in Circuits, Systems, Signal Processing, Communications and Computers*, 102–109.

Härder, T. (2005). DBMS Architecture – the Layer Model and its Evolution. *Datenbank-Spektrum*, *13*, 45–57.

Harris, S., Lamb, N., & Shadbolt, N. (2009). 4store: The design and implementation of a clustered RDF store. *Proceedings of the 5th International Workshop on Scalable Semantic Web Knowledge Base Systems*, 94-109.

Hecht, R., & Jablonski, S. (2011). NoSQL evaluation: A use case oriented survey. In *Proceedings of the 2011 International Conference on Cloud and Service Computing*. Hong Kong, China: IEEE. 10.1109/CSC.2011.6138544

He, L., Qiu, X., Wang, Y., & Gao, T. (2013). Design of policy language expression in SIoT. In *Wireless and Optical Communication Conference* (pp. 321-326). IEEE.

Helland, P. (2017, July). XML and JSON Are Like Cardboard. *ACM Queue; Tomorrow's Computing Today*.

Herrero, V., Abelló, A., & Romero, O. (2016). NOSQL Design for Analytical Workloads: Variability Matters. *Proceedings of ER Conf., LNCS 9974*, 50-64. 10.1007/978-3-319-46397-1_4

Hjaltason, G. R., & Samet, H. (2003). Index-driven similarity search in metric spaces. *ACM Transactions on Database Systems*, *28*(4), 517–580. doi:10.1145/958942.958948

Hoffart, J., Suchanek, F. M., Berberich, K., & Weikum, G. (2013). YAGO2: A spatially and temporally enhanced knowledge base from Wikipedia. *Artificial Intelligence*, *194*, 28–61. doi:10.1016/j.artint.2012.06.001

Horowitz, E. (2018). *MongoDB Drops ACID*. Retrieved from https://www.mongodb.com/blog/post/multi-document-transactions-in-mongodb.

Hu, V.C., Ferraiolo, D., & Kuhn, R. (2013). *Guide to attribute based access control (ABAC) definition and considerations.* NIST special publication 800.162.

Huang, H., Lee, C., & Lin, H. (2017). Nighttime vehicle detection and tracking base on spatiotemporal analysis using RCCC sensor. In *Proceedings of 2017 IEEE 9th International Conference on Humanoid, Nanotechnology, Information Technology, Communication and Control, Environment and Management,* Manila, Philippines (pp. 1-5). Piscataway, NJ: IEEE. 10.1109/HNICEM.2017.8269548

Huang, J., Abadi, D. J., & Ren, K. (2011). Scalable SPARQL querying of large RDF graphs. *Proceedings of the VLDB Endowment International Conference on Very Large Data Bases,* 4(11), 1123–1134.

Huang, X., Si, X., Yuan, X., & Wang, C. (2014). A dynamic load-balancing scheme for XPath queries parallelization in shared memory multi-core systems. *Journal of Computers,* 9(6), 1436–1445. doi:10.4304/jcp.9.6.1436-1445

Hua, X. Y., Wu, H., Li, Z., & Ren, S. P. (2014). Enhancing throughput of the Hadoop Distributed File System for interaction-intensive tasks. *Journal of Parallel and Distributed Computing,* 74(8), 2770–2779. doi:10.1016/j.jpdc.2014.03.010

Hu, J., Fan, J., Li, G., & Chen, S. (2012). Top-k fuzzy spatial keyword search. *Chinese Journal of Computers,* 36(2), 1930–1942.

Hurtado, C., & Vaisman, A. (2006). Reasoning with temporal constraints in RDF. *Proceedings of the 2006 International Conference on Principles and Practice of Semantic Web Reasoning,* 164-178. 10.1007/11853107_12

Husain, M. F., Khan, L., Kantarcioglu, M., & Thuraisingham, B. M. (2010). Data intensive query processing for large RDF graphs using cloud computing tools. *Proceedings of the 2010 IEEE International Conference on Cloud Computing,* 1-10. 10.1109/CLOUD.2010.36

Husain, M. F., McGlothlin, J. P., Masud, M. M., Khan, L. R., & Thuraisingham, B. M. (2011). Heuristics-based query processing for large RDF graphs using cloud computing. *IEEE Transactions on Knowledge and Data Engineering,* 23(9), 1312–1327. doi:10.1109/TKDE.2011.103

Hu, Y., & Dessloch, S. (2014). Defining Temporal Operators for Column Oriented NoSQL Databases. *Proceedings of the 18th East European Conference on Advances in Databases and Information Systems (ADBIS 2014),* 39-55. 10.1007/978-3-319-10933-6_4

Hu, Y., & Dessloch, S. (2015). Temporal Data Management and Processing with Column Oriented NoSQL Databases. *Journal of Database Management,* 26(3), 41–70. doi:10.4018/JDM.2015070103

Hwang, G.J. (2014). *Definition, Framework and Research Issues of Smart Learning Environments - A Context-Aware Ubiquitous Learning Perspective.* Academic Press.

Hypertable Inc. (2014). *Hypertable.* Retrieved November 10, 2018, from http://hypertable.org/

Idreos, S., Alagiannis, I., Johnson, R., & Ailamaki, A. (2011). Here are my Data Files. Here are my Queries. Where are my Results? *CIDR, 2011,* 57–68.

IEC. (2016). *IoT 2020: Smart & Secure IoT platform.* International Electro-technical Commission.

IEEE. (2000). *Recommended Practice for Architectural Description of Software-Intensive Systems. Standard Specification IEEE 1471-2000.* IEEE Computer Society.

IEEE. (2010). *ISO/IEC/IEEE 2010:2011, Systems and software engineering — Architecture description, the latest edition of the original IEEE Std 1471:2000.* Recommended Practice for Architectural Description of Software-intensive Systems.

IETF (Internet Engineering Task Force). (2013). *JSON Schema: interactive and non interactive validation.* Retrieved January 31, 2019, from http://tools.ietf.org/html/draft-fge-json-schema-validation-00

IETF (Internet Engineering Task Force). (2017). *The JavaScript Object Notation (JSON) Data Interchange Format.* Retrieved January 31, 2019, from https://tools.ietf.org/html/rfc8259

IETF (Internet Engineering Task Force). (2018). *JSON Schema: A Media Type for Describing JSON Documents.* Retrieved January 31, 2019, from https://json-schema.org/latest/json-schema-core.html

Indexing JSON Data in Oracle Database 12c Release 1 (12.1.0.2). (n.d.). Retrieved from https://oracle-base.com/articles/12c/indexing-json-data-in-oracle-database-12cr1

Intel. (2016). *Solution Brief, Intel IoT Platform, End-to-End IoT Reference Model and Products.* Author.

Introducing JSON. (n.d.). Retrieved from http://json.org/

Introducing JSON. (n.d.). Retrieved from https://www.json.org/

IoT Series. (2014). *Common requirements of the Internet of things, Series Y.2066: Global Information Infrastructure.* Internet Protocol Aspects and Next-Generation Networks – Frameworks and Functional Architecture Models.

Isele, R., Jentzsch, A., & Bizer, C. (2010, November). Silk server-adding missing links while consuming linked data. In *Proceedings of the First International Conference on Consuming Linked Data-Volume 665* (pp. 85-96). Aachen, Germany: CEUR-WS.org.

Isele, R. (2014). Methoden der Linked Data Integration. In T. Pellegrini, H. Sack, & S. Auer (Eds.), *Linked Enterprise Data* (pp. 103–120).

Itakura, F. (1975). Minimum prediction residual principle applied to speech recognition. *IEEE Transactions on Acoustics, Speech, and Signal Processing*, *23*(1), 67–72. doi:10.1109/TASSP.1975.1162641

ITU. (2014). *Study Report on IoT Reference Architectures/Frameworks.* ISO.

Izquierdo, J. L. C., & Cabot, J. (2016). JSONDiscoverer: Visualizing the schema lurking behind JSON documents. *Knowledge-Based Systems*, *103*, 52–55. doi:10.1016/j.knosys.2016.03.020

Jagadish, H. V., Ooi, B. C., Tan, K. L., Yu, C., & Zhang, R. (2005). iDistance: An adaptive B+-tree based indexing method for nearest neighbor search. *ACM Transactions on Database Systems*, *30*(2), 364–397. doi:10.1145/1071610.1071612

Jain, A., & Pandey, U.S. (2013). Role of Cloud Computing in Higher Education. *International Journal of Advanced Research in Computer Science and Software Engineering*, *3*(7), 966-972.

Jajodia, S., Samarati, P., & Subrahmanian, V. S. (1997). A logical language for expressing autho- rizations. In *Proceedings of IEEE Symposium on Security and Privacy.* IEEE.

Jaro, M. A. (1989). Advances in record-linkage methodology as applied to matching the 1985 census of Tampa, Florida. *Journal of the American Statistical Association*, *84*(406), 414–420. doi:10.1080/01621459.1989.10478785

Jensen, C. S. (2000). *Temporal Database Management* (PhD thesis). Department of Computer Science, Aalborg University, Aalborg, Denmark.

Jensen, C. S., Clifford, J., Gadia, S. K., Segev, A., & Snodgrass, R. T. (1992). A glossary of temporal database concepts. *SIGMOD Record*, *21*(3), 35–43. doi:10.1145/140979.140996

Jensen, C. S., & Snodgrass, R. T. (2018). Temporal Query Languages. In L. Liu & M. T. Özsu (Eds.), *Encyclopedia of Database Systems (2nd ed.).* New York: Springer-Verlag. doi:10.1007/978-1-4614-8265-9_407

Jeong, J. S., Kim, M., & Yoo, K. H. (2013). A Content-Oriented Smart Education System based on Cloud Computing. *International Journal of Multimedia and Ubiquitous Engineering*, *8*(6), 313–328. doi:10.14257/ijmue.2013.8.6.31

Jetlund, K. (2015). *Best practices for diagram design*. Retrieved from: https://github.com/ISO-TC211/UML-Best-Practices/wiki/Best-practices-for-diagram-design

Jiang, D., Ooi, B. C., Shi, L., & Wu, S. (2010). The performance of MapReduce: An in-depth study. *Proceedings of the VLDB Endowment International Conference on Very Large Data Bases*, *3*(1), 472–483. doi:10.14778/1920841.1920903

Jin, X., Sandhu, R., & Krishnan, R. (2012). RABAC: role-centric attribute-based access control. In *International Conference on Mathematical Methods, Models, and Architectures for Computer Network Security*. Springer.

Jingbo, W., Amir, A., Lesley, W., & Ben, E. (2017, April). *Providing Research Graph Data in JSON-LD Using Schema. org*. Paper presented at 2017 April 3-7 IW3C2 (International World Wide Web Conference Committee) conference.

JSON – Introduction. (n.d.). Retrieved from https://www.w3schools.com/js/js_json_intro.asp

JSON Alternate Serialization (RDF/JSON). (n.d.). Retrieved from https://dvcs.w3.org/hg/rdf/raw-file/default/rdf-json/index.html#bib-json-ld

JSON schema. (n.d.). Retrieved from http://json-schema.org/

JSON Types. (2018). Retrieved from https://www.postgresql.org/docs/devel/static/datatype-json.html

JSON. (n.d.). Retrieved from https://en.wikipedia.org/wiki/JSON

JSON. (n.d.). *Schema and Metadata*. Retrieved from https://en.wikipedia.org/wiki/JSON#JSONSchema

JSON-LD 1.1 Processing Algorithms and API. (2018). Retrieved from https://www.w3.org/2018/jsonld-cg-reports/json-ld-api/#data-round-tripping

Kagal, L., Finin, T., & Joshi, A. (2003). A policy language for a pervasive computing environment. In *Policies for Distributed Systems and Networks. Proceedings. POLICY 2003. IEEE 4th International Workshop on*. IEEE.

Kamble, R. S., & Nikam, D. A. (2013). Green cloud computing new approach of energy consumption. *International Journal of Latest Trends in Engineering and Technology*, *3*(2), 124–131.

Kankaanranta, M., & Makela, T. (2014). Valuation of Emerging Learning Solutions. *World Conf. on Educational Multimedia, Hypermedia and Telecommunications*, Tampere, Finland.

Kaoudi, Z., & Manolescu, I. (2015). RDF in the clouds: A survey. *The VLDB Journal*, *24*(1), 67–91. doi:10.100700778-014-0364-z

Karim, F., & Goodwin, R. (2013). Using Cloud Computing in e-learning Systems. *International Journal of Advanced Research in Computer Science & Technology*, *1*(1), 65–69.

Kaur, A. (2014). Green computing: Emerging Trends in Information and Communication Technology. *International Journal of Engineering Inventions*, *3*(9), 42–46.

Kaur, G., & Kumar, P. (2013). Compositional Framework of Green Cloud, *Intel. Journal of Emerging Trends in Engineering and Development*, *1*(3).

Kelly, J. (2014). *Big Data: Hadoop, Business Analytics and Beyond*. Wikibon. Retrieved November 20, 2018 from http://wikibon.org/wiki/v/Big_Data:_Hadoop,_Business_Analytics_and_Beyond

Keogh, E. J., & Pazzani, M. J. (2000, August). Scaling up dynamic time warping for datamining applications. In *Proceedings of the sixth ACM SIGKDD international conference on Knowledge discovery and data mining* (pp. 285-289). ACM. 10.1145/347090.347153

Keogh, E. J., & Pazzani, M. J. (2001, April). Derivative dynamic time warping. In *Proceedings of the 2001 SIAM international conference on data mining* (pp. 1-11). Society for Industrial and Applied Mathematics.

Keogh, E., & Ratanamahatana, C. A. (2005). Exact indexing of dynamic time warping. *Knowledge and Information Systems, 7*(3), 358–386. doi:10.100710115-004-0154-9

Khadilkar, V., Kantarcioglu, M., Thuraisingham, B. M., & Castagna, P. (2012). Jena-HBase: A distributed, scalable and efficient RDF triple store. *Proceedings of the 2012 International Semantic Web Conference.*

Khan, L., & Rao, Y. (2001). A Performance Evaluation of Storing XML Data in Relational Database Management Systems. In *Proceedings of the 3rd International Workshop on Web Information and Data Management* (pp. 31–38). Academic Press. 10.1145/502932.502939

Kim, H. S., Ravindra, P., & Anyanwu, K. (2013). Optimizing RDF(S) queries on cloud platforms, *Proceedings of the 2013 International World Wide Web Conference*, 261-264. 10.1145/2487788.2487917

Kim, S. W. (2006). Hybrid storage scheme for RDF data management in Semantic Web. *Journal of Digital Information Management, 4*(1), 32–36.

Kim, S. W., Park, S., & Chu, W. W. (2001). An index-based approach for similarity search supporting time warping in large sequence databases. In *Proceedings 17th International Conference on Data Engineering* (pp. 607-614). IEEE.

Kim, S., Song, S. M., & Yoon, Y. I. (2011). Smart Learning Services based on Smart Cloud Computing. *Sensors (Basel), 11*(8), 7835–7850. doi:10.3390110807835 PMID:22164048

Kim, W., Kim, Y., & Shim, K. (2016). Parallel computation of k-nearest neighbor joins using MapReduce. In *Proceedings of the IEEE International Conference on Big Data* (pp. 696-705). Washington, DC: IEEE. 10.1109/BigData.2016.7840662

Kim, Y., & Shim, K. (2012). Parallel top-k similarity join algorithms using MapReduce. In *Proceedings of the International Conference on Data Engineering* (pp. 510-521). IEEE Computer Society. 10.1109/ICDE.2012.87

Kitamoto, A. (2002). Spatio-temporal data mining for typhoon image collection. *Journal of Intelligent Information Systems, 19*(1), 25–41. doi:10.1023/A:1015560319636

Klettke, M., Störl, U., & Scherzinger, S. (2015). Schema extraction and structural outlier detection for JSON-based NoSQL data stores. *Datenbanksysteme für Business, Technologie und Web.*

Klyne, G., & Carroll, J. J. (2004). *Resource description framework (RDF): Concepts and Abstract Syntax.* W3C Recommendation. Retrieved from http://www.w3.org/TR/2004/REC-RDF-concepts-20040210/

Knolmayer, G. F., & Myrach, T. (2001). Concepts of bitemporal database theory and the evolution of web documents. In *Proceedings of the 34th Annual Hawaii International Conference on System Sciences* (p. 10). IEEE. 10.1109/HICSS.2001.927091

Kruskall, J. B. (1983). *The symmetric time warping algorithm: From continuous to discrete.* Time warps, string edits and macromolecules.

Kuhn, H. W. (1955). The Hungarian method for the assignment problem. *Naval Research Logistics Quarterly, 2*(1-2), 83-97.

Kuhn, D. R., Coyne, E. J., & Weil, T. R. (2010). Adding attributes to role-based access control. *Computer, 43*(6), 79–81. doi:10.1109/MC.2010.155

Kurte, K. R., Durbha, S. S., King, R. L., Younan, N. H., & Potnis, A. V. (2017). A spatiotemporal ontological model for flood disaster monitoring. In *Proceedings of 2017 IEEE International Geoscience and Remote Sensing Symposium*, Fort Worth, TX (pp. 5213-5216). Piscataway, NJ: IEEE. 10.1109/IGARSS.2017.8128176

Kyzirakos, K. (2013). The Spatiotemporal RDF Store Strabon. *Proceedings of the 13th International Symposium on Advances in Spatial and Temporal Databases*, 496-500. 10.1007/978-3-642-40235-7_35

Lahiri, T., Chavan, S., Colgan, M., Das, D., Ganesh, A., Gleeson, M., ... Zaït, M. (2015). Oracle Database In-Memory: A dual format in-memory database. *ICDE, 2015*, 1253–1258.

Lakshman, A., & Malik, P. (2010). Cassandra: A decentralized structured storage system. *ACM SIGOPS Operating System Review, 44*(2), 35–40. doi:10.1145/1773912.1773922

Lane, J., & Finsel, A. (2014). *Fostering Smarter Colleges and Universities Data, Big Data, and Analytics*. State University of New York Press.

Laney, D. (2001). *3D data management: Controlling data volume, velocity and variety*. Meta Group, Gartner. Retrieved from http://blogs.gartner.com/doug-laney/files/2012/01/ad949-3D-Data-Management-Controlling-Data-Volume-Velocity-and-Variety.pdf

Laney, D. (2001). *3D data management: Controlling data volume, velocity and variety*. Meta Group, Gartner. Retrieved November 6, 2018 from http://blogs.gartner.com/doug-laney/files/2012/01/ad949-3D-Data-Management-Controlling-Data-Volume-Velocity-and-Variety.pdf

Leloglu, E., Ayav, T., & Galip Aslan, B. (2013). A review of cloud deployment models for e-learning systems. *43rd Annual IEEE/IFIP International Conference on Dependable Systems and Networks (DSN)*, 1-2. 10.1109/DSN.2013.6575331

Levandoski, J. J., Lomet, D. B., & Sengupta, S. (2013). The Bw-Tree: A B-tree for new hardware platforms. *ICDE, 2013*, 302–313.

Levenshtein, V. I. (1966, February). Binary codes capable of correcting deletions, insertions, and reversals. *Soviet Physics, 10*(8), 707–710.

Li, G., Feng, J., & Xu, J. (2012). Desks: direction-aware spatial keyword search. In *Proceedings of the International Conference on Data Engineering (ICDE'12)* (pp. 474-485).

Li, J., Liu, C., Zhou, R., & Wang, W. (2011). Top-k keyword search over probabilistic XML data. In *Proceedings of the International Conference on Data Engineering (ICDE'11)* (pp. 673-684). 10.1109/ICDE.2011.5767875

Liagouris, J., Mamoulis, N., Bouros, P., & Terrovitis, M. (2014). An Effective Encoding Scheme for Spatial RDF Data. *Proceedings of the VLDB Endowment International Conference on Very Large Data Bases, 7*(12), 1271–1282. doi:10.14778/2732977.2733000

Lian, X., & Chen, L. (2011). Efficient query answering in probabilistic RDF graphs. *Proceedings of the ACM SIGMOD International Conference on Management of Data*, 157-168. 10.1145/1989323.1989341

Lian, X., Chen, L., & Huang, Z. (2015). Keyword Search Over Probabilistic RDF Graphs. *IEEE Transactions on Knowledge and Data Engineering, 27*(5), 1246–1260. doi:10.1109/TKDE.2014.2365791

Li, G., & Ma, Z. (2018). An efficient matching algorithm for fuzzy RDF graph. *Journal of Information Science and Engineering, 34*(2), 519–534.

Lihua, C. (2010). Comment on Latent Semantic Analysis of Retrieval Precision Rate Factors Based on the Impact of Natural Language. *Journal of Modern Information, 3*, 26–31.

Lin, B., Chen, Y., Chen, X., & Yu, Y. (2012). Comparison between JSON and XML in Applications Based on AJAX. In *Proceedings of the 2012 International Conference on Computer Science and Service System* (pp. 1174-1177). IEEE Computer Society. 10.1109/CSSS.2012.297

Li, R., Yang, D., Hu, H. B., Xie, J., & Fu, L. (2013). Scalable RDF graph querying using cloud computing. *Journal of Web Engineering*, *12*(1 & 2), 159–180.

Liu & Gawlick. (2015). Management of Flexible Schema Data in RDBMSs - Opportunities and Limitations for NoSQL. *CIDR 2015*.

Liu, X. P., Wan, C. X., Liu, D. X., & Liao, G. Q. (2016). Survey on spatial keyword search. *Journal of Software*, *27*(2), 329–347.

Liu, Y., Liu, C., Liu, B., Qu, M., & Xiong, H. (2016). Unified Point-of-Interest recommendation with temporal interval assessment. In *Proceedings of the ACM SIGKDD International Conference on Knowledge Discovery & Data Mining (KDD'16)* (pp.121-130) 10.1145/2939672.2939773

Liu, Y., Scharffe, F., & Zhou, C. (2008, December). Towards practical RDF datasets fusion. In *Workshop on Data Integration through Semantic Technology (DIST2008)*.

Liu, Z. H., Chang, H. J., & Sthanikam, B. (2012). Efficient Support of XQuery Update Facility in XML Enabled RDBMS. *ICDE*, *2012*, 1394–1404.

Liu, Z. H., Hammerschmidt, B., & McMahon, D. (2014). JSON data management: supporting schema-less development in RDBMS. *SIGMOD Conference 2014*, 1247-1258. 10.1145/2588555.2595628

Liu, Z. H., Hammerschmidt, B., McMahon, D., Liu, Y., & Chang, H. J. (2016, June). Closing the functional and performance gap between SQL and NoSQL. In *Proceedings of the 2016 International Conference on Management of Data* (pp. 227-238). ACM. 10.1145/2984356.2985239

Liu, Z. H., Hammerschmidt, B., McMahon, D., Lu, Y., & Chang, H. J. (2016). Closing the functional and Performance Gap between SQL and NoSQL. *SIGMOD Conference*, 227-238. 10.1145/2882903.2903731

Liu, Z. H., Lu, Y., & Chang, H. J. (2014). Efficient support of XQuery Full Text in SQL/XML enabled RDBMS. *ICDE*, *2014*, 1132–1143.

Li, W. (2015). *Research on the survey of spatial keyword query*.

Li, X., Liu, M., Ghafoor, A., & Sheu, P. C. (2010). A pattern-based temporal XML query language. In *Proceedings of the 2010 International Conference on Web Information Systems Engineering* (pp. 428-441). Berlin, Germany: Springer.

Li, Y., Katsipoulakis, N. R., Chandramouli, B., Goldstein, J., & Kossmann, D. (2017). Mison (2017). A Fast JSON Parser for Data Analytics. *PVLDB*, *10*(10), 1118–1129.

Li, Z., Hu, F., Schnase, J. L., Duffy, D. Q., Lee, T., Bowen, M. K., & Yang, C. (2017). A spatiotemporal indexing approach for efficient processing of big array-based climate data with MapReduce. *International Journal of Geographical Information Science*, *31*(1), 17–35. doi:10.1080/13658816.2015.1131830

Lohmosavi, V., Nejad, A. F., & Hosseini, E. M. (2013). E-learning ecosystem based on service-oriented cloud computing architecture. *International Conference on Information and Knowledge Technology (IKT)*, 24-29. 10.1109/IKT.2013.6620032

Lu, Y., Lu, J., Cong, G., Wu, W., & Shahabi, C. (2014). Efficient algorithms and cost models for reverse spatial-keyword k-nearest neighbor search. ACM Transactions on Database Systems, 39(2), 573–598.

Luo, Y., Picalausa, F., Fletcher, G. H. L., Hidders, J., & Vansummeren, S. (2012). *Storing and indexing massive RDF datasets. In Semantic Search over the Web* (pp. 31–60). Springer-Verlag Berlin Heidelberg. doi:10.1007/978-3-642-25008-8_2

Lu, W., Shen, Y., Chen, S., & Ooi, B. C. (2012). Efficient Processing of k Nearest Neighbor Joins using MapReduce. *Proceedings of the VLDB Endowment International Conference on Very Large Data Bases*, *5*(10), 1016–1027. doi:10.14778/2336664.2336674

Lv, Y., Ma, Z. M., & Yan, L. (2008). Fuzzy RDF: A data model to represent fuzzy metadata. In *IEEE International Conference on Fuzzy Systems*. Hong Kong, China (pp. 1439-1445).

Ma, A., & Sethi, I. K. (2007). Distributed k-median clustering with application to image clustering. In *Proceedings of the 7th International Workshop on Pattern Recognition in Information System* (pp. 215-220). Funchal, Portugal: INSTICC.

Ma, R., Ahmadzadeh, A., Boubrahimi, S. F., & Angryk, R. A. (2018, December). Segmentation of Time Series in Improving Dynamic Time Warping. In *2018 IEEE International Conference on Big Data (Big Data)* (pp. 3756-3761). IEEE. 10.1109/BigData.2018.8622554

Maciejewski, R., Hafen, R., Rudolph, S., Larew, S. G., Mitchell, M. A., Cleveland, W. S., & Ebert, D. S. (2011). Forecasting hotspots—A predictive analytics approach. *IEEE Transactions on Visualization and Computer Graphics*, *17*(4), 440–453. doi:10.1109/TVCG.2010.82 PMID:20498509

Maier, M. (2007). Internet of Things – Architecture (reference model for IoT). *European Commission within the Seventh Framework Programme*.

Maier, M. (2013). *Towards a Big Data Reference Architecture* (Master's Thesis). Eindhoven University of Technology, Department of Mathematics and Computer Science.

Malewicz, G., Austern, M. H., Bik, A. J. C., Dehnert, J. C., Horn, I., Leiser, N., & Czajkowski, G. (2010). Pregel: A System for Large-scale Graph Processing. *Proceedings of the PODS*. 10.1145/1807167.1807184

Manoj, P. (2013). Emerging Database Models and Related Technologies. *International Journal of Advanced Research in Computer Science and Software Engineering*, *3*(2), 264–269.

Manola, F., & Miller, E. (2004). *RDF Primer*. W3C Recommendation. Retrieved from http://www.w3.org/TR/2004/REC-rdf-primer-20040210/

Manyika, J., Chui, M., Brown, B., Bughin, J., Dobbs, R., Roxburgh, C., & Byers, A. H. (2011). *Big data: the next frontier for innovation, competition, and productivity*. McKinsey Global Inst. Retrieved November 6, 2018 from http://www.mckinsey.com/insights/business_technology/big_data_the_next_frontier_for_innovation

Ma, R., Ahmadzadeh, A., Boubrahimi, S. F., & Angryk, R. A. (in press). A Scalable Segmented Dynamic Time Warping for Time Series Classification. In *International Conference on Artificial Intelligence and Soft Computing Proceedings of the 18th International Conference on Artificial Intelligence and Soft Computing (ICAISC '19)*. 397-408.

MarkLogic Corp. (2018). *MarkLogic*. Retrieved November 10, 2018, from http://www.marklogic.com/

Maskare, P. R., & Sulke, S. R. (2014). E-learning using cloud computing. *International Journal of Computer Science and Mobile Computing*, *3*(5), 1281–1287.

Maso, J. (2017). *Testbed-12 JavaScript-JSON-JSON-LD Engineering Report (OGC 16-051)*. Retrieved from: http://docs.opengeospatial.org/per/16-051.html

Maso, J., Zabala, A., Serral, I., & Pons, X. (2018). Remote Sensing Analytical Geospatial Operations Directly in the Web Browser. *The International Archives of the Photogrammetry, Remote Sensing and Spatial Information Sciences*, *42*(4), 403–410. doi:10.5194/isprs-archives-XLII-4-403-2018

Masud, M. A. H., & Huang, X. (2012). An e-Learning System Architecture based on Cloud Computing. *World Academy of Science, Engineering and Technology*, *62*, 74–78.

Ma, Z., Capretz, M. A. M., & Yan, L. (2016). Storing massive Resource Description Framework (RDF) data: A survey. *The Knowledge Engineering Review*, *31*(4), 391–413. doi:10.1017/S0269888916000217

Ma, Z., Li, G., & Yan, L. (2018). Fuzzy data modeling and algebraic operations in RDF. *Fuzzy Sets and Systems*, *351*, 41–63. doi:10.1016/j.fss.2017.11.013

Ma, Z., & Yan, L. (2018). Modeling fuzzy data with RDF and fuzzy relational database models. *International Journal of Intelligent Systems*, *3*(7), 1534–1554. doi:10.1002/int.21996

Mazzieri, M., & Dragoni, A. F. (2008). A fuzzy semantics for the resource description framework. In *Uncertainty Reasoning for the Semantic Web I* (pp. 244–261). Berlin, Germany: Springer. doi:10.1007/978-3-540-89765-1_15

McBride, B. (2002). Jena: A Semantic Web toolkit. *IEEE Internet Computing*, *6*(6), 55–59. doi:10.1109/MIC.2002.1067737

Meijer, E., & Bierman, G. M. (2011). A co-relational model of data for large shared data banks. *Communications of the ACM*, *54*(4), 49–58. doi:10.1145/1924421.1924436

Mell, P., & Grance, T. (2009). *Definition: Cloud computing*. NIST Special Publication 800-145.

Mell, P., & Grance, T. (2011). *The NIST definition of cloud computing*. NIST Special Publication 800-145.

Melnik, Gubarev, Long, Romer, Shivakumar, Tolton, & Vassilakis. (2010). Interactive Analysis of Web-Scale Datasets. *VLDB 2010*.

Melnik, S., Garcia-Molina, H., & Rahm, E. (2002). Similarity Flooding: A Versatile Graph Matching Algorithm and Its Application to Schema Matching. In *Proceedings of the 18th IEEE Computer Society International Conference on Data Engineering* (pp. 117-128). IEEE. 10.1109/ICDE.2002.994702

Melton, J. (2003). *Advanced SQL, 1999: Understanding Object-Relational and Other Advanced Features*. Morgan Kaufmann.

Melton, J. (2003). *Information Technology-Database Languages-SQL-Part 14: XML-Related Specifications (SQL/XML) (ISO/IEC 9075-14: 2003)*. OASIS.

Memcached. (2018). Retrieved November 10, 2018, from http://memcached.org/

MemSQL Inc. (2018). *MemSQL*. Retrieved November 10, 2018, from http://www.memsql.com/

Mendelzon, A. O., Rizzolo, F., & Vaisman, A. (2004). Indexing temporal XML documents. In *Proceedings of the Thirtieth International Conference on Very Large Data Bases* (pp. 216-227). VLDB Endowment.

Merelo-Guervós, J. J., Castillo, P. A., Laredo, J. L. J., Garcia, A. M., & Prieto, A. (2008). Asynchronous distributed genetic algorithms with Javascript and JSON. In *Proceedings of the 2008 IEEE Congress on Evolutionary Computation* (pp. 1372-1379). IEEE. 10.1109/CEC.2008.4630973

MicroFocus International. (2018). *Vertica Analytic Database*. Retrieved November 10, 2018, from http://www.vertica.com/

Microsoft Azure. (2011). Retrieved from www.microsoft.com/windowsazure/

Microsoft. (2018). *Microsoft Azure*. Retrieved November 10, 2018, from https://docs.microsoft.com/en-us/azure/

Mircea, M., & Andreescu, A. I. (2011). Using cloud computing in higher education: A Strategy to Improve Agility in the Current Financial Crisis. *Communications of the IBIMA, 20*(11), 1–15. doi:10.5171/2011.875547

Mishra, A., Chavan, S., Holloway, A., Lahiri, T., Liu, Z. H., Chakkappen, S., ... Marwah, V. (2016). Accelerating Analytics with Dynamic In-Memory Expressions. *PVLDB, 9*(13), 1437–1448.

Mitsa, T. (2010). *Temporal Data Mining*. Chapman & Hall/CRC. doi:10.1201/9781420089776

Mohanapriya, M. (2016). IoT Enabled Futures Smart Campus with effective e-Learning. *i-Campus, 3*(4), 81– 87.

Monger, M. D., Mata-Toledo, R. A., & Gupta, P. (2012). Temporal Data Management in NoSQL Databases. *Journal of Information Systems & Operations Management, 6*(2), 237–243.

Monger, M. D., Mata-Toledo, R. A., & Gupta, P. (2012). Temporal Data Management in NoSQL Databases. *Romanian Economic Business Review, 6*(2), 237–243.

MongoD. B. (n.d.). Retrieved from https://www.mongodb.com/

MongoDB Inc. (2018). *MongoDB*. Retrieved November 10, 2018, from https://www.mongodb.org/

Moniruzzaman, A. B. M., & Hossain, S. A. (2013). NoSQL Database: New Era of Databases for Big data Analytics - Classification, Characteristics and Comparison. *International Journal of Database Theory and Application, 6*(4), 1–14.

Müller, M. (2007). *Information retrieval for music and motion* (Vol. 2). Heidelberg, Germany: Springer. doi:10.1007/978-3-540-74048-3

Murugesan, S. (2008). Harnessing Green IT: Principles and Practices. *IT Professional, 10*(1), 24–33. doi:10.1109/MITP.2008.10

MySQL 8.0 Reference Manual - The JSON Data Type. (2018). Retrieved from https://dev.mysql.com/doc/refman/8.0/en/json.html

MySQL 8.0 Reference Manual-JSON Functions. (2018). Retrieved from https://dev.mysql.com/doc/refman/8.0/en/json-functions.html

Nasser, T. & Tariq, R.S. (2015). Big Data Challenges. Journal of Computer Engineering & In-formation Technology. *SciTechnol, 4*(3).

Nedov, L. (2016). *JSON in Oracle Database 12c*. Retrieved from http://www.redstk.com/json-in-oracle-database-12c

Nejati, S., Sabetzadeh, M., Chechik, M., Easterbrook, S., & Zave, P. (2012). Matching and merging of variant feature specifications. *IEEE Transactions on Software Engineering, 38*(6), 1355–1375. doi:10.1109/TSE.2011.112

Neo Technology, Inc. (2018). *Neo4j*. Retrieved November 10, 2018, from http://www.neo4j.org/

Netmesh Inc. (2018). *InfoGrid – the Web Graph Database*. Retrieved November 10, 2018, from http://infogrid.org/trac/

Neuhaus, C., Polze, A., & Chowdhuryy, M. M. (2011). *Survey on healthcare IT systems: standards, regulations and security. No. 45*. Universitätsverlag Potsdam.

Neumann, T., & Weikum, G. (2008). RDF-3X: A RISC-style engine for RDF. *Proceedings of the VLDB Endowment International Conference on Very Large Data Bases, 1*(1), 647–659. doi:10.14778/1453856.1453927

Neumann, T., & Weikum, G. (2010). The RDF-3X engine for scalable management of RDF data. *The VLDB Journal*, *19*(1), 91–113. doi:10.100700778-009-0165-y

NGDATA. (2018). *Lily*. Retrieved November 10, 2018, from https://www.ngdata.com/platform/

Nicoara, D., Kamali, S., Daudjee, K., & Chen, L. (2015). Hermes: Dynamic partitioning for distributed social network graph databases. *Proceedings of the 18th International Conference on Extending Database Technology*, 25-36.

Niedermayer, J., Züfle, A., Emrich, T., Renz, M., Mamoulis, N., Chen, L., & Kriegel, H. P. (2013). Probabilistic nearest neighbor queries on uncertain moving object trajectories. *Proceedings of the VLDB Endowment International Conference on Very Large Data Bases*, *7*(3), 205–216. doi:10.14778/2732232.2732239

Niedermayer, J., Züfle, A., Emrich, T., Renz, M., Mamoulis, N., Chen, L., & Kriegel, H. P. (2013). Similarity search on uncertain spatiotemporal data. In *Proceedings of International Conference on Similarity Search and Applications* (pp. 43-49). Berlin, Germany: Springer. 10.1007/978-3-642-41062-8_5

Nikolov, A., Uren, V., & Motta, E. (2009). Towards data fusion in a multi-ontology environment. In *Proceedings of the www Workshop on Linked Data on the Web*.

Nishimura, S., Das, S., Agrawal, D., & Abbadi, A. E. (2011). MD-HBase: A scalable multidimensional data infrastructure for location aware services. In *Proceedings of the 2011 IEEE 12th Int. Conf. on Mobile Data Management*. IEEE Computer Society. 10.1109/MDM.2011.41

Ni, W., Gu, M., & Chen, X. (2016). Location privacy-preserving k nearest neighbor query under user's preference. *Knowledge-Based Systems*, *103*, 19–27. doi:10.1016/j.knosys.2016.03.016

NMC. (2015). New Media Consortium, Horizon Report: 2015. *Higher Education Edition*, 1–50.

Noh, S.-Y., & Gadia, S. K. (2006). A comparison of two approaches to utilizing XML in parametric databases for temporal data. *Information and Software Technology*, *48*(9), 807–819. doi:10.1016/j.infsof.2005.10.002

NuoDB Inc. (2018). *NuoDB*. Retrieved November 10, 2018, from http://www.nuodb.com/

Nurzhan, N., Michael, P., Randall, R., & Clemente, I. (2009). *Comparison of JSON and XML Data Interchange Formats: A Case Study*. Paper presented at CAINE 2009 conference.

O'Neil, P. E., Cheng, E., Gawlick, D., & O'Neil, E. J. (1996). The Log-Structured Merge-Tree (LSM-Tree). *Acta Informatica*, *33*(4), 351–385. doi:10.1007002360050048

OASIS XACML Technical Committee. (2013). *eXtensible access control markup langage (XACML) Version 3.0. Oasis Standard, OASIS*. Retrieved from http://docs.oasis-open.org/xacml/3.0/xacml-3.0-core-spec-os-en.html

Obrsta, L., McCandlessb, D., & Ferrella, D. (2012). Fast semantic Attribute-Role-Based Access Control (ARBAC) in a collaborative environment. *8th International Conference on Collaborative Computing: Networking, Applications and Worksharing*.

ODMS.org. (2013). *Big Data Analytics at Thomson Reuters. Interview with Jochen L. Leidner*. Retrieved November 10, 2018, http://www.odbms.org/blog/2013/11/big-data-analytics-at-thomson-reuters-interview-with-jochen-l-leidner/

OGC 07-011. (2015). *Abstract Specification Topic 6: Schema for coverage geometry and functions, version 7.0*. Retrieved from: http://portal.opengeospatial.org/files/?artifact_id=19820

Ogden, P., Thomas, D. B., & Pietzuch, P. R. (2013). Scalable XML query processing using parallel pushdown transducers. *Proceedings of the VLDB Endowment International Conference on Very Large Data Bases*, *6*(14), 1738–1749. doi:10.14778/2556549.2556558

Okabe, A., Boots, B., Sugihara, K., & Chiu, S. N. (2000). *Spatial tessellations, concepts and applications of Voronoi diagrams* (2nd ed.). John Wiley and Sons Ltd. doi:10.1002/9780470317013

Okcan, A., & Riedewald, M. (2011). Processing theta-joins using MapReduce. In *Proceedings of the ACM SIGMOD International Conference on Management of Data* (pp. 949-960). Athens, Greece: ACM.

Oracle. (2016). *Unified Query for Big Data Management Systems Integrating Big Data Systems with Enterprise Data Warehouses*. Oracle White Paper.

Oracle. (2017). *Big Data Appliance*. Retrieved November 10, 2018, from https://www.oracle.com/technetwork/database/bigdata-appliance/overview/bigdataappliance-datasheet-1883358.pdf

Oracle. (2018). *Oracle NoSQL Database*. Retrieved November 10, 2018, from http://www.oracle.com/technetwork/database/database-technologies/nosqldb/overview/index.html

Orient Technologies, Ltd. (2018). *OrientDB*. Retrieved November 10, 2018, from http://www.orientechnologies.com/orientdb/

Orrù, M. (2017). Demonstration of OpenGeoBase: The ICN NoSQL spatio-temporal database. *Proceedings of the 2017 IEEE International Symposium on Local and Metropolitan Area Networks*, 1-2. 10.1109/LANMAN.2017.7972184

Palanivel, K., & Chithralekha, T. (2017). Big Data Reference Architecture for e-learning Analytical Systems. *International Journal on Recent and Innovation Trends in Computing and Communication*, 6(1), 55–61.

Palanivel, K., & Kuppuswami, S. (2014). Towards Service-Oriented Reference Model and Architecture to e-Learning Systems. *International Journal of Emerging Trends & Technology in Computer Science*, 3(4), 146–155.

Pal, S., Cseri, I., Schaller, G., Seeliger, O., Giakoumakis, L., & Zolotov, V. V. (2004). Indexing XML Data Stored in a Relational Database. *VLDB*, *2004*, 1134–1145.

Papailiou, N., Konstantinou, I., Tsoumakos, D., Karras, P., & Koziris, N. (2013). H2RDF+: High-performance distributed joins over large-scale RDF graphs. *Proceedings of the 2013 IEEE International Conference on Big Data*, 255-263. 10.1109/BigData.2013.6691582

Papailiou, N., Konstantinou, I., Tsoumakos, D., & Koziris, N. (2012). H2RDF: Adaptive query processing on RDF data in the cloud. *Proceedings of the 21st World Wide Web Conference*, 397-400. 10.1145/2187980.2188058

Pasquale, L., & Raphaël, T. (2018, April). *Transforming the JSON Output of SPARQL Queries for Linked Data Clients*. Paper presented at 2018 IW3C2 (International World Wide Web Conference Committee) conference.

Pavlo, A., & Aslett, M. (2016). What's Really New with NewSQL? *SIGMOD Record*, 45(2), 45–55. doi:10.1145/3003665.3003674

Pavlo, A., Paulson, E., Rasin, A., Abadi, D., DeWitt, D. J., Madden, S., & Stonebraker, M. (2009). A Comparison of Approaches to Large-Scale Data Analysis. *Proceedings of SIGMOD/PODS'09*. 10.1145/1559845.1559865

Peixoto, D. A., Zhou, X., Hung, N. Q. V., He, D., & Stantic, B. (2018). A System for Spatial-Temporal Trajectory Data Integration and Representation. *International Conference on Database Systems for Advanced Applications*, 807-812. 10.1007/978-3-319-91458-9_53

Peng, Y., Cui, J., Li, H., & Ma, J. (2017). A reusable and single-interactive model for secure approximate k-nearest neighbor query in cloud. *Information Sciences*, *387*, 146–164. doi:10.1016/j.ins.2016.07.069

Petkovi'c, D. (2017a). JSON Integration in Relational Database Systems. *International Journal of Computers and Applications*, *168*(5), 14–19.

Petkovi'c, D. (2017b). SQL/JSON Standard: Properties and Deficiencies. *Datenbank-Spektrum Springer, 17*(3), 277–287. doi:10.100713222-017-0267-4

Petkovic, D. (2016). Temporal Data in Relational Database Systems: A Comparison. *Proceedings of the 4th World Conference on Information Systems and Technologies (WorldCIST'2016)*, 13-23. 10.1007/978-3-319-31232-3_2

Pezoa, F., Reutter, J. L., Suarez, F., Ugarte, M., & Vrgoc, D. (2016). Foundations of JSON Schema. In *Proceedings of the 25th international conference on World Wide Web* (pp. 263–273). Academic Press. 10.1145/2872427.2883029

Pfoser, D., Tryfona, N., & Jensen, C. S. (2005). Indeterminacy and Spatiotemporal Data: Basic definitions and case study. *GeoInformatica, 9*(3), 211–236. doi:10.100710707-005-1282-4

Phankokkruad, M. (2012). Implement of cloud computing for e-learning system. *International Conference on Computer & Information Science (ICCIS)*. 10.1109/ICCISci.2012.6297204

Pierre, B., Juan, L., Fernando, S., & Domagoj, V. (2016). *Foundations of JSON Schema.* Paper presented at 2016 IW3C2 Conference, April 11–15, 2016, Montréal, Québec, Canada.

Pierre, B., Juan, L., Fernando, S., & Domagoj, V. (2017). *JSON: Data model, Query languages and Schema specification.* Paper presented at 2017 ACM conference, PODS'17, Chicago, IL.

Pivert, O., Slama, O., & Thion, V. (2016). An extension of SPARQL with fuzzy navigational capabilities for querying fuzzy RDF data. In *IEEE International Conference on Fuzzy Systems*, Vancouver, Canada (pp. 2409-2416). 10.1109/FUZZ-IEEE.2016.7737995

Poçatilu, P. (2010). Cloud Computing Benefits for e-Learning Solutions. *Economics of Knowledge, 2*(1), 9–14.

Pocatilu, P., Alecu, F., & Vetrici, M. (2009). Using cloud computing for e-Learning systems. *Proc. of the 8th WSEAS International Conference on Data networks, communications, computers*, 54-59.

Pokorný, J. (2018) Integration of Relational and NoSQL Databases. Intelligent Information and Database Systems, ACIIDS 2018, Part II, LNCS 10752, 35-45. doi:10.1007/978-3-319-75420-8_4

Pokorný, J., & Stantic, B. (2016). Challenges and Opportunities in Big Data Processing. In Managing Big Data in Cloud Computing Environments. IGI Global.

Pokorny, J. (2011). NoSQL databases: A step to database scalability in web environment. *Proceedings of the 2011 International Conference on Information Integration and Web-based Applications and Services*, 278-283. 10.1145/2095536.2095583

Pokorný, J. (2013). NoSQL databases: A step to database scalability in web environment. *International Journal of Web Information Systems, 9*(1), 69–82. doi:10.1108/17440081311316398

Pokorný, J. (2015). Graph Databases: Their Power and Limitations. *Proc. of 14th Int. Conf. on Computer Information Systems and Industrial Management Applications (CISIM 2015)*, 58-69. 10.1007/978-3-319-24369-6_5

Pokorný, J. (2017). Big Data Storage and Management: Challenges and Opportunities. In J. Hřebíček, R. Denzer, G. Schimak, & T. Pitner (Eds.), *Environmental Software Systems. Computer Science for Environmental Protection. IS-ESS 2017. IFIP Advances in Information and Communication Technology* (Vol. 507, pp. 28–38). Cham: Springer. doi:10.1007/978-3-319-89935-0_3

Portele, C. (2007). *OpenGIS Geography Markup Language (GML) Encoding Standard. Ver 3.2.1, (OGC 07-036).* Retrieved from: http://portal.opengeospatial.org/files/?artifact_id=20509

Post, A. R., & Jr, H. J. (2008). Temporal data mining. *Clinics in Laboratory Medicine, 28*(1), 83–100. doi:10.1016/j.cll.2007.10.005 PMID:18194720

Postgre, S. Q. L. 9.4.18 Documentation: Data Types. (n.d.a). Retrieved from https://www.postgresql.org/docs/9.4/static/datatype-json.html

Postgre, S. Q. L. 9.4.18 Documentation: Functions and Operators. (n.d.b). Retrieved from https://www.postgresql.org/docs/9.4/static/functions-json.html

Pritchett, D. (2008). BASE: An ACID alternative. *ACM Queue; Tomorrow's Computing Today*, 6(3), 48–55. doi:10.1145/1394127.1394128

Prud'hommeaux, E., & Seaborne, A. (2008). *SPARQL Query Language for RDF*. W3C Recommendation. Retrieved from http://www.w3.org/TR/2008/REC-rdf-sparql-query-20080115/

Pugliese, A., Udrea, O., & Subrahmanian, V. S. (2008). Scaling RDF with time. *Proceedings of the 2008 International Conference on World Wide Web*, 605-614.

Qian, Z., Xu, J., Zheng, K., Zhao, P., & Zhou, X. (2017). Semantic-aware top-k spatial keyword queries. *World Wide Web*, 21(3), 573–594.

QueryingJ. S. O. N. in Postgres. (n.d.). Retrieved from https://link.springer.com/article/10.1007%2Fs13222-017-0267-4

Rabiner, L. R. (1989). A tutorial on hidden Markov models and selected applications in speech recognition. *Proceedings of the IEEE*, 77(2), 257–286. doi:10.1109/5.18626

Rabiner, L. R., Juang, B. H., & Rutledge, J. C. (1993). *Fundamentals of speech recognition* (Vol. 14). Englewood Cliffs, NJ: PTR Prentice Hall.

Raimond, Y., Sutton, C., & Sandler, M. B. (2008). Automatic interlinking of music datasets on the semantic web. In *Proceedings of the WWW2008 Workshop on Linked Data on the Web (LDOW 2008)* (pp. 137-145).

Rajaman, A., & Ullman, J. D. (2011). *Mining of Massive Datasets*. Cambridge University Press. doi:10.1017/CBO9781139058452

Ramanathan, A., & Chen, M. (2017). Spatiotemporal vehicle tracking, counting and classification. In *Proceedings of 2017 IEEE Third International Conference on Multimedia Big Data*, Laguna Hills, CA (pp. 246-247). Piscataway, NJ: IEEE. 10.1109/BigMM.2017.85

Ranacher, P., & Tzavella, K. (2014). How to compare movement? A review of physical movement similarity measures in geographic information science and beyond. *Cartography and Geographic Information Science*, 41(3), 286–307. doi:10.1080/15230406.2014.890071 PMID:27019646

Ratnasamy, S., Francis, P., Handley, M., Karp, R. M., & Shenker, S. (2001). A scalable content addressable network. In *Proceedings of SIGCOMM*. ACM.

Rawson, A., Pfleuger, J. & Cader, T. (2008). Green Grid Data Center Power Efficiency Metrics. Consortium green grid. *International Journal on Recent and Innovation Trends in Computing and Communication*.

Ray, P. P. (2018). A survey on Internet of Things architectures. *Journal of King Saud University - Computer and Information Sciences*, 30(3), 291-319.

RDF 1.1 Concepts and Abstract Syntax, W3C Recommendation. (2014). Retrieved from https://www.w3.org/TR/2014/REC-rdf11-concepts-20140225/

RDF Schema 1.1. (n.d.). Retrieved from https://www.w3.org/TR/rdf-schema/#ch_collectionvocab

Ré, C., Letchner, J., Balazinksa, M., & Suciu, D. (2008). Event queries on correlated probabilistic streams. In *Proceedings of the 2008 ACM SIGMOD international conference on Management of data,* Vancouver, Canada (pp. 715-728). 10.1145/1376616.1376688

Redis. (2018). Retrieved November 10, 2018, from http://redis.io/

Rehman, A. U., Abbasi, A. Z., & Shaikh, Z. A. (2008). Building a Smart University using RFID technology. *International Conference on Computer Science and Software Engineering.*

Resource Description Framework. (n.d.). Retrieved from https://www.w3.org/RDF/

reTHINK CSP Policy Engine. (2016). Retrieved from github.com/reTHINK-project/dev-msg-node- nodejs/tree/master/src/main/components/policyEngine

reTHINK Deliverable 6.4. (2016). *Assessment Report.* reTHINK H2020 Project.

reTHINK Project Testbed. (2016). *Deliverable D6.1: Testbed Specification.* Retrieved from https://bscw.rethink-project.eu/pub/bscw.cgi/d35657/D6.1%20Testbed%20specification.pdf

reTHINK Project. (2016). Retrieved from github.com/reTHINK-project/

Rizzolo, F., & Vaisman, A. A. (2008). Temporal XML: Modeling, Indexing, and Query Processing. *The VLDB Journal, 17*(5), 1179–1212. doi:10.100700778-007-0058-x

Robin, A. (2011). *OGC 08-094, OGC® SWE Common Data Model Encoding Standard, version 2.0.* Retrieved from: http://portal.opengeospatial.org/files/?artifact_id=41157

Rocha-Junior, J., Gkorgkas, O., Jonassen, S., & Nørvåg, K. (2011). Efficient processing of top-k spatial keyword queries. In *Proceedings of the International Symposium on Spatial and Temporal Databases* (pp. 93-104). 10.1007/978-3-642-22922-0_13

Roddick, J. F. (2018). Schema Versioning. In L. Liu & M. T. Özsu (Eds.), *Encyclopedia of Database Systems* (2nd ed.). New York: Springer-Verlag. doi:10.1007/978-1-4614-8265-9_323

Rosenfeld, A. (1975). In L. A. Zadeh, K. S. Fu, K. Tanaka, & M. Shimura (Eds.), *Fuzzy Graphs, Fuzzy Sets and Their Applications to Cognitive and Decision Processes* (pp. 77–95). New York: Academic Press. doi:10.1016/B978-0-12-775260-0.50008-6

Roy, S., & Chakrabarti, K. (2010). Location-aware type ahead search on spatial databases: semantics and efficiency. In *Proceedings* of the *ACM SIGMOD International Conference on Management* of *Data (SIGMOD'10)* (pp. 361-372). New York: ACM.

Rubiera, E., Polo, L., Berrueta, D., & Ghali, A. E. (2012). TELIX: An RDF-Based Model for Linguistic Annotation. *Proceedings of the 9th Extended Semantic Web Conference,* 195-209. 10.1007/978-3-642-30284-8_20

Sadalage, P. J., & Fowler, M. (2013). *NoSQL Distilled: A Brief Guide to the Emerging World of Polyglot Persistence.* Pearson Education, Inc.

Sakoe, H., & Chiba, S. (1973, December). Comparative study of DP-pattern matching techniques for speech recognition. *Tech. Group Meeting Speech, Acoust. Soc.*

Sakoe, H., & Chiba, S. (1978). Dynamic programming algorithm optimization for spoken word recognition. *IEEE Transactions on Acoustics, Speech, and Signal Processing, 26*(1), 43–49. doi:10.1109/TASSP.1978.1163055

Sakr, S., & Al-Naymat, G. (2009). Relational processing of RDF queries: A survey. *SIGMOD Record*, *38*(4), 23–28. doi:10.1145/1815948.1815953

Salvador, S., & Chan, P. (2007). Toward accurate dynamic time warping in linear time and space. *Intelligent Data Analysis*, *11*(5), 561–580. doi:10.3233/IDA-2007-11508

Sambhoos, K., Nagi, R., Sudit, M., & Stotz, A. (2010). Enhancements to high level data fusion using graph matching and state space search. *Information Fusion*, *11*(4), 351–364. doi:10.1016/j.inffus.2009.12.001

SAS Institute, Inc. (2018). *Big Data. What it is and why it matters*. Retrieved November 10, 2018, from https://www.sas.com/en_us/insights/big-data/what-is-big-data.html

Sato, S., Hao, W., & Matsuzaki, K. (2018). Parallelization of XPath queries using modern XQuery processors. In *Proceedings of the New Trends in Databases and Information Systems - ADBIS Short Papers and Workshops*, (pp. 54-62). Budapest, Hungary: Springer. 10.1007/978-3-030-00063-9_7

Saurabh, K. G., & Rajkumar, B. (2011). *Green Cloud computing and Environmental Sustainability, Cloud computing and Distributed Systems (CLOUDS)*. Laboratory Dept. of Computer Science and Software Engineering, The University of Melbourne.

ScaleArc. (2018). *ScaleArc*. Retrieved November 10, 2018, from http://scalearc.com/

Schonberger, V. S., & Cukier, K. (2013). *Big Data: A revolution that will transform how we live, work, and think*. Boston: Houghton Mifflin Harcourt.

Scriney, M., & Roantree, M. (2016). Efficient cube construction for smart city data. *Proceedings of the Workshops of the EDBT/ICDT 2016 Joint Conference*.

Selinger, M., Sepulveda, A., & Buchan, J. (2013). *Education and the internet of Everything*. Cisco Consulting Services and Cisco EMEAR Education Team.

Semantic Web. (n.d.). Retrieved from https://en.wikipedia.org/wiki/Semantic_Web

Senk, A., Valenta, M., & Benn, W. (2014). Distributed evaluation of XPath axes queries over large XML documents stored in MapReduce clusters. In *Proceedings of the 25th International Workshop on Database and Expert Systems Applications*, (pp. 253-257). Munich, Germany: IEEE.

Serra, J., & Arcos, J. L. (2014). An empirical evaluation of similarity measures for time series classification. *Knowledge-Based Systems*, *67*, 305–314. doi:10.1016/j.knosys.2014.04.035

Shalabh, A., & Asoke, N. (2011). Green Computing - a new Horizon of Energy Efficiency and Electronic waste minimization: a Global Perspective. *International Conference on Communication Systems and Network Technologies*, 688-693.

Sheth, A., Henson, C., & Sahoo, S. S. (2008). Semantic sensor web. *IEEE Internet Computing*, *12*(4), 78–83. doi:10.1109/MIC.2008.87

Shi, J. M., Wu, D. M., & Mamoulis, N. (2016). Top-k Relevant Semantic Place Retrieval on Spatial RDF Data. *Proceedings of the 2016 International Conference on Management of Data*, 1977-1990. 10.1145/2882903.2882941

Shukla, D., Thota, S., Raman, K., Gajendran, M., Shah, A., Ziuzin, S., ... Lomet, D. B. (2015). Schema-Agnostic Indexing with Azure DocumentDB. *PVLDB*, *8*(12), 1668–1679.

Shute, J., Vingralek, R., Samwel, B., Handy, B., Whipkey, Ch., Rollins, E.,... Apte, H. (2013). F1 A Distributed SQL Database That Scales. *PVLDB*, *6*(11), 1068-1079.

Shvachko, K., Kuang, H., Radia, S., & Chansler, R. (2010). The Hadoop Distributed File System, In *Proceedings of 2010 IEEE 26th Symposium on Mass Storage Systems and Technologies (MSST)*, Lake Tahoe, NV: IEEE. 10.1109/MSST.2010.5496972

Sindhu, S. (2014). Green Cloud Computing. *International Journal of Information and Computation Technology, 4*(4), 431–436.

Sintek, M., & Kiesel, M. (2006). RDFBroker: A signature-based high-performance RDF store. *Proceedings of the 3rd European Semantic Web Conference*, 363-377.

Slavov, V., Katib, A., & Rao, P. R. (2014). A tool for internet-scale cardinality estimation of XPath queries over distributed semistructured data. In *Proceedings of the IEEE 30th International Conference on Data Engineering*, (pp. 1270-1273). IEEE Computer Society. 10.1109/ICDE.2014.6816758

Slavov, V., & Rao, P. R. (2014). A gossip-based approach for internet-scale cardinality estimation of XPath queries over distributed semistructured data. *The VLDB Journal, 23*(1), 51–76. doi:10.100700778-013-0314-1

Smart. (2014). *New York Smart Schools Commission Report*. Retrieved from http://www.governor.ny.gov/ sites/ governor. ny.gov/ files/ archive/governor_files/SmartSchoolsReport.pdf

Smeros, P., & Koubarakis, M. (2016). Discovering Spatial and Temporal Links among RDF Data, *Proceedings of the 2016 Workshop on Linked Data on the Web*.

Smith, J., & Nair, R. (2003). *Virtual machines: Versatile Platforms for Systems and Processes*. Los Altos, CA: Morgan Kaufmann.

Snodgrass, R. T. (Ed.). (1995). The TSQL2 Temporal Query Language. Norwell, MA: Kluwer Academic Publishers.

Snodgrass, R. T., Dyreson, C. E., Currim, F., Currim, S., & Joshi, S. (2008). Validating Quicksand: Schema Versioning in τXSchema. *Data & Knowledge Engineering, 65*(2), 223–242. doi:10.1016/j.datak.2007.09.003

Snow, D. (2012). *Dwaine Snow's Thoughts on Databases and Data Management*. Retrieved from http://dsnowondb2. blogspot.cz/2012/07/adding-4th-v-to-big-data-veracity.html

Snow, D. (2012). *Dwaine Snow's Thoughts on Databases and Data Management*. Retrieved November 10, 2018, from http://dsnowondb2.blogspot.cz/2012/07/adding-4th-v-to-big-data-veracity.html

Soewito, B., Isa, S. M., Iskandar, K., Gaol, F. L., & Kosala, R. (2017, February). Server for SQLite database: Multithreaded HTTP server with synchronized database access and JSON data-interchange. In *Proceedings of the 19th International Conference on Advanced Communication Technology* (pp. 786-790). IEEE.

solid IT. (2018). *DB-engines*. Retrieved November 10, 2018, from http://db-engines.com/en/ranking

Solow, A. R. (1994). Time series prediction: Forecasting the future and understanding the past. *Science, 265*(5179), 1745–1747. doi:10.1126cience.265.5179.1745 PMID:17770902

Song, G., Rochas, J., Huet, F., & Magoules, F. (2015). Solutions for Processing K Nearest Neighbor Joins for Massive Data on MapReduce. In *Proceedings of the 23rd Euromicro International Conference on Parallel, Distributed, and Network-Based Processing* (pp. 279-287). Turku, Finland: IEEE Computer Society. 10.1109/PDP.2015.79

Song, K., & Lu, H. (2016). Efficient querying distributed big-XML data using MapReduce. *International Journal of Grid and High Performance Computing, 8*(3), 70–79. doi:10.4018/IJGHPC.2016070105

Song, K., & Lu, H. (2016). High-performance XML modeling of parallel queries based on MapReduce framework. *Cluster Computing, 19*(4), 1975–1986. doi:10.100710586-016-0628-z

Song, K., Lu, H., & Qin, X. (2016). An efficient parallel approach of parsing and indexing for large-scale XML datasets. In *Proceedings of the International Conference on IT Convergence and Security*, (pp. 1-2). Prague, Czech Republic: IEEE Computer Society. 10.1109/ICPADS.2016.0033

Spector, J. M. (2014). Conceptualizing the Emerging Field of Smart Learning Environments. *Smart Learning Environments*, *1*(1), 1–10. doi:10.118640561-014-0002-7

Sperka, S., & Smrz, P. (2012). Towards adaptive and semantic database model for RDF data stores. *Proceedings of the Sixth International Conference on Complex, Intelligent, and Software Intensive Systems*, 810-815.

Sporny, M., Kellogg, G., & Lanthaler, M. (2014). *W3C JSON-LD 1.0, A JSON-based Serialization for Linked Data.* Retrieved from: http://www.w3.org/TR/json-ld/

Srikantaiah, S., Kansal, A., & Zhao, F. (2009). Energy-aware Consolidation for Cloud Computing. *Cluster Computing*, *12*, 1–15.

Stamatios, T., & George, T. (2016). *RDF serialization from JSON Data: The case of JSON data in Diavgeia.gov.gr.* Paper presented at IISA 2016 conference.

Stantic, B., & Pokorný, J. (2014). Opportunities in Big Data Management and Processing. *Frontiers in Artificial Intelligence and Applications*, *270*, 15–26.

Steven, D., Bernard, B. & Leigh, G. (2013). *JSON-encoded ABAC (XACML) policies. FAME project of Waterford Institute of Technology.* Presentation to OASIS XACML TC concerning JSON-encoded XACML policies.

Stonebraker, M. (2013). *No Hadoop: The Future of the Hadoop/HDFS Stack.* Retrieved November 10, 2018, from http://istc-bigdata.org/index.php/no-hadoop-the-future-of-the-hadoophdfs-stack/

Stonebraker, M. (1986). Object Management in a Relational Data Base System. *COMPCON*, *1986*, 336–341.

Stonebraker, M., Wong, E., Kreps, P., & Held, G. (1976). The Design and Implementation of INGRES. *ACM Transactions on Database Systems*, *1*(3), 189–222. doi:10.1145/320473.320476

Straccia, U. (2009, October). A minimal deductive system for general fuzzy RDF. In *International Conference on Web Reasoning and Rule Systems* (pp. 166-181). Springer. 10.1007/978-3-642-05082-4_12

Stuart, J., & Barker, A. (2013). *Undefined By Data: A Survey of Big Data Definitions.* CoRR, abs/1309.5821

Sun, C. N., Zheng, C., & Xia, Q. S. (2013). Chinese text similarity computing based on LDA. *Computer Technology and Development*, *23*(1), 217–220.

Sun, J. L., & Jin, Q. (2010). Scalable RDF store based on HBase and MapReduce. *Proceedings of the 3rd International Conference Advanced Computer Theory and Engineering*, V1-633-V1-636.

Tahara, D., Diamond, T., & Abadi, D. J. (2014). a SQL system for multi-structured data. *SIGMOD Conference 2014*, 815-826

Tansel, A. U., Clifford, J., Gadia, S. K., Jajodia, S., Segev, A., & Snodgrass, R. T. (Eds.). (1993). *Temporal Databases: Theory, Design and Implementation.* Redwood City, CA: Benjamin/Cummings Publishing Company.

Tao, Y., Papadias, D., & Sun, J. (2003). The tpr*-tree: An optimized spatiotemporal access method for predictive queries. In *Proceedings of the 29th International Conference on Very Large Data Bases,* Berlin, Germany (pp. 790-801). .

Tauro, C., Aravindh, S., & Shreeharsha, A. B. (2012). Comparative Study of the New Generation, Agile, Scalable, High Performance NOSQL Databases. *International Journal of Computer Applications*, *48*(20).

Tear, A. (2014). SQL or NoSQL? Contrasting Approaches to the Storage, Manipulation and Analysis of Spatio-temporal Online Social Network Data. *Proceedings of the 14th International Conference on Computational Science and Its Applications*, 221-236.

The Apache Software Foundation. (2016). *Cassandra*. Retrieved November 10, 2018, from http://cassandra.apache.org/

The Apache Software Foundation. (2017). *Apache Solr™ 4.10*. Retrieved November 10, 2018, from http://lucene.apache.org/solr/

The Apache Software Foundation. (2018a). *Hadoop*. Retrieved November 10, 2018, from http://hadoop.apache.org/

The Apache Software Foundation. (2018b). *Apache HBase*. Retrieved November 10, 2018, from https://hbase.apache.org/

The Apache Software Foundation. (2018c). *Apache CouchDB™*. Retrieved November 10, 2018, from http://couchdb.apache.org/

The Apache Software Foundation. (2018d). *Mahout*. Retrieved November 10, 2018, from http://mahout.apache.org/

Thorsten, L. (2018). *Neo4j: A Reasonable RDF Graph Database and Reasoning Engine*. Retrieved from https://dzone.com/articles/neo4j-a-reasonable-rdf-graph-database-amp-reasonin

Thusoo, A., Sarma, J. S., Jain, N., Shao, Z., Chakka, P., Anthony, S., ... Murthy, R. (2009). Hive - a warehousing solution over a map-reduce framework. *PVLDB*, *2*(2), 1626–1629.

Tikhomirov, V., Dneprovskaya, N., & Yankovskaya, E. (2015). *Three Dimensions of Smart Education*. Academic Press.

Tiwari, S. (2011). *Professional NoSQL*. Indianapolis, IN: John Wiley & Sons, Inc.

Tossebro, E., & Nygård, M. (2002). Uncertainty in spatiotemporal databases. In *Proceedings of International Conference on Advances in Information Systems* (pp. 43-53). Berlin, Germany: Springer. 10.1007/3-540-36077-8_5

Trajcevski, G., Choudhary, A. N., Wolfson, O., Ye, L., & Li, G. (2010). Uncertain range queries for necklaces. In *Proceedings of 2010 Eleventh International Conference on Mobile Data Management*, Kansas City, MO (pp. 199-208). Piscataway, NJ: IEEE. 10.1109/MDM.2010.76

Trajcevski, G., Tamassia, R., Ding, H., Scheuermann, P., & Cruz, I. F. (2009). Continuous probabilistic nearest-neighbor queries for uncertain trajectories. In *Proceedings of the 12th International Conference on Extending Database Technology: Advances in Database Technology,* Saint Petersburg, Russian Federation (pp. 874-885). 10.1145/1516360.1516460

Udrea, O., Recupero, D. R., & Subrahmanian, V. S. (2010). Annotated RDF. *ACM Transactions on Computational Logic*, *11*(2), 10:1-10:41.

Ullmann, J. R. (1976). An algorithm for subgraph isomorphism. *Journal of the Association for Computing Machinery*, *23*(1), 31–42. doi:10.1145/321921.321925

Uskov, V., Howlett, R., & Jain, L. (2015). *Smart Education and Smart e-Learning. In Smart Innovation, Systems and Technologies, 41*. Cham: Springer. doi:10.1007/978-3-319-19875-0

Uszok, A., Bradshaw, J. M., & Jeffers, R. (2004). Kaos: A policy and domain services framework for grid computing and semantic web services. In *International Conference on Trust Management*. Springer. 10.1007/978-3-540-24747-0_2

Vattani, A. (2011). K-means requires exponentially many iterations even in the plane. *Discrete & Computational Geometry*, *45*(4), 596–616. doi:10.100700454-011-9340-1

Vecchiola, C., Chu, X., & Buyya, R. (2009). Aneka: A Software Platform for. NET-based Cloud Computing. In High Performance & Large Scale Computing, Advances in Parallel Computing. IOS Press.

Vernica, R., Carey, M. J., & Li, C. (2010). Efficient parallel set-similarity joins using mapreduce. In *Proceedings of the ACM SIGMOD International Conference on Management of Data* (pp. 495-506). Indianapolis, IN: ACM.

Vharkute, M., & Wagh, S. (2015). An architectural approach of the internet of things in E-Learning. In *International Conference on Communications and Signal Processing (ICCSP)*. IEEE. 10.1109/ICCSP.2015.7322827

Vinay, P. V., Chintan, M. B., & Hardik, S. J. (2014). Green Cloud: Implementation and Adoption of Green Data Center. *International Conference on Emerging Research in Computing, Information, Communication and Applications*, 163-167.

VoltDB Inc. (2018). *VoltDB*. Retrieved November 10, 2018, from http://voltdb.com/

W3C (World Wide Web). (2004). *XML Schema Part 0: Primer Second Edition*. W3C Recommendation. Retrieved January 31, 2019, from http://www.w3.org/TR/2004/REC-xmlschema-0-20041028/

W3schools. (n.d.). *JSON vs XML*. Retrieved from www.w3schools.com/js/js_json_xml.asp

Wang, J., Jin, B., & Li, J. (2004). An ontology-based publish/subscribe system. In *Proceedings of the 5th ACM/IFIP/USENIX international conference on Middleware* (pp. 232-253). Springer.

Wang, X., Zhang, X., Zhang, W., Lin, X., & Huang, Z. (2016). Skype: top-k spatial-keyword publish/subscribe over sliding window. In *Proceedings of the International Conference on Very Large Data Bases (VLDB'16)* (pp.588-599). 10.14778/2904483.2904490

Wang, D., Zhu, Y., & University, L. T. (2018). *Application of geojson in heterogeneous geographic information data integration. Geomatics & Spatial Information Technology.*

Wang, D., Zou, L., & Zhao, D. Y. (2014). gst-Store: An Engine for Large RDF Graph Integrating Spatiotemporal Information. *Proceedings of the 17th International Conference on Extending Database Technology*, 652-655.

Wang, F., & Zaniolo, C. (2004). XBiT: an XML-based bitemporal data model. In *Proceedings of the 2004 International Conference on Conceptual Modeling* (pp. 810-824). Berlin, Germany: Springer. 10.1007/978-3-540-30464-7_60

Wang, F., & Zaniolo, C. (2005). An XML-Based Approach to Publishing and Querying the History of Databases. *World Wide Web: Internet and Web Information Systems*, 8(3), 233–259. doi:10.100711280-005-1317-7

Wang, F., Zaniolo, C., & Zhou, X. (2008). ArchIS: An XML-based approach to transaction-time temporal database systems. *The VLDB Journal*, 17(6), 1445–1463. doi:10.100700778-007-0086-6

Wang, F., Zhou, X., & Zaniolo, C. (2004). Temporal information management using XML. In *Proceedings of the 2004 International Conference on Conceptual Modeling* (pp. 858-859). Berlin, Germany: Springer. 10.1007/978-3-540-30464-7_72

Wang, J., Wu, S., Gao, H., Li, J., & Ooi, B. C. (2010). Indexing multi-dimensional data in a cloud system. In *Proceedings of SIGMOD*. ACM. 10.1145/1807167.1807232

Wang, L., & Zhou, Z. (2017). Congestion prediction for urban areas by spatiotemporal data mining. In *Proceedings of 2017 International Conference on Cyber-Enabled Distributed Computing and Knowledge Discovery,* Nanjing, China (pp. 290-297). Piscataway, NJ: IEEE. 10.1109/CyberC.2017.61

Wang, X., Mueen, A., Ding, H., Trajcevski, G., Scheuermann, P., & Keogh, E. (2013). Experimental comparison of representation methods and distance measures for time series data. *Data Mining and Knowledge Discovery*, 26(2), 275–309. doi:10.100710618-012-0250-5

Wang, Y., Du, X. Y., Lu, J. H., & Wang, X. F. (2010). FlexTable: Using a dynamic relation model to store RDF data. *Proceedings of the 15th International Conference on Database Systems for Advanced Applications*, 580-594. 10.1007/978-3-642-12026-8_44

Wang, Z., Zhou, D., & Chen, S. (2017). An Analytical Database System for TrEE-structured Data. *PVLDB, 10*(12), 1897–1900.

Weather Underground. (2016). *Tracking Map and Storm Track Coordinates of Post-Tropical Cyclone Nicole*. Retrieved from https://www.wunderground.com/hurricane/atlantic/2016/Post-Tropical-Cyclone-Nicole?MR=1

Wei, H. C., & Elmasri, R. (2000). Schema versioning and database conversion techniques for bi-temporal databases. *Annals of Mathematics and Artificial Intelligence, 30*(1-4), 23–52. doi:10.1023/A:1016622202755

Weiss, C., Karras, P., & Bernstein, A. (2008). Hexastore: Sextuple indexing for semantic web data management. *Proceedings of the VLDB Endowment International Conference on Very Large Data Bases, 1*(1), 1008–1019. doi:10.14778/1453856.1453965

Weyrich, M., & Ebert, C. (2016). Reference Architectures for the Internet of Things. *IEEE Computers & Society*.

Why NoSQL Database. (n.d.). Retrieved from https://www.couchbase.com/resources/why-nosql

Wilkinson, K., Sayers, C., Kuno, H. A., & Reynolds, D. (2003). Efficient RDF storage and retrieval in Jena2. *Semantic Web and Databases Workshop*, 131-150.

Winkler, W. E. (1999). *The state of record linkage and current research problems*. Statistical Research Division, US Census Bureau.

Witayangkurn, A., Horanont, T., & Shibasaki, R. (2012). Performance comparisons of spatial data processing techniques for a large scale mobile phone dataset. In *Proceedings of the 3rd International Conference on Computing for Geospatial Research and Applications* (p. 25). ACM. 10.1145/2345316.2345346

Wright, A., & Luff, G. (2016). *JSON Schema Validation: A Vocabulary for Structural Validation of JSON* (Tech. Rep.). IETF Standard 2016. What Every Developer Should Know About CouchDB. Retrieved from https://www.dimagi.com/blog/what-every- developer-should-know-about-couchdb/

Wu, D., Yiu, M., Jensen, C., & Cong, G. (2011). Efficient continuously moving top-k spatial keyword query processing. In *Proceedings of the International Conference on Data Engineering (ICDE'11)* (pp. 541-552). 10.1109/ICDE.2011.5767861

Wu, H. (2014). Parallelizing structural joins to process queries over big XML data using MapReduce. In *Proceedings of the Database and Expert Systems Applications - 25th International Conference*, (pp. 183-190). Munich, Germany: Springer. 10.1007/978-3-319-10085-2_16

Wu, S. & Wu, K. (2009). An indexing framework for efficient retrieval on the cloud. *IEEE Data Engineering Bulletin, 1*(32), 75-82.

Wu, Y., Jin, R., & Zhang, X. (2014). Fast and unified local search for random walk based k-nearest-neighbor query in large graphs. In *Proceedings of the ACM SIGMOD International Conference on Management of Data* (pp. 1139-1150). Snowbird, UT: ACM. 10.1145/2588555.2610500

Xhafa, F., & Bessis, N. (2014). *Inter-cooperative Collective Intelligence: Techniques and Applications. In Studies in Computational Intelligence, 495* (pp. 39–67). Berlin, Germany: Springer-Verlag.

Xia, C., Lu, H., Ooi, B. C., & Hu, J. (2004). Gorder: an efficient method for knn join processing. In *Proceedings of the International Conference on Very Large Data Bases* (pp. 756-767). Toronto, Canada: Morgan Kaufmann.

XML Data Model. (n.d.). Retrieved from https://www.w3.org/XML/Datamodel.html

XML essentials. (n.d.). Retrieved from https://www.w3.org/standards/xml/core

XML Introduction. (n.d.). Retrieved from https://developer.mozilla.org/en-US/docs/XML_introduction

XML schema tutorial. (n.d.). Retrieve from https://www.w3schools.com/xml/schema_intro.asp

XML Schema. (n.d.). Retrieved from https://en.wikipedia.org/

Xu, K., Li, H., & Liu, Z. (2018). ISOMAP-based spatiotemporal modeling for lithium-ion battery thermal process. *IEEE Transactions on Industrial Informatics*, *14*(2), 569–577. doi:10.1109/TII.2017.2743260

Xu, X., Jager, J., & Kriegel, H. (1999). A fast parallel clustering algorithm for large spatial databases. *Data Mining and Knowledge Discovery*, *3*(3), 263–290. doi:10.1023/A:1009884809343

Xu, X., Zhang, B., & Zhong, Q. (2005). Text categorization using SVMs with Rocchio ensemble for internet information classification. In *Proceedings of the International Conference on Communications, Networking and Mobile Computing* (pp. 1022-1031).

Yaghob, J., Bednárek, D., Kruliš, M., & Zavoral, F. (2014). Column-oriented Data Store for Astrophysical Data. In *Proceedings of 25th International Workshop on Database and Expert Systems Applications*. Munich, Germany: IEEE Computer Society.

Yan Betts. (2014). *How JSON sparked NoSQL – and will return to the RDBMS fold*. Retrieved from https://www.infoworld.com/article/2608293/nosql/how-json-sparked-nosql----and-will-return- to-the-rdbms-fold.html

Yang, S. J. H., Okamoto, T., & Tseng, S. S. (2008). Context-Aware and Ubiquitous Learning (Guest Editorial). *Journal of Educational Technology & Society*, *11*(2), 1–2.

Yao, B., Li, F., & Kumar, P. (2010). K nearest neighbor queries and kNN-joins in large relational databases (almost) for free. In *Proceedings of the International Conference on Data Engineering* (pp. 4-15). Long Beach, CA: IEEE. 10.1109/ICDE.2010.5447837

Yavatkar, R., Pendarakis, D., & Guerin, R. (2000). *A Framework for Policy-based Admission Control*. IETF, RFC 2753.

Yazici, A., Zhu, Q., & Sun, N. (2001). Semantic data modeling of spatiotemporal database applications. *International Journal of Intelligent Systems*, *16*(7), 881–904. doi:10.1002/int.1040

Yeboah-Boateng, E. O., & Cudjoe-Seshie, S. (2013). Cloud Computing: The Emergence of Application Service providers (ASPs) in Developing Economies. *International Journal of Emerging Technology and Advanced Engineering*, *3*(5), 703–712.

Yi, B. K., Jagadish, H. V., & Faloutsos, C. (1998, February). Efficient retrieval of similar time sequences under time warping. In *Proceedings 14th International Conference on Data Engineering* (pp. 201-208). IEEE.

Yu, A., Agarwal, P., & Yang, J. (2010). Processing a large number of continuous preference top-k queries. In *Proceedings of the ACM SIGMOD International Conference on Management of Data (SIGMOD'10)* (pp. 397-408). New York: ACM.

Yu, C., Zhang, R., Huang, Y., & Xiong, H. (2010). High-dimensional kNN joins with incremental updates. *GeoInformatica*, *14*(1), 55–82. doi:10.100710707-009-0076-5

Yu, Z. (2011). Towards a Smart Campus with Mobile Social Networking. *Proceedings of International Conference on Cyber, Physical and Social Computing*, 162–169. 10.1109/iThings/CPSCom.2011.55

Zadeh, L. A. (1999). Fuzzy sets as a basis for a theory of possibility. *Fuzzy Sets and Systems*, *100*(1), 9–34. doi:10.1016/S0165-0114(99)80004-9

Zhang, D., Chan, C., & Tan, K. (2014). Processing spatial keyword query as a top-k aggregation query. In *Proceedings of the International ACM SIGIR Conference on Research and Development in Information Retrieval (SIGIR'14)* (pp. 355–364). New York: ACM. 10.1145/2600428.2609562

Zhang, D., Song, T., He, J., Shi, X., & Dong, Y. (2012). A Similarity-Oriented RDF Graph Matching Algorithm for Ranking Linked Data. In *IEEE 12th International Conference on Computer and Information Technology (CIT)* (pp.427-434). IEEE.

Zhang, C., Li, F., & Jestes, J. (2012). Efficient parallel kNN joins for large data in MapReduce. In *Proceedings of the International Conference on Extending Database Technology* (pp. 38-49). Berlin, Germany: ACM. 10.1145/2247596.2247602

Zhang, D. (2017). High-speed Train Control System Big Data Analysis Based on Fuzzy RDF Model and Uncertain Reasoning. *International Journal of Computers, Communications & Control*, *12*(4), 577. doi:10.15837/ijccc.2017.4.2914

Zhang, L., Zhu, G., Shen, P., & Song, J. (2017). Learning spatiotemporal features using 3DCNN and convolutional LSTM for gesture recognition. In *Proceedings of the IEEE Conference on Computer Vision and Pattern Recognition*, Venice, Italy (pp. 3120-3128). Piscataway, NJ: IEEE. 10.1109/ICCVW.2017.369

Zhang, S., Han, J., Liu, Z., Wang, K., & Xu, Z. (2009). SJMR: Parallelizing spacial join with MapReduce on clusters. In *Proceedings of the IEEE International Conference on Cluster Computing* (pp. 1-8). New Orleans, LA: IEEE Computer Society. 10.1109/CLUSTR.2009.5289178

Zhang, W. (2000) Depth-first branch-and-bound versus local search: a case study. In *Proceedings of 17th National Conference on Artificial Intelligence* (pp. 930–935).

Zhang, X., Ai, J., Wang, Z., Lu, J., & Meng, X. (2009). An efficient multi-dimensional index for cloud data management. In *Proceedings of CloudDB* (pp. 17–24). ACM. doi:10.1145/1651263.1651267

Zhao, G., Lin, Q., Li, L., & Li, Z. (2014). Schema Conversion Model of SQL Database to NoSQL. In *Proceedings of the 9th Int. Conf. on P2P, Parallel, Grid, Cloud and Internet Computing*. IEEE. 10.1109/3PGCIC.2014.137

Zhao, J., & Itti, L. (2018). Shapedtw: Shape dynamic time warping. *Pattern Recognition*, *74*, 171–184. doi:10.1016/j.patcog.2017.09.020

Zhao, W., Ma, H., & He, Q. (2009). Parallel k-means clustering based on MapReduce. In *Proceedings of the First International Conference CloudCom* (pp. 674-679). Beijing, China: Springer.

Zheng, K., Su, H., Zheng, B., Shang, S., Xu, J., Liu, J., & Zhou, X. (2015). Interactive top-k spatial keyword queries. In *Proceedings of the International Conference on Data Engineering (ICDE'15)*, (pp. 423-434).

Zheng, L., Zhou, L., Zhao, X., Liao, L., & Liu, W. (2017). The Spatio-Temporal Data Modeling and Application Based on Graph Database. In *Proceedings of the 4th International Conference on Information Science and Control Engineering* (pp. 741-746). IEEE. 10.1109/ICISCE.2017.159

Zhou, X., Zhang, X., Wang, Y., Li, R., & Wang, S. (2013). Efficient Distributed Multi-dimensional Index for Big Data Management. *Proceedings of WAIM 2013, LNCS 7923*, 130–141. 10.1007/978-3-642-38562-9_14

Zhu, H., Zhong, J., Li, J., & Yu, Y. (2002). An Approach for Semantic Search by Matching RDF Graphs. In *Proceedings of Fifteenth International Florida Artificial Intelligence Research Society Conference (FLAIRS-02)* (pp. 450-454).

Zhu, X., Song, S., Lian, X., Wang, J., & Zou, L. (2014). Matching heterogeneous event data. In *Proceedings of ACM SIGMOD International Conference on Management of Data* (pp. 1211-1222).

Zhu, Z. T., Yu, M. H., & Riezebos, P. (2016). A Research Framework of Smart Education, Springer Open Online. *Learning Environment*, *3*(1), 4. doi:10.118640561-016-0026-2

Zinn, D., Bowers, S., Kohler, S., & Ludascher, B. (2010). Parallelizing XML data-streaming workflows via MapReduce. *Journal of Computer and System Sciences*, *76*(6), 447–463. doi:10.1016/j.jcss.2009.11.006

Zou, L., & Özsu, M. T. (2017). Graph-Based RDF Data Management. *Data Science and Engineering*, *2*(1), 56–70. doi:10.100741019-016-0029-6

About the Contributors

Zongmin Ma is currently a Full Professor at Nanjing University of Aeronautics and Astronautics, China. He received his Ph.D. degree from the City University of Hong Kong, China. His research interests include databases, the semantic web, and knowledge representation and reasoning with a special focus on information uncertainty. He has published more than one hundred and seventy papers on these topics. He is also the author of four monographs published by Springer. He is a senior member of the IEEE.

Li Yan received her Ph.D. degree from Northeastern University, China. She is currently a Full Professor of College of Computer Science & Technology at Nanjing University of Aeronautics and Astronautics, China. Her research interests include database modeling, XML data management, as well as imprecise and uncertain data processing. She has published over 50 papers in international journals, conferences and books in these areas since 2008. She also authored and edited several scholarly books published by Springer-Verlag and IGI Global, respectively.

* * *

Azim Ahmadzadeh is currently a PhD student in Computer Science. His main interdisciplinary research interest centers in automatic detection of solar phenomena such as Filaments and Sun-Spots using Deep Neural Networks, prediction of M and X class flares through classical Machine Learning models, and selection and extraction of image parameters that can be used in detection and classification of solar events such as Active Regions and Coronal Holes. His research also explores time series analysis, specifically improving on a family of proximity measures based on Dynamic Time Warping, in terms of both accuracy and computation time. He received his Bachelor of Science in Computer Science from Warsaw University of Technology, and Associate's degree in Pure Mathematics from Guilan University.

Luyi Bai received his PhD degree from Northeastern University, China. He is currently an associate professor at Northeastern University at Qinhuangdao, China. His current research interests include uncertain databases and fuzzy spatiotemporal XML data management. He has published papers in several Journals such as Integrated Computer-Aided Engineering, Fuzzy Sets and Systems, Applied Intelligence, and Applied Artificial Intelligence, etc. He is also a member of CCF.

Peter Baumann obtained a degree in Computer Science (1987) from Technical University of Munich, a doctorate (1993) in Computer Science at Darmstadt University of Technology while working with Fraunhofer Institute for Computer Graphics. He has pursued post-doctoral activities in both industry and academia, working for Softlab Group in Munich (now Cirquent) and as Assistant Head of the Knowledge Bases Research Group of FORWISS (Bavarian Research Center for Knowledge-based Systems) / Technical University of Munich where he was deputy to Prof. Rudolf Bayer, Ph.D. Among Dr. Peter Baumann's entrepreneurial activities was founding of the spin-off company Rasdaman GmbH for commercialization of the world's first multi-dimensional array database system. In August 2004 he was appointed as Professor of Computer Science at Jacobs University Bremen. Baumann is active in many bodies concerned with scientific data access such as the Open Geospatial Consortium (OGC).

Ahmed Bouabdallah received his Ph.D. in Computer Science from the University of Franche-Comté (France) and joined IMT Atlantique. His research interests concern telecommunication services, IoT, eHealth, security and formal methods.

Rafik Bouaziz is full professor on computer science at the Faculty of Economic Sciences and Management of Sfax University, Tunisia. He was the president of this University during August 2014 – December 2017, and the director of its doctoral school of economy, management and computer science during December 2011 – July 2014. His PhD has dealt with temporal data management and historical record of data in Information Systems. The subject of his accreditation to supervise research was "A contribution for the control of versioning of data and schema in advanced information systems". Currently, his main research topics of interest are temporal databases, real-time databases, information systems engineering, ontologies, data warehousing and workflows. Between 1979 and 1986, he was a consulting Engineer in the organization and computer science and a head of the department of computer science at CEGOS-TUNISIA.

Safa Brahmia is currently a PhD student in Computer Science at the Faculty of Economics and Management of the University of Sfax, Tunisia. She is working on temporal and multi-schema-version JSON-based NoSQL databases. She is a member of the Multimedia, InfoRmation systems, and Advanced Computing Laboratory (MIRACL) since 2015. She received her MSc degree in Computer Science, in December 2014, from the Faculty of Economics and Management of the University of Sfax.

Zouhaier Brahmia is currently an Associate Professor of Computer Science in the Department of Computer Science at the Faculty of Economics and Management of the University of Sfax, Tunisia. He is a member of the Multimedia, InfoRmation systems, and Advanced Computing Laboratory (MIRACL). His scientific interests include temporal databases, schema versioning, and temporal, evolution and versioning aspects in emerging databases (XML, NoSQL, and NewSQL), ontologies, World Wide Web, and Semantic Web. He received his MSc degree in Computer Science, in July 2005, and a PhD in Computer Science, in December 2011, from the Faculty of Economics and Management of the University of Sfax.

Soukaina Filali Boubrahimi graduated from Al Akhawayn University in Ifrane with a Bachelor degree in computer science and a Master degree in software engineering. Currently she is a PhD student at Georgia State University where she is interested in the problem of time series classification and ensemble learning. Her research interests also includes solar event prediction and clustering, mining discriminative patterns from fMRI-based networks, and spatiotemporal interpolation methods.

Fabio Grandi is currently an Associate Professor in the School of Engineering of the University of Bologna, Italy. Since 1989 he has worked at the CSITE center of the Italian National Research Council (CNR) in Bologna in the field of neural networks and temporal databases, initially supported by a CNR fellowship. In 1993 and 1994 he was an Adjunct Professor at the Universities of Ferrara, Italy, and Bologna. In the University of Bologna, he was with the Dept. of Electronics, Computers and Systems from 1994 to 1998 as a Research Associate and as Associate Professor from 1998 to 2012, when he joined the Dept. of Computer Science and Engineering. His scientific interests include temporal, evolution and versioning aspects in data management, WWW and Semantic Web, knowledge representation, storage structures and access cost models. He received a Laurea degree cum Laude in Electronics Engineering and a PhD in Electronics Engineering and Computer Science from the University of Bologna.

Lubna Irshad from Pakistan is presently a master student in Nanjing University of Aeronautics and Astronautics (NUAA), China. She is researching on how JSON Data Stores and RDBMS can work hand-in-hand to get the best of both worlds. She has been working on RDBMS since long. She has studied JSON Data Stores in depth with different aspects and presented it in survey paper. She believes emergence of diversity occurs with incorporation of multiple technologies.

Hao Jiang serves as an SDN/NFV pre-research Engineer at New H3C Technologies. He just completed EIT Digital Dual Master Degree Programme with a major of Internet Technology and Architecture at KTH Royal Institute of Technology and a specialization of Internet of Things(IoT) at IMT Atlantique. He also minored in ICT Innovation and Entrepreneurship during his Master studies. Hao is a Cisco Certificated Internetwork Expert in Routing and Switching (CCIE R&S #40343).

Palanivel Kuppusamy received his Master of Technology in Computer Science & Engineering from Pondicherry University, India in 1999 and Bachelor of Engineering in Computer Science & Engineering from Bharathiar University in 1994. He was appointed as the Systems Analyst by the Computer Centre at Pondicherry University. He writes and presents widely on issues of network services, network design, network architecture, network security, applying new and latest technologies in campus network. His research coverage includes software architecture, advanced computer network, e-Learning and big data & analytics.

Guan-Feng Li received the M.S. degree in Computer Software and Theory from Ningxia University, China. He is currently pursuing the Ph.D. degree in the School of Computer Science and Engineering, Northeastern University, China. His research interests include RDF data and semantic web.

Zhen Hua Liu has been a DBMS veteran, industrial researcher and architect focus on developing industrial strength relational, object relational, XML, JSON, full text DBMS software products for 28 years upon his graduation from University of California at Berkeley with major in Computer Science. He is a senior Member of ACM/SIGMOD with 55 issued patents and 34 peer reviewed publications in SIGMOD, VLDB, ICDE, SIGPLAN etc conferences and journals. He is the semi-structured data management architect at Oracle and has established storage, query and index principles to address the challenge for RDBMS to enable schema-less development over flexible schema data. He is the originator and contributor of SQL/JSON standard. He has also contributed the development of SQL/XML standard and XQuery working group.

Ruizhe Ma is a Ph.D. student in the Computer Science Department at Georgia State University. Her research interests include sequential comparison, multidimensional data mining, clustering, and visualization. Her work has shown promising results with solar weather data and can be further applied to a variety of domains.

Joan Maso is a researcher at CREAF and GIS developer. Co-creator of the MiraMon compressed map: the first MiraMon technology for Internet distribution and data preservation. Creator of Remote Sensing imagery visualization and download web data portals with MiraMon owned technology. He is an active member of the TC of the Open Geospatial Consortium (OGC) since 2003 (editor OGC 07-057r7 WMTS, OGC 13-082r2 simple profile, OGC 12-108 GMLCOV for JPEG2000 and 08-085r2 GMLJP2 v2 standards), in several OGC Testbeds (recently in Testbed 12 resulting in several Public Engineering Reports such as OGC 15-053 JSON and GeoJSON), and member of the Opengeospatial Architecture Board OAB . He coordinated the GeoViQua FP7 project, the H2020 ConnectinGEO and the H2020 WaterInnEU and participated in H2020 ECOPotential and the H2020 ERAPlanet. Former Earth and Space Science Informatics (ESSI) division president in the European Geosciences Union (EGU). Active member in GEO-GEOSS.

Jaroslav Pokorny received his Ph.D. degree in theoretical cybernetics from Charles University, Prague, Czechoslovakia, in 1984. He is a full professor in the Faculty of Mathematics and Physics, Charles University in Prague. He has published more than 300 papers and books on data modeling, relational databases, query languages, XML technologies, and data organization. His current research interests include semi-structured data, Web technologies, database architectures, indexing methods, and Big Data. Jaroslav is involved as a chair and co-chair in the organization of conferences ADBIS-DASFAA, EDBT, Int. Workshop ClustWeb in conj. with EDBT, Web X.0 a Web Mining Workshop in conj. with IEEE ICDIM, ISD, IDEAS, ADBIS, IHCI, etc. He is a member of ACM and IEEE. He works also as the representative of Czech Republic in IFIP.

Bela Stantic is Professor in Computer Science and Head of School of Information and Communication Technology. He is also founder and Director of "Big Data and Smart Analytics" Lab within the Institute of Integrated and Intelligent Systems at Griffith University. Professor Stantic is internationally recognised in field of efficient management of complex data structures, such as found in Big Data, as well as data analytics. He successfully applied his research interdisciplinary, most prominently applying Big Data analytics to tourism as well as to health domain. He has published more than 130 journal and conference peer reviewed publications.

Wei Yan received his Ph. D. degree from Northeastern University, China. He is currently an associate professor at Liaoning University, China. His research interests include big data, massive XML data management, XML personalized and flexible query, as well as XML fuzzy query.

Alaitz Zabala is a researcher and assistant professor at the Department of Geography at Universitat Autónoma de Barcelona. Her main research lines are standardization of geographic information (metadata, geospatial user feedback, data models, web servers data distribution, Javascript and JSON web client using binary arrays,...) and the effect of lossy compressions in the generation of cartography from remote sensing images. Main developer of the GeMM metadata manager application, in the context of the

MiraMon GIS software. Participation in international standardization entities (ISO and OGC) providing comments on international standards through state representatives in these committees. Associate editor of GeoFocus magazine. Participant in previous FP7 (GeoPictures and GeoViQua) and H2020 projects (ECOPotential and NextGEOSS, the later as partner coordinator). She is part of the Research Group on Remote Sensing Methods and Applications and Geographical Information Systems (GRUMETS), a consolidated and quality research group recognized by the Generalitat de Catalunya (SGR N. 1511 in 2009, N. 1491 in 2104 and N. 1690 in 2017). The main objective of GRUMETS is the development of applications that allow progress in the geographic and environmental research both basic and applied.

Index

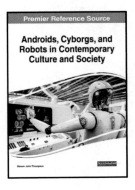

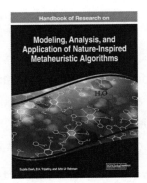

Ensure Quality Research is Introduced to the Academic Community

Become an IGI Global Reviewer for Authored Book Projects

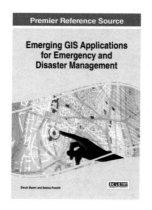

Premier Reference Source

Emerging GIS Applications for Emergency and Disaster Management

Premier Reference Source

Managerial Strategies and Green Solutions for Project Sustainability

Premier Reference Source

Comparative Approaches to Using R and Python for Statistical Data Analysis

Premier Reference Source

Solutions for High-Touch Communications in a High-Tech World

The overall success of an authored book project is dependent on quality and timely reviews.

In this competitive age of scholarly publishing, constructive and timely feedback significantly expedites the turnaround time of manuscripts from submission to acceptance, allowing the publication and discovery of forward-thinking research at a much more expeditious rate. Several IGI Global authored book projects are currently seeking highly qualified experts in the field to fill vacancies on their respective editorial review boards:

Applications may be sent to:
development@igi-global.com

Applicants must have a doctorate (or an equivalent degree) as well as publishing and reviewing experience. Reviewers are asked to write reviews in a timely, collegial, and constructive manner. All reviewers will begin their role on an ad-hoc basis for a period of one year, and upon successful completion of this term can be considered for full editorial review board status, with the potential for a subsequent promotion to Associate Editor.

If you have a colleague that may be interested in this opportunity, we encourage you to share this information with them.

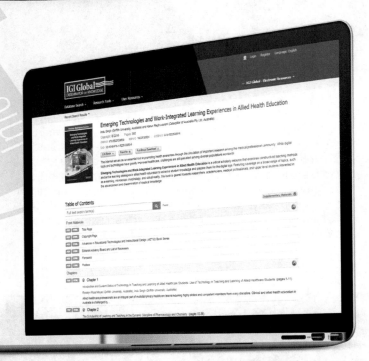

Printed in the United States
By Bookmasters